AF516179

# Integrated Pest Management

## Principles and Applications

## Volume 1: Principles

# Integrated Pest Management

## Principles and Applications

## Volume 1: Principles

**Amerika Singh**
M.Sc. (Ag.), Ph.D., FPSI, FSMPP
Director

**O.P. Sharma**
M.Sc., Ph.D.
Senior Scientist (Plant Pathology)

**D.K. Garg**
M.Sc., Ph.D.
Principal Scientist (Entomology)

National Centre for Integrated Pest Management,
LBS Building, Indian Agricultural Research Institute,
New Delhi - 110 012 (India)
E-mail: ipmnet@bol.net.in Website: www.ncipm.org.in

**CBS PUBLISHERS & DISTRIBUTORS**
NEW DELHI • BANGALORE

ISBN : 81-239-1254-4

First Edition : 2005



*Publishing Director :* Vinod K. Jain

*Published by :*
Satish Kumar Jain for CBS Publishers & Distributors,
4596/1-A, 11 Darya Ganj, New Delhi - 110 002 (India)
E-mail : cbspubs@del3.vsnl.net.in
Website : http://www.cbspd.com

*Branch Office :*
2975, 17th Cross, K.R. Road,
Bansankari 2nd Stage, Bangalore - 560 070
Fax : 080-26771680 • E-mail : cbsbng@vsnl.net

*Printed at :*
Asia Printograph, Delhi

## Foreword

The research and development efforts in the field of crop production and protection have significantly contributed towards attaining self-sufficiency in food production at national level. If the current growth in agricultural production has to be enhanced and sustained, mitigation of crop losses causes due to various stresses, especially the pests, which account for nearly 18% average reduction in yields obviously call for priority attention. Pest control has got the due attention of the farmers and researchers but indiscriminate and injudicious use of chemical pesticides has caused harm to human health and environment. Food security, food and environmental safety need to be viewed together. Therefore, environmentally safe option of Integrated Pest Management (IPM) as a cornerstone of crop protection is both a necessity and an eventuality. Appropriate strategic adjustments have become pertinent in view of implementation of WTO and new Sanitary and Phytosanitary (SPS) measures becoming globally effective. Research programmes are being implemented in different agro-ecological zones to meet the plant protection challenges keeping in view the strict standards in the world market. As a result of advancements in the information technology, Government initiatives and especially education, farmers in general have started adopting alternatives and eco-friendly plant protection measures to achieve sustainable yields. A number of bio-pesticides have been registered with the Central Insecticides Board and Registration Committee for use in agriculture. Successful examples of Integrated Pest Management have to be replicated widely and vigorously.

The present book entitled "*Integrated Pest Management: Principles and Applications*" has been presented in two volumes: Volume I covers the Principles and Volume II covers the Applications of Integrated Pest Management in economically important crops. Not only that the IPM strategies and technologies described in the book will help to increase crop yields but also enable the farmers to produce cleaner food for both domestic and international markets. The book is also expected to serve as standard reference book on IPM to students, researchers and policy makers involved with crop production and protection

I congratulate the editors for their valuable efforts.

**(MANGALA RAI)**
**Secretary,** Department of Agricultural Research & Education
and
**Director General,** Indian Council of Agricultural Research
Dr. Rajendra Prasad Road, Krishi Bhawan, New Delhi-110 001, India

March 23, 2005

# Preface

Injudicious and indiscriminate use of chemical pesticides has led to environmental pollution and health hazards through contamination of food chain. While the pesticide consumption has increased manifolds, the population of natural predators, parasitoids have gone down without checking the empirical growth of pests. Of late, a number of insect pests and plant pathogens have developed resistance against conventional chemical pesticides and pollution leading to reduced fertility, soil structure and water contamination. Declining efficiency of chemical pesticides, resurgence of minor pests, decreasing cost effectiveness, and environmental and health concerns have led to the development and adoption of alternative pest management strategies at various levels. A number of alternative biointensive technologies, coupled with biotechnology, have proven their effectiveness for pest management, and are making their respective places in some of the high value crops. Integrated Pest Management (IPM), based on the old, as well as emerging technologies, has been identified by the National Agricultural Policy of September 2001 as the cardinal principle of plant protection to minimize the indiscriminate and injudicious use of chemical pesticides in agriculture. The IPM strategies have proved a great boon as they are compatible with the stringent parameters of "organic agriculture". In view of the increasing importance of IPM for sustainable agriculture and absence of an authoritative book on its theory and practice under single cover, this edited book on the subject will fill the knowledge gap and meet the long awaited requirements of scientists, teachers, post-graduate students, extension workers, policy makers and all other concerned with pest management. The book has been divided in two volumes to cover the Principles (Volume I) and the examples of Applications (Volume II) of IPM in selected field and horticultural crops. The chapters have been written by well known specialists in the field.

We express our sincere thanks to all the contributors, who have made this book a reality. We are also thankful to Sh. S. Nagarajan, Sh. Sateesh Kumar Singh, Smt. Neelam Mehta and Sh. Satya Kumar, of NCIPM for their valuable assistance.

**Editors**

## List of Contributors

1. **A. Dhandapani**
National Centre for Integrated Pest Management,
LBS Building, Pusa Campus, New Delhi-110 012

2. **A. K. Sharma**
Directorate of Wheat Research,
P.B. No. 158, Agarsain Rd., Karnal-132 001

3. **Amerika Singh**
National Centre for Integrated Pest Management,
LBS Building, Pusa Campus, New Delhi-110 012

4. **Anushri Varshney**
National Research Centre on Plant Biotechnology,
Indian Agricultural Research Institute, New Delhi-110 012

5. **Ashok Gaur**
Div. of Seed Science and Technology,
Indian Agricultural Research Institute, New Delhi-110 012

6. **B. L. Meena**
National Centre for Integrated Pest Management,
LBS Building, Pusa Campus, New Delhi-110 012

7. **D. K. Das**
National Centre for Integrated Pest Management,
LBS Building, Pusa Campus, New Delhi-110 012

8. **D. S. Mishra**
Centre for Advance Studies in Pl. Pathology,
College of Agriculture,
Govind Ballabh Pant University of Agri. and Technology (GBPUA&T),
Pant Nagar-263 145

9. **Gita Kulshrestha**
Division of Agricultural Chemicals,
Indian Agricultural Research Institute, New Delhi-110 012

10. **H. S. Chaube**
Centre for Advance Studies in Pl. Pathology,
College of Agriculture,
Govind Ballabh Pant University of Agriculture and Technology (GBPUA&T),
Pant Nagar-263 145

11. **H. S. Gaur**
Division of Nematology,
Indian Agricultural Research Institute,
LBS Building IARI Campus, New Delhi-110 012

12. **J. Kumar**
Directorate of Wheat Research,
P.B. No. 158, Agarsain Rd., Karnal-132 001

13. **J. S. Mishra**
National Research Centre for Weed Sciences,
Maharajpur, Adhartal, Jabalpur-482 004

14. **Jameel Akhtar**
Centre for Advance Studies in Pl. Pathology,
College of Agriculture,
Govind Ballabh Pant University of Agriculture and Technology (GBPUA&T),
Pant Nagar-263 145

15. **K. P. Jayanth**
Biocontrol Research Laboratories,
P.O. Box 3228, H. M. T. Layout, R. T. Nagar,
Bangalore-560 032

16. **Kavita Gupta**
Plant Quarantine Division,
National Bureau of Plant Genetic Resources, New Delhi-110 012

17. **M. S. Saharan**
Directorate of Wheat Research,
P.B. No. 158, Agarsain Rd. Karnal-132 001

18. **Madhuban Gopal**
Division of Agricultural Chemicals
Indian Agricultural Research Institute, New Delhi-110 012

19. **N. S. Rao**
Project Directorate of Biological Control
P.O. Box No. 2491, H. A. Farm Post,
Bellary Road, Bangalore-560 024

20. **N. Sathiah**
Department of Entomology,
Tamil Nadu Agricultural University,
Coimbatore-641 003

21. **N. T. Yaduraju**
National Research Centre for Weed Sciences,
Maharajpur, Adhartal, Jabalpur-482 004

22. **Nasim Ahmad**
National Centre for Integrated Pest Management,
LBS Building, Pusa Campus, New Delhi-110 012

**23. Neelam Singh**
Centre for Advance Studies in Pl. Pathology,
College of Agriculture,
Govind Ballabh Pant University of Agri. and Technology (GBPUA&T),
Pant Nagar-263 145

**24. Najam Waris Zaidi**
Centre for Advance Studies in Pl. Pathology,
College of Agriculture,
Govind Ballabh Pant University of Agri. and Technology (GBPUA&T),
Pant Nagar-263 145

**25. Niranjan Singh**
National Centre for Integrated Pest Management,
LBS Building, Pusa Campus, New Delhi-110 012

**26. O. P. Sharma**
National Centre for Integrated Pest Management,
LBS Building, Pusa Campus, New Delhi-110 012

**27. O. M. Bambawale**
National Centre for Integrated Pest Management,
LBS Building, Pusa Campus, New Delhi-110 012

**28. Pankaj**
Division of Nematology,
Indian Agricultural Research Institute,
LBS Building IARI Campus, New Delhi-110 012

**29. Pratap S Birthal**
National Centre for Agricultural Economics and Policy Research,
Library Avenue Rd., New Delhi-110 012

**30. R. K. Khetarpal**
Plant Quarantine Division,
National Bureau of Plant Genetic Resources, New Delhi-110 012

**31. R. P. Sharma**
National Research Centre on Plant Biotechnology,
Indian Agricultural Research Institute, New Delhi-110 012

**32. R.J. Rabindra**
Project Directorate of Biological Control
P.O. Box No. 2491, H. A. Farm Post,
Bellary Road, Bangalore-560 024

**33. S. K. Jalali**
Project Directorate of Biological Control,
P.O. Box No. 2491, H.A. Farm Post,
Bellary Road, Bangalore-560 024

34. **S. S. Hussaini**
Project Directorate of Biological Control,
P.O. Box No. 2491, H. A. Farm Post,
Bellary Road, Bangalore-560 024

35. **Shekhar Varshney**
Centre for Advance Studies in Pl. Pathology,
College of Agriculture,
Govind Ballabh Pant University of Agri. and Technology (GBPUA&T),
Pant Nagar-263 145

36. **T. Mohapatra**
National Research Centre on Plant Biotechnology,
Indian Agricultural Research Institute, New Delhi-110 012

37. **T. P. Trivedi**
National Centre for Integrated Pest Management,
LBS Building, Pusa Campus, New Delhi-110 012

38. **Tarana**
Centre for Advance Studies in Pl. Pathology,
College of Agriculture,
Govind Ballabh Pant University of Agri. and Technology (GBPUA&T),
Pant Nagar-263 145

39. **U. R. Sangale**
National Centre for Integrated Pest Management,
LBS Building, Pusa Campus, New Delhi-110 012

40. **U. S. Singh**
Centre for Advance Studies in Pl. Pathology,
College of Agriculture,
Govind Ballabh Pant University of Agri. and Technology (GBPUA&T),
Pant Nagar-263 145

# Contents

1

# Ensuring Food Security

**Amerika Singh**

*"No nation can live with pride unless it has the capacity to feed its people."*

**—Smt. Indira Gandhi**

## INTRODUCTION

India's population is one billion and is expected to be around 1.3 billion by the year 2020. More than 69 per cent of the population lives in rural areas, where main occupation is agriculture, which contributes to India's GDP by 24.2 per cent and provides direct employment to 66.7 per cent population. Fourteen per cent of India's total export comes from agriculture. Two-third of the country's labour force and three fourth personnel of military and para forces come from rural areas (Sompal, 2003). Agriculture is not only the backbone of the India's economy and food security, but also a way of life and anchor of the overall livelihood of Indian people. Yet, India is home to one-fourth of the world's undernourished people. An estimated 208 million of the nearly 800 million undernourished people of the world live in India. The extent and intensity of hunger is closely linked with the extent, intensity and nature of poverty. In spite of the fact that the country is self-sufficient in food production and availability, but the poor households, most of them in rural areas, do not have sufficient economic access to food available in the market, hence remain food insecure. Therefore, the alleviation of food insecurity in India not only depends on the sustained food production but also on dismantling of the root cause, poverty (Singh, 2001).

## PRE-GREEN REVOLUTION SCENARIO

Attaining self-sufficiency in food had been the major objective of India since independence in 1947. In the early fifties, the total food grain production was about 50 million tonnes, which was not sufficient to feed the growing population. During mid-sixties it was necessary to import 8-10 million tonnes of food annually. In fact, India's food security was called "ship to mouth", highlighting the heavy dependence on food imports.

Through the mid-sixties, Indian agriculture was characterized by a rich diversity of crops and land races, high dependence on rainfall, very little use of fertilization and irrigation, good organic matter content and fertility of soil, low cropping intensity and almost no use of chemical fertilizers and pesticides on a sizeable scale. Farmers depended on use of farm wastes as manure; scanty irrigation from ponds, rivers and shallow wells; and managed insect pests, diseases and weeds through cultural and

*National Centre for Integrated Pest Management, LBS Building, Pusa Campus, New Delhi- 110 012.*

indigenous techniques. Although, pest outbreaks occurred, crop productivity was stabilized at low level and the losses caused by pests were usually unnoticed and tolerated by the farmers. The low yielding crop varieties, for instance in case of rice and wheat, were tall and lodged, if excessive manures and irrigation were provided. They, were however, able to survive pest attacks, except highly susceptible varieties lost heavily.

## GREEN REVOLUTION

Indian agriculture has undergone unique and spectacular technological transformations that gave rise to "Green Revolution". The success of Green Revolution resulted in four-fold increase in production of food grains from 51 million tonnes in 1950-51 to 211.32 million tonnes in 2001-2002. Similarly, production of oilseeds has more than doubled from 24.75 million tonnes in 1998-99 within a decade. There has also been a considerable increase in the production of vegetables and fruits, placing India among the leading producers at the global level, after China and Brazil (Paroda, 2003).

## POST-GREEN REVOLUTION SCENARIO

In spite of the impressive achievements, Indian agriculture continues to face infrastructural and technological constraints. For instance, only about 36 per cent

**TABLE 1.1:** PRODUCTION AND PRODUCTIVITY OF MAIN AGRICULTURAL PRODUCTS IN INDIA AND GLOBAL RANKING (2003)

| *Crop* | *Production* (*million tonnes*) | *Productivity* (*Kg/ha*) | *Global Rank* | |
|---|---|---|---|---|
| | | | *Production* | *Productivity* |
| Paddy | 107.60 | 2683 | 2 | 64 |
| Wheat | 72.77 | 2762 | 2 | 47 |
| Maize | 11.17 | 1676 | 7 | 102 |
| Total cereals | 206.50 | 2219 | 3 | 97 |
| Onion dry | 4.90 | 9423 | 2 | 94 |
| Potatoes | 23.92 | 19806 | 3 | 53 |
| Total pulses | 13.44 | 609 | 1 | 134 |
| Sugarcane | 297.21 | 67370 | 2 | 42 |
| Soybean | 4.56 | 777 | 5 | 73 |
| Sunflower seed | 0.90 | 551 | 9 | 60 |
| Rapeseed | 5.08 | 1002 | 2 | 40 |
| Groundnut | 4.36 | 733 | 2 | 87 |
| Sesame seed | 0.43 | 311 | 2 | 58 |
| Coffee (green) | 0.32 | 981 | 6 | 13 |
| Sweat potatoes | 0.85 | 8655 | 9 | 47 |
| Tea | 0.85 | 1970 | 1 | 9 |
| Tobacco leaves | 0.39 | 1185 | 4 | 84 |
| Linseed | 0.21 | 390 | 4 | 40 |
| Jute | 1.85 | 2145 | 1 | 5 |
| Cotton | 4.75 | 635 | 4 | 70 |

*Source:* FAOSTAT-Agriculture (online database).

of the total cultivated land is under assured irrigation system. Farmers on the remaining two-thirds of the land are completely dependent on rainfall, which is characterized by large variations in terms of precipitation both spatially and in time. For a large majority of farmers in different parts of India, gains from application of improved agricultural technology are yet to be realized (Hazra, 2001). In spite of the fact that India ranks next only to the top producers in the world in total production of paddy, wheat, onion, sugarcane, rapeseed, groundnut and sesame seed, its global rankings in productivity are amongst the lowest (Table 1.1). Productivity constraints are quite varied in different crops but generally include lack of high yielding pest resistant crop varieties, adverse growing condition, inadequate crop management, hostile climatic conditions and incidence of insect pests, diseases, weeds, etc.

Intensive agriculture, which led to the Green Revolution, has been featured by increased genetic uniformity of crops, dense plant population, mono-cropping, higher fertilization and irrigation, altered cropping systems with immediate profit motives and increased use of pesticides. The technology of intensive agriculture, no doubt, generated the Green Revolution with emphasis on producing more and more food from the available natural resources, it has also led to newer problems due to: (i) faulty soil and water management like over-exploitation of the land and excessive and untimely use of irrigation water, (ii) replacement of a rich diversity of traditional crop varieties with a fewer high yielding varieties and (iii) injudicious and indiscriminate use of chemical fertilizers and pesticides (Paroda, 1999, 2003).

The features of intensive agriculture not only enhance productivity of crops but also favour increased incidence of insect pests, diseases and weeds. Increasing trend in use of chemical pesticides during the Green Revolution years perhaps highlights the increasing concern of the farmers about insect pests, diseases and weeds (Fig. 1.1 to 1.5). The pesticide consumption increased from 2353 tonnes in 1955-56 to 75033 tonnes in 1990-91 and continues to be 48350 tonnes in 2002-2003.

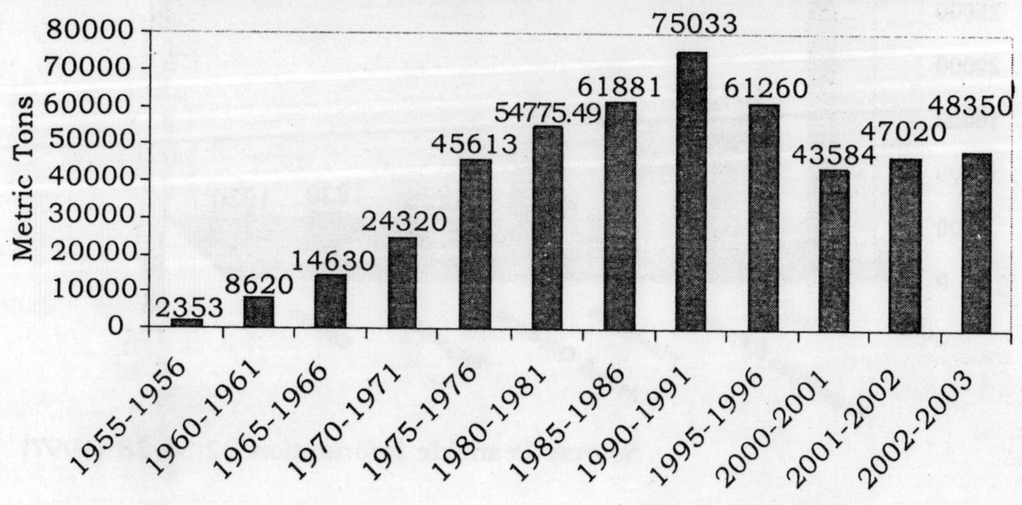


*Source*: DPPQ & S, Faridabad

**Fig. 1.1:** Pesticide consumption in India (1955-2003)

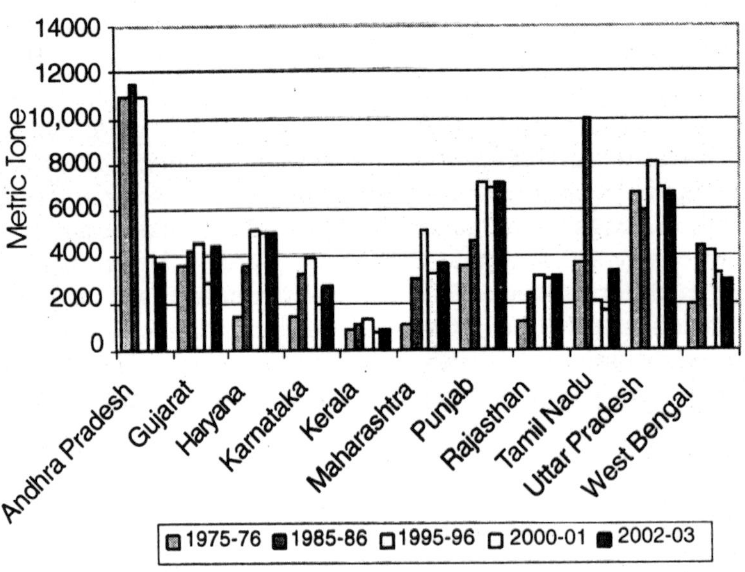


**Fig. 1.2:** Status of pesticide use in different states

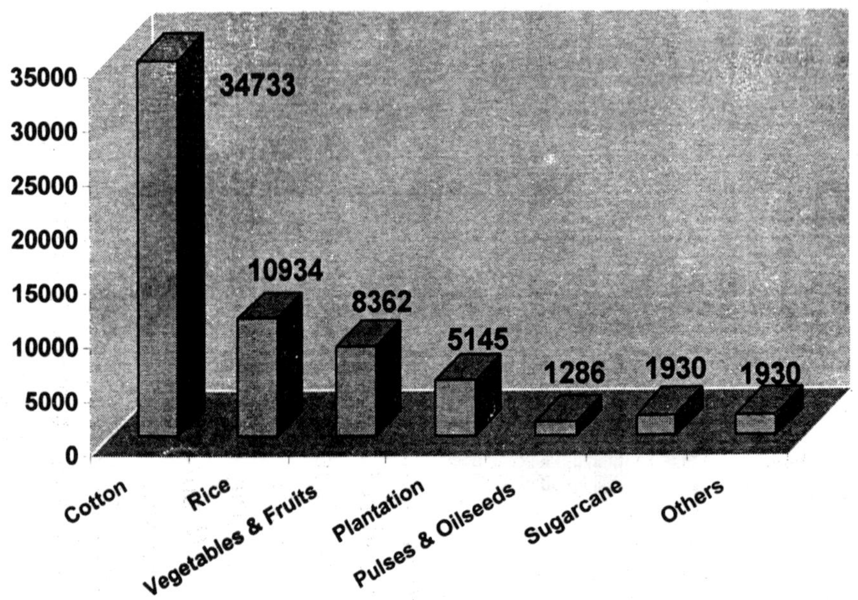


*Source*: Pesticide Information 22:36-38 (1997)

**Fig. 1.3:** Pesticide consumption on major crops in India (Metric Tonnes)

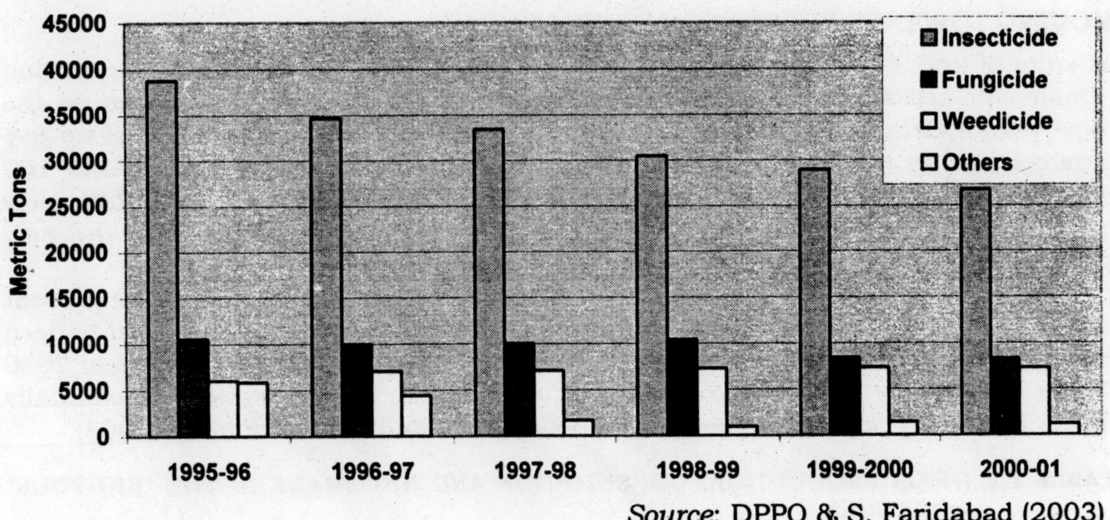


*Source*: DPPQ & S, Faridabad (2003)

**Fig. 1.4:** Groupwise pesticide consumption

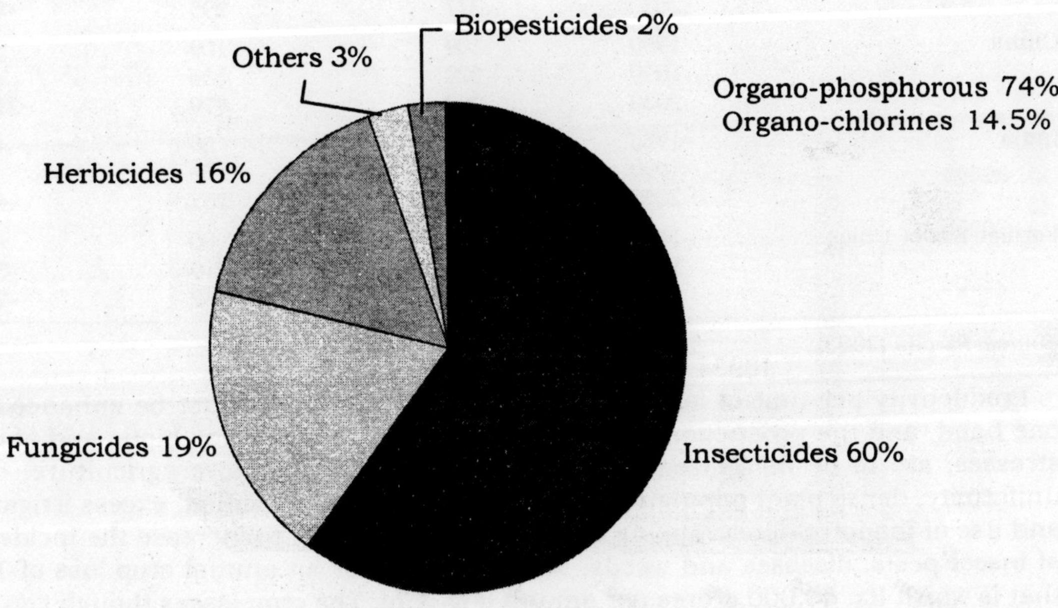


*Source*: DPPQ & S, Faridabad

**Fig. 1.5:** Pesticides being used in India (2000-01)

## MOVING TOWARDS EVERGREEN REVOLUTION

In spite of impressive gains of the green revolution, both poverty and malnutrition remain our serious concerns. Recently, growth of population has emerged as the most potent cause of widespread hunger. It is estimated that one out of every five persons still do not have means to buy two square meals a day and around 100 million children below 5 years of age are protein-energy malnourished (PEM). How to raise their income and access to food and nutritional security are the new paradigms of concern at the national level (Paroda, 2003).

World Watch Institute gave a wake up alarm in 1994 indicating that at the present rate of growth of food and population and also considering the consumption pattern for food, both China and India would face serious food grains deficit by the year 2030 (Table 1.2). Hence agricultural production will have to be accelerated substantially in the next 2-3 decades to meet the increasing demand of food (Paroda, 2003).

**TABLE 1.2:** GRAIN PRODUCTION, CONSUMPTION AND NET TRADE IN THE "BIG FOUR" COUNTRIES

| *Country* | *Year* | *Grain Production (million tonnes)* | *Grain Consumption (million tonnes)* | *Net Trade* |
|---|---|---|---|---|
| United States | 1950 | 133 | 121 | +12 |
| | 1990 | 290 | 214 | +76 |
| | 2030 | 377 | 295 | +82 |
| China | 1950 | 109 | 109 | 0 |
| | 1990 | 329 | 335 | –6 |
| | 2030 | 263 | 479 | –216 |
| India | 1950 | 57 | 55 | +2 |
| | 1990 | 158 | 158 | 0 |
| | 2030 | 222 | 267 | –45 |
| Former Soviet Union | 1950 | 79 | 80 | –1 |
| | 1990 | 182 | 219 | –37 |
| | 2030 | 237 | 262 | –25 |

*Source:* Paroda (2003).

Productivity per unit of land and other natural resources must be enhanced on one hand, and the production losses caused, on the other due to biotic and abiotic stresses, are to be minimized. In fact, the features of intensive agriculture, crop uniformity, dense plant population, excess unbalanced fertilization, excess irrigation and use of inappropriate cropping systems are well known to increase the incidence of insect pests, diseases and weeds, which account for an annual crop loss of 18% that is worth Rs. 60,000 crores per annum (Fig. 1.6). The crop losses though can not be eliminated altogether, these can be reduced significantly. Until recently, chemical pesticides were increasingly relied upon to limit the production losses. Pesticide use in India increased from a mere 15 g/ha of gross cropped area in 1955-56 to 90 g/ha in 1965-66. Introduction of green revolution technologies in mid-1960's gave a fillip to pesticide use and in 1975-76, it had increased to 266 g/ha, and reached a peak of 404 g/ha in 1990-91. However, pesticide use has started to decline since 1998-99, without much affecting the agricultural productivity (Birthal, 2003).

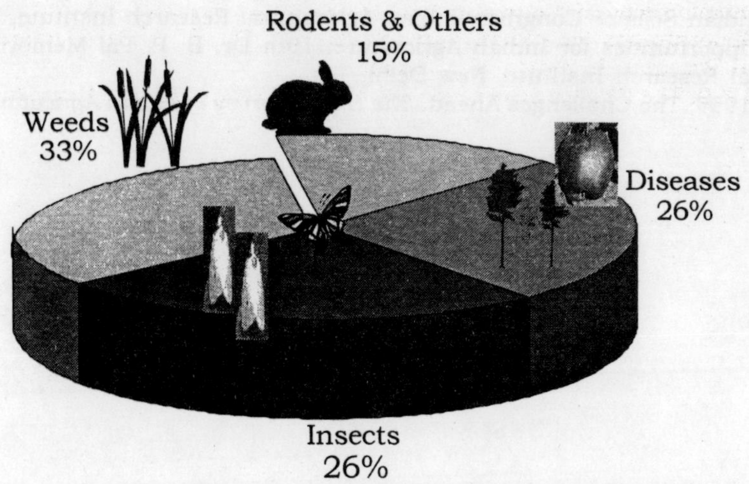


On an average 18% of the crop yield is lost due to pests

(Annual monetary loss: Rs. 60,000 crores)

*Source*: Working Subgroup on Plant Protection, Planning Commission, 2001

**Fig. 1.6:** Share of losses caused by different pests

Paroda (2003) stated "an assessment of the present scenario suggests that to meet the future challenges would not be an easy task, though not all that insurmountable. There are several uncommon opportunities which can, however, be harnessed to our advantage". He has listed a number of physical and technological options, which provide uncommon opportunities to meet the challenges of increasing agricultural productivity and production. Integrated management of natural resources using both Integrated Nutrient Management (INM) and Integrated Pest Management (IPM) have been included under the technological options. According to the noted agricultural scientist, M. S. Swaminathan (1999), agriculture production system in the 21st century need to be based on the appropriate use of biotechnology, information technology and ecotechnology. The IPM constitutes such a technology, which promotes and strengthens sustainable agriculture (Singh and Sharma, 2004).

## REFERENCES

Birthal, P. S. 2003. Economic potential of biological substitutes for agrochemicals. NCAP Poilcy Paper 18. National Centre for Agricultural Economics and Policy Research, New Delhi.

Hazra, C. R. 2001. Indian agriculture in the wake of globalization. *IPM Mitr.*, **2**: 1-7.

Paroda, R. S. 1999. For a food secure future. *The Hindu Survey of Indian Agriculture*, 1999.

Paroda, R. S. 2003. *Sustaining Our Food Security*. Konark Publishers, New Delhi.

Rabindra, R. J., Natarajan, N., Balagurunathan, R., Durairaj, C., Ramaraju, K. and Srinivasan, M. R. 2001. *Modern Trends in Integrated Pest Management*, TNAU, Coimbatore.

Singh, A. and Sharma, O. P. 2004. Integrated Pest Management for Sustainable Agriculture. *In*: Birthal, and Sharma (eds.), *Integrated Pest Management in Indian Agriculture*. Proceedings 11, NCAP and NCIPM, New Delhi.

Singh, R. B. 2001. A Hunger Free India. Presidential Address (Agricultural Science Section) at the 88th Session of Indian Science Congress, Indian Agricultural Research Institute, New Delhi.

Sompal 2003. New Opportunities for Indian Agriculture. 10th Dr. B. P. Pal Memorial Lecture, Indian Agricultural Research Institute, New Delhi.

Swaminathan, M. S. 1999. The Challenges Ahead. *The Hindu Survey of Indian Agriculture*, 1999.

## 2

# Concept and Philosophy of Integrated Pest Management

**Amerika Singh and O. P. Sharma**

## INTRODUCTION

The demands of a growing population for food and fibre require country to produce higher yields from cultivated land. On the basis of trends of consumption and income growth it is estimated that the total food grain requirements will be 240 million tonnes by 2006 AD. The production targets and required yield to feed the ever increasing current population in the present available resources will require the growth rate of 2.35 and 2.2 per cent in rice and wheat, respectively and as high as 4.45 and 3.38 per cent for pulses and oil seeds, respectively (APPARI, 1997). The average yield at national level will have to be increased by 30-50 per cent. The demand for certain food crops in 21st century warrants all out immediate remedial measures. Planner as well as policy makers are worried for tougher trade rules in the wake of implementation of WTO, however equally support the need and the aims of sustainable agriculture to produce sufficient food, in an environmentally and socially acceptable manner while maintaining the local natural resource base for future generations. Like other sensible gender we are equally committed to Integrated Pest Management (IPM) as defined by the FAO, as an economically viable and socially acceptable approach to crop protection. It is the top priority mission of the ICAR and other crop based institutes including the Govt. of India to provide safe and effective technologies to protect against unacceptable losses caused by weeds, diseases and pests, which to an estimate works out to Rs. 56,000 crores per annum at the price of Year 2000 and even exceeds in the time of epidemics.

To increase yields from existing land requires good crop protection against losses caused by pests. To be sustainable this must be achieved within the framework of IPM. IPM is an important principle and proved that sustainable crop protection can be based and relied on it. IPM policies and objectives are being adopted increasingly in developed and developing countries. IPM implementation is very much advanced in Western Europe and North America, and is expanding in developing countries in Southeast Asia, the Indian subcontinent and Africa. The goal is to achieve long-term sustainable systems of crop protection and production.

## ERA OF HIGH INPUT AGRICULTURE

A number of synthetic inorganic insecticides containing arsenic, mercury, tin and copper were developed towards the end of the nineteenth and the beginning of the

*National Centre for Integrated Pest Management, LBS Building, Pusa Campus, New Delhi-110 012.*

twentieth century. A number of synthetic inorganic insecticides, *viz.*, Paris green, lead arsenate, calcium arsenate and botanical insecticide, *i.e.*, rotenone, nicotine, etc. were developed during the end of nineteenth and beginning of 20th century. With the development of these insecticides the focus of research has shifted from ecological and cultural control practices to chemical control during the period 1920-1945 (Smith *et. al.*, 1976). Also organized use of both these groups of insecticides in India started on a limited scale during 1920s (Singh, 1986). Pesticides have made a great impact on human health, production of good, feed and forage and fibre crops by controlling diseases, insects and insect vectors and by keeping in check many unwanted species and weeds (Dhaliwal and Pathak, 1993). Gains achieved for the use of high yielding varieties of crops and application of increasing amounts of fertilizers have been made possible only due to the protection provided by the pesticide umbrella (Pradhan, 1983). However, excessive use of pesticides has resulted in emergence of new pest problems (Pimental, 1977, Jayaraj, 1988, Bramble, 1989).

With the development of these pesticides, the focus of research shifted from ecological and cultural control to chemical control, even before the development of synthetic organic insecticides (Perkins, 1980). The synthetic inorganic insecticides were broad-spectrum biocides and were highly toxic to all living organisms. The synthetic organic insecticides like alkyl thiocyanates, lethane, etc followed these in due course. The era of pesticides, however, began with the discovery of the insecticidal properties of DDT [2, 2-(p-chlorophenyl) -1, 1, 1-trichloroethane] by Paul Muller in 1939. The impact of DDT on pest control was unmatched and Muller was awarded Nobel Prize for this work in 1948. DDT was soon followed by HCH, chlordane, aldrin, dieldrin, heptachlor (organochlorine group); parathion, toxaphene, schradan, organophosphorus group and allethrin (synthetic pyrethroid) during the 1950s and a large number of other popularly used organophosphates and carbamates in the ensuing decade. Due to their efficacy, convenience, flexibility and economy, these pesticides played a major role in increasing crop production. The success of high yielding varieties of wheat and rice that ushered in the 'green revolution' was partially due to the protection umbrella of pesticides (Pradhan, 1983). The spectacular success of these pesticides masked their limitations. The intensive and extensive use, misuse and abuse of pesticides during the ensuing decades caused widespread damage to the environment. In addition, insect pest problems in some crops increased following the continuous application of pesticides. This, in turn, further increased the consumption of pesticides resulting in the phenomenon of the pesticide treadmill (Altieri, 1995). The combined impact of all these problems together with the rising cost of pesticides provided the necessary feedback for limiting the use of chemical control strategy and led to the development of the IPM concept.

## ERA OF IPM

Although many IPM programmes were initiated in late 1960s and early 1970s in several parts of the world, it was only in late 1970s that IPM gained momentum. The first major IPM project in USA, commonly called the Huffaker Project, spanned 1972-78 and covered six crops, *i.e.* alfalfa, citrus, cotton, pines, pome and stone fruits, and soybean. This was followed by another large scale IPM project called CIPM, the

Consortium for Integrated Pest Management (1979-85), which focussed on alfalfa, apple, cotton and soybean. The national IPM programmes were launched in late 1980s and early 1990s in several developing countries. The most outstanding success has been the FAO-IPM programme for rice in Southeast Asia. The recent development at FAO in support of IPM is the establishment of the Global IPM Facility, co-sponsored by UNDP, UNEP and the World Bank. The concept is in response to the UN Conference on Environment and Development, held at Rio de Janerio, Brazil in 1992, which assigned a central role for IPM in agriculture as part of "Agenda 21". The Facility will serve as a coordinating, consulting, advising and promoting agency for the advancement of IPM worldwide (Kogan, 1998).

## ORIGIN OF IPM CONCEPT

Basic tactics of IPM were proposed and used to protect crop plants against the ravages of pests long before the term was coined. In the absence of modern synthetic pesticides, crop protection specialists during late nineteenth and early twentieth centuries, relied on pest biology and cultural practices to propose multi tactical approaches, that could be considered as precursors of modern IPM systems. The idea of integrated control first appears to be conceived by Hoskins *et al.* (1939) when they said "biological and chemical control are considered as supplementing to one another or as the two edges of the same sword, nature's own balance provides the major part of the protection that is required for the successful pursuit of agriculture insecticides should be used so as to interfere with natural control of pests as little as possible". The credit for using the term 'integrated control' for the first time goes to Michelbacher and Bacon (1952), who while working on the control of codling moth, *Cydia pomonella* L., stressed "the importance of considering the entire entomological picture in developing a treatment for any particular pest. All efforts were directed towards developing an effective integrated control program of the important pests of walnut". Subsequently, Smith and Alien (1954) stated that "integrated control will utilize all the resources of ecology and give us the most permanent, satisfactory and economical insect control that is possible." Following this, it was the series of papers that established integrated control as a new trend in entomology. The integrated control was first defined by Stern *et al.* (1959) as "applied pest control, which combines and integrates biological and chemical control". This definition stood through late 1950s and early 1960s, but began to change soon to *Integrated Pest Management* in the early 1960s as the concept of pest management gained acceptance among crop protection specialists. The idea of managing insect pest populations was proposed by Geier and Clark (1961) who called this concept as "protective population management", which was later on shortened to "pest management" (Geier, 1966). By the mid-1970s both integrated control and pest management coexisted essentially as synonyms. However, a synthesis of two expressions had already become available when Smith and van den Bosch (1967) mentioned, "The determination of insect numbers is broadly under the influence of total agroecosystem and a background role of the principle elements is essential to integrated pest population management." It was, however, in 1972 when the term 'integrated pest management' was accepted by the scientific community after the publication of a report under the above title by the Council on Environmental

Quality (CEQ, 1972). In creating this synthesis between integrated control and pest management, no obvious attempts seemed to have been made to advance a new paradigm. Much of the debate had already taken place during 1960s and by then there was substantial agreement on the following issues (Kogan, 1998):

- 'Integration' means the harmonious use of multiple methods to control single pests as well as the impacts of multiple pests.
- 'Pests' are any organism detrimental to humans, including invertebrate and vertebrate animals, pathogens and weeds.
- 'Management' refers to a set of decision rules based on ecological principles and economic and social considerations. The backbone for the management of pests in an agricultural system is the concept of economic injury level (EIL).
- 'IPM' is a multidisciplinary endeavour.

## DEFINITIONS OF IPM

Since the first definition of integrated control (Stern *et al.*, 1959), there are over seventy-two definitions of IPM (Baweja and Kogan, 2002), issued by governments, research organisations, NGOs, and universities. Some assume that IPM will eliminate the use of crop protection products specially the chemical pesticides, which is most unlikely. Extreme views equating IPM with "pest free" farming will become increasingly marginalised and more balanced views will prevail. There is no reason not to support IPM as defined by the FAO International Code of Conduct on the Distribution and Use of Pesticides (Article 2). *Integrated Pest Management (IPM) means a pest management system that, in the context of the associated environment and the population dynamics of the pest species, utilises all suitable techniques and methods in as compatible a manner as possible and maintains the pest populations at levels below those causing economically unacceptable damage or loss* (FAO, 1967). It is not simply the juxtaposition or superimposition of two control techniques but the integration of all suitable management techniques with the natural regulating and limiting elements of the environment. According to National Academy of Sciences, IPM refers to an ecological approach in pest management in which all available necessary techniques are consolidated in a unified programme, so that pest populations can be managed in such a manner that economic damage is avoided and adverse side effects are minimized (NAS, 1969). Thus, IPM is the best combination of cultural, biological and chemical measures that provides the most cost effective, environmentally sound and socially acceptable method of managing diseases, insects, weeds and other pests. Therefore, an elementary principle of effective IPM is to develop strategies taking into account all relevant control tactics, and methods available locally. Experiences in southern Maharashtra show that the farmers are intelligent enough and evaluate the potential cost effectiveness of each alternative as well as the whole IPM strategy. This recognizes that the accountability for implementation of IPM ultimately rests with the farmer and others trying to control pests. They will only adopt and exploit IPM if it is seen to be practical and add value to their products.

Most of other contemporary definitions perpetuate the perception of an entomological bias in IPM because of the emphasis on pest populations and economic injury levels, of which the former is not always applicable to plant pathogens, and the latter is usually attached to the notion of an action threshold often incompatible with pathogen epidemiology or many weed management systems. Smith (1978) defined IPM as a multidiscipilinary ecological approach to the management of pest populations, which utilizes a variety of control tactics compatibly in a single coordinated pest management system. In its operation, integrated pest control is a multi-tactical approach that encourages the fullest use of natural mortality factors complemented when necessary by artificial means of pest management. In other words, IPM seeks to integrate multidisciplinary methodologies to develop pest management strategies that are practical, effective, economical and protective of both public health and the environment (Smith *et al.*, 1976). IPM has also been defined as a pest population management system that utilizes all suitable techniques in a compatible manner to reduce pest populations and maintain them at levels below those causing economic injury (Frisbie and Adkisson, 1985). Ray F. Smith and Perry Adkisson have been awarded the 1997 World Food Prize for their pioneering work in development and implementation of IPM concept.

## WHAT IS IPM?

IPM is a systematic approach to crop protection that uses increased information and improved decision-making paradigms to reduce purchased inputs and improve economic, social and environmental conditions on the farm and in society (Alien and Rajotte, 1990). IPM is a comprehensive approach to pest control that uses combined means to reduce the status of pests to tolerable levels while maintaining a quality environment (Pedigo, 1991). IPM is also defined as the intelligent selection and use of pest control tactics that will ensure favourable economical, ecological and sociological consequences (Luckman and Metcalf, 1994). IPM is a dynamic and constantly evolving approach to crop protection in which all the suitable management tactics and available surveillance and forecasting information are utilized to develop a holistic management programme as part of a sustainable crop production technology. Here it needs to be emphasized that the aim of future IPM programmes should not be restricted to mere efficient use of pesticides and product substitution (biorationals and botanicals in place of conventional insecticides), within an agricultural system that essentially remains unchanged. Rather, these programmes should aim at fundamental structural changes through a better understanding of ecological processes and synergy between crops (van Veldhuizen and Hiemstra, 1993). Kogan (1998) carried out a numerical analysis of various definitions spanning the last 35 years and found that most of the authors depended on the following issues to capture the essence of IPM concept:

- The appropriate selection of pest control methods, used singly or in combination;
- The economic benefits to growers and to society;
- The decision rules that guide the selection of the control action; and
- The need to consider impacts of multiple pests.

Taking into consideration all the above points and the current thought, Kogan (1998) put forth his definition: "IPM is a decision support system for the selection and use of pest control tactics, singly or harmoniously coordinated into a management strategy, based on cost/benefit analyses that take into account the interests of and impacts on producers, society and the environment."

IPM is the crop protection system, which best meets the requirements of sustainable development and sustainable agriculture. IPM is a component of Integrated Crop Management (ICM). ICM has been developed as a farming system to meet the requirements of long-term sustainability. It includes IPM and is a whole-farm strategy, which involves managing crops profitably, with respect for the environment, in ways, which suit local soil, climatic and economic conditions. It safeguards the farm's natural assets in the long term. It includes practices that avoid waste, enhance energy efficiency and minimise pollution. ICM is not a rigidly defined form of crop production but is a dynamic system, which adapts and makes sensible use of the latest research, technology, advice and experience.

Success of IPM requires three basic areas which includes; prevention, monitoring and timely intervention with need based pesticides with preference to bio-pesticides over the chemical pesticides.

## PREVENTION

It is an indirect measure and aims to reduce initial severity of pest infestation by way of removing inoculum. Many aspects of farm and crop management prevent the initial build-up of pest infestations and its secondary spread to adjoining crop and surrounding cropped areas. Prefer growing crops and varieties in appropriate locations where they fit to climate, soil and topography. Local conditions provides the crop with optimal growing conditions from the start which makes them strong enough to bear the injury to tolerable level. Avoid non locale crop.

### Crop Hygiene and Agronomic Practices

Mechanical and physical crop protection methods can be important in promoting good crop development, and prevent or minimise weed, disease and pest infestation. Traditional ploughing inverts the soil and buries crop residue and weeds before the preparation of a seed bed for the succeeding crop, which can also lead to increased erosion, so it should be combined with other conservation techniques such as the use of contour ploughing and ridging. Changes in soil disturbance, location of plant residue and weed ecology all influence the incidence of diseases and pests and should be taken into account in designing IPM programmes. Good crop hygiene is also important in reducing the build-up and carry-over of pest populations from one crop to another. Methods are often labour intensive (e.g. removal and destruction of crop residue), but may provide an essentially effective way of reducing the survival of some pests to the next season (e.g. in cotton, the carry-over of pink bollworm from one crop to another can be reduced by removing and destroying cotton trash well advance in sowing). Good fertiliser practice (INM) should be adopted to promote crop growth, but excessive use of nitrogen must be avoided—too much lush, vegetative growth encourages many diseases, insect pests (significantly proved in case of cotton) and weeds. Some of the agronomic practices which directly or indirectly influences the disease incidence and intensity has been listed below:

- Supply of water to the crop can enhance or reduce pest incidence. Flooding of some crops, particularly lowland rice, is important in checking weeds. However, flood irrigation can also adversely affect the survival of some soil-inhabiting natural enemies. In vegetables this can be lessened by growing the crop on ridges or raised beds, and should be taken into account in designing IPM systems.
- It is known that excess of nitrogen predisposes the host to rust and powdery mildew in wheat, blast in rice, tobacco mosaic, etc. Diseases like tomato wilt (*Fusarium oxysporum* f. sp. *lycopersici*), damping off (*Pythium* sp.) etc. are aggravated by low nitrogen. Excess of nitrogen attracts sucking pest, aphids in particular, which acts as vectors of many diseases.
- Application of potash and phosphate enhances the plant resistance against certain diseases. Application of K reduces the incidence of cotton wilt and stem rot in jute and rice. Application of superphosphate helps to overcome root weevil attack in rice crop. Application of potash, reduces the incidence of rice root weevil.
- Calcium deficiency predisposes tomato and pulses to *Fusarium* wilt.
- Deficiency of some trace elements also impairs plant resistance e.g. deficiency of zinc predisposes maize plants to downy mildew.
- Application of micronutrients like molybdenum and boron checks black vein of brassicae.
- *Fusarium* wilt of banana can be controlled by flooding the field. Flooding of rice nurseries helps in eliminating the attack of armyworm, *Spodoptera mauritia*.

There are many other instances where soil fertility or nutrient status plays a role in pest incidence. Faulty mechanical sowing may cause seed injury and thereby predispose it to attack by soil fungi. By delaying emergence, deep sowing prolongs the susceptible phase between germination and emergence and favours many disease and insect pests. So, sometimes shallow sowing favours the crop to escape disease infection. Sowing should always be as uniform as possible maintaining an optimum population per ha of that particular crop. Planting geometry affects plant density which is related to competition for available nutrients, moisture and sunlight and affects leaf wetness, etc. Plant nutrient status, interplant spacing, canopy structure, etc. affect pest behaviour in search of food, oviposition site, shelter and secondary spread. Plant density also affects natural enemies and results in greater pest control. *Nilaparvata lugens* incidence is always higher in closer plantings. Provision of alleys of 30 cm width after every 2-3 meters has proved beneficial in reducing pest incidence in endemic areas. Sometimes, the magnitude of spacing influences the incidence of insect pests and diseases.

- Seedling blight of groundnut (*Aspergillus niger*), soybean root rot (*Macrophomina phaseolina*) etc. may be reduced by shallow sowing.
- Blast of rice, sheath blight of rice, damping off, etc. can be reduced by wide spacing.
- *Verticillium* wilt of cotton, bacterial leaf blight of rice, tomato spotted wilt virus in groundnut, etc. can be checked by close spacing. Closer spacing or higher plant density in chickpea had higher incidence of *H. armigera.*
- Adoption of high seed rate in sorghum reduces shoot fly infestation.
- Nipping of leaves adjoining to grape bunches increases airflow preventing evelopment of *Botrytis* disease.

The non-availability of preferred host to adults certainly limits the future generation and aid in reduction of pest incidence. Some pest uses the weeds or the wild hosts as the means of their survival during the absence of the main crop. With the availability of crop and conducive climate the pest moves to the crop and sometimes appear in the empirical fashion. Therefore, proper weed management may check the perpetuation of many diseases/insect pests.

### Genetic Resistance

Selection of crop variety has always been a number one priority in crop protection, especially the growing of disease and pest resistant varieties. These may reduce the need for frequent treatments with crop protection products. Use of resistant varieties also encourages the survival of beneficial both in terms of microbes (fungal & bacterial) and insects. Developments in genetic engineering will increase the potential for developing novel opportunities and choices for pest resistant plants and herbicide tolerant crops as proved in case of Genetically Modified (GM) soybeans. Transgenic plants (e.g., Bt cotton ) offer a novel means of delivering biological agents, where insecticidal proteins are introduced genetically into the plant. The insect pest is killed only when it feeds on the plant and non-target organisms are unaffected but this particular scientific adventure needs further probing in terms of long term effectiveness and their residual effects on human beings as well as other fauna.

Growing different crops in a rotation helps in reducing the build-up of certain pests, especially those in the soil, such as root feeders, numerous fungal pathogens affecting the root system and nematodes. Rotations apart from reducing the weed problems increase the population of predators and parasites. Planting inter as well as cover crops increases the bio-diversity and helps in conservation of bio-agents in the field. In case of certain national emerging problems such as Cotton Leaf Curl Virus, alternative host crops (cucurbits, solanaceous vegetables and citrus orchards) should be avoided to possible extent.

### Habitat Management

Many natural enemy species require food sources in the form of pollen, nectar, or innocuous arthropods that are not present in particular crop habitats. These food requirements may be provided to support natural enemy populations by encouraging or deliberate development of certain wild vegetation habitats near plantings of the crop. Protection of natural habitats within the farm environment is recognized as a means of conserving many of the natural enemies of pests. Careful management of the margins of farm land, as well as growing tree crops or hedges, are particularly important because they provide habitat, cover and refuge for beneficial insects and other animals. In rice cropping systems, field bunds provide important refuges for predatory spiders which help control several important rice pests; and for snakes which help control rats. In case of cotton, growing of maize and cowpea on border increases the population of coccinellids which migrates to cotton in search of aphids and jassids and devour them.

**Trap Crops and Inter-cropping**

Small plantings of a susceptible or preferred crop may be established near a major crop to act as a 'trap'. After the pest has been attracted to the crop it is either treated with insecticides or ploughed under. It is intended for getting some return from an area, for example, when one crop is attacked by pests, the other escapes and comes up well. But sometimes, one component of mixed cropping directly inhibits or checks some pest(s) of the other crop. Sometimes a pest can be attracted away from a valuable sensitive crop by another crop which suffers less damage if attacked. In southern Maharashtra linseed is sown in rows every 10-15 m across chickpea fields to attract bollworms during critical periods of crop development, scattered tobacco crop attracts *Helicoverpa* on their growing shoots which can be nipped away. Traditionally, some farmers may sow different crops in alternate rows, or undersow a crop (e.g. maize) with a legume (e.g. beans) to help improve soil fertility and conserve beneficial bioagents. "Ashta" experience show that growing of *Setaria* as 10 row serve as live bird perch which attract the birds to predate on bollworms.

- Raising a crop of castor around chillies and tomatoes in citrus orchards for the control of fruit borer and sucking moths respectively.
- If *Crotolaria* is grown, it helps in checking the root knot nematodes. Eggs are hatched into larvae, but adults do not emerge out.
- Mixed cropping of marigold with tomato helps in reducing the nematode infestation.
- Mixed cropping of sorghum and tobacco checks tobacco wilt. Intercropping of pigeonpea with sorghum reduces the incidence of pigeon pea wilt (*Fusarium udum*).
- Mixed cropping of alfalfa and cocksfoot results in less incidence of alfalfa mosaic.

Time of sowing/harvesting: in cases, where the susceptible stage in the crop's life or infesting stage in the pest's life is brief, altering timings of sowing and harvesting can be effective as a control measure. Early sowing of chickpea (Oct., end) drastically reduces chances of occurrence of vascular wilt as well as *Ascochyta* blight disease.

- Cowpea wilt and wheat brown rust can be avoided by early sowing.
- Sugar beet damping off (*Rhizoctonia sp.*) and wheat "take all" disease can be controlled by late sowing.

If the crops are rotated, *i.e.*, the same crop is not grown successively on the same field, it aids in the control of pests by reducing population or breaking their life cycle. This is because the pest(s) of the preceding crop would not affect those of the following one. By the time the "cultivation of the crop" is repeated its pests would have perished for want of their host plants. Rotation should necessarily involve different kinds of crops, whose pests are not common.

- Lady's finger (bhindi) following a cotton crop will suffer from increased pest infestation because of pests common to both crops.
- A similar situation exists in areas of monoculture e.g., Thanjavur delta where rice is the main crop season after season.
- Crop rotation usually affects those insects, which have a limited host range and are relatively immobile in some stage of their development.
- Crop rotation is helpful in eradicating some soil borne diseases, specifically those are soil transient but not soil inhabiting (*Phoma* of Grapes). If the same crop is grown in the same field year after year, the pathogen is assured of its survival in soil especially in the crop debris. But crop rotation with unrelated plant species is detrimental to the survival of those pathogens e.g., vascular wilts.
- Crop rotation reduces the incidence of red rot of sugarcane, wilt of arhar (pigeon pea), wilt of pea and wheat mosaic, etc.
- Soil Amendments: Certain soil borne pests and diseases can be checked through incorporation of some amendments. Diseases like scab of potato (*Streptomyces scabies*), *Verticillium* wilts, wilt of pea (*Fusarium oxysponum* f.sp. *pisi* race-I), etc. are favoured by alkaline soil. Therefore, lowering of soil pH through application of elemental sulphur or gypsum reduces the incidence of these diseases.
- Club root of crucifers (*Plasmodiophora* sp.), bacterial wilt of potato (*Pseudomonas solanacearum*), cotton wilt (*Fusarium oxysporum* f. sp. *vasinfectum*) etc. are favoured by acidic soil. So, liming helps in checking these diseases.

In cultivated fields normal cultural practices enable addition of substantial quantities of organic matter in the form of crop residues. In addition to that, many farming practices such as green manuring, use of oil cakes, straw composting, etc. add organic matters to the soil. The decomposition of organic matter helps in alteration of physical, chemical and biotic conditions of the soil which reduces the inculum potential of certain pathogens.

- In "take all" disease of wheat, green manuring with mustard, rape or pea creates such antagonistic conditions which can destroy the pathogen.
- In potato scab, green manuring with soybean and pea gives good results.

- Potato black scurf (*Rhizoctonia solani*) can be checked by application of wheat straw compost.
- *Fusarium* wilt of banana can be checked by sugarcane residue compost.
- Nematodes can be controlled through use of neem cakes and FYM.

### Crop Monitoring

The aim is to determine WHEN and WHAT action is to be taken. Regular monitoring is crucial to effective pest management. An efficient monitoring programme can pay big dividends in lowering pest control costs. By detecting problems early, one can limit chemical inputs by treating at primary inoculum site and/or using reduced rates. It's usually not desirable or possible to examine every plant or square inch of ground. Standardised sampling should be used in the representative areas to gain enough information to guide decisions for an entire field or location. Management of any crop needs routine inspections to assess how well plants are growing and what actions need to be taken on cultivation's, pest and disease control. Monitoring for pests is an important part of the need to "walk" through a crop. Various tools, such as pheromone traps (*Helicoverpa* and PBW), diagnostics and forecasting systems (against apple scab disease) are available to assist in timing of management operations.

## INTERVENTION

The aim is to reduce the effects of economically damaging pest populations to acceptable levels. Mechanical, biological and chemical control measures may be applied individually or in combination, taking into consideration costs, benefits, timing, available labour force, machines/tools and control agents, as well as ecological and environmental effects. Some of the principal IPM intervention measures available for farmers to reduce the effects of pests include:

### Cultural and Physical Control

A number of cultural and physical techniques continue to be used in agriculture (e.g. weed control by manual methods or tractor cultivation; insect control by hand picking of egg masses or larvae; disease control by removing infected plant debris). Before including such methods in IPM recommendations their impact on yields and requirements for labour (family labour) inputs need to be critically assessed.

Dry fallowing is generally followed where other methods of disinfestations of soil pathogens are not economical. The field is kept fallow for a period of one season to kill the pathogen by starvation. Wet fallowing involves frequent irrigation during the fallow period. It is usually practised for some week. The main aim is to make pathogen germinate in the soil, which later dies due to lack of host plant. Wet fallowing reduces the pathogen population especially, of sclerotia, which retains viability in dry conditions for several years. It is also successful in reducing the population of *Pythium* and *Alternaria.* Flood fallowing is keeping the fallow land submerged. Under such condition the pathogens die due to lack of oxygen. Rotting of plant debris also releases the materials toxic to pathogens. Deep ploughing the hoeing help to bury resting propagules of pathogens present in soil or expose to harsh climate for inactivating as well as decay. Tillage operations tend to reduce soil pests by changing physical conditions of the soil, by eliminating the main or alternative host plants and by hastening the growth or increasing the vigour of crops. Ploughing also helps in reduction of pest inoculums. Disc ploughing does not open the furrows and, therefore, eggs/grubs are not exposed, to be picked up by predatory birds. However, the bullock drawn desi plough opens furrows and exposes the different stages of white grubs, which are eaten away by the friendly birds (predatory birds). Further, the ploughing with bullocks is generally started in the morning hours, when birds are awake and they are able to follow the track of the plough. On the other hand, the tractor ploughing is also done in the night when the birds are at rest. Some of the effective practices are as follows:

- In *Brassica* and millet downy mildew (*Peronospora* spp. and *Sclerospora graminicola*) and white rust (*Albugo candida*), oospores are harboured in the crop residues. Deep ploughing and soil inversion help in reducing the inoculum load of the pathogen.
- Incidence of foot rot of groundnut and chickpea (*Sclerotium rolfsii*) can be minimised with, deep ploughing which destroys sclerotia in the stubble.
- Soil tillage with repeated ploughing destroys the cysts of nematodes such as *Meloidogyne incognita.*

Sanitation and physical removal of inert plant materials, which are injurious to crop health is the key factor governing disease buildup. Removal of crop residues tends to kill pests like beetles and caterpillars that hibernate or pupate in plant debris. After the harvest, the leftover should be destroyed by deep burying in the soil. It has been successful in reducing the infesting pests, borers in particular (of the preceding crop) in order to protect the new one. Sanitary measures are more effective against pests (soil resident diseases), which are caused by high inoculums level at initial stage and have powerful secondary spread. Disease infected plants should be uprooted and burnt in case of viral diseases and other diseases, which have high potential secondary spread. But this is feasible only when the infection is sporadic.

Destruction of crop residues helps in reducing foot rot of groundnut and downy mildew of crucifers. Removal and destruction of infected plants check the secondary spread.

- Destruction of stubbles reduces the incidence of brown spot disease of rice caused by *Helminthosporium oryzae.*
- Deep burying of debris not only deprived the newly emerged nymphs of *Drosicha mangiferae* of their initial food and shelter but also exposed them to adverse conditions thus bringing their population to manageable level.
- Similarly caging of gin trash kill hibernating larvae/emerging adults of *Pectinophora gossypiella* in cotton at the same time allow conservation of emerging parasitoids from affected larvae.

- Black scurf (*Rhizoctonia solani*) of potato can be controlled by soil solarization. In summer months, the surface soil is exposed by light tillage/interculture and then covered by thin transparent polypropylene sheets. The heat, thus generated inside, kills many soil borne pests specially nematodes.

In case of trees, severely affected plant parts should be pruned and destroyed by deep burying. (e.g. citrus canker and scale insects). Tool contamination especially the pruners need to be avoided. During rainy season physical injury to foliar parts need to be avoided to reduce spread of bacterial diseases. Cutting knife is to be washed with formalin or disinfectant before cutting the fresh propagating materials. Composting of disease infested materials for leaf manure should be avoided. Decomposing organic matter acts as breeding sits for Rhinoceros beetles (*Oryctes rhinoceros*) in coconut gardens hence, maintenance of phytosanitary conditions helps in reducing the pest incidence, which injures plant to make way for fungal infection to be established.

Handpicking of egg masses, larvae or nymphs and sluggish adults is sometimes practicable. The egg masses of rice stem borer and groundnut red hairy caterpillar, gregarious larvae of *Amascta albistriga* and *Spodoptera litura* in their early stages, hairy caterpillars, snake gourd semilooper in their grown-up stages, the adults of *Epilachna* beetles on brinjal and cucurbits can be easily handpicked and killed. Insects like leafhoppers, ear head bugs and grasshoppers can be netted and killed. Adults of Rhinoceros beetle are hooked out from the coconut crowns by means of iron hook. Passing a rope across a rice crop is sometimes done so as to dislodge the case worms over the standing water, which is then drained out to collect and kill the pest.

Infection of *Pseudomonas sőlanacearum* in potato and banana and that of *Colletotrichum falcatum* in sugarcane can be significantly prevented adopting above-mentioned sanitary measures.

- Seed solarisation during the month of May and June is also effective in the smut of wheat (*Ustilago* sp.).

- In case of pigeon pea shaking of plants results in dislodging of overgrown larvae which in turn are collected for use in preparation HaNPV.

- In case of orchards one feet channels filled with water provides significant protection against ants and other beetles which not only cause the physical damage but also acts as vectors for viral disease.

Use of straw mulch or yellow polythene mulch repels certain insects, which are potential vectors of some viral diseases and thus helps in checking insect pests as well as viral diseases. Under balanced nutrition, a crop attains maximum resistance against pests and diseases. Due to excess application of nitrogenous fertilizers, plant foliage becomes sappy and it attracts insect pests. Adequate irrigation and proper drainage reduce the disease occurrence. In case of vegetable crops, ridge planting is helpful to avoid some diseases. Nursery bed should also be raised. Tomato leaf curl can be controlled by repelling white flies with plastic mulching. Trash mulching or earthing up a month or two after planting minimises shoot borer attack in sugarcane.

**Pheromones**

The use of pheromones has been instrumental in increasing the effectiveness of both monitoring insect populations and in providing adequate information to enable implementation of cost effective control. Since the discovery of pheromones, a term first used by Karlson and Luscher 1959, a multiplicity of uses has been found for them involving monitoring and control although no significant applied use was achieved for monitoring until the mid 1970's (Lewes, 1975). As with any management program it is important that knowledge of those factors hoping to be controlled is known. With regards to insect pest management, the population dynamics of a given species may not be precisely known, but long term monitoring can help to elucidate patterns in population life cycles. These patterns can then be combined with the known biology of the insect to define the parameters of an effective control campaign (Norton & Mumford, 1993). Over the last two or so decades, information collected from insect monitoring has led to the production of pest forecasting systems that allow farmers to begin spraying at precise time intervals for maximum impact. In the agricultural sense spraying may only be effective for a short period, for example when an insect stage is external on a crop plant, if this period is missed, and the larvae burrows into the plant then spraying is not cost effective. This short period when spraying should take place is termed the "open window." The use of pheromones in control is similar to methods used for monitoring but involves mechanisms which either kill the insect directly on contact with the trap, or serve to disseminate a chemical or pathogen which later renders them and, depending on the method others they contact, dead. The other method is mate disruption which involves the release of large amounts of synthetic female sex pheromone causing males to become confused and unable to locate females. Development and availability of pheromones offers interesting new possibilities for the farmer. Besides selective trapping techniques to monitor the movement of pests or changes in populations during the season, pheromones are also used in "lure and kill" strategies to attract the pest to localised insecticide deposits and reduce the need for overall crop spraying (as demonstrated against PBW in Punjab). Mating disruption to delay or reduce the population has been successfully demonstrated against PBW in Abohar area of Punjab.

**Biopesticides**

Biopesticides include all types of agents and products derived from biotic sources, with potential for the control of phytophagous insects, plant diseases and pests of public health importance. These products have been used for pest and disease control for many centuries, but it has been only in recent years that greater attention has been directed toward the discovery and development of natural products, phyto-chemicals, microbial control agents, antagonistic agents, genetically modified organisms, hormones, pheromones, kairomones and other agents of biological origin. In recent years we have seen a flurry of research activity in the area of genetic engineering of crop plants, human pests and vectors of diseases as well as that of currently available biological control agents. Thus, we are seeing a significant increase in fundamental and applied research activity on the development and potential use of biopesticides in pest management programs. Research groups in universities, national governments, research centers and institutes, international agencies and industrial firms have carried out these researches.

Currently, considerable amount of research is carried out in south and southeast Asia with emphasis on screening and development of plant products, phytochemicals and natural products. South and southeast Asia is blessed with great diversity of plants and biodiversity of microbes and it is here that the field of homeopathic medicine relying on herbal products is relatively advanced in contrast to other regions. With a great wealth of knowledge on herbal medicine, it is prudent to look for bioactive materials derived from plants that may have medicinal properties. In this regard, SE Asia and the Asia Pacific Region is in the forefront of this technology. In addition to identifying and evaluating plant products for pest control, a number of biotic agents such as bacteria amenable to fermentation technology have been developed and promoted for pest control. The area of antagonistic bacteria and fungal toxins is also explored for pest control properties and potential. Molecular and genetic techniques for modification and alteration of plants and pest targets have been found useful in some cases.

**Biological Control**

Biological control is use of a specially chosen living organism to control a particular pest. This chosen organism can be a predator, parasite, or disease, which will manage the harmful insect. It is a form of manipulating nature to increase a desired effect. A complete Biological Control program may range from choosing a pesticide which will be least harmful to beneficial insects, to raising and releasing one insect to have it attack another, almost like a 'living insecticide.' Cost effective technologies for a number of bioagents, such as the egg parasitoids *Trichogramma chilonis, T. japonicum,* larval parasitoids *Bracon hebetor, B. brevicornis, Goniozus* sp., *Brachymeria* sp, and predators *viz., Chrysoperla carnea, Chrysoperla incarnata, Coccinella septumpunctata, Menochilus sexmaculatus* have been standardised and are now available commercially. Apart from these entomopathogenic fungi *Metarhizium anisopliae, Beauveria bassiana, Nomuraea rileyi*, etc., had been widely used against several lepidopterous pests and specific success has been achieved in case of white grub. Viral pathogens, the Gv and NPV are now commerciallly available for the management of key pests such as *Spilosoma obliqua, Amsacta albistriga, Spodoptera litura, Helicoverpa armigera.* Commercial preparations of *Bacillus thuringiensis* has become popular for the management of *Plutella xylostella* and *H. armigera.* The bioagents and microbial pesticides (Bt., fungal and baculoviruses) have been widely used in the management of pests and avoiding the development of resistance. Entomopathogenic fungi and bacteria paralyse or kill their hosts by adversely affecting growth and development of host insects. These pathogens are now commercially available. However, their marketability is very negligible with total consumption of only 15-20 metric tonnes against the potential of 30 million tonnes. The production of bio-pesticides in the country is not even sufficient to cover 2% area under cultivation of single crop. Nevertheless, about 10-15% growth rate is envisaged for Bt. production in the country. There is sudden spurt and currently more than 300 units involved in production of various quality bio-control agents.

However, the potential of the bio-agents had not been exploited to the core. The natural enemies would keep 60% of the insect pest populations in nature under check, if there is no intervention by chemical pesticides. Conservation and augmentation of bioagents hence is of significance in IPM. The major constraints for promotion of the bioagents include the difficulties in mass rearing technologies, temporal variations, the shorter life span and delay in transit which often over runs the stage against which the bioagent is effective. Our research should aim to address these to tap their potential.

## Botanical and Chemical Control

Botanicals sources of secondary metabolites or allelochemicals that provide for the fundamental or physiological or biochemical process of the plant. As many as 2,121 plant species have been reported to possess pest control properties, 1,005 species have insecticidal, 384 antifeedants, 297 repellants, 27 attractants and 31 growth inhibiting properties but not many could find their way to commercialization. A number of plants such as Neem (*Azadiracta indica*), Pithraj or bullock's heart (*Amoora reticulate*), Mahua (*Madhuca longifolia*), Karanj (*Pongamia glabra*), Pinnae (*Calophyllum inophyllum*), Besharam (*Ipomoea sepiaria*), Gohkru (*Tribulus terristis*), Gandhigrass (*Parthenium hysterophorus*), Haldi (*Curcuma longa*), Sweetflag (*Acorus calamus*), Kusum (*Schleichera trijuga*), Custardapple (*Annona squamosa*), Lantana (*Lantana kamara*), Periwinkle (*Vinca rosea*), Garlic (*Allium sativum*), *Artemisia absinthium*, citrus grass (*Cymbopogan citratus*), Dhatura (*Dhatura metal*) *Cassica auriculata* and Kolingi (*Tephrosia purpurea*) have pesticidal properties. Amongst the botanical pesticides, 6 plants namely Neem, Pongamia, Cymbopogan, Annona, Chrysenthemum, Tobacco have been utilized and to some little extent poison vine or tuba root (*Derris elliptica*) as a source of Rotenone and Notchi (*Vitex negundo*) as fungicide have also been in use as botanical pesticides, though mostly in traditional pest control. Pure tri-terpenoids from neem oil has great potential as antifungal against *Dreschlera oryzae*, *F. oxysporum* and *Alternaria tenuis*. However, only the products based on Azadirachtin, Cymbopogon, Pyrethrum and Nicotine (currently banned for domestic use) are registered with Central Insecticides Board & Registration Committee. Around 735 botanical pesticide products from various companies stand registered and these include 443 Azadirachtin based, 290 Pyrethrum based and 1 Cymbopogan based products. In case of cruciferous vegetables crops the soap water of karanj soaps have proved significant over other chemical sprays. Other plants such as oscimum, melia, mahua, and calotropis are being explored for their pesticidal properties.

Insecticides formed the key tools for the management of pests and diseases over the years. Their misuse and abuse although incited several environmental hazards, the insecticides still continue to play a major role in all pest management programmes, as there is no alternative to compete their potent toxicity and yet times of emergency. However, with the growing concern about their ill effects and policies to promote IPM with bio-rational methods, their use would be reduced considerably in the years to come. Nevertheless, the development of new compounds, combination of two or more compounds is on the anvil to counteract the problems of resistance and resurgence of the pests. The concept of IPM needs a drastic reduction in the pesticide use and/or compounds that are compatible with bio-agents to sustain production with out degrading the ecological resource base.

**Decision Support and Area-wide Management Systems**

Farmers need assistance in interpreting pest monitoring data. Simple "expert systems" can be designed and made available to farmers in a range of ways, including simple pegboards or charts, special booklets, radio and television programmes or more advanced aids such as prediction models and computer-based systems (available for cotton, rice and wheat in USA). Development and provision of up-to-date information is a key factor enabling farmers to implement IPM programmes. IPM often requires collaborative decisions within a national or more localised area to provide effective control of pests. Some of these decisions need to be taken centrally by governments in relation to restriction of pest and infested movement through implementation of quarantine regulations and legislation. There should be adequate provision and training of advisory services. Establishment of resistance management strategies against highly mobile pests and diseases on major crop systems is the need of hour. Geographical Information Systems (GIS) and remote sensing techniques can also assist in implementation of area-wide management.

## CONCLUSION

The IPM Initiative will provide sustainable strategies by providing with pest control tools including chemical pesticides, biological control products or cultural tactics to replace agricultural chemicals which are under regulatory consideration; and by providing biologically-based and other sustainable strategies (genetic and cultural methods) for management of existing and emerging new pests in changing cropping systems. IPM approach of agriculture preserves biodiversity, maintains soil fertility and water purity, conserves and improves the chemical, physical and biological qualities of the soil, recycles natural resources and conserves energy. Application of proven IPM technology has increased the yield over the traditional calendar based chemical management. This has not only improved the socio-economic structure of the farming community but has also helped in saving of the environment from being polluted. In such fields, the increase in population of predators and parasitoids has been observed which is a positive trend of restoration of natural defense mechanism of the concerned agro ecosystem. Research work done by some of our major partners viz. NCIPM, DRR, PAU, GAU, TNAU, etc. have successfully demonstrated the effectiveness and compatibility of IPM with existing agricultural practices in some crops which is being adopted by the farmers in large areas. The principles of IPM are essential to sustainability of agricultural production systems and the priorities should take care of application of technologies to management of agroecosystems to maximize and planning of biological based technology (BBT) and inputs such as agrochemical while reducing problems of soil and water pollution. Decision support software needs to be developed so as to allow IPM practitioners to estimate cost/benefit for a variety of management inputs and examine profitability of a system. Genetically engineering to enhance potentiality of live modified organisms (LMO) to increase productivity by reducing damage due to pest (insects, diseases & weeds). Current examples include Bt cotton, Bt corn, glyphosate-resistant soybeans and transgenic wheat. Shifting of pest management strategies from unilateral control of pests with chemical pesticides to integrated methods that emphasize inspections and problem identification, with sanitation, traps, and other non-chemical controls employed to regulate pests.

To establish an integrated pest management program, the following basic guidelines should be followed.

- Understand the biology of the crop and identify the key pests, know their biology, recognize the damage they inflict, and evaluate their economic status.
- Identify the key environmental factors that affects pest and potential pest species in the ecosystem.
- Consider concepts, methods and materials that individually or in combination, will help to permanently suppress pest.
- Anticipate unforeseen developments and move with caution to face the changes that can occur within it.
- Seek the weak links in the lifecycle of the key pest species, and direct control practices as narrowly as possible at these weak links. Avoid broad impact on the resource ecosystem and consider and develop methods, which preserve, complement and augment the biotic and physical mortality factors that characterize the ecosystem, and
- Diversify the ecosystem.

Implementation of IPM programs is essential to economical and sustainable production of ecologically safe food supply while minimizing hazards of environmental pollution that could threaten entire ecosystems. To make the transition from chemically-based to ecologically-based pest management strategies, production and processing systems must be aggressive. Only through enhancement of research and education safety and profitability of food can be assured, and unique opportunity exists to bring great benefits to both agricultural and environment through IPM. Successful IPM implementation has three essential components: applicable research results, a policy change and a farmer participatory programme. Numerous IPM programmes have been implemented however, the successful implementation of IPM like "Ashta" has added a new dimension, not only to IPM but to extension in general. The IPM programs stress the responsibility of farmers for diagnosing pest problems and for participating in the development of solutions with their own means.

## REFERENCES

Annonymous. Annual Report, National Centre for IPM, (NCIPM), LBS Building, IARI Campus, New Delhi -110 012.

Ayyar, T. V. R. 1938. *Handbook of Economic Entomology for South India.* Government Press, Madras, India.

Bajwa, W. I. and Kogan, M. 2002. *Compendium of IPM Definitions* (CID)- *What is IPM and how is it defined in the Worldwide Literature*? IPPC Publication No. 998, Integrated Plant Protection Center (IPPC), Oregon State University, Corvallis, OR 97331, USA.

Bramble, B. J. 1989. An environmentalist's view of pest management and the green revolution. *Trop. Pest Mgt.*, **35**(3): 228-230.

Chakraborty, T . and Mallick, R. B. 1995. Concept of Sustainability in Agriculture Under Indian Context—Major Issues and Resource Recycling. *In*: M. K. Dasgupta, D. C. Ghosh, D. Das Gupta, D. K. Majumdar, G. N. Chattopadhyay, P. K. Ganguli, P. S. Munsi, and D. Bhattacharya (eds.), *Proceedings National Symposium on Sustainable Agriculture in Sub Humid Zone* (Mar. 1995). Visva-Bharati Birbhum India: Palli-Siksha Bhavana (Institute of Agriculture), pp. 12-19.

Dhaliwal, G. S. and Pathak, M. D. 1993. Pesticides in the developing world: A book in bane. *In*: G. S. Dhaliwal and B. Singh (eds.), *Pesticides: Their Ecological Impact in Developing Countries.* Commonwealth Publishers, New Delhi, India, pp. 1-29.

Herzog, D. C. and J. E. Funderburk. 1986. Ecological bases for habitat management and pest cultural control. *In*: M. Kogan (ed.), *Ecological Theory and Integrated Pest Management Practice.* John Wiley and Sons, New York, pp. 217-250.

Hrubovcak, J., Vasavada, U. and Aldy, J. E. 1999. *Green Technologies for a More Sustainable Agriculture*, U.S. Dept. of Agriculture, Economic Research Service, Washington DC.

Jayaraj, S. 1988. Accentuation of insect and mite problems in the changing agricultural scenario in India: An overview. National Seminar in changing pest situation in current agriculture scenario of India. July 14-16, 1988. IARI, New Delhi. India.

Mehrotra, R. S. 1980. Plant Pathology, 770 pp. 3. Rangaswamy, G. (1972): Diseases of crop Plants in India, 504 pp.

Park J. and Seaton, R. A. F. 1996. Integrative research and sustainable agriculture. *Agricultural Systems,* **50**(1): 81-100.

Piemental, D. 1977. Ecological basis of insect pests and weed problems. *In*: J. M. Cherrett and G. R. Sagar (eds.), *Origin of Pest Parasite, Disease and Weed Problems.* Blackwell Scientific Publications, Oxford, U.K., pp. 3-31.

Pradhan, S. 1983. Agricultural Entomology of Pest Control. Indian Council of Agricultural Research, New Delhi, India.

Rangaswamy, G. 1972. *Diseases of Crop Plants in India*, p. 504.

Roy, K. C., Sen, R. K., Tisdell, C. A. and International Institute for Development Studies 1996. *Environment and Sustainable Agricultural Development: Concepts, General Issues, Constraints and Strategies.* International Institute for Development Studies; New Age International, Calcutta; New Delhi.

Singh, R. S. 1984. *Introduction to Principles of Plant Pathology,* 3rd Edition, p. 533.

Singh, S. 1986. Plant Protecton in India. *In*: G. S. Venkataramana (ed.) *Plant Protection in the Year AD. 2000.* Indian National Science Academy, New Delhi, India, pp. 1-9.

Smith, R. I., Apple, J. L. and Bottrell, D. G. 1976. The origins of integrated pest management concepts for agricultural crops. *In*: J. L. Apple and R. F. Smith (eds.), *Integrated Pest Management.* Plenum Press, New York, USA, pp. 1-16.

# Molecular Markers and their Application in Breeding Crops for Pest Resistance

T. Mohapatra, Anushri Varshney and R. P. Sharma

## INTRODUCTION

Co-evolution of host plants and their pests is a continuous process. The host evolution in the nature is relatively slower than that of its pests. In this race, therefore, the host often loses out and thus remains in a disadvantageous position. In a few cases, the host somehow succeeds in managing to protect itself by evolving newer genetic mechanisms, but this happens at the cost of productivity. Weedy traits co-evolve with the host resistance/tolerance for imparting greater adaptability and thus increased fitness for survival, although with a penalty on yield performance. Plant breeders have been striving to improve crop productivity simultaneously by increasing yield potential and by reducing the losses due to pests through conventional means. With the development and use of novel biotechnological tools and techniques now available to the breeders, this process of developing high yielding and stable crop varieties with pest resistance is being greatly facilitated. One such area is the use of molecular markers. The objective of this brief review is to describe the important molecular markers and highlight their applications in breeding crop plants for pest resistance with specific examples.

## MOLECULAR MARKERS

Molecular markers can be defined as the differences in the nucleotide sequence of DNA at corresponding sites on the homologous chromosomes that follow a simple Mendelian pattern of inheritance. These differences are detected by employing various techniques such as Southern blot hybridization, Polymerase Chain Reaction (PCR) and DNA sequencing. Majority of the markers in use today are based on PCR. Depending on the method of detection of the sequence variation, the molecular markers have been given different names. The more important and frequently used molecular markers are described here.

### Restriction Fragment Length Polymorphisms (RFLP)

RFLP is the first molecular marker that was developed by Botstein *et al.*, (1980). It employs restriction enzymes that cut genomic DNA molecules at specific nucleotide sequences (restriction sites), thereby yielding variable size DNA fragments. The genomic DNA fragments thus generated are separated by electrophoresis and

*National Research Centre on Plant Biotechnology, I.A.R.I, New Delhi- 110 012, India.*

transferred to nitrocellulose or nylon filter (Southern, 1975). The filter-immobilized DNA is allowed to hybridize to radioactively labelled probe DNA. Through *X*-ray autoradiography, the hybridizing fragments are detected. The filter is placed against photographic film, where radioisotope disintegration from the probe results in visible bands. Variation in the position of the bands revealing the differences in the size of the hybridizing fragments is considered polymorphic. RFLP is a co-dominant marker in which the probes are usually small (500 to 3000 bp), cloned genomic or cDNA fragments. RFLP markers are highly reproducible and thus very robust. In the first decade of the use of molecular markers in plants, RFLP predominated. Even today, RFLP remains the most informative marker in comparative mapping of plant genomes. However, due to certain constraints such as low amenability to automation, requirement of larger amount of DNA per assay, use of radioisotopes, greater demand of time and labour, etc., RFLP markers are currently not being used so frequently in gene mapping and marker assisted selection programmes.

### Sequence Tagged Sites (STS)

This marker class was first conceived and used in human genome mapping (Olson *et al.*, 1989) and has been recently included in genome mapping in plants. STS markers are generated by an unmodified PCR. The primers are designed based on the sequence of cDNA (expressed sequence tags, EST), random genomic DNA and ends of large genomic DNA fragment cloned in cosmid, lambda or artificial chromosomes. The STS marker system has all the advantages of PCR technique. A limitation of STS is that considerable effort and time are needed to generate DNA sequence data for designing suitable primers. Besides, the fragments amplified by the primers may not show length variation between individuals. This problem however, is circumvented by restriction digestion of the PCR products, which detects polymorphism in the target site of a restriction enzyme internal to the two primer binding sites. This modification has led to a new marker system called cleaved amplified polymorphic sequence (CAPS, Koniecyzn and Ausubel, 1993). STS markers are considered robust. When these are based on gene sequences or ESTs, one directly deals with the expressed component of the genome, thereby completely ignoring the unexpressed repetitive sequences. Large number of EST databases available in the public domain can be used to design STS markers for simultaneous use in mapping and identification of candidates for the target gene(s) for pest resistance.

### Random Amplified Polymorphic DNA (RAPD)

RAPD is a dominant marker based on polymerase chain reaction (PCR). It employs a single decamer primer of arbitrary sequence, which is annealed to the template DNA typically at 37° C (Williams *et al.*, 1990). The variation in RAPD profile is in the form of presence or absence of a band resulting from variation in primer binding sites. This marker system requires less amount of DNA per assay. Being based on random primers, it does not need prior knowledge of the sequence of the genomes. A large number of such primers are commercially available that work across organisms starting from bacteria to human. RAPD marker is technically less demanding, and thus can be routinely used in a small laboratory set up by plant breeders/plant protection specialists with a little exposure to molecular tools and techniques. A major limitation of this marker system is non-reproducibility due to low annealing temperature. However, utility of a desired RAPD marker can be increased by sequencing its termini and designing longer primers for specific amplification of DNA (Paran and Michelmore, 1993). Such markers have been named as sequenced characterized amplified regions (SCARs).

### Sequence Tagged Microsatellite Sites (STMS)

Simple sequence repeats (SSR) or microsatellites are tandem repeats of mono-, di-, tri-, tetra- and penta-nucleotide units dispersed throughout the genome. These are ubiquitous in eukaryotes. These have been identified and characterized in many plant genomes including rice, wheat, barley, chickpea, soybean and *Brassica*. The frequency of repeats longer than 20 bp has been estimated to occur every 33 kb in plants. SSR polymorphism reflects variation in the number of repeat units in a defined region of the genome. Nucleotide sequence flanking the repeat is used to design primers to amplify different number of repeat units in different varieties. These primers are very useful for rapid and accurate detection of polymorphic loci and the information could be used for developing a physical map based on these sequence tags. This type of polymorphism is highly reproducible. STMS markers are codominant. These markers can be developed from the EST sequences and thus used to assay the expressed regions of the genome. Development of STMS markers is time and labour intensive since it requires large scale sequencing for discovery of microsatellites and their unique flanking sequences. Cross-species transfer of STMS that has been demonstrated in few cases may allow the use of such markers available in a closely related species without putting any effort in their development.

### Amplified Fragment Length Polymorphism (AFLP)

The AFLP markers are generated by selective amplification of DNA fragments obtained by restriction enzyme digestion (Vos *et al.*, 1995). High molecular weight DNA is digested by two restriction enzymes, one hexacutter (e.g. EcoRI) and one tetra cutter (e.g. Mse I). Adapter molecules are ligated to the ends of DNA fragments. Two primers possessing sequence complementarily to the adapter as well as few extra random nucleotides at their 3' ends are used for selective amplification of fragments employing PCR. The primers are labelled either by radioisotope or fluorescent dye so that the amplified products separated on sequencing gels/capillaries can be visualised by autoradiography or by laser based scanning in an automated fragment analysis system. Aletrnately the products can be separated even using ordinary Polyacrylamide Gei Electrophoresis (PAGE) and visualized by silver staining. Maximum number of amplified products is obtained as a single reaction in AFLP among all the DNA profiling systems. This increases the probability of detecting polymorphism many folds. The technique is, at present, lengthier and costlier than other PCR based techniques. It requires good quality DNA for ensuring complete digestion by enzymes. Partial digestion of DNA results in non-reproducible variation in DNA profiles. AFLP requires significant technical skills, laboratory facilities and also financial resources.

### Single/Simple Nucleotide Polymorphism (SNP)

Polymorphism observed between individuals/varieties may arise due to deletion/addition of multiple bases, or due to single nucleotide substitution. The detection of such variation has led to the development of a new sequence based molecular marker called single/simple nucleotide polymorphism (SNP; Brookes, 1999). SNPs are abundant in plant genomes. For instance, in maize, there has reported one SNP per every 48 base pairs in the 3' untranslated regions whereas in the coding regions its rate of occurrence is lower (one in every 130 base pairs). In rice, the rate of SNP is lower than in maize. The SNP markers are being used for genotyping human populations for certain genetic diseases. The cost of developing SNPs is very high, since for each locus, DNA has to be sequenced and suitable PCR primers designed. The primers must then be used to amplify the corresponding fragment from all other possible genotypes. These fragments must then be sequenced and the sequences compared with one another to determine the SNPs for each haplotype. The term 'haplotype' is used in the context of SNPs instead of the term 'allele'. There are a number of methods for identifying SNPs within a genetic locus namely direct sequencing, single-strand conformation polymorphism (SSCP), chemical cleavage of mismatches (CCM), enzyme mismatch cleavage (EMC) etc. Detection and assay of SNP has been automated that allows a large-scale genotyping in a far shorter period than the other markers.

## MOLECULAR MAPPING OF GENES FOR PEST RESISTANCE

Mapping and tagging of the genes conferring resistance on the host plant against pathogens, nematodes and insect pests is a prerequisite for their marker-assisted transfer to desired genetic backgrounds. Host plant resistance to the pests can be monogenic or polygenic. Molecular markers have been used for mapping genes for both monogenic and polygenic resistance. For mapping monogenic resistance, three approaches are being employed: (*i*) use of markers selected from a complete genome map and study of their co-segregation with the trait in a segregating population, (*ii*) use of random unmapped markers to differentiate near isogenic lines followed by validation of marker trait linkage in a segregating population, and (*iii*) use of random markers to differentiate two DNA bulks made from phenotypically different segregants identified in a mapping population followed by confirmation of linkage using the individual plants of the population. The first method is the most direct but needs a complete linkage map. The second method needs a pair of near isogenic lines, which have to be generated. This requires several years/seasons. The last method is considered fastest. Although RAPD markers were first used in conjunction with bulked segregant analysis (BSA) of a F2 mapping population, AFLP is more commonly being used in the recent years. Most of the genes for monogenic traits have been mapped using the third approach in crop plants. Reports on mapping of genes for qualitative pest resistance using different molecular markers during the last five years are listed in Table 3.1.

Polygenic pest resistance shows continuous variation. The individual genes controlling the expression of quantitative traits are called Quantitative Trait Loci (QTL). QTL with relatively strong effects are good targets for marker-assisted selection especially if the trait is difficult to measure. Many QTL have relatively small effects.

**TABLE 3.1:** RECENT REPORTS ON MOLECULAR MAPPING OF GENES FOR PEST RESISTANCE IN CROP PLANTS

1. DISEASE RESISTANCE

| *Crop* | *Pathogen/Trait* | *Gene/QTL* | *Marker(s)* | *Reference* |
|---|---|---|---|---|
| Rice | *Sclerotium oryzae* | — | AFLP, STMS | Ni *et al.* (2001) |
| | *Pyricularia grisea* | QTL | RFLP | Tabien *et al.* (2002) |
| | | Pi-b, Pi-k, Pi-ta | STMS | Fjellstrom *et al.* (2004) |
| | *Rhizoctonia solani* | Rsb1 | AFLP | Che *et al.* (2003) |
| Wheat | Yellow rust | YrMoro | AFLP-STS | Smith *et al.* (2002) |
| | | Yr5 | RGA | Yan *et al.* (2003) |
| | Leaf rust | Lr3 | EST | Danna *et al.* (2002) |
| | Powdery mildew | Pm24 | AFLP, STMS | Huang *et al.* (2000) |
| | | Pm22 | AFLP, STMS | Singrun *et al.* (2003) |
| | | MlG | SSR | Xie *et al.* (2003) |
| | Karnal bunt | — | STMS | Singh *et al.* (2003) |
| | *Fusarium* head blight | QTL | AFLP-STS | Guo *et al.* (2003) |
| | | QTL | RFLP, AFLP | Gervais *et al.* (2003) |
| | *Septoria tritici* blotch | QTL | STMS, AFLP | Erimsen *et al.* (2003) |
| | | Stb2, Stb3 | STMS | Adhikari *et al.* (2004) |
| | Tan spot | Tsn1 | AFLP | Haen *et al.* (2004) |
| Barley | *Cochliobolus sativus* | Vhv1 | AFLP | Zhong *et al.* (2002) |
| | *Pyrenophora graminea* | QTL | — | Arru *et al.* (2003) |
| | *Fusarium* head blight | QTL | RFLP, STMS, AFLP | Dahleen *et al.* (2003) |
| | BaMMV and BaYMV | Rym14 | AFLP-STS | Ruge *et al.* (2003) |
| | *Puccinia hordei* | Rph15 | AFLP-STS | Weerasena *et al.* (2004) |
| Maize | Sugarcane Mosaic Virus | Scmv1, Scmv2 | RGA-CAPS | Quint *et al.* (2002) |
| | | Scmv1, Scmv2 | AFLP, SSR | DuBle *et al.* (2003) |
| | Grey leaf spot | QTL | STMS | Gordon *et al.* (2004) |
| | Southern corn rust | RppQ | AFLP, STMS | Chen *et al.* (2004) |
| Rye | Rust | Lr26<br>Sr31<br>Yr9<br>SrR | AFLP, RGA, STS | Mago *et al.* (2002) |
| Sugar-cane | Brown rust | Bru1 | AFLP | Asnaghi *et al.* (2004) |
| Lentil | *Colletotricum truncatum* | LCt-2 | RAPD, AFLP | Tullu *et al.* (2003) |
| Pea | Seed borne mosaic virus | Sbm1 | cDNA-AFLP-EST | Gao *et al.* (2004) |
| Common bean | Angular leaf spot | — | AFLP-SCAR | Mahuku *et al.* (2004) |
| | Bean rust | Ur7 | RAPD | Park *et al.* (2003) |
| Soybean | Tobacco ringspot virus | QTL | STMS | Fasoula *et al.* (2003) |
| | *Phytophthora sojae* | Rps8 | STMS, RFLP | Burnham *et al.* (2003) |

| | | | | |
|---|---|---|---|---|
| Brassica | *Plasmodiophora brassicae* | Pb-Bn1, QTL | — | Dauleux *et al.* (2000) |
| | *Plasmodiophora brassicae* | CRb | AFLP-SCAR-CAPS | Piao *et al.* (2004) |
| | *Phoma lingum* | — | AFLP-STS | Plieske and Struss (2001) |
| | *Sclerotinia sclerotiorum* | | QTL RFLP, AFLP, SSR, RAPD | Zhao and Meng (2003) |
| | Turnip mosaic virus | TuRB03 | AFLP | Hughes *et al.* (2003) |
| | *Albugo candida* | Ac2(t) | CAPS, AFLP | Varshny *et al.* (2004) |
| Tomato | *Oidium lycopersicum* | Ol-1 | RFLP, RAPD, SCAR | Huang *et al.* (2000) |
| | *Alternaria solani* | QTL | RFLP, RGA | Foolad *et al.* (2002) |
| | Tomato mosaic virus | Tm-2 | RAPD-SCAR | Sobir *et al.* (2000) |
| Potato | Potato virus X | Nb | AFLP | Marano *et al.* (2002) |
| Pepper | Potato virus Y | Pvr4 | RAPD, SCAR | Andres-Arnado *et al.* (2002) |
| | *Xanthomonas campestris* pv *vesicatoria* | Bs3 | AFLP-STS | Pierre *et al.* (2000) |
| Apple | *Venturia inaequalis* | Vf | AFLP, SCAR | Xu *et al.* (2001) |
| | | | AFLP-SCAR | Huaracha *et al.* (2004) |
| | Powdery mildew | Pl-w | AFLP-SCAR | Evans and James (2003) |
| Apricot | Plum pox virus | — | AFLP, SSR | Vilanova *et al.* (2003) |
| Banana | Banana Streak Virus | — | AFLP | Lheureux *et al.* (2003) |
| Grape | Powdery mildew | Run1 | AFLP | Pauquet *et al.* (2001) |
| Cassava | Cassava Mosaic Virus | CMD2 | SSR, RFLP | Akano *et al.* (2002) |
| Cocoa | *Phytophthora palmivora* | | QTL AFLP | Flament *et al.* (2001) |
| Rubber | *Microcyclus ulei* | QTL | — | Lespinase *et al.* (2000) |
| | *Phyllochora herberi* | Phr | Isozyme | LeGuen *et al.* (2000) |
| Tobacco | *Ralstonia solanacearum* | QTL | AFLP | Nishi *et al.* (2003) |
| Rose | Diplocarpon | Rdr1 | RAPD, AFLP | Malik *et al.* (2000) |

2. INSECT, NEMATODE AND PARASITIC WEED RESISTANCE

| *Crop* | *Nematode/insect* | *Gene/QTL* | *Marker(s)* | *Reference* |
|---|---|---|---|---|
| Rice | *Orseolia oryzae* (Gall midge) | Gm7 | AFLP-SCAR | Sardesai *et al.* (2002) |
| | Brown plant hopper | Bph13(t) | RAPD-SCAR | Renganayaki *et al.* (2002) |
| Wheat | *Diuraphis noxia* | Dn2 | STMS | Miller *et al.* (2001) |
| | | Dn4Dn6 | STMS | Liu *et al.* (2002) |
| | Hessian fly | H6 | RAPD- STS | Dweikat *et al.* (2002) |
| | | H31 | AFLP | Williams *et al.* (2003) |
| | *Pratylenchus neglectus* | Rlnn1 | AFLP, RFLP | Williams *et al.* (2002) |
| | Wheat curl mite | Cmc3, Cmc4 | STMS | Malik *et al.* (2003) |
| Sorghum | *Schizaphids graminum* | QTL | RAPD, SSR | Agrama *et al.* (2002) |
| Maize | *Ostrinia nubilalis* | QTL | RFLP, SSR | Bohn *et al.* (2000) |
| Sun-flower | *Orobanche cumana* | Or5 | STMS | Tang *et al.* (2003) |

Table 3.1 (*contd. on* p. 34)

Table 3.1 (*contd. from* p. 33)

| | | | | |
|---|---|---|---|---|
| Potato | *Globodera pallida* | QTL | AFLP | Bryan *et al.* (2002) |
| | | QTL | RFLP, AFLP | Caromel *et al.* (2003) |
| | *Globodera rostochiensis* | H1 | AFLP | Bakker *et al.* (2004) |
| Cowpea | *Striga gesnerioides* | Rsg1 | AFLP-SCAR | Boukar *et al.* (2004) |
| Apple | *Dysaphis devecta* | Sd-1 | AFLP, SSR, RFLP | Cevik and King (2002) |
| Japanese black pine | Pine needle gall midge | Rpgm | AFLP | Hayashi *et al.* (2004) |

These QTL are difficult to accurately map, especially with population sizes typical of most mapping studies. So, now the population size for QTL mapping has increased to about 300-500 individuals. However, in order to have an understanding of what the gene does and how it interacts with other genes, it is useful to know where the genes are within the genome and in relation to other genes of interest. The number of QTL controlling a trait varies from 1 to more than 10. Since the environment in which the host grows influences the polygenic resistance, it is essential to replicate the mapping populations over locations and seasons. Use of recombinant inbred lines (RILs) and doubled haploids (DH) are very useful in precise mapping and estimation of the effects of the QTL. Three methods, which have more commonly used for mapping QTL are: (*i*) single marker analysis, (*ii*) simple interval mapping, and (*iii*) composite interval mapping. The first method does not require a genome map whereas the other two methods are based on mapped markers. The last method is considered most efficient in detection of QTL and estimation of their effects. Some recent examples of molecular mapping of loci for quantitative pest resistance are given in the Table 3.1.

**Experimental Approaches for Marker Assisted Breeding for Pest Resistance**

Molecular markers can be used in a variety of ways in different plant breeding schemes. In most of the cases reported so far, markers have been used in backcrossing programmes. There are not many attempts made so far to analyse the theoretical considerations and provide experimental steps in marker-assisted breeding. There can be three distinct situations in breeding for pest resistance using markers: (*i*) Transfer of the desirable gene/QTL from a donor to a suitable agronomic back ground through strict backcrossing, (*ii*) Recombining pest resistance gene from one of the parents with agronomic traits from both parents in pedigree breeding or a combination of limited back-crossing with pedigree method and (*iii*) Advanced backcross method particularly for simultaneous detection and transfer of QTL for pest resistance available in a related species. The first method has been highlighted in Fig. 3.1. Here, one has to use the markers for selection of the desirable segregants (heterozygous resistant in case of dominance of resistance over susceptibility or heterozygous carrier when resistance is recessive to susceptibility) in every backcross generation. The number of plants to be genotyped can be reduced by exercising selection for other phenotypic traits of the recipient parent such as plant height, flowering and maturity. After the third backcross, more than 99% of the recurrent parent genome can be recovered in case both foreground and background selections are practiced. When the objective is to combine desirable traits from both parents alongwith the pest resistance from one of them, it would be desirable to follow pedigree or a combination of initial backcrossing with pedigree selection. Here, the markers are to be used to identify homozygous resistant segregants in early generations. Several rounds of pedigree selection for agronomic characters may follow this. In the last generation, markers may be used to verify the presence of the gene(s) for pest resistance. The advance back cross method was designed to identify desirable QTL for pest resistance present in wild relatives that express when transferred to the nuclear genomic background of the cultivated variety through backcrossing (Tanksley and Nelson, 1996). Here, the phenotyping is carried out in BC2 or BC3 generation to identify the desirable QTL, which then is mobilized to the recipient genome through marker-assisted selection. This process leads to the development of Near Isogenic Lines (NILs) that are of immense use in isolation and functional analysis of the target locus.

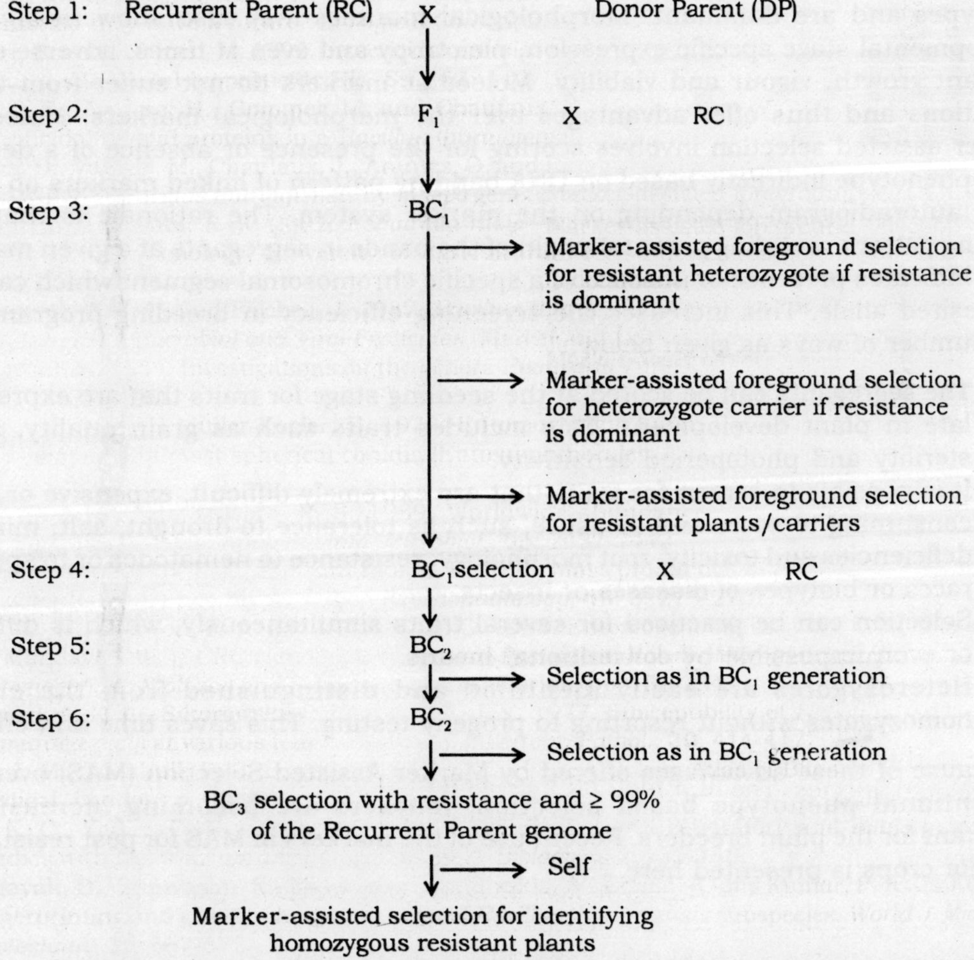


**Fig. 3.1:** Marker-assisted backcross breeding (MABB) scheme for transferring pest resistance gene to an agronomically superior variety

## USE OF MARKERS IN BREEDING FOR PEST RESISTANCE

Plant breeding involves creation of genetic variation and selection of the desirable variants/recombinants, which are subsequently evaluated and released for commercial cultivation. Selection of the desirable variants/recombinants has been based on the phenotype. Success of such selection largely depends upon the skill of the concerned plant breeder. Selection of a genotype carrying desirable gene or gene combination via linked marker(s) is/are called marker-assisted selection. Breeders sometimes practice marker-assisted selection when an important trait, that is difficult to assess phenotypically, is tightly linked to another Mendelian trait, which can be easily scored. For example, a gene for purple coleoptile color in some traditional rice varieties is closely linked to a gene that confers resistance to brown plant hopper (BPH). In a segregating population like F2, about 95% of the plants showing purple coleoptile are found resistant to BPH. In this case, coleoptile colour is a morphological marker, which is used to assist selection for BPH resistance. Morphological markers are however, limited in number, are specific to particular genotypes and are dominant. Morphological markers may also show tissue and developmental stage specific expression, pleiotropy and even at times, adverse effect on plant growth, vigour and viability. Molecular markers do not suffer from these limitations and thus offer advantages over the morphological markers. Molecular marker assisted selection involves scoring for the presence or absence of a desired plant phenotype indirectly based on DNA banding pattern of linked markers on a gel or on autoradiogram depending on the marker system. The rationale is that the banding pattern revealing parental origin of the bands in segregants at a given marker locus indicates presence or absence of a specific chromosomal segment which carries the desired allele. This increases the screening efficiency in breeding programmes in a number of ways as given below:

1. The segregants can be scored at the seedling stage for traits that are expressed late in plant development. This includes traits such as grain quality, male sterility and photoperiod sensitivity.
2. It is possible to screen for traits that are extremely difficult, expensive or time consuming to score and measure, such as tolerance to drought, salt, mineral deficiencies and toxicity, root morphology, resistance to nematodes or to specific races or biotypes of diseases or insects.
3. Selection can be practiced for several traits simultaneously, which is difficult or even impossible by conventional means.
4. Heterozygotes are easily identified and distinguished from the either homozygotes without resorting to progeny testing. This saves time and effort.

Because of these advantages offered by Marker Assisted Selection (MAS) over the conventional phenotype based selection, markers are becoming increasingly important for the plant breeders. Recent use of the markers in MAS for pest resistance in major crops is presented here.

### Rice

The on going significant efforts on marker-assisted breeding and gene pyramiding in rice include resistance to blast and bacterial blight. Bacterial blight (BB) caused by *Xanthomonas oryzae* pv. *oryzae* (Xoo) is one of the most destructive diseases of rice throughout the world and in some areas of Asia it can reduce crop yield by upto 50%. The most effective approach to combat BB is the use of resistant varieties (Khush *et al.,* 1989). So far, 19 resistant genes have been identified (Kinoshita, 1995) and some of these have been incorporated into modern rice varieties. However, the large-scale and long term cultivation of varieties carrying one of the most important resistant gene *Xa*-4 has resulted in significant shifts in the rice frequency of Xoo (Mew *et al.,* 1992). In many areas of Indonesia, India, China and Philippines, rice varieties with only *Xa*-4 for defense against Xoo have become susceptible to the pathogen. Thus, DNA marker-assisted selection was used to pyramid four bacterial resistance genes, *Xa*-4, *Xa*-5, *Xa*-13 and *Xa*-21. Breeding lines with two, three and four resistance genes were developed and tested for resistance to bacterial blight pathogen. The pyramid lines showed a wider spectrum and a higher level of resistance than lines with only a single gene. To speed up the gene pyramiding process and to facilitate future marker-aided selection, Huang *et. al.,* (1997) developed PCR markers for two recessive genes *Xa*-5 and X*a*-13, and used these to survey a range of rice germplasm. The results of the germplasm survey will be useful for the selection of parents in breeding programmes aimed at transferring these bacterial blight resistance genes from one varietal background to another. In India, at PAU, Ludhiana, three BB resistance genes *Xa*-5, *Xa*-13 and *Xa*-21 were pyramided in PR106 and Pusa 44 background. After multi-location and replicated testing, two PR106 pyramid lines were identified and these have been included in All India Coordinated Testing during 2002. This is the first ever marker-assisted product reaching testing at national level. Pusa 44 pyramid lines will be tested in multi-location replicated trials during 2002 (Singh *et al.,* 2001).

Basmati varieties of rice are highly susceptible to bacterial leaf blight (BLB). Since the disease is prevalent in the entire Basmati growing region of India, BLB is a severe constraint in Basmati rice production. In a recent study, the two-gene pyramid line IRBB55 carrying *Xa*13 and *Xa*21 was found equally effective as three/four gene pyramid lines (Josheph *et al.,* 2004). The two BLB resistance genes present in IRBB55 were combined with the Basmati quality traits of Pusa Basmati-1, the most popular high yielding Basmati rice variety used as recurrent parent. Phenotypic selection for disease resistance, agronomic and Basmati quality characteristics and marker-assisted selection for the two resistance genes were carried out in BC1F1, BC1F2 and BC1F3 generations. Background analysis using 252 polymorphic amplified fragment length polymorphism (AFLP) markers detected 80.4 to 86.7% recurrent parent alleles in BC1F3 selections. Recombinants having enhanced resistance to BLB, Basmati quality and desirable agronomic traits were identified, which can either be directly developed into commercial varieties or used as immediate donors of BLB resistance in Basmati breeding programs (Josheph *et al.,* 2004).

Blast caused by the fungus *Magnaportha grisea* is another devastating disease of rice. The most economical and effective approach to reduce the yield loss is to breed varieties that are resistant to the disease. However, the resistance often breaks down within a few years of cultivar release. Many genes for qualitative blast resistance have been mapped using molecular markers (Table 3.1) and some of those markers have also been tried in MAS for blast resistance. For example, RG64, a RFLP marker on chromosome 6 is tightly linked (2.8 cM) to *Pi*-2 (*t*), a major gene for blast resistance (Yu *et al.*, 1991). The RG64 rice genome clone was sequenced and primers based on the DNA sequences were found useful in producing polymorphism between the susceptible and resistant varieties after the monomorphic PCR product was digested with restriction enzymes (Williams *et al.*, 1991). The CAPS marker was then used to identify rice plants carrying *Pi*-2 (*t*) from an F2 population derived from the cross between CO39 and CO10151. The effectiveness of the selection for resistant plants based on linked DNA markers was then compared with phenotyping for blast resistance through progeny testing in the F3 families by blast inoculation. Results indicated that identification of plants carrying *Pi*-2 (*t*) in a large segregating population is possible using one linked marker as well as flanking markers. The accuracy of identification of homozygous resistant genotypes was 96% when RG64 marker was used. The accuracy of selection increased to 100% when two markers flanking the *Pi*-2 (*t*) were scored simultaneously. These results illustrate that marker-assisted identification of linked target gene in a segregating population is efficient in identifying resistant genotypes (Hittalmani *et al.*, 1994). This work has been extended further to pyramid three major genes (*Pi*-1, *Piz*-5 and Pita) for blast resistance (Hittalmani *et al.*, 2000). These genes located on chromosomes 11, 6 and 12, respectively, were fine-mapped and closely linked RFLP markers identified. New markers for *Pi*-1 and Pita were found flanking the genes. The three genes were pyramided using RFLP markers. A PCR-based SAP (sequence amplified polymorphism) marker was used to identify *Piz*-5 in the segregating population. The plants carrying two- and three-gene combinations that were tested for resistance to leaf blast in the Philippines and India indicated that combinations including *Piz*-5 have enhanced resistance than when it is present alone. The genes from the pyramided lines are at present being deployed into agronomically superior rice varieties by marker-aided selection.

**Wheat**

The wheat stem and leaf rusts are two major pathogens, which can potentially devastate wheat crops. Resistant cultivars have long been depended upon to control disease epidemics. Most of the genes for resistance have been mapped using molecular markers and currently being used in MAS at different National as well as International Centres. In India, RAPD markers linked to *Lr*19 (leaf rust) gene has been converted into SCAR markers. *Lr*28 gene was also tagged by two flanking RAPD marker $S464_{700}$ and $S326_{350}$. These linked molecular markers are further in use in pyramiding of rust resistance genes, which is difficult, and time consuming by conventional breeding procedures (K. V. Prabhu and coworkers, personal communication). A population of 220 BC1F2 plants segregating for two genes *Cre*1 and *Cre*3 was evaluated with three molecular markers Xglk605, Xcdo588 and Cd2.2 and the markers were found to provide a reliable means of gene pyramiding and selecting plants carrying the genes in wheat breeding programmes (Ogbonnaya *et al.*, 1998).

**Potato**

A breeding scheme has been reported to overcome the interspecific barriers existing between the cultivated *Solanum tuberosum* and the wild species *S. commersonii*. Both the foreground and background selections were carried out to introgress only limited chromosomal regions of the wild species carrying the genes of interest to the cultivated genetic background (Barone *et al.*, 2001). Three backcross generations were obtained that were analyzed by means of molecular markers in order to verify the occurrence of recombination between homeologous chromosomes, the extent of the wild genome carried in each backcross, and the efficiency of introgressing useful genes. Twenty *commersonii*-specific RFLPs provided evidence for recombination on 5 out of 12 chromosomes; for the others no more than 1 *commersonii*-specific marker was found. Thirty-four *commersonii*-specific RAPDs and 61 *commersonii*-specific AFLPs were used to estimate the wild genome content in the BC1, BC2, and BC3 generations. The mean value of *commersonii*-specific markers was 93% and 91% in the BC1, 74% and 76% in the BC2, and 31% and 26% in the BC3 using RAPDs or AFLPs, respectively. Efficiency of the breeding scheme was evaluated by monitoring across these progenies the introgression of *S. commersonii* resistance to tuber soft rot caused by *Erwinia carotovora*. Eleven and five resistant genotypes were found among BC2 and BC3 hybrids, respectively. The same progenies were also evaluated for chromosome number and tuber traits. For all analyzed traits except stolon length, all BC2 and BC3 hybrids resembled the *tuberosum* type. In order to choose the best genotypes to obtain the following backcrosses, a negative molecular-assisted selection against the wild genome was performed, in each generation, combined with selection for resistance to *Erwinia* spp. and other traits.

**Tomato**

Marker Assisted Selection has been carried out for several traits including fruit characteristics in tomato. More recently, MAS has been demonstrated for QTL influencing blackmold resistance. Blackmold, caused by the fungus *Alternaria alternata*, is a major ripe fruit disease of processing tomatoes. Five QTLs were selected for introgression from *Lycopersicon cheesmanii* into cultivated tomato using marker-assisted selection. RFLP and PCR-based markers flanking and within, the chromosomal regions containing QTLs were used for MAS during backcross and selfing generations (Robert *et al.*, 2001).

**Soybean**

Marker Assisted Selection offers the potential to reduce linkage drag and to pyramid genes with similar phenotypic effects into elite genotypes. One such example was seen in soybean breeding programme where a QTL conditioning corn earworm resistance in the accession PI229358 and a synthetic *Bacillus thuringiensis cry1Ac* transgene from the recurrent parent 'Jack-Bt' were pyramided into BC2F3 plants by marker-assisted selection. Segregating individuals were genotyped at SSR markers linked to an antibiosis/antixenosis QTL on linkage group M, and were tested for the presence of *cryAc*1. MAS was used during and after the two backcrosses to develop a series of BC2F3 plants with or without *cryAc*1 transgene and the QTL conditioning for resistance in BC2F3 plants that were homozygous for parental alleles at markers. This work by Walker *et al.,* (2002) demonstrated the usefulness of SSR for MAS in soybean, and showed that combining transgene and QTL-mediated resistance to lepidopteran pests might be a viable strategy for insect control.

### Sunflower

Marker Assisted Selection for two rust resistance genes in sunflower was reported using RAPD markers $Ox20_{600}$ and $OO04_{950}$ linked to the gene $R_{A}dv$ responsible for rust resistance in the proprietary inbred line $P_2$. This gene confers resistance to most of the pathotypes of *Puccinia helianthi* identified in Australia. These RAPD markers were converted into SCAR markers and the robustness of these markers were demonstrated through the amplification in a diverse range of sunflower germplasm. This will be useful in further attempts for molecular-assisted breeding to produce durable resistance in sunflower to *P. helianthi* (Lawson *et al.,* 1998).

### Mustard

White rust, caused by *Albugo candida,* is a very serious disease in crucifers. In Indian mustard (*Brassica juncea*), it can cause a yield loss to the extent of 89.9%. The locus *Ac2*(t) controlling resistance to white rust in BEC-144, an exotic accession of mustard, was mapped using RAPD markers. A CAPS marker was developed from the tightly linked RAPD marker and used to carry out MAS in two different F2 populations. The marker was validated in both populations, which established its utility in marker-assisted selection (MAS) for white rust resistance. The use of both flanking markers in MAS is expected to allow only 0.25% misclassification and thus provide greater efficiency to selection (Varshney *et al.,* 2004).

### Apple

Marker Assisted Selection is also a promising method to select resistant individuals in horticultural crops like apple. Molecular tools have the potential to give very early information on the genetics of apple seedlings. The aims of apple breeding such as high fruit quality, consistently high yields and durable disease and pest resistance can be achieved more efficiently. Progress in MAS for apple breeding is being achieved mainly in the area of disease resistance especially in the durable incorporation of scab and mildew resistance. The AL07-SCAR and M18-CAPS molecular analysis in progenies, in which both parents are heterozygous for the resistance gene, made it possible to identify clearly the homozygous plants for the *Vf* gene (resistance for apple scab) and these plants showed higher level of resistance than the heterozygous one. Progenies were developed from crosses with parents that carry different resistance genes such as *Vf, Vm, Vb, Pl*1 and QTLs in different combinations (Markussen *et al.,* 1995; Gianfranceschi *et al.,* 1996; Tartarini *et al.,* 1999).

## FUTURE CHALLENGES AND OPPORTUNITIES

The above review of the available literature reveals that during the last 17 years since the publication of the first paper on the use of RFLP markers for construction of linkage maps in tomato and maize in 1986, molecular markers have been extensively used for mapping and tagging of different pest resistance genes/QTL in various crop species. With the availability of linked markers, the first requirement for successful use of markers in breeding for pest resistance has been fulfilled. Besides, its feasibility of the use of markers in MAS has been demonstrated in several crops both for qualitative as well as quantitative pest resistance.

Utility of the MAS in crop plants is currently limited by factors such as recombination between the marker and the target gene, low level of polymorphism between parents with contrasting traits and lower resolution of QTLs due to interaction with the environment. With the recent developments in both structural and functional genomics, it would not be difficult to find solutions to these problems. Availability of high-density genetic and physical maps will enable finding markers physically closer to the target gene that would not allow failure of MAS due to genetic recombination. Moreover, cloning and characterization of the target genes, which are possible based of their position on the linkage map, would allow development of allele-specific markers. Use of such markers would completely eliminate the possibility of breakdown of the marker-trait linkage. Besides, markers based on the sequences of the genes would facilitate allele mining in the germplasm resources, thereby leading to identification and utilization of newer alleles in crop improvement. Different alleles of a gene would differ for a number of nucleotides at different positions in their sequence that would be the basis of developing highly polymorphic single nucleotide polymorphism (SNP) markers. The problem of low level of polymorphism in narrow crosses can thus be circumvented.

Use of MAS for QTL, particularly those having little effect on trait expression and highly interacting with environment would require greater amount of research efforts and newer experimental strategies. Detection of QTL and its validation has to be carried out using a large population (>200 individuals) across several locations. Their expression needs to be confirmed in the target/new genetic backgrounds. More than one population may be used in parallel to understand the effect of different genetic backgrounds. It would be essential to understand the kind and the extent of epistatic interactions to identify desirable QTL combinations to be used in different situations.

Complete integration of MAS with the conventional breeding for pest resistance demands consideration of two important factors: (a) size of population and (b) cost. Plant breeding experiment requires screening of large segregating populations routinely over generations. Genotyping of large number of samples manually is an extremely difficult task. MAS to be practicable should be amenable to automation that would allow handling of large number of samples. Development and use of PCR based markers such as STS and SCAR will be a key to success of MAS in crop improvement. As the technology develops and gets modified to analyze large number of samples, the cost will automatically go down. The investment in gene tagging, and selection based on molecular markers should be weighted against the overall cost and time involved in traditional breeding program. Even though, the cost of MAS is higher at present level of estimation, its integration with traditional plant breeding is desirable because of immense possibilities it offers.

## REFERENCES

Adhikari, T. B., Wallwork, H., Goodwin, S. B. 2004. Microsatellite markers linked to the *Stb2* and *Stb3* genes for resistance to *Septoria tritici* Blotch in wheat. *Crop Sci.*, **44**: 1403-1411.

Agrama, H. A., Widle, G. E., Reese, J. C., Campbell, L. R. and Tuinstra, M. R. 2002. Genetic mapping of QTLs associated with green bug resistance and tolerance in *Sorghum bicolor*. *Theor. Appl. Genet.*, **104**: 1373-1378.

Akano, A. O., Dixon, A. G. O., Mba, C., Barrera, E. and Fregene, M. 2002. Genetic mapping of a dominant gene conferring resistance to cassava mosaic disease. *Theor. Appl. Genet.*, **105**: 521-525.

Andres-Arnedo, M. S., Ortega-Gill, R., Arteaga-Luis, M. and Hormaza, J. I. 2002. Development of RAPD and SCAR markers linked to the Pvr4 locus for resistance to PVR in pepper (*Capsicum annuum* L.). *Theor. Appl. Genet.*, **105**: 1067-1074.

Arru, L., Faccini, N., Govoni, C., Cattivelli, L., Pecchioni, N., Delogu, G., Stanca, A. M. and Valè, G. 2003. The PCR-based marker MWG2018 linked to the *RDG2*A leaf stripe resistance gene is a useful tool for assessing barley resistance in breeding programs. *Crop Sci.*, **43**: 1036-1042.

Arru, L., Francia, E., and Pecchioni, N. 2003. Isolate-specific QTLs of resistance to leaf stripe (*Pyrenophora graminea*) in the 'Steptoe' x 'Morex' spring barley cross. *Theor. Appl. Genet.*, **106**: 668-675.

Asnaghi, C., Roques, D., Ruffel, S., Kaye, C., Hoarau, J. Y., Télismart, H., Girard, J. C., Raboin, L. M., Risterucci, A. M., Grivet, L. and Hont, A. D. 2004. Targeted mapping of a sugarcane rust resistance gene (*Bru*1) using bulked segregant analysis and AFLP markers. *Theor. Appl. Genet.*, **108**: 759-764.

Bakker, E., Achenbach, U., Bakker, J., van Vliet, J., Peleman, J., Segers, B., van der Heijden, S., van der Linde, P., Graveland, R., Hutten, R., van Eck, H., Coppoolse, E., van der Vossen, E., Bakker, J., Goverse, A. 2004. A high-resolution map of the *H*1 locus harbouring resistance to the potato cyst nematode *Globodera rostochiensis*. *Theor. Appl. Genet.*, **109**: 146-152.

Barone A., Sebastiano A., Carputo D., Della Rocca F. and Frusciante, L. 2001. Molecular marker-assisted introgression of the wild *Solanum commersonii* genome into the cultivated *S. tuberosum* gene pool. *Theor. Appl. Genet.*, **102**: 900-907.

Bohn, M., Schulz, B., Kreps, R., Klein, D. and Melchinger, A. E. 2000. QTL mapping of resistance against the European corn borer (*Ostrinia nubilalis* H.) in early maturing European dent germplasm. *Theor. Appl. Genet.*, **101**: 907-917.

Botstein, B., White, R. L., Skolnick, M. and Davis, R. W. 1980. Construction of a genetic linkage map in man using restriction fragment length polymorphisms. *Am. J. Hum. Genet.*, **32**: 314-331.

Boukar, O., Kong, L., Singh, B. B., Murdock, L. and Ohm, H. W. 2004. AFLP and AFLP-derived SCAR markers associated with *Striga gesnerioides* resistance in cowpea. *Crop Sci.*, **44**: 1259-1264.

Brookes, A. J. 1999. The essence of SNPs. *Gene,* **234**: 177-186.

Bryan, G. J., McLean, K., Bradshaw, J. E., DeJong, W. S., Phillips, M., Castelli, L. and Waugh, R. 2002. Mapping QTLs for resistance to the cyst nematode *Globodera pallida* derived from the wild potato species *Solanum vernei*. *Theor. Appl. Genet.*, **105**: 68-77.

Burnham, K. D., Dorrance, A. E., Francis, D. M., Fioritto, R. J. and St. Martin, S. K. 2003. *Rps*8, a new locus in soybean for resistance to *Phytophthora sojae*. *Crop Sci.*, **43**: 101-105.

Caromel, B., Mugniéry, D., Lefebvre, V., Andrzejewski, S., Ellissèche, D., Kerlan, M. C., Rousselle, P. and Rousselle-Bourgeois, F. 2003. Mapping QTLs for resistance against *Globodera pallida* (Stone) Pa2/3 in a diploid potato progeny originating from *Solanum spegazzinii*. *Theor. Appl. Genet.*, **106**: 1517-1523.

Cevik, V. and King, G. J. 2002. High-resolution genetic analysis of the Sd-1 aphid resistance locus in *Malus* sp. *Theor. Appl. Genet.*, **105**: 346-354.

Che, K. P., Zhan, Q. C., Xing, Q. H., Wang, Z. P., Jin, D. M., He, D. J. and Wang, B. 2003. Tagging and mapping of rice sheath blight resistance gene. *Theor. Appl. Genet.*, **106**: 293-297.

Chen, C. X., Wang, Z. L., Yang, D. E., Ye, C. J., Zhao, Y. B., Jin, D. M., Weng, M. L. and Wang, B. 2004. Molecular tagging and genetic mapping of the disease resistance gene *RppQ* to southern corn rust. *Theor. Appl. Genet.*, **108**: 945-950.

Dahleen, L. S., Agrama, H. A., Horsley, R. D., Steffenson, B. J., Schwarz, P. B., Mesfin, A. and Franckowiak, J. D. 2003. Identification of QTLs associated with Fusarium head blight resistance in Zhedar 2 barley. *Theor. Appl. Genet.*, **108**: 95-104.

Danna, C. H., Sacco, F., Ingala, L. R., Saione, H. A. and Ugalde, R. A. 2002. Cloning and mapping of genes involved in wheat-leaf rust interaction through gene-expression analysis using chromosome-deleted near-isogenic wheat lines. *Theor. Appl. Genet.*, **105**: 972-979.

Dauleux-Manzanares, M. J., Delourme, R., Baron, F. and Thomas, G. 2000. Mapping of one major gene and of QTLs involved in resistance to clubroot in *Brassica napus*. *Theor. Appl. Genet.*, **101**: 885-891.

Duble, C. M., Quint, M., Melchinger, A. E., Xu, M. L. and Lubberstedt, T. 2003. Saturation of two chromosome regions conferring resistance to SCMV with SSR and AFLP markers by targeted BSA. *Theor. Appl. Genet.*, **106**: 485-493.

Dweikat, I., Zhang, W. and Ohm, H. 2002. Development of STS markers linked to *Hessian* fly resistance gene H6 in wheat. *Theor. Appl. Genet.*, **105**: 766-770.

Eriksen, L., Borum, F. and Jahoor, A. 2003. Inheritance and localisation of resistance to *Mycosphaerella graminicola* causing septoria tritici blotch and plant height in the wheat (*Triticum aestivum* L.) genome with DNA markers. *Theor. Appl. Genet.*, **107**: 515-527.

Evans, K. and James, C. 2003. Identification of SCAR markers linked to Pl-w mildew resistance in apple. *Theor. Appl. Genet.*, **106**: 1178-1183.

Fasoula, V. A., Harris, D. K., Bailey, M. A., Phillips, D. V. and Boerma, H. R. 2003. Identification, mapping, and confirmation of a soybean gene for bud blight resistance. *Crop Sci.*, **43**: 1754-1759.

Fjellstrom, R., Conaway-Bormans, C. A., McClung, A. M., Marchetti, M. A., Shank, A. R. and Park, W. D. 2004. Development of DNA markers suitable for marker-assisted selection of three *Pi* Genes conferring resistance to multiple *Pyricularia grisea* pathotypes. *Crop Sci.*, **44**: 1790-1798.

Foolad, M. R., Zhang, L. P., Khan, A. A., Liu-Nino, D. and Liu, G. Y. 2002. Identification of QTLs for early blight (*Alternaria solani*) resistance in tomato using backcross populations of a *Lycopersicon esculentum* x *L. hirsutum* cross. *Theor. Appl. Genet.*, **104**: 945-958.

Gao, Z., Eyers, S., Thomas, C., Ellis, N. and Maule, A. 2004. Identification of markers tightly linked to *sbm* recessive genes for resistance to *Pea seed-borne mosaic virus*. *Theor. Appl. Genet.*, **109**: 488-494.

Gervais, L., Dedryver, F., Morlais, J. Y., Bodusseau, V., Negre, S., Bilous, M., Groos, C. and Trottet, M. 2003. Mapping of quantitative trait loci for field resistance to *Fusarium* head blight in an European winter wheat. *Theor. Appl. Genet.*, **106**: 961-970.

Gianfranceschi, L., Koller, B., Seglias, N., Kellerhals, M. and Gessler, C. 1996. Molecular markers in apple for resistance to scab caused by *Venturia inaequalis*. *Theor. Appl. Genet.*, **93**: 199-204.

Gordon, S. G., Bartsch, M., Matthies, I., Gevers, H. O., Lipps, P. E. and Pratt, R. C. 2004. Linkage of Molecular markers to *Cercospora zeae-maydis* resistance in maize. *Crop Sci.*, **44**: 628-636.

Guo, P. G., Bai, G. H. and Shaner, G. 2003. AFLP and STS tagging of a major QTL for *Fusarium* head blight resistance in wheat. *Theor. Appl. Genet.*, 1011-1017.

Haen, K. M., Lu, H., Friesen, T. L. and Faris, J. D. 2004. Genomic targeting and high-resolution mapping of the *Tsn*1 gene in wheat. *Crop Sci.*, **44**: 951-962.

Hayashi, E., Kondo, T., Terada, K., Kuramoto, N. and Kawasaki, S. 2004. Identification of AFLP markers linked to a resistance gene against pine needle gall midge in Japanese black pine. *Theor. Appl. Genet.*, **108**: 1177-1181.

Hittalmani, S., Foolad, M., Mew, T., Rodrigues, R. and Huang, H. 1994. Identification of blast resistance gene, *Pi*-2(t) in rice plants by flanking DNA markers. *Rice Genetics Newsletter*, H. I. Oka, G. S. Khush (eds.), a publication of Rice Genetics Cooperative Genetic Resources Section, National Institute of Genetics, Misima, Japan. Vol. **11**: 144.

Hittalmani, S., Parco, A., Mew, T. V., Zeigier, R. S. and Huang, N. 2000. Fine mapping and DNA marker-assisted pyramiding of the three major genes for blast resistance in rice. *Theor. Appl. Genet.*, **100**: 1121-1128.

Huang, N., Angeles, E. R., Domingo, J., Magpantay, G., Singh, S., Zhang, G., Kumaravadivel, N., Bennett, J. and Khush, G. S. 1997. Pyramiding of bacterial blight resistance genes in rice: marker-assisted selection using RFLP and PCR. *Theor. Appl. Genet.*, **95**: 313-320.

Huang, C. C., Cui, Y. Y., Weng, C. R., Zabel, P. and Lindhout, P. 2000. Development of diagnostic PCR marker is closely linked to the tomato powdery mildew resistance gene Ol-1 on chromosome 6 of tomato. *Theor. Appl. Genet.*, **101**: 918-924.

Huang, X. Q., Hsam, S. L. K., Zeller, F. J., Wenzel, G. and Mohler, V. 2000. Molecular mapping of the wheat powdery mildew resistance gene *Pm*24 and marker validation for molecular breeding. *Theor. Appl. Genet.*, **101**: 407-414.

Huaracha, E., Xu, M. and Korban, S. S. 2004. Narrowing down the region of the *Vf* locus for scab resistance in apple using AFLP-derived SCARs. *Theor. Appl. Genet.*, **108**: 274-279.

Hughes, S. L., Hunter, P. J., Sharpe, A. G., Kearsey, M. J., Lydiate, D. J. and Walsh, J. A. 2003. Genetic mapping of the novel *Turnip mosaic virus* resistance gene *TuRB*03 in *Brassica napus. Theor. Appl. Genet.*, 1169-1173.

Joseph, M., Gopalakrishnan, S., Sharma, R. K., Singh, V. P., Singh, A. K., Singh, N. K., Mohapatra T. 2004. Combining bacterial blight resistance and Basmati quality characteristics by phenotypic and molecular marker-assisted selection in rice. *Molecular Breeding,* **13**: 377-387.

Khush, G. S., Mackill, D. J. and Sidhu, G. S. 1989. Breeding rice for resistance to bacterial blight. *In: Bacterial Blight of Rice.* International Rice Research Institute, Los, Banos, Manila, Philippines, pp. 207-217.

Kinoshita, T. 1995. Report of committee on gene symbolization, nomenclature and linkage groups. *Rice Genet. Newsl.*, **12**: 9-153.

Konieczny, A. and Ausubel, F. M. 1993. A procedure for mapping *Arabidopsis* mutations using co-dominant ecotype-specific PCR based markers. *The Plant Journal,* **4**(2): 403-410.

Lawson, W. R., Goutler, K. C., Henry, R. J., Kong, G. A. and Kochman, J. K. 1998. Marker-assisted selection for two rust resistance genes in sunflower. *Mol. Breed.*, **4**: 227-234.

Le Guen, V., Seguin M. and Mattos, C. R. R. 2000. Qualitative resistance of *Hevea* to *Phyllachora huberi* P. Henn. *Euphytica,* **112**: 211-217.

Lespinase, D., Grivet, L., Troispoux, V., Rodier-Goud, M., Pinard, F. and Sequin, M. 2000. Identification of QTLs involved in the resistance to South American leaf blight (*Microcyclus ulei*) in the rubber tree. *Theor. Appl.Genet.*, **100**: 975-984.

Lheureux, F., Carreel, F., Jenny C., Lockhart, B. E. L. and Caruana-Iskra, M. L. 2003. Identification of molecular markers linked to banana streak disease expression in inter-specific *Musa* hybrids. *Theor. Appl. Genet.*, **106**: 594-598.

Liu, X. M., Smith, C. M. and Gill, B. S. 2002. Identification of microsatellite markers linked to Russian wheat aphid resistance genes Dn4 and Dn6. *Theor. Appl. Genet.*, **104**: 1042-1048.

Mago, R., Spielmeyer, W., Lawrence, G. J., Lagudah, E. S., Ellis, J. G. and Psyor, A. 2002. Identification and mapping of molecular markers linked to rust resistance genes located on chromosome 1RS of rye using wheat-rye translocation lines. *Theor. Appl. Genet.*, **104**: 1317-1324.

Mahuku, G., Montoya, C., Henríquez, M. A., Jara, C., Teran, H. and Beebe, S. 2004. Inheritance and characterization of angular leaf spot resistance gene present in common bean accession G 10474 and identification of an AFLP marker linked to the resistance gene. *Crop Sci.*, **44**: 1817-1824.

Malek, B., Weber, W. E. and Debener, T. 2000. Identification of molecular markers linked to Rdr1, a gene conferring resistance to blackspot in roses. *Theor. Appl. Genet.*, **101**: 977-983.

Malik, R., Brown-Guedira, G. L., Smith, C. M., Harvey, T. L. and Gill, B. S. 2003. Genetic mapping of wheat curl mite resistance genes *Cmc*3 and *Cmc*4 in common wheat. *Crop Sci.*, **43**: 644-650.

Marano, M. R., Malcuit, I., De Jong, W. and Baulcombe, D. C. 2002. High-resolution genetic map of Nb, a gene that confers hypersensitive resistance to potato virus X in *Solanum tuberosum. Theor. Appl. Genet.*, **105**: 192-200.

Markussen, T., Kruger, J., Schmidt, H. and Dunemann, F. 1995. Identification of PCR-based markers linked to the powdery mildew gene Pl1 from *Malus robusta* in cultivated apple. *Plant Breed.*, **114**: 530-534.

Mew, T. W., Vera, Cruz, C. M. and Medalla, E. S. 1992. Changes in race frequency of *Xanthomonas oryzae* pv. *oryzae* in response to the planting of rice cultivars in the Philippines. *Plant Dis.*, **76**: 1029-1032.

Miller, C. A., Altinkut, A. and Lapitan, N. L. V. 2001. A microsatellite marker for tagging *Dn*2, a wheat gene conferring resistance to the Russian wheat aphid. *Crop Sci.*, **41**: 1584-1589.

Ni, J., Colowit, P. M., Oster, J. J., Xu, K. and Mackill, D. J. 2001. Molecular markers linked to stem rot resistance in rice. *Theor. Appl. Genet.*, 511-516.

Nishi, T., Tajima, T., Noguchi, S., Ajisaka, H. and Negishi, H. 2003. Identification of DNA markers of tobacco linked to bacterial wilt resistance. *Theor. Appl. Genet.*, **106**: 765-770.

Ogbonnaya, F. C., Moullet, O., Eastwppd, R. F., Kollmorgen, J., Eagles, H., Appels, R. and Lagudah, E. S. 1998. The use of molecular markers to pyramid cereal cyst nematode resistance genes in wheat. *In:* A. E. Slinkard, (ed.), Proc. 9th Int. *Wheat Genet. Symp.*, Vol. **3**, 138-139. Univ. Extension Press, Univ. of Saskatchewan, Saskatoon.

Olson, M., Hood, L., Cantor, C. H., Botstein, D. 1989. A common language for physical mapping of the human genome. *Science*, **24**: 1434-1435.

Paran, I. and Michelmore, R. W. 1993. Development of reliable PCR-based markers linked to downy mildew genes in lettuce. *Theor Appl Genet.*, **85**: 985-993.

Park, S. O., Coyne, D. P., Steadman, J. R. and Skroch, P. W. 2003. Mapping of the *Ur*-7 gene for specific resistance to rust in common bean. *Crop Sci.*, **43**: 1470-1476.

Pauquet, J., Bouquet, A., This, P. and Blondou-Adam, A. F. 2001. Establishment of a local map of AFLP markers around the powdery mildew resistance gene Run 1 in grapevine and assessment of their usefulness for marker assisted selection. *Theor. Appl. Genet.*, **103**: 1201-1210.

Piao, Z. Y., Deng, Y. Q., Choi, S. R., Park, Y. J. and Lim, Y. P. 2004. SCAR and CAPS mapping of *CRb*, a gene conferring resistance to *Plasmodiophora brassicae* in Chinese cabbage (*Brassica rapa ssp. pekinensis*). *Theor. Appl. Genet.*, **108**: 1458-1465.

Pierre, M., Noël, L., Lahaye, T., Ballvora, A., Veuskens, J., Ganal, M. and Bonas, U. 2000. High-resolution genetic mapping of the pepper resistance locus *Bs*3 governing recognition of the *Xanthomonas campestris pv vesicatora AvrBs*3 protein. *Theor. Appl. Genet.*, **101**: 255-263.

Plieske, J. and Struss, D. 2001. STS markers linked to *Phoma* resistance genes of the *Brassica* B-genome revealed sequence homology between *Brassica nigra* and *Brassica napus*. *Theor. Appl. Genet.*, **102**: 483-488.

Quint, M., Mihaljevic, R., Dussle, C. M., Xu, M. L., Melchinger, A. E. and Lubberstedt, T. 2002. Development of RGA-CAPs markers and genetic mapping of candidate genes for sugarcane mosaic virus resistance in maize. *Theor. Appl. Genet.*, **105**: 355-363.

Renganayaki, K., Fritz, A. K., Sadasivam, S., Pammi, S., Harrington, S. E., McCouch, S. R., Kumar S. M. and Reddy, A. S. 2002. Mapping and progress toward map-based cloning of brown plant hopper biotype-4 resistance gene introgressed from *Oryza officinalis* into cultivated rice, *O. sativa. Crop Sci.*, **42**: 2112-2117.

Robert, V. J. M., West, M. A. L., Inai, S., Caines, A., Arntzen, L., Smith, J. K. and St Clair, D. A. 2001. Marker-assisted introgression of blackmold resistance QTL alleles from wild *Lycopersicon cheesmanii* to cultivated tomato (*L. esculentum*) and evaluation of QTL phenotypic effects. *Mol. Breed.*, **8**: 217-233.

Ruge, B., Linz, A., Pickering, R., Proeseler, G., Greif, P. and Wehling, P. 2003. Mapping of *Rym*14Hb, a gene introgressed from *Hordeum bulbosum* and conferring resistance to BaMMV and BaYMV in barley. *Theor. Appl. Genet.*, **107**: 965-971.

Sardesai, N., Kumar, A., Rajyashri, K. R., Nair, S. and Mohan, M. 2002. Identification and mapping of an AFLP marker linked to Gm7, a gall midge resistance gene and its conversion to a SCAR marker for its utility in marker aided selection in rice. *Theor. Appl. Genet.*, **105**: 691-698.

Singh, S., Sidhu, J. S., Huang, N., Vikal, Y., Li, Z., Brar, D. S., Dhaliwal, H. S. and Khush, G. S. 2001. Pyramiding three bacterial blight resistance genes (Xa5, xa13 and Xa21) using marker-assisted selection into indica cultivar PR106. *Theor. Appl. Genet.*, **102**: 1011-1015.

Singh, S., Guedira, G. B., Grewal, T., Dhaliwal, H., Nelson, J., Singh, H. and Gill, B. 2003. Mapping of a resistance gene effective against Karnal bunt pathogen of wheat. *Theor. Appl. Genet.*, **106**: 287-292.

Singrün, C., Hsam, S. L. K., Hartl, L., Zeller, F. J. and Mohler, V. 2003. Powdery mildew resistance gene *Pm22* in cultivar Virest is a member of the complex *Pml* locus in common wheat (*Triticum aestivum* L. em Thell.). *Theor. Appl. Genet.*, **106**: 1420-1424.

Smith, P., Koebner, R. and Boyd L. 2002. The development of STS marker linked to a yellow rust resistance derived from the wheat cultivar Moro. *Theor. Appl. Genet.*, **104**: 1278-1282.

Sobir, Ohmori, T., Murata, M. and Motoyoshi, F. 2000. Molecular characterization of the SCAR markers tightly linked to the Tm-2 locus of the genus *Lycopersicon. Theor. Appl. Genet.*, **101**: 64-69.

Southern, E. M., 1975. Detection of specific sequences of DNA fragments separated by gel electrophoresis. *J. Mol. Bio.*, **98**: 503-517.

Tabien, R. E., Li, Z., Paterson, A. H., Marchetti, M. A., Stansel, J. W. and Pinson, S. R. M. 2002. Mapping QTLs for field resistance to the rice blast pathogen in improved varieties. *Theor. Appl. Genet.*, **105**: 313-324.

Tang, S., Heesacker, A., Kishore, V. K., Fernandez, A., Sadik, El S., Cole, G. and Knapp, S. J. 2003. Genetic mapping of the $Or_5$ gene for resistance to Orobanche race E in sunflower. *Crop Sci.*, **43**: 1021-1028.

Tanksley, S. D. and Nelson, T. C. 1996. Advanced backcross QTL analysis: a method for the simultaneous discovery and transfer of valuable QTLs from unadapted germplasm into elite breeding lines. *Theor. Appl. Genet.*, **92**: 191-203.

Tartarini, S., Sansavini, S., Vinatzer, B. A. and Gennari, F. 2000. Development of reliable PCR markers for the selection of the *Vf* gene conferring scab resistance in apple. *Plant Breed.*, **118**: 183-186.

Tullu, A., Buchwaldt, L., Warkentin, T., Taran, B. and Vandenberg, A. 2003. Genetics of resistance to anthracnose and identification of AFLP and RAPD markers linked to the resistance gene in PI 320937 germplasm of lentil (*Lens culinaris* Medikus). *Theor. Appl. Genet.*, **106**: 428-434.

Varshney, A., Mohapatra, T. and Sharma, R. P. 2004. Development and validation of CAPS and AFLP markers for the white rust resistance genes in *Brassica juncea. Theor. Appl. Genet.*, **109**: 153-159.

Vilanova, S., Romero, C., Abbott, A. G., Llácer, G. and Badenes M. L. 2003. An apricot (*Prunus armeniaca* L.) F2 progeny linkage map based on SSR and AFLP markers, mapping plum pox virus resistance and self-incompatibility traits. *Theor. Appl. Genet.*, **107**: 239-247.

Vos, P., Hogers, R., Bleeker, M., Reijans, M., van de Lee, T., Hornes, M., Frijters, A., Pot, J., Peleman, J., Kuipers, M. and Zabeau, M. 1995. AFLP: a new technique for DNA fingerprinting. *Nucl Acids Res.*, **23**: 4407-4414.

Walker, D., Boerma, H. R., All, J. and Parrott, W. 2002. Combining *cry1*Ac with QTL alleles from PI 229358 to improve soybean resistance to lepidopteran pests. *Mol. Breed.*, **9**: 43-51.

Weerasena, J. S., Steffenson, B. J. and Falk, A. B. 2004. Conversion of an amplified fragment length polymorphism marker into a co-dominant marker in the mapping of the *Rph*15 gene conferring resistance to barley leaf rust, *Puccinia hordei* Otth. *Theor. Appl. Genet.*, **108**: 712-719.

Williams, G. K., Kubelik, A. R., Livak, K. J., Rafalski, J. A. and Tingey, S. V. 1990. DNA polymorphisms amplified by arbitrary primers are useful as genetic markers. *Nucl. Acids Res.*, **18**: 6531-6535

Williams, M. N. V., Pande, N., Nair, S., Mohan, M. and Bennett, J. 1991. Restriction length polymorphism analysis of polymerase chain reaction products and amplified from mapped loci of rice (*Oryza sativa* L.) genomic DNA. *Theor. Appl. Genet.*, **82**: 489-498.

Williams, K. J., Taylor, S. P., Bogacki, P., Pallotta, M., Bariana, H. S. and Wallwork, H. 2002. Mapping of the root lesion nematode (*Pratylenchus neglectus*) resistance gene Rlnn1 in wheat. *Theor. Appl. Genet.*, **104**: 874-879.

Williams, C. E., Collier, C. C., Sardesai, N., Ohm, H. W. and Cambron, S. E. 2003. Phenotypic assessment and mapped markers for *H*31, a new wheat gene conferring resistance to Hessian fly (Diptera: Cecidomyiidae). *Theor. Appl. Genet.*, **107**: 1516-1523.

Xie, C., Sun, Q., Ni, Z., Yang, T., Nevo, E. and Fahima, T. 2003. Chromosomal location of a *Triticum dicoccoides*-derived powdery mildew resistance gene in common wheat by using microsatellite markers. *Theor. Appl. Genet.*, **106**: 341-345.

Xu, M., Huaracha, E., Korban, S. S. 2001. Development of sequence characterized amplified regions (SCARs) from amplified fragment length polymorphism (AFLP) markers tightly linked to the *Vf* gene in apple. *Genome*, **44**: 63-70.

Yan, G. P., Chen, X. M., Line, R. F. and Wellings, C. R. 2003. Resistance gene-analog polymorphism markers co-segregating with the YR5 gene for resistance to wheat stripe rust. *Theor. Appl. Genet.*, **106**: 636-643.

Yu, Z. H., Mackill, D. J., Bonman, J. M. and Tanksley, S. D. 1991. Tagging genes for balst resistance in rice via linkage to RFLP markers. *Theor. Appl. Genet.*, **81**: 471-476.

Zhao, J. and Meng, J. 2003. Genetic analysis of loci associated with partial resistance to *Sclerotinia sclerotiorum* in rapeseed (*Brassica napus* L.). *Theor. Appl. Genet.*, **106**: 759-764.

Zhong, S. and Steffenson, B. J. 2002. Identification and characterization of DNA markers associated with a locus conferring virulence on barley in the plant pathogenic fungus *Cochliobolus sativus*. *Theor. Appl. Genet.*, **104**: 1049-1054.

# Role of Regulatory Measures in Controlling Spread of Plant Pests

**Kavita Gupta, Ashok Gaur and R. K. Khetarpal**

## INTRODUCTION

Plant quarantine is a regulatory measure enforced to restrict the movement of agricultural commodities in order to prevent introduction and spread of pests and diseases. International movement of plants/planting material has led to spread of associated pests resulting in heavy crop losses. The Destructive Insects and Pests Act (1914) and the Plant Quarantine Order (Regulation of Import into India), 2003 issued under the Act are legislative measures to regulate the introduction of plants/ planting material from other countries and also their interstate movement. Also, the New Policy on Seed Development (1988) recently revised as a National Seeds Policy (2002) calls for quality and safe movement of seed. With the advent of World Trade Organization (WTO), and the Convention on Biological Diversity (CBD), India needs to update its quarantine set-up to compete in the world market. The Agreement on Application of Sanitary and Phytosanitary (SPS) Measures under the WTO is aimed to protect plants, animals and human beings from risks associated with pests and diseases. The task of developing standards for food safety, animal and plant health has been assigned to three international organizations, which also advise WTO dispute settlement panels. A pest risk analysis now needs to be undertaken before import/ export as decisions regarding entry status of agricultural commodities have to be based on risk analysis. One of the key activities that need to be expedited is the establishment of a Central Co-ordination Unit to review and mitigate repercussions of SPS Agreement. In addition, up-gradation and strengthening of quarantine set-up along with research, networking and revision of policies would surely facilitate India in becoming a strong contender in world trade.

The word 'Quarantine' means forty days which was the period of time for which a person or animal suspected to carry communicable diseases were kept in isolation so as to prevent the spread of the disease causing organisms. In 19th century or till the first half of 20th century even, cholera caused by *Vibrio comma* in Asia and yellow fever caused by Tsetse fly in Africa were considered to be the most dreaded diseases by the Americans and Europeans. Hence, any person traveling from Asia or Africa to Europe or America was kept in isolation at the airport for a period of 40 days so that

*National Bureau of Plant Genetic Resources, Pusa, New Delhi.-110 012.*

any latent infection being carried by him might get expressed during that period. With the development of vaccines, etc. the practice has been discontinued in case of several diseases. However, the term quarantine now applies more to movement of plants/planting materials rather than to human beings and animals.

In the present context, plant quarantine is a government endeavour enforced through legislative measures to regulate the introduction of planting materials, plant products, soil, living organisms, etc. in order to prevent inadvertent introduction of pests (including fungi, bacteria, viruses, nematodes, insects and weeds) harmful to the agriculture of a country/state/region, and if introduced, prevent their establishment and further spread (Kahn, 1989). The plant quarantine measures act as filters against the entry of exotic species and check or delay the introduction of unwanted organisms. Therefore, practicing plant quarantine *i.e.* protection of plants by observing quarantine measures will go a long way in protecting our agriculture from the ravages of exotic pests and diseases and also from further spread of those present in a particular region.

The devastating effects resulting from diseases and pests introduced along with international movement of planting material, agricultural produce and products are well documented. (Ram Nath *et al.*, 1988). The Irish famine of 1845, which forced the people to migrate *en masse* from Europe, was the result of almost total failure of potato crop due to attack of late blight pathogen (*Phytophthora infestans*) introduced from Central America. Powdery mildew (*Uncinula necator*), root eating aphid (*Viteus vitifoliae*) and downy mildew (*Plasmopara viticola*) of grape were introduced in succession into France in mid nineteenth century from North America. These pests caused extensive damage to the grapevines and virtually annihilated the wine industry of the country. Coffee rust (*Hemileia vastatrix*) appeared in Sri Lanka in 1875, was so severe that production went down from 400 million pounds in 1870 to just 5 million pounds in 1889. The disease entered India in 1876 from Sri Lanka and within a decade, the coffee industry of South India was badly affected. Germany put embargo in 1875 on the import of potatoes from USA to keep out the dreaded Colorado potato beetle (*Leptinotarsa decemlineata*). In 1898, most European countries put embargo on American import directed mainly to keep out the San Jose´ scale (*Quadraspidiotus perniciosus*). Among the first few countries to promulgate comprehensive plant quarantine regulations were France, Germany, USA, UK and Australia.

In India, heavy losses in grain yield of *Cicer arietinum* crop in states of Haryana, Madhya Pradesh, Punjab and adjoining areas occurred during 1981-82 due to the introduction of virulent biotype of Aschochyta blight from the Middle East. Bunchy top of banana entered India from Sri Lanka and causes loss to banana of over Rs. 4 crores annually (Khetarpal and Ram Nath, 1998). The dreaded golden nematode (*Heterodera rostochiensis*) introduced from UK along with exotic seed material in 1960s has been causing severe infestation of potato tubers in the Nilgiris. Bunchy top of banana was reported for the first time in 1943 in Kottayam area of Travancore (Verghese, 1945). The disease has been introduced from Sri Lanka. Similarly, potato wart caused by *Synchytrium endobioticum* was first reported from the Darjeeling area of West Bengal by Ganguly and Paul, (1973). Jones (1961) reported for the first time the golden nematode of potato caused by *Heterodera rostochiensis* from Ooty (Tamil Nadu). Both these diseases were introduced in India from Europe. A noxious weed *Lantana camara* was introduced in 1809 from Central America, which spread to wastelands and pastures causing displacement of native species. All these examples clearly demonstrate that imported seed/planting material, especially bulk imports, without proper quarantine may result in introduction and establishment of quarantine pests into new areas which may severely damage the crop production and economy of a nation.

There is a need to protect our agriculture against the losses from introduction of these pests without restricting the international movement of people or commodities. One of the primary missions of plant protection organizations/institutions is to identify exotic pests of crops that are important in Indian agricultural scenario and assessing the potential damage that those pests could cause if introduced in our country.

## REGULATORY MEASURES

The first plant quarantine law was promulgated in Rouen, France in 1860 to suppress and prevent the spread of common berberry, which is the alternate host for wheat rust. Other countries to establish the quarantine laws after France, were Germany, USA, UK and Australia. In 1881, a California Pest Act was passed to prevent the spread of grape Phylloxera. However, subsequently, a number of countries became aware of the necessity and importance of plant quarantine for the safety and health of their agriculture. The first effort towards an International Agreement on Plant Protection was made in 1914 under the auspices of the International Institute of Agriculture, Rome. This was followed by an International Convention of Plant Protection with over 50 member countries of the Institute in 1919 under which Agreements regarding the issue and acceptance of phytosanitary certificates were finalized. The project got a set back due to Second World War and was later appreciated by Food and Agriculture Organisation (FAO) and in 1951, an International Plant Protection Convention (IPPC) was convened by the FAO (http//www.ippc.com). India became a party to this agreement in the year 1956 along with Australia, Sri Lanka, UK, Netherlands, Indonesia, Portugal and Vietnam. At present there are 156 signatory members of the IPPC.

### Destructive Insects and Pests Act (1914)

The quarantine measures are of utmost relevance to a country like India whose economy is largely agriculture based. The awareness to quarantine measures in India started in early 20th century when the Indian Government in 1906 ordered compulsory fumigation of imported cotton bales to prevent introduction of Mexican cotton boll weevil (*Anthonomus grandis*). The policy of using government authority to prevent entry of dangerous exotic pests is based on the ground that it is preferable to undergo and tolerate some inconvenience in an effort to exclude pests than to submit to the expenses of controlling them for an indefinite period. The quarantine law was implemented for the first time in India by the then Governor General of India on 3rd February, 1914. It was known as Destructive Insects and Pests (DIP) Act. A gazette notification entitled Rules for Regulating the Import of Plants, etc. into India was published in 1936 and Custom authorities were entrusted to enforce the plant quarantine regulations. Within a span of 20 years, from 1937 to 1956, the DIP Act was revised 8 times and amended in 1967 (Raychaudhuri,

1973), yet it needs to be further amended to meet the emerging scenario. The Central Plant Protection Organization was formed in 1946, under the Ministry of Food and Agriculture and a Plant Protection Advisor to Govt. of India was appointed as its Director. The first Plant Quarantine and Fumigation station was established in Bombay in 1949, followed by the second one in Madras in 1950. Later, a number of such stations were established at various ports. In 1962, the first land frontier station was established at Khalra at Indo-Pak border. Subsequently, in 1970, another land frontier station was established at Sukhiapokhri on Indo-Nepal border, which was later shifted to Panitanki. In 1966 the Indian Parliament also passed the Seed Act, which came into being in October, 1969 but unfortunately the Seed Act is also silent about the seed health (Gaur and Dev, 1988). In 1968, the Central Plant Protection Organization was raised to the status of a full-fledged Directorate of Plant Protection, Quarantine and Storage (DPPQS) with its headquarter at Faridabad in Haryana State.

The DIP Act (1914) provides for the following:

1. It authorizes the Central Government to prohibit or regulate the import into India or any part thereof or any specific place therein or any article or class of articles.
2. It authorizes the officers of the customs at every port to operate as if the rules under the DIP Act are made under the Sea and Custom Act.
3. It authorizes the Central Government to prohibit or regulate the export from a State or the transport from one State to another State in India of any plants and plant materials, diseases or insects, likely to cause infection or infestation. It also authorizes the control of transport and carriage and gives power to prescribe the nature of documents to accompany such plants and plant materials and articles.
4. It authorizes the State Government to make rules for the detention, inspection, disinfection or destruction of any pest or class of pests or of any article or class of articles, in respect of which the Central Government have issued notifications. It also authorizes the State Government for regulating the powers and duties of the officers whom it may appoint on its behalf
5. It provides penalty for persons who knowingly contravene the rules and regulations issued under the Act.
6. It also protects the persons from a suit or prosecution or other legal proceedings for anything done or intended to be done in good faith under the Act.

### Plants Fruits and Seeds Order (1984)

In 1984, a notification was issued under DIP Act namely Plants, Fruits and Seeds (Regulation of Import into India) Order popularly known as the PFS Order which was revised in 1989 after the announcement of the New Policy on Seed Development by the Government of India in 1988, proposing major modifications for smooth quarantine functioning. This order has been further revised and notified as Plant Quarantine (Regulation of Import into India) Order (2003).

### Plant Quarantine (Regulation of Import into India Order 2003)

This Order came into force due to the urgent need to fill-up the gaps in existing PFS order regarding import of germplasm/GMO's/transgenic plant material/bio-control agents etc., to fulfill India's legal obligations under the international Agreements, to protect the interest of the farmers of the country by preventing the entry, establishment and spread of destructive pests, and to safeguard the national bio-diversity from threats of invasions by alien species. Under this Order, the need for incorporation of Additional/Special declarations for freedom of import commodities from quarantine and invasive alien species (IAS), on the basis of standardized pest risk analysis (PRA), particularly for seed/planting materials is also taken care of. Further, the scope of plant quarantine activities has been widened with incorporation of additional definitions. The other salient features of the Order are:

- Prohibition on import of commodities with weed/alien species contamination as per Schedule VIII, and restriction on import of packaging material of plant origin unless treated.
- Provisions included for regulating the import of soil, peat and sphagnum moss; germplasm/GMOs/transgenic material for research, live insects/microbial cultures & biocontrol agents and import of timber and wooden logs.
- Agricultural imports have been classified as (a) Prohibited plant species (Schedule IV); (b) Restricted species where import permitted only by authorized institutions (Schedule V); (c) Restricted species permitted only with additional declarations of freedoms from quarantine/regulated pests and subject to specified treatment certifications (Schedule VI) and; (d) Plant material imported for consumption/industrial processing permitted with normal Phytosanitary Certificate (Schedule VII).
- Permit requirement enforced on imports of seeds including flower seeds, propagating material and mushroom spawn cultures.
- Additional declarations being specified in the Order for import of 144 agricultural commodities with specific lists of more than 590 quarantine pests and 61 weed species.
- Notified points of entry increased to 130 from the existing 59.
- Certification fee and inspection charges have been rationalized.

So far, *i.e.*, till November 2004, four amendments of the Plant Quarantine (PQ) Order 2003 have been notified to the WTO revising definitions, clarifications regarding specific queries raised by quarantine authorities of various countries, with revised lists of crops under the Schedules IV, V VI and VII. The revised list under Schedule VI and VII now include 392 and 296 crops/commodities, respectively.

To facilitate the import of germplasm for research and development of new crop varieties, the Plant Introduction Division was created in 1961, at Indian Agricultural Research Institute, New Delhi. This Division was raised to the status of National Bureau of Plant Genetic Resources (NBPGR) in 1976 with its headquarters at IARI Campus, New Delhi. It is the responsibility of NBPGR to issue import permit for the germplasm coming from different countries to be used by ICAR institutes and other state Agricultural Universities and to do quarantine of small samples of germplasm/transgenics meant for research purposes. Similarly, inspection and clearance of the germplasm required by the International Crop Research Institute for Semi-Arid Tropics, Pattancheru, Andhra Pradesh, was being taken care of by the Central Plant Protection Training Institute (CPPTI), Hyderabad since 1973 but in 1986, a Regional Plant Quarantine Laboratory (now Regional Station) of NBPGR was established at Hyderabad which took over the responsibilities of CPPTI, and now also caters to the quarantine needs of public and private sector organizations of certain parts of south India.

## New Policy on Seed Development (1988)

The New Policy on Seed Development (NPSD) came into force on 1st October, 1988 with an objective to provide the Indian farmers with the best genetic material available anywhere in the world to increase agricultural productivity, farm income and export earnings. This policy is a result of a positive and progressive attitude of the government towards seeds. To encourage an export-oriented horticultural industry the government wanted to provide best seed or other planting material like bulbs, cuttings, saplings and bud woods freely to the farming community, which would produce exportable surpluses of the best quality. Simultaneously, the government wanted to take all precautions so that there is no introduction of new insects or diseases in the country. Keeping in view the indigenous capabilities, the policy takes a differentiated approach to the import of various categories of seeds and planting materials. The quarantine policy for different categories of seeds is also different. Thus, the policy aimed at liberalization of imports along with streamlining of plant quarantine procedures and encouragement to domestic seed industry through incentives.

## National Seeds Policy (2002)

The Seeds Act, 1966 and Seeds Control Order promulgated there under, and the New Policy on Seeds Development, 1988 forms the basis of promotion and regulation of the Seed Industry. Far-reaching changes, however, have taken place in the national economic and agricultural scenario and in the international environment since the enactment of the existing seed legislation and the announcement of the 1988 Policy. Globalization and economic liberalization have opened up several new opportunities as well as challenges. While providing the appropriate climate for the seed industry to utilize available and prospective opportunities, safeguarding the interests of Indian farmers, protecting and conserving agro-biodiversity and traditional knowledge, are the main objectives of the policy. The National Seeds Policy has come into force which encompasses quality assurance mechanisms coupled with facilitation of a vibrant and responsible seed industry. Major thrust areas for quarantine of imported seeds and planting material in the policy includes the following points.

- It would be ensured that there are no deleterious effects on the environment, health and bio-safety.
- Compulsory fulfillment of requirements under prevailing plant quarantine procedures would be required to prevent entry into the country of exotic pests, diseases and weeds detrimental to the Indian agriculture.
- All imports of seeds would require a permit granted by the Plant Protection Advisor to the Government of India and a small specified quantity of imported seeds would be sent to the Gene Bank maintained by NBPGR.
- All import of seeds and planting material, etc. will be allowed freely subject to EXIM Policy guidelines and the requirements of PFS Order, 1989 as amended from time to time.
- Tubers and bulbs of flowers would additionally be subjected to post-entry quarantine. However, the existing policy which permits free import of seeds of

vegetables, flowers and ornamental plants, cuttings, saplings of flowers, tubers and bulbs of flowers by certain specified categories of importers would continue.

- After the arrival of consignments at the port of entry, quarantine checks would be undertaken; which include visual inspection, laboratory inspection, fumigation and grow-out tests.

In India, private companies are more active in seed trade while government's role is more in proactive policy development. A harmonious interaction between the two can put Indian seed industry at par with the best in the world by preventing the introduction of exotic pests through effective quarantine measures.

## NATIONAL PLANT QUARANTINE SET-UP

The Directorate of Plant Protection, Quarantine and Storage (DPPQS) of Ministry of Agriculture is the apex body for implementation of plant quarantine regulation. It has a national network of 29 plant quarantine stations at different airports (10), seaports (10) and land frontiers (9). In all, three categories of materials being imported under the PFS Order, 1989: (a) bulk consignments of grains/pulses for consumption, (b) bulk consignments of seeds/planting materials for sowing/planting, and (c) samples of germplasm in small quantities for research purposes. The Plant Quarantine Stations under the DPPQS undertake quarantine processing and clearance of consignments of the first two categories, while, NBPGR undertakes the quarantine processing of all plant germplasm and transgenic planting material under exchange. NBPGR has developed well-equipped laboratories and green house complex (Mathur and Lal, 1997). Recently, a containment facility has also been established for processing transgenics (Khetarpal and Pandey, 2001) in Delhi.

Out of the three different categories of material being imported, bulk imports for sowing/planting carry maximum risk as thorough examination and treatment becomes difficult and planting area required is also far too large. Quarantine processing is often restricted to smaller samples derived from them and based on results of these samples the whole consignment is rejected/detained or released after giving fumigation treatment or fungicidal/insecticidal treatments. The bulk consignments meant for consumption pose lesser hazards. However, certain small samples meant for research purposes are of immense quarantine importance. These samples usually comprise of germplasm material or wild relatives or landraces of a crop, and are thus more likely to carry diverse biotypes/races/strains of the pest/pathogen. Besides, in case of true seed, generally, risks are more with deep-seated infections than with surface-borne contamination. However, import of vegetative propagules present a much higher order of risk than true seeds.

## SIGNIFICANT INTERCEPTIONS IN IMPORTED MATERIAL

Over the years, a large number of pests and pathogens have been intercepted in imported material and germplasm during quarantine processing. Significant interceptions, many of which are yet not reported from India are enumerated below.

**TABLE 4.1:** IMPORTANT INSECTS AND MITES INTERCEPTED IN GERMPLASM UNDER EXCHANGE

| *Insects/ Mites* | *Crop* | *Origin/ Source* |
|---|---|---|
| *Acanthoscelides* sp. | *Leucaena* sp. | Guatemala, Mexico, UK, |
| | *Phaselous vulgaris* | USA, Italy |
| *Anthonomus africanum* | *Hibiscus* | Italy |
| *A. pullus* | *Hibiscus* sp., *Pennisetum* sp., *Sesamum* sp. | Nigeria, Zambia |
| *Bruchidius* spp. | *Acacia albida, Cassia* sp. | Australia, Ethiopia |
| | *Cordia* sp. | UK |
| | *Glycyrrhiza glabra, Trifolium* sp. | Iran, Iraq, Senegal |
| | *T. alexandrinum,* | USSR |
| | *Lablab purpureus* | Australia |
| | *Sesbania* sp. | Philippines |
| *Callosobruchus subinmotatus* | *Voandezia* sp. | Nigeria |
| *Cryptolestes* sp. | *Helianthus annus* | USSR |
| *Ephestia cautella* | *Gmelina arborea* | Thailand |
| *Eriococcus araucaria* | *Araucaria angustifolia* | Argentina |
| *Eurytoma* sp. | *Medicago sativa, Sesamum* sp. (pods), *Trifolium pratense* | Italy, USA, Zambia |
| *Mycetophagus quadriguttatus* | *Cocos nucifera* | Ivory Coast |
| *Oryzaephilus mercator* | *Arachis hypogaea, Bauhinia* sp., Zea mays | Philippines, Thailand, USA |
| *O. surinamensis* | *Beta vulgaris, Triticum* spp., *Lycopersicon esculentum* | Italy, Mexico USA |
| *Prostephanus truncates* | *Triticum aestivum* | Syria |
| *Rhizopertha dominica* | *Allium sativum, Beta vulgaris, Hordeum vulgare, Oryza sativa, Vigna* sp., *Triticale, Triticum* sp., *Zea mays* | Bhutan, Egypt, Germany, Italy, Mexico, Philippines, Swedan, Syria, Thailand, UK, USA |
| *Sitophilus granaries* | *Avena sativa, Triticale, Triticum* spp. | France, Hungary, Mexico, Syria, Turkey, UK, USA, Upper Volta |
| *S. zemais* | *Zea Mays* | USA |
| *Tribolium castaneum* | *Beta vulgaris, Gladiolus* sp., *Hordeum vulgare, Seasamum indicum, Simmondsia clunensis, Vigna* sp., *Triticum* sp., *Zea mays* | Myanmar, China, Germany, Italy, Mexico, Pakistan, Philippines, Poland, Romania, Sweden, Syria, Thailand, UK, USA |
| *Trogoderma granarium* | *Atropa belladonna, Beta vulgaris, Carthamus tinctorius, Hordeum vulgare, Triticum* sp. | Afghanistan, France, Iran, Israel, Germany |
| *T. inclusum* | *Beta vulgaris* | Italy |

**Insects and Mites**

This include *Acanthoscelides obtectus* on *Cajanus cajan* introduced from Brazil and Columbia, in *Phaseolus vulgaris* introduced from Italy and Nigeria; *Anthonomus grandis* on *Gossypium* spp. introduced from USA; *Ephestia cautella* on Macadamia (nuts) and *Vigna* spp. from USA; *Pachymerus lacerdae* on nuts of *Orbynya phalerata* introduced from Brazil; *Quadrastichodella eucalypti* on *Eucalyptus* spp. from Australia. Apart from this other interceptions of insects and mites are given in Table 4.1 (Plate 4.1).

## Nematodes

This include interceptions of *Ditylenchus dipsaci* in *Allium cepa* (bulbs) from UK, *Heterodera schachtii* in *Beta vulgaris* (soil clods) from Germany, Denmark and Italy (Sethi *et al.*, 1972) and *Rhadinaphelenchus cocophilus* in *Cocos nucifera* (husked nuts) from Guyana and *Aphelenchoides fragariae* in strawberry (rooted plants) from Australia. *Heterodera schachtii*, the sugarbeet nematode and *Heterodera rostochiensis*, the golden nematode were intercepted at Madras port in a bulk consignment of potato from Scotland, Northern Ireland and West Germany during 1965-68, the consignment of which was destroyed by dumping into the sea (Renjhen, 1973). Twelve thousand cuttings of hops (*Humulus lupulus*) were unauthorisedly imported into India in 1974 from Australia were intercepted at New Delhi Airport as they were carrying the nematode *Heterodera humuli*. Other nematodes intercepted in germplasm have been listed in Table 4.2.

**TABLE 4.2:** IMPORTANT NEMATODES INTERCEPTED IN GERMPLASM UNDER EXCHANGE

| *Nematode* | *Crop (Planting Material or Soil on which Intercepted)* | *Source/Origin* |
|---|---|---|
| *Anguina tritici* | *Triticum aestivum* (Seed galls) | Italy, Turkey, UK |
| *Aphelenchoides besseyi* | *Digitaria smutsii*, *Oryza glaberrima*, *O. sativa*, *Setaria italica*, *Stylosanthes hamata* (Seeds) | Cameroon, Australia, Bangladesh, Brazil, Myanmar, Costa Rica, (seeds) Indonesia, Italy, Madagascar, Nigeria, Philippines, UK, USA, Turkey |
| *Bursaphelenchus* spp. | *Elaeis guineensis* | Indonesia |
| *Ditylenchus angustus* | *Oryza sativa* (seeds) | Madagascar, Philippines, USA |
| *D. destructor* | *Humulus lupulus* (rooted plants) *Solanum tuberosum* (tubers) | Australia, Germany, Philippines, UK, USA, Peru |
| *Ditylenchus* spp. | *Euphorbia tirucalli*, *Humulus lupulus* (rooted plants), *Microchloa caffra* (plants), *Narcissus* sp. (bulbs), *Pepper* (plants), *Prunus americana* *Rosa* sp. (plants), *Stylosanthes* sp. (seeds), *Tulipa* sp. (bulbs), *Helianthus* sp. | Australia, Denmark, The Netherlands, Indonesia, Philippines |
| *Helicotylenchus erythrinae* | *Sorghum halpense* (plants) | USA |
| *Heterodera goettingiana* | *Pisum sativum* (soil clods) | UK |

| | | |
|---|---|---|
| *Heterodera* spp. | *Cynodon dactylon* (soil clods), *Ipomoea batatas* (tubers), *Pinus oocarpa* (soil clods), *Saccharum officinarum* (soil with cuttings), *Solanum tuberosum* (soil with tuber), *Triticum aestivum* (soil) | Brazil, Mexico, Puerto Rico, Turkey, USA |
| *Hirschmanniella* sp. | *Zizania cauducifolia* (plants) | Thailand |
| *Paratylenchus* sp. | *Mentha* sp. (rhizomes), *Triticum aestivum* (soil clods) | Syria, Vietnam |
| *Pratylenchus hamatus* | *Mentha spicata* (rooted material) | Brazil |
| *Pratylenchus brachyurus* | *Fragaria* sp., *Strawberry* (plants) | USA |
| *P. crenatus* | *Maltls* sp., *Rosa* sp., *Rubus* sp. (rooted plants) | The Netherands, UK |
| *P.penetrans* | *Cynodon dactylon, Mentha* spp., *Prunus* sp., *Pyrus* sp., *Rubus* sp. (rooted plants) | Bulgaria, Japan, USA |
| *P. vulnus* | *Annona* sp., *Fragaria* sp., *Musa* sp. (suckers), *Prunus* sp., *Pyrus* sp. (plants), *Pyracantha* sp. | Australia, Canada, Italy, Surinam, USA, UK |
| *P. zeae* | *Saccharum officinarum* (cuttings), *Sorghum halpense* (rooted plants); | USA |
| *Radopholus similis* | *Musa* spp. (suckers) | Jamaica |
| *Rotylenchulus reniformis* | *Gladilous* spp. (bulbs), *Pisum sativum* (soil clods) | Hungary, USA |
| *Scutellonema bradys* | *Dioscorea alata* (tubers) | USA |
| *Xiphinema* spp. | *Beta vulgaris* (soil clods), *Carya* sp. (plants), black berry, raspberry (plants), *Malus* sp. (plants), *Prunus* sp. (plants), *Pistacia vera*, *Persia americana* (plants), *Ribes* sp. (plants), *Rubus* sp. (plants), *Vitis vinifera* (plants) | Australia, Bangladesh, USA |

**Fungi**

This include *Peronospora manshurica* (downy mildew of soybean) from more than 16 countries, *Uromyces betae* from UK; *Fusarium nivale* in wheat (from Italy, Mexico, Sweden, UK), on barley (from Italy and Hungary) and on *Aegilops* (from East Germany), safflower rust, *Puccinia carthami* from USA; *Ascochyta pisi* from Europe and USA; *Botryodiplodia theobromae* from several Asian countries; *Drechslera maydis* from minor millets imported from Africa and Americas and *Ustilago maydis* from USA (Khetarpal *et al.*, 2001b).

*Phoma betae* and *Heterodera schachtii* were intercepted in a 6 metric tonne consignment of sugar beet from Denmark in 1971 at Bombay port (Sethi *et al.*, 1972). In 1973, 1,20,000 seeds of oil palm (*Elaeis guineensis*) were imported from Nigeria. When the seeds were sown in post entry quarantine, they were found to have severe infection of *Fusarium oxysporum* f. sp. *elaedis* causing the vascular wilt. Another pathogen of oil palm *Schizophyllum commune* was intercepted in a consignment of oil palm from Papua New Guinea at Madras port in 1978. A consignment of oil palm from Malaysia showed the incidence of *Marasmius* bunch rot caused by *Marasmius palmivorus* when seeds were sown in post-entry quarantine nursery at Andamans and Nicobar islands in 1985. One lakh gladioli bulbs from Netherlands were found to have the incidence of *Fusarium* rot caused by *Fusarium oxysporum* f. sp. *gladioli* in 1980. *Tilletia contraversa* and *Claviceps purpurea* causing dwarf bunt and ergot, respectively, in wheat were intercepted in a consignment from USA in 1988-89. Reddy and Muthaiyan (1982) reported the interception of *Fusarium moniliforme* f. sp. *subglutinans* in seed of *Pinus carabaea* var. *hondurensis* from Fiji. The pathogen causes pitch canker of Pines.

**TABLE 4.3:** IMPORTANT PATHOGENS INTERCEPTED FROM GERMPLASM UNDER EXCHANGE

| *Pathogen* | *Crop* | *Source/Origin* |
|---|---|---|
| *Alternaria brassicae* | *Brassica* spp. | Italy, Sweden, Taiwan, USA, Bangladesh, Ethiopia, Canada |
| *A. brassicicola* | *Allium* spp. | Philippines, UK, Germany, Denmark, Canada, Ethiopia, France, Japan, N. Korea, Nepal |
| *A. helianthi* | *Lycopersicon esculentum* | Taiwan |
| *A. padwickii* | *Oryza sativa,* | Philippines, USA |
| | *Gossypium* sp. | France |
| *A. ricini* | *Ricinus communis* | France, Italy, USA, USSR, |
| | *Capsicum* spp. | Romania, USA |
| *A. solani* | *Hibiscus* sp. | Nigeria |
| | *Carthamus tinctorius,* | Italy, USA |
| | *Solanum melongena* | Bangladesh |
| *A. pinodella* | *Pisum sativum, Lens esculentum, Medicago* sp. | Germany, Hungary, UK, USA, Syria, Canada |
| *A. sojicola* | *Glycine max* | USA |
| *Botrytis cinerea* | *Aegilops* spp. | Greece, Germany, USA |
| | *Amaryllis* sp. | USA |
| | *Brassica* spp. | Sweden |
| | *Calligonum* spp. | USSR |
| | *Carthamus tinctorius* | Italy, USA |
| | *Cucumis* sp. | USA |
| | *Daucus carota* | UK |
| | *Ferula assafoetida* | USSR |
| | *Ficus* spp. | USA |
| | *Helianthus annus* | France, Italy, USA, USSR |
| | *Hordeum vulgare* | Italy |
| | *Pisum sativum* | Germany, Sweden |

| | | |
|---|---|---|
| | *Psophocarpus tetragonolobus* | Papua New Guinea |
| | *Rosa* spp. | Germany, The Netherlands, |
| | *Trifolium* spp. | USA, UK |
| | *Triticum* sp. | Czechoslovakia |
| | *Vitis* spp. | Italy, Belgium, Czechoslovakia, Switzerland, USA, USSR |
| | *Zea mays* | USA |
| *Cercospora corchori* | *Corchorus olitorius* | Bangladesh |
| *C. kikuchii* | *Glycine max* | Sri Lanka, Taiwan, USA |
| *C. sesame* | *Sesamum* sp. | Korea, Nepal, Thailand |
| *Claviceps purpurea* | *Aegilops* spp. | Germany |
| | *Avena sativa* | USA |
| | *Agropyron* spp. | Germany, USA |
| | *Dactylis glomerata* | Italy |
| | *Festuca* sp. | USA |
| | *Hordeum vulgare* | USA |
| | *Lolium* sp. | Italy |
| | *Secale cereale* | Canada, USA |
| | *Triticum* spp. | Hungary, Italy, Syria, USA |
| *C. lagenarium* | *Cucumis melo* | USA |
| *Drechslera maydis* | *Capsicum* spp. | USA |
| | *Corchorus* sp. | UK |
| | *Hordeum vulgare* | Taiwan |
| | *Lycopersicon esculentum* | Mexico |
| | *Sorghum* sp. | Australia |
| | *Stylosanthes* sp. | USA |
| | *Tripsacum* sp. | Argentina, China, Nigeria |
| | *Zea mays* | Mexico, Pakistan, Thailand, USA |
| *D. nodulosa* | *Eleusine* spp. | Bhutan, Italy, Malawi, UK, Zimbabwe |
| | *Oryza sativa* | The Netherlands, Philippines, USA |
| | Wild rice | Philippines |
| *D. setariae* | *Echinochloa* spp. | Japan |
| | *Panicum maximum* | Australia |
| | *Setaria* spp. | China, Korea, UK |
| | *Sorghum vulgare* | USA |
| *D. sorokiniana* | *Aegilops* spp. | China, Germany Japan |
| | *Agropyron* spp. | USA |
| | *Atriplex* sp. | Australia |
| | *Atropa belladona* | Portugal |
| | *Avena sativa* | Canada, Hungary, Japan, USA, USSR |
| | *Beta vulgaris* | Germany, USA |
| | *Carthamus tinctorius* | Italy, USA |
| | *Capsicum* sp. | Hungary, Philippines, Taiwan |
| | *Cucumis* sp. | USA |

Table 4.3 (*contd. on* p. 60)

Table 4.3 (*contd. from* p. 59)

| | | |
|---|---|---|
| | *Corchorus* sp. | Bangladesh |
| | *Daucus carota* | Germany |
| | *Echniochola* spp. | Japan |
| | *Eleusine* spp. | Italy, Japan, UK, Zambia, Zimbabwe |
| | *Fagopyrum* sp. | USSR |
| | *Glycine max* | Taiwan |
| | *Gossypium* sp. | USSR |
| | *Goynaldia* sp. | China |
| | *Helianthus annus* | USA |
| | *Hibiscus cannabinus* | Bangladesh |
| | *Hordeum* sp. | Canada, Italy, Mexico, Sweden, Syria, USA, USSR |
| | *H. vulgare* | Mexico |
| | *Lesquerella* sp. | USA |
| | *Luffa* sp. | Philippines |
| | *Lycopersicon esculentum* | Taiwan |
| | *Panicum miliaccum* | Mexico, USA |
| | *Secale cereale* | Canada, USA |
| | *Setaria* spp. | Mexico, South Africa, UK |
| | *Solanum melongena* | Japan |
| | *Sorghum* spp. | USA |
| | *Triticum* spp. | Australia, Brazil, Canada, Italy, Israel, Korea, Mexico, Norway, Poland, Sweden, UK, USA, USSR |
| | *Zea mays* | Nepal, South Africa, USA |
| | *Hordeum* spp. | Italy, Hungary |
| | *Triticum* spp. | Italy, Sweden, UK, Mexico |
| *E. poae* | *Aegilops* spp. | Germany, USA |
| | *Agropyron* spp. | USA |
| | *Avena sativa* | Hungary, Japan, USA |
| | *Hordeum* spp. | Italy |
| | *Triticum* spp. | Italy, USA, UK |
| *Gloeocercospora sorghi* | *Sorghum vulgare* | Nigeria, Philippines |
| | *S. biclor* | USA |
| *Macrophomina phaseolina* | *Vigna radiate* | Taiwan |
| | *Gescentia alata* | UK |
| | *Solanum melongena* | Bangladesh |
| | *Leucaena* spp. | USA, Taiwan |
| | *Corchorus* spp. | Bangladesh |
| | *Sesamum indicum* | South Africa, USA |
| *Pestalotiopsis mangiferae* | *Alocasia delludata* | Singapore |
| *Phomopsis sajae* | *Glycine max* | Poland, Taiwan, USA |
| *P. helianthi* | *Helianthus annuus* | USA, Canada, Indonesia, Ethiopia, USSR, Argentina, Australia, Hungary, Italy, Spain |
| *Pyricularia grisea* | *Echinochloa* spp. | Japan |
| | *Eleusine* spp. | Italy, Kenya, Malawi, Nepal, Sri Lanka, UK, Zambia, Zimbabwe |

| | | |
|---|---|---|
| | *Setaria* spp. | UK |
| *P. oryzae* | *Eleusine* spp. | Nepal |
| *Tolyposporium penicillariae* | *Pennisetum* sp. | UK, USA |
| *Ustilago hordei* | *Hordeum vulgare* | Argentina |
| *Xanthomonas campestris pv. campestris* | *Brassica* spp. | UK, Canada, USA, Sweden, France, Pakistan, Taiwan |

## Bacteria

Important bacterial interceptions include *Xanthomonas campestris* pv. *campestris* from brassicas imported from Australia and Canada; *Burkholderia solonacearum 'biovar3'* in association with groundnut imported from Australia and *Pseudomonas syringae* pv. *syringae* from *Hibiscus cannabinus* imported from Bangladesh.

## Viruses

The important viruses intercepted include soybean mosaic potyvirus in soybean, pea seed-borne mosaic potyvirus in pea and frenchbean, peanut stripe potyvirus in groundnut, cowpea mottle comovirus in cowpea, barley stripe mosaic hordeivirus in wheat, bean common mosaic potyvirus and broadbean stain comovirus in faba bean (Khetarpal *et al.*, 2001a) (Plate 4.1). Peanut mottle virus (PMV) was intercepted by CPPTI, Hyderabad during post-entry quarantine inspection of ground nut germplasm imported by ICRISAT.

**TABLE 4.4**: IMPORTANT VIRUSES INTERCEPTED FROM THE GERMPLASM UNDER EXCHANGE

| *Pathogen* | *Crop* | *Source/Origin* |
|---|---|---|
| Unidentified filamentous virus | Adzuki bean | Germany |
| Cowpea-aphid borne mosaic potyvirus | Cowpea | USA |
| Unidentified filamentous virus | Cowpea | USA |
| Bean yellow mosaic potyvirus | Faba bean | Bulgaria |
| Broad bean stain comovirus | Faba bean | Bulgaria |
| Bean common mosaic potyvirus | Frenchbean | Columbia, CIS, Hungary, USA |
| Carla-virus like particles | *Lilium* spp. | Israel |
| Unidentified isometric virus | Mungbean | Germany, Indonesia, AVRDC (Taiwan) |
| Unidentified filamentous virus | *Phaseolus acutifolius* | USA |
| Unidentified filamentous virus | Savibean | France |

## Weeds

In the early years of 19th century *Lantana camara* was introduced from Central America. Similarly, *Phalaris minor* and *Parthenium hysterophorus* were introduced into India from Mexico and South America in the middle of 20th century (Plate 4.1).

## PRESENT INTERNATIONAL SCENARIO

The recent biologic and economic development in International trade activities and the thrust of the World Trade Organization (WTO) Agreements and the Convention on Biological Diversity (CBD) suggest that countries need to update their quarantine or plant health services to improve health status of their exports.

### World Trade Organization

The establishment of the WTO in 1995 has provided unlimited opportunities for international trade of agricultural products. History has witnessed the devastating effects resulting from diseases and pests introduced along with the international movement of planting materials, agricultural produce and products. It is only recently however, that legal standards have been promulgated in the form of Sanitary and Phytosanitary (SPS) Measures for regulating the international trade. The WTO Agreement on the Application of SPS measures concerns the application of food safety and animal and plant health regulations. It recognizes government's rights to take SPS measures but stipulates that they must be based on science, should be applied only to the extent necessary to protect human, animal or plant life or health and should not arbitrarily or unjustifiably discriminate between members where identical or similar conditions prevail (http://www.wto.org, Khetarpal and Gupta, 2002).

The SPS Agreement aims to overcome health-related impediments of plants and animals to market access by encouraging the "establishment, recognition and application of common SPS measures by different members". The primary incentive for the use of common international norms is that these provide the necessary health protection based on scientific evidence and improve trade flow at the same time.

SPS measures are defined as any measure applied:

(a) to protect animal or plant life or health within the territory of the Member State from risks arising from the entry, establishment or spread of pests, diseases, disease-carrying organisms or disease causing organisms;

(b) to protect human or animal life or health within the territory of the Member State from risks arising from additives, contaminants, toxins or disease causing organisms in food, beverages or foodstuffs;

(c) to protect human life or health within the territory of the Member State from risks arising from diseases carried by animals, plants or products thereof, or from the entry, establishment or spread of pests; or

(d) to prevent or limit other damage within the territory of the Member State from the entry, establishment or spread of pests.

Prior to the establishment of WTO, governments on a voluntary basis could adopt international standards, guidelines, recommendations and other advisory texts. Although these norms remain voluntary, a new status has in effect been conferred upon them by the SPS Agreement. A WTO member adopting such norms is presumed to be in full compliance with the SPS Agreement.

**Existing International Organizations for Developing Standards**

In order to achieve the targets international standards need to be developed for which WTO has assigned the responsibility as follows:

(a) *For food safety:* The Codex Alimentarius Commission (CAC) based in Rome is a subsidiary organ of the Food and Agricultural Organization (FAO) of United Nations and the World Health Organization (WHO). The SPS Agreement designates Codex as the authority for all matters related to international food safety evaluation and harmonization. Codex also develops methodologies relating to food additives, veterinary drugs, pesticide residues, and contaminants, methods of analysis and sampling, and codes and guidelines of hygienic practice.

(b) *For animal health and zoonosis:* Zoonosis is animal diseases transmittable to humans. The standards, guidelines and recommendations are developed under the auspices of the International Office of Epizootics (IOE), Paris. The IOE develops manuals on animal diseases, standards for diagnosis, vaccination, disease control, disinfection and certification.

(c) *For plant health:* The International Plant Protection Convention (IPPC), Rome plays a vital role in trade as it is the organization recognized by the WTO under the SPS Agreement, as the source for International Standards for the Phytosanitary Measures (ISPMs) affecting trade. The guidelines and recommendations are developed under the auspices of the Secretariat, IPPC.

The above three organizations commonly called as the 'three sisters' are observers and important contributors to SPS committee meetings. They are also called in as experts to give advice to WTO dispute settlement panels. For matters not covered by the above organizations, appropriate standards, guidelines and recommendations are promulgated by other relevant international organizations open for membership to all members of WTO, as identified by the SPS Committee. The WTO agreements suggest that countries not only update their quarantine or plant health services to improve health status of their exports; they should also incorporate pest risk analysis (PRA) for making regulatory decisions during imports and exports. To this end FAO has been working in consultation with various Regional Plant Protection Organizations such as that of Europe and North America. It has published ISPM Part 1 on Guidelines for pest risk analysis, dated February, 1996 under the provisions of SPS Measures. The standards, guidelines and recommendations for SPS have been developed under the auspices of the secretariat of the IPPC. The essence of the ISPM and SPS documents is regulatory action for International trade. Imports should be based on an acceptable level of risk through PRA and take transparent action having the least negative effect on the flow of international trade but still commensurate with the level of risk.

Quarantine services of most countries determine the entry status of imported agricultural commodities based on perceived risk. The entry status is the combination of a country's law, regulations, guidelines, policy and decisions of inspectors at ports or points of entry. A biologically based position about entry status is that if the risk (*i.e.*

chances of pest entry) is perceived to be high, the entry status of imported articles should be conservative, or conversely if the risk is perceived to be low, the entry status should be liberal. The entry status is also influenced by the use of effective and practical safeguards. If the risk of introduction is low but the entry status is conservative, then it is not based on scientific facts but alleged to be a trade barrier. If the risk is high and the entry is liberal, again the status is not scientifically sound.

A PRA conducted according to international standards can provides the basis for our national planners to allocate resources to areas facing the highest risk and thereby, enabling them to better protect our agriculture and environment from the entry and establishment of exotic pests. PRA offers an improved method for assessing and managing risk by providing a format to consider and perhaps weigh the relative importance of the various factors leading to a more biologically sound approach to pest risk and mitigation. PRA, which consists of risk assessment and risk management, is a procedure by which quarantine services can technically justify new regulations, phytosanitary guidelines or safeguards, operational procedures, entry status of imported articles and resource allocations (Gupta *et al.* 2002a).

The IPPC requirement for a PRA consists of three stages (viz., Initiation, Risk Assessment and Risk Management) whose compilation should be fully documented in the event a review or dispute arises. The PRA should clearly document information sources and the rationale used in reaching a management decision regarding mitigation measures that have been taken or are to be taken. PRA consists of risk assessment (scientific estimation of likelihood and magnitude of risk of establishment of a given pest) and impact assessment (estimation of the consequences of the establishment of pest). Therefore, to ensure that imported commodity present a minimal pest or disease risk to our agriculture and forestry, PRA must be conducted.

**Convention on Biological Diversity**

The Convention on Biological Diversity (CBD), affirms that conservation of biodiversity is a common concern of humankind and reaffirms that nations have sovereign rights over their own biological resources. The treaty states as major objectives the conservation of biological diversity and sustainable use of its components; fair and equitable sharing of the benefits arising out from the use of genetic resources; and appropriate transfer of relevant technologies (http://www.cbd.org).

The quarantine related commitments made by parties to the Convention are:

- to establish means to regulate, manage or control risks associated with use and release of living modified organisms from biotechnology with likely adverse environmental effects (Article 8g).
- to prevent introduction of species from outside a country which could threaten native ecosystems or species (Article 8h).

Although CBD covers all types of organisms (including plants), the scope of IPPC appears broader. The IPPC covers all organisms injurious to plants and plant products, whereas the coverage under the CBD is subject to their sustainable use. The ISPM 11 (supplement) on Analysis of Environmental risks is being developed by IPPC to address the environmental safety issues. This would give an independent framework of rules for WTO members who are not signatories to CBD (Gupta *et al.*, 2002b).

## CHALLENGES AHEAD

India is slowly emerging as a participant in the world's agricultural trade. Nevertheless, it is necessary to watch this sector carefully from both import and export fronts in order to protect the interest of domestic consumers, traders and producers. It is essential to fine tune the balance between domestic demand, exportable surplus and imports. With this aim, India needs to gear up certain key activities as given below:

### Establishment of a Central Coordination Unit

To meet the challenges of liberalization of trade posed by the WTO, there is a need to have a Central Co-ordination Unit to act as the nodal agency of the SPS Agreement, under the Ministry of Agriculture. An SPS Committee needs to be set-up to coordinate activities regarding setting up of national standards for SPS measures adopted/to be adopted and notify the same to the WTO. This would also facilitate periodic review of its implications and to take necessary actions to mitigate its repercussions in order to eventually harmonize our trade policies. Preparation of a database on endemic pests would be the first step in this direction.

A PRA cell under the central unit needs to be established on priority, so as to play a critical role in decision making prior to import. It would also boost the export of the country, as the importers would be assured of the health status of the material. Well-equipped laboratories with trained manpower are the backbone of any inspection and certification system. The PRA submitted by any other government or agency should be thoroughly reviewed for its scientific and technical justifications. A good example is the PRA of soybean import into India initially prepared by the US but which had a number of anomalies and could be technically challenged.

For carrying out a PRA for the commodities of trade, a database on endemic pests is necessary. Steps taken by Regional Plant Quarantine Station, Chennai in this direction is commendable and needs to be further supported. Also, a database on the potential quarantine pests for India is being compiled at NBPGR, New Delhi to supplement the information. An effective risk analysis would indeed minimize or eliminate the utilization of techniques for detection of pests and would facilitate the quick release of the material from quarantine based on sound scientific and logical decisions as per WTO norms.

### Upgrading the National Quarantine Set-up

The establishment of WTO coupled with the liberalization policies of the government has provided unlimited opportunities for flow of materials. Quarantine set-up needs to be upgraded as this could result in globalization of pests. In the light of removal of quantitative restrictions in trade since April 1, 2001, the issue of seed health has assumed paramount importance in order to prevent the entry of exotic seed borne diseases and pests along with the imported material into new areas. Further, the increase in import of transgenic planting material and the stipulation of WTO under its SPS Agreement has brought about additional elements of challenge to be faced by quarantine personnel.

Looking at our National Plant Protection Organization in totality, there is a need to upgrade its manpower, infrastructure and capabilities to bring it up to the international standards. The DPPQS, which is charged with the responsibility of quarantine has initiated upgradation activities at all the major airports and seaports. Particularly with the ratification of WTO treaty, the responsibilities have increased manifold but infrastructural facilities did not improve to commensurate with the additional responsibilities. Recently, four state-of-art facilities have been established at Delhi, Chennai, Kolkata and Amritsar with the UNDP/FAO assistance, but these laboratories lack qualified technical manpower and resources to effectively perform all the assigned functions. For a country of our size, having more than 50 ports of entry, many more such facilities are required.

The domestic quarantine regulations already promulgated for eight destructive pests (fluted scale, San José scale, coffee berry borer, codling moth, banana bunchy top and mosaic viruses, potato cyst nematode, potato wart and apple scab) seem to be a complete failure as there are reports of spread of these pests to neighboring states and also to different parts of the country. Extensive eradication measures and surveys are needed in regions of different states that would finally contribute in identifying the pest free areas, a task that is also required to be accomplished as per the international norms for fulfilling the commitments made under the SPS Agreement.

There is also a dire need to check not only spread of above pests but also to promulgate domestic quarantine against certain important pests which have been introduced/detected in the country in the recent years and which are likely to spread fast. The important examples of reports of such pests are American serpentine leaf miner (*Liriomyza trifolii*) from Karnataka in 1991, spiralling white fly (*Aleurodiscus dispersus*) recorded from Tamil Nadu in 1993, papaya ring spot virus in Maharashtra and Madhya Pradesh in 1994, and banana bract mosaic potyvirus and banana streak mosaic badnavirus in Trichy area of Tamil Nadu in 1995. Similarly, sunflower downy mildew (*Plasmopara halstedii*) recorded for the first time from Maharashtra in 1984 and peanut stripe potyvirus initially recorded at Raichur in Karnataka in 1987 are now being reported from certain other States. Unlike in USA and Australia, there is a total lack of organised services of plant quarantine at State level in India. It is essential to set-up plant quarantine check-posts at inter-state border roads/inland container depots/rail roads manned by trained personnel to control the movement of planting material, transport carriers and containers so as to have effective check of the pests.

There are a large number of beneficial organisms such as insect pathogenic viruses, bacteria, fungi and protozoa, silkworms, honeybees and pollinators, lac insects, earthworms, entomo-pathogenic nematodes and weed control arthropods and pathogens, which are potential biocontrol agents. Two types of negative effects have been observed in import of such organisms which become invasive *i.e.* either they colonize and become a pest or such colonizing species lead to extinction of native species. At present we do not have clear-cut guidelines in the DIP Act, 1914 for regulating their import and export. A Core Committee of experts was constituted by ICAR to draft exhaustive guidelines for safe export and import of beneficial organisms

## Plate 4.1

Necrotic Line Pattern on Pea due to Pea Seed-borne Mosaic Virus

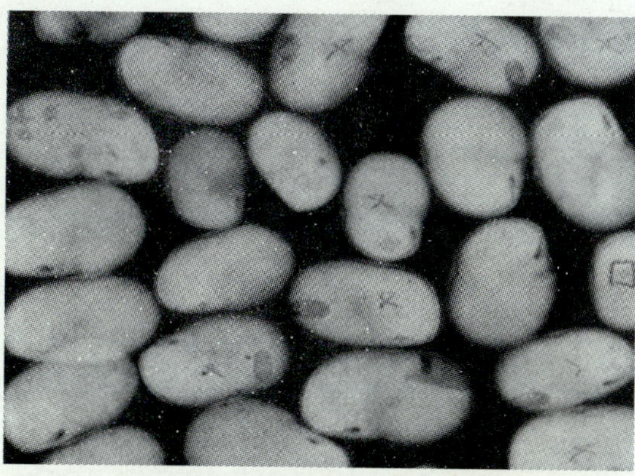

Detection of Hidden Infestation of Pests in Cowpea by X- ray Radiography

Bruchid Infestation in Horsegram

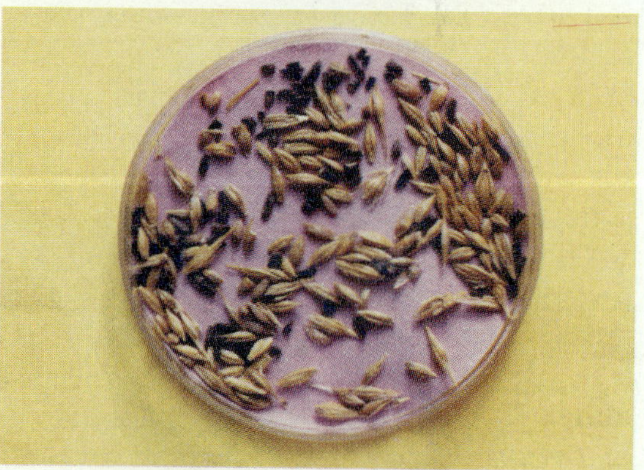

Sclerotia Mixed with Barley Seed

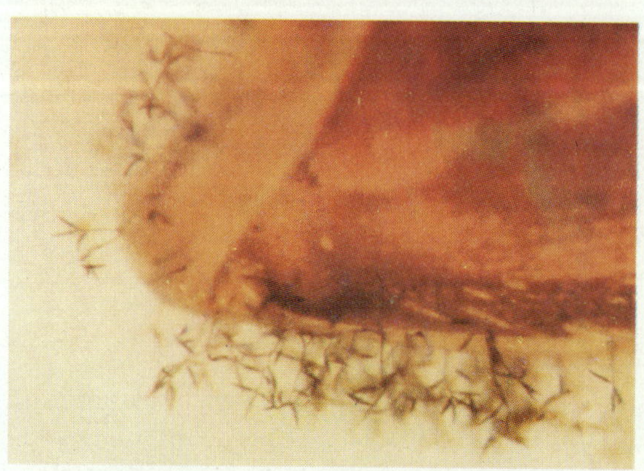

*Drechslera oryzae* on *Oryza sativa* Seeds

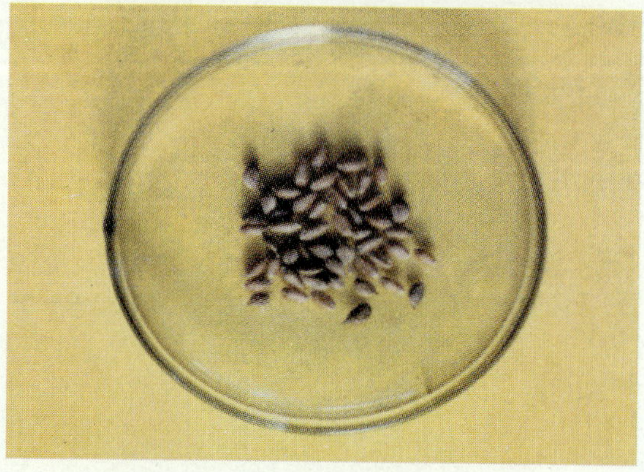

Weed Seeds Mixed with Wheat Seeds

and to identify nodal agencies for quarantine which would be notified under PFS Order of DIP Act once the draft recommendations submitted are approved.

## Generation of Public Awareness

Most of the problems of quarantine are because of lack of proper appreciation of risks involved with introduction of exotic pests and the damage they could do to Indian agriculture including the export of agricultural commodities. There is, therefore, an urgent need for an aggressive mass education programme through press, television, radio and other publicity channels for farmers, custom and postal officials, scientists and all others connected with movement/introduction of plant materials about observing plant quarantine requirements in the interest of the country.

For international passengers, there is a need for declaration either through a separate 'Plant quarantine declaration card' or in the disembarkation card of Govt. of India itself for declaring the plant/plant product being carried. Further, display boards should be placed at arrival halls indicating the requirement of passenger baggage declaration. All baggage's/couriers/mail at cargo stations should be invariably scanned through a high efficiency X-ray machine which can detect both organic and inorganic material based on colour changes on the screen. After the arrival of the material at the port of entry, the custom officials should work hand in hand with quarantine staff to ensure quick release of material.

## Re-prioritization and Focus

Development of detection techniques and alternative salvaging techniques for diagnosis and treatment of destructive pests especially to test samples of bulk consignments in batches getting preference. In the post CBD era, access to germplasm material is not as it was before. Therefore, more efforts need to be made to salvage as far as possible the infected or infested material through suitable treatments so that precious material is available to our researchers. Most of the presently used chemical fumigants would be phased out as per WHO norms in the coming years. Therefore, research needs to be focused on the feasibility of use of electron beam, or ionising radiations and alternate fumigants as quarantine disinfestation treatments. Similarly, more physico-chemical treatments have to be worked out for controlling fungi, bacteria and nematodes.

SPS Agreement at present does not deal in transgenics/genetically modified organisms. There are certain inherent risks to the ecology and environment in the use of these especially for biodiversity rich countries like India. Therefore, the biosafety issues need to be addressed properly before trading in GMOs (Khetarpal and Pandey, 2001).

Extensive research programmes also needs to be undertaken to review status of pests and to bring the current quarantine regulations in harmony with the SPS Agreement. In order to prepare an updated list of endemic pests, authentic survey/ surveillance is indispensable. There is a need to develop certification protocols as per international standards to increase our share in export market as these international protocols and agreements do not recognize the internal problems of any member country.

**Revision and Harmonization of Policies**

To overcome the plant health related impediments to market access, there is a need to harmonize our national sanitary and phytosanitary regulations to be consistent with international standards, guidelines and recommendations. The Indian SPS measures need to be in harmony with international standards and measures followed by neighbouring and other countries, which have a similar agricultural system. Not only this, India can play an important role in debating and suggesting approaches to harmonization of procedures, by sending technical representatives to the international meetings related to WTO/SPS, so that international standards do not become disguised barriers to trade. But this can be done only after we have developed our own well defined SPS measures.

Also to have complete understanding of the SPS measures of our target markets, direct technical contact with the concerned authorities in those countries is required. This can be achieved only if India posts a technically qualified Agricultural Attache at our diplomatic missions in the countries of interest.

All the 'Regulations' directly or indirectly concerning agricultural trade viz., DIP Act, 1914; PFS Order, 1989; Seeds Act, 1966; NPSD (1988); National Seeds Policy (2002); Insecticides Act, 1968; Environmental Protection Act, 1986 etc. need to be thoroughly reviewed and updated periodically as per the emerging scenario.

## REFERENCES

Destructive Insects and Pests (DIP) Act, 1914 and the Plants, Fruits and Seeds (Regulation of Import into India) Order, 1989 of Government of India.

Ganguli, A. and Paul, D. K. 1973. Wart disease of potato in India. *Sci. & Cult.*, **19**: 605-606.

Gaur, Ashok and Dev, Usha 1988. Detection techniques for seed-borne fungi, bacteria and viruses. *In*: V. P. Agnihotri, A. K. Sarabhoy and Dinesh Kumar (eds.), *Perspectives in Mycology and Plant Pathology*. Malhotra Publishing House, New Delhi, pp. 591-609.

Gupta, Kavita, Pandey, B. M and Khetarpal, R. K. 2002a. Pest risk analysis and its significance to India in WTO regime. *Seed Tech News.*, **32**(2&3): 266-269.

Gupta, Kavita, Rajan and Khetarpal, R. K. 2002b. Importance of Phytosanitation in WTO and CBD Regimes. *In*: Asian Congress of Mycology and Plant Pathology, University of Mysore, Mysore and Indian Society of Mycology and Plant Pathology, October 1-4, 2002. pp 141-142.

http://www.cbd.org

http://www.ippc.org

http://www.plantquarantineindia.com

http://www.wto.org

Jones, F. G. W. 1961. The potato root eel worm, *Heterodera rostichiensis* in India. *Curr Sci.*, **30**: 187.

Kahn, R. P. 1989. *Plant Protection and Quarantine: Selected Pest and Pathogens of Quarantine Significance* Vol II, CRC Press Inc., Florida, p. 265.

Khetarpal, R. K. 2002. Role of plant quarantine in safe movement of germplasm. *In*: *Trainers Training Programme on Sustainable Management of Plant Biodiversity under NATP (Mission Mode)*, NBPGR, New Delhi, January 8-31, 2002.

Khetarpal, R. K. and Gupta, Kavita 2002. Implications of Sanitary and Phytosanitary Agreement of WTO on plant protection in India. *Annual Review of Plant Pathology*, **1**: 1-26.

Khetarpal, R. K. and Pandey, B. M. 2001. Plant quarantine and safe exchange of transgenics. *In*: *Transgenic Crops and Biosafety Concern*. NBPGR, New Delhi. pp. 101-109.

Khetarpal, R. K. and Ram Nath 1998. Evolving national plant quarantine system: harmonisation of current quarantine regulations with sanitary and phytosanitary (SPS) agreement. *In*: National

Dialogue (ISPGR Dialogue 1998): Issues on Plant Genetic Resources, December 1-2, 1998, NBPGR, New Delhi.

Khetarpal, R. K., Shamsher Singh, D. B. Parakh, A. K. Maurya and V. Celia Chalam 2001a. Virus intercepted in exotic germplasm during 1991-2000 in quarantine. *Indian Journal of Plant Genetic Resources*, **14**(2): 127-129.

Khetarpal, R. K., Varaprasad, K. S., Lal, A., Agarwal, P. C. and Lal, B. 2001b. Plant quarantine of germplasm under exchange. *In*: B. S. Dhillon, K. S. Varaprasad, Kalyani Srinivasan, Mahendra Singh, Sunil Archak, Umesh Srivastava and G. D. Sharma (eds.), *National Bureau of Plant Genetic Resources: A Compendium of Achievements*. NBPGR, New Delhi, pp. 90-115.

Mathur, V. K. and Arjun Lal (eds.) 1997. Plant Quarantine Activities at NBPGR (1976-96). *Sci. Monogr.*, No. 6. NBPGR, New Delhi, p. 96.

Plant Quarantine (Regulation of Import into India) Order 2003. The Gazette of India Extraordinary, Part II Section 3 Sub-section (ii) No. 1037 Published by Authority. p. 105.

Ram Nath, Mathur, V. K. and Verma, B. R. 1988. Plant quarantine activities in Indian context. *In*: R. S. Paroda, R. K. Arora and K. P. S. Chandel (eds.), *Plant Genetic Resources-Indian Perspective. NBPGR*. New Delhi, pp. 470-480.

Raychaudhuri, S. P. 1973. Seed pathology in relation to plant quarantine and seed industry in India. *Indian Phytopath.*, **26**: 185-196.

Reddy, O. R. and Muthaiyan, M. C. 1982. Interception of *Fusarium moniliforme* var. *subglutinans* in seeds of *Pinus caribaea* var. *hondurensis* imported from Fiji. *Indian J. mycol. Res.*, **20**: 99-101.

Renjhen, P. L. 1973. History of plant quarantine and its functioning in India. Deptt. of Plant Protection, Quarantine and Storage, Faridabad. Min. of Agri., Govt. of India.

Sethi, C. L., Nath, R. P., Mathur, V. K.and Ahuja, S. 1972. Interception of plant parasitic nematodes from imported seeds & plant material. *Indian J. Nemato.*, **2**: 89-93.

Verghese, M. K. 1945. Bunchy top disease of plantains. *Indian Farming*, **6**: 239-240.

5

# Cultural Practices and their Role in Crop Pest Management

**H. S. Chaube and Jameel Akhtar**

## INTRODUCTION

Adjustment in crop management practices to prevent or minimize disease development represents the oldest and most broadly applicable approach to plant disease control (Anonymous, 1968). These measures are mainly directed at avoiding disease or suppressing the causal agents. Cultural practices are an integral part of disease control programmes in most agricultural crops. A pathogen, its host and suitable environmental conditions must coincide for an infectious disease to develop. Cultural practices often offer the opportunity to alter the environment, the condition of the host, and/or the behaviour of the causal agent, to economically achieve a measure of disease control.

Most cultural practices used to control plant disease are preventive in nature (Anonymous, 1968). They may reduce the amount or activity of pathogen inoculum, as in the use of disease-free seed or planting stock, crop rotation, green manuring, ploughing, sanitation, and rouging; or they may help to avoid disease by, for example, the choice of field location, time of planting, seed bed preparation, plant spacing and host nutrition. Integration of cultural practices, host resistance, and pesticides or biocontrol agents may be necessary to provide optimal level of control for economically important plant diseases (Andrews, 1983; Baker, 1983).

Whetzel was the first to classify methods, including cultural practices, for the control of diseases (Apple, 1977). His list included exclusion, eradication, protection, and immunization. Subsequent authors have expanded or modified the list of include avoidance and therapy (Anonymous, 1968), as well as environmental manipulation, biological control, and genetic engineering. Several compilations of cultural control strategies have been published (Engel-hard, 1989; Fry, 1982; Jarvis, 1992; Kahn 1991; Kupers 1979; Schippers and Gams, 1979; Sterems, 1960; Zentmeyer and Bald, 1977). In addition, Cowling (1978) prepared a list of agricultural and forest practices that can favour plant disease epidemics, and which warrant attention when considering the use of cultural control methods.

## THE CONCEPT AND APPLICATION

The definition of cultural practices (CP) in the context of disease control is complicated. Katan (1996) has classified CP into three categories:

*Department of Plant Pathology, GBPUA & T, Pantnagar-263 145.*

(*i*) CP which are usually applied for agricultural purposes not connected with crop protection, such as fertilization and irrigation. They may or may not have a positive or a negative side-effect on disease incidence.

(*ii*) CP which are used solely or mainly for disease control, such as sanitation and flooding.

(*iii*) CP which are used for both agricultural purposes and disease control, such as crop-rotation, grafting and composting.

It is rather difficult to draw clear lines between the categories. CP from category (*i*) might also be used specifically for disease control. Thus, planting date, irrigation and ploughing can be adjusted to escape or avoid a disease. Composts have been used in the past primarily to improve plant nutrition and soil structure. It is now realized that suppressive compost can serve as an effective tool for the control of soil-borne pathogens (Hoitink and Fahy, 1986). Mulching of soil with transparent or black plastic was introduced for water conservation and raising of horticultural crops, but it was found later that plastic mulching can affect the incidence of diseases (Waggoner *et al.*, 1960). Moreover, since 1976, soil mulching with transparent polyethylene has been used for the control of soil-borne diseases by soil solarization (Katan *et al.*, 1976, Katan and DeVay, 1991). Traditionally, crop rotation was used to maintain good soil fertility and structure but also apparently with the knowledge that the lower the frequency of cropping a susceptible crop, the lower the probability of an outbreak of a severe disease (Katan, 1996). Grafting is traditionally a horticultural practice, which has also been adopted as a tool for controlling diseases by grafting susceptible scion on resistant stocks. In an era where agriculture is adopting biotechnology, such an approach should also be regarded as CP for disease control (Katan, 1996). Similarly, according to Keel *et al.*, (1990) the use of beneficial bacteria which both promote plant growth and serve as biocontrol agents may become in the future a standard CP for disease control.

The interest in studying the effect of CP on disease has dual purpose: to develop CP as control methods whenever and wherever possible, and to obtain information regarding their impact on diseases when they are used as agricultural practices in order to avoid negative side-effects. CP may be employed at, or after planting, at various frequencies. Deep ploughing and flooding are used before planting, while irrigation and fertilization can be applied several times during the crop season for disease management. CP can be applied by the individual farmer in his own plot, on a regional scale—as in the case with sanitation, or on a national scale—as for the production of healthy propagation material. As with any control measure, CP for disease control should be evaluated according to several criteria: effectiveness and spectrum of control, ease of application, reproducibility, simplicity, range of application and cost.

## THE PROCEDURES FOR DISEASE MANAGEMENT THROUGH CP

Singh (2000) has described and discussed procedures for disease control through cultural practices under three categories as shown in Fig. 5.1. In the present commercial agriculture where sustainability and integrated approach are guiding principles, few methods listed in Fig. 5.1 are very relevant and are described here.

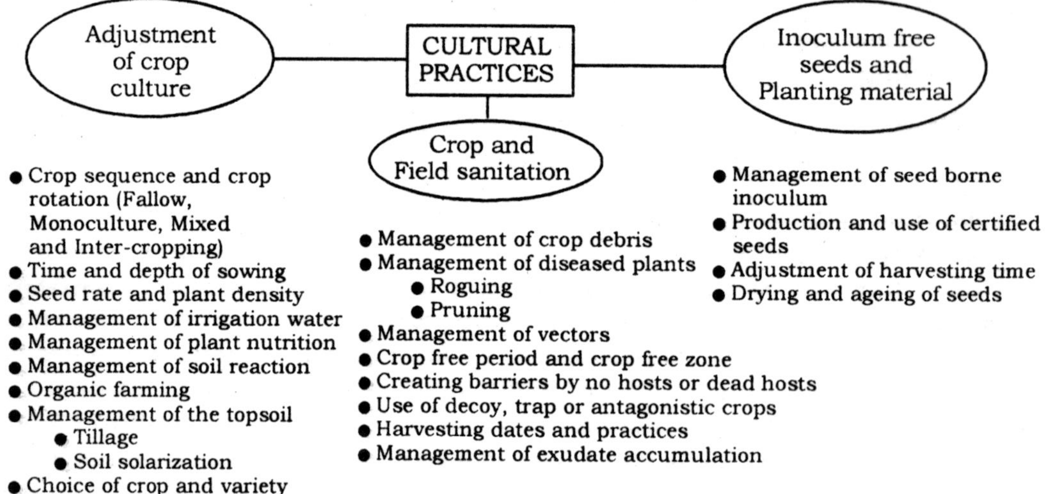


**Fig. 5.1:** Procedures for disease control through cultural practices

## THE PRACTICES

### Inoculum Free Seeds and Planting Materials

A large number of biotic and mesobiotic agents survive and get introduced in the crop or field or an area through true seed or through vegetative planting material such as seed tubers, cuttings, bulbs, grafts, rhizomes, etc. The inoculum is present either as contaminant or admixture (Ear cockle of wheat-*Arguina tritici*, cysts of golden nematode of potato, oospores of *Albugo candida*, sclerotia of ergot fungi), or as internally seed borne (loose smuts of wheat and barley, *Ascochyta* blight of chickpea, *Phomopsis* blight of brinjal, etc.) or as externally seed borne (covered smut of barley, grain smut of sorghum, covered smut of oats, bunt of cereals, etc.), or through nursery raised planting stocks.

Today in agriculture sector, several seed producing agencies both in public and private sectors are engaged in production and distribution of certified seeds of almost all the crops. Even then there are huge areas in India where farmers grow crops from their own produced seed. Some cultural practices such as cleaning, drying and ageing of seed and proper adjustment of harvesting time are the practices, which if followed, would reduce the introduction, survival and spread of inoculum.

Cleaning of seed is done by hot air blast or by hand. In hand cleaning, seed is submerged in salt solution (20% common salt solution) and floating impurities are removed by hand. Sometimes pathogens may be present in the dust accompanying the seed. Thus, removal of dust is also an essential part of this procedure. The germinability of seeds not properly dried before storage is reduced. Such seeds harbor several types of parasitic fungi and bacteria. For example, fungus causing downy mildew in maize has been found in freshly harvested seed but once the seeds are thoroughly dried, the mycelium present in seed tissues collapses and is destroyed. Prolonged storage of seed also eliminates many pathogens. *Xanthomonas axonopodis* pv. *malvacearum* causing blight and black arm of cotton survives in the seed for a year or so. Storage of seed for more than a year reduces seed-borne inoculum. *Fusarium solani* f. sp. *cucurbitae* which is internally seed borne, is inactivated when the seed is stored for two years before sowing. Similar eradication of pathogen has been reported in anthracnose of cotton. In such methods, proper storage conditions must be maintained to avoid harm to the seed.

Time and condition of harvesting affects cleanliness of the seed. Delayed harvesting of grain crops in temperate climate gives the pathogens more time for contaminating the seed. Grain crops harvested in wet weather often produce contaminated seed. Potatoes harvested when the leaves are still green easily get contaminated by the late blight fungus present on leaves. To avoid such situations, it is best to first remove the tops and let them dry before digging the tubers. Drying kills spores and tubers are not contaminated.

Vegetable seedlings, tree seedlings and grafts raised in infested nurseries when used for transplanting, carry inoculum to main field or orchard. Vegetable seedlings infected in nursery with root knot nematode are an important source of introduction of *Meloidogyne* spp. in clean field. In bacterial canker of tomato-(*Clavibacter michiganense* subsp. *michiganense*) bacterium which has caused seedlings infection from the seed is carried in symptom less seedlings (Gitatis *et al.*, 1991), and such seedlings are major source of dissemination of the bacterium (Chang *et al.*, 1991). Transmission of parasitic fungi (*Pythium, Phytophthora*) is common in papaya through seedlings raised in infested soils. According to Naqvi (1994) in citrus major source of inoculum of *Phytophthora* root and collar rot is the nursery infected planting stock and infested nurseries. Nursery stock infected with powdery mildew fungus (*Podosphaera leucotricha*) is a major source of introduction of disease in apple orchard.

### Crop and Field Sanitation

Sanitation is a major part of disease management through cultural practices. It consists of all activities aimed at eliminating or reducing the amount of inoculum present in a plant, a field, or a warehouse, and at preventing the spread of the pathogen. Regular removal of diseased plants from a population is an important sanitary precaution. It is one of the effective recommendations in the management of virus diseases of field crops. For the control of loose smut of wheat and production of disease free seed, rouging is always recommended in seed plots. Roguing is effective only if the smutted ears are removed before spores have been dispersed. In many varieties particularly Sonalika, appearance of smutted heads is preceded by yellowing of flag leaves. This indicator facilitates effective roguing in such varieties. Roguing of infected plants is recommended for several other diseases e.g. smut of sugarcane, red rot of sugarcane, downy mildews of sorghum and maize, wilts of pigeon pea and cotton, etc.

Management of weeds, collateral and volunteer host plants is another important sanitation practice. Plant pathogens usually have a wide host range. These additional hosts ensure carry over of the pathogen from one season to the next, and also provide a base on which inoculum multiplies and reaches epidemic proportions early in the season of main host/crop. Cucumber mosaic virus, powdery mildew fungi (*Erysiphe* spp.), and root knot nematodes have over 700 plant species as their host (Singh, 2000). Keeping the field free from additional hosts of the pathogen is a major sanitary cultural practice.

The destruction of crop debris especially the roots to reduce source of survival and multiplication of inoculum helps in control of many diseases. The oospores of fungi causing downy mildew of pearl millet, maize, sorghum, pea, grapevines and white rust of crucifers perennate in soil through crop debris. In cooler regions, the fungus causing powdery mildew of wheat and pea also survive through their peritheeia in crop refuse and locally produced conidial inoculum on infected hosts for dispersal by wind to distant places. In certain areas, the linseed rust fungus, the rice blast and leaf spotting fungi, and the pathogen causing early blight of potato and tomato also perennate through dormant stages in diseased crop debris. In rice growing areas, paddy straw harbors many pathogens such as true sclerotia of *Ustilaginoidea virens* (false smut), the sheath blight fungus (*R. solani*) the stem rot fungus (*S. oryzae*) and rice bunt fungus (*Neovossia horrida*) as well as spore of leaf smut (*Entyloma oryzae*). In temperate climate, fungus causing late blight of potato besides surviving in seed tubers also survives as mycelium and sporangia in crop debris. In apple scab (*V. inaequalis*) also the scab bearing fallen leaves play the most important part of providing inoculum in the next spring.

Use of fire and flame has been recommended as one method of destroying infected crop debris (Hardison, 1976). Deep ploughing, especially during summer in the tropics, buries the debris to such depths where the pathogens are automatically destroyed. Fallows also help in the reduction of inoculum through sanitary effects of decomposition of crop debris in absence of a host. The principle of flood fallowing is also a method of cleaning the soil of pathogens.

## Adjustment of Crop Culture

During green revolution, high yielding varieties particulary of wheat and paddy occupied larger and contiguous areas with alarming increase in production and productivity of the crops. There has been similar increase in diseases of both biotic and abiotic origin. The success of green revolution was based on use of chemicals. Chemicalization of agriculture created problems and to tackle them without loosing production, concepts such as sustainability, integration (IPM, INM), biocontrol, ecologically safe, etc. have become most "sought after" areas for research and development. In pre green revolution period, our total approach was based on systems of ecosystems. It was in fact an era of cultural practices. Different sets of crop cultures were used. Every approach was biological, be it production technology or protection technology. Today, too we are endeavoring to develop technologies which are biological and then to sustain such concepts, sets of cultural practices must be part of operations to sustain effectivity of such system(s). Cultural operations include cropping systems, crop rotations, monocropping, mixed or inter cropping, sowing factors, soil factors particularly tillage, irrigation practices, source and amount of nutrients, organic farming, etc. In our effort to develop practical IPM modules for crops/ pests, it is natural to try best component from each practice and integrate them.

### *Crop Rotation, Cropping Systems and Crop Sequence*

Crop rotation is the growing of economic plants in recurring succession and in definite sequence on the same land, as distinguished from a one-crop system usually lacking a definite plan (Curl, 1963). Cook and Baker (1983) defined the cropping system as the sequence or combination of crops grown in a single field. The term 'crop sequence' is to be preferred, according to Palti (1981), since it covers monoculture also. The sequential sowing of crops may or may not include fallow or green manure. The crop rotation programme determines the frequency of growing each crop, the list of crops (and fallow periods) during a defined period (cycle), the order (history) of crops and the agricultural practices which will be employed during the whole cycle (Katan, 1996). Monoculture is the opposite of such a practice and is applied for agroclimatic reasons and economic considerations.

Originally, crop rotation was employed for nutritional reasons and to improve the physical conditions of the soil. However, the value of this practice in controlling soil-borne pathogens and improving plant health was noted and crop rotation became an integral part of cropping systems.

Crop rotation, especially as a tool for disease control has been thoroughly discussed in many review and books, e.g. Burehl, 1987; Cook and Baker, 1983; Curl, 1963; Garrett, 1970; Katan, 1996; Palti, 1981; Schippers *et al.*, 1987. The effectiveness of crop rotation in disease control will depend on the nature of the pathogen and the crop, on the agricultural practices involved, on soil properties and on other biotic and abiotic factors. The factors that reduce effectiveness of crop rotation in controlling soil borne diseases include (1) wide host range of the pathogen (2) pathogens having multiple and lasting mechanisms for survival in the absence of host, (3) pathogens producing large inoculum densities as resting structures, (4) crops that are susceptible to several diseases, (5) crops which stimulate formation of resting structures, (6) frequent infestation of soil with pathogen form external sources, (7) soils that are conducive to diseases, and (8) poor control of weeds and volunteer crops. In planning for crop rotation various factors to be taken into considerations are (1) in soils conducive to disease, frequency of growing susceptible crop should be reduced, (2) include crops from different botanical families which do not have many common diseases in cropping system, (3) integrate crop rotation with other management practices, such as resistant cultivars, biological control, etc. and (4) attempts should be made to include in the cropping systems crops that induce biological control.

Most of the diseases caused by soil borne pathogens can be significantly reduced by proper crop rotation (Curl, 1963; Jacobsen and Backman, 1993). Examples are wilt diseases of pigionpea, pea, cotton, linseed, red rot and wilt of sugarcane, ergot cyst nematode (Singh, 2000). Vegetables are rotated with grain crops such as rice or with highly resistant cultivar of the same vegetable to control pathogens like root knot nematode. When potato is grown in two consecutive seasons in infested soil, there is 35.5% rise in the incidence of common scab (*Streptomyces scabies*) in the first year and 65.5 in the second year. Keeping two crops of cereals (wheat and rice) or a legume and millet between two potato crops significantly reduces the disease incidence (Singh and Jeswani, 1986). Generally, a 4 year rotation is recommended against this desease avoiding beet and fleshy rooted crucifers. Long rotations with graminaceous crops between potatoes are a major recommendation against bacterial wilt caused by *Ralstonia solanacearum* (Verma and Shekhawat, 1991). A crop of rice taken after cotton reduces inoculum of *Verticillium dahliae* and that of pea taken after wheat reduces the inoculum of the take-all fungus. Even virus diseases are suppressed by suitable crop rotations and cropping practices (Thresh, 1982; Thomas *et al.*, 1983).

### Monoculture

According to Palti (1981) monoculture means cultivation of a single or closely allied crop species in annual or seasonal succession, with interruption only by fallow or intermittent growing of green manure crop or application of soil amendments, not necessarily after each crop. It is generally agreed that in each agro-ecosystem, diversity is a stabilizing factor and prevents excessive pressure on any part of the system. This applies to crop disease system also (Singh, 2000). From the general biological aspects, monoculture is, therefore, clearly dangerous because it does not permit diversity. Monoculture may also exert selection pressure on pathogens, resulting in emergence of new pathotypes. However, monoculture is advantageous to some farmers from the viewpoint of economic gain and ease to operate the cropping system. In general, monoculture is viewed as a disease perpetuating system because diversity is lacking, the host is available periodically, and the pathogen can subsist on crop remains under stabilized conditions. There are examples however, when continued monoculture resulted in development of soil suppressiveness (Baker, 1980).

### Tillage

This is a major agricultural practice which affects many physical properties of soil, such as water infiltration, bulk density, aeration, temperature, moisture, compacting, and resistance to root penetration. These affect biological activities in the soil, root growth, pathogen activity, and the capacity of the plant to withstand pathogen action (Katan, 1996). In addition, tillage affects the spatial distribution of crop residues in the soil. There are various tillage practices, including deep ploughing, reduced cultivation, subsoiling, chiseling, conservation tillage, minimum tillage, and zero or no tillage (Palti, 1981 and Summer *et al.*, 1981). It would be unrealistic to generalize the effect of a given tillage practice on soil borne pathogens. Deep plouging is practiced to reduce the contact between plant roots and pathogen propagules or to expose the propagules to natural heating and desiccation. According to Worley *et al.*, (1966), the incidence of southern blight of tomato was lower after deep ploughing (25 cm depth) compared to shallow tillage by means of a harrow. Newhall (1955) had described several cases where ploughing during the hot season in order to expose it to the rays of sun, resulted in a decrease in disease incidence, apparently due to physical killing of pathogen propagules of elevated temperatures. This can be regarded as dry soil solarization. Another typical example of the effect of tillage on a soil borne disease was given by Burke *et al.*, (1972). Loosing the soil by subsoiling to reduce soil compaction after seed bed preparation increased yields of bean plants whose roots were infected by *F. Solani* f. sp. *phaseoli.* The increase in yields redulted not from reduced infection but from counteraction of the effects of disease through greater regeneration of roots as the season progressed. These results were further supported by Miller and Burker (1975, 1985). Minimum tillage practice may increase, decrease, or have no effect on plant diseases. Leaving crop debris on the surface or partially buried in the soil may allow numerous pathogens to survive until the next crop is planted, but conditons favourable for biological control may also be increased (Katan, 1996). As advocated by Summer *et al.*, (1981), tillage practices also directly influence chemical properties of soil, root growth and nutrient uptake, and populations of vectors and susceptibility or resistance of the host. In a long-term study, the intensity of common root rot disease caused by *Cochliobolus sativus* was generally lower under zero than conventional tillage (Tinline and Spurr, 1991). Unfortunately, although some pathogens can be controlled by reduced tillage systems, many others are favoured if the soil is not tilled adequately (Cook and Baker, 1983).

### *Organic Amendment of Soil*

Sun and Huang (1985) had rightly observed that continuous extensive agricultural practices that depend heavily on use of chemicals have resulted in loss of organic matter, an increase in acidity, and accumulation of toxic elements in cultivated soils creating an environment favourable for development of certain soil borne pathogen. One of the cheapest hazard-free and ecofriendly, effective methods of modifying soil environment is amendment of soil with decomposable organic matter. The reduction in common scab of potatoes (*S. scabies*) by green manuring through prevention of the build-up of inoculum was the first report of organic amendments as a means of disease suppression. Since this observation of Sanford (1926), numerous reports have appeared regarding the beneficial effects of organic and inorganic amendments of soil (Baker, 1981; Chen and Close, 1987; Chang and Hsu, 1988; Chaube and Singh, 1991; Hoitnik and Fahy, 1986; Linduman, 1979; Muller and Gooch, 1982; Nelson and Hoitnik, 1983; Singh, 1965; Singh and Sitaramaiah, 1973; Singh *et al.*, 1972, Stover, 1962; Sun and Huang, 1983, 1985; Yang and Hsieh, 1985).

The list of soil-borne diseases that have been controlled in glasshouse, microplots or field plots by organic amendment of soil, is quite exhaustive. Some of the important ones are given in Table 5.1. Crop residue decomposition in soil is known to encourage microbial activities both quantitatively and qualitatively. The enhanced microbial

**TABLE 5.1:** EXAMPLES OF SOIL-BORNE DISEASES SUPPRESSED BY ORGANIC AMENDMENT OF SOIL

| *Pathogen* | *Crop and Disease* |
|---|---|
| **Fungal diseases** | |
| *Aphanomyces euteiches* | Root rot of peas |
| *Fusarium oxysporum* f. sp. *udum* | Wilt of pigeonpea |
| *F. oxyporum* f. sp. *cubense* | Wilt of banana |
| *F. oxysporum* f. sp. *lini* | Wilt of linseed |
| *F. oxysporum* f. sp. *pisi* | Wilt of pea |
| *F. oxysporum* f. sp. *corianderi* | Wilt of coriander |
| *F. oxysporum* f. sp. *ciceri* | Wilt of chickpea |
| *F. solani* f. sp. *phaseoli* | Wilt and root rot of bean |
| *F. coeruleum* | Wilt and root rot of guar |
| *Helminthosporium sativum* | Root rot of wheat |
| *Macrophomina phaseolina* | Root rot of cotton |
| *Ophiobolus graminis* | Take-all disease of wheat |
| *Phymatotrichum omnivorum* | Root rot of cotton |
| *Phytophthora* sp. | Root rots of ornamentals |
| *Phytophthora cinnamoni* | Root rot of avocado |
| *Pythium* spp. | Browning root rot of wheat |
| *Pythium aphanidermatum* | Soft rot of ginger |
| *Pythium ultimum* | Seedling blight of alfalfa |
| *Rhizoctonia solani* | Black scurf of potato |
| *Sclerotium rolfsii* | Wilt of piper beetle |
| *S. graminis* | Foot rot of wheat |
| *Streptomyces scabies* | Common scab of potato |
| *Thielaviopsis* spp. | Root rots of ornamentals |
| *Thielaviopsis basicola* | Root rot of bean and sesamum |
| *Verticillium albo-atrum* | Wilt of potato, tomato and cotton |
| **Diseases caused by nematodes** | |
| *Belanolaimus longicaudatus* | Sting nematode |
| *Heterodera avenae* | Cereal cyst nematode |
| *H. major* | Cereal cyst nematode |
| *H. rostochidensis* | Potato cyst nematode |
| *H. schachtii* | Sugarbeet cyst nematode |
| *H. tabacum* | Tobacco cyst nematode |
| *Hoplolaimus indicus* | Lance nematode |
| *Hoplolaimus tylenchiformis* | Lance nematode |
| *Meloidogyne javanica* | Root knot nematode of vegetables |
| *M. incognita* | Root knot nematode of vegetables |
| *Pratylenchus penetrans* | Lesion nematode |
| *Tylenchulus semipenetrans* | Citrus nematode |

activity has two effects: it increases the variety of complex organic compounds in soil and promotes the population of antagonists in soil. Together these two factors increase the biological buffering capacity of the soil. This capacity of the soil helps in disease prevention in areas where the pathogen is not yet established. Amendments act against a disease through (1) direct effect on the active pathogen on the root or in the rhizosphere, (2) direct effect on the pathogen during its survival in the absence of the host and (3) indirect effect on the pathogenesis through the host. In the latter are included all these consequences of amendment which result from uptake of organic compounds by plant root, changed host physiology and possible development of resistance (Singh and Sitaramaiah, 1973). Therefore, the amendments can reduce inoculum density, inoculum capacity, host proneness and can also increase host resistance; the net result being reduction in disease severity.

***Irrigation and Water Management***

Irrigation affects both soil-borne and foliar diseases (Rotem and Palti, 1969). It alters soil's moisture content and consequently influences its aeration and temperature, and these in turn affect soil-borne diseases through their actions on biotic and abiotic processes in soil. Irrigation also affects disease incidence indirectly due to change in agricultural regimes, such as intensification of cropping, changes in date of sowing and growing seasons (Katan, 1996). Irrigation results in a dramatic rise in crop production which may also lead to increased loading stress on the plant and to a predisposition to certain diseases on the other hand, irrigation alleviates water stress which predisposes the plants to certain diseases. Irrigation occasionally makes it possible to avoid diseases by growing crops out of season (Rotem and Palti, 1969). Irrigation water is often a means of transport of inoculum through the field and to different fields in the area. Also, all irrigated crops, if infected, may be the source of inoculum for other crops reached by irrigation or drainage water. Transfer of conidia and appresoria of *Colletotrichum falcatum*, sporangia of downy mildew fungi, sporangia and zoospores of *Pythium* and *Phytophthora*, cells of bacteria, can all be moved in and outside the field through irrigation or running water. The crop debris carrying active or dormant inoculum of pathogens is also transported by irrigation and drainage water in channels through infested field.

Soil moisture is related to many diseases. For example, wet soil favours club root of crucifers, silver scurf of potatoes, and *Cercosporella* on wheat while dry soil increases severity of white mold of onion, common scab of potatoes and fusarium diseases of cereals (Colhoun, 1973). Damping-off diseases caused by *Pythium* spp. can be decreased by maintaining a dry soil surface zoosporic fungi such as *Pythium* and *Phytophthora* depend on soil water for zoospores release and motility. Diseases caused by these fungi have invariably been reported to be favoured by heavy or frequent irrigations. The incidence of root rot of chilli peppers caused by *P. capsici* in plants receiving alternate row irrigation was significantly less than in plants with irrigation of every row (Biles *et al.*, 1992). According to Ristaino (1991) *Phytophthora* root and crown rot in bell pepper were greater in plots irrigated more frequently with a deep system. Weekly light irrigation aggravated *Pythium* rot of ground nut pods, as compared with an equal amount of water applied in heavier irrigation at longer (every two weeks) intervals, since the top soil dried out between irrigations (Frank, 1967). Growing plants in raised beds which provide good drainage and aeration will reduce diseases favoured by wet conditions. This practice of reducing the number of irrigations decreases the incidence of root rot caused by *S. sclerotiorum* in lettuce (Steadman, 1979). Sclerotia of *S. sclerotiorum, S. minor, S. cepvoirum,* dried for short periods and remoistened in soil leak nutrients, are rapidly colonized by microorganisms, particularly the antagonists and rot within 3 weeks (Smith, 1972). This finding gives a potential tool for biocontrol of plant pathogens via management/manipulations of soil moisture. Irrigation will be especially useful for management of diseases favoured by water stress such as charcoal rots caused by *M. phaseolina*, as shown with cotton (Gaffar and Erwin, 1969). Moisture status of soil affects microflora and their interactions in soil and thus irrigation can be a tool for biological control. For instance, common scab of potatoes (*S. cabies*) can be managed by maintaining soil water near field during tuberization which according to Lapwood and Hering (1970) stimulates antagonistic bacteria.

In addition to amount of irrigation, the timing of irrigation is also important. The principles governing the timing of irrigation, its beginning and its frequency, from the aspect of disease management are (1) providing the crop with as uniform a water supply as possible to obviate stresses of water deficit or excess, (2) timing of giving water in relation to periods of heightened susceptibility of host to disease, and (3) minimizing hours of continuous leaf wetness, e.g., avoidance of sprinkling in continuation of dew period (Chaube and Singh, 1991).

### *Management of Plant Nutrition*

The plants absorb mineral nutrition from soil and the parasites attacking them take nutrition and energy from the plants. The macronutrients (N, P, K), are needed in large amounts by plants while the micronutrients are needed in smaller quantities. Maintenance of optimum plant health with sufficient, but not excessive, levels of fertility can be beneficial in crop resistance to stress from infection. Soil nutrients could affect diseases by direct effects on the pathogen or by their effects on the nutrition of the plant host or through their influence on soil microflora particularly antagonists (Fig. 5.2)

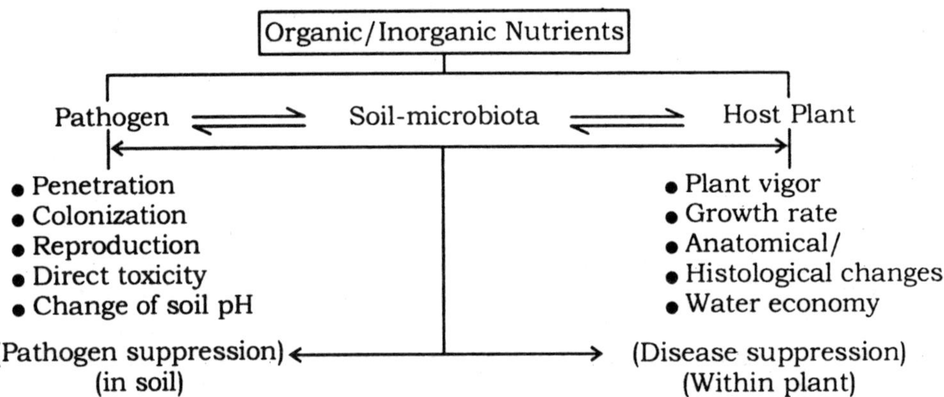


**Fig. 5.2:** Soil fertility and disease management

**Nitrogen:** It is one of the major essential elements for plant growth and markedly affects cell size. The forms of nitrogen influence the severity of diseases. Cortical and root diseases caused by *Fusarium, Rhizoctonia, Aphanomyces, Cercosporela, Amillaria*, etc. may be reduced by $NO_3$-N or increased by $NH_4$-N, while diseases caused by *Ophiobolus, Diplodia, Pythium*, and *Streptomyces* respond in an opposite manner.

Cereal rusts and mildews generally increase with $NO_3$-N and are reduced with $NH_4$-N (Huber and Watson, 1974).

Dosages of nitrogen influence plant susceptibility. The late blight of potato is severe when due to high nitrogen nutrition crop canopy is dense, resulting in high humidity. In sheath blight of rice (*R. solani*) high nitrogen promotes disease. In the false smut disease of rice (*U. virens*) also high nitrogen enhances disease incidence. According to Patel *et al.*, (1992) since there is no difference in yield of crop receiving 100 to 200 kg/ha nitrogen, the low dose of 100 kg/ha is recommended to suppress the disease. Excess of nitrogen predisposes the host to rusts, powdery mildew and Karnal bunt of wheat, tobacco mosaic, and potato tubers to soft rot.

When nitrogen is deficient, the plant is week, its development is incomplete and its maturity is hastened. Pathogen favoured by slow growth of the host are favoured by low nitrogen. In this category are tomato wilt (*F. oxysporum* f. sp. *lycopersicae*), bacterial wilt caused by *Ralstonia solanacearum*, root rot caused by *S. rolfsii*, and damping-off caused by *Pythium* spp. Increased nitrogen application reduces the apparent infection rate of early blight of potato (*Alternaria solani*).

**Phosphorus:** Phosphorus is one of the major elements utilized by plants; largely used in membranes, cell division, nucleic acids and high energy compounds. Its deficiency is second in importance next only to nitrogen. The development of roots is likely to be subnormal. Leaves tend to be under sized, erect, and somewhat necrotic, and relatively few lateral buds are formed. Foliage may be red or purple tinge. Phosphate and potassium generally have the tendency to decrease susceptibility. Results of investigation reveal that effects of phosphates on plant diseases appear to be connected with one of the two situations: (1) either the crop grown on soil markedly deficient in P, and correction of imbalance contributes to its health or (2) maturity of the crop is somewhat advanced by liberal supply of P, and this helps it escape from biotrophs preferring younger tissues (Palti, 1981). Effects of P on some important diseases have been summarized by Palti (1981) and Huber (1980). According to them, diseases such as damping-off of pea (*R. solani*) downy mildews of cabbage and grapes, flag smut of wheat (*U. tritici*), root rot of tobacco (*T. basicola*), root rot of soybean (*R. solani*) and take-all of wheat (*G. graminis*) decrease as a result of phosphate application.

**Potassium:** Usually high potassium (K) has been reported to reduce incidence of diseases. The mechanism by which K affects disease differs greatly, and includes both direct and indirect effects (Chaube and Singh, 1991). Direct effects include reduction or stimulation of pathogen penetration multiplication, survival, aggressiveness and rate of establishment in the host. Indirect effects include promotion of wound healing, increase in resistance to frost injury and delay in maturity in some crops. Among the diseases reported to be reduced include ascochytosis of chickpea, blast of rice, brown spot of rice, downy mildews of lettuce, grapes and cauliflower, early blight of tomato, gray mold of grape, late blight of potatoes, northern blight of corn, powdery mildew of cereals, root rot of pea, pine apple, cotton and jute, rusts of cereals, sheath blight of rice, stalk rot of maize, wilts of cotton, melon and tomato (Palti, 1981; Huber, 1980).

**Balance and Imbalanced Nutrition:** It has invariably been observed that in fields having unequal levels of NPK, the plants are predisposed to the attack of pathogens than in the fields having balanced levels of nutrients (Kartha and Nema, 1969; Sharma and Basu Chaudhary, 1985). Imbalanced fertilizers, compared to balanced or no fertilizer and high levels of nitrogen generally decrease resistance (Smalley, 1963; Sivaprakasham and Rajagopalan, 1974; Wolts and Engel-hard, 1973). High levels of N (120 kg/ha) to soil increase the wilt and root rot incidence in cauliflower while it was not so with phosphate/potassium. A balanced dose of NPK (120:80:40 kg/ha) was most suitable for reducing plant mortality (Sharma and Basu Chaudhary, 1985). High nitrogen generally increases susceptibility, whereas high potassium and phosphorus levels decrease susceptibility (Sivaprakasham *et al.*, 1975). In general, susceptibility is most evident when there is a potash deficiency. Phosphorus deficiency also leads to reduce resistance. Plant of *Vigna mungo* receiving sub-optimal N and high P-developed less powdery mildew than those under other regimes (Nawaz and Narayanswami, 1983). Incidence of bacterial stalk rot of maize increased with high N applications without P or K but decreased with high doses of P and K (Saxena and Lal, 1981). According to Carnegie and Colhoun (1983), a complete NPK fertilizer applied at planting but not afterwards influenced the resistance of potato leaves to infection by *P. infestans* and subsequent growth of lesions. Increasing rates of phosphate or potash, applied separately, did not significantly affect the development of blight lesions but a linear increase in lesion size was associated with increasing rates of nitrogen application. In general, it can be surmised that the behaviour of the plant towards parasite attack is largely determined by the main nutrients, NPK, depending on the quantities available. Practically, application of varying levels of commercial fertilizer in a balanced way helps to maintain the health of plants (Basu Chaudhary and Gupta, 1988).

### *Soil Solarization*

Soil solarization is the most advanced field technology for the control of soil-borne pathogens. It represents one of the very few cases where a new nonchemical control procedure has been adopted by farmers in several parts of the world, within a rather short period of time. The first report on use of solar energy for the control of soil-borne diseases was published by Katan *et al.*, (1976). Since then hundreds of papers have been published, covering the subject in over 38 countries around the globe (Chaube and Singh, 1991; Tjamos, 1996). Soil solarization is based on trapping solar irradiation by tightly covering the soil, usually with transparent polyethylene sheets. This results in a significant increase (10-15° C above normal depending on the soil depth) of soil temperature up to the point where most pathogens are vulnerable to heat effects.

Soil solarization offers multiple pest control (Plate 5.1). It controls parasitic diseases, soil-borne pests, weeds and improves soil suppressivity and fertility. Major parasitic fungi and diseases managed successfully include damping-off, root rots, stem rots, fruit rots, wilts, blights, etc. caused by *Pythium* spp., *Phytophthora* spp. *Fusarium* spp. *S. rolfsii, R. solani, Sclerotinia, Sclerotiorum, T. basicola,* and *Verticillium* spp. (Katan, 1981; Chaube and Singh, 1991, 2000; Tjmos, 1996). Among the nematodes *Ditylenchus dipsci, Globodera rostochiensis, Heterodera* spp., *Meloidogyne* spp, etc. have been managed successfully. Bacterial canker of tomato caused by *Clavibacter*

**Plate 5.1**

*Effect on soil solarization on weeds and antagonists*

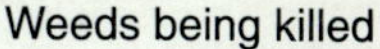

Weeds being killed

Weeds killed

Growth of antogonists in solarized soil

*Effect on soil solarization on weeds and antagonists*

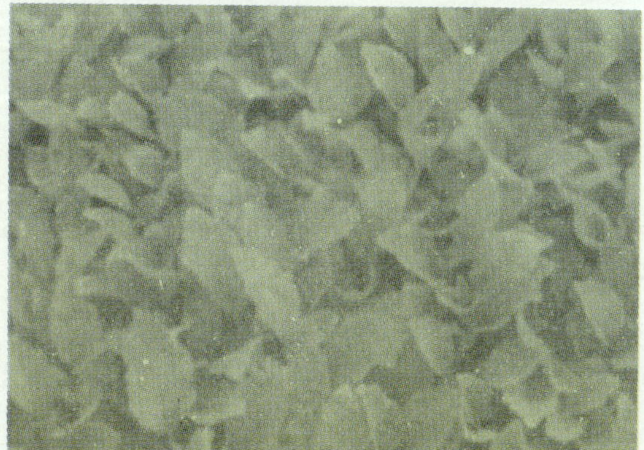

Effect of soil solarization on damping off and plant growth

*michiganensis* sub sp. *michiganensis* successfully controlled by soil solarization for 1-2 months (Tjmos, *et al.*, 1992). In general, most of the annual and many perennial weeds (Plate 5.1) such as *Amaranthus* spp., *Amsickia donglasiana, Anagallis* sp., *Avena fauta, Chaenopodium* spp., *Convolunalus* spp., *Cynodon dactylon, Digitaria sanguinalis, Echinochloacrus-galli, Eleusine* sp., *Fumaria* sp., *Lactuca* sp. *Lanium amplexicaule, Molueella, Montia, Notabaris* sp., *Phalaris* spp., *Poa* sp., *Portulaca oleraceae, Sisymbrium* sp., *Senecio valgaris, Solanum halpense, Sorghum stellaria,* and *Xanthium pensylvanicum* have been controlled, many graminae are especially sensitive, while others like *Melilotus*, remain unaffected. *Cyperus rotundus* is only partially controlled (Katan, 1981; 1987, Chaube and Singh, 1991; Esfahini, 1991; Khulbe, *et al.*, 2001, Chaube, 2002).

Soil solarization has been observed to improve plant growth and yield increase (Chen *et al.*, 1991; Gamliel and Katan, 1991; Stapleton *et al.*, 1991; Khulbe *et al.*, 2001; Chaube, 2002). Increased growth response has been attributed to altered/ increased concentrations and availability of macro and micronutrients (Chen *et al.*, 1991; Khulbe, 2000). Abdel-Rahim *et al.*, (1980) reported reduction in soil salinity due to solarization. Electrical conductivity increases significantly (Arora, 1998; Arora and Yaduraju, 1989; Patel and Patel, 1997; Khulbe, 2000; Chaube, 2002). Total soil nitrogen increases significantly (Gruntzweig *et al.*, 1998; Patel and Patel, 1997; Khulbe, 2000). During solarization increased amounts of nitrogen (principally $NH_4$-N and/or $NO_3$-N) usually are liberated (Chen and Katan, 1980; Stapleton *et al*, 1985; Chauhan *et al.*, 1988). Increased levels of phosphorus and potash have also been recorded (Arora, 1989; Gruntzweig, *et al.*, 1998; Patel and Patel, 1997; Ahamed *et al.*, 1996; Khulbe, 2000). According to Stapleton and DeVay (1984) solarization increased KCl, extractable $NO_3$-N, $NH_4^+$-N, $Mg^{2+}$, $Fe^{2+}$, $Cl^-$, and EC. However, solarization did not consistently affect available K, Fe, Mn, Zn, Cu concentrations, soil pH, and total organic matter (Stapleton *et al.*, 1985). Nitrogen appears to be one of the major elements whose availability most consistently increased in solarized soil (Stapleton *et al.*, 1985)

**Mechanisms:** Reduction in disease incidence occurring in solarized soils, results from the effects exerted on each of the three living components (Fig. 5.3) involved in diseases (host, pathogen, and soil-microbiota), as well as the physical and chemical environments which, in turn affect the activity and interrelationships of the organisms. Although these processes occur primarily during solarization, they may continue to various extents and in different ways, after the removal of sheets and planting. The most pronounced effect of soil mulching with polythene is a physical one, *i.e.* an increase in soil temperatures for several hours of the day. However, other accompanying processes such as shift in microbial populations, changes in chemical composition and physical structure of the soil, high moisture levels maintained by the mulch, and changes in gas composition of the soil should also be considered when analyzing mechanisms of disease control.

In the Fig. 5.3 multicital effects of solarization and the consequent effects on soil ecosystem, giving integrated management are explained.

### *Indirect Management of Microbial Populations*

When examining Baker and Cook's definition of biological control (Baker and Cook, 1974; Cook and Baker, 1983) and IPM as a new hat for an old concept, thousands of

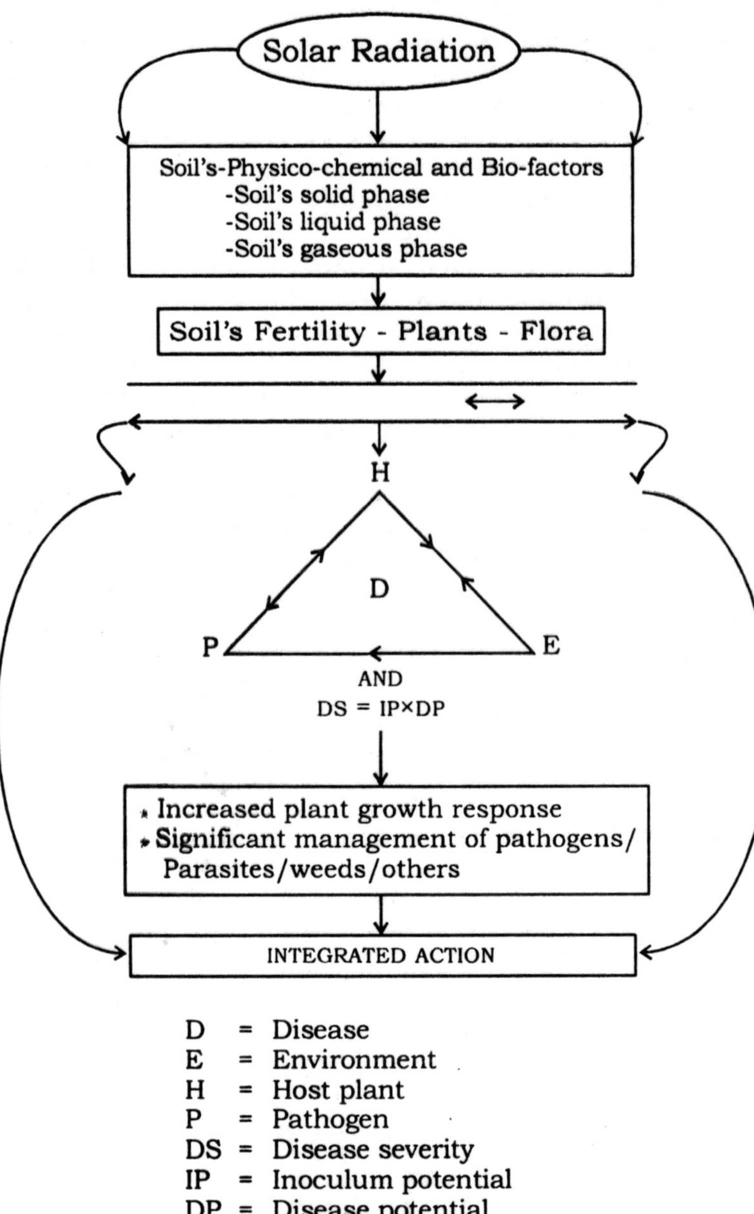


D = Disease
E = Environment
H = Host plant
P = Pathogen
DS = Disease severity
IP = Inoculum potential
DP = Disease potential

**Fig. 5.3:** Diagrammatic representation of the multicital effects of solarization and integrated management of crop health

papers, including books the many examples presented, it is clear why plant pathologists generally consider have been written on the control and management of plant diseases by biological means involving the manipulation of the host and environment. Knowledge from these studies has led to the development of unique and effective methods to manage disease. For example, Horsfall and Cowling's (1977) *Plant Diseases: An Advanced Treatise,* Vol. 1, features at least six chapters dealing with disease management. Baker and Cook (1984) in their book on biological control also emphasizes the relationship between management and biological control. Effective control tactics have involved such approaches as crop rotation, altering soil pH, use of certain fertilizers and organic amendments, tillage methods that modify soil structure, irrigation practices, planting dates, use of trap or inhibitory plants, and manipulation of the environment to promote maximum resistance of the host. Table 5.2 lists various methods used to control diseases with a few examples selected from hundreds where these methods have been used. Plant pathologists and farmers for centuries have used these approaches because of economic reasons and the general lack of effective chemical controls. Whether or not all these practices are forms of biological control depend on ones definition of biological control. We prefer the more restricted definition that attributes disease reduction directly or indirectly to the means of living microorganism or macroorganisms. Therefore, we would consider as biological control tactics those practices (Table. 5.2) which result in the manipulation of antagonistic microflora to disfavour disease.

**TABLE 5.2:** SOME OF CULTURAL PRACTICES THAT PROMOTE CONTROL OF DISEASE

| *Method* | *Pathogen Managed* | *Crop* |
|---|---|---|
| Crop rotation | *Cephalosorium gramineum* | Wheat |
| | *G. graminis* var. *tritici* | Wheat |
| Crop spacing | *Sclerotinia sclerotiorum* | Dry beans |
| Decoy crop | *Spongospora subterranea* | Potato |
| Fallow | *Pseudomnas solanacearum* | Banana |
| Fertilizer practices | *F. oxyporum* f. sp. *phaseoli* | Dry bean |
| Flooding | *F. oxysporum* f. sp. *cubense* | Banana |
| Monoculture | *Streptomyces scabies* | Potato |
| | *G. graminis* var. *tritici* | Wheat |
| Organic amendments | Several parasitic fungi and nematodes | Many Crops |
| pH adjustment | *Plasmodiophora brassicae* | Crucifers |
| | *Streptomyces scabies* | Potato |
| Tillage | *Sclerotium rolfsii* | Peanut |
| Time of planting | *Fusarium roseum 'culmorum'* | Wheat |
| | *Tilletia controversa* | Wheat |
| Trap crop | *Meloidogyne* spp. | Crops |
| Water management | *Phytophthora* spp. | Walnut, Cherry |
| | *Macrophomina phaseolina* | Sorghum |

## CONCLUSION

Modern agriculture involves numerous practices used in various ways and under different conditions. Every CP should be evaluated as a potential tool for disease management. A thorough familiarity with the ecology and crop husbandry is absolutely necessary; for disease management, appropriate modification or innovations in crop husbandry practices have furnished the foundations for success of all types of crop cultivation (Garrett, 1970). There are several justifiable reasons for reducing pesticides, beyond legislation, social issues and political pressures, the continuous use of pesticides frequently results in a concomitant reduction in pesticidal activity. However, the task of replacing pesticides is enormous because of their effectivity. What in fact is needed that the society, through the appropriate institution must support research and development of nonchemical methods of disease and pest management. There are many potential promising methods. The renaissance of CP for disease management is a fact. Our march towards ecologically harmonious and sustainable agriculture has already commenced. We must continue it, CP can and should play an important role in achieving this goal (Katan, 1996). "The main objective of cultural practices is to plant healthy seed in pathogen free soil or in soil with minimal contamination and obtain healthy stand of the crop".

## REFERENCES

Abdel-Rahim, M. F., Satour, M. M., Meckali, K. Y., EL-Eraki, S. A., Grinstein, A., Chen, Y. and Katan, J. 1988. Effectiveness of sol solarization in furrow irrigated soils. *Plant Dis.*, **72**: 143-146.

Ahmad, Y. Hameed, A. and Aslam, M. 1996. Effect of soil solarization on corn stalk rot. *Plant and soil,* **179**: 17-24.

Andrews, J. A. 1983. Future strategies for integrated control. Chapter 40 *In*: T. Kommedahl and P. H. Williams (eds.), *Challenging Problem in Plant Health.* American Phytopathological Society. St. Paul, Minnesota. pp. 538.

Anonymous, 1968. *Plant Disease Development and Control*, Vol I, Principles of plant and animal pest control, Publ. 1596. Nat, Acad. Sci. Washington, D.C. pp. 250.

Apple, J. L. 1977. The theory of disease management. *In*: J. G. Horsfall and E. B. Cowling (eds.), *Plant Disease—An Advanced Treatise* Vol I. Academic Press, New York, pp. 79-102.

Arora, A. and Yaduraju, M. I. 1989. High temperature effects of germination and viability of weed seeds in soil. *J. Agron. Crop Sci.*, **181**: 35-43.

Arora, R. K. 1989. Distribution of healthy and late blight infected tubers in potato ridges. *Indian. J. Mycol. Plant Pthol.*, **19**: 232.

Baker, K. R. 1980. Microbial antagonists—The potential for biological control. *In*: D. C. Euwood, M. J. Lethern, J. N. Hedger, J. M. Lyneh and J. H. Slater (eds.), *Center Porany Microbiolecology.* Academic Press, London, pp. 327-347.

Baker, K. E. and Cook, R. J. 1974. *Biological Control of Plant Pathogens.* Freeman, San Francisco.

Baker, K. F. 1983. The future of biological and cultural control of plant diseases. *In*: T. Kommedahl and P. H. Williams (eds.), *Challenging Problem in Plant Health.* American Phytopathological Society, APS Press. St. Paner, Minnesota, pp. 217.

Baker, R. 1980. Pathogen suppressive soils in biocontrol of plant pathogens. *Plant Prot. Bull.* (Taiwan), **22**: 183.

Baker, R. 1981. Biological control: Eradication of plant pathogen by adding organic amendments to soil. *In*: D. Pimental (ed.), *Handbook of Pest Management in Agriculture,* Vol. 2. CRC Press, Boca Raton. pp. 137-157.

Basuchaudhary, K. C. and Gupta, D. K. 1988. Role of fertilizers in plant disease management. *In*: V. P. Agnihotri, A. K. Sarbhoy and Dinesh Kumar (eds.), *Prospectives in Mycology and Plant Pathology.* Malhotra Publishing House, New Delhi, pp. 84-91.

Biles, C. L. Lindsey, D. L. and Leddell, C. M. 1992. Control of Phytophthora root rot of chilli peppers by irrigation practices and fungicides. *Crop Protection,* **11**: 225-228.

Bruehl, G. W. 1987. *Soil Borne Plant Pathogens*. McMillan Publishing Company. New York, p. 368.

Chang, M. L. and Hsu, S. T. 1988. Supprevision of bacterial wilt of tomato by soil amendment. *Plant Prot. Bull.*, **30**: 349.

Chang, R. J., Ries, S. M. and Patakay, J. K. 1991. Dissemination of *Clavibacter michiganensc* subsp. *michiganense* by practices used to promote transplants. *Phytopathology,* **81**: 1276.

Chaube, H. S. 2001. Soil solarization and management of seedling deseases of horticultural crops. *Technical Bulletin, Directorate of Exp. Sta. G.B.P.U.A. & T.*, Pantnagar. p. 142.

Chaube, H. S. and Singh, U. S. 1991. *Plant Disease Management:Principles and Practices*. CRC Press, New York, p. 329.

Chauhan, Y. S. Nene, Y. L. Johonson, C. Haware, M. P. Saxena, N. P. Singh S. Sharma, S. B. Sahrawat, K. L. Burford, J. R. Rupela, O. P. Kumar, J. V. Rao, D. K. and Sithanantham, S. 1988. Effect of soil solarization on pigeonpea and chickpea. *Research Bull II. ICCRISAI,* Patoncheru. p. 16.

Chen, M. K. Y. and Close, R. C. 1987. Aphanomyces root rot of pea. 3. control by the use of enviuferous amendments. *N. Z. J. Agric. Res.*, **30**: 325.

Chen, Y. and Katan, J. 1980. Effect of solar heating of soils by transparent polyethylene mulching on their chemical properties. *Soil Sci.*, **130**: 271-277.

Chen, Y., Gamliel, A., Stepleton, J. J. and Aniad. T. 1991. Chemical, physical and microbial changes related to plant growth in disinfested soil. 103-129. *In*: J. Katan and J. E. DeVay (eds.), *Soil Solarization*. CRC Press. Boca Rato, pp. 103-129.

Colhoun, J. 1973. Effect of environmental factors on plant diseases. *Ann. Rev. Phytopathol.*, **11**: 345.

Cook, R. J. and Baker, K. F. 1983. The nature and practrice of biological control of plant pathogens. American Phytopatholocgical Society, St. Paul, p. 539.

Cornegie, S. F. and Colhoun, J. 1983. Effect of plant nutrition on susceptibility of potato leaves to *Phytophthora infestans. Phytopath. Z.*, **108**: 248-250.

Cowling, E. B.1978. Agricultural and forest practices that favours epidemics. *In*: G. Horsfall and C. B. Cowling (eds.), *Plant Diseases: An Advanced Treatise*, Vol. II, How Disease Develops in Populations. Academic Press, New York. p. 436.

Curl, E. A. 1963. Control of plant diseases by crop rotation. *Bot. Rev.*, **29**: 413-479.

Engel-hard, A. W. 1989. *Soil-borne Plant Pathogens: Management of Disease with Macro and Microelements.* APS Press. St. Paul, Minnesota, p. 217.

Esfahani, Mehdi Naser. 1991. Effect of soil solarization an soil-borne seedling diseases of some vegetable crops. *Thesis, Ph.D. G. B. Pant Univ. Agric. Tech*. Pantnagar. India.

Frank, Z. R. 1967. Effect of irrigation procedure in *Pythium* rot of groundnut pods. *Plant Dis. Rep.*, **51**: 414-416.

Fry, W. E. 1982. *Principles of Plant Diseases Management*. Academic Press. Orlando, p. 578.

Gaffar, A and Erwin, D. C. 1969. Effect of soil water stress on root rot of cotton caused by *Maenephomina phasoli. Phytopathology,* **59**: 795-797.

Garrett, S. D. 1970. *Pathogenic Root Infecting Fungi*. Cambridge University Press, Cambridge, p. 294.

Gitatis, R. D., Beaver, R. W. and Voloudakis, A. E. 1991. Detection of *Clavibacter michiganense* subsp. *michiganense* in symptomless tomato transplants. *Plant Dis.*, **75**: 834.

Glamiel, A. and Katan, J. 1991. Involvement of fluorescent *Pseudomonas* and other microorganisms in increased growth response of plants in solarized soils. *Phytopathology,* **81**: 494-502.

Gruntzweig, J. M., Katan, J., Ben-Tal, Y. and Rabinowieh, H. D. 1998. The role of mineral nutrients in the increased growth response of tomato plants in solarized soil. *Plant and Soil.*, **206**: 21-27.

Hardison, J. R. 1976. Fire and flame for plant disease control. *Annu. Rev. Phytopathol.*, **14**: 355-279.

Hoitink, H. A. J. and Fahy, P. C. 1986. Basis for the control of soil-borne plant pathogen with composts. *Annu. Rev. Phytopahol.,* **24**: 93-114.

Horsfall, J. G. and Cowling, E. B. 1977. The sociology of plant pathology. *In*: J. G. Horsfall and E. B. Cowling (eds.), *Plant Disease—An Advanced Treatise*, Vol I, *How Disease is Managed*, Academic Press, New York, p. 465.

Huber, D. M. 1980. Role of nutrients in defume. *In*: J. G. Horsfall and E. B. Cowling (eds.), *Plant Pathology—An advanced Treatise* Vol. V Academic Press, New York. pp. 163-118.

Huber, D. M. and Watson, R. D. 1974. Nitrogen form and plant disease *Annu. Rev. Phytopathol.*, **12**: 139.

Jacobsen, B. J. and Backman, P. A. 1993. Biological and cultural plant disease control: Alternatives and supplements to chemical in IPM strategy. *Plant Dis.*, **77**: 311.

Jarvis, W. R. 1992. Managing Diseases in Greenhouse crops. APS Press Amr. Phytopathol. Soc., St. Paull, Minnesota, p. 288.

Kahn, R. P. 1991. Exclusion as a plant disease control strategy. *Annu. Rev. Phytopathaol.*, **29**: 219-246.

Kartha, K. K. and Nema, K. G. 1969. Effect of host nutrition on the incidence and severity of a *Rhizoctonia* disease of *Phseolus aureus*. *Indian Phytopath.*, **22**: 471-475.

Katan, J and DeVay, J. E. (eds.) 1991. *Soil Solarization*. CRC Press. Boea Raton, p. 267.

Katan, J. 1987. Soil solarization. *In*: I. Chet (ed.), *Innovation Approaches to Plant Diseases Control*. John Wiley and Sons, New York, pp. 77-105.

Katan, J. 1996. Cultural practices and soil borne disease management. *In*: R. S. Utkhde and V. K. Gupta (eds.), *Management of Soil-Borne Diseases*. Kalyani Publichers, India, pp. 100-120.

Katan, J., Greenberger, A, Alon, H. and Grinstein, A. 1976. Solar heating by polyethylene mulching for the control of diseases caused by soil-borne pathogens. *Phytopathology*, **66**: 683-688.

Keel, C., Koller, B. and Defago, G. (eds.) 1990. Plant Growth promoting Rhizobactria. *Union Biol. Sci.*, p. 418.

Khuble, D., Chaube H. S. and Sharma, J. 2001. Soil solarization: An ecofriendly method to raise healthy crops. *In*: A. Sinha (ed.), *Microbes and Plants*. Campus Book, pp. 158-187.

Khulbe, D. 2000. Soil solarization: Effect on soil's nutrients, microorganisms and plant growth response. *Thesis, Ph.D. G. B.Pant Univ. Agric. Tech.* Pantnagar.

Kupers, L. J. P. 1979. Agronomic aspects of soil-borne plant pathogens. *In*: B. Schippers and W. Games (eds.), *Soil-borne Plant Pathogens*. Academic Press, New York, p. 686.

Lapwood, U. H. and Hering, T. F. 1970. Soil moisture and the infection of young potato tubers by *Streptomyces scabies* (common scab). *Potato Res.*, **13**: 296-304.

Linderman, R. G. 1970. Plant residue decomposition products and their effect on host roots and fungi pathogenic to roots. *Phytopathology*, **60**: 19.

Miller, D. E. and Burkey, D. W. 1985. Effect of soil physical factors on resistance in beans to *Fusarium* root rot. *Plant Dis.*, **69**: 324-327.

Miller, D. E. and Burkey, D. M. 1975. Effect of soil aeration on *Fusarium* root rot of beans. *Phytopathol.*, **65**: 519-523.

Muller, R. and Gooch, P. S. 1982. Organic amendments in nematodes control. An examination of the literature. *Nematropica*, **12**: 319.

Naqui, S. M. 1994. Effect of some fungicides in control of Phytophthora diseases of Nagpur mandarin in central India. *Indian Phytopath.*, **47**: 430.

Nawaz, R. M. S. and Narayanaswamy, P. 1983. Influence of host nutrition no powdery mildew disease development in black gram. *Madras Agric. J.*, **70**: 57-58.

Nelson, E. G. and Hoitink, H. A. J. 1983. The role of microorganisms in the suppression of *Rhizoctonia solani* in container media amended with composted hardwood bark. *Phytopathology*, **73**: 272

Newhall, A. G. 1955. Disinfestation of soil by heat, flooding and fumigation. *Bot. Rev.*, **21**: 189.

Palti, J. 1981. *Cultural Practices and Infection Crop Diseases*. Springer-Verlag, Borlin, p. 243.

Patel, B. K. and Patel, H. R. 1997. Effect of nematicides, soil solarization, rabbing, green manuring on some physical and chemical properties of soil in nematode infested bidi tobacco nursery. *Tabacco Research*, **23**: 19-26.

Patel, K. V., Vala, D. G., Mehta, B. P. and Patel, T. C. 1992. Effect of nitrogen doses on incidence of false smut of rice. *Ind. J. Mycol. Pl. Pathol.*, **22**: 250.

Ristaino, J. B. 1991. Influence of rainfall, drip irrigation, and inoculum density on the development of Phytophthora root and crown rot epidemic and yield in bell pepper. Phytopathology, **81**: 922-929.

Rotem, J. and Palti, J. 1969. Irrigation and plant diseases. *Annu. Rev. Phytopathol.*, **7**: 267-288.

Sanford, G. B. 1926. Some factors affecting the pathogenicity of *Actinomyces scabies*. *Phytopathology,* **16**: 525.

Saxena, S. C. and Lal, S. 1981. Effect of fertilizer application on the incidence of bacterial stalk rot of maize. *Indian J. Myco. Plant Patho.*, **11**: 164-168.

Schippers, B. and Games, W. 1979. *Soil-borne Plant Pathogens*. Academic Press, Incl., (London) Ltd. p. 686.

Schippers, B., Baker, A. W. and Baker P. A. H. M. 1987. Interactions of detections and beneficial rhizosphere microorganisms and the effect of cropping practices. *Annu. Rev. Phytopathol.*, **25**: 339-358.

Sharma, Y. and Basuchaudhary, K. C. 1985. Effect of inorganic fertilizers on the incidence of wilt and root rot of cauliflower. *Indian J. Plant Pathol.*, **3**: 259-262.

Singh, B. P. and Jeswani, M. D. 1986. Managing common scab of potato through chemicals and cultural practices. *Indian Phytopath.*, **39**: 152.

Singh, R. S. 1965. Control of root knot nematodes with organic soil amendments *FAO Plant Prot. Bull.*, **13**: 35.

Singh, R. S. 2000. *Plant Disease Management*. Oxford IBH Publishing Co. Pvt. Ltd. New Delhi.

Singh, R. S. and Sitaramaiah, K. 1973. Control of plant parasitic nematodes with organic amendments of soil. *Exp. Sta. Res. Bull. No-6.* G.B. Pant Univ. Agric. Tech., Pantnagar, India.

Singh, R. S., Chaube, H. S. and Singh, N. 1972. Studies on the control of black scurf disease of potato. *Indian Phytopath.*, **25**: 343.

Sivaprakasham K. and Rajagopalan, C. K. S. 1974. Effect of nitrogen on the incidence of Verticillium wilt disease of egg plant caused by *Verticillium dahliae. Plant and Soil.*, **40**: 217-220.

Sivaprakasham, K., Pillayaswamy, K. and Rajaram. J. 1975. Effect of NPK on root rot disease incidence in sunflower. *Madras Agric. J.,* **62**: 308-309.

Smalley, E. V. 1963. Seasonal fluctuations in susceptibility of young seedlings to Dutch Elm Disease. *Phytopathology,* **53**: 846-853.

Smith, A. M. 1972. Biological control of fungal scleortia in soil. *Soil Biol. Biochem.*, **4**: 131-134.

Stapleton, J. J. and DeVay, J. E. 1985. Thermal components of soil solarization as related to changes in soil and root microflora and increased plant growth response. *Phytopathology,* **74**: 255.

Stapleton, J. J. DeVay, J. E. and Lear, B. 1991. Simulated and field effected of ammonia based fertilizers and soil solarization on pathogen survival, soil fertility and crop growth. *In*: J. E. DeVay, J. J. Stapleton and C. L. Elmone (eds.), Soil Solarization. *Plant Prot. Paper,* 109 FAO, Rohme pp. 331-342.

Stapleton, J. J. Quick, J. and DeVay, J. E. 1991. Soil solarization: Effect on soil properties, crop fertilization and plant growth. *Soil Biol. Biochem.*, **17**: 369.

Steadman, J. R. 1979. Control of plant disease caused by Sclerotinia disease. *Phytopathology,* **69**: 904-907.

Sterems, R. B. 1960. Cultural practices in diseases control. *In*: J. G. Horsfell and A. E. Dimond (eds.), *Plant Pathology: An Advanced Treatise* Vol. III. *The Diseased Population: Epidemics and Control.* Academic Press, New York, p. 675.

Stover, R. H. 1962. Rusarial wilt (Panama diseases) of bananas and other *Musa* species. *Phytopathological Paper No.* 4 CMI. Surrey, p. 117.

Summer, D. R. Doupink, B. Jr. and Boodalis, M. G. 1981. Effect of reduced tillage and multiple cropping on plant diseases. *Annu. Rev. Phytopathol.*, **17**: 167-187.

Sun, S. K. and Huang, J. W. 1983. Effect of soil amendments on *Fusarium* wilt of watermelon. *Plant Prot. Bull.* (Taiwan), **25**: 117.

Sun, S. K. and Haung. J. W. 1985. Formulated soil amendment for controlling *Fusarium* wilt and other soil-borne disease. *Plant Dis.*, **69**: 917.

Thomas, P. E., Heng, A. N., Reed, G., Gilliland, G. C. and Reisenauor, G. 1993. Potential role of winter rapeseed culture on the epidemiology of potato leaf role disease. *Plant Dis.*, **77**: 420.

Thresh, J. M. 1982. Cropping practices and virus spread. *Annu. Rev. Phytopathol.*, **20**: 193.

Tinline, R. D. and Spurr, D. T. 1991. Agronomic practices and common root rot in spring wheat: Effect of tillage on disease and inoculum density of *Cochliobolus sativus* in soil. *Can. J. Pl. Pthol.*, **13**: 258-266.

Tjamos, E. C. 1996. Chemical treatment and soil solarization for mangement of soil-borne diseases. *In*: R. S. Utkhede and V. K. Gupta (eds.), *Management of Soil-borne Disease*. Kalyani Publishers,. India, pp. 261-281.

Tjamos, E. C., Antonou, P. and Panago Pulos, C. G. 1992. Control of bacterial canker of tomato by application to soil solarization. Phytopathology, **82**(10): 1076 (abst.)

Verma, R. K. and Shekhawat, G. S. 1991. Effect of crop rotation and chemical soil treatment on bacterial wilt of potato. *Indian Phytopathol.*, **44**: 5.

Waggoner, P. E. Miller, P. M. and DeRao, H. 1960. Plastic mulching principle and benefits. *Can. Agric. Exp. Sta. Bull.*, 623

Wolts, S. S. and Engelhard, A. W. 1973. Fusarium Wilt of Chrysanthemum: Effect of nitrogen source and lime on disease development. *Phytopathol.*, **63**: 155-157.

Worley, R. E., Modern, D. J. and Jarmon, S. A. 1966. Reduction of southern blight on tomato by deep ploughing. *Plant Dis. Reptr.*, **50**: 443-444.

Yang, C. H. and Hsich, W. H. 1985. Effect of soil amendments on clubroot of curcifers. *Plant. Prot. Bull.* (Taiwan), **27**: 225.

Zentmeyer, G. A. and Bard, T. G. 1977. Management of the environment. pp. 132-144. *In*: J. G. Horsfell and E. B. Cowling (eds.), *Plant Disease: An Advanced Practice*, vol. I. Academic Press, New York. p. 465.

6

# Predators and Parasitoids of Commercial Potential in Management of Pests of High Input Crops

**N. S. Rao and S. K. Jalali**

## INTRODUCTION

Predators and parasitoids are one of the important components of Integrated Pest Mangement (IPM) and have been proved to be an excellent alternative to chemical pesticides in many ecosystems. In the native field, both abiotic factors and natural enemies are responsible in reducing the pest population by upto 60 per cent. The history of biological control dates back to the seventeenth century and since then a great deal of information has been generated on biological methods of pest suppression. Biological control has been accepted as an important component of IPM. Much of the information developed on IPM remains at the level of researchers and information flow from researchers to farmers has not received due attention. Unfortunately, biological control has not been practised to the extent it should be due to various reasons and the voluminous research findings have not percolated down to the farmers' level. The folly of sole dependence on pesticides has been realised the world over now and the concern for preserving a cleaner world for posterity has increased. Still, it has been a challenge to implement biological control in the field for the benefit of the small and marginal farmers, especially in the developing world.

## PREDATORS AND PARASITOIDS OF COMMERCIAL POTENTIAL IN PEST MANAGEMENT

### Sugarcane

Biological control has gained maximum acceptance among sugarcane farmers of India. A number of insects dominated by borers and sucking pests attack sugarcane from sowing to harvest. Use of *Trichogramma* species for the management of sugarcane borers has been followed in a major way. Sugar mills have their own coperative parasitoid production units and have contributed in a big way in adoption of biological control. Doomra *et al.* (1994) recorded least infestation of *Scirpophaga excerptalis* and highest yield in areas where *T. japonicum* was released @ 50,000/ha/10 days during April-June with mechanical control of top borer infested shoots compared to carbofuran treated areas in Punjab. Some of the earlier work for two decades on the releases of *T. chilonis* evolved around *Emmalocera depressella* due to which highly satisfactory control was achieved (Narayanan and Mukherji, 1953). Gupta (1951)

*Project Directorate of Biological Control, P. B. No. 2491, H. A. Farm Post, Bellary Road, Bangalore-560 024.*

reported that releases of *T. chilonis* controlled de *E. depressella* in U.P. Similarly, for *Chilo sacchariphagus indicus* releases of *T. chilonis* @ 40,000/ha at fortnightly interval six times resulted in lower borer infestation in treated area (Kalyanasundram *et al.*, 1993). Varma *et al.*, (1991) released *T. chilonis* in an area of 500 hectares and reported highly significant results in reducing incidence of *C. auricilius* in Punjab. Releases of *Sturmiopsis inferens* has decreased the population of *C. infuscatellus* in Tamil Nadu, Orissa and on *C. auricilius* in Haryana (David, 1980). Similarly, inoculative releases of *Isotima javensis* have given good results in the control of top borer in many parts of the country.

Amongst sucking pests, notable success has been achieved in the biosuppression of the hopper, *Pyrilla perpusilla* in some states by the colonisation/redistribution of the lepidopteran parasitoid, *Epiricania melanoleuca.* Misra and Pawar (1983) released 8000-12000 cocoons or 800000-1000000 eggs/ha when pest density was 5-7 individuals/leaf and obtained significant control all over India. The releases of *Chilocorus nigrita, Pharoscymnus horni* and *Sticholotis madagassa* @ 800 adults/acre reduced infestation by 48 per cent (Ansari *et el.*, 1989).

**Cotton**

Cotton is another crop which suffers from number of insect pests, major ones being bollworms, sucking pests and leaf eating caterpillar. Therefore, management becomes very difficult because these pests are associated with the crop till harvest. The farmers spray approximately 10 rounds in rainfed cotton and 20 rounds of insecticide in irrigated cotton especially in northern India. Therefore, attempts were made to develop IPM schedules. IPM schedule comprising the use of trap crop, releases of *Trichogramma chilonis, Chrysoperla carnea* (Plate 6.1), spray of Ha nuclear polyhedrosis viruses (HaNPV) and neem based formulations integrated with insecticides when tried in Karnataka, Maharashtra and Gujarat has given better results against pest complex compared to insecticidal sprays alone. The results indicated that insecticidal sprays were reduced by half and yield was increased by up to 10 q/ha in Bio-intensive Integrated Pest Management (BIPM) area (Lingappa *et al.*, 2001). These findings could convince the farmers that they could obtain higher returns by adopting bio-intensive than purely calendar based insecticidal control measures.

**Tobacco**

In tobacco, combinations of several natural enemies were tried to control pest complex. An IPM strategy comprising castor as a trap crop, NPV of *S. litura*, neem seed kernel extract, *Bt*, release of *C. carnea, Telenomus remus* and *Cotesia africanus* (Plate 6.1) for the management of *S. litura* and the aphid, *Myzus persicae*, has been formulated and found effective in Andhra Pradesh. The results of IPM trial showed cost-benefit ratio of 1 : 1.92-1 : 2.74 compared to 1 : 1.52-1 : 2.25 in insecticidal treatment both in nursery and open field (Anonymous, 1995-2001). In Karnataka, BIPM was compared to a recommended insecticidal approach. In BIPM castor was grown as trap crop, 0.05% quinalphos was sprayed on 30th day after transplanting, *Sl* NPV was sprayed on 45th day and NSKE 1.0% on 60th day after dransplanting. In the chemical control, 3 sprays of quinalphos were given. The yield obtained was 1311 kg/ha in BIPM compared to 980 kg/ha in insecticidal treated area (Shivayogeshwara *et al.*, 1991). Tobacco IPM has been successfully field demonstrated in farmers' fields in Andhra Pradesh.

## Fruits

### *Apple*

*Quadraspidiotus perniciosus* is one of the most serious pests of apple and many other deciduous fruit trees in Kashmir, Himachal Pradesh and Uttar Pradesh. A number of coccinellid beetles such as *Chilocorus infernalis (C. bijugus), C. rubidus, Pharoscymnus flexubilis* and *Sticholotis marginalis* have been recorded feeding on this pest, but these beetles are unable to give the desired natural control. These beetles have been introduced from Jammu and Kashmir to Thanedhar area of Himachal Pradesh. Both the predators have established and provided reasonable control of San Jose scale (Rao *et al.*, 1971; Singh, 1989).

In 1958 and 1960, three strains of *Encarsia perniciosi viz.* Californian, Russian and Chinese, were introduced. In addition, *Aphytis diaspidis* (origin: Japan) was introduced from California. All the strains were established; the Russian strain of the parasitoid gave 89 per cent parasitism in Himachal Pradesh. *A diaspidis* in combination with *E. perniciosi* gave 86.5 per cent parasitism. In the beginning, low parasitism by Chinese strain was attributed to small number of parasitoids released. In Kashmir, the Russian and Chinese strains appeared to be superior to Californian and Hinois strains. American and Chinese strains of *E. perniciosi* were also released in the Kumaon hills of Uttar Pradesh; the population of the pest was reduced by about 95 per cent. In Kashmir, release of *E. perniciosi* and *A. proclia* resulted in an increase of parasitism from 8.9 to 64.3 per cent. Studies on the biology of *E. perniciosi* revealed that the multiplication rate of the parasitoid was over 10 times. In apple, release of *Encarsia perniciosi* or *Aphytis proclia* @ 2000/infested tree and *Chilocorus infernalis* @ 20/infested tree gave effective control of San Jose scale (Rao *et al.*, 1971; Singh 1989).

In India, the first consignment of the exotic parasitoid *Aphelinus mali* to control woolly aphid was imported in 1930 from England. The parasitoid was not effective in Kumaon hills due to the activity of *Coccinella septempunctata*, which fed on parasitised and unparasitised aphids alike and provided nearly complete control. But the parasitoid was quite effective in Kullu valley of Himachal Pradesh. The parasitoid has since then spread to Kashmir valley. *A. mali* was also released around Shimla and it has established well. However, the current status of this parasitoid indicates that it gives good control in valleys, but is less effective on slopes. It has established in most of the woolly aphid infested orchards (Rao *et al.*, 1971; Singh, 1989).

*Cydia pomonella* is a serious pest of apple and other fruits in Ladakh district of Jammu & Kashmir. Two exotic egg parasitoids *Trichogramma embryophagum* and *T. cacoaciae pallidum* were evaluated. Based on the results, weekly releases of the egg parasitoids are recommended. A survey for two consecutive years brought out the need to initiate control measures by monitoring the pest by large scale use of pheromones, conservation of natural enemies, synchronization of the first release of *T. embryophagum* with the first appearance of the moth, and subsequent releases at weekly intervals at 2000 per tree. Fortunately, the codling moth has not crossed the Zojila Pass and it may be possible to check the pest in Ladakh region itself if proper measures are adopted (Rao *et al.*, 1971; Singh, 1989).

Indian Gypsy moth, *Lymantria obfuscata* is a common pest of apple, poplar, willow, walnut, peach, plum, cherry, etc. in Kashmir. It has been found to cause severe damage to many tree and fruit crops in temperate regions of Himachal Pradesh and Uttar Pradesh. Egg parasitoid *Anastatus kashmirensis*; larval parasitoids *Glyptapanteles indiensis, G. flavicoxis, G. liparidis, Cotesia melanoscela, Hyposoter lymantriae, Rogas indiscretus, Exorista rossica, Palexorista conspicua*; pupal parasitoids *Brachymeria intermedia* and *B. lasus* are the dominant parasitoids of Indian gypsy moth. In addition to these pupal parasitoids, *Pimpla laothoe, Theronia atalantae* and *Calosoma himalyanum* have been recorded as population regulatory factors of the Indian gypsy moth (Rao *et al.*, 1971).

*Amblyseius finlandicus* was the most common predator on mite *Tetranychus urticae* attaching apple in Kashmir. The life cycle of the host synchronised with that of the predator (Rao *et al.*, 1971).

### Citrus

On citrus butterfly *Papilio demoleus*, egg parasitoid *Trichogramma chilonis* parasitised up to 75.86 per cent and *Telenomus* sp. nr. *incommodus* 78 per cent in February (Krishnamoorthy and Singh, 1988; Jalali and Singh, 1990). *Distatrix papilionis* is the dominant parasitoid of caterpillars and *T. chilonis, T. incommodus* and *D. papilionis* caused a cumulative parasitism of 88 per cent (Krishnamoorthy and Singh, 1988). Most of the parasitoids of *P. demoleus* also attack another common species of butterfly *P. polytes* L. in other places. *T. chilonis, Melalophacharops* sp. and *D. papilionis* could be utilised for the biological suppression of butterflies attacking citrus.

The eggs of fruit sucking moth, *Othreis fullonia* (C1.) are successfully parasitised by *Trichogramma chilonis*, which suggests the possibility of utilising *T. chilonis* for the control of this pest (Dodia *et al.*, 1986).

*Coccus viridis* can be controlled by releases of *Cryptolaemus montrouzieri* @ 10 beetles/tree. *Aneristus ceroplastae* and *Encyrtus lecaniorum* caused 43 per cent parasitism in July (Tandon, 1985). These can be utilised to achieve control of this pest.

Mealybug *Planococcus citri* can be controlled in the fields by releasing *C. montrouzieri* and preventing patrolling of ants on the plants by applying 5% diazinon granules about one foot around the trunk. Ten beetles (starved overnight) per plant were released 24 hours after the application of diazinon. The impact was visible within a week and by the 5th week the population of mealybugs was reduced to a negligible level (Singh, 1989). Releases of the predator may have to be repeated annually whenever the mealybugs appear.

An exotic parasitoid, *Leptomastix dactylopii* was introduced from the West Indies in 1983. It is a fairly specific parasitoid of *P. citri*, possessing excellent host searching ability. Field release of *Leptomastix* resulted in its establishment in mixed plantations of citrus and coffee, and also in citrus orchards in several parts of Karnataka, resulting in control of *P. citri* within 3-4 months. No insecticidal sprays were required subsequently for the control of *P. citri* in the following season (Manjunath, 1985; Krishnamoorthy and Singh, 1987; Nagarkatti *et al.*, 1992).

Over a dozen parasitoids have been recorded on the mealybug *Nipaecoccus viridis*. However, *Anagyrus dactylopii* was dominant parasitising up to 90 per cent in the field (Ali, 1957; Subba Rao *et al.*, 1965). A severe infestation of *N. viridis* on citrus was completely controlled by releasing *C. montrouzieri* @ 10 beetles per tree in Andhra Pradesh (Tirumala Rao and David, 1958).

*Icerya purchasi* was reported to be under control by the introduced ladybird predator *Rodolia cardinalis* (Rao and Kamath, 1966). Release of 8-10 beetles on each moderately infested plant has been suggested whenever required.

### *Guava*

The striped mealybug *Ferrisia virgata* is a very serious pest of guava in south India. *Cryptolaemus montrouzieri* (Plate 6.1) has controlled the pest effectively within 30 days of its release (Mani *et al.*, 1989). The efficacy of *Cryptolaemus* when released @ 20 adults per tree in controlling green shield scale. *Chloropulvinaria psidii* was demonstrated in farmer's field (Mani and Krishnamoorthy, 1990a). In another trial, the parasitoid, *Aenasius advena* and the *coccinellid Scymnus coccivora* complimented the performance of *C. montrouzieri* in the complete control of *F. virgata* (Mani *et al.*, 1989). *Planococcus citri* can be brought under effective control by releasing 10 *C. montrouzieri* per plant (Mani and Krishnamoorthy, 1990b).

### *Grape*

*Maconellicoccus hirsutus* has become a major pest in south India in recent years. Release of 10 beetles of *C. montrouzieri* per vine could effectively suppress the grape mealybugs in about 75 days of release (Mani and Thontadarya, 1988a). Dichlorvos, chlorpyriphos and all the commonly used fungicides at recommended concentrations were safe to all the stages of *C. montrouzieri*. Application of these pesticides can be combined with *Cryptolaemus* in the pest management programme (Mani and Thontadarya, 1988b; Babu, 1986).

## Plantation Crops

### *Cashew*

Egg parasitoids, *Telenomus* sp., *Chaetostricha* sp. and *Erythmelus helopeltidis* have been found promising against tea mosquito bug (Singh, 1996).

### *Arecanut*

On arecanut scales (*Chrysomphalus* spp. and *Lepidosaphes* spp.), extensive releases of *Chilococrus nigrita* have shown effective management over other practices (Singh, 1996).

### Cardamom

On shoot and capsule borer of cardamom (*Conogethes punctiferalis*), *Friona* sp., *Eriborus trochanteratus, Agrypon* sp. and *Xanthopimpla australis* are important parasitoids (Singh, 1996).

### Tea

On tea, *Micromus timidus, Calleida nilgiriensis, Opistoplatys* sp., *Pseudopachybrachius guttus, Jauravia pubescens* and *Cheilomenes sexmaculata* are the predators, which regulate the population of tea flushworm, *Cydia leucostoma*. On leaf roller of tea, *Caloptilia theivora, Sympiesis dolichogaster* parasitises up to 67 per cent larvae. *Telenomus* spp. is a very important parasitoid of tea mosquito bug, *Helopeltis theivora*. Combined action of reduviid bug and parasitoids (*Aphytis* sp.) keeps the diaspine scale (*Fiorinia theae*) population very low. *Comperiella bifasciata* and *Aphytis chrysomphali* are important parasitoids and *Chilocorus circumdatus* is the most efficient predator of purple scale *Chrysomphalus aonidum* on tea. Syrphids and coccinellids play a mojor role in the natural regulation of *Toxoptera aurantii*. Parasitoids—*Aphidius, Lipolexis, Trioxys, Aphelinus*, etc.—regulate the aphid population in different seasons. Coccinellid *Stethorus gilvifrons* and predatory mites *Agistemus* sp. are very efficient predators of phytophagous mites on tea (Singh, 1996).

### Coffee

On coffee, parasitoids *Coccophagus bogoriensis, C. cowperi*, and predator *Chilocorus nigrita* are effective on green scale, *Coccus viridis. Coccidoxenoides peregrinus* on *P. citri, Tetracnemoidea indica* on *P. lilacinus, Blepyrus insularis* on *F. virgata* and *Anagyrus dactylopii* on *Nipaecoccus viridis* are the potential parasitoids. Exotic coccinellid predator *C. montrouzieri* and exotic parasitoid *L. dactylopii* have been found to be effective against *P. citri* on coffee (Singh, 1996).

### Pepper

On black pepper scales, *Aspidiotus destructor* and *Lepidosaphes* sp., predatory beetles, *Cybocephalus* sp. and *Chilocorus circumdatus* and the parasitoid *Encarsia lounsburyi* can be released for effective management (Singh, 1996).

## Vegetables

### Cabbage

*Cotesia plutellae* is the most common parasitiod of *Plutella xylostella* on cabbage and cauliflower in plains. *Diadegma fenestrale* and *D. semiclausum* are the dominant larval parasitoids at high altitudes. On cabbage butterfly, *Pieris brassicae, Cotesia glomerata* parasitises up to 65 per cent larvae. Coccinellids *Coccinella septempunctata, Hippodamia variegata* and *Harmonia dimidiata*, Parasitoids *Diaeretiella rapae* and the syrphid, *Eupeodes confrater* are important bioagents of cabbage aphids. The pest management strategy adopted for cabbage and cauliflower pest *P. xylostella*, includes raising Indian mustard as trap crop. Neem seed kernel extract (4%) and pongamia oil can be sprayed twice to control the pest infestation in cabbage. Larval parasitoid *C. plutellae* and egg parasitoid *Trichogrammatoidea bactrae* can be conserved in the plains and *Diadegma semiclausum* in the higher altitudes by avoiding pesticidal sprays (Singh, 1993; Jalali *et al.*, 2001).

### Tomato

*Trichogramma* spp. and *Campoletis chlorideae* are important biotic agents of *Helicoverpa armigera. H. armigera* can be suppressed through inundative releases of egg parasitoid, *T. chilonis/T. brasiliense/T. pretiosum* @ 50,000/ha/week. A nucleopolyhedrovirus of *H. armigera* at $10^9$ POBs./ha/week and *Bacillus thuringiensis* var. *kurstaki* at 0.5 kg/ ha can also be used. Trap crop of African marigold (yellow-tall) can be utilised in the management of *H. armigera* on tomato in 1 : 14 row combination. *H. armigera* females prefer to lay eggs on marigold buds which also attract parasitoids or *T. brasiliense/T. pretiosum/T. chilonis* Bio $H_1$ could be released (Krishnamoorthy and Mani 1990; Singh, 1993).

### Beans

Pod borers *Adisura atkinsoni* and *H. armigera* on field beans can be suppressed by applying *NOPV of A. atkinsoni* $10^9$ at weekly interval. *Tetranychus* spp. can be controlled by releasing the predator; *Phytoseiulus persimilis* @ ten adults per plant, 30 days after germination or as and when infestation is noticed (Singh, 1993).

## Future Prospects of Bio-control

Several natural enemies have been recorded on most of the crop pests but only few can be utilised for pest management as potential predators and parasitoids alone or as a component of IPM. In India, predators, which are commonly employed for pest management are chyysopids, coccinellids and predatory mites. Amongst parasitoids most potential ones are trichogrammatids, tachinids, braconids, encyrtids and aphelinids. Natural enemies have been successfully used in pest management on crops like sugarcane, fruit crops, cotton, tobacco, vegetables and spices. The combined use of natural enemies leads to reduction of pesticide application drastically on crops like cotton, tomato, tobacco, etc. Dissemination of knowledge obtained regarding use of predators and parasitoids of commercial potential for mangement of pests of high input crops would help in widespread adoption of biological control by farmers which is an important component of Integrated Pest Management.

## REFERENCES

Ali, M. S. 1957. Some biological studies on *Pseudococcus vastator* (Maskell). *Indian J. Ent.*, **19**: 54-58.

Anonymous, 1995-2001. Annual Report. All India Co-ordinated Research Project on Biological Control of Crop Pests and Weeds. Project Directorate of Biological Control (PDBC), Bangalore.

Ansari, M. A., Pawar, A. D., Murthy, K. R. K. and Ahmed, S. N. 1989. Sugarcane scale, *Melanaspis glomerata* Green and its biocontrol prospects in Karnataka. *Plant Prot. Bull.*, **41**: 21-23.

Babu, T. R., 1986. Population density of grape mealybug *Maconellicoccus hirsutus* (Green) and its control by a predator *Cryptolaemus montrouzieri* Muls. Ph.D. Thesis, APAU, Hyderabad.

David, H. 1980. Tachnid parasites to control moth borers in India. *In*: S. Sithanantham and A. R. Solayappan (eds.), *Biological Control of Sugarcane Pests in India*. Tamil Nadu State Federation of Cooperative Sugar Factories Ltd., Chennai, pp. 61-66.

Dodia, J. F., Yadav, D. N. and Patel, R. C. 1986. Management of fruit sucking moth, *Othreis fullonica* L. (Lepidoptera: Noctuidae) in citrus orchards at Anand (Gujrat). *GAU. Res. J.*, **11**: 72-73.

Doomra, S., Maninder, S. and Varma, G. C. 1994. Studies on the effect of *Trichogramma japonicum* Ashnead (Hymenoptera: Trichogrammatidae) on the control of *Scirpophaga excerptalis* (Walker) (Lepidoptera: Pyralidae). *In*: *Biological Control of Insect Pests*. PAU, Ludhiana, pp. 143-144.

Gupta, B. D. 1951. A note on the scope of biological control of sugarcane pests. *In*: Proceedings of the 2[nd] Biennial Conference of Sugarcane Research and development Workers, India, Part 2, pp. 229-235.

Jalali, S. K. and Singh, S. P. 1990. A new record of *Ooencyrtus papilionis* (Hymenoptera: Encyrtidae) on the eggs of *Papilio demoleus* (Linn.) from India. *J. Biol. Control.*, **4**: 1, 59-60.

Jalali, S. K., Singh, S. P. and Venkatesan, T. 2001. Choice of suitable *Trichogrammatid* species for suppression of diamond back moth *Plutella xylostella* (Linnaeus) (Lepidoptera: Yponomeutidae) on cabbage. *Shashpa,* **8**:161-166.

Kalyanasundram, M., Justin, C. G. L., Swamiappan, M., Sujdarababu, P. C. and Jayaraj, S. 1993. Efficacy of *Trichogramma chilonis* against sugarcane internode borer *Chilo sacchariphagus indicus* in Tamil Nadu. *Indian J. Plant Prot.*, **21**.

Krishnamoorthy, A. and Mani, M. 1990. Feasibility of managing *Heliothis armigera* through parasitoids. *In*: S. Jayaraj, S. Uttamasamy, M. Gopalan, and R. J. Rabindra (eds), *Heliothis Management—Proceedings of National Workshop*. Centre for Plant Protection Studies, Tamil Nadu Agricultural University, Coimbatore, pp. 195-205, 328.

Krishnamoorthy, A. and Singh, S. P. 1987. Biological control of citrus mealybug with an introduced parasite, *Leptomastix dactylopii* in India. *Entomophaga,* **32**: 143-148.

Krishnamoorthy, A. and Singh, S. P. 1988. Observational studies on the occurrence of parasitoids of *Papilio* spp in citrus. *India J. Plant. Prot.*, **16**: 79-81.

Lingappa, S., Yadav, D. N. and Brar, K. S. 2001. Augmentative biocontrol within cotton IPM-Indian scenario. *In*: S. P. Singh, S. T. Murphy and C. R. Ballal (eds.), *Augmentative Biocontrol—Proceedings of the ICAR-CABI Workshop*. PDBC, Bangalore, pp. 57-92.

Mani, M. and Krishnamoorthy, A. 1990a. Evaluation of the exotic predator *Cryptolaemus montrouzieri* Muls. (Coccinellidae, coleoptera) in the suppression of green shield scale *Chloropulvinaria psidii* (Maskell) (Coccidae, Homoptera) on guava. *Entomon,* **15**: 45-48.

Mani, M. and Krishnamoorthy, A. 1990b. Natural suppression of mealybugs in guava orchards. *Entomon,* **15**: 245-247.

Mani, M. and Thontadarya, T. S. 1988a. Field evaluation of *Cryptolaemus montrouzieri* Muls. in the suppression of *Macanellicoccus hirsutus* (Green) on grapevine. *J. Biol. Control,* **2**: 14-16.

Mani, M. and Thontadarya, T. S. 1988b. Response of *Crytolaemus montrouzieri* Muls. (Coccinellidae, Coleoptera) to commonly used pesticides in vineyards. *J. Biol. Control,* **2**: 1720.

Mani, M., Krishnamoorthy, A. and Singh, S. P. 1989. The impact of the predator, *Cryptolaemus montrouzieri* Muls. on the pesticide resistant populations of the striped mealybug *Ferrisia virgata* (Ckll.) on guava in India. *Insect Sci. Applic.*, **11**: 167-170.

Manjunath, T. M. 1985. *Leptomastix dactylopii* in India. *Biocontrol News Inform.*, **6**: 297.

Misra, M. P. and Pawar, A. D. 1983. Biocontrol trials against sugarcane pyrilla, *Pyrilla perpusilla* Walker in eastern Uttar Pradesh and elsewhere in India. *In*: S. Sithananthan and A. R. Solayappan (eds.), *Biological Control of Sugarcane Pests in India*. Tamil Nadu State Federation of Cooperative Sugar Factories Ltd., Chennai, pp. 75-78.

Nagarkatti, S., Singh, S. P., Jayanth, K. P. and Bhumannavar, B. S. 1992. Introduction and establishment of *Leptomastix dactylopii* How against *Planococcus* spp. in India. *Indian J. Plant Prot.*, **19**: 102-104.

**Plate 6.1**

*Tricho* card for field release of *Trichogramma*

Wasp parasitizing host egg

Adult *Chyrosoperla*

*Chyrosoperla* grub feeding on aphids

*Cotesia* egg mass in cotton ecosystem

Lady bird beetle grub feeding on aphids

Narayanan, E. S. and Mukherji, P. B. 1953. Two decades of field trials in India with *Trichogramma* against the sugarcane stem borer *Argyria* sp. and the root borer, *Emmalocera depresella*. *In*: *Proceedings of the 40th Indian Science Congress*, **10**: 148-149.

Rao, V. P., Ghani, M. A., Sankaran, T. and Mathur, K. C. 1971. A review of the biological control of insects and other pests in South East Asia and the pacific region. *CIBC Tech. Communication*, **6**: 149.

Rao, V. P. and Kamath, S. M. 1966. Record of cottony cushion scale *Icerya purchasi* Maskell in the Cannore district of Kerala and its control. *Indian J. Ent.*, **27**: 552.

Shivayogeshwara, B., Mallikarjunaiah, H., Krishnaprasad, N. K. and Shetty, M. V. N. 1991. Integrated pest management (IPM) of *Spodoptera litura* (Fab.) (Noctuidae: Lepidoptera) in FCV tobacco crop. *Tob. Res.*, **17**: 59-61.

Singh, S. P. 1989. Achievements of AICRP on Biological Control. *Tech. Bull.* No. 2. Biological Control Centre, NCIPM, Faridabad, p. 20.

Singh, S. P. 1993. Biological control of vegetable pests. *In*: K. L. Chadha and G. Kalloo (eds.), *Advances in Horticulture, Vol. 6—Vegetable Crops*: Part 2 (1993), Malhotra Publishing House, New Delhi, pp. 887-920.

Singh, S. P. 1996. Biological control. *In*: R. S. Paroda and K. L. Chadha (eds.), *50 Years of Crop Science Research in India— Goldern Jubilee Year of India's Independence 1947-1996*. Indian Council of Agricultural Research, New Delhi, pp. 89-116, 796.

Singh, S. P. 1996. Biological control in India. *In*: Rajiv K. Upadhyay, K. G. Mukherjee and R. L. Rajak (eds.), *IPM System in Agriculture Volume 2 Biocontrol in Emerging Biotechnology*. Aditya Books Pvt. Ltd. New Delhi, India, pp. 216-328, 620.

Subba Rao, B. R., Sangwar, H. S. Abbasi, O. A. Singh, Y. and Ksheer Sagar, A. M. 1965. New records of hymenopterous parasiter of *Nipaecoccus vastator* (Maskell) (Homoptera: Coccidae), a serious pest of citrus sp. from India. *Indian J. Ent.*, **27**: 109-110.

Tondon, P. L. 1985. Spatial distribution sampling technique and population dynamics of citrus green scale *Coccus viridis* (Green) on mandarin. Ph.D. thesis, UAS, Bangalore.

Tirumala Rao, V. and David, L. A. 1958. The biological control of a coccid pest in South India by the use of beetle *Cryptolaemus montrouzieri* Muls. *Indian J. Agric. Sci.*, **28**: 545-552.

Varma, G. C., Rataul, H. S., Shenmar, M., Singh S. P. and Jalali, S. K. 1991. Role of inundative releases of *Trichogramma chilonis* Ishii in the control of *Chilo auricilius* Dudgeon on sugarcane. *J. Insect Sci.*, **4**: 165-166.

# Potential of Fungal and Bacterial Pathogens in the Management of Key Lepidopteran Pests

O. M. Bambawale, U. R. Sangale, Nasim Ahmad and B. L. Meena

## INTRODUCTION

Lepidopteran pests constitute one of the major concerns in crop protection. Rapid progress has been made in their management in the past twenty years or so with the sole reliance on chemical pesticides getting replaced in part with other means of management such as utilization of various cultural practices, botanicals and biologicals, mechanical practices, etc.. Greater awareness on the part of the farmers has resulted in replacing organophosphates and pyrethroids which are detrimental to the natural enemies. Before we could use alternative options in any sizable proportions there is further technological development of transgenics, and now, we have cotton transgenic hybrids commercialized in India which, though, further reduced the dependence on pesticides for the management of Lepidopteran pests, have created additional pest problems requiring non-chemical management. With such varied options being increasingly used, there are still several pest problems, which need attention, and harnessing the full potential of biopesticides in the category of bacterial and fungal insect pathogens is warranted. This chapter deals with their status and scope in the key Lepidopteran pest management.

In India several key Lepidopteran pests are known to cause major losses in different crops (Table 7.1) with majority of them being crop specific and a few others polyphagous in nature. The fungal and bacterial lepidopteran pathogens are often wide spectrum in their action, cutting across Lepidopteran families, though evaluation for specific purposes is necessary before their commercial use.

## MICROBIALS FOR LEPIDOPTERAN PEST MANAGEMENT

The microbials that cause disease in insects fall into four main groups. They are: viruses, bacteria, fungi and protozoa. These microbials or their toxins are formulated for application as sprays, dusts, or granules. Though hundreds of microbials are known to cause disease in insect pests, only a few microbial agents have been used on a widespread basis as operational control agents and bacterial and fungal pathogens hold high promise as these are amenable to industrial fermentation processes for their mass production unlike the viral or protozoan pathogens which are obligate and require living systems that limit their large scale production and utilization.

*National Centre for Integrated Pest Management, IARI Campus, Pusa, New Delhi-110 012.*

**TABLE 7.1:** KEY LEPIDOPTERAN PESTS OF CROP PLANTS IN INDIA

| *Crop* | *Name of the Pest* | *Scientific Name & Family* |
|---|---|---|
| Rice | Yellow stem borer | *Scirpophaga incertulas* Pyralidae |
| | Pink borer | *Sesamia inferens* Noctuidae |
| Maize | Maize borer | *Chilo partellus* Pyralidae |
| | European corn borer | *Ostrilica nubilalis* Pyralidae |
| Wheat | Army worm | *Mythimma separate* Noctuidae |
| Pulse | Gram pod worm | *Helicoverpa armigera* Noctuidae |
| | Plume moth | *Exelastis atomosa* Pterophoridae |
| | Lentil pod borer | *Etiella zinckenella* Phycitidae |
| Oil Seeds | Castor semilooper | *Achaea janata* Noctuidae |
| | Castor hairy caterpillar | *Euproctis lunata* Lymantriidae |
| | Til leaf and pod caterpillar | *Antigastra catalaunalis* Pyralidae |
| | Til Hawk moth | *Acherontia styx* Spingidae |
| | Tobacco caterpillar | *Spodoptera litura* Noctuidae |
| | Semi looper | *Thysanoplusia orichaleca* Noctuidae |
| | Bihar hairy caterpillar | *Spilosoma oblique* Arctiidae |
| Cotton | Pink bollworm | *Pectinophora gossypiella* Noctuidae |
| | Spotted bollworm | *Earias insulana, E. vittella* Noctuidae |
| | American bollworm | *Helicoverpa armigera* Noctuidae |
| Sugarcane | Sugarcane top borer | *Scirpophaga novella* Pyralidae |
| | Sugarcane shoot borer | *Chilo infuscatellus* Pyralidae |
| | Sugarcane root borer | *Emmalocera depressella* Pyralidae |
| Vegetables | Cabbage caterpillar | *Pieris brassicae* Pyralidae |
| | Diamond back moth | *Plutella zylostella* Yponomeutidae |
| | Cabbage semi looper | *Thysanopulsia orihalcea* Noctuidae |
| | Potato tuber moth | *Phthorimaea operculeua* Gelechiidae |
| | Tomato fruit borer | *Helicoverpa armigera* Noctuidae |
| | Pea Pod borer | *Etiella zinckenella* Pyralidae |
| | Brinjal fruit borer | *Leucinodes orbonalis* Pyralidae |
| | Brinjal stem borer | *Euzophera perticella* Pyralidae |

## Fungal Pathogens

Some 700 species of entomopathogenic fungi have been reported from over 100 genera, but only about 10 of these have been used or currently being developed for insect control. A broad range of biologies from obligate parasitism to opportunistic pathogens that can survive saprophytically in the absence of living hosts, have been documented. Reviews dealing with entomopathogenic fungi and their development and use as microbial control agents include those of McCoy *et al.* (1988), Ferron *et al.* (1991), Tanada and Kaya (1993), Hajek and St Leger (1994), Boucias and Pendland (1998), Wraight and Carruthers (1999), Goettel *et al.* (2000) Lacey *et al.* (2001) and Singh *et al.* (2004). Specific reviews deal with *Nomuraea rileyi* (Ignoffo, 1981), and *Metarhizium anisopliae* and *Beauveria bassiana* (Ferron, 1981). A recent book (Butt *et al.*, 2001) deals extensively in the status and prospects of the fungal biocontrol agents in insect pest management. A technical bulletin (Lingappa and Patil, 2002) enumerates development, mass production and use of *N. rileyi* under Indian conditions.

Of the entomopathogenic fungi, deuteromycete fungi have received most attention as they are among the easiest to produce *in vitro* and several have a broad host range. Another group of fungi (zygomycetes) act as important natural pest regulators but are rarely used commercially due to inherent difficulties in mass production.

**Entomophthora**

Entomogenous zygomycetes are located principally in the order Entomophthorales. Entomophthorales have potential for biological control of aphids and bollworms. The genera *Entomophthora, Neozygites* and *Pandora* have species which cause epizootics in arthropod populations. The insect hosts of these fungi occur in more than 32 families in the orders Hemiptera, Homoptera, Diptera, Lepidoptera, Coleoptera, Orthoptera and Hymenoptera (MacLeod and Muller-Kogler, 1973). *Helicoverpa armigera* larvae overgrown with sporulated *Entomophthora* spp. in cotton fields can be frequently seen during August-September in Central India.

In the genus *Entomophthora*, the conidiophore forcibly discharges the conidium, which is covered with a mucilaginous sticky substance. When the conidium lands on a moist substrate other than the host, it may produce a secondary conidiophore and secondary conidium, which may produce tertiary conidiophores and conidia. This process may continue until the protoplasm is depleted or a suitable host is found (Tanada and Kaya, 1993). Secondary and tertiary conidia may become resting spores. Secondary conidia (capilliconidia) may be borne on narrow capillary conidiophores. The surface of the capilliconidia has sticky substances, which adhere the spores to objects with which they come in contact. Upon germination, the conidium produces a germ tube that penetrates the insect cuticle and enters the haemocoele. Inside the haemocoele, the fungus forms protoplasts, hyphal bodies and hyphae. The protoplasts appear early in infection and have amoeboid movement. The reason for the production of protoplasts by certain species of Entomophthorales is not well understood. The time required for entomophthorous species to kill an insect is dependent upon many factors such as the host it infects, temperature, moisture and developmental stage of the insect. At the time of death, nearly all of the internal organs of the insect are utilized by the fungus. The period from infection to death of the insect takes from 3 to 12 days. After death of the insect, conidiophores grow out from the hyphal bodies and emerge through the less resistant portions of the exoskeleton. Terminally-borne conidia are produced via septum formation. Entomophthorous fungi produce various types of resistant or resting structures such as chlamydospores, zygospores, thick-walled hyphae, and azygospores. Zygospores may be produced when two hyphal bodies of opposite mating types fuse. Thick-walled zygospores are important for survival in temperate climatic zones. Germinating resting zygospores produce a germ tube, which may produce infectious primary-discharge conidia or secondary adhesive spores.

The use of the Entomophthoraceae as microbial control agents has been hindered by the poor survival of conidia (McCoy *et al.*, 1988). Most species of entomophthoralean fungi are relatively difficult to produce and their primary conidia are short lived, making timing of inundative applications difficult or impossible. This group of fungi has been tested for microbial control of aphids with some degree of success in the former U.S.S.R. and Australia (McCoy *et al.*, 1988). In the United States, Hajek *et al.* (1996) successfully introduced Entomophthora maimaiga into areas more recently colonized by the gypsy moth (*Lymantria dispar*).

**Fungi Imperfecti–Hyphomycetes**

Most of the entomopathogenic fungi belong to Deuteromycetes. About 30 genera have been reported to contain one or more species that infect insects. The members of this class are characterized by mycelial forms that bear asexual spores, termed 'conidia', borne on specialized conidiogenous cells. Conidiogenous cells are often formed on simple or branched hyphae, termed 'conidiophores', or form aggregations of conidiophores, reffered to as synnemata or sporodochia. Since these fungi apparently lack a sexual or perfect stage, they are known as imperfect fungi. They may have parasexual reproduction in which nuclear fusion occurs but not meiosis proper. The parasexual process provides a mechanism for genetic exchange among imperfect fungi. Fungi that produce conidia on more or less loose, cottony hyphae are often termed 'Hyphomycetes'. As a group, the hyphomycetous fungi are facultative pathogens. Almost all can be cultured on artificial media. Fungi imperfecti that show potential as microbial control agents for commercial development include *B. bassiana, M. anisopliae*, and *N. rileyi.*

A number of fungi in this class cause muscardine diseases in insects, including *H. armigera* larvae. The term was first applied to the white muscardine of the silkworm caused by *B. bassiana.* Other muscardine diseases associated with heliothine larvae are the green muscardine caused by *M. anisopliae*, the red muscardine by *Sorosporella uvella*, and yellow muscardine by *Aspergillus flavus.* On *H. armigera* several fungal pathogens have been recorded viz., *Fusarium oxysporium* var. *orthoceras, Aspergillus parasiticus* and *Scopulariopsis brevicaulis* from Russia (Singh, 1972), and *M. anisopliae, B. bassiana* and *N. rileyi* from Indonesia (Van der Laan, 1981). Larval diseases of *H. armigera* caused by *N. rileyi* and *B. bassiana* were recorded from all the nine Indian states recently surveyed (S. K. Jalali, unpublished data Singh *et al.*, 2002). Local isolates of *B. bassiana* and *M. anisopliae*, virulent against two of the major pests of cotton (*S. litura* and *H. armigera*) and Bean crop (*S. litura* ) were developed and found to be highly effective under field conditions (Padmaja, *In*: Bambawale *et al.*, 2003).

Hyphomycetous fungi infect their hosts primarily through the external cuticle, although a few taxa are able to invade through the alimentary canal. Conidia strongly adhere to insect cuticles, and their attachment to cuticles is thought to involve non-specific adhesion mechanisms mediated by the hydrophobicity of the conidial cell wall (*Boucias et al.*, 1988). Once a propagule comes in contact with an appropriate insect cuticle, it may germinate and it may produce penetration structures (e.g., germ-tube swelling, appressorium or extracellular sheath) from which penetration hyphae are formed. Even if germination does occur, the fungus may not be able to penetrate the cuticle, due to a number of factors, such as an inappropriate environment (e.g., conditions of moisture), and/or the presence of inhibitory factors, such as fatty acids or melanin, within the cuticle. To penetrate the cuticle, the entomopathogenic Hyphomycetes utilize a combination of enzymatic and mechanical mechanisms. The production of exoproteases are important in penetration by *M. anisopliae* and other fungi, but other enzymes, such as endoproteases, esterases, lipases, chitinases and chitobiases, are involved as well (Boucias and Pendland, 1998).

Pathogenicity and epizootiology of the Hyphomycetes has been described in detail by Inglis *et al.* (2001). After reaching the haemocoele, the fungus grows as hyphal bodies, which are single or multicelled structures that lack a formal cell wall but contain a thin, fibrillar layer on the plasma membrane (some forms are often referred to as blastospores). Before the fungus can proliferate in the haemocoele, it must often overcome the insect's defence response, and the production of toxins by the fungus can debilitate the efficacy of the defence response mounted by the insect. Insect death may result from a combination of actions, including depletion of nutrients, physical obstruction or invasion of organs and toxicosis. For example, *B. bassiana* produces a number of toxic compounds, including beauvericin, bassianolide and oosporein. Perhaps the best-studied toxins produced by entomopathogenic Hyphomycetes are the destruxins produced by *M. anisopliae.* Several of these are known to induce titanic paralysis, while others can be immunosuppressive. Following death, the fungus often grows saprotrophically within the host, and metabolites produced by the various taxa may be involved in the competitive exclusion of competing microorganisms from the cadaver. After the death of the host and under favourable conditions, hyphae emerge from the cadaver; they produce conidiogenous cells, sporulation occurs on the host surface and the conidia are liberated.

A complex set of interacting processes, both environmental and biotic, is necessary for development of epizootics caused by entomopathogenic fungi. These include sensitivity to solar radiation; microbial antagonists; host behaviour, physiological condition, and age; pathogen vigor and age; presence of pesticides; and appropriate temperature, humidity, and inoculum thresholds. We need to understand not only the factors critical in fungal virulence and infection but also the techniques to exert control over them through optimization of culture methods, formulation and environmental manipulation.

### *Beauveria bassiana*

The first microorganism to be recognized as a disease causing agent was the fungus *B. bassiana* (Bassi, 1835). The genus *Beauveria* has been monographed by MacLeod (1954), who recognized two species, *B. bassiana* and *B. brongniartii,* that attack all stages of insects of all groups. They have also occasionally been found in the lungs of wild rodents and nasal passages of horses, man, and giant tortoises. *B. bassiana* occurs worldwide and has one of the largest host lists among the imperfect fungi and occurs in soil as a ubiquitous saprophyte (McCoy *et al.*, 1988; Tanada and Kaya, 1993).

The pathogen is of cosmopolitan nature. The hosts include mainly Lepidoptera, Coleoptera, Hemiptera, Diptera and Hymenoptera. The fungus has been recorded to cause infection of the lungs of wild rodents, nasal passages of humans, horses and giant tortoises and, therefore, caution in use is necessary. Some of the pests of economic importance, which can be targeted for control through this pathogen are *H. armigera, Spodoptera* spp., *P. xylostella, Pieris brassicae, Odontotermes obeuss, Chilo infuscatellus, Idioscopus* spp., *Ostrinia nubilalis, Laspeyresia pomonella, Bemisia tabaci,* etc.. *B. bassiana* also produces mycotoxins and the secondary metabolites that prevent bacterial contamination and leads to fungal mummification of the infected insect. In India, the important fungal pathogens isolated from *H. armigera* include *Beauveria bassiana* and *B. brongniartii* (Jayaramaiah, 1981). *Beauveria* sp. was found infecting *H. armigera* on cotton (Plate 7.1), pigeon pea and other legumes in Andhra Pradesh in October-December, 1987 (Abbaiah *et al.*, 1988). The pathogen is readily amenable to mass production (Mazumdar *et al.*, 1995, Puzari *et al.*, 1997) and is commercially available in India.

### *Nomuraea rileyi*

The fungus *Nomuraea rileyi* (= *Spicaria prasina* = *Spicaria rileyi*) is pathogenic to a number of economically important lepidopterous pests, including *H. zea* and *H. virescens* (Ignoffo *et al.*, 1976). Infected hosts are covered with a dense white mat of hyphae that, upon conidia formation, turn pale green (Plate 7.1).

Sprenkel and Brooks (1975) reported that *N. rileyi* infects all of the major lepidopterous pests of soybean in North Carolina. Mohamed *et al.* (1977) reported that the third to fifth instars were more susceptible to infection than were those in the first and second instars. They also reported that the fungus was most effective at 20° C and 25° C, with a mortality of 80% and 71%, respectively. Epizootics severe enough to eliminate a population of heliothines in localized areas are common in Mississippi. Such epizootic outbreaks are usually associated with a humid, cool environment and a dense host population, frequently present during autumn in this state.

In India, natural occurrence of the pathogen has been recorded on *Spodoptera* spp. (*exigua* and *litura*), *Helicoverpa armigera, Trichoplusia ni, Plusia orichalcea, Diacrisia obliqua, Achaea janata, Acontia graellsii, Agrotis ipsilon, Junonia orithiya, Hypocala rostrata, Thysanoplusia orichalcea,* etc. (Rao and Phadke, 1977; Phadke and Rao, 1978; Phadke *et al.*, 1978; Gopalakrishnan and Narayanan, 1988a & b, 1989; Singh and Gangrade, 1975; Agarwal and Rajak, 1985; Rajak *et al.*, 1991; Vimla Devi *et al.*, 1996; Lingappa and Patil, 2002; Vimla Devi *et al.*, 2003; Deshpande *et al.*, 2004). A detailed global list of the Lepidopteran hosts of *N. rileyi* is presented by Lingappa and Patil (2002). Naturally occurring epizootics by *N. rileyi* have been noted in cotton, corn, sorghum, soybean and other crops. Epizootiology studies of *N. rileyi* in field populations of *H. armigera* in India (Karnataka) have revealed higher rates of fungal infection in *H. armigera* on *Cajanus cajun* (37%) compared to *Phaseolus vulgaris* (28.2%) and tomato (20.5%) (Gopalakrishnan and Narayanan, 1989). In Andhra Pradesh in 1998 when outbreak of *H. armigera* occurred on cotton and chickpea, naturally occurring epizootics by *N. rileyi* was recorded. More than 35% of the larvae infected yielded mycelium and spores of *N. rileyi* and only about 6% yielded *B. bassiana.* The availability of *H. armigera* and *Spodoptera litura* in exceptionally large numbers and favourable climatic conditions appeared to have triggered the infection (Singh, 1999).

*N. rileyi* was noticed in epidemic proportions on *H. armigera* at the end of the epizootics of the pest on cotton and chickpea in 1987 and 1997 in the central and south regions of India and appear to be largely responsible for containing the carryover of the pest to the next season (Bambawale *et al.*, 2002). The subsequent years of epizootics were invariably found to have very low incidence of the pest. The pathogen, therefore, deserves to be critically studied for ways of proper utilization. The pathogen has a wide host range in Lepidopteran pests, which can help it to get established in the fields much before the flare up of the main pests. Epizootiological perspective of the pathogen is important (Carruthers and Soper, 1987) to utilize it logically in the IPM programmes. The fungus is also known to cause natural epizootics in soybean loopers (*Pseudoplusia includens*) and velvet-bean caterpillars (*Anticarsia gemmatalis*) in soybean.

The fungus is recommended for use at $2 \times 10^{11}$ conidia/l spray solution for foliar application. The pathogen holds a high promise in utilization as a component of IPM for management of some of the most economically important and polyphagous noctuid pests. Soil treatment has been reported to be an effective (Vimala Devi, 1995) technique for the management of *S. litura* on groundnut crop. *N. rileyi* has a high market potential, and the production technology is now available for commercialization (Vimala Devi, 1994; Vimala Devi *et al.*, 2001; Lingappa *et al.*, 2002). Vimala Devi *et al.* (2003) screened a large number of *N. rileyi* and found out highly virulent isolates against *H. armigera* and *S. litura*.

### *Metarhizium anisopliae*

*M. anisopliae* (Green muscardine fungus) is a widely distributed pathogen (Plate 7.1) and is capable of infecting more than 100 different insect species belonging to a variety of insect orders such as Coleoptera, Lepidoptera, Hemiptera, Hymenoptera and Orthoptera (McCoy *et al.*, 1988). The important economic pests controlled by the pathogen are: the coconut rhinoceros beetle (*Oryctes rhinoceros*), spittle bug (*Mahanarva posticata*) on sugarcane, *Nilaparvata lugens* on rice, scarabaeids (*Popillia japonica* and *Rhizotrogus majalis*), diamond back moth (*Plutella xylostella*), etc. *M. anisopliae* was reported on *H. armigera* (Urs and Govindu, 1971). Several secondary metabolites (cyclodepsipeptides, destruxins A, B, C, D and E and desmethyldestruxin B) are produced by the pathogen in culture which act as mycotoxins. They are also produced in the fungus-infected larvae and are important in development of symptoms. The rapid production of destruxins in the larvae causes death. *M. anisopliae* also produces toxic proteolytic enzymes. *M. anisopliae* has two types of conidia, the short-spored (3.9-9.0 μm) and long-spored (9.0-18.0 μm). The pathogen can be used for both soil application and aerial spray and is readily amenable to mass production (Fargues *et al.*, 2002; Patel *et al.*, 1990).

### Mass Production of Fungal Bioagents

More than 30 trade-named mycoinsecticide products are now registered or are under development worldwide (Wraight *et al.*, 2001). Conidial production is important in field efficacy of entomopathogenic fungi because conidia are the means of dispersal and infection under natural conditions and also conidia of many species have strong hydrophobic walls, which confer environmental stability to the product. Since the fungal conidia are rarely able to cause infection singly even under favourable environmental conditions, there is a requirement of high doseses ($10^{13}$ - $10^{14}$ spores per ha) for pest control under field situations.

Most of the deuteromycete fungi can be mass-produced on locally available organic substrates such as grains of millets (jowar, bajra), molasses and grain husks. These can be either produced through submerged fermentation procedure or on semi-solid substrates. In submerged fermentation, a diphasic procedure is followed. The mycelial mass is first produced in the broth cultures and then the harvested mass is placed under humid conditions on inert substrate with sufficient aeration for sporulation. In case of semi-solid fermentation procedure, the sporulation occurs sufficiently on the substrate itself and such substrate is pulverized with a wet grinder and after spore count the desired formulation is prepared using a carrier such as talk powder.

Currently only a few private entrepreneurs are known to produce fungal bioagents in India using submerged fermentation procedure. These include Agriland Biotech Ltd., Baroda and International Panacea Ltd., New Delhi and their range of bioagents include *B. bassiana* and *Paecelomyces lilacinus*.

A thorough review (Wraight *et al.*, 2001) is available on the mass production of fungal biocontrol agents, product efficiency, quality, formulation and stabilization of the product. A list of the fungi available commercially for the management of Lepidopteran pests is presented in Table 7.2.

**TABLE 7.2:** FUNGI DEVELOPED FOR THE BIOLOGICAL CONTROL OF LEPIDOPTERAN PESTS

| *Product* | *Fungus* | *Target* | *Producer* |
|---|---|---|---|
| Ostrinil | *Beauveria bassiana* | Corn-borer | Natural Plant Protection (NPP), France |
| CornGuard | *B. bassiana* | European corn-borer | Mycotech, USA |
| Naturalis-L | *B. bassiana* | Cotton pests including bollworms | Troy Biosciences, USA |
| Proecol | *B. bassiana* | Army worm | Probioagro, Venezuela |
| Mycotol/ BotaniGard | *B. bassiana* | Diamondback moth | Mycotech, USA |
| Biosoft | *B. bassiana* | *Helicoverpa armigera*, Spodoptera, Plutella and other Lepidopteran pests | Agriland Biotech Ltd, Baroda, Gujrat, India |
| Daman | *B. bassiana* | *H. armigera, Spodoptera*, Diamondback moth | International Panacea Limited, New Delhi, India |
| Bravegard | *B. bassiana* | *H. armigera, Spodoptera*, Diamondback moth | National Biocontrol Laboratories, Nagpur, India |
| Biorin | *B. bassiana* | Lepidopteran pests of vegetables | Biotech International Limited, New Delhi |
| Meta-Sin | *Metarhizium anisopliae* | Sugarcane borer | Agrobionsa, Mexico |

(supplemented from Burges, 1998; Butt and Copping, 2000)

Many public institutions and private entrepreneurs also produce such microbials:

***B. bassiana*:**

Pesticides India Ltd., Udaipur
Division of Plant Protection, Sugarcane Breeding Institute, Coimbatore
Green Tech Agro Products Pvt. Ltd. Coimbatore
Shri Durga Agro Services, Coimbatore

***M. anisopliae*:**

Department of Entomology, Gujarat Agricultural University, Anand
Division of Entomology and Nematology, CPCRI, Kayangulam
Shri Durga Agro Services, Coimbatore
Division of Plant Protection, Sugarcane Breeding Institute, Coimbatore
Jeypee BioTechs, Virudhunagar

***Nomuraea rileyi*:**

Division of Entomology and Nematology, IIHR, Bangalore

Entomopathogenic fungi need to be targeted in areas where the microclimate provides high humidity with temperatures between 20° and 30° C. Such situations occur particularly during the rainy season and mild winters in major parts of the country. These could be usefully employed for area wide management to reduce the overall pest population and involves moving from regular application of the biopesticide to strategic application early in the crop season, to establish populations that recycle over the whole season and check the growth of invading pest populations. This strategy greatly extends the utility of fungal bioagents and can be much cheaper for farmers.

## Bacteria

*Bacillus thuringiensis* (*Bt*) is the only important bacterial pathogen used in Lepidopteran pest management. *Bt* is a rod-shaped (1.0-1.2 by 3-5 micron), gram-positive, facultative anaerobic, spore forming bacterium belonging to morphological group I along with *Bacillus cereus*, *Bacillus anthracis*, and *Bacillus laterosporus* (Parry *et al.*, 1983), and a facultative pathogen of some insect species commonly used as a biopesticide. *Bt* is a ubiquitous soil bacterium isolated from soil, stored grain, insect cadavers and the phylloplane (plant surface) (Martin and Travers, 1989). *Bt* is recognized by its parasporal body (known as the crystal) that is proteinaceous in nature and possesses insecticidal properties. Considerable amount of information with respect to various aspects of *Bt* such as fermentation (Bryant, 1994), biology and genetics (Aronson *et al.*, 1986), molecular biology (Hofte and Whiteley, 1989; Kumar *et al.*, 1996), mechanism of action (Knowles, 1994) and application as biopesticide (Federici, 1999) is available. The classification and nomenclature of *Bt* toxins has been recently described (Crickmore *et al.*, 1998). Recent information about *Bt* proteins/genes can be obtained from http://www.biols.susx.ac.uk/Home/Neil_Crickmore/Bt/. Kumar and Bambawale (2002) have recently reviewed *Bt* crystal proteins and their application in agriculture. Several websites provide useful information on development of *Bt* as a biopesticide and its expression in the transgenic crops: (*Bacillus thuringiensis*– Based Biological Control (http://ippc.orst.edu/dir/

microbial/Bt/); *Bt* (*Bacillus thuringiensis*) Toxin Resources (http://www.nal.usda.gov/bic/BTTOX/Bttoxin.htm); Transgenic Plants and Genetic Engineering (http://www.nal. usda.gov/bic/BTTOX/Bttoxin.htm#gen); 100 Years of *Bacillus thuringiensis*: A Critical Scientific Assessment," American Academy of Microbiology, 2002, p.12. (http://www.asm.org/ASM/files/CCPAGECONTENT/docfilename/0000003782/Btreport[1]).

### *Classification of Bt Subspecies*

Based on the serotype (serological analysis of flagella antigens) supplemented by morphological and biochemical criteria, over 67 subspecies and eight non-flagellated biotypes have been identified (Federici, 1999). *Bt* subspecies *kurstaki* (*Bt* k) controls various types of lepidopterous insects. Currently over 60,000 isolates of *Bt* are being maintained in culture collections worldwide. *Bt* strains can be characterized by a number of techniques including serotyping, crystal serology, crystal morphology, protein profiles, peptide mapping, DNA probes, AFLP and insecticidal activity (Pattanayak *et al.*, 2000). Known *Bt* toxins kill subsets of insects among the Lepidoptera, Coleoptera, Diptera (Hofte and Whiteley, 1989). By virtue of the lack of toxicity toward other species of animals, human beings, and plants, there is tremendous potential for exploiting *Bt* as a biological control agent.

The most useful scheme for classification of *Bt* toxins is based primarily on homology of toxin gene sequences and the spectrum of insecticidal activity (Hofte and Whiteley, 1989). Hofte and Whiteley (1989) classified 42 *Bt* genes into 14 distinct types and grouped them into four major classes. Many more *Bt* genes have since been sequenced and analyzed. Following the analysis of toxin domains of 29 distinct *Bt* toxin proteins, Feitelson *et al.* (1992) added two new major classes, *cryV* and *cryVI*. Several novel genes were also added within the previously defined classes. The nomenclature of Hofte and Whiteley (1989), based mainly on insecticidal activity, failed to accommodate genes that were highly homologous to known genes but with a different insecticidal spectrum. Based on amino acid identity of full-length gene products, Crickmore *et al.* (1998) have introduced a systematic nomenclature for classifying the cry genes and their protein products.

Insecticidal Crystal Proteins (ICP) are also called as delta-endotoxin. They are protoxin (it must be activated before it has any effect). Commonly designated as "Cry" proteins encoded by "cry" genes. The genes that encode ICP are mostly on plasmids; each ICP is the product of a single gene. A subspecies can synthesize more that one type of ICP. ICPs have various forms (bipyramidal, cuboidal, flate rhomboid, or a composite with two or more crystal types). Most susceptible insects are killed by ingestion of the crystals alone; a mixture of spores and crystals is required for a toxic effect in only a small number of insects. Cry proteins are classified according to their insect specificity (Host spectrum is designated in roman numerals):

- CryI Lepidoptera-specific
- CryII Lepidoptera- and Diptera-specific
- CryIII Coleoptera-specific
- CryIV Diptera-specific
- CryV Coleoptera- and Lepidoptera-specific.

ICP Gene and Protein Nomenclature

cryIA(a)- an ICP gene
CryIA(a)- Crystal Protein

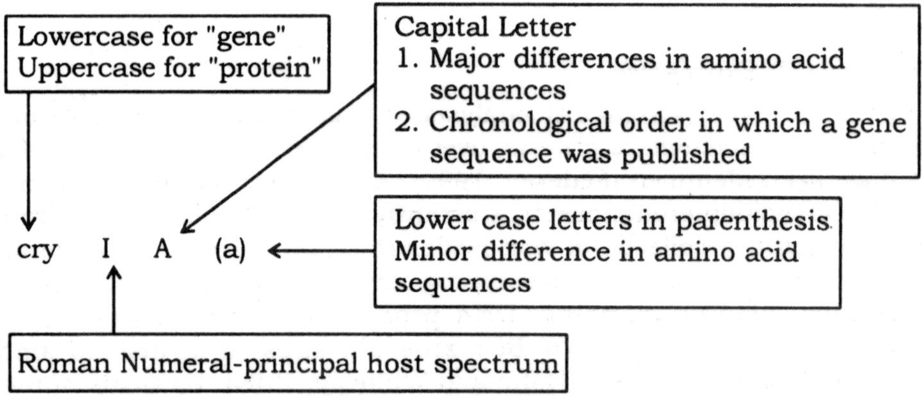


(After Bajwa and Kogan http://ippc.orst.edu/dir/microbial/Bt/)

A mixture of different Cry toxins results in a synergism of insecticidal activity. A mixture of Cry toxins and *Bt* spores results in a synergism of insecticidal activity in several insect pests including Indian meal moth, *Plodia interpunctella* (due to either additional toxins in the spore coat or the outgrowth of vegetative cells from ingested spores). *Bt* crystals are highly insoluble in normal digestive system conditions—safe to humans, higher animals, and most insects. It is soluble in reducing conditions of high pH (above pH 9.5)—a condition commonly found in the mid-gut of lepidopteran larvae. For this reason, *Bt* is a highly specific insecticidal agent. The midgut of susceptible insects contains the correct pH and enzymes to transform the crystal into an active toxin. Different domains of the ICP are responsible for host susceptibility (receptor recognition) and toxicity (pore formation).

After ingestion of spores and ICPs by a susceptible insect larva, ICP dissolves in the alkaline midgut, activation of the ICP by proteases; takes place, there is irreversible binding of the C-terminal domain of activated ICP to specific receptors in the midgut cell membrane followed by insertion of the N-terminal domain of activated toxin in the cell membrane and formation of pores and channels in the gut membrane. This leads to destruction of epithelial cells and paralysis of the digestive system. Spore which find entry into the haemocoel germinate and cause septicemia. Immediate cessation of feeding occurs with general paralysis of the larval midgut. Subsequent symptoms include vomiting, diarrhoea, general sluggishness, and general paralysis. Death may follow immediately or in an hour to a few days from starvation or septicemia. Sublethal effects may include reduction in feeding, larval and adult longevity, fecundity, larval and adult body weight.

### *Beta exotoxin*

During vegetative growth, some *Bt* subspecies (*thuringiensis, galleriae,* and *darmstadiensis*) produce Beta exotoxin, an ATP analogue, which is a water soluble and heat stable secondary metabolite. Beta-exotoxin is an inhibitor of RNA polymerase and acts competitively with ATP in various biological processes. It is, therefore, toxic to almost all forms of life. Products with Beta exotoxin are prohibited for commercial use and manufacturing processes monitor and prevent Beta exotoxin from the final product.

### *Using Bt in Lepidopteran Pest Management*

*Bt* is the most popular biological control agent with a world-wide sales of about $90 million during 1995 (Lambert and Peferoen, 1992). There were nearly 200 registered *Bt* products having more than 450 uses and formulations (Schnepf *et al.*, 1998).

The earliest commercial production of *Bt* began in France in 1938 under the trade name Sporeine (Luthy *et al.*, 1982). During the 1960s, several industrial formulations of *Bt* were manufactured in the United States, France, Germany and Soviet Union. The isolation of the highly potent *kurstaki* variety by Kurstak in 1962 and by Dulmage in 1967 (Dulmage, 1970) provided a much-needed boost to the commercialization of *Bt*. The HD 1 isolate of Dulmage is still the active ingredient in most *Bt* products used against caterpillar pests in agriculture, horticulture and forestry. The discovery of new strains of *Bt* widened the toxicity spectrum of bioinsecticides. The use of conventional *Bt* insecticides, however, was found to have limitations like narrow specificity, short shelf life, low potency, lack of systemic activity, and the presence of viable spores. These problems are now overcome by various approaches that utilize the tools of molecular biology and genetic engineering as well as conventional microbiological methods (Kumar *et al.*, 1996). The plasmid location of *Bt* toxin genes enabled the construction of novel *Bt* strains with microbial genetic approaches such as plasmid curing and conjugal transfer. Ecogen Corporation (USA) produced several bioinsecticides with broadened spectrum of toxicity (Baum *et al.*, 1998); the product "Foil" is made from a strain that carries toxin genes active against European corn borer (*Lepidoptera*) and Colorado potato beetle (Coleoptera).

Using the conjugational approach, Bora *et al.* (1994) transferred the *crylAa* gene of *Bt* into *Bacillus megaterium*, which resides in the cotton phyllosphere. Leaf bioassays of cotton plants, inoculated with a single spray of the transcipient, showed that there was protection to the cotton plants from *H. armigera*. Enhanced production of insecticidal proteins occurs in *Bt* strains carrying an additional crystal protein gene in their chromosomes (Kalman *et al.*, 1995).

Another interesting approach to expand the insecticidal host range of *Bt* is to make use of the *in vivo* genetic recombination property (Baum *et al.*, 1990). Lereclus *et al.* (1992) used insertion sequence IS232 to deliver *cry3A* gene into an isolate producing CrylAc toxin. Expression of the introduced gene did not alter the composition of the polypeptides normally produced by the strain. Novel *Bt* mutants, defective in sporulation but overproducers of toxin, have been isolated (Lereclus *et al.*, 1995). They can be used safely as a biopesticide in silkworm-rearing areas.

*Bt* is primarily a pathogen of insect larval stages. Younger larvae are more susceptible than older larvae. There are different strains or varieties of *Bt* available that have been selected for the control of specific insects. It is compatible with many pesticides and can be used mixed with chemical insecticides.

The larval stages of many Lepidopteran families are sensitive to *Bt* toxin (Table 7.3) after Kumar and Bambawale, 2002). A large number of commercial products of *Bt* are available the world over, and most of them are based on *Bt* var. *kurstaki* (Table 7.4).

**TABLE 7.3:** EXAMPLES OF LEPIDOPTERAN INSECTS SUSCEPTIBLE TO BT TOXIN

| *Family* | *Example* |
|---|---|
| Spingidae | Hawkmoths |
| Pieridae | Cabbage worms |
| Lymantriidae | Tussock moths |
| Tortricidae | Leafroller moths |
| Noctuidae | Cutworms/armyworms, cotton bollworms, etc. |

Management of lepidopteran pests, *Bt* is applied to the surfaces of the plants. Many *Bt* insecticides show poor stability under field conditions, and so frequent reapplication is required. *Bt* ICPs are degraded quickly by solar radiation. *Bt* endospores are inactivated rapidly when exposed to UV radiation. Half-life is from a few hours to about 10 days depending on the season and the crop involved. Vegetative cells and spores may persist at gradually decreasing concentrations for weeks, months, or years as a component of the natural microflora. Endospores are resistant to inactivation by heat and desiccation, persist in the environment under adverse conditions and provide a mechanism for long-term survival of *Bt*.

**TABLE 7.4:** *Bacillus thuringiensis* PRODUCTS FOR THE MANAGEMENT OF LEPIDOPTERAN PESTS

| *Crop** | *Product* | *Bt subspecies* | *Producer* |
|---|---|---|---|
| Vegetables | Biobit | *Bt kurstaki* (H3a3b) | Abbott Laboratories |
| | Condor | *Bt kurstaki* (H3a3b) | Ecogen |
| | Cutlass | *Bt kurstaki* (H3a3b) | Ecogen |
| | Dipel | *Bt kurstaki* (H3a3b) | Abbott Laboratories |
| | Thuricide | *Bt kurstaki* (H3a3b) | Thermo-Trilogy |
| | Javelin | *Bt kurstaki* (H3a3b) | Thermo-Trilogy |
| | Toarow CT | *Bt kurstaki* (H3a3b) | Toagosei Chemical |
| | Xentari | *Bt aizawai* (H7) | Abbott Laboratories |
| Flowers | Clorbac | *Bt aizawai* (H7) | Abbott Laboratories |
| Field crops and | Bioasp | *Bt Kurstaki* (H3a3b) | Biotech International |
| Vegetables | Biolep | *Bt kurstaki* (H3a3b) | Limited |
| Vegetables and field crops | Delfin | *Bt kurstaki* (H3a3b) | Sandoz (I) Ltd. |
| Field crops and vegetables | Halt | *Bt kurstaki* (3a3b) | Wodkhardt Limited |
| Field crops and vegetables | Dipel | *Bt kurstaki* (3a3b) | Lupin Laboratories Ltd. |
| Field crops and vegetables | Spicturin | *Bt galleriae* (5a5b) | Turicorin Alkali Chemicals and Fertilizers Ltd. |
| Field crops and vegetables | HIL BTK | *Bt kurstaki* (3a3b) | Hindustan Insecticides Ltd. |

(List partly adapted from Federici, 1999)

***Field crops and vegetables include**: cotton, paddy, wheat, mustard, tobacco, groundnut, soybean, sunflower, gram, pigeonpea, millets, maize , tomato, cabbage, cauliflower, cole-crops, peas, etc. on which *Bt* formulations are recommended for management of a number of Lepidopteran pests such as *H. armigera, Spodoptera* spp., *Plutella*, cutworms, borers, army worms, hairy caterpillars, leaf rollers and defoliators, etc.

A few other entrepreneurs are also producing commercial *Bt* products in India:

Rallis India Ltd.; Indore Biotech Inputs & Research (Pvt.) Ltd.; Hindustan Insecticides Ltd.; Tuticorin Alkali Chemicals and Fertilizers Ltd.

### Advantages of Bt

*Bt* is essentially non-toxic to humans, pets, birds, aquatic organisms and wildlife, however, inhalation or contact with eyes or open wounds should be avoided. There is no waiting period from time of application before re-entering the field. Different strains of *Bt* are class-specific, meaning beneficials such as predators, parasites, honey bees etc., or non-target insects are not harmed. The insects that ingest *Bt* and later die from it, are not considered dangerous to birds or other animals that may feed on the dead insects. *Bt* is not known to be phytotoxic and is not considered harmful to the environment. There may be only a few cases of *Bt* resistance reported to date; overuse must be avoided. Relying on any one pesticide can lead to the build up of resistance in the pest population. Pesticide rotation and cultural control methods should be used to slow down or eliminate the possibility of resistance development. *Bt* use can integrate well with other natural controls and IPM.

### Disadvantages of Bt

*Bt* acts as a stomach poison; consequently good coverage is essential; *Bt* must be eaten to be effective. It is only effective against immature stages of Lepidoptera feeding on exposed plant surfaces. This limits its usefulness against the Lepidopteran pests that tunnel into the plants or plant parts. Examples include *H. armigera, Earias* spp. and *P. gossypiella* on cotton, which are susceptible to *Bt* but rarely have an opportunity to eat it in field use. It lacks transmission and spreading facilities, it must be applied like a chemical insecticide. *Bt* does not induce epizootics (disease outbreak) except in cases where insects are in confined or crowded area such as bee-hives, insect rearing facilities, or stored grain bins. Due to short residual effect more frequent applications are required compared with chemical insecticides. *Bt* is susceptible to degradation by sunlight and most formulations persist on foliage less than a week following application. The highly specific activity of *Bt* insecticides might limit their use on crops where problems with several pests occur, including non-susceptible insects (aphids, jassids, thrips, whiteflies, etc.). *Bt*-based products tend to have a shorter shelf life than other insecticides. Manufacturers generally indicate reduced effectiveness after two to three years of storage, with liquid formulations being more perishable than dry formulations. Shelf-life is greatest when storage conditions are cool, dry and out of direct sunlight.

## STRATEGIES FOR UTILIZATION OF FUNGAL AND BACTERIAL BIOPESTICIDES

Strategies for the use of entomopathogenic organisms for insect control are basically the same as those for other biological control agents. There are three basic approaches for use of entomopathogens as microbial control agents. They may be used to augment naturally occurring pathogens (augmentation), conserved or activated in nature (conservation), introduced into pest populations as classical biological control agents to become established and exert long-term regulation of the pest (inoculative release), or used inundatively for rapid short term control (inundative release).

Although the market for microbial insecticides is growing, it represents only approximately 1-1.5% of the total crop protection market and most of this is due to sales of *B. thuringiensis*. Not only new products, but new approaches to use, registration, marketing, end-user training and distribution will be required to create a dependable supply of high quality biological control technologies as components of sustainable IPM. Other aspects which require greater attention are: (a) increased pathogen virulence and speed of kill; (b) improved pathogen performance under challenging environmental conditions (cool weather, dry conditions, etc.); (c) greater efficiency in their production; (d) improvements in formulation that enable ease of application, increased environmental persistence, and longer shelf life; and (e) better understanding of how they will fit into integrated systems and their interaction with the environment and other integrated pest management (IPM) components.

Biopesticides offer a transition route to IPM. The role of microbial pesticides in the integrated management of insect pests has been recently reviewed (Lacey *et al.*, 2001) and the Indian scenario is available from the proceedings of a winter school (Rabindra *et al.*, 2001). In most cases no single microbial control agent will provide sustainable control of an insect pest or complex of pests. As components of an integrated approach, entomopathogens can provide significant and selective insect control. The use of pathogens to suppress populations of pests over large areas containing multiple agricultural and wild host plants has not been adequately explored. Such an area wide management (AWM) concept could take advantage of controlling populations of pests before they become economically important in crop plants. An effort has been initiated in Australia in AWM and would also be useful in India for the polyphagous pest like *H. armigera* (Bambawale *et al.*, 2001; 2003).

Technology of the mass production of most of the microbial biocontrol agents is simple and the activity can be taken up as a cottage industry in India. It is now mandatory for microbials to have registration and involves sizable expenditure. An organized effort is the logical solution for this situation where the small entrepreneurs can collectively generate information and share it for registration purposes. An effort has been made by the bioagent producers of Maharashtra who have formed Vidarbha-Marathwada Agro Biotech Association (personal communication) with > 20 members and taken up the process of registration collectively. More such joint efforts would be required in different regions for the spread of the mass production units. Excellent quality production of fungal microbes is now possible through biofermenters in India (Agriland Biotech Ltd, Baroda/International Panacea Limited, New Delhi) and in the near future more such units are likely to be established. Along with the establishment of production units, there is an urgent need for establishing quality control units

## Plate 7.1

Culture of *Beauveria bassiana*

*Helicoverpa* larvae infected with *B. bassiana*

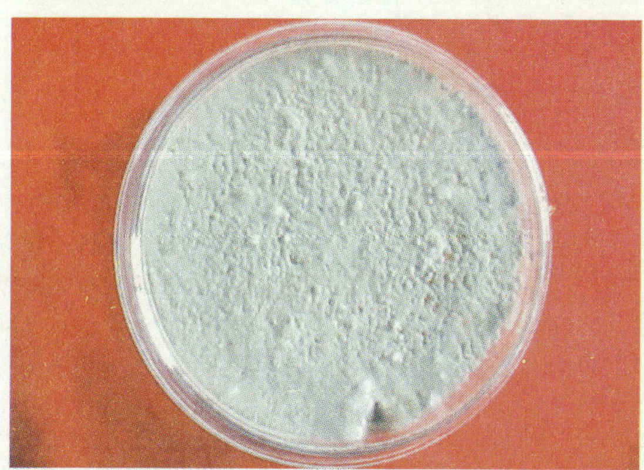

Culture of *Nomuraea rileyi*

Chickpea Pod borer larvae infected with *N. rileyi*

Culture of *Metarhizium anisopliae*

*Metarhizium* mass multiplication using sorghum grains

(referral labs) powered by SAUs/public sector institutes so as to keep a check on supply of standard bioagents to the farmers. Department of Biotechnology, Govt. of India is spearheading the microbial crop protection movement in the country by generation of data for registration of biopesticides through its various funded projects in the ICAR and SAUs and is also actively promoting the use of biopesticides (Wahab, 2003).

Lepidopteran pests constitute one of the major challenges in improvement of crop production. Technological advances are being experienced in terms of ecosafe and multifaceted management options including the development of semiochemicals, soft, improved, and targeted chemical pesticides, insect resistant transgenics, etc. Matching progress is also taking place in better understanding and utilization of fungal and bacterial pathogens. Efforts now need to be directed to optimize the utility of these agents by integrating them with other novel crop protection strategies.

## REFERENCES


Abbaiah, K., Satyanarayana, A., Rao, K. T. and Rao, N. V. 1988. Incidence of a fungal disease on *Heliothis armigera* larvae in Andhra Pradesh, India. *International Pigeonpea Newslettr* No. **8**. p. 11.

Agarwal, G. P. and Rajak, R. C. 1985. A list of entomopathogenic fungi of insect pests of crop and forest nurseries of Jabalpur (M.P.). *Biol. Bull. India,* **7**: 67-69.

Aronson, A. I., Beckman, W. and Dunn. P. 1986. *Bacillus thuringiensis* and related insect pathogens. *Microbiol. Rev.*, **50**: 1-24.

Bajwa, W. I. and Kogan, M. *Bacillus thuringiensis*- Based Biological Control of Insect Pests http://ippc.orst.edu/dir/microbial/bt/, Integrated Plant Protection Center (IPPC), Oregon State University, Corvallis.

Bambawale, O. M., Sheo Raj, Kumar, P., Taneja, N. K. and Sharma, O. P. 2001. Holistic approach in the production and utilization of HaNPV for managing *Helicoverpa armigera. National J. Pl. Improvement,* **3**: 56-60.

Bambawale, O. M., Ahmad, N. and Gautam, R. 2002. *Current status of microbials in Helicoverpa armigera management.* Souvenir cum abstracts. National symposium on perspectives in integrated plant disease management (Feb. 13-14, 2002), NRC for Citrus, Nagpur, pp. 16-18.

Bambawale, O. M., Raj, S., Mahadevan, N. R. and Padmaja, V. 2003. Development and validation of IPM in cotton based cropping system. *In*: Amerika Singh, T. P. Trivedi, H. R. Sardana, O. P. Sharma and Naved Sabir (eds.), *Recent Advances in Integrated Pest Management* (Proceedings and recommendations of the NATP interactive workshop on IPM, Feb. 26-28, 2003. NCIPM, New Delhi, pp. 71-83.

Bassi, A. 1835. Del mal del segno calcinaccio moscardino malattia che affleigge bachi de seta. 1. Teorica. Orcesi, Lodi.

Baum, J. A., Coyle, D. M., Gilbert, M. P., Jany, C. S. and Gawron-Burke, C. 1990. Novel cloning vectors for *Bacillus thuringiensis. Appl. Environ. Microbiol.*, **56**: 3420-3428.

Baum, J. A., Johnson, T. B. and Carlton, B. C. 1998. Natural and recombinant bioinsecticide products. *In*: F. R. Hall and J. J. Menn (eds.), *Biopesticides: Use and Delivery.* Humana Press, Totowa, pp. 189-209.

Bora, R. S., Murthy, M. G., Shenbagarathai, R. and Sekar, V. 1994, Introduction of a lepidopteran-specific insecticidal crystal protein gene of *Bacillus thuringiensis subsp kurstaki* by conjugal transfer into a *Bacillus megaterium* strain that persists in the cotton phyllosphere. *Appl. Environ. Microbiol.*, **60**: 214-222.

Boucias, D. G. and Pendland, J. C. 1998. *Principles of Insect Pathology.* Kluwer Academic Publishing, Massachusetts.

Boucias, D. G., Penland, J. C. and Latge, J. P. 1988. Nonspecific factors involved in attachment of entomopathogenic Deuteromycetes to host insect cuticle. *Appl. And Environmental Microbiology,* **54**: 1795-1805.

Bryant, J. E. 1994, Commercial production and formulation of *Bacillus thuringiensis*. *Agric. Eco. Environ.*, **49**: 31-35.

Burges, H. D. 1998. *Formulation of Microbial Pesticides.* Kluwer Academic Publishers, Dordrecht, The Netherlands.

Butt, T. M. and Copping, L. 2000. Fungal biological control agents. *Pesticide Outlook*, **11**: 186-191.

Butt, T. M., Jackson, C. W. and Magan, N. (eds.) 2001. Fungi as Biocontrol Agents, Progress, Problems and Potential. CABI Publishing, Oxford, UK. pp. 395.

Carruthers, R. I. and Sopers, R. S. 1987. Fungal diseases. *In*: J. R. Fuxa and Y. Tanada (eds.), *Epizootiology of Insect Diseases*. John Wiley & Sons, New York, pp. 357-416.

Crickmore, N., Zeigler, D. R., Feitelson, J., Schnepf, E., Van Rie, J., Lereclus, D., Baum, J. and Dean, D. H. 1998, Revision of the nomenclature for the *Bacillus thuringiensis* pesticidal crystal proteins. *Microbiol. Mol. Biol. Rev.*, **62**: 807-813.

Deshpande, M. V., Hassani, M., Keller, S and Jurg, E. 2004. Microbial control of pests: Entomopathogenic fungi as mycoinsecticides. Annual Report, National Chemical Laboratory, Pune. http://www.biotech.biol.ethz.ch/India/Projects/3_ project_bp1.html.

Dulmage, H. T. 1970, Insecticidal activity of HD-1, a new isolate of *Bacillus thuringiensis* var *alesti. J. Invertebr. Pathol.*, **15**: 232-239.

Fargues, J., Smits, N., Vidal, C., Vey, A., Vega, F., Mercadier, G. and Quimby, P. 2002. Effect of liquid culture media on morphology, growth, propagule production and pathogenic activity of the *Hyphomycete, Metarhizium flavoviride. Mycopathologia*, **154**: 3, 127-138.

Federici, B. A. 1999. *Bacillus thuringiensis* in biological control. *In*: *Handbook of Biological Control.* Academic Press, New York, pp. 575-593.

Feitelson, J. S., Payne, J. and Kim, L. 1992. *Bacillus thuringiensis*: insects and beyond. *Bio/Technol.*, **10**: 271-275.

Ferron, P. 1981. Pest control by the fungi *Beauveria* and *Metarhizium*. *In*: H. D. Burges (eds.), *Microbial Control of Pests and Plant Diseases 1970-1980.* Academic Press, New York, USA, pp. 465- 482.

Ferron, P., Fargies, J. and Riba, G. 1991. Fungi as microbial insecticides against pests. *In*: D. K. Arora, L. Ajell and K. G. Mukerjee (eds.), *Handbook of Applied Mycology.* Marcel Kekker, New York, pp. 665-706.

Goettel, M. S. Inglis, G. D. and Wraight, S. P. 2000. Fungi. *In*: L. A. Lacey and H. K. Kaya (eds.), *Field Manual of Techniques in Ivertebrate Pathology.* Kluwer Academic Press. Netherlands, pp. 255-282.

Gopalakrishnan, C. and Narayanan, K. 1988a. Occurrence of two entomofungal pathogens *Metarhizium anisopliae* (Metschnikoff) Sorokin var minor Tulloch and *Nomuraea rileyi* (Farlow) Samson, on *Heliothis armigera* Hubner (Noctuidae: Lepidoptera). *Curr. Science*, **57**: 867-868.

Gopalakrishnan, C. and Narayanan, K. 1988b. Occurrence of entomopathogenic fungi *Nomuraea rileyi* (Farlow) Samson on *Acontia graellis* F. (Noctuidae: Lepidoptera) and *Beauveria bassiana* (Balsamo) Vuill. On *Myllocerus subfasciatus* G. (Curculionidae: Coleoptera). *J. Biol. Cont.*, **2**: 58-59.

Gopalakrishnan, C. and Narayanan, K. 1989. Epizootiology of *Nomuraea rileyi* (Farlow) Samson in field populations of *Helicoverpa* (=*Heliothis*) *armigera* (Hubner) in relation to three host plants. *J. Biol. Cont.*, **3**: 50-52.

Hajek, A. E., Elkinton, J. S. and Witcosky, J. J. 1996. Introduction and spread of the fungal pathogen *Entomophaga maimaiga* (Zygomycetes: Entomophthorales) along the leading edge of the gypsy moth (Lepidoptera: Lymantriidae) spread. *Environ. Entomol.*, **25**: 1235-1247.

Hajek, A. E. and St Leger, R. J. 1994. Interactions between fungal pathogens and insect host. *Ann. Rev. Ent.*, **39**: 293-322.

Hofte, H. and Whiteley, H. R. 1989. Insecticidal crystal proteins of Bacillus thuringiensis. *Microbiol. Rev.*, **53**: 242-255.

Ignoffo, C. M., Marston, N. L. D. L. Hostetter, B. Puttler and J. V. Bell. 1976. Natural and induced epizootics of *Nomuraea rileyi* in soybean caterpillars. *J. Invertebr. Pathol.*, **27**: 191-198.

Inglis, G. D., Goettel, M. S., Butt, T. M. and Strasser, H. 2001. Use of Hyphomycetous fungi for managing insect pests. *In*: T. M. Butt, C. Jackson and N. Magani (eds.), *Fungi as Biocontrol Agents*. CAB International. pp. 23-69.

Jayaramaiah, M. 1981. Studies on the entomogenous fungus, *Beauveria brongniartii* (Sacc.) petch in relation to white grub, *Holotrichia serrata* Fab. and silkworm, *Bombyx mori* Linn. and possibilities of its use in the management of the white grub. Ph.D. thesis, University of Agricultural Sciences, Bangalore, India, p. 112.

Kalman, S., Kiehne, K. L., Cooper, N., Reynoso, M. S. and Yamamoto, T. 1995. Enhanced production of insecticidal proteins in *Bacillus thuringiensis* strains carrying an additional crystal protein gene in their chromosomes. *Appl. Environ. Microbiol.*, **61**: 3063-3068.

Knowles, B. H. 1994. Mechanism of action of *Bacillus thuringiensis* insecticidal d-endotoxins. *Adv. Insect Physiol.*, **24**: 275-308.

Kumar, P. A. and Bambawale, O. M. 2002. Insecticidal proteins of *Bacillus thuringiensis* and their application in agriculture. *In*: R. K. Upadhyay (ed.), *Advances in Microbial Toxin Research and its Biotechnological Exploitation*. Kluwer Academic Publishers, USA, pp. 259-280.

Kumar, P. A., Sharma, R. P. and Malik, V. S. 1996, Insecticidal proteins of *Bacillus thuringiensis*. *Adv. Appl Microbiol.*, **42**: 1-43.

Lacey, L. A., Frutos, R. Kaya, H. K. and Vail, P. 2001. Insect pathogens as biological control agents: do they have a future? *Biological Control*, **21**: 230-248.

Lambert, B. and Peferoen, M. 1992, Insecticidal promise of *Bacillus thuringiensis*. Facts and mysteries about a successful biopesticide.*Bio. Sci.*, **42**: 112-122.

Lereclus, D., Agaisse, H., Gominet, M. and Chaufaux, J. 1995, Overproduction of encapsulated insecticidal crystal proteins in a *Bacillus thuringiensis spOA* mutant. *Bio/Technol.*, **13**: 67-71.

Lereclus, D., Vallade, M., Chaufaux, J., Arantes, O. and Rambaud, S. 1992. Expansion of insecticidal host range of *Bacillus thuringiensis* by *in vivo* genetic recombination. *Bio/Technol.*, **10**: 418-421.

Lingappa, S. and Patil, R. K. 2002. *Nomuraea rileyi*—a potential mycoinsecticide. Department of Agricultural Entomology, University of Agricultural Sciences, Dharwad, Karnataka, India. p. 30.

Luthy, P., Cordier, J. and Fischer, J. 1982. *Bacillus thuringiensis* as a bacterial insecticide. *In*: E. Kurstak, (ed.), *Microbial and Viral Pesticides*, Marcel and Decker, New York, pp. 35-74.

MacLeod, D. M. 1954. Investigations on the genera *Beauveria* Vuill. and *Tritirachium* Limber. *Can. J. Bot.*, **32**: 818-890.

MacLeod, D. M. and Muller-Kogler, E. 1973. Entomogenous fungi: Entomophthora species with pear-shaped to almost spherical conidia (Entomophthorales: Entomophthoraceae). *Mycologica*, **65**: 823-893.

Martin, P. A. W. and Travers, R. S. 1989. Worldwide abundance and distribution of *Bacillus thuringiensis* isolates. *Appl. Environ. Microbiol.*, **55**: 2437-2442.

Mazumdar, D., Puzari, K. C. and Hazarika, L. K. 1995. Mass production of *Beauveria bassiana* and its potentiality on rice hispa. *Indian Psychopathology*, **48**: 3, 275-278.

McCoy, C. W., Samson, R. A. and Boucias, D. G. 1988. Entomogenous fungi. *In*: C. Ignoffo and N. B. Mandava (eds.), *CRC Handbook of Natural Pesticides*, Vol. 5. *Microbial Insecticides, Part A*: *Entomogenous Protozoa and Fungi*. CRC Press, Florida. pp. 151-234.

Mohamed, A. K. A., Sikorowski, P. P. and Bell, J. V. 1977. Susceptibility of *Heliothis zea* larvae to *Nomuraea rileyi* at various temperatures. *J. Invertebr. Pathol.*, **30**: 414-417.

Parry, J. M., Turnbull, P. C. B. and Gibson, J. R. 1983. A Colour Atlas of Bacillus Species. Wolfe Medical, London, p. 99.

Patel, K. C., Yadav, D. N., Dube, H. C. and Patel, R. J. 1990. Laboratory and mass production studies with *Metarhizium anisopliae*. *Annals of Biology*, **6**: 2, 135-140.

Pattanayak, D., Srinivasan, K., Mandaokar, A., Shukla, A., Bhalla, R. ans Kumar, P. A. 2000. AFLP fingerprinting and genetic characterization of *Bacillus thuringiensis* subspecies. *World J. Microbiol. Biotechnol.*, **16**: 667-672.

Phadke, C. H. and Rao, V. G. 1978. Studies on the entomogenous fungus *Nomuraea rileyi* (Farlow) Samson. *Curr. Science*, **47**: 511-512.

Phadke, C. H., Rao, V. G. and Pawar, S. K. 1978. Natural outbreak of the muscardine fungus *Nomuraea rileyi* (Farlow) Samson on leaf eating caterpillar, Spodoptera exigua HB in Maharashtra. *Curr. Science,* **47**: 476.

Puzari, K. C., Sarmah, D. K. and Hazarika, L. K. 1997. Medium for mass production of *Beauveria bassiana* (Balsamo) Vuillemin. *Journal of Biological Control,* **11**: 1-2, 97-100.

Rabindra, R. J. Kennedy, J. S., Sathiah, N., Rajasekaran, B. and Srinivasan, M. R. 2001. Microbial control of crop pests. Deptt. of Agricultural Entomology, TNAU, Coimbatore. p. 321.

Rajak, R. C., Sandhu, S. S., Mukherjee, S., Khare, S. and Gupta, A. 1991. Natural outbreak of *Nomuraea rileyi* (Farlow) Samson on *Junonia orthyia* (Nymphaldae: Lepidoptera). *J. Biol. Cont.*, **5**: 123-124.

Rao, V. G. and Phadke, C. H. 1977. A muscardine disease of tobacco leaf eating caterpillar. *Curr. Science,* **46**: 648-649.

Schnepf, E., Crickmore, N., Van Rie, J., Lereclus, D., Baum, J., Feitelson, J., Zeigler, D. R. and Dean, D. H. 1998. *Bacillus thuringiensis* and its pesticidal crystal proteins. *Microbiol. Mol. Biol. Rev.*, **62**: 775-806.

Singh, A., Bambawale, O. M. and Sharma, O. P. 2004. Entomopathogen biopesticides in integrated pest management. *In:* Nutan Kaushik (ed), *Biopesticides for Sustainable Agriculture—Prospects and Constraints.* The Energy and Resources Institute Press, New Delhi, pp. 41-66.

Singh, O. P. and Gangrade, G. A. 1975. Parasites, predators and diseases of larvae of *Diacrisia oblique* Walker (Lepidoptera: Arctiidae) on soybean. *Curr. Sci.*, **44**: 481-482.

Singh, S. P. 1972. Cotton bollworm in Kuban and basis for its biological control. Ph.D. thesis, Kuban Agricultural Institute, Krasnodor, USSR, p. 186.

Singh, S. P. 1999. Pest management—The ecofriendly approach. *In:* N. Ravi (ed), *The Hindu Survey of Indian Agriculture.* National Press, Chennai, pp. 175-184, 208.

Singh, S. P., Ballal, C. R. and Poorani, J. 2002. Old world bollworm *Helicoverpa armigera*, associated Heliothinae and their natural enemies. Project Directorate of Biological Control, Bangalore, India, *Technical Bulletin No.* **31**, pp. iii + 135.

Sprenkel, R. K., and W. M. Brooks. 1975. Artificial dissemination and epizootic initiation of *Nomuraea rileyi* an entomogenous fungus of lepidopterous pests of soybeans. *J. Econ. Entomol.*, **68**: 847-851.

Tanada, Y. and H. K. Kaya. 1993. *Insect Pathology.* Academic Press, Inc., New York, NY.

Urs, N. V. R. R. and Govindu, H. C. 1971. *Metarhizium anisopliae* (Metschnikoff) Sorokin and its host range. *Mycopathological and Mycological Application,* **44**: 317-320.

Van Der Laan, P. A. 1981. L. G. E. Kalshoven pests of crops in Indonesia. *P.T. Ichtiar Baru-Van Hoeve, Jakarta,* p. 701.

Vimala Devi, P. S. 1994. Conidia production of the entomopathogenic fungus *Nomuraea rileyi* and its evaluation for the control of *Spodoptera litura* (Fab) on *Ricinus communis. J. Invert. Pathol.*, **63**: 145-150.

Vimala Devi, P. S. 1995. Soil treatment with *Nomurae rileyi*: a promising technique for the control of *Spodoptera litura* on groundnut. *Biocont. Sci. Technol.*, **5**: 361-364.

Vimla Devi, P. S., Prasad, Y. G., Rajeswari, B. and Vijay Bhaskar, L. 1996. Epizootic of the entomofungal pathogen, *Nomuraea rileyi,* on lepidopterous pests of oilseeds. *J. Oilseeds Res.*, **13**: 144-148.

Vimala Devi, P. S., Chowdary, A. and Prasad, Y. G., 2001. Cost effective multiplication of the entomopathogenic fungus *Nomuraea rileyi* (F) *Samson Mycopathologia,* **151**(1): 35-39.

Vimala Devi, P. S., Prasad, Y. G., Chowdhary D. A., Rao L. M. and Balakrishnan, K. 2003. Identification of virulent isolates of the entomopathogenic fungus *Nomuraea rileyi* (F) Samson for the management of *Helicoverpa armigera* and *Spodoptera litura* (identification of virulent isolates of *N. rileyi*). *Mycopathologia,* **156**: 365-373.

Wahab, S. 2003. Development, quality and availability of Bio-pesticides in India. *In*: Amerika Singh, T. P. Trivedi, H. R. Sardana, O. P. Sharma and Naved Sabir (eds.), *Recent Advances in Integrated Pest Management.* Proceedings and recommendations of the NATP interactive workshop on IPM. 26-28 Feb. 2003, NCIPM, New Delhi.

Wraight, S. P. and Carruthers, R. I. 1999. Production, delivery and use of mycoinsecticides for control of insect pests of field crops. *In*: F. R. Hall and J. J. Menn (eds), *Methods in Biotechnology Vol.* 5, *Biopesticides: Use and Delivery*. Humana Press, Totowa, New Jersey, pp. 233-269.

Wraight, S. P., Jackson, M. A., Kock, S. L. 2001. Production, stabilization and formulation of fungal biocontrol agents. *In*: T. M. Butt, C. W. Jackson and N. Magan (eds.), *Fungi as Biocontrol Agents*. CABI Publishing, Wallingford, Oxon, U.K. pp. 385.

# Role of Baculoviruses in the IPM of Lepidopteran Pests

R. J. Rabindra[1], N. Sathiah[2] and K. P. Jayanth[3]

## INTRODUCTION

Insect pests causing economic damage to crops fall under the orders Hemiptera, Isoptera, Diptera, Coleoptera, Hymenoptera and Lepidoptera. Among these, the Lepidopteran pests are of major concern since they cause devastating damage in several food and fiber crops. The bollworms are the major cause for the enormous quantities of chemical pesticides being applied to cotton. The pesticide consumption on cotton in India is estimated to be around 40-45 per cent of the total pesticides marketed and it may be safely stated that 60 per cent of this is often used for the management of lepidopteran pest complex attacking both foliage and fruiting parts. *Helicoverpa armigera, Spodoptera litura* and *Plutella xylostella* are of national importance since outbreak of these lepidopteran pests have invited indiscriminate use of chemical insecticides leading to the development of resistance to several chemical insecticides in insect pests. Pests like *S. litura* are a serious problem in polyhouses and the cucurbit caterpillar *Diaphania indica* is emerging as a serious problem in gherkins, an important export commodity.

Fortunately, the lepidopterans are susceptible to several entomopathogens particularly the baculoviruses which play a major role in the natural regulation of pest populations. If properly exploited, baculoviruses can be useful augmentative biocontrol agents. Their high specificity to target pest groups and safety to higher animals make them attractive candidates in sustainable pest management.

## THE BACULOVIRUSES

The occluded group of baculoviruses, the nuclear polyhedrosis (NPV) and granulosis (GV) viruses are potent pathogens infecting several insect species particularly of the order Lepidoptera. They are characterized by rod shaped nucleocapsids assembled singly or in bundles of two or more into virions. The capsids enveloped by a lipoprotein envelope contain the double stranded closed circular DNA genome of size ranging from 85-130 kb. The virions are embedded in the occlusion body protein, the polyhedrin in the case of NPV and granulin in GV. Upon ingestion by the insects, the occlusion body protein is dissolved due to the alkaline gut proteases, and the virions, the infectious units of the virus are released. These virions enter the columnar epitheral cells of the mid gut and after prolific replication in the nuclei as in the case

[1]*Project Directorate of Biological Control, P. O. Box No. 2491, H. A. Farm Post. Bellary Road, Bangalore-560 024.*
[2]*Department of Entomology, Tamil Nadu Agriculture University, Coimbatore-641 003.*
[3]*Biocontrol Research Laboratories, P. O. Box No. 3228, H.M.T. Layout, R. T. Nagar, Bangalore-560 032.*

of *H. armigera* NPV (*Ha*NPV), they enter the blood stream as extra cellular virions and start infecting the nuclei of various tissues like fat body, epithelium of trachea, hypodermis and gonads, sarcolemma, neurilemma and salivary glands. In the case of GV, after the collapse of the infected nuclei, the virus may continue to replicate in the cytoplasm and the capsules are seen in the entire cell. Fat body provides the major substrate for the multiplication of these viruses (Plate 8.1). In the case of NPV, due to infection of the hypodermis (Plate 8.1), the skin of infected larvae ruptures in later stages of infection releasing a turbid fluid containing liquefied body tissues carrying millions of the polyhedral occlusion bodies (POB). In most of the cases of infection by GV, the skin does not rupture since the hypodermal epithelium is not infected. Larvae killed by NPV are often found hanging head downwards from plant substrate or rearing containers (Plate 8.1). The virosed cadavers are often fed upon by other larvae spreading the infection horizontally. Larvae feeding on contaminated leaves also pick up infection. Infected adults transmit the virus vertically by either transovum or transovarial transmission. Cadavers falling to the ground or virus-infected larvae entering the soil for pupation and subsequently dying leave abundant quantities of the virus in the soil, which can persist for several months (Godge and Patil, 1979; Hugar *et al.*, 1995). Virus from soil subsequently reach the crop foliage due to the splashing action of the rain. Birds feeding on infected larvae may spread the virus through their droppings (Gitay and Polson, 1971; Vyas *et al.*, 1988). Parasitoids attacking virus—infected larvae are also known to spread the virus as they parasitise healthy larvae (Trang *et al.*, 2002).

### Baculoviruses as Microbial Pesticides

The NPV and the GV are potential insect pathogens and if properly used can be effective tools in integrated pest management programs.

### Diversity of Baculoviruses

Baculoviruses particularly NPV are known to occur extensively in different groups of insects though predominantly among the lepidopterans. World over about 525 insect species in 52 families and eight orders are known to be infected by NPV and of this large number of species, 455 belong to Lepidoptera. Among the lepidopterans, noctuids comprise of the largest family with 107 species. In India, NPV has been recovered from several insects, many of them of economic importance (Table 8.1) and a majority of them under noctuidae (Table 8.2). A rich genetic diversity also exists within each of these viruses as documented in the case of HaNPV (Somasekar *et al.*, 1993; Rabindra *et al.*, 1998; Geetha and Rabindra, 2000) (Plate 8.2), *Amsacta albistriga* NPV (AaNPV) (Rabindra, 2000) (Plate 8.2) and *Chilo infuscatellus* granulosis virus (CiGv) and *S. litura* NPV (SlNPV). The widespread occurrence of baculoviruses and their diversity make them attractive candidates as microbial insecticides.

## NUCLEAR POLYHEDROSIS VIRUSES

Nuclear polyhedrosis viruses have enormous potential as viral biopesticides as they are highly virulent with shorter incubation period than the GV. The virus has been

**TABLE 8.1:** NUCLEAR POLYHEDROVIRUSES OF INSECT PESTS REPORTED FROM INDIA

| *Host Insect* | *Family* | *References* |
|---|---|---|
| *Helicoverpa armigera* Hb. | Noctuidae | Patel *et al.* (1968) |
| *Spodoptera litura* F. | Noctuidae | Ramakrishnan and Tiwari (1969) |
| *Pericallia ricini* F. | Arctiidae | Jacob *et al.* (1972) |
| *Diacrisia obliqua* Wlk. | Arctiidae | Chand (1979); Battu *et al.* (1977) |
| *Amsacta albistriga* Wlk. | Arctiidae | Jacob and Subramaniam (1972) |
| *Mythimna separata* Wlk. | Noctuidae | Neelgund and Mathad (1972) |
| *Spodoptera mauritia* Boisd. | Noctuidae | Jacob *et al.* (1973) |
| *Antheraea mylitta* (Dru.) | Saturniidae | Pattar and Mathad (1972) |
| *Corcyra cephalonica* Stnt. | Pyralidae | Rabindra and Subramaniam (1973) |
| *Dasychira mendosa* (Hb.) | Lymantriidae | Rabindra and Subramaniam (1974a) |
| *Anadevidia peponis* (F.) | Noctuidae | Rabindra and Subramaniam (1975a) |
| *Chrysodeixis chalcites* Esp. | Noctuidae | Rabindra *et al.* (1975) |
| *Trichoplusia ni* Hb. | Noctuidae | Pawar *et al.* (1983) |
| *Nymphula depunctalis* Gn. | Pyralidae | Jacob *et al.* (1978) |
| *Plusia signata* (F.) | Noctuidae | Godse and Patil (1979b) |
| *Anomis sabulifera* (Gn.) | Noctuidae | Bakwad and Pawar (1981) |
| *Sesamia inferens* Wlk. | Noctuidae | Nayak and Srivastava (1979) |
| *Scirpophaga incertulas* (Wlk.) | Pyralidae | – |
| *Pelopidas mathias* (F.) | Hesperiidae | – |
| *Amsacta moorei* Btlr. | Arctiidae | Rao and Amonkar (1989) |
| *Eupterote cardamomi* Renga | Eupterotidae | Rabindra *et al.* (1990) |
| *Adisura atkinsoni* Moore | Noctuidae | Narayanan, (1985, 1986) |
| *Diaphania indica* (Saunders) | Pyralidae | Narayanan and Veenakumari (2002a) |
| *Lymantria obfuscata* Walkers | Lymantriidae | Dharmadikari *et al.* (1985) |
| *Pygaera fulgurita* Walk. | Notodontidae | Ahmad *et al.* (1983) |
| *Agrotis ipsilon* (Hufnagel) | Noctuidae | Santharam and Kumaraswamy (1984) |
| *Perigea capensis* (Guen) | Noctuidae | Paliwal and Jakhmola (1981) |
| *Hyblaea puera* (Cramer) | Hyblaeidae | Nair *et al.* (1998) |
| *Thysanoplusia orichalcea* F. | Noctuidae | Men and Thakare (1998a, b) |
| *Trabala vishnou* (Lefebvre) | Lasiocampidae | Battu (1991) |
| *Hellula undalis* (Fab.) | Pyralidae | Battu *et al.* (1989) |
| *Euproctis lunata* (Walk) | Lymantriidae | Battu *et al.* (1990) |
| *Boarmia selenaria* Denis & Schiffermuller | Geometridae | Rabindra *et al.* (2002) |
| *Agrotis segetum* Denis & Schiffermuller | Noctuidae | Narayanan and Sharma (2001) |
| *Gangara thyrsis* (Fabricius) | Hesperiidae | Narayanan and Veenakumari (2002b) |
| *Diaphania pulverulentalis* (Hampson) | Pyralidae | Narayanan and Veenakumari (2003a) |
| *Spodoptera exigua* Hubner | Noctuidae | Narayanan and Veenakumari (2003b) |
| *Opisina arenosella* Walker | Oecophoridae | |
| *Chilo partellus* Swinhoe | Pyralidae | Narayanan (2002) |

isolated from several important crop pests like the gram pod borer *H. armigera*, the tobacco cutworm *S. litura*, the groundnut red hairy caterpillar *A. albistriga*, the cutworm *Mythimna separata*, the Bihar hairy caterpillar *Spilosoma obliqua*, the teak defoliator *Hyblea peura* and several others. Several field experiments have shown that the virus at doses ranging from 1.5 – 3 × $10^{12}$ polyhederal occlusion bodies (POB)/ha could bring about substantial reduction in pest numbers and increased yield in several agricultural and horticultural crops.

**TABLE 8.2:** REPORTS OF NPV IN INDIA: FAMILY-WISE DISTRIBUTION OF LEPIDOPTERAN HOSTS

| *Family* | *No.* | *Family* | *No.* |
|---|---|---|---|
| Noctuidae | 18 | Hesperiidae | 2 |
| Arctiidae | 4 | Geometridae | 1 |
| Satuniidae | 1 | Eupterotidae | 1 |
| Lymantriidae | 3 | Notodontidae | 1 |
| Plutellidae | 1 | Lasiocampidae | 1 |
| Hyblaedae | 1 | Oecophoridae | 1 |
| Pyralidae | 8 | | |

### *Helicoverpa armigera*

Research over the last three decades on the NPV of *H. armigera* (HaNPV) has been focussed on the natural occurrence of the virus, virus-host relationship, mass production and formulation, field-testing and safety evaluation against several non-target species. The following review traces some of the research and developmental activities, which have led to the commercial scale production and registration of HaNPV as a microbial pesticide in India.

### *Occurrence of the Virus*

The occurrence of the virus was first reported by Patel *et al.* (1968) in Gujarat. Rabindra and Subramaniam (1974 b) subsequently described a very virulent NPV which was singly occluded (Plate 8.3). Sudhakar and Mathavan (1999) reported a multiply occluded NPV from *H. armigera.* Natural occurrence of the virus was also reported from Maharashtra by Chundurwar and Pawar (1991).

### *Diversity of HaNPV*

Genomic variation among the different geographic isolates of HaNPV was reported by Somasekar *et al.* (1993). Rabindra *et al.* (1998) found that an isolate from Negamum had a lower $LC_{50}$ value when compared to those of a few other isolates. Geetha and Rabindra (2000) using restriction endonuclease analysis, characterized several isolates of *Ha*NPV and found genetic variations among them. Bioassays against second instar *H. armigera* larvae revealed variations in their virulence. As in the earlier report of Rabindra *et al.* (1998), the Negamum isolate recorded the lowest $LC_{50}$ among the several geographic isolates (Table 8.3). These reports indicate the scope for selecting a strain of virus with high virulence for development as a microbial pesticide.

**TABLE 8.3:** COMPARATIVE VIRULENCE OF HANPV ISOLATES AGAINST *H. armigera* LARVAE

| *HaNPV isolates* | $LC_{50}$ (*POB/cm*$^2$) | |
|---|---|---|
| | *II instar* | *III instar* |
| Coimbatore | 0.291 | 1.751 |
| Anthiyoor | 0.372 | 1.682 |
| Ooty | 0.237 | 1.363 |
| Negamum | 0.175 | 0.761 |
| Iruttapallam | 0.381 | 1.766 |
| Hyderabad | 0.520 | 2.050 |
| Bangalore | 0.236 | 1.730 |
| New Delhi | 0.596 | 2.122 |
| Rajasthan | 1.444 | 4.988 |
| Rajahmundry | 0.474 | 1.775 |

*Source*: Geetha and Rabindra, 2000.

### *Spread of the Virus*

Baculoviruses spread among the field populations in many ways. Apart from vertical spread of the virus through transovarial transmission, cannibalism (Dhandapani *et al.*, 1993a) and predation by ants (Dhandapani *et al.*, 1994a) are known to contribute to the spread of the virus. Viruses can persist in soil and subsequent to rains, plant foliage may become contaminated. Virus may also be spread through wind. When adults of *H. armigera* were fed with NPV ($10^8$ POB/ml) they transmitted the virus to the progeny (Dhandapani *et al.*, 1993b). The rate of transmission was greater when both sexes were fed. Singh *et al.* (1990) observed that in berseem, highest population of *H. armigera* as well as highest incidence of NPV was seen on crop following cutting in late February. Several species of birds predominantly *Acridotheres gingiam* and *Passer domesticus* were found to predate on *H. armigera* larvae and these birds would also spread the virus through their droppings, as active NPV has been recovered from bird droppings. The birds were not affected by feeding on NPV- infected *H. armigera* larvae (Vyas *et al.*, 1988).

### *Mass Production*

Being an obligate pathogen, the virus can be mass produced only in *H. armigera* larvae. Sathiah (2001) manipulating the inoculum dose, temperature of incubation and stage of larvae could obtain a maximum yield of $1.2 \times 10^{10}$ polyhedral occlusion bodies (POB)/larva. Earlier reports have indicated lower yields of $2 \times 10^9$ POB/larva. Obtaining a high yield/larva is critical to economic production of the virus. A successful technique of mass production of *H. armigera* for *in vivo* production of the virus has also been developed (Sathiah, 2001). Comparing different semisynthetic diets for *H. armigera* mass production for *in vivo* NPV production, Srinivasan *et al.* (1998) found that a chickpea flour-based diet was significantly better than cowpea or french bean-based diets. However, french bean flour substituted at 75% was the most cost-effective diet for NPV production. Kalia *et al.* (2001) obtained a high yield of 1.2 × $10^{10}$ POB/larva by optimizing the virus dose and stage of *H. armigera* larvae. Topical spiracular application of alkali-liberated virus on 8-day old larvae could also give a high yield of 1.5 × $10^{10}$ POB/larva.

### *Waste Recycling in Mass Production of NPV*

The unutilized semisynthetic diet and frass after rearing of *H. armigera* for mass production of NPV could be utilized for either biogas generation or oyster mushroom production (Baskaran *et al.*, 1996). This recycling of waste would contribute to reducing the cost of production of the virus and increasing the profitability of commercial scale production of HaNPV.

### *Formulation*

While crude NPV preparations were found to be effective in the control of *H. armigera* (Rabindra *et al.*, 1986), development of stable basic formulations of the virus would become critical for commercial scale production of the virus. In India, Ethiraju *et al.* (1988) developed the first wettable powder formulation of HaNPV and in laboratory as well as field tests, the formulation was found effective (Rabindra *et al.*, 1990). Rabindra *et al.* (1998) developed a formulation, which can be applied with a controlled droplet applicator. The formulation gave good control of *H. armigera* on chickpea when applied with UV protectant adjuvants (Rabindra *et al.*, 1989). Wettable powder formulation applied by a backpack hydraulic sprayer and a VLV (very low volume) formulation applied using a controlled droplet applicator were found to be effective in controlling *H. armigera* on pigeonpea (Muthiah and Rabindra, 1991). Freeze-dried preparation, oilbased formulation as well as a simple liquid formulation were also found to be effective (Cherry *et al.*, 2000).

### *Adjuvants Enhancing the Efficacy of the Virus*

Several adjuvants with phago-stimulant and possible UV protectant property were found to increase the efficacy of the virus (Table 8.4). Dhandapani *et al.* (1994) incorporated NPV into different bait formulations containing various combinations of maize, soybean or chickpea flour, crude sugar, cotton seed kernel and extracts of larvae of *H. armigera*. Results of bioassays revealed that baits containing chickpea or maize flour along with *H. armigera* larval extracts were the most effective. Adjuvants may also protect the virus from inactivation by the leaf environment. These results indicate the role of adjuvants in increasing the persistence of the virus on the crop plants.

### *Botanicals Enhancing the Efficacy of the Virus*

Aqueous crude extracts of leaves of several plants were found to enhance the activity of HaNPV (Table 8.5) (Anon., 1994). These botanicals probably acted as stressors and increased the mortality caused by the virus. Rabindra *et al.* (1994) found that 10% aqueous leaf extracts of *Tagetus patula* and *Calotropis gigantea* when fed to apparently healthy *H. armigera* larvae, expressed latent NPV infections resulting in mortality ranging from 36-50 per cent. Aqueous leaf extract (10%) of *Vitex negundo* when applied with HaNPV @ 1.5 × $10^{12}$ POB/ha gave better control of *H. armigera* and increased the yield of grain significantly than did the virus applied alone (Rabindra and Jayaraj, 1992).

**TABLE 8.4:** ADJUVANTS INCREASING THE EFFICACY AGAINST *H. armigera*

| *Adjuvant* | *Reference* |
|---|---|
| Crude sugar 10% cotton seed kernel extract 5% | Rabindra and Jayaraj (1988b) |
| *H. armigera* larval extract 4% | Rabindra and Jayaraj (1988c) |
| Egg white 1% | Sonalkar and Deshmukh (1999) |
| *Vitex negundo* leaf extract 10% | Rabindra *et al.* (1991) |
| Maize flour + *H. armigera* larval extract | Dhandapani *et al.* (1994b) |
| Sunflower leaf extract | Jadhav *et al.* (1992) |
| Boric acid 0.1% | Bijjur *et al.* (1991b) |
| Robin blue 0.1% | Reddy and Divakar (2001) |
| Crude sugar 5% + starch 5% | Chand Asaf and Rabindra (1999) |

**TABLE 8.5:** LEAF EXTRACTS OF BOTANICALS ENHANCING THE MORTALITY OF *H. armigera* SECOND INSTAR LARVAE CAUSED BY NPV (5 × $10^4$ POB/ML) BY CHICKPEA LEAF DIP ASSAY

| *Plant sp.* | *% Concentration* | *% Mortality due to* | | *Potency ratio* |
|---|---|---|---|---|
| | | *NPV* | *NPV + Botanical* | |
| *Tagetus patula* | 10 | 42.6 | 91.2 | 2.1 |
| | 10 | 12.6 | 80.4 | 1.9 |
| | 10 | 42.6 | 85.4 | 2.0 |
| *Prosopis juliflora* | 10 | 48.3 | 100.0 | 2.1 |
| *Argemone mexicana* | 5 | 45.2 | 95.2 | 2.0 |
| | 5 | 45.2 | 8.05 | 1.8 |
| | 5 | 45.2 | 82.3 | 1.8 |
| *Achyranthes aspera* | 5 | 40.3 | 81.7 | 2.0 |
| *Acasia arabica* | 5 | 40.3 | 79.7 | 2.0 |
| *Allium cepa* | 5 | 37.2 | 69.6 | 1.9 |
| *Citrus limon* | 5 | 40.67 | 82.3 | 2.0 |
| *Ocimum basilicum* | 5 | 40.67 | 83.7 | 2.1 |
| *Carica papaya* | 5 | 40.67 | 82.0 | 2.2 |

*Source*: Anon, 1994.

### *Effect of Host Plant Surface Environment and Compatibility with Host Plant Resistance*

Host plant surface environment was shown to reduce the activity of the virus enormously. Cotton followed by chickpea leaf environment was found to be the most detrimental to the virus (Rabindra *et al.*, 1994). The $LC_{50}$ was lowest on lablab followed by sunflower but highest on cotton. A more or less a similar trend was observed with $LT_{50}$ (Table 8.6). Among the different plant parts of cotton, the leaf environment was the most detrimental. This detrimental effect, however, could be offset by the addition of an adjuvant mix consisting of cotton seed kernel extract 10% + crude sugar 10%.

**TABLE 8.6:** PROBIT ANALYSIS OF DOSAGE AND TIME MORTALITY RESPONSES OF SECOND INSTAR LARVAE OF *H. armigera* TO HaNPV EXPOSED TO THE LEAF SURFACE OF DIFFERENT CROP PLANTS

| *Host Plant* | $LC_{50}$ *(PIB/ml)* | $LT_{50}$ *(h)* |
|---|---|---|
| Chickpea | $1.29 \times 10^6$ | 121.97 |
| Pigeonpea | $4.97 \times 10^5$ | 129.99 |
| Lablab | $1.37 \times 10^3$ | 90.50 |
| Sunflower | $4.52 \times 10^3$ | 107.125 |
| Cotton | $4.96 \times 10^6$ | 121.41 |
| Untreated NPV | $8.26 \times 10^4$ | 111.82 |

*Source*: Rabindra *et al.*, 1994.

The compatibility of NPV with host plant resistance was studied by Rabindra *et al.* (1992). The mortality caused by NPV in *H. armigera* larvae was much higher on a susceptible chickpea (Shoba ) than on a resistant variety ICC506. Similar observations were made by Cowgill and Bagwat (1996).

Dhandapani *et al.* (1993c) studied the efficacy of HaNPV in the control of *H. armigera* on five varieties of sorghum with different head morphologies. *H. armigera* was controlled better on sorghum cultivars with compact earheads than on those with loose panicles. Studies with different cotton species showed that mortality due to NPV was much higher on *barbadense* (cv DCH 32) than either *hirsutum* (cv LRA 5166) or *arboreum* (cv K10) (Dhandapani *et al.*, 1993d).

### *Time of Application*

It is well known that the performance of NPV can be increased when sprayed in the evening hours through enhanced persistence. But not many field experiments have been conducted with HaNPV. Pokharkar and Chaudhary (1999) found that application of the virus in the evening was significantly better than application in the morning hours in reducing the larval population and increasing the yield of chickpea.

### *Baculovirus Combinations*

A combination of NPV of *H. armigera* and *S. litura* each at $1.5 \times 10^{12}$ POB/ha applied along with 10% cotton seed kernel extract and 10% crude sugar using a controlled droplet applicator successfully controlled mixed population of the homologous pests on groundnut (Muthuswamy *et al.*, 1993) and tomato (Devraj *et al.*, 2001).

### *NPV Enhances the Susceptibility to Insecticides*

When larvae of *H. armigera* sub-lethally infected with NPV were exposed to insecticides, their susceptibility to fenvalerate, cypermethrin, endosulfan and monocrotophos was enhanced significantly (Rabindra and Jayaraj, 1990). It was found that NPV infection reduced the levels of the pesticide detoxifying enzymes like carboxyl esterase (Table, 8.7) and glutathion-S transferase resulting in enhanced susceptibility to insecticides (Geetha *et al.*, 1999). NPV would have to be integrated with insecticides like endosulfan for the management of *H. armigera* on crops like pigeonpea and cotton, which are infested with other lepidopterous pests and in such an event, the NPV would be expected to enhance the susceptibility of *H. armigera* to pesticides. This phenomenon would make NPV a powerful component of IPM and an important tool in insecticide resistance management.

**TABLE 8.7:** ACTIVITY OF CARBOXYL ESTERASE IN LARVAE OF *Helicoverpa armigera* EXPOSED TO BOTH CHLORPYRIPHOS AND NUCLEAR POLYHEDROSIS VIRUS

| *Hours after Treatment* | *Enzyme Activity ($n$ moles $min^{-1}$ $mg^{-1}$ of protein)* | | | |
|---|---|---|---|---|
| | *Control* | *Chlorpyriphos* | *NPV* | *Chlorpyriphos + NPV* |
| 36 | 1627.2 | 1830.11 | 1169.6 | 872.5 |
| 48 | 1788.3 | 2044.3 | 1231.3 | 753.5 |
| 60 | 1987.1 | 2417.8 | 1274.0 | 718.3 |
| 72 | 2102.4 | 2601.9 | 1304.8 | 698.2 |

*Source*: Geetha *et al.*, 1999.

### *Insecticide Resistance and Susceptibility to NPV*

Goud *et al.* (1997) made an interesting observation that fenvalerate and endosulfan - resistant *H. armigera* larvae were much more susceptible to HaNPV than those which were not resistant. This finding has immense relevance to insecticide resistance management through the use of NPV.

### *Genetic Engineering of HaNPV*

In order to enhance the activity of HaNPV, Xin Wen *et al.* (2000) successfully deleted the gene for ecdysteroid UDP-glucosyl transferase (EGT) and engineered the AaIT, the Australian Scorpion (*Andractonus australis*) venom gene into the genome of HaNPV. The recombinant virus no longer produced EGT but expressed the AaIT. One recombinant HacXWI had a significantly smaller log $LC_{50}$. The recombinant HaC × W2 however recorded the shortest $LC_{50}$.

### *Safety of HaNPV to Non-target Species*

The baculoviruses are known to be highly specific and are not known to infect non-target species. The safety of semi-purified as well as wettable powder formulations of HaNPV to several non-target organisms has been demonstrated. The virus did not produce any deleterious effect on silkworm, honey bees, parasitoids and predators (Table. 8.8).

**TABLE 8.8:** SAFETY OF HaNPV TO CERTAIN NON-TARGET SPECIES

| *Organisms* | *NPV/Preparation* | *Reference* |
|---|---|---|
| *Bombyx mori* | Semi purified<br>Wettable powder | Bijjur *et al.* (1991)Muthiah and Rabindra (1991) |
| *Samia cynthia ricini*<br>*Apis cerana indica*<br>*Steinernema feltiae* | Semipurified | Bijjur *et al.* (1991a) |
| *Apanteles* sp., *Bracon* spp.<br>*Chelonus blackburni*<br>*Eriborus* sp.<br>*Campoletis chlorideae*<br>*Eucelaboria bryani* | Semi purified virus | Srinivas (1987) |
| *Chrysoperla* sp.<br>*Cotesia* sp. | Wettable powder formulation | Geetha and Rabindra (2001) |

### *Field efficacy of HaNPV and IPM*

A large number of field experiments on the efficacy of NPV against *H. armigera* on chickpea in different states of India have been conducted (Table 8.9). The results revealed that the virus at 1.5 × $10^{12}$ POB/ha applied 4-5 times when the larval population is in the early stages gave effective control of the pest and increased the grain yield (Table 8.10). Ultra low volume application of the virus at 1.5 × $10^{12}$ POB/ha along with 20 per cent crude sugar gave control equivalent to that of endosulfan (Rabindra and Jayaraj, 1988a). The virus at a concentration of 1.5 × $10^{12}$ POB/ha was found to control the population of *H. armigera* and increase the yield of other crops like pigeonpea (Muthiah and Rabindra, 1991), sunflower (Rabindra *et al.*, 1990), tomato (Satpathy *et al.*, 1999; Mahalingam and Hanifa, 2001), groundnut (Dhandapani *et al.*, 1993; Muthuswamy *et al.*, 1993) and Egyptian clover (Battu *et al.*, 2001). On cotton a higher dose of 3 × $10^{12}$ POB/ha was required (Dhandapani *et al.*, 1987; Sathaiah and Rabindra, 2001) (Table 8.11). The virus had to be applied along with an adjuvant mix of crude sugar (1.25 kg/ha) and cotton seed kernel extract (1.25 kg/ha) to prevent the inactivation of the virus on the cotton leaf surface. Virus applied alone often resulted in poor control of the pest on cotton. On sorghum variable results were reported. While Dhandapani *et al.* (1993c) found the virus effective in the control of the pest particularly on compact type of earheads, Mote and Murthy (1989) could not obtain satisfactory control of *H. armigera* on sorghum. The panicle morphology may have a strong influence on the efficacy of the virus.

### *NPV and IPM*

The virus has been used in combination with other components of pest management like *Bacillus thuringiensis*, chemical insecticides, azadirachtin, neem seed kernel extract, *Chrysoperla carnea* and bird perches (Table 8.12). Such integration would be necessary when mixed population of different instars particularly of grown up larvae of *H. armigera* or different species of pests occur along with *H. armigera* on crops like pigeonpea or cotton.

**TABLE 8.9:** FIELD EFFICACY OF NPV AGAINST *H. armigera* ON CHICKPEA IN DIFFERENT PARTS OF INDIA

| *State* | *Reference* |
|---|---|
| Tamil Nadu | Rabindra and Jayaraj (1988a) |
| Maharashtra | Misra *et al.* (1991) |
| Karnataka | Bijjur *et al.* (1991b) |
| Haryana | Satishkumar *et al.* (1998) |
| Bihar | Singh *et al.* (1999) |
| Madhya Pradesh | Sharma *et al.* (1997) |
| Rajasthan | Balasubramanian *et al.* (1989) |

**TABLE 8.10:** FIELD EVALUATION OF NPV FORMULATIONS AGAINST *H. armigera* ON CHICKPEA

| *Treatment** | *Larval Population/ 10 plants (7 days after spray)* | | *Pod Damage (%)* | *Yield* (kg/ha) |
|---|---|---|---|---|
| | *I* | *II* | | |
| NPV Unformulated | 5.67a | 1.67ab | 14.33b | 902.33a |
| NPV Liquid formulation | 4.67a | 1.33ab | 10.99a | 1003.33a |
| *Bacillus thuringiensis* 1 kg/ha | 5.00a | 2.33b | 11.94a | 939.00a |
| Endosulfan 350 g ai/ha | 3.33a | 0.33a | 12.89ab | 966.67a |
| Control | 16.00b | 7.67c | 22.46c | 669.00b |

*NPV treatments were applied @ $1.5 \times 10^{12}$ POB/ha in Tween 0.1%.
In a column, means followed by similar letters are not statistically different by DMRT (p = 0.05).

**TABLE 8.11:** EFFICACY OF NPV FORMULATIONS AGAINST *H. armigera* ON COTTON

| *Treatment** | *Larvae/5 plants* | *% square damage* | *% Boll damage* | *Seed cotton yield (Kg/ha)* |
|---|---|---|---|---|
| NPV unformulaed | $4.67^{b}$ | $11.02^{b}$ | $10.35^{c}$ | $1850.17^{b}$ |
| NPV liquid formulation | $4.67^{b}$ | $10.19^{b}$ | $8.20^{b}$ | $1910.73^{b}$ |
| NPV liquid formulation + adjuvant | $2.00^{a}$ | $6.65^{a}$ | $5.56^{a}$ | $2124.00^{a}$ |
| Endosulfan 700 g ai/ha | $2.67^{ab}$ | $5.25^{a}$ | $5.46^{a}$ | $2074.80^{a}$ |
| Control | $7.67^{c}$ | $18.96^{c}$ | $14.27^{d}$ | $1505.10^{c}$ |

*NPV treatments were applied @ $3 \times 10^{12}$ POB/ha in Tween 0.1%.
In a column, means followed by similar letters are not statistically different by DMRT (p = 0.05).

**TABLE 8.12:** USE OF NPV IN COMBINATION WITH OTHER AGENTS IN THE MANAGEMENT OF *H. armigera* ON DIFFERENT CROPS

| *NPV Combination* | *Crop* | *References* |
|---|---|---|
| NPV 1.5 × $10^{12}$ POB/ha + endosulfan 350 g ai/ha | Tomato | Ganguli and Dubey (1998)<br>Chandrakar *et al.* (1999)<br>Satpathy *et al.* (2000) |
| NPV 1.5 × $10^{12}$ POB/ha – Malathion | Cotton | Nimbalkar *et al.* (1996) |
| NPV + bird perches | Chickpea | Suganthy and Kumar (2000) |
| NPV + *Trichogramma pretiosum* | Chickpea | Balasubramanian *et al.* (1989) |
| NPV + Bt | Pigeonpea | Nagrare and More (1998) |
| NPV (1.5 × $10^{12}$ POB/ha) + Azadirachtin 2% | Cotton | Reddy and Manjunath (2000)<br>Lingappa *et al.* (2000) |
| NPV + *Chrysoperla carnea* | Sunflower<br>Chickpea | Venkatesan *et al.* (1997)<br>Rabindra *et al.* (1994) |
| NPV (3.0x1012 POB/ha) + NSKE 5% | Pigeonpea | Sarode *et al.* (1997) |
| NPV + Bt + *C. carnea* | Pigeonpea | Santharam *et al.* (1994) |

### *Spray Equipment for Application of HaNPV*

Various spray equipment have been used for applying the virus. Controlled droplet application of the virus with 20% crude sugar as an adjuvant was found to give very good control of *H. armigera* on chickpea (Rabindra and Jayaraj, 1988a). There were no significant differences in efficacy when the virus was applied with either the backpack hydraulic sprayer, mist blower or controlled droplet applicator (CDA) on chickpea (Rabindra and Jayaraj, 1995). Satisfactory control of *H. armigera* could also be demonstrated by CDA application of NPV at the rate of 3 × $10^{12}$ POB/ha along with 10% crude sugar and 10% cotton seed kernel extract (Dhandapani *et al.*, 1987).

Application of the virus with the controlled droplet applicator (CDA) was found effective against *H. armigera* on pigeonpea (Muthiaha and Rabindra, 1991). These reports indicate that the virus may be applied with any of the spray equipment. Parnell *et al.* (1999) however reported that CDA application of the virus was better than the mist blower for *H. armigera* control on rainfed cotton. For best results, the plant canopy should be covered properly and the application should be made when the pests are in the early stages.

### *Use of HaNPV in Other Countries*

**Thailand, Indonesia and Taiwan:** *H. armigera* NPV is used effectively in cotton IPM in Thailand (Ketunuti and Prathomrat, 1989) at a dosage of 1.3 × $10^{12}$ to 1.95 × $10^{12}$ OB/ha. Also, it has been recommended as a part of IPM in cotton in Indonesia and in Taiwan. The commercial product Elcar, was reported to give good control of the pest on maize. Investigations on the efficiency of spray equipment indicated that the spinning disk ULV treatments were more effective (50-100% mortality) than mist blower treatments at Sakaeo, Thailand on cotton. The efficacy was determined by conducting bioassays to neonate larvae (Parnell *et al.*, 1999).

**Africa:** *H. armigera* is an important pest of sorghum, maize, cotton, chickpeas and tomatoes. The HaNPV is probably the most widely tested baculovirus in Africa. Results have been highly variable but generally poorer on cotton than on other crops. The Canadian biopesticide company BioTEPP is collaborating on development of *H. armigera* NPV in Burkina Faso with the cotton industry (Sofitex) and the National Agricultural Research Institute (INERA). The French company Natural Plant Protection (NPP) tested *Mamestra brassicae* (L.) NPV on Togo on a medium scale against *H. armigera* and although the results were excellent, the project was abandoned for logistical and technical reasons (Langewald and Cherry, 2000). And in cote d Ivoire, *H. armigera* NPV was successfully tested in cotton at dosage of more than $5 \times 10^{12}$ OB/ha. In Botswana NPV at a rate of 100 LE/ha with 0.6% molasses or 200 LE/ha alone gave season long control in sorghum with high activity upto 30 days (Roome, 1975).

Field trials in Eastern Cape Provice of South Africa showed that application of HaNPV @ $7.26 \times 10^5$ POB/ml by a hydraulic backpack sprayer resulted in 100% reduction of *H. armigera* population in Naval orange within two weeks and damage to fruits was reduced to an extent of 84 per cent resulting in the saving of US$ 339/ha. The efficacy of NPV was better than Bt or chemical insecticides (Moore *et al.*, 2004).

In Uganda, application of $5 \times 10^8$ POBs in 20 ml or $1.5 \times 10^9$ in 60 ml per plant resulted in 56.6 and 70.0% control respectively on cotton. A local isolate of HaNPV was compared with the commercial preparation of *H. zea* (Biocontrol VHF). The results revealed poor field performances and field trials using local isolate in Tchad was not successful. In Cameroon, combination of Mamestrin ($1 \times 10^{13}$ OB/ha) and triazophos at 250 g ai/ha or cypermethrin at 5 g/ha at every 3 or 7 days interval gave increased yields and addition of phagostimulant Gustol R (1 kg/ha) was recommended by Montaldo (1991).

**Australia:** A commercial *Helicoverpa* nuclear polyhedrosis virus, ElcarTM, was investigated for the control of *H. armigera* on sorghum panicles together with two larval parasitoids, *Microplitis demolitor* and *Cotesia kazak* at Dalby, Queensland, Australia. The virus was sprayed at 75, 150 and 300 g Elcar $ha^{-1}$ and rates of infection ranging from 52.5 to 96.5% were recorded in larvae sampled after five days. The virus showed considerable potential for use against insecticide-resistant *H. armigera* in IPM programs on grain sorghum (Franzmann *et al.*, 1996).

### *Spodoptera litura*

### *Occurrence of the Virus*

The NPV of *S. litura* was first reported in India by Ramakrishnan and Tewari (1969). An epizootic occurrence of the virus was recorded by Dhandapani *et al.* (1982) on *S. litura* larvae migrating to *Sesbania bispinosa*. Younger larvae were more susceptible to the virus and mortality increased with dose of virus (Jacob and Subramanian, 1972).

### *Effect of Host Plants*

The infectivity of a nuclear polyhedrosis virus to larvae of *S. litura* on knolkhol (kohlrabi), beetroot, tobacco, cotton (*Gossypium barbadense* and *G. hirsutum*), cauliflower, cabbage and castor (*Ricinus communis*) was studied in pot experiments in Tamil Nadu, India. Maximum larval mortality was obtained on tobacco (96.67%), cauliflower (96.67%) and cabbage (93.33%) with a minimum incubation period of 7.67-8.67 days. Application of the virus to the lower leaf surface of tobacco or cotton caused higher mortality than application to the upper leaf surface (Santharam, 1986).

### *Diversity of SlNPV*

Genomic variation among the isolates of SlNPV was studied by comparing the restriction profiles of the isolates with PstI, HindIII, BamH1 and EcoRI and the genomic size was found to range from 127.37-132.54 kbp (Subramanian, 1998). The Bangalore isolate was found to be 100 times more virulent than an isolate from Rajamundry to *S. litura* lavae (Table 8.13).

**TABLE 8.13:** PROBIT ANALYSES CONCENTRATION-MORTALITY RESPONSE OF *Spodoptera litura* TO SlNPV ISOLATES

| *SlNPV isolates* | $LC_{50}$ *POB/cm²* | | |
|---|---|---|---|
| | *I instar* | *II instar* | *III intar* |
| Bangalore | 0.02 | 16.69 | 30.13 |
| Rajahmundry | 2.44 | 123.69 | 357.67 |
| Coimbatore I | 0.17 | 18.42 | 26.85 |
| New Delhi | 1.64 | 100.88 | — |

### *Dispersal of SlNPV*

Trang *et al.* (2002) found that the larval parasitoid *Cotesia angaleti* exposed to NPV-infected larvae of *S. litura* was able to transmit the virus to new host larvae of *S. litura* through oviposition. When the common sparrow *Passer domesticus* was fed with NPV-infected larvae of *S. litura*, the droppings contained active polyhedra upto $6.4 \times 10^6$ POB/g (Chaudhary and Ramakrishnan, 1983).

### *Mass Production of SlNPV*

Evaluation of different host plant leaves for growing *S. litura* larvae to be used for SlNPV production revealed that castor, groundnut, soybean and mulberry leaves produced higher mortality of larvae indicating that these plants can be used for mass production of SlNPV (Kulkarni and Hugar, 2000). NPV production could be maximized (upto $6 \times 10^9$ POB/larvae) by inoculating fifth instar larvae of *S. litura* and incubating at 25° C (Subramanian, 1998).

### *Development of Formulations*

A wettable powder formulation of SlNPV was developed using indigenously available ingredients which was as effective as the unformulated virus against the larvae of *S. litura* in pot culture test on groundnut (Sachithanandam *et al.*, 1989).

### *Persistence of SlNPV in Different Host Plants*

The relative persistence of SlNPV was studied on soybean, cabbage, cotton, castor bean, groundnut, mulberry, potato, strawberry, sunflower and tomato plants by Kulkarni and Hugar (1999). Results of bioassays showed that three days after spray, persistence was highest on soybean and groundnut but lowest on cotton.

### *Increasing the Efficacy and Persistence*

Field experiments conducted at different locations in Tamil Nadu on tobacco indicated that two rounds of application of NPV at $1.5 \times 10^{12}$ POB + 2.5 kg crude sugar/ha at 10 days interval gave effective control of *S. litura* (Dhandapani *et al.*, 1992). In a laboratory experiment, the additives SDS, PEG, lecithin and boric acid in combination with NPV reduced the $LC_{50}$ (Jayachandran and Chaudhari, 1997). In tobacco nurseries addition of boric acid or tannic acid at 25% to SlNPV enhanced the efficacy of the virus and reduced the leaf damage (Rao *et al.*, 1987). The $LC_{50}$ of NPV was reduced by about 10 times by the addition of 0.5% boric acid and about 20 times with 1.0% boric acid and also the $LT_{50}$ was reduced by 40% (Chaudhari, 1992).

Polyflavonoids extracted from mango and guava leaves using 80% of methanol and then lyophilized were shown to increase the persistence of SlNPV upto 60% (Asokan, 1998) and the concentration from 0.001 to 1% increased the retention of viral activity from 14.8 to 99.97 and 10.8 to 99.9% for Ranipal BVN and 2B, respectively (Baskaran *et al.*, 1998). Neem biller, a preparation from the neem seeds when combined with crude sugar as an adjuvant enhanced the mortality caused by the NPV (Rabindra *et al.*, 1997).

### *Field Efficacy of SlNPV*

Control of *S. litura* has been studied on banana, blackgram, castor, cauliflower, cotton and tobacco using the NPV alone (Table 8.14) or in combination with low concentrations of insecticides (Table 8.15). Reduction in plant damage was assessed in some experiments. The leaf damage index (0-5 scale) in cotton was reduced from 3.84 in control to 2.03 following the application of NPV at $1.5 \times 10^{12}$ POB/ha (Jayaraj *et al.*, 1981). The use of virus at $6 \times 10^{11}$ POB/ha, along with castor as a trap crop on the borders, was suggested as a tobacco nursery management practice. In a more recent field trial, a liquid formulation of SlNPV was found by Subramanian (1998) to be as effective as chlorpyriphos in reducing the larval population of *S. litura* and increasing the yield of the flower heads (Table 8.16). Two applications of the SlNPV at $1.5 \times 10^{12}$ POB/ha at 7 and 10 days interval were as effective as endosulfan on groundnut (Dhandapani *et al.*, 1993). The efficacy of the cirus against *S. litura* was also observed in chillies (Dhandapani and Jayaraj, 1989).

### *Mythimna separata*

The NPV of *M. separata* was characterized biochemically and its field efficacy has been investigated. On sorghum the virus at $2.5 \times 10^{6}$ OB/ml and $1 \times 10^{7}$ OB/ml caused 43.9% and 71.4% mortality respectively. Both tran-ovarial and trans-ovum transmission to progeny were observed. A concentration of $6 \times 10^{9}$ POB/ml was found to be optimum for transmission of NPV (Rahman *et al.*, 1997). Hugar *et al.* (1996) reported that a dose of $1.5 \times 10^{12}$ POB/ha produced 76 per cent mortality of *M. separata* larvae while endosulfan produced 90 per cent mortality. In another field trial on sorghum, Mallapur *et al.* (1997) found that mechanical removal of dried leaves and spraying of NPV followed by chlorpyriphos was effective in the management of *M. separata*. Like other viruses, MsNPV did not persist long on sorghum. A study designed to determine the persistence of the virus showed that 5 days after application of $1.5 \times 10^{12}$ POB/ha on sorghum, no virus activity could be found (Hugar *et al.*, 1996). Studies on the persistence of MsNPV in the soil by Hugar *et al.* (1995) revealed that the half life of the virus was 9 months in black soil and 13 months in red soils.

**TABLE 8.14:** EFFICIENCY OF NPV AGAINST *S.litura* ON VARIOUS CROPS IN INDIA

| *Crop* | *Dosage (POB)* | *Efficacy* | *Reference* |
|---|---|---|---|
| Banana | $8.4 \times 10^{12}$/ha | 80.1-90.4% mortality | Santharam *et al.* (1978) |
| Tobacco nursery | $93 \times 10^{6}$/ml | 14.48% (damage reduction) | Ramakrishnan *et al.* (1981) |
| Cotton | 1.5-3 $\times 10^{12}$/ha | 80.6-87.7% mortality | Jayaraj *et al.* (1981) |
| Blackgram | $9.0 \times 10^{12}$/ha | Yield increase 16.2% | Krishnaiah *et al.* (1984, 1985) |
| Groundnut | $9.0 \times 10^{12}$/ha | Yield increase 66.0% | Krishnaiah *et al.* (1984) |
| | $1.5 \times 10^{12}$/ha | Increased yield | Dhandapani and Babu (1995) |
| Cauliflower | $26 \times 10^{6}$ PIB/ml | 56.4% (damage reduction) | Chaudhari and Ramakrishnan, (1980) |
| Strawberry | $1.5 \times 10^{12}$/ha | Good larval kill | Kulkarni *et al.* (1999) |
| Chillies | $1.5 \times 10^{12}$/ha | Reduced fruit damage | Dhandapani and Jayaraj (1989) |

**TABLE 8.15:** INTEGRATION OF SlNPV WITH INSECTICIDES

| *Crop* | *Dosage POB/ha* | *Insecticide* | *Effect* | *Reference* |
|---|---|---|---|---|
| Tobacco | Half the dose of NPV ($9.3 \times 10^{2}$/ml) | 0.02% carbaryl | Synergistic | Ramakrishnan *et al.* (1981) |
| Cauliflower | Half the recommended dose | 50 ppm endosulfan | No effect | Chaudhari and Ramakrishnan (1980) |
| | Half the recommended dose | 10 ppm DAT | less synergistic | |
| Banana | $1.55 \times 10^{12}$ | Sub lethal dose of dichlorvos 0.01% + DDT 0.01% | Increased synergism | Mahadevan (1978) |
| Tobacco | $7.5 \times 10^{11}$ | 0.04% chlorpyriphos | Synergistic | Santharam & Balasubramanian (1980) |
| | $7.5 \times 10^{11}$ | 100 gai/ha chlorpyriphos | Synergistic | Dhandapani (1994) |
| Chilli | $7.5 \times 10^{11}$ | Fenpropathrin 100 gai/ha | Synergistic | Dhandapani and Jayaraj (1989) |
| Crucifers | $3.0 \times 10^{12}$ | Endosulfan | Synergistic | Pawar *et al.* (1991) |
| Cotton | $1.5 \times 10^{12}$ | Half of the dose of chlorpyriphos and fenitroon | Synergistic | Jayaraj *et al.* (1981) |
| Cowpea | $1.5 \times 10^{12}$ | Followed by chlorpyriphos | Increased yield | Sivaprakasam *et al.* (1988) |

**TABLE 8.16:** FIELD EFFICACY OF SlNPV FORMULATION ON CAULIFLOWER (cv. KRISHNA)–IRUTUPALLAM

| *Treatment** | *Pre treatment Count*** | *Number of Larvae per 20 Plants 7 days after Spray**** | | | *Yield (tons/ha)* |
|---|---|---|---|---|---|
| | | *I* | *II* | *III* | |
| NPV-unformulated | 6.67 | 0.3a | 0.33 | 1.3abc | 21.93a |
| NPV-Liquid formulation G25 | 8.00 | 1.0ab | 1.33 | 1.7abc | 21.17a |
| Chlorpyriphos 20 EC 1 l/ha) | 8.67 | 2.3ab | 0.0 | 1.7abc | 20.97a |
| Control | 7.33 | 4.70b | 2.00 | 5.00d | 16.42b |

*All the virus treatments were applied @ $1.5 \times 10^{12}$ POB/ha.
**Differences between means are not significant (P = 0.05) by DMRT.
***Similar letters means not significantly different (P = 0.05) by DMRT.

### *Spilosoma obliqua*

Application of *S. obliqua* (SoNPV) @ $10^9$ POB/ml recorded 0.1 larvae/plant as against 2.10 in control and the virus persisted on the foliage of cowpea for a period of 5 days with 53.3% of its original activity and the $LC_{50}$ for 4, 12 and 16-day old larvae were $2.6 \times 10^4$, $1.1 \times 10^6$ and $3.16 \times 10^6$ POB/ml (Chaudhari, 1997). In Punjab, field trials on groundnut by Arora *et al.* (1996) showed that application of SoNPV @ $1.5 \times 10^{12}$ POB/ha can bring about significant control of the pest within five days on groundnut. The virus in combination with endosulfan gave good control of the pest (Khan *et al.*, 2001).

### *Amsacta albistriga*

The red hairy caterpillar *A. albistriga* is a notorious pest devastating groundnut crop in several parts of South India. A nuclear polyhedrosis virus was reported to infect this insect by Jacob and Subramaniam (1972) (Plate 8.3). Investigating the host-pathogen relationship Rabindra and Subramaniam (1975a) found that the virus multiplied in the nuclei of fat bodies, hypodermis, gonadal epithelium, haemocytes, neurilemma and oesophageal value. Younger larvae of *A. albistriga* were found to be more susceptible to the virus when compared to the older ones (Rabindra and Subramaniam, 1975b).

The field efficacy of the virus against *A. albistriga* on groundnut was demonstrated by Chandramohan and Kumaraswamy (1979). Rabindra and Balasubramaniam (1980) could induce an epizootic of NPV in *A. albistriga* population in ground nut field resulting in collapse of the entire population leading to long term control of the pest. Anuradha *et al.* (1995) constructed a restriction map of AaNPV using four restriction enzymes. The size of the genome was estimated to be 120 ± 4 kbp. Genetic diversity through DNA restriction endonuclease analysis did not reveal major genetic variations among the few geographic isolates of AaNPV (Rabindra, 2000).

Baskaran *et al.* (2001) studying the variation in biological activity of four isolates of AaNPV found the Dharwad isolate to be the most virulent followed by Madurai, Narikudi and Pavagada isolates to II to IV instar larvae of *A. albistriga*. The effect of nine host plants on the *in vivo* production of AaNPV in *A. albistriga* larvae was studied by Baskaran *et al.* (2001). Larvae inoculated through the leaves of *Calotropis* recorded the highest mortality of larvae followed by castor and sesamum. Highest yield of virus was also obtained when *Calotropis* leaves were used for growing the larvae of *A. albistriga.*

### *Hyblea peura*

The teak defoliator *Hyblea peura* is a serious pest of teak causing extensive defoliation. Being a forest plantation, spraying of chemical pesticides is not a good preposition in view of the potential ecological hazards. Sudheendrakumar *et al.*, (1988) identified a nuclear polyhedrosis virus (HpNPV) infecting this insect. Epizootiological studies revealed that the virus did not persist for long in the environment. But both horizontal and vertical transmission of the virus was seen among the field populations of *H. peura.* Application of a high volume spray of HpNPV @ 1.75 liter of spray fluid per tree containing $1 \times 10^5$ POB/ml gave appreciable control of the pest and prevented the leaf damage to an extent of 76 per cent (Nair *et al.*, 1996, 1998). These studies indicate the usefulness of the virus in the management of *H. peura* and being host specific (Rabindra *et al.*, 1997) is unlikely to cause any ecological disruption.

### NPV of *Galleria mellonella*

The NPV of the wax moth *Galleria mellonella* (GmNPV) is known to infect several lepidopteran insect pests. Parthasarathy (2002) made detailed investigations in the laboratory as well field to explore the potential of GmNPV. Cross-infectivity studies revealed the susceptibility of 16 insect species to GmNPV. It included important crop pests like *P. xylostella, Chilo partellus, C. infuscatellus, Chilo sacchariphagus indicus, Maruca vitrata, Cnaphalocrocis medinalis, Opisina arenosella, A. albistriga, Diaphania pulverulentalis, Spodoptera exigua* and other pests like *Crocidolomia binotalis, Hellula undalis, Pericallia ricini, Ergolis merione, Exelastis atomosa* and *Marasmia patnalis.* The cross-infectivity was confirmed by DNA characterization and reciprocal inoculation studies. Serial passaging of GmNPV five times through alternate hosts increased its virulence to *P. xylostella.*

Second, third and fourth instar larvae of *P. xylostella* were equally susceptible to two isolates of GmNPV viz., Coimbatore and Bangalore. Serial passages of GmNPV through *P. xylostella* 15 times enhanced the virulence of GmNPV to *P. xylostella* by decreasing the $LC_{50}$ 12.76 fold.

Application of GmNPV @ $5 \times 10^7$ POB/ml was effective against the lepidopteran pest complex of cauliflower viz., *P. xylostella* , *C. binotalis* and *H. undalis* in pot culture experiments. Four sprays of GmNPV @ $7.5 \times 10^{13}$ POB/ha at eight day intervals effectively reduced the population of *P. xylostella* and *C. binotalis* under field conditions. GmNPV was safe to *Trichogramma chilonis, Chrysoperla carnea, Apis* spp., and six different races of *Bombyx mori.* These results highlight the possibility of developing GmNPV as a microbial insecticide for the management of several economically important lepidopteran pests.

## GRANULOSIS VIRUSES

Granulosis viruses like the NPV, belong to the baculovirus group and have been reported from several insect pests in India (Table 8.17). Unlike the NPV, the GV has only a single virion inside the occlusion bodies. They are also not as virulent as the NPV but the GV has been found to be effective at least against three agriculturally important insects.

**TABLE 8.17:** SOME INSECT PESTS WHICH HAVE BEEN REPORTED TO CARRY GV INFECTION

| *Pest* | *Reference* |
|---|---|
| *Chilo infuscatellus* | Easwaramoorthy and David (1979) |
| *C. sacchariphagus indicus* | Mehta and David (1980) |
| *Spodoptera exigua* | Narayanan (2003) |
| *S. litura* | Narayanan (1985) |
| *Plutella xylostella* | Rabindra *et al.* (1998) |
| *Cnaphalocrocis medinalis* | Jacob *et al.* (1971) |
| *Agrotis ipsilon* | Rabindra *et al.* (1990) |
| *Phthorimaea operculella* | Amonkar *et al.* (1979) |
| *Achaea janata* | Singaravelu and Ramakrishnan (1988) |
| *Pericallia ricini* | Jacob *et al.* (1972) |

### The Sugarcane Early Shoot Borer (*Chilo infuscatellus*)

A granulosis virus infection on *C. infuscatellus* was first reported by Easwaramoorthy and David (1979). (Plate, 8.3). The virus was found to be widely prevalent in Tamil Nadu causing upto 30 per cent mortality in larvae (Easwaramoorthy and Santhalakshmi, 2000). The *C. infuscatellus* GV (CiGV) was cross infective to the sugarcane internode borer, *Chilo sacchariphagus indicus* (Easwaramoorthy and Jayaraj, 1987). But the virus was found to be safe to the Indian honey bee *Apis cerana indica* (Easwaramoorthy and Jayaraj, 1987), silkworm *Bombyx mori* (Easwaramoorthy and Jayaraj, 1988) and albino rats (Easwaramoorthy and Jayaraj, 1990).

Easwaramoorthy and Santhalakshmi (1999) developed a wettable powder formulation of the CiGV and in laboratory bioassays, the virus formulation was as effective as that of the unformulated virus against the early shoot borer of sugarcane. In several field trials, the CiGV was found to be effective in controlling the shoot borer in sugarcane field. In Tamil Nadu, when the GV was applied at the rate of $5.5 \times 10^{12}$ occlusion bodies (OB)/ha as high volume spray, 70 per cent of the plants were protected (Easwaramoorthy and Jayaraj, 1991). The efficacy of the virus was also reported from Karnataka (Patil *et al.*, 1996) and Madhya Pradesh (Chaudhary and Singh, 1998).

### The Potato tuber Moth (*Phthorimaea operculella*)

A GV was isolated from diseased larvae of *P. operculella* (PoGV) and glass house experiments showed that the virus could be used for the management of this pest

(Amonkar *et al.*, 1979). Restriction endonuclease analysis of DNA from 8 isolates of PoGV, including the Maharashtra isolate revealed minor genotypic variations (Vickers *et al.*, 1991). Spraying the GV in potato fields in Maharashtra @ 5.5 × $10^{13}$ OB/ha + endosulfan 0.035% three times at 10 days interval gave excellent protection to the tubers and increased the tuber yield (Gorkpade and Pokharkar, 1997). The pest could also be controlled with GV in stored potatoes (Pokharkar and Jogi, 2000).

### The Diamondback Moth (*Plutella xylostella*)

Rabindra *et al.* (1998) isolated a very virulent GV from the larvae of the diamond back *P. xylostella.* Detailed investigations were made on the mass production, formulation and field evaluation of the PxGV against the DBM on cauliflower under a project funded by the Department of Biotechnology, Government of India at the Tamil Nadu Agricultural University, Coimbatore between 1997 and 2000. Laboratory studies showed that there were variations in the susceptibility of different geographic populations of *P. xylostella* to the GV. Pot culture studies showed that the persistence of the virus on cauliflower could be increased by the addition of lampblack 0.1%. Aqueous leaf extract of *Vitex negundo* significantly increased the mortality caused by the PxGV in larvae of *P. xylostella.* Laboratory studies showed that the GV infection significantly increased the susceptibility of *P. xylostella* larvae to endosulfan and chlorpyriphos. The virus was found to be safe to beneficial insects like the honeybees and the silk worms and the entomophagous insects like *C. carnea* and *T. chilonis.*

The virus was mass produced in III instar *P. xylostella* larvae. The virus was developed into a liquid formulation and in field experiments, the GV gave good control of *P. xylostella* and increased the yield of flower heads (Kennedy *et al.*, 2002.). Alternate application of Gv (1.5 × $10^{13}$ OB/ha) with Bt @ 0.5 kg/ha gave better control of *P. xylostella* than the virus applied alone on cauliflower. When different doses of virus were evaluated, a dose of 1.5 × $10^{13}$ OB/ha was found to be optimum. In GV sprayed plots, the population of the parasitoids Cotesia plutellae was found to be significantly higher than in plots applied with quinalphos. When used in conjunction with some of the new insecticides like abamectin and indoxacarb, it was found that application of PxGV at 0.75 × $10^{13}$ OB in combination with abamectin 4.75 g a.i./ha was the most effective against *P. xylostella* on cauliflower (Rajagopal Babu *et al.*, 2001). Application of GV at 1.5 × $10^{13}$ OB gave better control than Bt 0.5 kg/ha.

## COMMERCIAL SCALE PRODUCTION OF NPV

With several field trials highlighting the usefulness of NPV in pest control and the subsequent large-scale demonstrations, the NPVs were recommended for the management of pests and the demand for the viral pesticides particularly HaNPV and SlNPV increased enormously. As a consequence, several agencies attempted large-scale production of these NPVs. The resource inventory in IPM (Puri *et al.*, 1996) lists dozens of agencies including several private companies commercially producing these two viruses. Under the centrally-sponsored programmes, several state governments received subsidy grants for procurement and supply of NPVs to the farmers. This encouraged several small-scale producers into the business of NPV production. However, most of the products were found to be of poor quality in terms of viral counts, virulence and contaminants. A survey by Kennedy *et al.* (1998) revealed that out of the 11 products tested none had the minimum expected viral count of $1 \times 10^9$ POB/ml. While two samples did not contain any virus at all, seven had extremely low concentrations ranging from $10^6$-$10^8$ POB/ml.

Subsequently, two training programmes for commercial entrepreneurs were organized at the International Crops Research Institute for Semi Arid Tropics (Hyderabad) under a Tamil Nadu Agricultural University-Natural Resources Institute, collaborative project. A careful study of their methods and procedures revealed many difficulties and bottlenecks in the process of production of quality viral insecticides. This scenario highlighted the need for developing protocols for cost-effective commercial scale production of quality NPVs. Realising the importance of the role of the industry, a collaborative project involving the Department of Entomology of the Tamil Nadu Agricultural University and the Biocontrol Research Laboratory (BCRL) of the Pest Control India Ltd. funded by the National Agricultural Technology Project (NATP) under the competitive grant programme of the Indian Council of Agricultural Research was implemented successfully. Protocols for economic production of the host insects *H. armigera, S. litura* and their viruses and processing and formulation were developed. The efficacy of the viruses were evaluated in field trials and demonstrated in farmers fields.

## Mass Production of Host Insects

Mass production of both *H. armigera* and *S. litura* is the key to successful commercial scale production of the NPVs. Establishment of a disease-free insect colony and standardisation of a suitable semisynthetic diet and economic handling of the various steps in mass production are essential to cost-effective product development.

### *Establishment of Disease-free Host Insect Colony*

Both HaNPV and SlNPV are produced in their respective host insects and therefore establishment of a disease-free colony of *H. armigera* and *S. litura* is a key to successful virus production.

### *Selection of the Colony*

Wild colonies of *H. armigera* and *S. litura* should be collected from the field during the early season, as insects colleced in the late season are likely to harbour persistent infections like the microsporidians and viral infections. The initial colony should also consist of atleast three geographic populations in order to ensure genetic fitness.

### *Elimination of Diseases*

Wild population of insects often carry infectious diseases caused by *Vairimorpha* and *Nosema* species as well as granulosis, nuclear and cytoplasmic polyhedrosis viruses. Insects should be properly quarantined to eliminate these diseases. Mother-moth examination can help in ridding the culture of the microsporidians. Some of these chronic infections can reduce the fertility of the host insects as well as virus yield and contaminate the final product.

***Semisynthetic Diet and Host Nutrition***

A semisynthetic diet with proper blend of nutrients to supply the protein, vitamins and mineral requirement of the larvae is essential to get a vigorous colony with a high fecundity and fertility. This has been achieved in the current NATP-sponsored TNAU-BCRL Collaborative Project entitled "Improving commercial scale production and formulation of NPV of *Helicoverpa armigera* and *Spodoptera litura*. The productivity of *H. armigera* as well as *S. litura* host culture was improved through supplementation of the diet with vitamins and oil. The fecundity of *S. litura* could be increased significantly by the addition of these components (Table 8.18).

In the case of *H. armigera*, combination of corn flour + agar agar (6 : 4), vitamin 0.4% + Sunflower oil 0.8% recorded the highest fertility of 1125 eggs.

**TABLE 8.18:** EFFECT OF VITAMINS AND KOH ON THE FECUNDITY OF *S. litura*

| *Diet* | *No. of Eggs/Female* |
|---|---|
| Vitamin mix 0.8% | 1426 |
| KOH 6.72% | 1379 |
| Standard diet | 930 |

***Development of Multicavity Rearing Tray***

After studying four different prototypes, a multi-cavity rearing tray made up of ABS plastic was developed for rearing of *H. armigera* as well as virus-inoculated *S. litura* larvae. The efficiency in terms of saving time involved in diet dispensing, larval handling, pupae or virosed cadaver collection, cleaning and sterilizing was demonstrated.

***Development of a Large Volume Blender***

A nine litrè heavy duty, stainless steel blender was fabricated and tested for preparing large volume of diet. A comparative study in preparing diet for 10,000 larvae revealed that there was a 400% saving of time and labour with the new blender when compared to the kitchen blender.

***Pressure Washing of Trays***

A pressure washing system to clean the multicavity trays was developed which resulted in labour efficiency and 63 per cent saving in time.

**Economic Mass Production of Virus**

Intensive studies were undertaken to improve the commercial scale production of virus. The viruses have to be produced *in vivo* in the host insects and the process could be expensive in term of consumables for the diet as well as labour. In order to cover 20,000 ha of a crop like tomato for example, with three rounds of spray of HaNPV at the rate of $1.5 \times 10^{12}$ POB/ha, the total virus required would be $9 \times 10^{16}$ POB. A modest estimate put the total cost of production at Rs. 94.85 lakhs with the assumed productivity of $2 \times 10^9$ POB/larva (Table 8.19). The cost of production can be reduced if we can increase the productivity of the virus by various manipulations.

**TABLE 8.19:** COST OF PRODUCTION OF HaNPV TO SPRAY 20,000 HA, THREE TIMES @ $1.5 \times 10^2$/HA

Total virus required $9 \times 10^{16}$ POB
Larval No. required at a productivity rate of $3 \times 10^9$ PoB/larva = $3 \times 10^7$

| *Recurring Costs* | *(Rs. in lakhs)* |
|---|---|
| Diet | 57.30 |
| Labour | 15.00 |
| Consumables | 6.06 |
| Sub total | 78.36 |
| Interest on investment 10% | 12.16 |
| Depreciation on equipments | 4.33 |
| Total | 94.85 |
| Cost of 3 rounds of treatment @ $1.5 \times 10^{12}$ POB/ha | Rs. 474.00 |

### *Manipulation of Diet*

Out of the total cost of production, more than 50 per cent goes for the diet. While the full compliments of the diet would be essential for the production of host culture, there could be some deletions or changes in the diet for virus production. Studies revealed that we can reduce the cost of diet by the following methods:

(*i*) Supplementation of brown channa in place of white kabuli type which is more expensive
(*ii*) Using a combination of corn flour and agar agar in the ratio of 60 : 40 instead of 100% agar
(*iii*) Using an optimum quantity of 4.5 g of diet for the virus—inoculated larvae to avoid wastage
(*iv*) Supplementing the diet with coconut oil at 0.6 per cent and multivitamins of 0.4% enhanced the production of SlNPV
(*v*) In the case of HaNPV, sunflower oil at 0.8 per cent and vitamin at 0.4% gave significantly higher yield of virus.
(*vi*) Deletion of yeast did not affect the production of both SlNPV and HaNPV

### *Choice of Larval Stage and Incubation Conditions*

In both species inoculation of early fifth instar larvae and incubation at 25° C gave the highest yield of virus increasing the overall productivity.

### *Labour-Saving Methods*

In order to reduce the cost of labour, several labour- saving techniques were evolved.

- A simple suction mechanism was developed for efficient collection of virosed cadavers

- A special grinder was used instead of the kitchen mixie for maceration of the cadavers for extraction of the virus
- The volume of water to be used and the speed of centrifugation cycles standardized for cost effective recovery of the virus
- A semi-automatic bottling machine has been fabricated and the bottles are sealed by using a shrink-wrap machine

### *Improvement of Productivity of HaNPV at BCRL*

Increasing the productivity of the virus would reduce the cost of production and hence several investigations were undertaken to increase the virus yield from larvae. By manipulation of stage of the larvae for inoculation, inoculum dose and incubation temperature and time, the productivity of the virus was increased phenomenally. From a very low productivity of $10^8$ POB/larva during 1999 before the initiation of the project, the productivity slowly increased and is currently at a mean of $3 \times 10^9$ at BCRL, a phenomenal 30 fold increase (Table 8.20). Productivity level as high as $1.2 \times 10^{10}$ has been seen in certain cadavers which indicates the scope for increasing the productivity to a mean of $6 \times 10^9$ POB/larva. At this target level only 250 larvae will be required to produce NPV for one ha of gram or tomato.

**TABLE 8.20:** INCREASE IN THE PRODUCTIVITY OF HaNPV DUE TO THE NATP

| *Year* | *Productivity Pod/ larva* | *No. of Larvae Required to Produce Virus for one ha* |
|---|---|---|
| 1999 | $1 \times 10^8$ | 15,000 |
| 2000 | $8 \times 10^8$ | 1875 |
| 2001 | $1 \times 10^9$ | 1500 |
| 2002 | $2 \times 10^9$ | 750 |
| 2003 | $3 \times 10^9$ | 500 |
| Target | $6 \times 10^9$ | 250 |

### *Development of Formulations of NPV*

Liquid formulation of both HaNPV and SlNPV were developed and tested in the laboratory as well as field. The liquid formulation of HaNPV did not lose its virulence even after 14 months of storage under the room temperature which is a significant development. The crude virus began to loose the virulence beyond 12 months (Table 8.21). The liquid formulation was also as stable as the unformulated NPV and contained only a very low bacterial population.

### *Quality Assurance*

A quality control laboratory has been set up at BCRL with all necessary equipment including a phase contrast research microscope and all the batches of the viral formulation are verified for POB counts and bacterial contaminants. Virulence is checked by conducting bioassays periodically. Efforts are underway to get the ISO9001 certification for the formulation.

**TABLE 8.21:** STORAGE STABILITY OF LIQUID FORMULATION OF HaNPV

| *Period of Storage (months)* | *$LC_{50}$ POB/cm$^2$* | |
|---|---|---|
| | *Liquid Formulation* | *Crude* |
| 0 | 0.024 | 0.014 |
| 4 | 0.050 | 0.014 |
| 8 | 0.026 | 0.015 |
| 10 | 0.034 | 0.045 |
| 12 | 0.088 | 0.064 |
| 14 | 0.051 | 2.733 |

Since both HaNPV and SlNPV have been brought under the schedule of the insecticide act, these viruses have been registered with the Central Insecticides Board and a 9-3(B) registration obtained.

### *Use of NPV in IPM in Tomato*

The HaNPV produced under the NATP at BCRL was supplied to the Indian Institute of Horticultural Research, Bangalore for use in the NATP on Validation and Promotion of IPM of *H. armigera* on tomato. Three sprays of HaNPV at 28, 35 and 42 days of transplanting reduced the borer damage to 2.6 per cent. In non-IPM plots the borer damage was 18% inspite of 14 rounds of sprays of chemical pesticides. The IPM plots receiving NPV sprays recorded a fruit yield of 46.16 t/ha as against 30 t/ha in non-IPM plots (IIHR, 2002).

## FUTURE RESEARCH NEEDS IN COMMERCIAL SCALE PRODUCTION OF NPV

Through the NATP activity, significant progress has been made in development of formulation and improving the commercial scale production of the virus. However, it is important that the process of production of host insects as well as virus is semi mechanized in order to reduce the drudgery and cost of manual labour. This would improve the efficiency and reliability of the production system and reduce the cost of production. The following are some important research areas.

(*i*) Mechanisation of host egg separation and dispensing on diet

(*ii*) Development of low cost disposable multicavity trays for rearing of host larvae

(*iii*) Development of an automatic diet preparation and dispensing machine

(*iv*) Automatic virus inoculation unit

(*v*) In the case of SlNPV, due to the large size of the polyhedra, the productivity of the virus is rather low (Ca $2 \times 10^9$ POB/larva). There is a need to clone small polyhedra virus to increase the productivity.

## ROAD MAP FOR INCREASING THE UPTAKE OF BACULOVIRUSES FOR PEST MANAGEMENT

The value and potential of baculoviruses in insect pest management is well recognized. Despite this fact, the uptake of viral pesticides is still meagre due to the fact that these are fragile organisms which require great care in production, formulation and field application.

### Some of the Constraints which need to be Addressed

- Non availability of baculoviral biopesticides
- Poor quality of the available products and poor enforcement of quality control
- Slow action of the microbials making them poor competitors against the more aggressive chemical pesticides
- Narrow host range of the viruses providing only niche market
- Lack of expertise with the commercial producers
- High cost of production
- Cumbersome and expensive registration requirements
- Subsidy providing an undue advantage for chemical pesticides and weakens the biopesticide industry.

### Future Road Map for Research and Development for Increasing the Uptake of Baculoviral Pesticides

- Identification of highly potent strains of baculoviruses to make them more effective
- Economic mass production and formulation for competitive pricing
- Development of UV-tolerant strains with increased persistence on crop foliage
- Development of formulations with enhanced persistence on host plants particularly cotton
- Determine threshold levels for different pests with reference to use of NPV to enable need-based application.

### Government Support and Policy Issues

The Central and State Governments should encourage the production and uptake of microbial pesticides. Following are some of the issues to be addressed.

- Encourage public sector-private enterprise joint research and development for commercial scale production and formulation of baculoviral pesticides through liberal funding.
- Enable reduction in cost of registration through simplification of registration requirements and protocols.
- Extend appropriate tax concession to the bio pesticide producers.

## CONCLUSION

The usefulness and value of baculoviral insecticides in the management of lepidopteran pests is well recognized. Baculoviruses can be used intensively without the possibility of development of resistance. In view of their specificity and safety, there will not be any environmental, ecological or health hazards either to beneficial organisms, man, or animals. The use of these microbials is highly sustainable and can contribute to increasing the productivity and profitability in agriculture. Particular focus has to be given to lepidopteran pests of cotton and pulses. Cotton consumes majority of the pesticides marketed in India and hence it is important that we substitute these hazardous chemical pesticides with microbial pesticides. Productivity of pulses in India is very low and hence pulse production has to be increased phenomenally to meet the nutritional security of the Indian population through the use of microbial pesticides. Intensive commercial scale production and formulation of viral pesticides and strict enforcement of quality control requirements should be important activities in order to promote microbial pesticides for sustainable crop production in India.

## REFERENCES

Ahmad, S. I., Sen Sarma, P. K. and Sarma, P. K. S. 1983. Investigation on a newly recorded nuclear polyhedrosis virus of *Pygaera fulgurita* Wlk. (Notodontidae: Lepidoptera). I. Nature of disease and insect-virus interactions. *Journal of Entomological Research*, **7**: 150-153.

Amonkar, S. V., Pal, A. K., Vijayalakshmi, L. and Rao, A. S. 1979. Microbial control of potato tuber moth (*Phthorimaea operculella* Zell.). *Indian Journal of Experimental Biology*, **17**(10): 1127-1133.

Anonymous 1994. Development and use of indigenous microbial pathogens for the control of *Heliothis armigera* and *Spodoptera litura* in different cropping systems in South India. *Final Research Report of the USIF project, Tamil Nadu Agricultural University, Coimbatore*, pp . 99.

Anuradha, S., Ramakrishnan, N. and Srinivasan. 1995. Restriction map of genomic DNA of a nuclear polyhedrosis virus isolated from *Amsacta albistriga* (Walker). *Proceedings of the Indian National Science Academy, Part B, Biological Sciences*, **61**(2): 119-125.

Arora, R., Battu, G. S., Bath, D. S., Mohinder Singh, Arora, R. and Singh, M.1996. Management of Bihar hairy caterpillar, *Spilosoma oblique* (Walker) with a nuclear polyhedrosis virus. *Indian Journal of Ecology*, **23**(2): 138-140.

Asokan, R. 1998. Plant derived polyflavanoids as "sun screens" for nuclear polyhedrosis viruses. *Insect Environment*, **4**(3): 65-66.

Bakwad, D. G., Pawar, V. M. 1981. A new record of nuclear polyhedrosis virus (NPV) of jute semilooper, *Anomis sabulifera* (Guenee). *Indian Journal of Entomology*, **43**: 39-43.

Balasubramanian, S., Arora, R. S. and Pawar, A. D. 1989. Biological control of *Heliothis armigera* (Hubn.) using *Trichogramma pretiosum* Riley and nuclear polyhedrosis virus in Sriganganagar district of Rajasthan. *Plant Protection Bulletin, Faridabad*, **41**(3-4): 1-3.

Baskaran, R. K. M., Venugopal, M. S. and Mahadevan, N. R. 1996. Recycling of wastes obtained particularly from semi-synthetic diet during mass production of nuclear polyhedrosis virus of *Helicoverpa armigera* (Hubner) in biocontrol laboratory for biogas production and cultivation of mushroom, *Pleurotus sajor-caju* (Fr.) Singer. *Journal of Entomological Research*, **20**(1): 13-18.

Baskaran, R. K. M., Venugopal, M. S. and Mahadevan, N. R. 1998. Optical brightners as UV protectants and their influence on the virulence of nuclear polyhedrosis virus of *Spodoptera litura* (Fabricius) (Lepidoptera: Noctuidae). *Journal of Biolological Control*, **11**(1/2): 17-22.

Baskaran, R. K. M., Srinivasan, T. R., Muthumeena, K., Muthulakshmi, S. and Mahadevan, N. R. 2001. Biological activity of four geographic isolates of baculovirus on groundnut redhairy caterpillar, *Amsacta albistriga* (Lepidoptera: Arctiidae). *Indian Journal of Agricultural Sciences*, **71**(3): 212-214.

## Plate 8.1

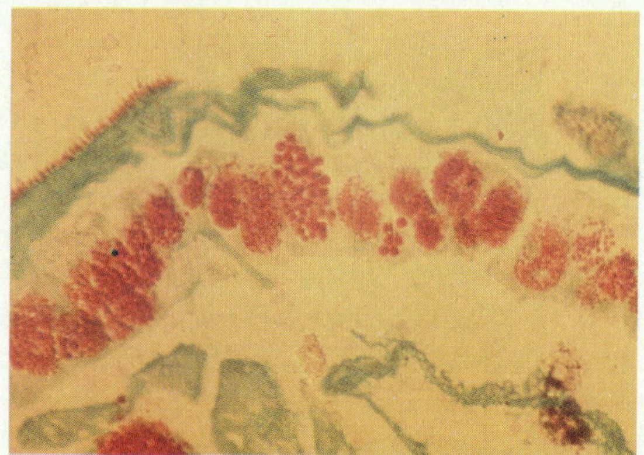

Photomicrograph of section of fat body lobe of larva of *Dasychira mendosa* showing nuclei loaded with polyhedra

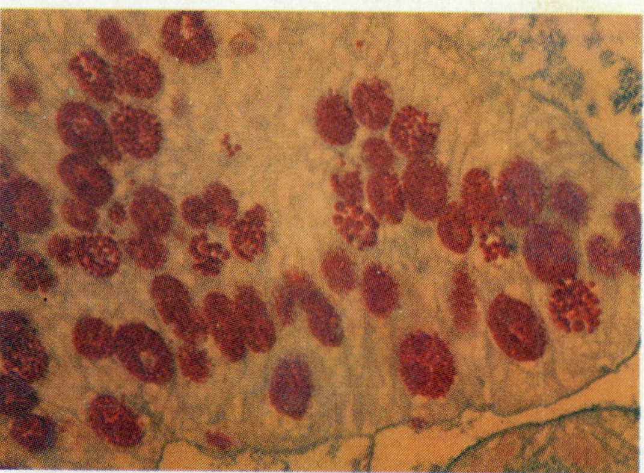

Photomicrograph of cross section larva of Dasychira mendosa showing virus infection and polyhedra in the epithelial nuclei of the hypodermis resulting in the rupturing of the larval cuticle

Grown-up final larva of *Helicoverpa armigera* killed by NPV on cotton showing the characteristic symptoms

## Plate 8.2

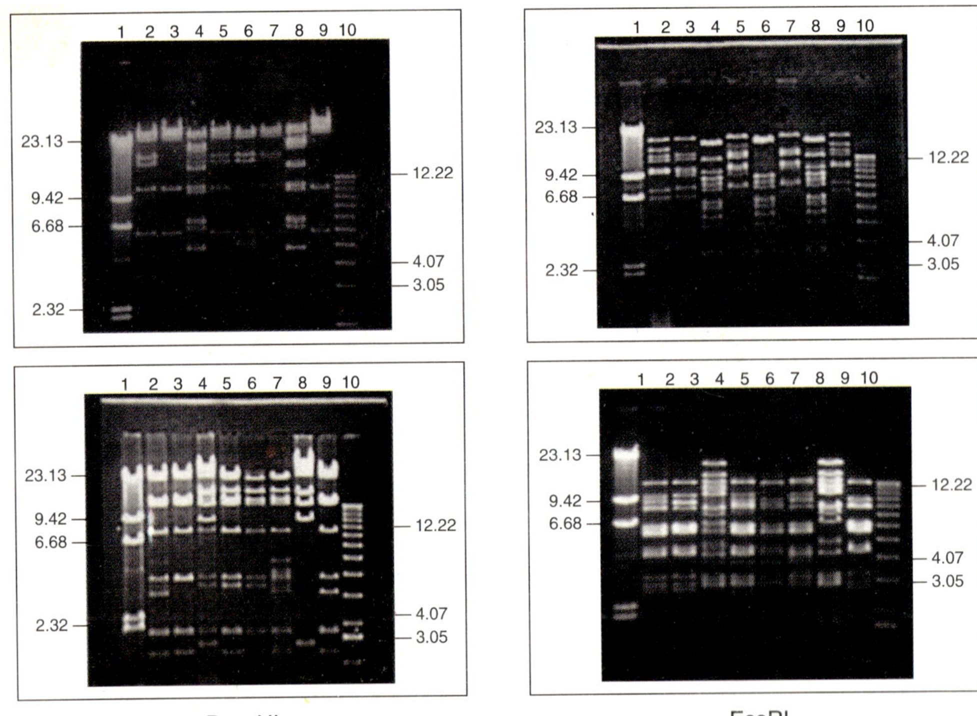


Restriction endonuclease analysis of eight isolates of NPV of *H. armigra* (Tracks 2-9) showing the genomic heterogeity

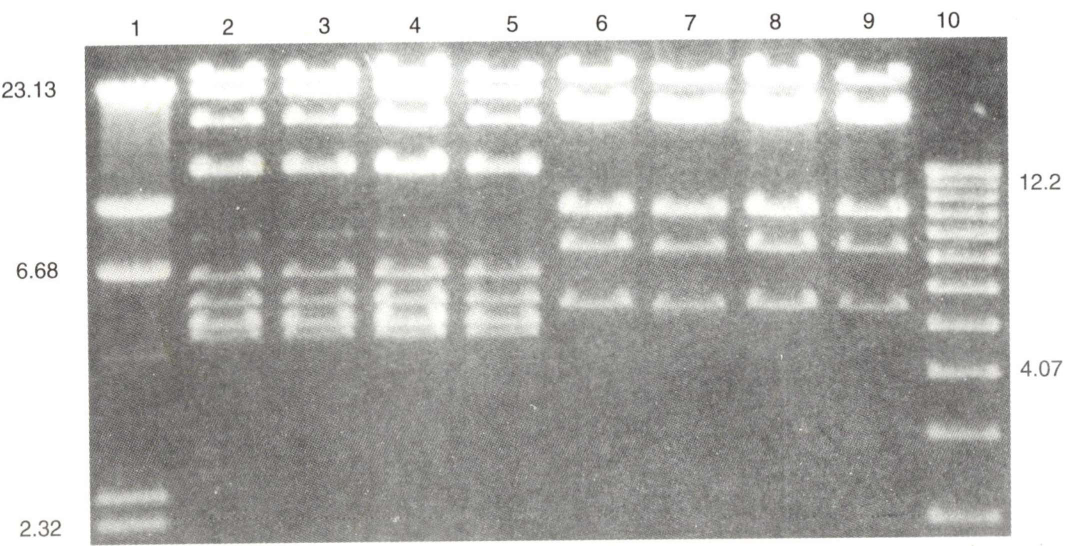


Restriction endonuclease analysis of DNA of HaNPV isolated Coimbatore (Tracks 2 and 6), Maduri (Tracks 3 and 7), Hyderabad (Tracks 4 and 8) and Kanchepuram (Tracks 5 and 9) cut with Pst 1 (Tracks 2-5) and Hind III (Tracks 6-9) Tracks 1 = l DNA cut with Hind III Track 10 = 1 kb ladder

## Plate 8.3

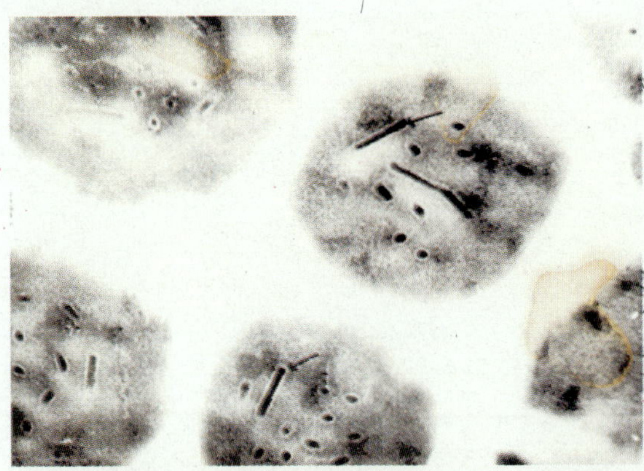

Electron micrograph of ultra thin section of nuclear polyhedrosis virus of *Helicoverpa* showing the singly occluded virus (Photo: J. R. Adams)

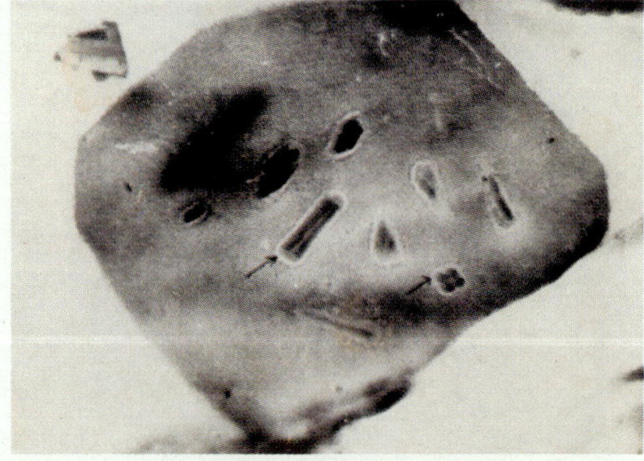

Electron micrograph of ultra thin section of nuclear polyhedrosis virus of *Amsacta albistriga* showing multiple virus (Photo: J. R. Adams)

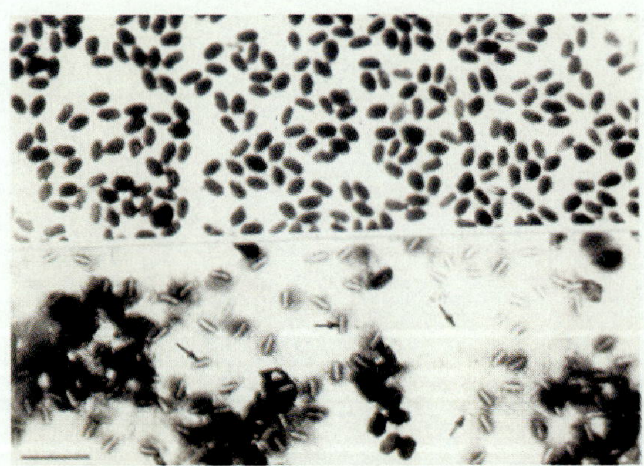

Electron micrograph of (A) of granulsis of *Agrotis ipsilon* showing single virions in capsules (B)

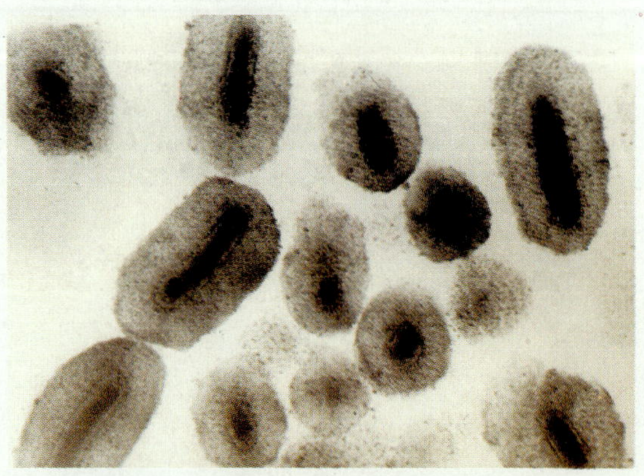

Electron micrograph of ultra thin section of Granulosis Virus of *Chilo infuscatellus* showing single virions in capsules (Courtesy: S. Eswaramoorthy)

Baskaran, R. K. M., Srinivasan, T. R., Muthumeena, K., Muthulakshmi, S., Mahadevan and N. R. 2001. Influence of host plants on infectivity and *in vivo* production of nuclear polyhedrosis virus of red hairy caterpillar (*Amsacta albistriga*) (Lepidoptera: Arctiidae). *Indian Journal of Agricultural Sciences*, **71**(11): 742-744.

Battu, G. S. 1990. New record of the nucleopolyhedrosis of *Euproctis lunata* (Walk.) from India. *Journal of Insect Science*, **3**: 111-112.

Battu, G. S. 1991. Bioassay of the nuclear polyhedrosis virus of *Trabala vishnou* (Lefevere). *Indian Journal of Entomology*, **53**: 73-75.

Battu, G. S. Dilawari, V. K. and Bindra, O. S. 1977. Investigations on microbial infections of insect pests in the Punjab-II. *Indian-Journal-of-Entomology*. publ.1978, **39**: 3, 271-280; 2 fig.; 19 ref.

Battu, G. S. Harjapinder Singh, Labh-Singh. 1989. Nuclear polyhedrosis virus infection of *Hellula undalis* Fab. *Journal-of-Insect-Science*, **2**: 1, 60-61; 2 ref.

Battu, G. S., Arora, R. and Bath, D. S. 2001. Field evaluation of nucleopolyhedrovirus for the management of *Helicoverpa armigera* (Hubner) on egyptian clover. pp.146. *In*: Symposium on Biocontrol based pest management for quality crop protection in the current millenniun, July 18-19, 2001, PAU, Ludhiana, pp. 146, 224.

Bijjur, S., Kulkarni, K. A. and Lingappa, S. 1991a. Safety of *Heliothis armigera* (Hubner) NPV to some non-target beneficial organisms. *Indian Journal of Entomology*, **53**(3): 475-478.

Bijjur, S., Kulkarni, K. A. and Lingappa, S. 1991b. Evaluation of nuclear polyhedrosis virus with certain adjuvants for the control of *Heliothis armigera* (Hubner). *Indian Journal of Entomology*, **53**(3): 479-483.

Chand Asaf and Rabindra, R. J. 1999. Efficacy of NPV applied with certain adjuvants in the management of the gram pod borer *Helicoverpa armigera* (Hubner) on chickpea. *Madras Agricultural Journal*, **86** (4/6): 335-337.

Chand, P. 1979. Polyhedrosis of *Diacrisia obliqua* Walker. *Indian Journal of Entomology*, **41**: 194.

Chandrakar, Ganguli, R. N., Kaushik, U. K., Dubey, V. K. and Chandrakar, G. 1999. Management of tomato fruit borer, *Heliothis armigera* Hubn. using biopesticides. *Journal of Applied Zoological Researches*, **10**(2): 105-107.

Chandramohan, M. and Kumarswami, T. 1979. Comparative efficacy of chemical and nuclear polyhedrosis virus in the control of groundnut red hariy caterpillar, *Amsacta albistriga* (Walker). *Science and Culture*, **45**(5): 202-204.

Chaudhari, S. 1992. Formulation of nuclear polyhedrosis virus of *Spodoptera littoralis* with boric acid. *Indian Journal of Entomology*, **54**: 202-206.

Chaudhari, S. 1997. Effect of age of *Spilosoma obliqua* larvae on their susceptibility to nuclear polyhedrosis virus. *Indian Journal of Entomology*, **59**(1): 59-61.

Chaudhari, S. and Ramakrishnan, N. 1983. A note on the recovery of a virulent nuclear polyhedrosis virus of *Spodoptera litura* (F.) from the birds droppings. *Indian Journal of Entomology*, **45**(4): 491-492.

Chaudhari, S. and Ramakrishnan, N. (1980). Field efficacy of baculovirus and its combination with sub-lethal dose of DDT and endosulfan on cauliflower against tobacco caterpillar (*Spodoptera litura* (Fabricius). *Indian Journal of Entomology*, **42**: 592-596.

Cherry, A. J., Rabindra, R. J., Parnell, M. A., Geetha, N., Kennedy, J. S. and Grzywacz, D. 2000. Field evaluation of *Helicoverpa armigera* nucleopolyhedrovirus formulations for control of the chickpea pod-borer, *H. armigera* (Hubn.), on chickpea (*Cicer arietinum* var. Shoba) in southern India. *Crop Protection*, **19**(1): 51-60.

Choudhary, A. K. and Singh, S. N. 1998. Efficacy of granulosis virus against the infestation of early shoot borer, *Chilo infuscatellus* Sneller and yield of sugarcane. *Annals of Plant Protection Sciences*, **6**(2): 211-213.

Chundurwar, T. D. and Pawar, V. M. 1991. Natural incidence of nuclear polyhedrosis virus infection in *Heliothis armigera* (Hub.) on chickpea. *Journal of Maharashtra Agricultural Universities*, **16**(3): 420-421.

Cowgill, S. E. and Bhagwat, V. R. 1996. Comparison of the efficacy of chemical control and *Helicoverpa* NPV for the management of *Helicoverpa armigera*/UL/(Hubner) on resistant and susceptible chickpea. *Crop Protection*, **15**(3): 241-246.

Devaraj, R., Rabindra, R. J., Kennedy, J. S. and Sathia, N. 2001. Combined application of SINPV and HaNPV against *Spodoptera litura* (F.) and *Helicoverpa armigera* (Hbn.) Populations on Tomato. *In*: S. Ignachimuthu and A. Sen, (eds.), *Microbials in Insect Pest Management*. Oxford and IBH Co. Pvt. Ltd., New Delhi, pp. 53-58.

Dhandapani, N. 1994. Efficacy of nuclear polyhedrosis virus and chlorpyriphos against tobacco caterpillar (*Spodoptera litura*) on tobacco (*Nicotiana tabacum*). *Indian Journal of Agricultural Sciences*, **64**(5): 346-348.

Dhandapani, N. and Babu, P. C. S. 1995. Efficacy of nuclear polyhedrosis virus against *Spodoptera litura* on groundnut in different locations of Tamil Nadu. *Madras Agricultural Journal*, **82**(9-10): 531-533.

Dhandapani, N. and Jayaraj, S. 1989. Efficacy of nuclear polyhedrosis virus formulation for the control of *Spodoptera litura* (Fab.) on chillies. *Journal of Biological Control*, **3**(1): 47-49.

Dhandapani, N., Jayaraj, S. and Rabindra, R. J. 1987. Efficacy of ULV application of NPV with certain adjuvants for the control of *Heliothis armigera* on cotton. *Journal of Biological Control*, **1**: 111-117.

Dhandapani, N., Babu, P. C. S. and Jayaraj, S. 1992. Field evaluation of nuclear polyhedrosis virus with adjuvant for the control of *S. litura* (Fb.) on tobacco. *Tobacco Research*, **18**: 5-8.

Dhandapani, N., Janarthanan, R. and Kumaraswami, T. 1982. Epizootic occurrence of nuclear polyhedrosis virus on *Spodoptera litura* F. *Current Science*, **51**(16): 793-794.

Dhandapani, N., Jayaraj, S. and Rabindra, R. J. 1993a. Cannibalism on nuclear polyhedrosis virus infected larvae by *Heliothis armigera* (Hubn.) and its effect on viral infection. *Insect Science and its Application*, **14**(4): 427-430.

Dhandapani, N., Jayaraj, S. and Rabindra, R. J. 1993b. Transmission of nuclear polyhedrosis of *Heliothis armigera* (Hbn.) to progeny through adult feeding. *Indian Journal of Experimental Biology*, **31**(8): 721-722.

Dhandapani, N., Babu, P. C. S., Jayaraj, S. and Rabindra, R. J. 1993c. Field efficacy of nuclear polyhedrosis virus against *Heliothis armigera* (Hbn.) and *Spodoptera litura* (Fb.) on different host crops. *Tropical Agriculture*, **70**(4): 320-324.

Dhandapani, N., Jayaraj, S. and Rabindra, R. J. 1993d. Laboratory studies on the efficacy of nuclear polyhedrosis virus against *Heliothis armigera* (Hbn.) on some cotton cultivars. *Anzeiger fur Schadlingskunde, Pflanzenschutz, Umweltschutz*, **66**(5): 96-100.

Dhandapani, N., Jayaraj, S. and Rabindra, R. J. 1994a. Activity of ants on cotton plants sprayed with nuclear polyhedrosis virus and adjuvants against *Heliothis armigera* (Hubner). *Journal of Entomological Research*, **18**(1): 65-68.

Dhandapani, N., Jayaraj, S. and Rabindra, R. J. 1994b. Nuclear polyhedrosis virus bait formulations against larvae and adults of *Heliothis armigra* (Hbn.). *Indian Journal of Experimental Biology*, **32**: 294-295.

Dharmadhikari, P. R., Ramaseshiah, G. and Achan, P. G. 1985. Survey of *Lymantria obfuscata* and its natural enemies in India. *Entomophaga*, **30**: 399-408.

Dhandapani, N., Sundara Babu, P. C., Sathiah, N. and Jayaraj, S. 1993. Combined use of nuclear polyhedrosis viruses of *Spodoptera litura* (Fb.) and *Heliothis armigera* (Hb.) on groundnut (*Arachis hypogaea L.*). *Journal of Applied Entomology*, **116**: 523-526.

Easwaramoorthy, S. and David, H. 1979. A granulosis virus of sugarcane shoot borer, *Chilo infuscatellus Snell.* (Lepidoptera: Crambidae). *Current Science*, **48**(15): 685-686.

Easwaramoorthy, S. and Jayaraj, S. 1987. Environmental persistence of granulosis virus infecting sugarcane shoot borer, *Chilo infuscatellus* Snellen. *Journal of Biological Control*, **1**(1): 31-36.

Easwaramoorthy, S. and Santhalakshmi, G. 1999. Laboratory evaluation of a wettable formulation of granulosis virus of *Chilo infuscatellus* Snell. *Insect Environment*, **5**(1): 3-5.

Easwaramoorthy, S. and Santhalakshmi, G. 2000. The granulosis virus of the sugarcane borer, *Chilo infuscatellus* Snellen. *Sugarcane International*, **May**: 5-8.

Easwaramoothy, S. and Jayaraj, S. 1987. Lack of susceptibility of Indian honey bee, *Apis cerana indica* Fabr. to two granulosis viruses infecting sugarcane borers. *Indian Bee Journal*, **49**: 1-4, 1-2.

Easwaramoothy, S. and Jayaraj, S. 1987. Cross infectivity of granulosis viruses infecting *Chilo infuscatellus* Snell and *C. sacchariphagus indicus* (Kapur). *Journal of Entomological Research*, **11**(2): 170-174.

Easwaramoothy, S. and Jayaraj, S. 1988. Effect of two granulosis viruses on the silkworms, *Bombyx mori meridionalis* F. and *Philosamia ricini, B. Entomon*, **13**(1): 57-59.

Easwaramoothy, S. and Jayaraj, S. 1990. Safety of two granulosis viruses infecting sugarcane borers to albino rats. *Journal of Biological Control*, **4**(1): 35-39.

Easwaramoothy, S. and Jayaraj, S. 1991. Influence of spray fluid volume and purity on the effectiveness of a granulosis virus infecting sugarcane shoot borer, *Chilo infuscatellus* Snellen. *Tropical Pest Management*, **37**(2): 134-137.

Ethiraju, S., Rabindra, R. J. and Jayaraj 1988. Laboratory evaluation of certain formulations of nuclear polyhedrosis virus against the larvae of *Heliothis armigera*. *J. Biol. Control*, **2**: 21-25.

Franzmann, B. A., Monsour, C. J., Teakle, R. E. and Murray, D. A. H. 1996. A small plot trial on the management of *Helicoverpa armigera* (Hubner) (Lepidoptera: Noctuidae) on sorghum with nuclear polyhedrosis virus and larval parasitoids. *Proceedings of the Third Australian Sorghum Conference, Tamworth*, 20-22 February 1996. AIAS-Occasional-Publication. No. **93**: 353-357; 10 ref.

Ganguli, R. N. and Dubey, V. K. 1998. Management of tomato fruit borer, *Helicoverpa armigera* Hubner in Chhattisgarh region of Madhya Pradesh. *Insect Environment*, **4**(1): 25.

Geetha, N. and Rabindra, R. J. 2000. Genetic variability and comparative virulence of some geographic isolates of nuclear polyhedrosis virus of *Helicoverpa armigera* Hubner. *In*: S. Ignachimuthu, A. Sen and S. Janarthanan (eds.), *Biotechnological Applications for Integrated Pest Management*. Oxford & IBH Publishing Co. Pvt.Ltd., New Delhi. pp. 65-80.

Geetha, N. and Rabindra, R. J. 2001. Safety of newly developed formulations of nuclear polyhedrosis virus of *Helicoverpa armigera* to a parasitoid and a predator. *Entomon*, **26**: 104-109.

Geetha, N., Rabindra, R. J., Muthukumar, B., Thayumanavan, B., Regupathy, A. and Sundarababu, P. C. 1999. Effect of nuclear polyhedrosis virus infection on the activity of carboxylesterase and glutathione S-transferase in *Helicoverpa armigera* (Hbn). *Tropical Agricultural Research*, **11**: 408-424.

Gitay, H. and Polson, A. 1971. Isolation of a granulosis virus from *Heliothis armigera* and its persistence in avian feces. *Journal* of *Invertebrate Pathology*, **17**(2): 288-290.

Godse, D. B. and Patil, R. B. 1979a. Persistance of nuclear polyhedrosis virus of tobacco caterpillar *Spodoptera litura* Fabr. in Karnatak soil. *Indian Journal of Experimental Biology*, **17**(11): 1286-1287.

Godse, D. B., Patil, R. B. 1979b. Nuclear polyhedrosis of *Plusia signata* (Lepidoptera: Noctuidae). *Current Science*, **48**(9): 405-406.

Gorpade, V. P. and Pokharkar, D. S., 1997. Biologcial control of potato tuber moth *Phthorimea operculella* (Zeller) on potato. *Journal of Maharashtra Agricultural University*, **22**: 187-189.

Goud, K. B., Lingappa, S. and Kulkarni, K. A. 1997. Effectiveness of *Helicoverpa armigera* nuclear polyhedrosis virus against insecticide resistant strains of *Helicoverpa armigera* (Hubner) (Lepidoptera: Noctuidae). *Journal of Biological Control*, **11**: 1-2, 1-4.

Hugar, P., Kulkarni, K. A. and Lingappa, S. 1996. Effectiveness of the nuclear polyhedrosis virus against field populations of the armyworm, *Mythimna separata* (Walker) on sorghum. *Karnataka Journal of Agricultural Sciences*, **9**(1): 47-50.

Hugar, P., Kulkarni, K. A. and Lingappa, S. 1995. Persistence of the nuclear polyhedrosis virus of sorghum armyworm, *Mythimna separata* (Walker) in soil. *Karnataka Journal of Agricultural Science*, **8**(1): 5-9.

I.I.H.R. 2002. Annual Report of the National Agricultural Technology Project on Validation and Promotion of IPM in selected crops. Indian Institute of Horticultural Research, Bangalore.

Jacob, A. and Subramaniam, T. R. 1972. Nuclear polyhedrosis on some lepidoptera. *Current Science.*, **41**: 536.

Jacob, A., Das, N. M. and Thomas, M. J. 1971. A granulosis virus of the rice leaf roller, *Cnaphalocrocis medinalis* Guenee (Pyraustidae, Lepidoptera). *Agricultural Research Journal of Kerala*, **9**(2): 103.

Jacob, A., Pillai, K. S. and Asari, P. A. R. 1978. A nuclear polyhedrosis virus from rice case worm, *Nymphula depunctalis* (Guen.) (Lepidoptera: Pyralidae). *Current Science*, **47**(23): 928-929.

Jacob, A., Subramaniam, T. R. 1972. Effect of larval age and dosage of virus on the susceptibility of *Spodoptera litura* F. to a nuclear polyhedrosis. *Agricultural Research Journal of Kerala. Publ.* 1973, **10**(2): 176-178.

Jacob, A., Thomas, M. J. and Chandrika, S. 1972. Occurrence of two virus diseases in *Pericallia ricini* Fabr. (Arctiidae, Lepidoptera). *Agricultural Research Journal of Kerala., Publ.* 1973, **10**(1): 65.

Jadhav, R. G., Khaire, V. M. and Mote, U. N. 1992. Evaluation of adjuvants for nuclear polyhedrosis virus of gram-pod-borer (*Helicoverpa armigera*) on sunflower (*Helianthus annuus*). *Indian Journal of Agricultural Sciences*, **62**(7): 494-496.

Jayachandran, G. and Chaudhari, S. 1997. Combination effect of additives on the activity of nuclear polyhedrosis virus of *Spodoptera litura*. *Indian Journal of Entomology*, **59**(1): 110-118.

Jayaraj, S., Santharam, G., Narayanan, K., Soundararajan, K. and Balagurunathan, R. 1981. Effectiveness of the nuclear polyhedro virus against field populations of the tobacco caterpillar, *Spodoptera litura* on cotton. *Andhra Agricultural Journal*, **27**: 26-29.

Kalia, V., Chaudhari, S. and Gujar, G. T. 2001. Optimization of production of nucleopolyhedrovirus of *Helicoverpa armigera* throughout larval stges. *Phytoparasitica*, **29**(1): 23-28.

Kennedy, J. S., Sairabanu, B. and Rabindra, R. J. 2002. Management of *Plutella xylostella* (Linnaeus) with granulosis virus. Abstract No. III-P-02 of Proceedings of the symposium on Biological Control of Lepidopteran Pests, July 17-18, 2002, pp.32, Soceity for Biological Control, Bangalore.

Kennedy, J. S., Rabindra, R. J., Sathiah, N. and Grzywacz, D. 1998. The role of standardization and quality control in the successful promotion of NPV insecticides. *In: Proceedings of National Symposium on Biopesticides and Insect Pest Management*, Chennai, February 26-27, 1998, pp.170-174.

Ketunuti, U. and Prathomrat, S. 1989. Cotton bollworm larvae control by *Heliothis armigera* nuclear polyhedrosis virus. Abstracts of the First Asia-Pacific Conference of Entomology, 8-13 November 1989. Chang Mai. Thailand, Bangkok: *The Secretariat*, APCE, p.16.

Khan, M. A., Rohitashwa, Meena, A. and Agnihotri, M. 2001. Efficacy of NPV and its compatibility with different insecticides against *Spilosoma oblique* Walker. *Shashpa*, **8**(1): 69-74.

Krishnaiah, K., Ramakrishnan, N. and Reddy, P. C. 1984. Further trials on control of *Spodoptera litura* Fab. By nuclear polyhedrosis virus on black gram and groundnut. *Indian Journal of Plant Protection*, **12**(1): 81-83.

Krishnaiah, K., Ramakrishnan, N. and Reddy, P. D. 1985. Control of *Spodoptera litura* Fabr. on blackgram by nuclear polyhedrosis virus. *Indian Journal of Agricultural Sciences*, **55**: 775-776.

Kulkarni, G. G. and Hugar, P. S. 1999. Persistence of nuclear polyhedrosis virus on different host plants of *Spodoptera litura* Fab. *Haryana Agricultural Unversity Journal of Research*, **29**(3-4): 95-99.

Kulkarni, G. G. and Hugar, P. S. 2000. Standardization of inoculum dose for mass multiplication of *Spodoptera litura* nuclear polyhedrosis virus (SlNPV) on different host plants. *Karnataka Journal of Agricultural Sciences*, **13**(1): 51-54.

Kulkarni, G. G., Kumar, S. S. R., Hugar, P. S. and Kulkarni, K. A. 1999. Persistence of NPV against *Spodoptera litura* Fab. on strawberry in transitional tract of Karnataka. *Annuals of Agri. Bio-Research*, **4**: 45-47.

Langewald, J., Cherry, A. 2000. Prospects for microbial pest control in West Africa. *Biocontrol News and Information*, **21**: 2.

Lingappa, S., Rajendra Hegde, Udikeri, S. S. and Hegde, R. 2000. Efficacy of econeem with microbial insecticides against *Helicoverpa armigera* (Hubner) in cotton. *Karnataka Journal of Agricultural Sciences*, **13**(3): 597-600.

Mahadeva, N. R. 1978. Studies on biology and control of the tobacco caterpillar *S. litura* with NPV. M.Sc. (Ag.) Thesis, TNAU, Madurai.

Mahalingam, C. A. and Hanifa, A. M. 2001. Efficacy of HaNPV in combination with insecticides against tomato fruit borer *Helicoverpa armigera* Hubner. *In: Symposium on Biocontrol based Pest Management for Quality Crop Protection in the Current Millenniun*, July 18-19, 2001, PAU, Ludhiana, pp. 210-211, 224.

Mallapur, C. P., Kulkarni, K. A. and Lingappa, S. 1997. Integrated management of the armyworm, *Mythima separata* (Walker), on sorghum. *In:* G. S. Dhaliwal, R. Arora, N. S. Randhawa and A. K. Dhawan, (eds.), *Proceedings of International Conference on Ecological Agriculture Towards Sustainable Development, Chandigarh.* 15-17 November, pp. 334-339.

Mehta, U. K. and David, H. 1980. A granulosis virus disease of sugarcane internode borer. *Madras Agricultural Journal*, **67**(9): 616-619.

Men, U. B. and Thakare, H. S. 1998a. Basic studies on nuclear polyhedrosis virus of sunflower semilooper, *Thysanoplusia orichalcea* Fabricius. *Insect Environment*, **4**(1): 18.

Men, U. B. and Thakre, H. S. 1998b. Parasitoids, predators and pathogens recorded on sunflower semilooper, *Thysanoplusia orichalcea* F. in Vidarbha: *PKV Research Journal*, **22**(2): 218-219.

Misra, M. P., Pawar, A. D. and Ram, N. 1991. Use of NPV in management of the insect pest, *Heliothis armigera* (Hubner) in gram. *Journal of the Andaman Science Association*, **7**(1-2): 75-78.

Montaldo, T. 1991. Microbiological control in cotton crops in North Cameroon: conclusions from studies carried out from 1979 to 1988. *Coton-et-Fibres-Tropicales*, **46**(3): 217-229.

Mote, U. N. and Murthy, D. K. 1989. Control of *Heliothis armigera* on sorghum by chemical and nonchemical means. *Plant Protection Bulletin Faridabad*, **41**(1-2): 12-20.

Moore, S. D. Pittaway, T., Gustav Bouwer, G. and Fourie, J. G. 2004. Evaluation of *Helicoverpa armigera* Nucleopolyhedrovirus (Hear NPV) for control of *Helicoverpa armigera* (Lepidoptera: Noctuidae) on citrus in South Africa. *Biocontrol Science and Technology*, **14**: 239-250.

Muthiah, C. and Rabindra, R. J. 1991. Control of gram pod borer *Heliothis armigera* on pigeonpea *Cajanus cajan* with controlled droplet application of nuclear polyhedrosis virus and effect of oral feeding of virus on mulberry silkworm, *Bombyx mori. Indian Journal of Agricultural Sciences*, **61**: 449-452.

Muthuswami, M. Rabindra, R. J. and Jayaraj, S. 1993. Use of baculovirus mixture for the control of *Helicoverpa armigera* (Hbn) and Spodoptera litura (F) on groundnut. *Journal of Biological Control*, **7**: 105-108.

Nagrare, V. S. and More, G. D. 1998. Economics in using bioagents against *Helicoverpa armigera* on pigeonpea. *Indian Journal of Entomology*, **60**(2): 203-206.

Nair, K. S. S., Biju, B., Sajeev, T. V., Sudheendrakumar, V. V., Ali, M. I. M., Varma, R. V., Mohanadas, K. and Babajan, B. 1996. Field efficacy of nuclear polyhedrosis virus for protection of teak against the defoliator, *Hyblaea puera* Cramer (Lepidoptera: Hyblaeidae). *Journal of Biological Control*, **10**(1-2): 79-85.

Nair, K. S. S., Varma, R. V., Sudheendrakumar, V. V., Mohanadas, K. and Ali, M. I. M. 1998. Management of the teak defoliatior. (Hyblaea puera) using nuclear polydedrosis virus (NPV). *KFRI Research Report*, p. 64.

Narayanan, K. 1985. The occurrence of mixed infection of viruses in *Spodoptera litura* F. *Current Science, India*, **54**(22): 1190-1191.

Narayanan, K. 1986. Studies on the cross-infectivity of nuclear polyhedrosis virus of *Adisura atkinsoni* Moore (Noctuidae: Lepidoptera). *Current Science, India*, **55**: 372-373.

Narayanan, K. (2003). Occurrence, cross infectivity and safety of nuclear polyehdrosis virus of beet army worm *Spodoptera exigua* "Biopesticides and Pest Management" Ed. by Opender Koul, G. S. Dhaliwal, S. S. Marwaha and Jatinder K. Arora. Pub. *Society of Biopesticide Sciences, India Vol.* **2**: 198-203.

Narayanan, K. 2003. Occurrence of granulosis virus of *Spodoptera exigua* (Hubner) (Lepidoptera: Noctuidae). *In:* P. L. Tandon, C. R. Ballal, S. K. Jalali and R. J. Rabindra, (eds.), *Biological Control of Lepidopteran Pests.* Proceedings of the Symposium of Biological Control of Lepidopteran Pests. pp. 139-142.

Narayanan, K., Sharma, K. K. 2001. Effect of Nuclear polyhedrosis virus on *Agrotis segetum* and its safety towards *Bombyx mori* and *Chrysoperla carnea*, Symposium on Biological Control based pest management for quality crop protection in the current millenium at the Punjab Agricultural University, Ludhiana, July 18-19, 2001.

Narayanan, K. and Veenakumar, K. 2002a. Report on the occurrence of nuclear polyhedrosis virus on gherkin caterpillar *Diaphania indica* (Lepidoptera: Pyralidae). *In*: Proceedings "Symposium on Biological Control of Lepidopterous Pest" held 17th to 18th July (PDBC, Bangalore), p. 34.

Narayanan, K. and Veenakumari, K. 2002b. Report on the occurrence of nuclear polyhedrosis virus of the coconut skipper *Gangara thyrsis* (Fabricius) (Lepidoptera: Hesperiidae). *Indian Coconut Journal*, **33**: 3-4.

Narayanan, K. and Veenakumari, K. 2003b. Nuclear polyhedrosis viruses from coconut blackheaded caterpillar, *Opisina arenosella* Walker and sorghum spotted stem borer, *Chilo partellus* (Swinhoe); *Journal of Biological Control*, **17**(1): 97-98.

Narayanan, K. and Veenakumari, K., 2003a. Report on the occurrence of nuclear polyhedrosis virus on gherkin caterpillar, *Diaphania indica* (Saunders) (Lepidoptera: Pyralidae). *In*: P. L. Tandon, C. R. Ballal, S. K. Jalali and R. J. Rabindra, (eds.), Biological Control of Lepidopteran Pests. *Proceedings of the Symposium of Biological Control of Lepidopteran Pests*, **17**(1): 169-170.

Nayak, P, and Srivastava, R. P. 1979. Nuclear polyhedroses on certain insect pests of rice. *Current-Science*, **48**(3): 122-123.

Neelgund, Y. F. and Mathad, S. B. 1972. Nuclear polyhedrosis of *Pseudaletia separata* (Lepidoptera: Noctuidae). *Annals of the Entomological Society of America*, **65**(3): 763-764.

Nimbalkar, S. A., Kulat, S. S., Dhurve, S. B. and Tambe, V. J. 1996. Bioefficacy of insecticides and biocides for the bollworm management of cotton. *Journal of Soils and Crops*, **6**(2): 162-164.

Paliwal, K. C. and Jakhmola, S. S. 1981. Role of parasites and pathogens in the natural control of safflower caterpillar, *Perigea capensis* Guen, *Journal of the Bombay Natural History Society*, **78**: 2, 410-412.

Parathasarthy, R. 2002. Evaluation of baculoviruses for the management of diamondback moth, *Plutella xylostella* (L.) (Lepidoptera: Plutellidae) Ph.D. thesis (unpublished), submitted to TNAU, Coimbatore.

Parnell, M. A., King, W. J., Jones, K. A., Ketunuti, U. and Wetchakti, D. 1999. A comparison of motorized knapsack mist blower, medium volume application and spinning disk, very low volume application of *Helicoverpa armigera* nuclear polyhedrosis virus on cotton in Thailand. *Crop Protection*, **18**(4): 259-265

Patel, R. C., Singh, R, and Patel, P. B. 1968. Nuclear polyhedrosis of the gram pod borer, *Heliothis armigera*. *Journal of Economic Entomology*, **61**: 191-193.

Patil, S. B., Jayarao, K. and Khot, R. S. 1996. Bioefficacy of granulosis virus in the management of early shoot borer *Chilo infuscatellus* Snell, of sugarcane. *Bharatiya Sugar*, **22**(5): 7-10.

Pattar, G. L. Mathad, S. B. 1972. Nuclear polyhedrosis of *Antheraea mylitta* Drury (Lepidoptera: Saturniidae). *Indian Journal of Entomology*, **34**: 2.

Pawar, V. M. Waghmare, U. M and Bilapate, G. G. 1983. Studies on nuclear polyhedrosis virus infections in *Heliothis armigera* (Hubner) and *Trichoplusia ni* (Fabricius). *Journal of Entomological Research*, **5**(2): 147-151.

Pawar, V. M., Chundurwar, R. D., Thombre, U. T. and Dhawandkar, S. D. 1991. Effectiveness of NPV against *Spodoptera litura* (F.) on cabbage. *Journal of Maharashtra Agricultural Universities*, **16**(3): 430.

Pokharkar, D. S. and Jogi, R. R. 2000. Biological suppression of potato tubermoth, *Phthorimaea operculella* (Zeller) with exotic parasitoids and microbial agents under field and storage conditions. *Journal of Biological Control*, **14**(2): 23-28.

Pokharkar, D. S. and Chaudhary, S. D. 1999. Application time of nuclear polyhedrosis virus against *Helicoverpa armigera* (Hubner) on tomato. *Journal of Maharashtra Agricultural Universities*, **24**(2): 147-151.

Puri, S. N., Murthy, K. S. and Sharma, O. P. 1996. *Resource Inventory for IPM-I*, National Centre for Integrated Pest Management, ICAR, New Delhi.

Rabindra, R. J. 2000. Characterization of four geographic isolates of nuclear polyhedrosis virus of *Amsacta albistriga* by restriction endonuclease analysis *In*: S. Ignachimuthu, A. Sen and S.

Janarthanan (eds.), *Biotechnological Applications for Integrated Pest Management.* Oxford & IBH Publishing Co. Pvt.Ltd., New Delhi, pp. 49-50.

Rabindra, R. J. and Balasubramanian, M. 1980. Observations on an induced epizootic of nuclear polyhedrosis of *Amsacta albistriga* Walker. *Current Sciences*, **49**: 279.

Rabindra, R. J. and Jayaraj, S. 1988a. Efficacy of NPV with adjuvants as high volume and ultra low volume applications against *Heliothis armigera* (Hbn.) on chickpea. *Tropical Pest Management*, **34**: 441-444.

Rabindra, R. J. and Jayaraj, S. 1988b. Evaluation of certain adjuvants of NPV of *Heliothis armigera* (Hbn.) on chickpea. *Indian Journal of Experimental Biology*, **26**: 60-62.

Rabindra, R. J. and Jayaraj, S. 1988c. Larval extracts and other adjuvants for increased efficacy of nuclear polyhedrosis virus against *Heliothis armigera* larvae. *Journal of Biologicl Control*, **2**: 102-105.

Rabindra, R. J. and Jayaraj, S. 1990. Effect of nuclear polyhedrosis virus infection on the insecticide susceptibility of *Heliothis armigera* and *Spodoptera litura* larvae. *Journal of Biological Control*, **4**(1): 31-34.

Rabindra, R. J. and Jayaraj, S. 1992. Efficacy of extracts of certain host plants as adjuvants of nuclear polyhedrosis virus of *Helicoverpa armigera* Hbn. and its dust formulation. *Journal of Biological Control*, **6**: 80-83.

Rabindra, R. J. and Jayaraj, S. 1995. Management of *Helicoverpa armigera* with nuclear polyhedrosis virus on cotton using different spray equipment and adjuvants. *Journal of Biological Control*, **9**: 34-36.

Rabindra, R. J., Subramaniam, T. R., 1973. A nuclear polyhedrosis of rice moth *Corcyra cephalonica* St. (Lepidoptera: Galleriidae). *Current Science*, **42**: 21, 757.

Rabindra, R. J. and Subramaniam, T. R., 1974a. A nuclear polyhedrosis of *Dasychira mendosa* Hb. (Lepidoptera: Lymantriidae). *Current Science*, **43**: 22, 721-722.

Rabindra, R. J. and Subramaniam, T. R. 1974b. Studies on Nuclear polyhedrosis of *Heliothis armigera* (Hbn): Susceptibility and gross pathology. *Madras Agricultural Journal*, **61**: 217-220.

Rabindra, R. J. and Subramaniam, T. R. 1975a. Studies with a virus disease of red hairy caterpillar, *Amsacta albistriga* W. I. Susceptibility of gross pathology. *Madras Agriculture Journal*, **62**: 453-455.

Rabindra, R. J. and Subramaniam, T. R. 1975b. Studies with a virus disease of red hairy caterpillar, *Amsacta albistriga* W. *Madras Agriculture Journal.*, **62**: 114-117.

Rabindra, R. J., Subramaniam, T. R. 1975a. Nuclear polyhedrosis of *Plusia peponis* F. (Lepidoptera: Noctuidae). *Current Science*, **44**: 17, 634.

Rabindra, R. J. and Jayaraj, S. 1988. Control of *Heliothis armigera* on chickpea with CDA application of nuclear polyhedrosis virus in combination with endosulfan and boric acid. *Jounral of Biological Control*, **1**: 122-125.

Rabindra, R. J., Balasaraswathy, S. and Jayaraj, S. 1991. Combined use of NPV with certain botanicals for the control of *Heliothis armigera* on chickpea. *Jounral of Biological Control*, **5**: 85-87.

Rabindra, R. J., Ethiraju, S. and Jayaraj, S. 1990. Efficacy of nuclear polyhedrosis virus formulations against *Heliothis armigera* (Hbn.) on sunflower. *Journal of Biological Control*, **4**: 130-131.

Rabindra, R. J., Jayaraj, S. and Balasubramanian, M. 1986. Efficacy of nuclear polyhedrosis virus for the control of *Heliothis armigera* (Hubner) infesting sunflower. *Journal of Entomology Research*, **9**: 246-248.

Rabindra, R. J., Muthaiah, C. and Jayaraj, S. 1988. Laboratory evaluation of a CDA formulation of nuclear polyhedrosis virus against *Heliothis armigera* (Hbn.). *Journal of Entomological Research*, **12**(2): 166-168.

Rabindra, R. J, Muthuswami, M. and Jayaraj, S. 1994. Feasibility of nuclear polyhedrosis virus and *Chrysoperla carnea* Stephen use in *Helicoverpa armigera* (Hubner) management on chickpea. *Pest Management and Economic Zoology*, **2**(1): 31-34.

Rabindra, R. J., Rajasekaran, B. and Jayaraj, S. 1997. Combined action of nuclear polyhedrosis virus and neem bitter against *Spodoptera litura* (Fabricius) larvae. *Journal of Biological Control*, **11**: 1-2.

Rabindra, R. J., Sathiah, N. and Jayaraj, S. 1992. Efficacy of nuclear polyhedrosis virus against *Helicoverpa armigera* (Hbn.) on *Helicoverpa*-resistant and susceptible varieties of chickpea. *Crop Protection*, **11**(4): 320-322.

Rabindra, R. J., Muthuswami, M. and Jayaraj, S. 1994. Influence of host plant surface environment on the virulence of nuclear polyhedrosis virus against *Helicoverpa armigera* (Hbn.) (Lep., Noctuidae) larvae. *Journal of Applied Entomology*, **118**(4-5): 453-460.

Rabindra. R. J. and Arivudai Nambi, S. and Jayaraj, S. 1994. Evaluation of certain botanicals as stressors of nuclear polyhedrosis virus in larvae of *Helicoverpa armigera. J. Biol. Control*, **8**: 129-130.

Rabindra, R. J., Sathiah, N., Muthaiah, C. and Jayaraj, S. 1989. Controlled droplet application of nuclear polyhedrosis virus with adjuvants and UV protectants for the control of *Heliothis armigera* Hbn. on chickpea. *Journal of Biological Control*, **3**(1): 37-39.

Rabindra, R. J., Paul, A. V. N., David, B. V. and Subramaniam, T. R. 1975. On the nuclear polyhedrosis of *Plusia chalcytes* Esp. (Lepidoptera: Noctuidae). *Current Science*, **44**(8): 273-274.

Rabindra, R. J., Geetha, N., Renuka, S. and Regupathy, A. 1998. Occurrence of a granulosis virus from two populations of *Plutella xylostella* (L) in India. The management of Diamondback Moth and other Cruciferous pests. Proceedings of Third international workshop, Kualalumpur, Malaysia, 29 Oct. to 1 Nov. 1996. [A. Sivapragasam, W. H. Loke, A. K. Hussan and G. S. Lim (eds.)], Malaysian Plant Protection Society, 1996, pp. 113-115.

Rabindra, R. J., Jayaraj, S., Parameswaran, S., Natarajan, K. and Huger, A. M. 1990. Baculoviruses from two lepidopterans: *Eupterote cardamomi* and *Agrotis ipsilon. Current Science*, **59**: 12, 610-612.

Rabindra, R. J. Geetha, N., David Grzywacz, Margaret Brown and Jayaraj, S. 1998. Comparative efficacy of two isolates of NPV against *Helicoverpa armigera.* Abstract of papers in National Symposium on Development of Microbial Pesticides and Insect Pest Management, Bhabha Atomic Research Centre and Hindustan Antibiotics Ltd., Pune, Nov. 12-13, 1998, p. 32.

Rabindra, R. J., Swamiappan, M., Parthasarathy, R., Subramanian, S., Kennedy, J. S., Sathiah, N. and Rajasekaran, B. 2003. Isolation and DNA characterisation of a nuclear polyhedrosis virus from the looper *Boarmia* (=*Ascotis*) *selenaria* (Lepidoptera: Geometridae). *Pest Management in Horticultural Ecosystems*, **9**: 49-53.

Rabindra, R. J., Varma, R. V., Ali, M. I. and Sudheendrakumar, V. V. 1997. Tests of cross infectivity of the Nuclear polyhedrosis virus of teak defoliator. *Hyblaea purea* to some lepidopterans insects. *Pest Management in Horticultural Ecosystem*, **3**: 109-111.

Rahman, S. M., Kulkarni, K. A. and Lingappa, S. 1997. Transmission of NPV in sorghum armyworm from *Mythimna separata* from generation to generation. *Advances in Agricultural Research in India*, **7**: 87-93.

Rajagopal Babu, S., Rabindra, R. J. and Kennedy, J. S. 2001. Efficacy of granulosis virus (GV) used in conjuction with abamectin and indoxacarb in the management of *Plutella xylostella* (L.) (Yponomeutidae: Lepidoptera) on cauliflower. *The Madras Agricultural Journal*, **89**(4-6): 207-210.

Ramakrishnan, N., Chaudhari, S., Kumar, S., Rao, R. S. N. and Satyanarayanan, S. V. V. 1981. Field efficacy of nuclear polyhedrosis virus against the tobacco caterpillar, *Spodoptera litura* (F.). *Tobacco Research*, **7**: 129-134.

Ramakrishnan, N. S. and Tiwari, L. D. 1969. Polyhedrosis of *Prodenia litura.* Fabr. (Noctuidae: Lepidoptera). *Indian Journal of Entomology*, **31**: 191-192.

Rao, A. S. and Amonkar, S. V. 1980.. Nucleopolyhedrosis of *Amsacta moorei*, Buttler (Lepidoptera: Arctiidae). *Current Science*, **49**: 709-710.

Rao, R. S. N., Gunneswararao, S. and Chandra, I. J. 1987. Biochemical potentiation of nuclear polyhedrosis virus of *Spodoptera litura* (F.). *Journal of Biological Control*, **1**(1): 36-39.

Reddy, A. R. and Divakar, B. J. 2001. Effect of Robin blue on the efficacy of nuclear polyhedrosis for the management of *Helicoverpa armigera* (Hub.) in groundnut crop. *In: Perspectives in Biotechnology. Proceedings of a National Symposium, Warangal, India, 26-27 February 1999*, pp. 41-43.

Reddy, G. V. P. and Manjunath, M. 2000. Laboratory and field studies on the integrated pest management of *Helicoverpa armigera* (Hubner) in cotton, based on pheromone trap catch threshold level. *Journal of Applied Entomology,* **124**(5-6): 213-221.

Roome, R. E. 1975. Field trials with a nuclear polyhedrosis virus and *Bacillus thuringiensis* against larvae of *Heliothis armigera* (Hb.), *Bulletin of Entomological Research,* **65**: 507-514.

Sachithanandam, S., Rabindra, R. J. and Jayaraj, S 1989. Pot culture studies on the efficacy of NPV formulations against the tobacco cut worm *Spodoptera litura* (F.) larvae on groundnut. *Journal of Biological Control,* **3**(1): 44-46.

Santharam, G. 1986. Studies on the nuclear polyhedrosis virus of *Spodoptera litura* F. (Lepidoptera: Noctuidae). P.G. Thesis, Unpub., Tamil Nadu Agricultural University, Coimbatore.

Santharam, G. and Balasubramanian, M. 1980. Note on the control of *Spodoptera litura* Fabricius (Lepidoptera:Noctuidae) on tobacco with nuclear polyhedrosis virus and diflubenzuron. *Indian Journal of Agricultural Sciences,* **50**(9): 726-727.

Santharam, G. and Jayaraj, S. 1989. Studies on the transmission of nuclear polyhedrosis virus of *Spodoptera litura* (Fabricius) to its progenies. *Journal of Biological Control,* **3**(1): 40-43.

Santharam, G. and Kumaraswami, T. 1984. Nuclear polyhedrosis virus of *Agrotis ipsilon* (Hufnagel) (Noctuidae: Lepidoptera), the black cutworm of cabbage. *Current Science,* **53**: 1, 49.

Santharam, G., Regupaty, A., Easwaramoorthy, S. and Jayaraj, S. 1978. Effectiveness of nuclear polyhedrosis virus against field populations of *Spodoptera litura* Fabricius on banana. *Indian Journal of Agricultural Sciences,* **48**: 676-678.

Santharam, G., Victoria, D. R., Rabindra, R. J. and Jayaraj, S. 1994. Studies on biological control of pigeonpea pod borers in India. *Anzeiger fur Schadlingskunde, Pflanzenschutz, Umweltschutz,* **67**(5): 103-106.

Sarode, S. V., Jumade, Y. S. and Borkar, S. L. 1997. Efficacy of Heliothis nuclear polyhedrosis virus and neem seed kernel extract combinations against *Helicoverpa armigera* (Hb) on pigeonpea. *PKV Research Journal,* **21**(2): 227-229.

Sathiah, N. 2001. Studies on improving production and formulation of the Nuclear PolyhedrosisVirus of cotton bollworm *Helicoverpa armigera* (Hubner),. Ph.D. thesis Tamil Nadu Agricultural University, Coimbatore.

Sathiah, N. and Rabindra, R. J. 2001. Field efficacy of certain improved formulations of the nuclear polyhedrosis virus against the bollworm *Helicoverpa armigera* (Hubner) on cotton. *In* : *Symposium on Biocontrol based Pest Management for Quality Crop Protection in the Current Millenniun,* July 18-19, 2001, PAU, Ludhiana, pp. 82-83, 224.

Satish Kumar, Malik, V. S. and Kumar, S. 1998. Management of gram pod borer, *Helicoverpa armigera* (Hubner), by nuclear polyhedrosis virus in chickpea. *In:* G. S. Dhaliwal, R. Arora, N. S. Randhawa and A. K. Dhawan, (eds.), *"Ecological Agriculture and Sustainable Development Vol. 2. Proceedings of International Conference on Ecological Agriculture: Towards Sustainable Development, Chandigarh, India"* 15-17 November, 1997. 1998, pp. 329-333.

Satpathy, S., Samarjit Rai and Rai, S. 2000. Preliminary field evaluation of NPV and insecticides against tomato fruit borer, *Helicoverpa armigera* (Hubner). *Insect Environment,* **6**(1): 21-22.

Satpathy, S., Samarjit Rai, Chattopadhyay, M. and Rai, S. 1999. Field evaluation of NPV and insecticides against tomato fruit borer, *Helicoverpa armigera* (Hubner). *Insect Environment,* **5**: 117-118.

Sharma, M. L., Rai, H. S. and Verma, M. L. 1997. Biopesticides for management of *Helicoverpa armigera* (Hubner) in chickpea. *International Chickpea and Pigeonpea Newsletter,* No. **4**: 26-27.

Singaravelu, B. and Ramakrishnan, N. 1998. Characterization of a granulosis virus form the castor semilooper, *Achaea janata* L. *Journal of Invertebrate Pathology,* **71**(3): 227-235.

Singh, J., Sidhu, A. S., Dhindsa, M. S. and Saini, H. K. 1990. The effect of fodder cuttings on larval population, disease incidence and bird predation of *Helicoverpa armigera* in berseem. *Annals of Biology Ludhiana,* **6**(2): 153-159.

Singh, P. P., Monobrullah, M. and Singh, B. 1999. Field efficacy in some microbial pesticides against gram pod borer (*Helicoverpa armigera* Hubner) in chickpea. *Shashpa,* **6**(1): 63-66.

Sivaprakasam, N., Balasubramanian, G., Venkatesan, S and Chandrasekran, J. 1988. Control of *Spodoptera litura* F. with nuclear polyhedrosis virus and chlorpyriphos on cowpea. *Madras Agricultural Journal*, **75**(9-10): 366-368.

Somasekar, S., Jayapragasam, M., Rabindra, R. J. 1993. Characterization of five Indian isolates of the nuclear polyhedrosis virus of *Helicoverpa armigera. Phytoparasitica*, **21**(4): 333-337.

Sonalkar, V. U. and Deshmukh, S. D. 1999. Evaluation of certain adjuvants in increasing the efficacy of nuclear polyhedrosis virus against *Helicoverpa armigera* (Hub.). *Journal of Experimental Zoology*, **2**(1): 89-91.

Srinivasan, G., Sundarababu, P. C., Sathiah, N. and Balasubramanian, G. 1998. Standardization of diet for mass culturing of *Helicoverpa armigera* (Hubner) and its nuclear polyhedrosis virus. *Pest Management and Economic Zoology*, **6**(1): 49-54.

Subramanian, S. 1998. Studies on the nuclear polyhedrosis virus of *Spodoptera litura* (Fabricius). Unpublished thesis, Tamil Nadu Agricultural University, Coimbatore, India.

Sudhakar, S. and Mathavan, S. 1999. Electron microscopical studies and restriction analysis of *Helicoverpa armigera* nucleo polyhedrosis virus. *Journal of Biosciences*, **24**(3): 361-370.

Sudheendrakumar, V. V., Mohamed Ali, M. T. and Varma, R. V. 1988. Nuclear polyhedrosis virus of the teak defoliator, *Hyblaea puera. Journal of Invertebrate Pathology*, **51**: 307-308.

Suganthy, M and Kumar, S. T. 2000. Integrated pest management strategies against gram pod borer, *Helicoverpa armigera* (Hubner). *Annals of Plant Protection Sciences*, **8**(2): 136-139.

Trang, T. T. K., Chaudhari, S. and Gautam, R. D. 2002. A note on the spread of *Spodoptera litura* (Fab.) nuclear polyhedrosis virus through Cotesia (Apanteles) angaleti Muesbeck (Hymenoptera: Braconidae). *Shashpa*, **9**(1): 93-94.

Venkatesan, S., Balasubramanian, G., Babu, P. C. S. and Sivaram, M. R. 1997. Use of nuclear polyhedrosis virus and green lacewing, *Chrysoperla carnea* Stephens for *Helicoverpa armigera* (Hubner) management on sunflower. *Pest Management and Economic Zoology*, **5**(1): 63-66.

Vickers, J. M., Cory, J. S. and Entwistle, P. F. 1991. DNA characterization of eight geographic isolates of granulosis virus from the potato tuber moth (*Phthorimaea operculella*) (Lepidoptera, Gelechiidae). *Journal of Invertebrate Pathology*, **57**(3): 334-342.

Vyas, R. V., Parasharya, B. M. and Yadav, D. N. 1988. Transmission of nuclear polyhedrosis virus of *Heliothis armigera* (Lepidoptera: Noctuidae) through insectivorous birds. *Indian Journal of Agricultural Sciences*, **58**(8): 661-663.

Xinwen, C., Xiulian, S., Zhihong, H., Mei, L., Reilly, D. R. O., Zuidema, D. and Vlak, J. M. 2000. Genetic engineering of *Helicoverpa armigera* single-nucleocapsid nucleo polyhedrovirus as an improved pesticide. *Journal of Invertebrate Pathology*, **76**(2): 140-146.

9

# Potential and Effectiveness of Fungi and Bacteria as Biocontrol Agents for Plant Disease Management

**U. S. Singh, D. S. Mishra, Shekhar Varshney, Najam Waris Zaidi, Tarana & Neelam Singh**

## INTRODUCTION

Biological control is a principle of cultural control of plant pathogens that primarily involves alteration of biotic and abiotic environments from one that favours disease/ pathogen to one that discourages accumulation of infective or parasitic material and reduces the activity of the pathogen. Broadly speaking, biological control could be defined as "*any condition under which, or practice whereby, survival and activity of a pathogen is reduced through the agency of any other living organism (except man himself) with the result that there is a reduction in the incidence of disease caused by the pathogen*" (Garret, 1965). Biological control was defined by Baker and Cook (1974) as the "*reduction of inoculum density or disease producing activities of a pathogen or parasite in its active or dormant state, by one or more organisms, accomplished naturally or through manipulation of the environment, host, or antagonists, or by mass introduction of one or more antagonists*". Subsequently, they (Cook and Baker, 1983) revised the definition to '*biological control is the reduction of the amount of inoculum or disease producing activity of a pathogen accomplished by one or more organisms other than man*'.

Biological control as a strategy and philosophy for reducing crop losses from diseases is not new to agriculture. Even the earliest farmers practiced biological control by rotating their crops, burrowing disease infested crop residues and fertilizing with organic manures. These and many other traditional practices give effective disease control by allowing the time and opportunity for biological destruction of disease causing organisms. It is based on the natural phenomenon that every biological entity has its adversary in nature. Darwin had said that in the struggle for life everything is born to eat and get eaten (Stone, 1980). This maintains the biological balance under natural conditions The challenge today is how to achieve not only food security but also food safety by employing effective measures for biological control of plant pathogens in agriculture where farmers must specialize with one or two crops, use minimal or no-till to save fuel and stop soil erosion, and where organic fertilizers are unavailable, inconvenient or too expensive. Pesticides may be necessary at present but are not a long-term solution to crop health.

## HISTORICAL PERSPECTIVES

The work on biological control of plant diseases initiated during early 20th century. Ever since in 1874, W. Roberts demonstrated antagonistic action of microorganisms

*Department of Plant Pathology, College of Agriculture, G. B. Pant University of Agriculture & Technology, Pantnagar-263 145.*

in liquid cultures between *Penicillium glaucum* and bacteria and introduced word 'antagonism' (Baker, 1987), enough data have been produced to show that biological control is a feasible proposition for disease management. L. Hiltner in 1904 studied the zone of intensified microbiological activity around plant roots, and named it the 'Rhizosphere'. C. F. von Tubeuf used the term "biological control" for the first time in relation to plant pathogens in 1914 and to insect by H. S. Smith in 1919. The first attempt at control of a root disease with microorganisms introduced into the soil was by C. Hartley in 1921. In a classic study, he introduced 12 isolates of saprophytic fungi and one of bacteria and obtained significant reduction in severity of damping-off of pine seedlings caused by *Pythium debaryanum*. He found that *Pythium* inoculated in non-treated nursery soil resulted in 35.8% damping-off, but 100% in the same soil when autoclaved (Baker, 1987). The introduction of these saprophytes resulted in better initial emergence and better seedling survival. In 1926, G. B. Sanford observed that potato scab (*Streptomyces scabies*) was suppressed by green manuring through activities of antagonists. W. A. Millard and C. B. Taylor were more successful in 1927 in controlling scab of potato by adding *S. praecox* (an obligate parasite without *in-vitro* antibiosis) plus green grass clippings to sterilized soil. The discovery of Penicillin by A. Fleming in 1928 and its purification and use in medicine in 1939, greatly stimulated studies of antagonists of plant pathogens. G. B. Sanford and W. C. Broadfoot demonstrated in 1931 a "suppressive effect" on the take-all pathogen (*Gaeumannomyces graminis* var. *tritici*) in pots of sterilized soil amended with any of six fungi, fifteen bacteria, or one actinomycete. Culture filtrates of some of these microorganisms also somewhat reduced infection. A. W. Henery in 1931 reported that *Fusarium graminearum* or *Helminthosporium sativum* gave a much higher percentage of wheat plant with foot rot when inoculated into sterilized soil. Adding a trace of non-sterilized soil to sterilized pathogen inoculated soil in pots decreased infection by *H. sativum* from 47.6% to 7.8%. This experiment was the first successful transfer of a total antagonistic soil micro-flora to produce a suppressive soil. In 1932, R. Weindling reported the parasitic nature of *Trichoderma lignorum* on several plant pathogens, including *Rhizoctonia solani, Phytophthora parasitica, Pythium* spp., and *Sclerotium rolfsii*. This was the first report of use of a known antibiotic-producing antagonist in plant disease control. E. Grossbard in 1948-1952, J. M. Wright in 1952-1957, and others demonstrated that *Penicillium, Aspergillus, Trichoderma*, and *Streptomyces* spp. produced antibiotics in soil. In classical studies from 1950 to 1970 J. Rishbeth inoculated freshly cut pine stumps with the weak pathogen *Peniophora gigantea*, which prevented their invasion by the important pathogen *Heterobasidion annosum* and the spread of *H. annosum* to nearby trees. This inoculation was the first use of an introduced antagonist for commercial control of a pathogen of aerial parts, and *P. gigantea* was the first antagonist registered for biocontrol use in United States. Control is achieved by pre-emption of the cut surface by the antagonist and by hyphal interference with the pathogen. Since then, the species of fungal biocontrol agents mainly *Trichoderma* and *Gliocladium* spp. have received more attention not only against soil borne root pathogens (Chet, 1987; Chet *et al.*, 1981; Elad *et al.*, 1980) but also of foliage pathogens (Elad, 1994; Elad *et al.*, 1998 a,b; Harman, 2000). Use of bacteria to increase plant growth and yield got a poor start in Russia in the late 1950s during the Lysenko era, with extravagant claims that were critically examined by R. Cooper, E. N. Mishustin & A. N. Naumova, and by A. D. Rovira in 1959-1965. Although there appeared to be a factual base for the phenomenon, its validity was clearly established only in the 1970s (Kloepper and Schroth, 1981). The mode of action of these biocontrol agents includes all the attributes of a successful antagonist such as competition for space and nutrients on the same energy source as the pathogen, production of enzymes (glucanases, proteases and chitinases) to lyse fungal cell walls, antibiotic and inhibitory metabolite production, predatory effect or direct parasitic action against the pathogen, and indirect effect resulting in modification of the environment adverse to the pathogen (Dennis and Webster, 1971a,b). The natural populations of these antagonists are increased by organic amendment of soil. Classical studies by A. G. Lochhead and associates in 1938-1957 explored the nutritional grouping of soil and rhizosphere bacteria; the rhizosphere generally required amino acids excreted by roots, but they less stimulated the soil microflora outside the rhizosphere. An extensive series of papers by A. D. Rovira from 1956 to 1969 clarified the composition of root exudates, factors that affected their production, and their dominant influence on the rhizosphere microbiota. Some important observations in this area are as follows:

- Both resident and introduced antagonists are able to diminish plant disease (Wells *et al.*, 1972; Gindrat, 1979; Sivan and Chet, 1986; McLaren *et al.*, 1994; Desai and Schlosser, 1999).
- The ecological balance of soil microorganisms can be manipulated by modifying the organic matter content, temperature or pH of the soil (Menzies, 1959; Hornby, 1983; Ko, 1985).
- Microorganisms compete for limited available nutrients (Chet, 1987; Paulitz *et al.*, 1990; Elad *et al.*, 1998b; Harman, 2000).
- Some microorganisms may parasitize other microorganisms (Chet, 1987; Harman *et al.*, 1989; Mukherjee *et al.*, 1995a&b; Harman, 2000; Sharon *et al.*, 2001).
- Antagonists produce antibiotics that may play a part in biocontrol of plant pathogens (Mukherjee, 1991; Howell, 1998; Woo *et al.*, 1999; Elad, 2000; Gupta *et al.*, 2001).
- Some soils are naturally suppressive to some soil-borne plant pathogens, or become so following prolonged occurrence of disease caused by a pathogen (Mathre *et al.*, 1999; Harman, 2000).
- The total micro-flora of some suppressive soils can be transferred to conducive soils, making them suppressive (Menizies, 1959; Schneider, 1982; KO, 1985; Elad and Baker, 1985).
- Inoculation of a plant with a mild strain of a virus can protect it against subsequent inoculation with a more virulent strain (cross protection). Fungal and bacterial biocontrol agents may induce silent defense genes that make plant system resistant against plant pathogens {Induced Systemic Resistance (ISR)} (Kuc, 1982; 1987; 1995; Van Loon *et al.*, 1998; De Meyer *et al.*, 1998; Elad *et al.*, 1998b, 1999; Howell *et al.*, 1999; Van Wees *et al.*, 1999; Elad, 2000;

Harman, 2000). Although ISR may not provide absolute protection, it enhances tolerance of the plant towards both target and non-target diseases. It plays an important role under natural conditions to protect plants against infections (Singh *et al.*, 2002).

- Application of more than one biocontrol agents (mixed formulations) could be a reliable means of reducing the variability and increasing the reliability of biological control (Janisiewicz, 1988; Paulitz *et al.*, 1990; Datnoff *et al.*, 1993; Duffy and Weller, 1995; Duffy *et al.*, 1996; Leeman *et al.*, 1996; Hassan *et al.*, 1997; Fukui *et al.*, 1999; Guetsky *et al.*, 1998a, b, 2001).
- Genes from biocontrol agents can be a good source for improving plant resistance to pathogens (Hayes *et al.*, 1994; Lorito *et al.*, 1996a&b, 1998; Bolar *et al.*, 2000).
- Transformation of biocontrol agents with extra-genes could increase the anti-microbial activity of the strains (Flores *et al.*, 1997; Harman and Bjoorjman, 1998; Lo *et al.*, 1998; Limon *et al.*, 1995).

## BIOCONTROL AGENTS

Biocontrol agents are the one that adversely affect the population of another micro-organism (e.g. target pathogen) growing in association with them. Generally biocontrol agents have potential to interfere in the life process of pathogens both directly as well as indirectly. Biocontrol agents include virtually all classes of organisms' e.g. fungi, bacteria, nematodes, protozoa, viruses and seed plants. However, only the fungal and bacterial biocontrol agents are within the scope of this chapter.

### Fungal Biocontrol Agents

Fungi are by far the most extensively researched group of biocontrol agents. They have been used against aerial, root and soil borne pathogens. These potential biocontrol fungi are mostly saprophytic in nature and proliferate abundantly in various natural soils. However, little information is available on their ecology on the aerial surfaces. Interest in the use of biocontrol agents against aerial plant pathogens has developed more slowly than root pathogen. The important fungal biocontrol agents used against plant pathogens are:

#### *Trichoderma*

*Trichoderma* spp. (Plate 9.1) are most extensively studied fungal biocontrol agents for management of fungal pathogens. They have been also shown to be effective against nematode diseases like root knot of vegetable and rice root lesion nematode (Singh & Tarana, personal observation). They have shown excellent performance when applied to sterile soil or soil less mix in the greenhouse and also in normal field soil. Within the genus *Trichoderma* different species aggregates have been reported. These are *Trichoderma piluliferum* Webster & Rifai, *T. polysporum* (Link) Rifai, *T. virens* Gidden & Foster, *T. hamatum* (Bon.) Bain., *T. koningii* Oudem, Apud Oudem, Et Koning, *T. aureoviride* Rifai, *T. harzianum* Rifai, *T. longibrachiatum* Rifai, *T. pseudokoningii* Rifai and *T. viride* Pers.: Fr. Several commercial formulations of *Trichoderma* spp. are available in the market as mentioned in the later part of text.

Earlier *T. virens* was considered as a member of *Gliocladium* group and was named as *Gliocladium virens* (Papavizas, 1985). On purely morphological grounds, there are justifications for including *T. virens* in either *Gliocladium* or *Trichoderma*. Characteristic of *Gliocladium* is that the conidia are held in drops of liquid on a penicillus of phialides that form at the tips of branches of more or less discrete phialides. However, (i) the green conidia (ii) compact phialides (iii) essentially indeterminate conidiophores that branch at right angles that are often joined in hemispherical tufts on agar media (iv) production of chlamydospores in culture (v) the rapid growth rate and overall colony characters are indicative of *Trichoderma*. von Arx (1987), without providing justifications, transferred *G. virens* to *Trichoderma*. This placement was followed more recently by Bissett (1991a&b) in his monograph of *Trichoderma*. The result of rDNA analysis (28S rDNA) and its internal transcribed spacer (ITS) sequences supported the taxonomic usage of von Arx and of Bissett and it was shown conclusively that *T. virens* is phylogenetically distinct from the type species of *Gliocladium*, *G. penicillioides* and is in close proximity to *T. harzianum* (Rehner and Samuels, 1994; 1995; Samuels *et al.*, 1999).

### Coniothyrium

*Coniothyrium minitans* is a mycoparasite that appears to have great potential for biological control of a number of plant diseases caused by *Sclerotinia* species and *Sclerotium cepivorum*. This mycoparasite is quite common in both coarse and fine textured soils. Field tests have demonstrated conclusively that this mycoparasite has the potential to be an effective biocontrol agent. A sand-cornmeal culture of *C. minitans* mixed thoroughly into soil resulted in death of 85-90% of the sclerotia of *S. trifoliorum* within 11 week (Aylor, 1990). Two commercial formulations (Contans WG & KONI) containing this BCA are available in the world market.

### Talaromyces

*Talaromyces flavus* is a mycoparasite of *Rhizoctonia solani* and *Sclerotinia sclerotiorum*. Good control of *Sclerotinia* wilt of sunflowers was obtained when *T. flavus* and *S. scleritiorum* were buried together in the soil (McLaren *et al.*, 1994). Very little is known about the ecology of this mycoparasite in soil and much more research is needed to develop this promising fungus into a practical biocontrol agent.

### Sporidesmium

*Sporidesmium sclerotivorum* appears to be a nearly perfect biocontrol agent (BCA). In nature, the fungus behaves as an obligate parasite of sclerotia of *Sclerotinia scleritiorum, S. minor, S. trifolium, Sclerotium cepivorum* and *Botrytis cineria*. The fungus produces macroconidia, microconidia, chlamydospores, microsclerotia and mycelium in culture.

### Laetisaria

*Laetisaria* is a mycoparasite that has attracted attention as a biocontrol agent for diseases caused by *Pythium* and *Rhizoctonia* spp. This potential BCA suppressed damping-off of beets caused by *Pythium ultimum* when applied to soil at the rate of 5 or 10% (v/v). Addition of *L. arvalis* to soil at the rate of 100 sclerotia/g of soil ($2.24 \times 10^{11}$ sclerotia/ha 15 cm) gave better disease control in steamed soil than in raw soil (Adams, 1990).

### *Phlebiopsis (Peniophora)*

*Phlebiopsis gigantia* is common wood-rotting saprotroph that is applied to freshly cut stumps of pine to prevent their colonization by the root rotting fungus *Heterobasidion annosum*. It is not a biocide that kills the target organism rather it competes for the food base that the pathogen would otherwise use. Commercial products containing oidia as active material are available in the world market.

### *Ampelomyces*

It is the first biocontrol fungus developed for controlling powdery mildew. The range of plants protected includes strawberry, tomato, grape, fruit trees and ornamentals.

### *Aspergillus*

*Aspergillus flavus* has shown a great promise for the management of a number of fungal diseases in a wide range of crops (Sen, 2000). It is also reported to have growth promoting and plant resistance inducing activity. Only apprehension with this fungus is that some isolates of *A. flavus* causes seed rot in ground nut and may produce aflatoxin. It is also reported to be toxic to silkworm. Therefore, there is an urgent need to critically investigate biocontrol strain of *A. flavus* for its disease causing and mycotoxin producing ability.

### Others

Some other important fungal biocontrol agents of plant pathogens are:

<u>Biocontrol agents</u> <u>Pathogens</u>

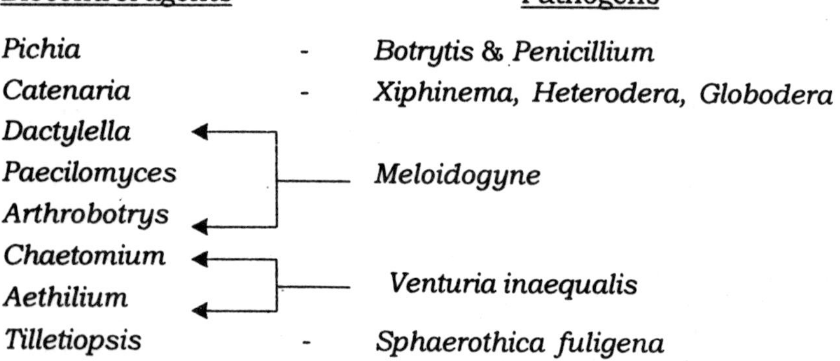


### Bacterial Biocontrol Agents

Use of bacteria for the management of plant diseases and yield improvement started in the early part of this century (Cook and Baker, 1983). However, intensified researches on biocontrol aspects accelerated in mid 1960's and experimental application in many crop pathogen systems have now been reported (Weller, 1988). There are number of positive properties with bacterial biocontrol agents such as (*i*) high bacterial population in rhizosphere/rhizoplane, (*ii*) rapid breeding potential and thus high population dynamics, (*iii*) capacity to colonize rhizosphere, (*iv*) easy to handle and manage, (*v*) easy and rapid response to external or internal treatments and above all comparatively easy to manipulate by available genetic engineering technologies (Goto, 1990; Klein, 1993). In addition, bacterial biocontrol agents produce antibiotics, siderophores, ammonia, cyanide and hydrolytic enzymes (Lam and Gaffney, 1993). They may also provide protection through induction of host plant defense mechanisms, elimination of plant signals that trigger pathogen development or competition for nutrients (Lam and Gaffney, 1993). A number of bacterial strains have so far been tried as biocontrol agents. These are:

### *Agrobacterium*

The premier example of a bacterial biocontrol agent is *A. radiobacter* strain 84, which controls crown gall caused by *A. tumefaciens* (Kerr, 1972). Strain 84 is the first bacterium used commercially for biocontrol and is successful worldwide.

### *Alkaligenes*

*Alkaligenes* sp. MFA1 isolated from the roots of carnations grown in a suppressive soil has been reported to significantly reduce wilt severity by 30% (Yuen *et al.*, 1985). It inhibits carnation root colonization and delays systemic development of the pathogen and wilt symptoms.

### *Arthrobacter*

Chitinolytic activity of *Arthrobacter* sp. has been demonstrated extensively. Introduction of *Arthrobacter* strain $P_{35}$ to the rhizosphere protected the carnation seedlings from wilt caused by *Fusarium oxysporum* f. sp. *Dianthi* (Sneh, 1981). Although the protection mechanisms of the rhizosphere chitinolytic activity may be explained by lysis of *Fusarium* hyphae, yet it might have also induced production of phytoalexins by the host resulting in increased host resistance to infection.

### *Bacillus spp.*

*Bacillus* spp. have been tested successfully for their ability to control plant diseases as well as plant growth response. Of greatest interest is *Bacillus subtilis*, tolerant to heat and desiccation and produces endospores. *B. subtilis* A13, was isolated by Broadbent *et al.* (1971) from lysed mycelium of *S. rolfsii.* Strain A13 is inhibitory *in-vitro* to several plant pathogens and has improved the growth of many plant species in steamed and natural soils (Broadbent *et al.*, 1971; Broadbent *et al.*, 1977; Yuen *et al.*, 1985). As a seed treatment it increased the yield of carrots by 48%, oats by 33% (Merriman *et al.*, 1974), and peanuts up to 37% (Turner and Backman, 1986).

### *Enterobacter*

One of the more abundant bacteria widely distributed in nature, is *Enterobacter cloacae.* Its wide application in biological control is well known. Hadar *et al.* (1983) demonstrated partial control of pea and cucumber seedling rots caused by *Pythium* spp. with *E. cloacae.* In this instance, the antagonist was not found to produce an antibiotic against *Pythium* spp. but formed a sheath around the hyphae and lysed them. Later, Howell *et al.* (1988) supported the absence of any detectable antibiotic production by *E. cloacae*. They showed that *E. cloacae* produced strong antifungal compound inhibitory to many fungi and this inhibitor was ammonia. In a different study, *E. cloacae* (isolate D-3) delayed the onset and reduced the development of rot in artificially wounded peaches inoculated with *Rhizopus stolonifer*.

### *Pseudomonas spp.*

Fluorescent *Pseudomonas* spp., make up a diverse group of bacteria that can generally be distinguished from other pseudomonads by their ability to produce water-soluble yellow green pigment. They are typically gram negative, chemoheterotrophic motile rods with polar flagella and are grouped in r-RNA homology group-I (Palleroni *et al.*, 1973). They are known to produce a large number of secondary metabolites, which may affect the growth, and health of plants (Dube, 2001). Fluorescent pseudomonads have simple nutritional requirements, and this is reflected by the relative abundance of these organisms in nature.

### *Serratia*

In a study conducted by Sneh *et al.* (1984), *Serratia liquifasciens*, a chitinolytic bacteria, provided moderate protection (56% of the control) to cucumber seedlings from *Fusarium* wilt. Chitinases produced by *S. marcecscens* have been associated with biocontrol of fungal diseases of pea and bean.

## MECHANISM OF ACTION

The biocontrol agents provide protection against plant diseases either by direct action against the pathogen (*i.e.* antagonism) and/or indirectly by reducing host susceptibility towards the pathogen (Fig. 9.1).

As an antagonist, biocontrol agent may directly kill the pathogen by mycoparasitism and/or antibiosis. It may adversely affect the growth and development of the pathogen either by antibiosis or by competing for the nutrient, oxygen or space. Antagonist like *Trichoderma* is not only capable of colonizing and killing the hyphae but also hard sclerotia of the fungal plant pathogens. Mechanism of action of different antagonists against various plant pathogens/diseases has been summarized in Table 9.1.

### Parasitism

It is an important mechanism of action of fungal biological control agents. This is a complex process involving tropic growth of the biocontrol agent towards the target organism, coiling and finally dissolution of the target organism's cell wall/cell membrane by the activity of enzymes (Weindling, 1932; Chet, 1987; Elad, 1995; Mukherjee *et al.*, 1995a&b; Sharon *et al.*, 2001). Findings within the last few years indicate that hyperparasitism is one of the main mechanisms involved in the antagonism of *Trichoderma* as a biocontrol agent (Mukhopadhyay, 1994, 1987; Howell, 1987; Mukherjee *et al.*, 1995a&b; Sharon *et al.*, 2001) (Fig 9.2). *Trichoderma harzianum exhibits* excellent mycoparasitic activity against *R. solani* hyphae whereas *T. virens* relies more on antibiosis against hyphae of this pathogen (Roy, 1977). Nature of antagonism not only depends on antagonist but also on target pathogen. Parasitism is more common against *R. solani* (Plate 9.3), while antibiosis is the predominant mechanism of antagonism against *Sclerotium* and *Fusarium* spp. (Plate 9.4). *T. harzianum* have been found to colonize second stage juveniles of *Meloidogyne* spp. It forms loops to trap nematode, coils around nematode body, penetrates by forming haustoria like structures, colonize and kills nematode (Plate 9.5 ; Singh, U.S. and Tarana, unpublished; Sharon *et al.*, 2001). Egg masses are also penetrated by hyphal growth of *T. harzianum* (Plate 9.6). Some species of *Aspergillus* also parasitize, directly on the pathogen hyphae (Chattopadhyay and Sen, 1996; Mishra, 1998; Sen, 2000).

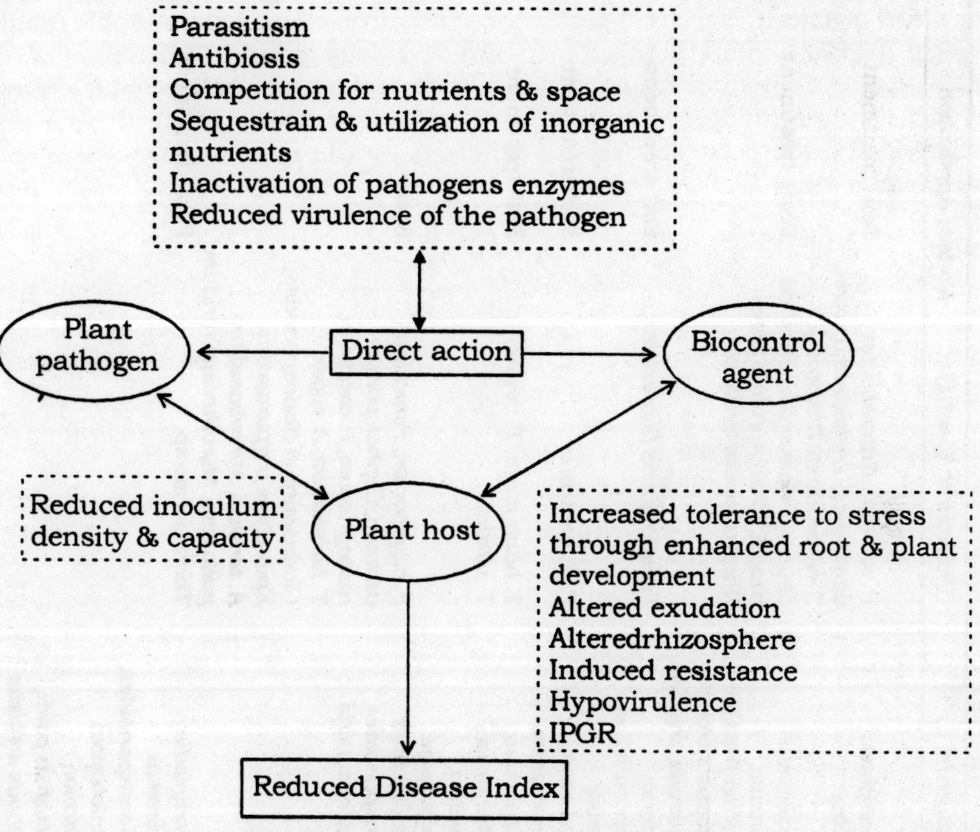


**Fig. 9.1:** Modes of action of bioagents

Numerous separate genes and gene products have been proposed to be involved in mycoparasitic interactions. Harman *et al.* (1989) tested the involvement of "chitinase and β-1,3-glucanase" in *Trichoderma* mediated biological control by inactivating these two enzymes and within each class, there are distinctly different enzymes. In 1998, Lorito listed 10 separate chitinolytic enzymes alone. Similar levels of diversity exist in β-1,3 glucanases (Benftez *et al.*, 1998). In addition β-1,6 glucanases and proteases are also likely to be involved (Geremia *et al.*, 1993; Lora *et al.*, 1995). For mycoparasitism of pythiaceous fungi, β-1,4 glucanases may also be important (Thrane *et al.*, 1997). Ait-Lahsen (2001) isolated and characterized an exo-α-1,3 glucanase (AGN 13.1) enzyme

**TABLE 9.1:** MANAGEMENT OF PLANT PATHOGENS/DISEASE BY FUNGAL AND BACTERIAL BIOCONTROL AGENTS

| *Crop* | *Disease* | *Pathogen(s)* | *Biocontrol Agent(s)* | *Mode of Application* | *Reference(s)* |
|---|---|---|---|---|---|
| **Fruit Crops** | | | | | |
| Apple | White root rot | *Dematophora necatrix* | *B. subtilis, Enterobacter aerogenes, Trichoderma viride, T. harzianum, T. virens* | Soil Treatment | Sharma and Gupta, 1996; Gupta, 2000 |
| Apple | Fruit rot | *Penicillium expansum, Monilinia fructigena, Rhizopus stolonifer, Glomerella cingulata* | *Leucosporium scotti, Candida rhaggi, Rhodotorula glutinis, Rhodosporium toruloies* | Fruit treatment | Gupta, 2000 |
| Banana | Panama disease | *Fusarium oxysporum* f. sp. *cubense* | *Pseudomonas fluorescens* | Soil treatment | Sakthivel *et al.*, 1987 |
| | Wilt | *Pseudomonas solanacearum* | *P. fluorescens* | Soil treatment | Sivamani *et al.*, 1987 |
| Citrus (Mandarin) | Root rot | *Phytophthora nicotianae* pv. *parasitica, P. colocasiae* | *T. harzianum, T. virens, T. viride* | Soil treatment | Sawant *et al.*, 1995b |
| Guava | Anthracnose | *Colletotrichum gloeosporioides, Pestalotia psidii* | *F. oxysporum, Penicillium citrinum, Cephaloporium roseogriseum, P. oxalicum, T. harzianum, A. niger, Cladosporium cladosporiodes, Epicoccum purpurascens, A. terreus, Aureobasidium pullulans, Myrothecium roridum* | Spray | Pandey *et al.*, 1993 Sharma and Gupta, 1982; Dhiman, 1993 |
| | Fruit rot | *Lasiodiplodia theobromae, C. gloeosporioides, Pestalotiopsis versicolor, Phomopsis psidi, Rhizopus arrhizus* | *Trichoderma* sp. | Fruit treatment | Majumdar and Pathak, 1995 |
| Mango | Fruit rot | *Lasiodiplodia theobromae, Rhizopus arrhinus* | *Trichoderma* spp. | Fruit treatment | Patil, 1992 |

| | | | | | |
|---|---|---|---|---|---|
| Melon | Wilt | *F. oxysporum* | *T. viride* | Seed treatment | Chattopadhyaya and Sen, 1996 |
| Muskmelon | Wilt | *F. oxysporum* | *T. harzianum* | Seed treatment | Sivan and Chet, 1986 |
| Orange | Blue mould | *Penicillium italicum* | *T. harzianum* | Fruit dip | Godara and Pathak, 2000 |
| Peanut | Seed rot | *S. rolfsii* | *P. fluorescens* | Seed treatment | Ganesan and Gnanamanickam, 1987 |
| Peanut | Collar rot | *A. niger* | *Fluorescent pseudomonads* | Seed treatment | Dileep *et al.*, 1999 |
| Plum | Fruit rot | *A. niger* | *P. fluorescens* | Fruit treatment | Ray *et al.*, 1990 |
| Strawberry | Grey mould | *B. cineria* | *T. harzianum* | Thruugh hone bees | Waraitch, 1987 |
| Watermelon | Wilt | *F. oxysporum* f. sp. *solani* | *T. viride* | Seed & Soil treatment | Fugro *et al.*, 2000 |
| **Vegetables** | | | | | |
| Bean | Seedling rot | *Phythium* sp.; *S. sclerotiorum*, *B. cineria*, *R. solani* | *T. koningii*, *G. catenulatum* | Seed treatment | Mukhopadhayay and Mukherjee, 1998 |
| Cabbage | Seed borne | *Alternaria brassicicola* | *Penicillium corylophisum* *T. virens*, *T. longiberachiatum* | Seed treatment | Bhargava, 1993 |
| | Damping off | *Rhizoctonia solani* | *T. harzianum* *Streptomyces koningii* | Seeds treatment | Das *et al.*, 2000 |
| Cauliflower | Damping-off | *R. solani*, *Phythium aphanidermatum* | *T. harzianum* *Streptomyces asenae*, *S. chibaensis* | Seed & soil treatment | Kundu and Nandi, 1993; Dohroo and Gupta, 1995 |
| Chilli | Root rot | *S. rolfsii* | *T. harzianum* | Soil treatment | Sreenivasa, 1994 |
| | Fruit rot and die back | *Colletotrichum capsici* | *T. viride*, *T. harzianum*, *T. koningii*, *T. pseudokoninqii*, *T. hamatum*, *T. longibrachiatum*, *T. pileatus*, *Fluorescent pseudomonands* | Seed and seedling treatment | Sreenivasa, 1994 |
| Egg plant | Wilt,, damping off | *F. solani*, *Pythium aphanidermatum* | *T. harzianum* *T. viride* | Seed & Soil treatment | Sheela *et al.*, 1995 |
| | Collar off | *Sclerotinia sclerotiorum* | *T. virens*, *T. viride* | Soil treatment | Phookan & chalia, 2000 |
| Fenugreek | Root rot | *R. solani* | *Trichoderma* spp. | Seed treatment | Rajan *et al.*, 1991 |
| French bean | Root rot | *R. solani* | *T. virens*, *T. harzianum*, *T. hamatum*, *T. viride*, | | Abraham Mathew and Gupta, 1998 |
| Pea | Seed and collar rot | *Pythium* sp. *R. solani* | *T. harzianum*. *T. hamatum* | Seed treatment | Harman *et al.*, 1980; Hubbard *et al.*, 1983 |
| | White rot | *Sclerotinia sclerotiorum* | *T. harzianum*, *T. viride*, *T. virens* | Soil treatment | Sharma and Singh, 1990 |

Table 9.1 (*contd. on* p. 168)

Table 9.1 (*contd. from* p. 167)

| Potato | Bacterial wilt | *P. solanacearum* | *P. flurescens* | Seed treatment | Sekhawat *et al.*, 1993 |
|---|---|---|---|---|---|
| | Black scurf | *R. solani* | *T. virens. T. viride* | Tuber treatment | Bari and Mukhopadhyay 1988 |
| Radish | Seedling rot Damping off | *Pythium* ap., *R. solani* | *T. harzianum, T. hamatum* | Seed treatment | Harman *et al.*, 1980 |
| | Seed rot | *R. solani* | *T. harzianum* | Seed treatment | Marshal, 1982 |
| Tomato | Damping off | *Pythium indicum* | *T. viride, T. harazianum* | Seed & soil treatment | Krishnamoorthy and Bhaskaran, 1990 |
| | Grey mould | *B. cineria* | *T. harzianum* | Foliar spray | Elad, 2000 |
| | Wilt | *Pseudomonas solanacearum* | *Penicillium purpurescens* | Soil treatment | Krishnamoorthy and Bhaskaran, 1990 |
| | Damping off | *Pythium aphanidermatum, R. solani* | *T. viride, T. koningii, T. pseodokoningii* and *P. fluorescens* | Seed & soil treatment | Hadwan and Khara, 1990; Dinakoran and Ramakrishnan, 1996 |
| | Seedling disease and wilt | *F. oxysporum f.* sp. *lycopersici* | *Trichoderma* sp., *Pseudomonas* sp. | Seed treatment | Padmodya and Reddy, 1996; 1998 |
| | Root knot | *Meloidogyne incognita, M. javanica* | *T. harzianum, Paecilomyces lilacinus, Beauveria bassiana, Paecilomyces lilacinus, Verticillium lacanii* | Soil treatment | Sharon *et al.*, 2001 |
| **Oil Seed Crops** | | | | | |
| Groundnut | Wilt complex seed rot | *Sclerotium rolfsii, F. solani, F. oxysporum, S. rolfsii* | *T. harzianum, T. virens, T. viride, P. fluorescens* | Soil treatment | Ganeshan and Gnanamanickam, 1987; Mukhopadhyay *et al.*, 1992 |
| | Root and stem rot | *R. solani* | *T. virens, T. longibrachiatum* | Soil treatment | Bhattacharya and Mukherjee, 1990; Sreenivasaprasad and Manibhusanrao, 1993; Maheswari and Ramakrishanan, 1994 |
| | Leaf rust | *Puccinia arachidis* | *Acremonium obclavatum, Myrothecium verrucaria, Fusarium solani, T. harzianum* | Spray | Gowda and Balasubramanian, 1991; 1993 |
| | Collar rot Root rot crown rot Stem rot Pod rot | *A. flavus, S. rolfsii, A. niger* | *T. harzianum, T. viride, T. viride* | Soil treatment | Ebenezar *et al.*, 1996 1991; Kartikeyyan, 1996; Rajappan *et al.*, 1996; Muthamilan and Jeyarajan, 1996 |

| | | | | | |
|---|---|---|---|---|---|
| Mustard | Damping off | *Pythium aphanidermatum,* | *T. harzianum, T. viride,* | Seed & soil treatment | Ebenezar *et al.*, 1996 |
| Safflower | Root blight | *M. phaseolina* | *T. viride,* | Soil treatment | Prashanthi *et al.*, 1997 |
| Seasamum | Blight | *Phytophthora* sp. | *T. harzianum, T. viride, P. fluorescens* | Seed treatment | Jharia and Singh, 2000 |
| | Root rot | *M. phaseolina* | *T. harzianum, T. viride, T. longibrachiatum, T. virens* | Seed & soil treatment | Gaikwad and Kapgate, 1990; Gupta and Cheema, 1990 |
| Sunflower | Blight | *Alternaria helianthii* | *T. virens* | Seed treatment | Narayan and Behira, 2000 |
| | Rust | *Puccinia helianthii* | *Pseudumonas* spp. | Foliar spray | Patil *et al.*, 2000 |
| | Root/collar rot | *Sclerotium rolfsii, R. solani, Sclerotinia sclerotiorum* | *T. harzianum, T. hamatum, P. fluorescens, P. putida,* | Seed treatment | Prasad *et al.*, 1999; Rangeshwaran and Prasad, 2000b |
| **Fibre Crops** | | | | | |
| Cotton | Bacterial blight | *Xanthomonas capmpestris* pv. *malvacearum* | *P. fluorescens; P. putida, P. alcaligenes,* Bacteriophages | Spray | Verma *et al.*, 1983; Sakthivel *et al.*, 1987 Verma *et al.*, 1983 |
| | Damping-off (Post emergence) | *R. solani* | *P. fluorescens* | – | Alagesaboopathi, 1994; Laha and Verma, 1998 |
| | Root rot | *M. phasiolina* | *T. harzianum, T. virens* | Seed treatment | Gangopadhyay and Joshi, 2000; Mongia and Sheoraj, 2000 |
| | Wilt | *F. oxysporum* f. sp. *vasinfectum, S. rolfsii, R. solani* | *T. harzianum,* fluorescent pseudomonads | – | Laha *et al.*, 1992; Katragadda and Murugesan, 1996 |
| **Plantation crops** | | | | | |
| Aracanut palm | Fruit rot | *Phytophthora* spp. | *Asperigillus terreus Myrothecium verrucaria Trichoderma* spp.; *Pseudomonas fluorescens* | Fruit treatment | Saraswathy, 2000 |
| Coffee | Collar rot | *R. solani* | *T. harzianum* | Seed & Soil treatment | Venkatasubbaiah and Safeeulla, 1984; Venkatasubbaiah, 1985 |
| Mulberry | Leaf spot | *Cercospora moricola* | *T. harzianum, T. viride* | Foliar spray | Shivapratap *et al.*, 1996 |

Table 9.1 (*contd. on* p. 170)

Table 9.1 (*contd. from* p. 169)

| | | | | | |
|---|---|---|---|---|---|
| | Stem canker & die-back | *Botryodiploidia* spp. | *T. harzianum, T. virens, T. pseudokoningii* | Cutting and Soil treatment | Gupta and Sarkar, 2000 |
| | Cutting rot | *F. solani* | *T. harzianum, T. virens, T. pseudokoningii* | Cutting and soil treatment | —do— |
| | Collar rot | *Phoma sorghina* | *T. harzianum, T. virens, T. pseudokoningii* | Cutting and soil treatment | —do— |
| Rubber | Brown root | *Phellinus noxius* | *T. harzianum, T. viride, T. hamatum* | Soil treatment | Jacob *et al.*, 1991 |
| **Sugar Crops** | | | | | |
| Sugarbeet | Damping off | *Phythium aphanidermatum* | *T. harzianum, T. viride,* | Soil treatment | Sawant and Mukhopadhyay, 1991 |
| | Root rot/wilt | *S. rolfsii* | *T. harzianum,* | Soil treatment | Upadhayay and Mukhopadhyay, 1986 Waraitch, 1987 |
| Sugarcane | Red rot | *Collectotrichum falcatum* | *T. harzianum, T. virode, P. fluorescens* | Soil treatment and Spray | Sharma and Gupta, 1982, Sharma and Sinha, 1982 |
| | Seedling rot | *Pythium graminicola* | *T. viride* | Soil treatment | Padmanabhan and Alexander, 1983 |
| | Wilt | *F. moniliformae* | *T. harzianum, T. viriede, T. longibrachiatum,* | Soil treatment | Gohil and Vala, 1996, |
| | Rust | *Puccinia melanocephala,* | *Mycodiplosia* sp. | Spray | Kapadia *et al.*, 1997 |
| **Condiments, Spices, Narcotics, Stimulants, etc.** | | | | | |
| Cardamom | Capsule rot | *Phytophthora meadii* | *T. harzianum, T. viride* | Soil treatment | Bhai *et al.*, 1994 |
| | Damping-off | *Fusarium moniliforme, Pythium vexans, Rhizoctonia* sp., *Pythium aphanidermatum* | *Glomus fasciculatum T. harzianum, T. viride* | Soil treatment | Mani and Marimuthu, 1994; Thomas *et al.*, 1994, 2000 |
| Coriander | Wilt | *F. oxysporum* f. sp. *corianderii* | *T. viride, T. harzianum, P. fluorescens* | Seed treatment | Ghandhikumar and Rangnathan, 2000b. |
| Ginger | Rhizome rot | *F. oxysporm* f. sp. *zingiberi* | *T. harzianum, G. virens* | Rhizome treatment | Sharma and Dohroo, 1991 |

| | | | | | |
|---|---|---|---|---|---|
| | Rhizome rot | *Pythium pleroticu, f. equiseti, Pythium myriothylum, F. solani* | *T. viride* | Seed treatment | Dohroo and Sharma, 1984; Rathore *et al.*, 1992 |
| | Yellows | *F. oxysporum* f. sp. *zingiberi* | *T. harzianum, T. virens, T. hamatum* | Seed treatment | Dohroo, 1995 |
| | Rhizome rot | *S. rolfsii, Fusarium solani, Pythium* sp. | *T. harzianum, Tricoderma* sp. *T. virens, P. fluorescens* | Soil treatment | Rem *et al.*, 1997 Mukherjee *et al.*, 1997 |
| Pepper | Collar rot | *Phytophthora capsici* | *T. virens, Trichoderma* spp. | Spray | Anandraj and Sharma, 1994; Jubina and Girija, 1998 |
| Poppy | Downy mildew | *Peronospora arborescens* | | Seed treatment | |
| Tea | Brown light disease | *Glomerella cingulata* | *A. nidulans, A. niger Penicillium oxalicum, Pseudomonas* sp. *Flavobacterium, Bacillus Micrococcus, Alcaligenes, Aureobacterium* spp. | | Bezbarruah and Patgiri, 1992; Chakraborthy *et al.*, 1994 |
| Tobacco | Damping off | *Pythium aphanidermatum* | *T. harzianum* | Seed treatment | Patel *et al.*, 1996 |
| **Cereals** | | | | | |
| Barley | Foot and root rot | *Sclerotium rolfsii, Fusarium, Curvularia, Pythium, Aspergillus, Penicillium* | *T. viride, T. pseudokoningii* | Seed treatment | Bari *et al.*, 2000 |
| | Leaf spot | *Alternaria alternata* | *Sterptomyces rochei* | Spray | Sharma and Gupta, 1982 |
| Maize | Charcoal rot, Banded blight | *M. phaseolina, R. solani* | *Trichoderma spp.* | Seed treatment and foliar spray | Singh and Kaiser, 1996 |
| Rice | Blast | *Magnaporthe grisea* | *Pseudomonas fluorescens* | Spray | Vidhyasekaran, *et al.*, 1997 |

Table 9.1 (*contd. on* p. 172)

Table 9.1 (*contd. from* p. 171)

| | | | | | |
|---|---|---|---|---|---|
| | Bacterial leaf blight | *Xanthomonas Compestris* pv. *oryzae* | *Pseudomonas acidovorus, A. ochraceus, A. flavus, A. niger Fusarium pollidoroseum, F. chalamydosporum, P. fluorescens, Bacillus megaterium, B. subtilis, Erwinia herbicola* | Seed treatment and foliar spray | Islam Andnandi, 1985; Anuratha and Gnanamanickam, 1987; Gajbe and Lanjewar, 1991; Saikia and Chawdhury, 1993; Sindhan *et al.*, 1997a |
| | Banded blight | *R. solani* | *T. virens, T. harzianum, T. viride* | Seed, Soil, Seedling treatment | Gnanamanickam *et al.*, 1990, 1992; Dubey, 1998 |
| | Kernel smut | *Tilletia barclayana* | *T. harzianum, T. viride, T. virens, T. deliquescens* | – | Sharma *et al.*, 2000 |
| | Bunt | *Neovossia indica* | *T. harzianum, T. viride, T. virens, T. deliquescens* | Seed treatment | Sharma *et al.*, 2000 |
| | Brown spot | *Drechaslera oryzae* | *T. viride* | Seed treatment | Kumar and Mishra, 194 |
| | Sheath blight | *R. solani* | *T. viride, T. harzianum, A. terreus T. longibrachiatum, T. aureoviride, P. fluorescens, P. putida* | Soil treatment, seed treatment and foliar spray | Gokullapalan and Nair, 1992; Bhuyan *et al.*, 1994; Das *et al.*, 1995a, b; Gogoi and Roy, 1996; Mishra and Sinha, 1997, 2000a, c; Mishra, 1998 |
| | Brown spot | *Cochliobolus miyabianus* | *P. fluorescens* | Spray | Nanda and Gangopadhyay, 1983; Ray *et al.*, 1990 |
| | Sheath rot | *Sarocladium oryzae* | *P. fluorescens* | Seed treatment | Sakthivel *et al.*, 1987; Sakthivel and Gnanamanickam, 1986 1987 |
| Sorghum | Seed pathogens | *A. flavus, A. niger, Alternaria, Cladosporium, Collectotricum, Curvularia lunata, Exserohilum, F. moniliforme, Phoma sogina* | *T. harzianum, T. viride* | Seed treatment | Deshmukh *et al.*, 1994 |
| Wheat | Root rot | *S. rolfsii,* f. *oxysporum* | *T. harzianum* | Seed & Soil treatment | Sivan and Chet, 1986 |

| | | | | | |
|---|---|---|---|---|---|
| | Take-all | *Gaeumanomyces graminis* var. *tritici* | *T. harzianum, P. fluorescens* | Seed treatment | Weller, 1988 |
| | Karnal bunt | *Neovossia indica* | *T. viride, T. harzianum, T. koningii T. virens, T. deliquescens,* *Fluorescent pseudomonads* | Seed treatment | Sharma *et al.*, 1996, Amer *et al.*, 1998, Aggarwal *et al.*, 2000, Singh and Srivastava, 2000, Aggarwal, 2000 |
| | Loose smut | *Ustilago segatum* | *T. viride, T. koningii, T. harzianum, T. virens, T. deliquescens, Fluorescent pseudomonads* | Seed treatment | Sharma *et al.*, 1996, Amer *et al.*, 1998, Aggarwal *et al.*, 2000, Singh and Srivastva, 2000, Aggarwal, 2000 |
| Wheat | Loose smut | *Ustilago segatum tritici* | *T. viride, T. koningii, T. harzianum, T. lignorum, P. fluorescens* | Seed treatment | Mondal *et al.*, 1996, Aggarwal, 2000; Selvakumar *et al.*, 2000 |
| Wheat | Spot blotch | *Drechslera srokiniana* | *T. reesei, T. pseudokoningii, T. viride, Talaromyces flavus, Chaetomium globossum, Triocholthesium roseum* | Spray | Mondal *et al.*, 1996, Selvakumar and Srivastva, 2000 |
| **Flowering Plants** | | | | | |
| Gladiolus | Yellows and Corm rot | *F. oxysporum gladiolii* | *T. virens* | Corm and soil treatment | Mishra, 1996 |
| Jasmine | Root rot | *M. phaseolina* | *T. harzianum, T. viride* | Cutting treatment | Alice *et al.*, 1996 |
| Rose | Grey mould | *Botrytis cinera* | *T. harzianum, T. viride, P. fluorescens* | Spray | Prasad *et al.*,, 1998 |
| **Pulse** | | | | | |
| Blackgram | Dry root rot | *Macrophomina phaseolina* | *Trichoderma harzianum* | Soil treatment | Mani and Marimuthu, 1994 |
| | Damping-off | *Sclerotium rolfsii* | *T. viride* | Seed treatment | Pande, 1985 |
| Chickpea | Wilt, Seed rot, Root rot | *F. oxysporum* f. sp. *ciceris, R. bataticola, Pythium* sp. | *P. fluorescens* NBRI 1303, *T. harzianum a. flaviceps, Penicillium funiculosum, Bacillus* sp. *Paecilomyces lilacinus, A. niger, Epicoccum purpurascens* | Seed & soil treatment | Haral and Konde, 1983; Parakhia and Vaishnav, 1986; Nautiyal, 1997; Vidhyasekaran Muthamilan, 1995; Singh *et al.*, 1997 |
| | Wilt-complex | *F. oxysporum* f. sp. *ciceris, R. solani, S. rolfsii* | *P. fluorescens, T. virens, T. harzianum, T. viride* | Seed & soil treatment | Kaur and Mukhopadhyay, 1992; Mukhopadhyay *et al.*, 1995 |

Table 9.1 (*contd. on* p. 174)

Table 9.1 (*contd. from* p. 173)

| | | | | | |
|---|---|---|---|---|---|
| | Root-rot complex | *Meloidogyne incognita, M. phaseolina* | *Paecilomyces lilacinus, A. flavus, A. niger, Alternaria brassicicola, Alternaria triticina, F. solani Pseudomonas fluorescens Coryophilum, B. subtilis, Curvularia tuberculata Pseudomonas, Coryophilum, B. subtilis, Curvularia tuberculata* | Seed & soil treatment | Siddiqui and Mahmood, 1993 ab; 1995b |
| | Gray mould | *Botrytis cineria* | *Trichoderma* sp. | Spray | Mukherjee and Haware, 1993; Mukherjee *et al.*, 1995, 1997 |
| | Collar rot | *S. rolfsii, R. solani* | *T. harzianum, T. viride* | Seed treatment | Sugha *et al.*, 1993; Prasad and Rangeswaran, 1997 |
| | Seed & root rot | *R. solani, M. phaseolina, F. oxysporum, Aspergillus* sp., *Curvularia* sp., *Pythium aphanidermatum* | *Pseudomonas* sp., | Seed treatment | Nagina and Dadarwal, 1997 |
| | Root rot | *Fusarium solani and M. phaseolina* | *T. viride, T. harzianum, T. harzianum, P. fluorescens* | Seed and soil treatment | Jayarajan *et al.*, 1993 |
| | Stem rot | *Sclerotinia sclerotiorum* | *T. harzianum* | Seed treatment | Sharma *et al.*, 1999 |
| | Wilt complex | *Meloidogyne incognita, F. oxysporum* | *Glomus fasciculatum* | Soil treatment | Rao and Krishnappa, 1995 |
| | Wilt | *F. oxyporum* f. sp. *ciceris* | *T. virens, T. harzianum, T. viride* | Seed treatment | De *et al.*, 1996 |
| Cowpea | Bacterial blight | *Xanthomonas campestris* pv. *vignicola* | *A. flavus, A. fumigatus, Epicoccum, nigrum, F. equiseti, Penicillium citrinum, Penicillium oxalium, Rhizopus oryzae B. subtilis, Enterobacter cloacae, Erwinia herbicola, Flavobacterium* sp., *Micrococcus luteus P. ocidovorans, P. fluorescens* | Seed treatment | Jindal and Thind, 1990; 1993 |

| | | | | | |
|---|---|---|---|---|---|
| | Seed-borne | *Xanthomanas campestris* pv. *vignicola* | *Aceitobacter calcoaceticus, Erwinia herbicola, P. acidovorans, Fusarium semitectum P. oxalicum, Trichothecium roseum P. acidovorans, P. oxalicum* | Seed treatment | Jindal and Thind, 1990 |
| | Anthracnose | *Colletotricum lindemuthianum* | *Penicilium* sp., *Pestalotiopsis* sp. | –do– | Naik and Anil Kumar, 1992 |
| | Wilt | *Fusarium oxysporum* f. sp. *tracheiphilum* | *T. harzianum* and *T. viride* | Seed treatment | Ushamalini *et al.*, 1997b |
| Green gram | Leaf spot | *P. oxalicum, canmpestris* pv. *vignaeradiatae* | *Xanthomonas Flavobacterium* sp. *Erwinia herbicola, Serratia marcescens, Rhizopus oryzae* | Spray | Jindal and Thind, 1994 |
| Horse gram (chickpea) | Damping-off | *M. phaseolina* | *T. viride* | Seed & soil treatment | Pandey, 1985 |
| Lentil | Wilt comples; *Collar rot* | *R. solani, F. oxysporum, S. rolfsii* | *T. virens* | Seed treatment | Agarwal *et al.*, 1977; Mukhopadhyay *et al.*, 1992 |
| Moth bean | Blight | *M. phaseolina* | *T. harzianum, T. viride* | Foliar spray | Majumdar and Singh, 1995; Majumdar *et al.*, 1996 |
| Mung bean | Root rot | *M. phaseolina* | *T. viride, T. harzianum* | Seed & Soil treatment | Kehri *et al.*, 1991;. Ranghuchander *et al.*, 1993 |
| | Bacterial leaf spot | *Xanthomonas campestris* pv. *vignae radiatae* | *Erwinia herbicola, Flavobacterium* sp., *Micrococcus luteus, Serratia marcescens, Pencillium oxalicum, Epicocum purpurascens, T. harzianum, T. viride* | Spray | Bora *et al*, 1993 |
| Pigeon pea | Seed borne disease | *Alternaria alternata, Cladosporium, Curvularia lunatra* | *T. viride* | Seed treatment | Lokesh *et al.*, 1987 |
| | Seed borne fungi | *A. flavus, A. niger, Penicillium* sp. | *T. harzianum, T. longibrachiatum* | Seed treatment | Nakkeeran and Devi, 1997 |

Table 9.1 (*contd. on* p. 176)

Table 9.1 (*contd. from* p. 175)

| | | | | | |
|---|---|---|---|---|---|
| | | *Cladosporium* sp. *Rhizopus stoloniter, Alternaria alternata, M. phaseolina, F. udum* | | | |
| | Wilt | *F. udum* | *T, viride T. hamatum, T. harzianum, T. koningii,* | Seed & seedling treatment | Chakraborthy and Gupta, 1995; Bhatnagar, 1996; Somasekhara *et al.* 1996; Bidari and Gundappagol, 1997 Prasad and Rangeshwaran, 2000 |
| | Wilt complex | *Heterodera cajani* and *F. udum* | *T. harzianum* | Seed & soil treatment | Siddiqui and Mahmood, 1995a; Sumitha and Gaikwad, 1995 |
| **Others** | | | | | |
| Betelvine | Foot and root rot | *Phytophthora parasitica* var. *piperina* | *T. viride* | Soil treatment | Chaurasia and Bhatt, 2000. |
| Casuarina | Root-rot | *Rhizoctonia solani* | *Trichoderma* sp. *Frankia* sp. (Actinomycete) | Seed treatment | Gopinathan, 1995 |
| Chir pine | Damping-off | *F. solani* | *T. viride* | Soil treatment | Kuma, 1993 |
| Finger millet | Blast | *Magnaporthe grisea* | *P. fluorescens* | Spray | Sitther and Gnanamanickha, 1996 |
| Menthol mint | Stolon decay | *Sclerotinia sclerotiorum* | *T. harzianum, T. virens* | Sucker treatment | Singh *et al.*, 2000 |
| Moth bean | Blight | *M. phaseolina* | *T. harzianum, T. viride* | Foliar spray | Majumdar and Singh 1995; Majumdar *et al.*, 1996 |
| Passion fruit | Collar rot | *R. solani* | *T. harzianum, Trichoderma* spp. | Seed treatment | Sawant *et al.*, 1995a |
| Pearl millet | Ergot | *Claviceps fusiformis* | *T. viride, T. harzianum, T. virens* | Soil treatment | Mohan and Jeyarajan, 1990 |
| Coffee | Collar rot | *R. solani* | *T. harzianum* | Seed & soil treatment | Venkatasubbaiah and Safeeulla, 1984 |

from *T. harzianum* that degrade α- glycosidic linkages of polysaccharides of cell wall of fungi. To add even more complexity, peptibol antibiotics are specifically produced by *T. harzianum* in the presence of fungal cell walls, so they probably also should be considered as part of the mycoparasitic complex (Schirmbock *et al.*, 1994). Zeilinger *et al.*, (1999) reported that the regulation of individual genes presumably involved in mycoparasitism differs in their function. They showed that the 42-kDa endochitinase is induced before *T. harzianum* comes into contact with *Botrytis cineria*, while the 72-kDa N-acetylhexosaminidase is induced only after the two fungi are in direct contact. Therefore, a single step in the mycoparasitic process of *T. harzianum* may involve more than 20 separate genes and gene products under complex regulatory control. Most of these gene products are synergistic with one another (Lorito, 1998). Given this entire arsenal of synergistic gene products that are part of only one mechanism by which *Trichoderma* species attack and gain nutrition from other fungi, it is not surprising that this genus has been reported to be pathogenic against, and provide control of, very diverse groups of fungi (Chet, 1987; Harman, 2000). Nevertheless recent studies have demonstrated some degree of host specificity in different isolates of *T. harzianum*. Some isolates may be highly effective against one fungal plant pathogen while exhibiting poor efficacy against other pathogens. In one of the study most effective isolates of *T. harzianum* against *R. solani, S. rolfsii, Macrophomina phaseolina* and *Fusarium* were found to be different.

## Non-parasitic Actions

### *Antibiosis*

The antagonistic organisms release antibiotics and other metabolites that are harmful to the pathogen and inhibit their growth. Many antibiotics have been isolated and characterized from fungal as well as bacterial biocontrol agents. These include gliotoxin and glyoviridin from *T. virens* (Sharma and Dohroo, 1991; Sivan and Chet, 1989); viridin, alkyl pyrones, isonitriles, polyketides, peptaibols, diketopiperazines, sesquiterpenes and some steroids from *Trichoderma* spp. (Upadhyay and Mukhopadhyay, 1986; Howell, 1998); compounds of hydroxamate and catecholate group e.g. -trans & *-cis*-4-(3-acetoxy-6-methoxy-2-hydroxyphenyl)-2-methoxy-butanolide, etc. from *Aspergillus* spp. (Sen, 2000) and some from bacterial biocontrol agents like pyoverdin, 2, 4-diacetylphloroglucinol from *Pseudomonas fluorescens*, azotobactin from *Azotobacter vinclandii*, agrobactin from *Agrobacterium tumifaciens*, agrocin-84 from *Agrobacterium radiobacter* (Jones and Kerr, 1989; Dube, 2001; Gupta *et al.*, 2001), rhizobactin from *Rhizobium meliloti* (Parasher *et al.*, 1992b; Johari *et al.*, 1997). These antibiotics are effective against a large number of plant pathogens. A particular antibiotic that may be important in activity of one strain may not even be produced by another highly effective strain of biocontrol agent. Some mutants developed without activity of a specific component expected to be involved in biocontrol, have shown more activity than the parental strain (Mukherjee, 1991; Rajappan *et al.*, 1996; Woo *et al.*, 1999). These mutants may develop the ability to produce different antibiotics/metabolites, which may be due to arising of an alternate biosynthetic pathway of antibiotic by mutations, to produce a new product. So, it may be assumed that there are several silent pathways for production of antibiotics and mutation may suppress/eliminate or activate these pathways. This alternation of expression indicates that biocontrol agents have genes that may only be expressed if some changes in regulatory processes occur. Therefore, studies with knockout mutants, no matter how carefully the study is done to avoid changes to other than the gene of interest, may identify the phenomena that act, by analogy, like "snake's teeth." If a snake's fang are lost or removed, others take their place, if activity of one gene is deleted and a mechanism of biocontrol is lost, another may take its place.

### *Siderophoress*

Siderophores (Gr. "iron-bearers") are defined as 'low molecular weight, virtually ferric specific legends, the biosynthesis of which is carefully regulated by iron and the function of which is to supply iron to the cell' (Neilands, 1981). The structural diversity among the different siderophores is quite considerable and depends on the producing microorganisms. However, a common feature of all siderophores is that they form six coordinate octahedral complexes with ferric iron (Raymond *et al.*, 1984). Iron is generally present in the microbial environment as the ferric ion ($Fe^{+3}$), which is virtually insoluble in the presence of $O_2$ and therefore, is not available for microbial growth. Siderophore chelate Fe (III) and microbial membrane receptor proteins specifically recognize and take-up the siderophore-Fe-complex (Neilands, 1981; Leong, 1986; Hemming, 1986; Neilands and Leong, 1986). This results in making iron unavailable to rhizosphere microorganisms, including plant pathogens, which produce less or different siderophores with lower binding coefficients. The result is less pathogen infection and biological control.

Soil pseudomonads generally produce fluorescent, yellow green, water-soluble siderophores with both a hydroxamate and phenolate group. Siderophores from different fluorescent pseudomonads strains have shown that the principal difference is the composition, number, and configuration of the amino acids in the peptide backbone (Neilands and Leong, 1986). The production of these siderophores has been linked to the disease suppression ability of certain fluorescent *Pseudomonas* spp. (Loper and Buyer, 1991). Altman (1970) first suggested the involvement of these compounds in plant growth promotion and disease suppression by these strains. However, the first real substantiation of this concept was studied by Kloepper *et al.*, (1980) who isolated fluorescent siderophores from strain B-10 and showed its disease suppression ability.

Different fungi are also reported to produce siderophores involved in iron uptake and these are commonly short peptides containing non-protein amino acids. *T. virens* produces three types of hydroxamate siderophores: a monohydroxamate (*cis*-and trans-fusarinines), a dipeptide of *trans*-fusarinine (dimerum acid), and a trimer disdepsipeptide (copragen) (Lorito *et al.*, 1993b). *Aspergillus niger* strain AN-27 is reported to produce hydroxamate and catecholate groups of siderophores that helps in improving antagonistic activities, rhizosphere competence and plant growth (Mondal *et al.*, 1999a; Sen, 2000).

### *Competition*

Competition is considered as a 'classical' mechanism of biological control. It involves competition between antagonist and plant pathogen for space and nutrients (Chet, 1987). It seems to be an important mechanism of biocontrol, but it is difficult to assess its actual contribution in biological control. This mechanism is assumed to be involved if no evidence for mycoparasitism or antibiosis is found in a particular interaction (Alexander, 1982; Cook and Baker, 1983). Pseudomonads catabolize diverse nutrients and have fast generation times in the root zone and, they are logical candidates for biological control by competition for nutrients, especially against the slow growing pathogenic fungi (Weller, 1988). Suslow and Schroth (1982) reported that PGPR prevented deleterious bacteria from colonizing sugar beet to their full potential presumably because the PGPR occupied and excluded deleterious rhizobacteria from cortical cell junctions, at which exudation of nutrients is maximal. Competition for infection sites by fluorescent pseudomonads was implicated as a mechanism for biological; control by Osburn *et al.* (1989). Paulitz (1990), in his review on "biochemical and ecological aspects of competition" has given in depth account of competition for nutrients and infection sites on root surface. O'Sullivan and O'Gara (1992) suggested that nutrient completion varies at different rhizosphere depending on the available sources of C, N, S, phosphates and other micronutrients.

The omnipresence of *Trichoderma* in agricultural and natural soils throughout the world proves that it must be an excellent competitor for space and nutritional resources. Elad *et al.*, (1999) presented the information regarding biocontrol of *B. cineria* by *T. harzianum* strain T-39. *B. cineria* conidia require external nutrients for germination and infection. When conidia of T-39 were applied to leaves, germination of the pathogens conidia was slowed, an effect attributed in part to competition (Elad, 2000). The competitive ability of *Trichoderma* and thus its biocontrol potential has shown to be affected by soil properties. Weindling (1934) noted that pH affected the relative value of *Trichoderma* as an effective antagonist to *R. solani* by affecting the growth and development of each fungus. Backman *et al.* (1975) showed that when fungicides toxic to *Trichoderma* were applied for peanut spot control, there was an increase in disease caused by *Sclerotium rolfsii*, a pathogen susceptible to biocontrol by *Trichoderma*. Thus there was a wide array of factors that affect *Trichoderma's* competitive ability to be present and active as a biocontrol agent. Papavizas (1985) indicated that soil antagonism plays a direct role in reducing the efficacy of *Trichoderma* as a biocontrol agent.

### *Induction of Systemic Resistance (ISR)*

Elicitation of resistance in plants by biocontrol agents is becoming a more researched topic amongst scientists (Bailey and Lumsden, 1998). Some strains of bacterial biocontrol agent like *Pseudomonas* are clearly potent inducers of systemic resistance responses in plants (Van wees *et al.*, 1999; Meena *et al.*, 2000). The evidence for involvement of psudomonads in ISR was observed when lipopolysaccharides extracted from the outer membrane of *P. fluorescens* caused more accumulation of phytoalexins, increased amount of salicylic acid, phenolics and pathogenesis related (PR) proteins. Bacterial lipopolysaccharides contributes to growth and survival of bacteria in plants by aiding colonization in creating a favourable micro-environment, acting as a barrier to plant defensive compounds, and by modulating host reactions. Siderophores may induce resistance to the same level as the bacterial LPS (Leeman *et al.*, 1996). Because siderophore mediated competition for iron occurs in the rhizosphere, it must be inferred that iron limitation commonly occurs around plant roots, making it likely that bacteria can produce siderophores at the root surface. Different siderophores thus seem to trigger ISR. Experiments with *P. aeruginosa* 7NSK 2 as the inducing rhizobacterium and tobacco mosaic virus (TMV) as the challenging leaf pathogen suggest that bacterially produced SA contributes to the induction of systemic resistance. The SA producing rhizobacterial strain *Serratia marcescens* 90-166 induced resistance to wildfire disease caused by *P. syringae* pv. *tabaci* ( Press *et al.*, 1997).

Pieterse *et al.* (1996) showed that ISR induced by PGPR in *Arabidopsis* occurs without induction of transcripts for PR-proteins, which indicates that, in this case, resistance is likely to be based on features other than PR-proteins accumulation. In radish, *Pseudomonas* mediated ISR is not associated with the accumulation of PR-proteins (Carver *et al.*, 1994). However, in bean and tobacco, colonization of the roots by fluorescent bacteria is correlated with induction of PR-proteins and systemic resistance. In the studies on protection of rice plants against sheath blight pathogen (*R. solani*) by strains of *P. fluorescens* 7-14 and *P. putida* V-14i, there was up to 18% reduction in disease severity as compared to untreated control (Krishnamoorthy and Gnanamanickam, 1997). Meena *et al.* (2000), reported that seed inoculation of *P. fluorescens* induced systemic resistance against leaf spot fungus, *Cercosporidium personatum*, in groundnut. Maximum disease protection was observed after 30 days of inoculation and there was an increase in the activity of phenylalanine ammonia-lyase (PAL), phenolic content and lytic enzymes (defense related compounds) in the treated plants.

Some *Trichoderma* strains are potent inducers of induced resistance like responses. It was reported that xylanase from *Trichoderma* spp. is responsible for induction of systemic resistance in cotton, tobacco, grapevine, etc. (Anderson *et al.*, 1993; Calderon *et al.*, 1993; Bailey and Lumsden, 1998; Howell *et al.*, 1999; Yedidia *et al.*, 1999; Elad, 2000). Seed treatment with *T. virens* can stimulate defense responses by the synthesis of terpenoids in cotton roots. Terpenoid synthesis and peroxidase activity is increased in the roots of *T. virens* treated plants but not in the hypocotyls of these plants or the untreated controls. Bioassay of the terpenoids for toxicity of *R. solani* showed that the pathway intermediates desoxyhemigossypol and hemigossypol were strongly inhibitory to the pathogen. Studies further proved that a major mechanism of biocontrol of cotton seedlings damping off by *T . virens* appear to be the induction of host resistance as indicated by the observation that there was increased peroxidase activity and terpenoid synthesis in seedling roots by biological control agent prior to attack by pathogen (Howell *et al.*, 1999). Assay of *T. virens* culture filtrate for terpenoid induction indicate that the inducers are synthesized by the fungus and released to the environment. Efforts are currently underway to isolate and characterize these inducers.

*T. harzianum* strain T-39 when inoculated on to roots or leaves of grapes provided control of disease caused by *B. cineria* on leaves spatially separated from the site of application of the biocontrol agent (De Meyer *et al.*, 1998). Analysis of protected leaves to which T-39 was not applied revealed the biocontrol agent was not present. The level of protection afforded by T-39 applied to roots was similar to the known bacterial induced systemic resistance inducing organism *Pseudomonas aeruginosa* KMPCH (De Meyer *et al.*, 1998). Elad *et al.*, (1999) consider induced resistance to be primary method by which T-39 controls powdery mildews, because T-39 is not a mycoparasite or a producer of inhibitory compounds that can affect powdery mildew fungi. Therefore, another mode of action must be responsible for the effect of this biocontrol agent on powdery mildew. The significant effect of soil application of T-39 on the disease of the upper parts of various crops demonstrated the involvement of induced resistance in disease suppression and explains the phenomenon of powdery mildew control (Elad, 2000). In another recent study (Yedidia *et al.*, 1999) cucumbers were grown in the presence or absence of strain T-203 in an axenic hydroponic system. Plants were always larger in the presence of T-203 than in its absence and, unlike T-22, this strain penetrated root cortical tissue. Cell walls of the roots were strengthened in the area of penetration. Both chitinase and peroxidase activities were increased in both root and leaf tissues of treated seedling, which is an indication of induced systemic resistance (Yedidia *et al.*, 1999). Howell *et al.* (1999), have also demonstrated the presence of induced systemic resistance induced by *T. virens* that usually produce gliotoxin or glioviridin. Mutants were prepared that lacked both mycoparasitic ability and the capacity to produce these or other detectable antibiotics. Many of the mutants were as effective as or more effective than the parental strains in biocontrol of *R. solani* (Howell, 1987; Howell and Stipanovic, 1995). This high level of protection was associated with significantly enhanced levels of the various terpenoids phytoalexins known to be involved in disease resistance in cotton (Howell *et al.*, 1999). Levels of phytoalexin production induced by the mutants were significantly greater than the parental antibiotic-producing strains. Thus at least a portion of the mechanism of action of the mutant strains of *T. virens* is probably induction of systemic resistance (Howell *et al.*, 1999). Elad (2000) reported that cellulase produced by *T. harzianum* act as elicitor by triggering peroxidase and chitinase activity to induce SAR. *Fusarium oxysporum* f. sp. *melonis* and powdery mildew infections on green house melon plants were reduced in plants treated with cellulase.

Sen (2000) demonstrated ISR in muskmelon by *Aspergillus niger* strain AN-27. Muskmelon seedlings raised from *A. niger* treated seeds showed 56% less disease without the physical presence of the bioagents in the root zone. These seedlings also exhibited higher peroxidase, polyphenol oxidase and phenylalanine ammonia lyase (PAL) activity and lignin. Similarly, rice plants raised from *A. niger* treated seeds exhibited 30% less sheath blight disease as compared to control. Nevertheless, since seeds/seedlings are soaked in spore suspension overnight, direct involvement of antifungal metabolites produced by *A. niger* in disease suppression cannot be ruled out. Sathiabama and Balasubramanian (2001) observed induction of defense responses in the leaves of groundnut when they were treated with a compound 'glucan' extracted from *Acremonium obclavatum*, a biocontrol agent of the rust pathogen. There were enhanced activities of apoplastic chitinases, β-1, 3-glucanases and salicylic acid.

### *Growth Promotion*

Biocontrol agents, both fungal and bacterial, are reported to induce the growth of various crops. These responses may be due to—(*i*) suppression of deleterious root micro-flora including those not causing obvious disease, (*ii*) production of growth stimulating factors (hormones or growth factors) and/or (*iii*) Increased nutrient uptake through solubilization and sequestration of nutrients and/or enhanced root growth. Enhanced root development is also helpful in tolerating the biotic and abiotic stresses by the plants. The first report of growth promotion by rhizosphere bacteria was confined to root crops such as radish (Kloepper and Schroth, 1978), potato (Burr *et al.*, 1978; Kloepper *et al.*, 1980) tomato (Varshney, 1997) and sugar beet (Suslow and Schroth, 1982) (Table 9.2). Subsequent reports indicate that these bacteria could exert positive effects on diverse host; including barley (Pierson and Weller, 1994), bean (Anderson and Guerra, 1985), canola (Kloepper *et al.*, 1988), gram and wheat (Pandey, 1997), rice (Mishra and Sinha, 2000a,b,c), and vegetables (Elad *et al.*, 1987) (Table 9.2). These bacteria are ideally suited as soil inoculants because of their potential of rapid and aggressive colonization. Direct growth promotion occurs when a rhizobacteria produces metabolites that directly promote plant growth without interactions with native soil micro-flora (Kloepper *et al.*, 1989, 1991; Dube, 2001). In contrast, antibiotics, siderophores and HCN, which decrease activities of pathogens or deleterious microorganisms and, thereby, increase plant growth, are examples of indirect growth promotion by biocontrol agents (Table 9.2). Knowledge of bacterial genes involved in plant association has been widely established. As a result of rather intensive work carried out with *Trichoderma*, several independent research groups have noticed that the addition of antagonist *Trichoderma* spp. induced the growth of various crops (Chet, 1987, Kleifeld and Chet, 1992). *Trichoderma* preparations have been reported to increase vigour and emergence of oat seedlings (Wu, 1977) and germination in radish (Henis *et al.*, 1978). Application of *T. harzianum* grown on wheat bran significantly increased growth and dry weight of tomato, pepper and cucumber and height and flowering of *petunias*, *chrysanthemum* and *periwinkle* (Chang *et al.*, 1986). Seeds coated with *T. viride* increased fresh and dry weight of shoots, roots and nodules of broad bean (Yehia *et al.*, 1985). Conway and Khan (1990) reported an increase in weight of stem and root of broccoli transplants by addition of *T. harzianum* chlamydospores @ 5 kg mixture per hectare. There was a significant increase in germination, seedling length and weight when rice seeds were treated with powdered formulations of *T. harzianum*. *T. virens* and *Aspergillus niger* (Mishra and Sinha, 2000a,b,c). The enhanced rooting by *T. harzianum* T-22 induces tolerance to drought and enhanced nitrogen utilization. It also induces tolerance to pests that it does not directly control, as it was shown that *T. harzianum* T-22 don't have ability to control *Phytophthora* spp. because it has no mechanism to intercept or attack zoospores (Harman, 2000). However growers have indicated that *Phytophthora*-attacked plants were larger in the presence of T-22 than in its absence. It might be due to the larger root systems of plants colonized by T-22 were able to withstand the damaging effects of the pathogen (Harman, 2000). *Aspergillus niger* strain AN-27 was reported to produce growth promotory compounds, 2-carboxy-methyl-3-hexyl-maleic anhydride and 2-methylene-3-hexyl-butanedioic acid (hexylitaconic acid) that were directly responsible for increased root and shoot length and biomass of the crop plants (Sen, 2000).

**TABLE 9.2:** PLANT GROWTH PROMOTION BY FUNGAL AND BACTERIAL BIOCONTROL AGENTS

| *Crop* | *Biocontrol Agents* | *Special Features* | *References* |
|---|---|---|---|
| Bean | *Pseudomonas putida* | Increase in shoot and root length and plant weight | Anderson and Guera, 1985 |
| Brinjal | *T. harzianum* | Promotion of shoot and root length | Chaturvedi, 1986 |
| Cauliflower | *T. harzianum, P. fluorescens* | Increase in root and shoot growth | Mukherjee *et al.*, 1989 |
| Chick pea | *T. harzianum, P. fluorescens* | Increase in root and shoot growth | Kaur and Mukhopadhyay 1992; Pandey, 1996 |
| Cotton | *P. fluorescens* | Increase in plant growth | Sakthivel *et al.*, 1987 |
| Cucumber | *T. harzianum* | Increase in dry weight | Ahmed and Baker, 1988 |
| Lentil | *T. harzianum, T. virens* | Increase in plant growth | Shrestha, 1992 |
| Melon | *P. fluorescens* | Increase in germination by >30% and in dry weight upto 165% | Ahmed and Baker, 1988 |
| Pepper | *T. harzianum* | Increase in seedling height, leaf area and plant dry weight | Anderson and Guera, 1985 |
| Pigeon pea | *T. harzianum, P. fluorescens* | Increase in root and shoot growth | Mehrotra, 1988 |
| Rice | *T. virens, T. longibrachiatum, T. harzianum, T. virens, P. fluorescens* | Increase in plant growth | Baby and Manibhushanrao, 1993; Mishra and Sinha, 1997; 1998, 1999, 2000 b |
| Sugar beet | *P. fluorescens* | Increased seedling emergence by 13% | Rath and Wolf, 1992 |
| Tomato | *T. harzianum, P. fluorescens* | Promotion of shoot and root length and increase in seed germination by 10-31% | Gupta *et al.*, 1995; Varshney, 1997 |
| Wheat | *P. fluorescens* | Shoot and root growth promotion | Pierson and Weller, 1994; Pandey, 1996 |

### *Solubilization and Sequestration of Inorganic Plant Nutrients*

In soil, various plant nutrients undergo complex transition from soluble to insoluble forms that strongly influence their accessibility and absorption by roots. Microorganisms may strongly influence these transitions (Altomare *et al.*, 1999; Sen, 2000). Iron and manganese in particular have been investigated with regard to both microbial solubilization of oxidized forms of these elements and their influence on plant disease (Graham and Webb, 1991). *Pseudomonas* spp. produces some compounds (siderophores) with very high affinities for iron (Pandey, 1996; Varshney, 1997). Iron chelated with these siderophores is unavailable to plant pathogens, thereby reducing their activity, but plant roots can take up iron in this form either directly or after reduction of $Fe^{3+}$ to $Fe^{2+}$ (Pandey, 1996). *Aspergillus niger* strain AN-27 produced hydroxamate and catecholate groups of siderophores that helps in improving antagonistic activities, rhizosphere competence and plant growth (Mondal *et al.*, 1999a). Manganese is a microelement essential for diverse physiological functions in plants, including both plant growth and disease resistance (Graham and Webb, 1991). Only $Mn^{2+}$ form of this element is soluble, the more highly oxidized forms are insoluble. Several plant pathogens can oxidize manganese and thereby inactivate a major part of the plant defense mechanisms (Huber and Wilhelm, 1988; Huber and McCay-Buis, 1995). It was reported that some strains of *Trichoderma* could solubilize rock phosphate, Zn-metal, $Mn^{4+}$, $Fe^{3+}$ and $Cu^{2+}$ by producing a large number of chemicals (Harman, 2000).

### *Inactivation of Pathogens' Enzyme*

Some pathogens depend upon production of cell wall degrading enzymes to infect living plants. *B. cineria* depends upon production of pectolytic, cutinolytic, and cellulolytic enzymes to infect living plants (Kapat *et al.*, 1998). Secondary metabolites or proteolytic enzymes produced by biocontrol agents may inactivate these enzymes resulting in reduced ability of the pathogen to infect the plant. For instance, one member of the group of hydrolytic enzymes that are believed to play an important role in mycoparasitism was purified and bio-chemically characterized as serine-protease (Geremia *et al.*, 1993). Inactivation of enzymes of pathogens by means of protease produced by antagonistic microorganisms has been demonstrated in several systems: proteolytic activity of *T. viride* was claimed to be involved in biocontrol of *Sclerotium rolfsii* in autoclaved soil (Rodriguez-Kabana *et al.*, 1978). Endoproteinase of *Bacillus megaterium* can inactivate extracellular enzymes of *Rhizoctonia solani* (Bertagnolii *et al.*, 1996). Conidia of two strains of *T. harzianum* (T39 and NCIM 1185), when applied to the leaves, produce a serine protease that is capable of degrading the pathogen's plant cell wall degrading enzymes and thereby reducing the ability of the pathogen to infect the plant. The biocontrol ability of T-39 could be enhanced by adding additional quantities of its protease; further, several protease inhibitors like trans-epoxysuccyinyl-L-leucylamido-(4-guanidino)-butane (E-64), antipain hydrochloride, and a mixture of inhibitors, but not pepstanin-A reduced the biocontrol activity of T-39 while, the proteases of T-39 could be detected on the leaf surfaces, no activity of chitinolytic or β-1,3-glucanolytic enzymes, which are presumed to involved in mycoparasitism, could be detected (Zimand *et al.*, 1996; Kapat *et al.*, 1998; Elad and Kapat, 1999; Elad, 2000). Thus there is a solid case for the role of proteases from *T. harzianum* in inactivation of the pathogen's primary modes of ingress into plants. The author suggests that the proteases might be directly toxic to germination of the pathogen and also may inactivate its enzymes (Zimand *et al.*, 1996; Elad and Kapat, 1999).

There is almost bewildering array of mechanisms by which a biocontrol agent exert its biocontrol potential. Thus it is not surprising that different strains of biocontrol agents have very different capabilities, even mutants of the same original strain may exhibit very different biocontrol mechanisms.

## IMPROVEMENTS IN BIO-EFFICACY

### Strain improvement

Once soil isolates with desired traits are obtained, they may be used as a commercial strain or improved further through laboratory manipulation. Naturally this will depend upon the specific goals of each research programme. Biocontrol agents can be improved for desirable characteristics like better antagonistic ability, wider host range, tolerance to pesticides, survival ability in the environment, rhizosphere-competence, tolerance to adverse environmental conditions, vigorous growth and long shelf life. Different methods in use for strain improvement are as follows:

#### *Mutation*

N-methyl-N-nitro-N-nitrosoguanidine (*NTG*) has been the most widely used chemical for mutating biocontrol fungi (Katan *et al.*, 1984; Chang *et al.*, 1986). By exposing the conidia of *Trichoderma* spp. to NTG, Ahmad and Baker (1987, 1988) generated mutants that are rhizosphere competent and superior to wild types in respect of controlling *Pythium ultimum* in barley, radish, cucumber, pea and tomato and also in increasing fruit weight of cucumber. These mutants were insensitive to up to 100 mg/ml of benomyl. Liu (1988) used several chemicals (diethyl sulphate, ethyl methane sulphonate, sodium nitrate) to reduce benomyl resistant mutants of *T. koningii* which could tolerate up to 1000 mg/ml of benomyl and also without decreased mycoparasitic ability including lyses and antibiosis against *R. solani* and *S. rolfsii*. Mukherjee *et al.*, (1997) developed benomyl-tolerant mutants of *T. viride* through chemical mutagenesis. The stable mutants produced more antifungal substances and were equally effective as the wild type strain in disease control potential. A vinclazolin tolerant strain of *T. viride* was also developed showing better potential than the wild one (Mukherjee *et al.*, 1995a).

Using radiations has also developed several genetic variants of fungal biocontrol agents. Troutman and Matejka (1978) made the first attempt of this kind by inducing benomyl tolerant strains of *T. viride* by exposing the conidia to gamma radiation. The application of ultraviolet (UV) radiations for this purpose has been most extensive (Papavizas and Lewis, 1983, 1991; Papavizas, 1987). Several genetic variants of *T. harzianum* and *T. viride* have been developed. Mukherjee and Mukhopadhyay (1993) developed seven stable mutants of *T. virens* by exposing the cultures to 125 k rad of gamma radiation. The mutants differed from the wild type strain in phenotype, growth rate, sporulation and antagonistic potential. Ultraviolet (UV) irradiation of *T. viride* induced mutants with increased biomass, conidia and chlamydospores at higher pH levels (Rajappan, 1997). Selvakumar and co-workers (2000) developed carboxin tolerant mutants of *Trichoderma viride* by exposing the culture to UV-light and ethyl methane sulfonate. Triazole (tebuconazole) tolerant biotypes of *T. viride* developed by UV-irradiation showed a wide variation in enzyme activity especially β-1,3-glucanase, β-1,4-endoglucanase and chitinases (Kumar and Gupta, 2000).

### Protoplast Fusion

*Trichoderma* is well known as a producer of chitinases, glucanases, cellulases and various other mycolytic enzymes. Combination of these desirable traits from different species/strains can give rise to superior strains. Various biotechnological methods can be used for the development of improved strains to suit the modern integrated disease management. The strain improvement of biocontrol agents by protoplast fusion may be one of them. The advantage of which is that there is higher possibility of obtaining recombinants, and testing their large numbers in a short time (Stasz *et al.*, 1988; Harman *et al.*, 1989; Harman and Stasz, 1989). This technology also allows the induction of the para sexual cycle at high frequency not only for the strains of same species but also for different species. Sundaram (1996) developed fusants of two isolates of *T. harzianum* (Th-1 & Th-2), among them some showed morphological characteristics intermediate between Th-1 and Th-3. In majority of the fusants, dominance of characteristics of Th-1 over Th-3 was observed. Protoplast fusants of two different species of biocontrol agents used as parent were also developed. When *T. harzianum* (Th-3) was fused with *T. virens* many fusants were developed and few of them exhibited improved biocontrol potential over parent isolates (Ghosh, 1996). Protoplast fusants developed by taking 10 isolates of *Trichoderma* spp, *T. harzianum* and *T. longibrachiatum* as parent strains exhibited an enhanced antagonistic potential against *R. solani, Fusarium oxysporum* f. sp. *lycopersici, Venturia inaequalis, Curvularia lunata* and *Cochliobolus miyabeanus* (Lalithakumari *et al.*, 1996; Lalithakumari, 2000).

### Genetic Engineering

Genetic modifications can introduce or improve desirable traits in fungal and bacterial biocontrol agents and this is, therefore, an attractive option for the commercialization of these strains. The biosynthesis of cell wall degrading enzymes like chitinases, glucanases, proteases, etc., which are involved in mycoparasitism, is controlled mainly at transcriptional level (De la Cruz *et al.*, 1995) and responsible genes are present as single copy genes (Lora *et al.*, 1995; Limon *et al.*, 1999). To overproduce these enzymes, their gene copy number has been increased by transformation (Harman and Bjöorjman, 1998). Transformants overproducing these enzymes are more efficient as biocontrol agents. Biocontrol efficiency of *Trichoderma* has been improved by transformation with genes *prb1* (basic protease), *egl1* (β-1,4-glucanase) and *chit33* (chitinase) (Flores *et al.*, 1997; Migheli *et al.*, 1998; Limón *et al.*, 1995). Lo *et al.*, (1998) developed transformant of *T. harzianum* strain 1295-22 by integrating β-glucuronidase (GUS) and hygromycin B (hygB) phospho-transferase genes, that exhibited increased biocontrol activity against *R. solani* as compared with the wild type.

Transgenic microorganisms, in which specific strains are constructed to express genes from another microorganism whose products are inhibitory to plant pathogens, are likely to have high utility as biocontrol agents. The gene encoding the detoxification of fusaric acid (FA), a pathogenesis related metabolite from vascular wilt *Fusarium* species, was cloned in *Escherichia coli* and detoxification activity was expressed (Utsumi *et al.*, 1988).

The best-documented success story of biocontrol has been management of crown gall caused by *Agrobacterium tumefaciens* using *A. radiobacter* strain K84. Strain K84 contains the plasmid pAgK84, which harbours genes encoding agrocin-84 biosynthesis and agrocin-84 resistance (Ryder *et al.*, 1987). Plasmid pAgK84 is readily mobilizable into virulent strain of *A. tumifaciens* by conjugation (Ferrand *et al.*, 1985). In such case virulent strain would become resistant to agrocin-84 resulting in failure of biocontrol. Therefore, a strategy was developed to construct conjugal transfer deficient deletion mutants in which part of the transfer region of pAgK84 was deleted. The resultant strain was designated K1026. It possessed all of the traits of the parental K84 with the exception of its inability to transfer pAgK84 (Jones and Kerr, 1989). Strain K-1026 was registered in Australia in 1988 under the trade name '*Nogall*' for the control of crown gall on stone fruits, nuts and roses. To date, *A. radiobacter* strain K1026 is the only genetically engineered biocontrol agent registered for the management of plant diseases.

## Formulation Improvement

### *Development of Mixed Formulations of Biocontrol Agents*

Most of the studies on biological control of plant diseases deal with single biocontrol agent as antagonist to a single pathogen. Considering the fact that there is some degree of host-specificity in biocontrol agents even at sub-species level, this may partially account for the reported inconsistent performance of biocontrol agent preparations. Single biocontrol agent is not likely to be active in all soil environments or against all pathogens that attack the host plant. Control of a wide spectrum of pathogens under a wide range of environmental conditions by applied antagonists largely remains an unfulfilled goal for biological control. There are four main approaches to achieve this goal: (1) select strain of biocontrol agent with wide host range, (2) modify the genetics of the biocontrol agent to add mechanisms of disease suppression that are operable against more than one pathogen, (3) alter the environment to favour the biocontrol agent and to disfavour competitive micro-flora, and (4) develop strain mixtures with superior biocontrol activity (Janisiewicz, 1988). Several strategies for developing mixtures of biocontrol agents could be envisioned including mixtures of organisms with different plant colonization patterns, mixtures of antagonists that control different pathogens, mixtures of antagonists with different mechanisms of disease suppression, mixtures of taxonomically different organisms, mixtures of organisms (antagonists) with different optimum temperature, pH, or moisture conditions for rhizosphere/phyllosphere colonization.

It is likely that most cases of naturally occurring biological control results from mixtures of antagonists, rather than from high population of a single antagonist. For example, mixtures of antagonists are considered to account for protection in disease suppressive soils (Lemanceau and Alabouvette, 1991; Chaube and Singh, 1991). Consequently, application of a mixture of introduced biocontrol agents would more closely mimic the natural situation and might broaden the spectrum of biocontrol activity, enhance the efficacy and reliability of control (Duffy and Weller, 1995), and allow the combination of various mechanisms without need for genetic engineering (Janisiewicz, 1988).

Previous studies on combinations of biocontrol agents for plant diseases have included mixtures of fungi (Paulitz *et al.*, 1990; Datnoff *et al.*, 1993; Budge *et al.*, 1995; Datnoff *et al.*, 1995), mixtures of fungi and bacteria (Janisiewicz, 1988, 1996; Park *et al.*, 1988; Duffy and Weller, 1995; Duffy *et al.*, 1996; Leeman *et al.*, 1996; Hassan *et al.*, 1997; Guetsky *et al.*, 2001), and mixtures of bacteria (Johnson *et al.*, 1993; Pierson and Weller, 1994; Janisiewicz and Bors, 1995; Mazzola *et al.*, 1995; Raaijmakers *et al.*, 1995; Stockwell *et al.*, 1996; De Boer *et al.*, 1997; Roberts *et al.*, 1997; Schisler *et al.*, 1997; Sung and Chung, 1997; Wei *et al.*, 1996; Raupach and Kloepper, 1998). Most of these reports on mixtures of biocontrol agents showed that combining antagonists resulted in improved biocontrol. However, there are also reports of combinations of biocontrol agents that do not result in improved suppression of disease compared with the separate antagonists (Dandurand and Knudsen, 1993; Hubbard *et al.*, 1983; Miller and May, 1991; Sneh *et al.*, 1984). Incompatibility of the co-inoculants can arise because biocontrol agents may also inhibit each other as well as the target pathogen or pathogens (Leeman *et al.*, 1996). Thus an important prerequisite for successful development of strain mixtures appears to be the compatibility of the co-inoculated microorganisms (Baker, 1990; De Boer *et al.*, 1997; Guetsky *et al.*, 2001).

In most of the investigations conducted so far, screening these agents against a single isolate of the target pathogen assessed the efficacy of individual biocontrol strains or strain combinations. This could be another reason why selected biocontrol agents fail to be commercially successful, because often there is no consideration for the genetic diversity of the target pathogen. Little emphasis has been placed on identifying the potential effects of pathogen diversity on the efficacy of biocontrol agents. Significant genotypic variation in a fungal pathogen population may exist among geographic regions, within a given field, or even among lesions on the same plant. In addition, classical reaction of biocontrol agents has focused on a single target pathogen and has not accounted for non-target pathogens causing diseases on the host plants.

## ANTAGONISTIC GENES FROM BIOCONTROL AGENTS FOR DEVELOPING DISEASE RESISTANCE IN PLANTS

The antifungal mechanism of *Trichoderma* spp., involves cell wall degrading enzymes. Several different classes of hydrolytic enzymes (for example, cellulases, endo-chitinase, chitobiosidase, N-acetyl-β-glucosaminidase, glucan 1,3-β-glucosidase, xylanase and protease) have been purified from *Trichoderma* spp. (Harman *et al.*, 1993; Goldman *et al.*, 1994; Jebakumar *et al.*, 2000). The purified enzymes from *T. harzianum*, which have an antagonistic and nutritional role, are strong inhibitors of many important plant pathogens and lyse not only the soft hyphal tips but also the 'hard' chitin wall of mature hyphae, conidia, chlamydospores, and sclerotia. They are active on a much wider range of pathogens and non-toxic to plants even at high concentrations (Vidhyasekaran and Balasubramanium, 1995; Vidhyasekaran *et al.*, 1996; Lorito *et al.*, 1998; Krishnamoorthy *et al.*, 1999). The plant defense system against microbial pathogens may be modified to produce high constitutive levels of anti microbial compounds. Plant genes encoding cell wall degrading enzymes, especially chitinases, have been used to alter plant resistance to fugal pathogens, but no single genes have produced an adequate level of resistance. Reasons for this may be that plant chitinases: (*i*) usually affect only the hyphal tip and are unable to effectively degrade harder chitin structures, (ii) have weak antifungal activity, (*iii*) are inhibitory only to a limited number of fungal species, and (iv) have no effect on several important pathogens (Broglie *et al.*, 1991; Punja and Raharjo, 1996). In terms of antifungal activity, chitinase genes from biocontrol fungi such as *Trichoderma* are clearly an improvement over corresponding plant genes. These fungal genes encode for chitinolytic enzymes that can reach the antifungal activity level of some chemical fungicides based on $ED_{50}$ values (Lorito *et al.*, 1993a; 1994). Furthermore, extensive testing *in vitro* has shown that there are virtually no chitinous pathogens resistant to *Trichoderma* chitinases (Lorito *et al.*, 1994). For these reasons, the genome of mycoparasites, which has evolved specifically to attack other pathogens but not plants, represents a potential source of powerful antifungal genes. Genes encoding a serine protease and endochitinase (*ThEn-42, ech42, Chit-42*) have been cloned and characterized (Hayes *et al.*, 1994). Recently, transgenic potato and tobacco plants expressing chitinase *Chit-42* from *Trichoderma* were shown to be highly tolerant or resistant to foliar pathogens (*Alternaria alternata, A. solani* and *Botrytis cineria*) and to the soil borne pathogen, *Rhizoctonia solani* (Lorito *et al.*, 1998). On the basis of result obtained from this experiment they have pointed out that: (i) there was a very high level of chitinolytic activity in some transgenic lines; (ii) the endochitinase concentrated in the extracellular space had a strong antifungal activity; (iii) the *Trichoderma* enzyme is highly synergistic with antifungal pathogenesis-related proteins in plants, such as tobacco osmotin (Lorito *et al.*, 1996); and the *Trichoderma* endochitinase in plant tissues may release from the cell-wall of invading fungal compounds that elicit the plant defense response (Lorito, *et al.*, 1998). Apple transgenic lines expressing *ech42* gene exhibited lesser susceptibility to apple scab (*Venturia inaequalis*) (Bolar *et al.*, 2000). In India, little work has been done on these lines. Jebakumar *et al.* (2000) purified and determined the N-terminal sequence of the extracellular chitinase (ASGYABAVYF) of molecular weight 42-kDa from *T. viride*. This chitinase inhibited the growth of the rice sheath blight isolate of *R. solani in vitro*.

## MASS MULTIPLICATION

One of the greatest obstacles to biological control by introduced antagonists has been the lack or scarcity of methods for mass culturing and delivering the biocontrol agents (Papavizas and Lewis, 1982; Mukhopadhyay, 1996). The unique problem in developing bio-pesticides is that it represents a living system, which must be able to stand the process of formulation and should remain sufficiently viable for a period until it reaches the farmers (Vidhyasekaran and Muthamilan, 1995). Despite the limited progress, scientists are engaged in developing effective experimental systems for growth and delivery of antagonists. The most widely used fungal antagonist *Trichoderma* spp. have been grown on solid substrates like sorghum grain, wheat straw, wheat bran, spent tea leaf waste, coffee husk, wheat bran-saw dust, diatomaceous earth granules impregnated with molasses, etc. for their mass multiplication (Henis *et al.*, 1978; Chet *et al.*, 1979; Lewis and Papavizas, 1984; Gogoi and Roy, 1996; Mishra, 1998). Papavizas *et al.*, (1984) produced biomass of fungal antagonists by liquid fermentation consisting of molasses and brewer's yeast. Montealegre *et al.*, (1993) proposed liquid fermentation method consisting of molasses, wheat bran and yeast for large-scale production of *T. harzianum*. The bacterial biocontrol agent *Pseudomonas* has been used as cell-suspension for experimental purpose. For commercial production of these antagonists' different technologies has been adopted on industrial scale (Mukhopadhyay and Mukherjee, 1998; Vidhyasekaran and Muthamilan, 1995). It was reported that large-scale production of *T. virens; T. harzianum* and *T. viride* could be achieved by liquid fermentation (Lewis and Papavizas, 1985; Lewis *et al.*, 1987; Mcquilken *et al.*, 1990; Mukhopadhyay (1994). The system stimulated industrial conditions by utilizing commercially available ingredients. Fermented biomass of *Trichoderma* consisted mainly of chlamydospores and conidia with some amount of mycelial fragments. Air-dried mats were ground and mixed with a commercially available carrier (Table 9.3). The formulation thus developed, contained $10^8$ to $10^9$ propagules/g. Commercial formulation of *P. fluorescens* was developed using a mixture of carboxy methyl cellulose and talc (1 : 100, w/w) and the commercial formulation, contained about $10^8$ colony forming unit (*cfu*) per g. This formulation was used as seed treatment and foliar spray against many plant diseases (Vidhyasekaran and Muthamilan, 1995; Vidhyasekaran *et al.*, 1997; Mishra *et al.*, 2001).

Bio-efficacy of solid fermentation based (sorghum grain) formulation of *T. harzianum* was better than liquid fermentation (potato-dextrose broth). Solid substrate based formulations contain only conidia whereas liquid fermentation based formulations contain mixture of chlamydospores, hyphal fragments and conidia (Lewis and Papavizas 1985; Dandurand and Knudsen, 1993; Mishra, *et al.*, 2001b). Bio-efficacy of formulations based on conidia and chlamydospores and hyphal fragments is likely to be different even at same *cfu*. Therefore, there is need to properly define the *cfu* for different types of formulations and as far as possible formulations must indicate relative numbers of different propagules.

## SHELF LIFE

One of the critical obstacles to commercialization of a biopesticidal preparation is the loss of viability of the biocontrol agents over time. Several attempts have been made to determine the viability of biocontrol agents in their preparations when stored at room temperature and in refrigerator. Most of the results are variable and it appears that shelf life is also dependent upon species/isolate/strain.

**TABLE 9.3:** BASE MATERIALS/CARRIERS USED FOR MASS PRODUCTION OF FUNGAL AND BACTERIAL BIOCONTROL AGENTS

| *Base Material* | *Biocontrol Agent* | *Formulation* | *References (form)* |
|---|---|---|---|
| Black gram shell, Shelled maize cob, coir-pith, Peat, Gypsum, Barley grains | *T. viride, T. harzianum* | Powder | Kumar and Marimuthu, 1997; Gandhikumar and Rangnathan, 2000a |
| Coffee fruit skin+Biogas slurry | *T. harzianum* | Pellets | Sawant *et al.*, 1995 |
| Coffee husk | *T. harzianum, T. viride, T. virens* | Pellets | Bhai *et al.*, 1994 |
| Coffee-cherry husk | *T. harzianum, T. viride, T. virens* | Powder | Sawant *et al.*, 1995 |
| Fruit skin and berry mucilage | *T. harzianum, T. viride, T. virens* | Pellets | Sawant *et al.*, 1995 |
| Farm Yard Manure | *T. harzianum, T. viride, T. virens* | Pellets | Sangeetha *et al.*, 1995 |
| Groundnut shell | *T. viride* | Powder | Raghuchander *et al.*, 1993 |
| Molases + yeast, Molases + soy, Molases + $NaNO_3$ Molases + $KNO_3$ | *T. harzianum* | Powder | Papavizas *et al.*, 1984; Montealegre *et al.*, 1993; Prasad and Rangeshwaran, 2000 |
| Mushroom-grown waste | *T. harzianum, T. viride, T. virens* | Powder | Sawant *et al.*, 1995 |
| Mustard oil cake | *T. viride* | Pellets | Chaurasia and Bhatt, 2000 |
| Neem cake + cowdung | *T. viride, T. harzianum, T. virens* | Pellets | Prasad and Rangeshwaran, 2000 |
| Peat | *P. fluorescens* | Powder | Vidhyasekaran and Muthamilan, 1995 |
| Poultry manure | *T. harzianum, T. viride, T. virens* | Powder | Sawant *et al.*, 1995 |
| Soil | *T. harzianum, T. viride* | Powder | Chet, 1987 |
| Sorghum grain | *T. harzianum, T. virens* | Powder | Upadhyay and Mukhopadhyay, 1986, Mishra, 1998 |
| Spent tea leaf waste | *T. harzianum, T. viride, T. virens* | Pellets | Bhai *et al.*, 1994 |
| Sugarcane straw | *T. harzianum, T. viride, T. reesei, T. koningii* | Pellets | Singh *et al.*, 2000 |

Table 9.3 (*contd. on* p. 192)

Table 9.3 (*contd. from* p. 192)

| | | | |
|---|---|---|---|
| Talc | *P. fluorescens, P. putida* | Powder | Vidhyasekaran and Muthamilan, 1995; Krishnamoorthy and Gnanamanickam, 1998 |
| Talc | *T. virens, T. viride, T. harzianum, T. longibrachiatum* | Powder | Sanker and Jayarajan, 1996; Nakkeeran and Devi, 1997; Prasad and Rangeswaran, 2000 |
| Tapioca refuse + FYM | *T. harzianum* | Granules & Powder | Sanker and Jayarajan, 1996 |
| Vermiculite + Wheat bran + HCl | *T. viride* | Powder | Nakkeeran and Devi, 1997 |
| Wheat bran | *T. virens* | Powder | Henis *et al.*, 1978; Chet *et al.*, 1979; Lewis and Papavizas, 1984; Khilari, 1994 |
| Wheat bran + biogas manure (1 : 1) | *T. harzianum* | Powder | Jagadeesh and Geeta, 1994 |
| Wheat bran-saw dust | *T. virens, T. longibrachiatum* | Powder | Elad *et al.*, 1980, 1981; Mukhopadhyay *et al.*, 1986; Baby & Manibhushanrao, 1993 |
| Wheat-bran, kaolin | *T. harzianum* | Granules | Prasad and Rangeshwaran, 2000 |
| Wheat bran + sand + water (1 : 1 : 2 w/w/v) | *T. harzianum* | Granules | Lewis and Papavizas, 1984; Papavizas, 1985 |

A talc based preparation of *T. virens* conidia retained 82% viability at 5° C in refrigerator after 6 months, while at room temperature (25-35° C) same level of viability was observed only up to 3 months. Shelf life was same, when *T. virens* treated chickpea (Tewari, 1996) or soybean treated seeds were stored at room temperature. Viability was better for CMC based formulations (Tewari, 1996). Conidia of *Trichoderma* in pyrophyllite survived better than fermenter biomass propagules alone at –5 to 30° C. The most suitable temperature to prolong shelf life of conidia and fermenter biomass propagules in pyrophyllite were –5° C to 5° C (Mukherjee, 1991). Talc based formulations of *T. harzianum* retained more than $10^8$ viable propagules per g up to 90 days and by 120 days propagules declined below the optimum level (Prasad and Rangeshwaran, 2000).

Chlamydospores based formulations of *Trichoderma* sp. exhibited longer shelf life (80 % viability for 9 months) than conidia based formulations (80% viability for 4 months) at room temperature (Mishra *et al.*, 2001b). A preparation of *T. virens* (mainly in the form of chlamydospores obtained from peat moss Czapeks broth culture) stored at 25° C for six months without loss of viability (Howell, 1982). Commercial formulations of *Aspergillus niger* AN-27 showed an extraordinary long shelf-life of more than two years at room temperature (15-35° C) when packed in polyethylene bags and stored under less than 80% relative humidity (Sen, 2000).

In the past, many attempts have been made to assess the viability of biocontrol agents on coated seed. Mihuta-Grim and Rowe (1986) estimated viability of *Trichoderma* spp. on coated seeds of radish by plating the seeds on malt-extract agar every week. Mukherjee (1991) quantitatively assessed the viability of *T. virens* and found that it maintains almost constant on coated chickpea seeds when the seeds were stored at low temperature (5° C). Even at room temperature (15-35° C), 88% of the propagules remained viable for up to 4 months, a time sufficient for reaching the coated seeds to the farmers. In our experiment similar type of results have been observed, where formulations have shown shelf life up to 9 months on the seed of different crops. Mixed formulation exhibited longer shelf life as compared to individual ones when stored at room temperature, while at low temperature there was no significant difference among them. The higher shelf life of mixed formulation at room temperature on coated seeds might be due to the reason that the biocontrol agents are reported to stimulate the exudation from the seeds (Barber and Lynch, 1977) that may serve as nutrients for the biocontrol agents (Dandurand and Knudsen, 1993). In that way there might be stimulation of production of some compounds from biocontrol agents also that could increase the growth and activity of biocontrol agents of mixed formulation, but at lower temperature they may remain inactive, so there will not be the chance of such type of activities.

## APPLICATION

One of the areas of biocontrol research has been the delivery system. It is rather necessary to have an efficient, economic and ecologically viable mode of application of biocontrol agents in soil ecosystem. A good amount of work has been done on this aspect under different conditions.

### *Seed Treatment*

Seed coating with biocontrol agents has emerged as a feasible way of delivering the antagonist for the management of plant diseases. As this technique of disease management represents a living system, the viability of the biocontrol agent may pose a limitation to its commercialization. One approach for this might be supplying the coated seeds to the farmers directly by the seed companies/agencies. A considerable time gap between coating seeds by the seed supply agencies and sowing such seeds by farmers is bound to occur and it should be ensured that sufficient propagules remain viable on coated seeds at the time of sowing. Inoculation of seeds, corms, bulbs, tuber, etc. with antagonists prevents seed/corm decay and seedling blight. This also takes care of seed borne inoculum, particularly externally seed borne, of even diseases affecting above ground plant parts. Even internally seed borne disease like loose smut of wheat is suppressed by seed treatment with *Trichoderma* (Agarwal, 2000; Selvakumar *et al.*, 2000; Singh, 2000). This could be due to action of metabolites produced by *Trichoderma*, which may penetrate seeds to affect growth of internally seed borne inoculum (Table 9.1). When applied through seeds, antagonists not only colonize spermoplane and spermosphere, but also rhizoplane and rhizosphere.

Spore/cell suspension as well as dry powder has been used to coat the seeds with potential antagonists (Harman *et al.*, 1980; Chao *et al.*, 1986; Mukhopadhyay *et al.*, 1992). The widely used practice for experimental purpose is to harvest the conidia/bacterial colony from a fully grown culture plate making suspension of desired concentration with some sticker, soaking the seeds in the suspension and air drying before sowing (Harman *et al.*, 1980; Mukherjee, 1991; Pandey, 1996). Propagules of biocontrol agents germinate on the seed surface and colonize roots of germinated seedlings (Tiwari, 1996). For commercial purpose dry powder of antagonists are used @ 3 to 8 g powder per kg seed, based on seed size and formulations of antagonist (Mukhopadhyay *et al.*, 1992; Mukherjee and Mukhopadhyay, 1995; Vidhyasekaran and Muthamilan, 1995). Haral and Konde (1983) coated chickpea seeds with spores of *Aspergillus flaviceps* and *Penicillium funiculosum* and observed that the treated seeds increased nodulation in roots by *Rhizobium* and protected the seeds from the attack of pathogens. In pre-emergence seed rot of pea caused by *Pythium ultimum*, the pathogen derives nutrients for colonization of seed and subsequent invasion from seed exudates released during swelling of the seed in soil. If the seed is coated with spores of *Penicillium oxalicum*, the antagonist exhausts this source of nutrients before the pathogen could utilize it (Sankar and Jeyarajan, 1996). *T. hamatum*, *T. harzianum*, *T. virens* and *T. viride* are effective seed protectants against *Pythium* spp. and *Rhizoctonia solani* (Mukherjee and Mukhopadhyay, 1995). A large number of seed, seedling, root, stem, foliar and panicle diseases have been suppressed by seed treatment with antagonists as mentioned in Table 1.

### *Normal Seed Treatment vs. Seed Bio Priming*

Seed bio priming (treating of seeds with biocontrol agents and then incubating under warm and moist conditions until just prior to radicle emergence) has potential advantages over simple coating of seeds as it results in rapid and uniform seedling emergence (Mathre *et al.*, 1999). It might be useful under adverse soil conditions. Callan *et al.*, (1997) conducted experiments on sweet corn during 1989-1996 and reported that by bio-priming with *P. aureofaciens* AB 254, seed protection was almost equal to metalaxyl treatment. They conclusively showed that bio priming had potential advantages over simply coating seed with AB254. The greatest advantage of bio priming over coating was seen when seeds were planted in excessively wet soil infested with *Pythium ultimum*. Emergence from bio-primed seeds was 38%, compared with only 5% for seed coated with AB 254 and no emergence from untreated seed (Mathre *et al.*, 1994). Bio priming could also reduce the amount of biocontrol agents that must be applied to the seed. Vidhyasekaran and Muthamilan (1995) showed that when chickpea seeds were given bio-priming treatment with *P. fluorescens*, the population of biocontrol agent was significantly higher in the rhizosphere than those without bio priming. Callan *et al.* (1997) demonstrated that a minimum of $10^7$ *cfu* per seed was needed for protection of sweet corn seed from *Pythium* seed rot, but the rapid rate of multiplication of *P. aureofaciens* AB 254 on seed during bio-priming enabled an initial population of $10^4$ to $10^5$ cfu per seed to increase to $10^7$ *cfu* per seed during bio-priming. Population of *T. harzianum* and *T. virens* on the surface of treated seeds of tomato, brinjal, soybean and chickpea increases from @ $10^4$ *cfu* per seed up to $10^6$-$10^7$ *cfu* per seed after bio priming (Mishra *et al.*, 2001a).

### Seedling Treatment

Treatment of planting materials with beneficial microorganisms is becoming increasingly important. Seedling roots can be treated with spore or cell suspension of antagonists. This method is generally used for vegetable crops, rice, etc. where transplanting is practiced. Seedling root dipping in the suspension of *Azospirillum* spp. controlled shoot die back of chilies (Kolte *et al.*, 1994; Jeyalashmi *et al.*, 1998). There are also reports on the reduction of sheath blight disease severity in rice by treatment of seedlings in the suspension of antagonists before transplanting. Root dipping of tomato seedlings in solution of antagonists reduces the severity of root knot caused by nematode *Meloidogyne incognita*. Root dipping in antagonist's suspension not only reduces disease severity but also enhances seedling growth in rice, tomato, brinjal, chili and capsicum (Mishra and Sinha, 2000b; Mishra *et al.*, 2001a).

### Soil Treatment

There are several reports on the application of biocontrol agents to the soil and other growing media either before or at the time of planting for control of a wide range of soil-borne fungal pathogens (Baby and Manibhushanrao, 1993, 1996). Such applications are ideally suited for green house and nursery but because of the bulk requirement, cost and problem of uniform distribution, feasibility of field application is less. However, biocontrol agents are capable of colonizing farmyard manure (FYM). Therefore, for soil application, first biocontrol agents are added to moist FYM, incubated for 3 to 4 days to allow colonization and colonized FYM is distributed in field followed by irrigation. Granular or pellets preparations have been used directly for soil application and they have provided effective control of diseases both under green house and field conditions (Raghuchander *et al.*, 1993; Prasad and Rangeshwaran, 1999).

### Foliar Application

Existence of epiphytic micro-flora on plant surface including leaves and flowers is a natural phenomenon. There are many studies where phyllosphere microflora has been implicated in reduction of foliar diseases (Chattopadhyay and Nandy, 1982; Bora *et al.*, 1993; Haware *et al.*, 1996). Antagonists isolated from phyllosphere can be introduced on the host surface by spraying their propagules. Bacteria are better colonizer than fungi in this respect (Parasher *et al.*, 1992a). There are several reports showing effectiveness of biocontrol agents applied as foliar spray against different plant pathogens as mentioned in Table 9.1. However, success of any antagonists on leaf/sheath surface depends largely on its ability to colonize these surfaces. Even environmental factors (humidity, temperature and sun light) affecting this colonization affect bio efficacy of antagonists. Because of these reasons foliar application is preferred during evening hours and it is more successful in rainy season crops.

## MONITORING POPULATION OF BIOCONTROL AGENTS

Biocontrol agents differ fundamentally from chemical fungicides in that they must grow and proliferate to be effective. Therefore, effective antagonist must become established in crop ecosystems and remain active against target pathogens during periods favourable for plant infection. The survival ability of biocontrol agents including population size, survival period, and distribution in or on crops, needs to be surveyed and associated with biocontrol effects.

For estimation of the behaviour of resident as well as introduced antagonists in the system/ecosystem, invariably soil dilution and soil plate technique has been used with semi selective/selective media, but problems arise from the inability to detect, monitor, and recover specific microorganisms. On selective media it is very difficult to distinguish between introduced and indigenous microorganisms. More recently this problem has been partially overcome by utilizing antibiotic/fungicide resistance as the marker for their introduced microorganisms. Vidhyasekaran *et al.* (1997) used antibiotic-resistance markers to monitor the presence of *Pseudomonas fluorescens* 7-14 and reported that the strain survived in rice phylloplane for 40 days after the seed treatment. Recently, molecular approaches have enabled reporter and marker genes to be integrated into the genome of microorganisms. Such strains can be monitored after introduction into natural environments (Ishii, 1995; Ryder, 1995). Bacteria carrying *xyl E*, a gene which codes for catechol-2,3-dioxygenase, can be readily identified by a yellow colour reaction in colonies of the marked strain. This marker has been used to study the survival of *Pseudomonas putida* in water and in soil (Ryder, 1995). Apart from its use as a reporter gene, β-glucuronidase from *E. coli* can be used as a marker for detection of bacteria in the environment. The hygromycin (*hyg B*) phosphotransferase gene coding for *hyg B* resistance (*hyg B$^R$*) has been used to detect the survival of *T. harzianum* on tomato phylloplane (Migheli *et al.*, 1998). The β-glucuronidase (GUS) reporter gene from *E. coli* is also promising for use in ecological studies (Bae and Knudsen, 2000) because of its stability and it can also be assayed easily by different methods (Green and Jensen, 1995). GUS-transformants of several plant pathogenic fungi has been used for detection and biomass quantification in infected plant tissue.

## DISEASE MANAGEMENT

Most of the efforts on biological control of plant diseases were diverted against pre- and post-emergence seedling and root rot and wilt diseases and only a few reports deals with the foliar pathogens. Major pathogens targeted are *R. solani, Sclerotium rolfsii, Fusarium* (particularly *F. oxysporum*), *Sclerotinia, Macrophomina, Pythium,* and *Phytophthora,* etc. It is due to the fact that other means of disease management are either not so effective or economically feasible against these soil-borne pathogens. Because of their wide host range, sources of resistance are not available against these pathogens. Soil application of fungicides is neither economically feasible nor so effective due to their poor persistence in soil as a result of microbial breakdown and binding with soil organic matter. Almost all present generation fungicides are fungi static in their action. Therefore, they are unable to kill resting structures like sclerotia, chlamydospores, etc. formed by many soil-borne pathogens. Higher dosages and more frequent application of chemicals to soil disturb ecological balance. Therefore, biological control alone or in combination with cultural and other practices seems to be only practical answer for these types of pathogens. A critical review of the literature reveal that soil-borne diseases such as pre- and post- emergence damping off, root rots, wilts, collar rots and other complex diseases are successfully suppressed by biocontrol agents under glass-house/field conditions (Table 9.1).

In India, pioneering work on this aspect was done at G. B. Pant University of Agriculture and Technology, Pantnagar under leadership of Dr. A.N. Mukhopadhyay and at Tamil Nadu Agriculture University, Coimbatore under leadership of Dr. S. Jeyarajan. The pace of work on biological control of soil borne plant pathogens through introduction of the antagonists got required momentum with generous grants from Department of Biotechnology (DBT). Dr. Mukhopadhyay and his team isolated more than 100 different genera and species of fungi from different agro-climatic regions and tested their efficacy as fungal antagonists. Among the fungi isolated, three cultures of *T. harzianum*, two cultures of *T. viride*, two cultures of *T. koningii* and one culture of *T. virens* (=*Gliocladium virens*) showed antagonistic activity against *P. aphanidermatum*, *Phytophthora* spp., *S. rolfsii, R. solani, F. oxysporum* f.sp. *ciceri, F. oxysporum* f.sp. *lini* and *Sclerotinia sclerotiorum* . Diseases and pathogens reported to be managed under different conditions are listed in Table 9.1.

## INTERACTIONS AMONG BIOCONTROL AGENTS

Microorganisms inoculated in the rhizosphere or developing there are known to have positive and/or negative interactions with various members of the rhizosphere community. Various interactions among microorganisms in the rhizosphere affect the various organisms of concern, but also other microorganisms as well as the plants. These interactions are extremely important in the ecological study of the rhizosphere, yet they are among the least well-understood ones in the rhizosphere ecology.

Working with various biocontrol agents (*Bacillus subtilis, Pseudomonas fluorescens, Serratia plymuthica, Streptomyces griseoviridin* and *Trichoderma, Gliocladium, Aspergillus, Penicillium*, etc.) for their survival and compatibility with the mycorrhizal fungus (*Glomus intraradices*), Nemec (1997) provided evidences for the *G. intraradices* having no influence of numbers of these bioagents/genera except on *P. fluorescens* as the *cfu* of *Pseudomonas* isolates were greater when mixed with *G. intraradices* than when alone. In his experiment, he found *Bacillus* and *Trichoderma* were the best survivors for potential use as biocontrol agents. Varshney (1997) studied the effect of strains of fluorescent *Pseudomonas* spp. (PGPR), *T. harzianum* and *Glomus* sp. (VAM) in different combinations on growth of tomato. Individually strains of PGPR caused stimulation of plant growth followed by VAM and *Trichoderma*. PGPR with VAM was the most effective treatment and increased growth of tomato plants compared to PGPR and VAM alone. PGPR+ *Trichoderma* as well as *Trichoderma* +VAM were almost similar to PGPR alone, respectively. Combinations of all the three microbes (PGPR + VAM +

*Trichoderma*) were found stimulatory but were not different from PGPR + VAM treated plants (Varshney and Chaube, 2001).

### *Trichoderma* and VAM

The interaction effects of these two fungi may generally be attributed to antagonistic, synergistic and neutral actions. Kichadi and Srinivasa (1998) reported not only the increased plant growth and yield but also improved 'P' nutrition in tomato besides the least disease severity index (by *Sclerotium rolfsii*) in dual inoculated tomato plants by *Glomus fasciculatum* and *T. harzianum*. The percentage mycorrhizal root colonization and mycorrhizal spore counts were highest in the rhizosphere soil of plants inoculated with both fungi symbolizing the synergistic effects of the two fungi. The population of two different species of *Trichoderma* may be decreased (*T. harzianum*) or increased (*T. pseudokoningii*) in the presence of *G. mosseae* (Fracchia *et al.*, 1998). McAllister *et al.* (1994) made some interesting observations. They reported that plant dry weight of non-AM inoculated maize and lettuce were unaffected by the presence *T. koningii* and *Fusarium solani*. In contrast, *T. koningii* decreased plant dry weight and VAM colonization when inoculated in the rhizosphere before or at the same time as *G. mosseae*.

### Rhizobacteria and *Trichoderma*

Combined inoculation of *Pseudomonas striata* and *Trichoderma harzianum* in sorghum increased the size and weight of ear head, number of spikelets per ear, straw and grain yield as well as 'P' and 'N' uptake significantly over uninoculated control and single inoculated treatments (Jisha and Alagawadi, 1996). The population of both the interacting organisms and soil available 'P' were highest in combined inoculation treatments indicating a synergistic interaction between the inoculated organisms. Recently, some excellent work has been done by Duffy *et al.* (1996). They have proved experimentally that *T. koningii* was generally more suppressive to take all than *P. fluorescens* Q29z-80 or a mixture of *P. fluorescens* and *P. putida* strains in field trials. Varshney (1997) reported that strain TR20 of fluorescent *Pseudomonas, in vitro,* inhibited the growth of *T. harzianum* significantly.

### Pathogen-Host-Biocontrol Agent

In developing effective preparations for the biological control, one should take in to account the antagonistic activity, inoculum potential, inoculum formulation, mode of application and the site of interaction. It would be pertinent to precisely mention the very important findings of Fahima and Henis (1990). They studied the capacity of two facultative mycoparasites, *Trichoderma harzianum* and *Talaromyces flavus*, to multiply on roots of diseased and healthy plants using radish-*Rhizoctonia solani* and eggplant -*Verticillium dahaliae* systems respectively. It was clearly shown that not only these antagonists protected the plants against their respective pathogens but they also multiplied on roots, especially of the diseased plants. These results agree with the report that both pathogen and host were needed before soil suppressiveness to *R. solani* developed. On the basis of these findings, the following hypothesis was suggested (Fig. 9.2).

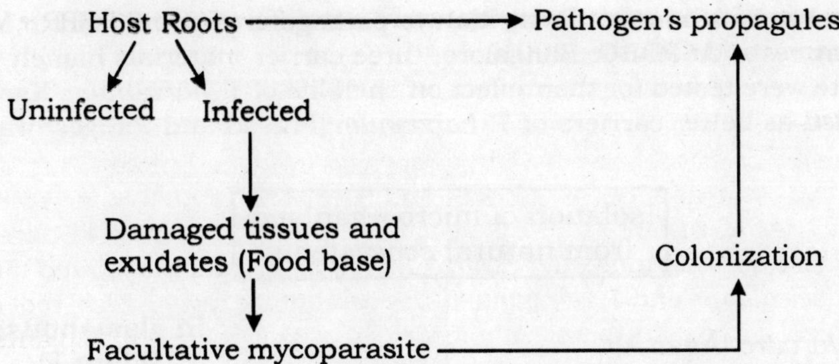


**Fig. 9.2:** Interactions among host, pathogen and biocontrol agent

## COMMERCIALIZATION OF BIOCONTROL AGENTS

It is the next logical step of the above sequence. In recent years, many small and large entrepreneurs have entered into commercial production of biocontrol agents resulting in entry of several products into world market. Commercialization of biopesticides is a multi-step process involving a wide range of activities (Fig. 9.3) (Mukhopadhyay and Mukherjee, 1998; Mathre *et al.*, 1999).

### Discovery

Development of a new soil microbial product begins with discovery of a useful naturally occurring organism. This is not generally serendipitous, but instead, occurs as a result of extensive screening of natural soil isolates for strains having the desired traits

### Formulation

The best technology is of no value unless it can be placed easily in the consumer's hand for use. Hence, developing a safe, easy to use, cost-effective formulation that will keep the microorganism alive is one of the most important steps in developing a biological product. Formulation is the blending of active ingredients such as fungal spores with inert carriers such as diluents and surfactants in order to alter the physical characteristics to a more desirable form. Lethbridge stated that the final formulation must have a minimum shelf-life of 2 years at room temperature, be easy to handle, insensitive to abuse and must be stable over a range of –5 to 35° C. This is the ideal situation and should be kept as an ultimate aim for developing a formulation. Failure to meet these rigid standards, however, should not stop the commercialization of biologicals. Few of the biological products currently on the market meet all of Lethbridge's requirements.

What is needed currently that too urgently is the development of drying techniques, which allows retention of maximum number of viable propagules in dried products? The method should be quick and safe without compromising on the bioagent's viability and efficacy. Adverse drying conditions lead to the death of bioagent's propagules, which may serve as a source of nutrition to pathogens and will lead to inconsistent results during tests. At PDBC, Bangalore, three carrier materials namely talc, kaolin and bentonite were tested for their effect on shelf life of *T. harzianum*. Kaolin and talc were identified as better carriers of *T. harzianum* (Prasad and Rangeshwaran, 2000).

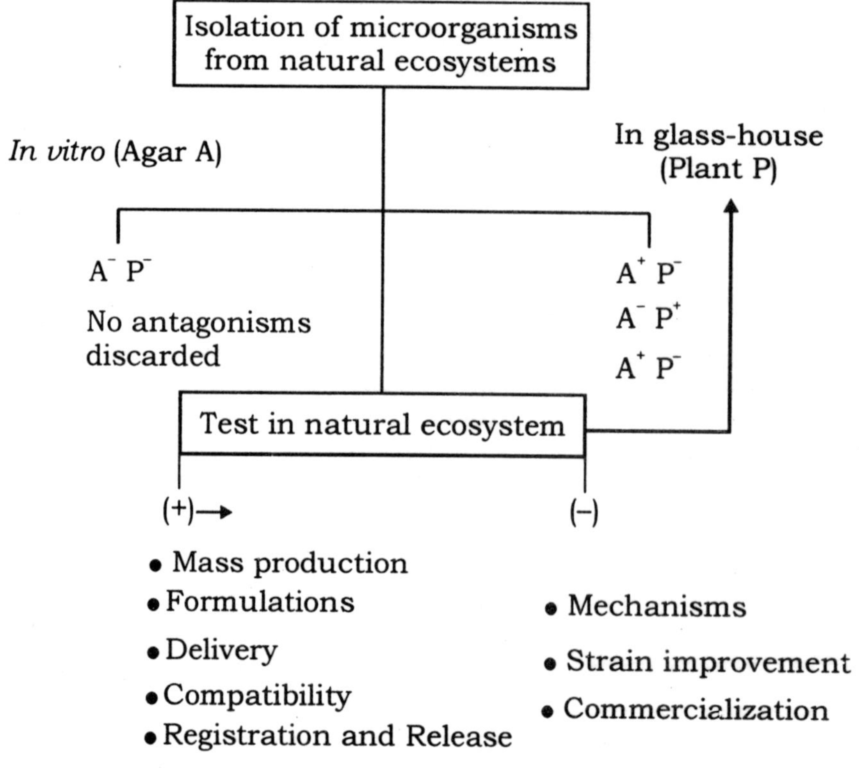


(+) = Antagonism/Disease suppression
(–) = No evidence of antagonism/Disease suppression

**Fig. 9.3:** Components and sequence of assays in screening for biocontrol activity

## Green House and Field Testing

All agricultural products must be tested in situations that approximate actual farming conditions. Testing usually begins in green houses or growth chambers. Although green house testing often provide a useful preliminary screening for selecting candidate microorganisms for the testing, it is very difficult to mimic true farming conditions. Therefore, well-designed field trials are necessary to prove the efficacy of any product. Field programmes generally start with limited trial in one or a very few locations that are designed to provide a preliminary test of efficacy or to screen several candidate products. Once promising results are obtained they are tested in larger area. It is important that field tests ultimately be conducted at several different locations to prove efficacy under varying climatic conditions.

## REGULATION AND REGISTRATION

Current legislation demands that new products are subjected to detailed study of their environmental impact and toxicological effects and they are registered. As current legislation stands, there are certain categories of biocontrol agents that have an easier and quicker passage for registration. Indigenous microorganisms that are never recorded as being plant, animal or human pathogens and which are specific to a defined group of targets have a comparatively straightforward progress. Under the Section 9(3) of Pesticide Act of India (1968) information required for registration of any bio-pesticides are: systematic name and common name; natural occurrence and morphological descriptions; details of manufacturing process (active and inert ingredients of formulation); Test methods (dual culture or pathogenecity); Quantitative analysis (*cfu* on selective media, Absence of Gram(-ve) bacteria contaminants); moisture content; shelf life; mammalian toxicity; bioefficacy; environmental toxicity and residue analysis.

### Registration of Antagonistic Organisms

The following antagonistic organisms have been registered on provisional basis with commercialization for promoting IPM

(1) *Trichoderma*

(a) *Trichoderma viride* W .P
(b) *Trichoderma viride* 1% W.P
(c) *Trichoderma viride* 0.50% W.S
(d) *Trichoderma harzianum* 0.50% W.S
(e) *Trichoderma harzianum* 1.15% W.P

(2) *Pseudomonas*

(a) *Pseudomonas fluorescens* 1.15% WP

## MANUFACTURE

The characteristics of biocontrol agents that might be successful in market place include: (a) Longer shelf-life (b) high performance and consistency (c) persistence of effect (d) safety, (e) stability (f) product differentiation (g) indigenous microbes (h) minimal capital cost, (i) cheap and easy to manufacture and apply using conventional technologies and above all (j) viable market size. Manufacture of microbial products requires fermentation of the microorganisms in commercial quantities. Aqueous fermentation has historically been the preferred approach. However, several companies have developed other approaches such as semi-solid fermentation. Some complex submerged cultural fermentation media for soil inoculants evaluated for *Trichoderma, Pseudomonas, Bacillus, Aspergillus, Penicillium* spp. include molasses, brewer's yeast, soy digest, soybean meal, starch, corn steep liquor, molasses, etc. Recent studies have shown that parasite fitness of *T. harzianum* is better when grown on solid substrate than in liquid culture.

## QUALITY CONTROL STANDARDS OF ANTAGONISTIC ORGANISMS

1. *cfu* on selective medium, minimum of $2 \times 10^6$/ml of TH
2. Microbial contaminants should not increase $1 \times 10^4$
3. Maximum moisture content not more than 8% for dry formulations of fungi and 12% for bacteria.
4. Stability of *cfu* bacteria counts at 30° C and 65% for relative humidity.

## COMMERCIALIZATION

The efforts under way today to commercialize a biocontrol agent can be grouped into three categories based on both increasing level of difficulty and decreasing potential for repeated sales.

The first group, which follows the lead of Rishketh and Kerr is to apply the antagonist directly and precisely to the infection court when and where needed. This group also exemplifies the strategy based on an inundative application, where the antagonist is applied at an instantly high and timely population with the intent to preempt or swamp the pathogen (Cook *et al.*, 1996). This includes examples of seed applied antagonists for protection of germinating seeds against damping-off, to fruits against fruit decay in storage, and ice-minus bacteria to frost injury (Lindow, 1983). Nearly all bioagents commercialized till date fall in to this group. The second group includes antagonists applied at one place, e.g., on seeds, with the intent that they will spread and protect the plant at one or more distant places. Plant growth promoting rhizobacteria (PGPR) fall into this category (Kloepper *et al.*, 1980). This group of antagonists can include cases that exemplify the strategy of inundative application, but more likely, their use exemplifies the strategy of augmentative application, where the antagonist is expected to multiply, persist for part or all of the life of the plant, and augment a background but inadequate population of a related or similar antagonist (Cook *et al.*, 1996). This category of examples obviously represents a much more challenging approach to biological control because of the greater vulnerability of the introduced agent to the effects of competition and environmental conditions. No antagonist that fits nearly into this group has been commercialized. On the other hand, this group continues to attract attention because these agents, like the first group, represent the potential for repeat sales, and because of the competing commercial products, if they exist, are soil fumigants or foliar applied chemicals but can not be used for seed treatments.

The third category of antagonists includes cases that would exemplify the strategy of effective biological control following a one time or occasional inoculative release (Cook *et al.*, 1996). Most of the successful examples of biological control of perennial weeds and insects with microorganisms (other than Bt) are of this type, because the microbial biocontrol agents are pathogens dependent for their ability to multiply and persist on the target pest, their host, and because the perennial nature of the target pests gives them time to become effective. Certain hyperparasites of the reproductive structures of pathogens of perennial plants could fit into this category (Baker and Cook, 1974). While it is too early in the research, it will be interesting to determine whether the toxigenic strain of *Aspergillus flavus* that is showing such potential for biological control of toxigenic strains might become established over time and therefore fit somewhat into this category of biological control. Aside from these kinds of examples, our third category is more hypothetical than actual as an approach to commercial products for biological control of a plant pathogen, nor would there be potential for repeat sales. Development of this category of biological control, where it can be effective, will obviously depend on public sector research since it will not likely attract private sector investment, other than possibly from grower and commodity groups and cooperatives. The commercial formulations available for commercial field use in world market are listed in Table 9.4.

## BIOCONTROL AGENTS AS A MAJOR COMPONENT OF INTEGRATED DISEASE MANAGEMENT SYSTEM

An integrated pest management (IPM) system entails simultaneous or sequential use of several methods of control. Biological control is of particular interest as a component of, and can best be exploited within the framework of an IPM system. Biocontrol agents have distinct advantages in being compatible with most of the agricultural practices and hence, can be successfully utilized as a part of total crop management practices or broadly, as a component of the agro-ecosystem management. Different biocontrol agents have been integrated with cultural practices, soil solarization, fungicides and disease resistant varieties for managing different crop diseases. Combination of the seed/root application of *T. harzianum* or *P. fluorescens* with soil solarization was very effective in management of seed and seedling diseases of tomato, brinjal and capsicum in nursery at farmers field (Singh, U.S., unpublished). Wilt and root-rot complex of chickpea, lentil and pigeon pea were successfully managed by integration of *T. harzianum* or *T. virens* with Vitavax (Mukhopadhyay, 1996). Integration of fertilizers or herbicides with biocontrol agents to control plant diseases has also been attempted. Bacterial biocontrol agents are compatible with most of the fungicides. Even fungal biocontrol agents like *Trichoderma* spp. are insensitive to fungicides like carboxins, oxycarboxins, metalaxyl, tricyclazoles, carpropamid, host defense inducers (e.g. benzothiadiazole) etc. Therefore, they could be integrated easily. Integrating biocontrol agents with reduced doses of fungicides seems to be a very promising way of controlling pathogens with minimal interference with biological equilibrium. This would not only reduce the use of fungicides but also improve the efficacy of a biocontrol system with reduced cost and lessen the chances of development of fungicide resistant strains of the pathogen. Integration of biocontrol agents and fungicides for seed treatment is very effective even against high population of fast growing pathogens like *R. solani* in soil. Under such conditions biocontrol agent alone may not be very effective as by the time it gets activated in soil pathogen is able to penetrate the host. Integration of fungicide with biocontrol agents helps in early protection by fungicide and later protection by biocontrol agent. Fungicide also provide congenial environment to insensitive biocontrol agent to multiply and colonize spermosphere and rhizosphere by suppressing other microbes sensitive to the fungicide.

**TABLE 9.4:** LIST OF AVAILABLE COMMERCIAL PRODUCTS OF FUNGAL AND BACTERIAL BIOCONTROL AGENTS*

| *Product* | *Biocontrol Agent* | *Target Pathogen/ Disease* | *Crop* | *Formulation* | *Application Method* | *Manufacturer/ Distributor* |
|---|---|---|---|---|---|---|
| **AVAILABLE IN INDIA** | | | | | | |
| **Biocon** | *T. viride* | Root and stem diseases | Tea | Liquid and dust | Soil treatment, cutting treatment, foliar spray | Tocklai Experimental Station, Tea Research Association, Jorhat, Assam |
| **Bioderma** | *T. viride* + *T. harzianum* | Fungal pathogens | Vegetables, pulses, cereals and sugar crops | Wettable powder | Seed treatment, soil treatment, seedling dip and foliar spray | Biotech International Limited, New Delhi |
| **Bioguard** | *T. viride* | Seed and soil borne diseases | Vegetables & pulses | Wettable powder | Seed and soil treatment | Krishi Rasayan Export Pvt. Ltd., Solan (H.P.) |
| **Bioshield** | *Pseudomonas fluorescens* | Fungal pathogens | Cereals, pulses, sugar crops and vegetables | Wettable powder | Seed, soil and seedling dip | Anu Biotech International Ltd., Faridabad |
| **Biotok** | *Bacillus subtilis* | Black rot disease caused by *Corticium invisum* and *C. theae* | Tea | Liquid | Soil treatment, cutting treatment, foliar spray | Tocklai Experimental Station, Tea Research Association, Jorhat, Assam |
| **Defence-SF** | *T. viride* | Seed & soil-borne diseases | Cereals, pulses and vegetables | Wettable powder | Seed & soil treatment | Wockhardt Life Science Limited, Mumbai |
| **Ecoderma** | *T. viride* + *T. harzianum* | Fungal pathogens | Vegetables and pulses | Wettable powder | Seed, soil and seedling dip | Margo Biocontrol Pvt. Ltd., Bangalore |
| **Ecofit** | *Trichoderma viride* | Soil-borne plant pathogens | Vegetables and pulses | Wettable powder | Seed treatment | Hoechst and Schering AgrEvo Ltd., Mumbai |

| | | | | | | |
|---|---|---|---|---|---|---|
| **Funginil** | *T. viride* | Soil-borne plant pathogens | Vegetables and pulses | Wettable powder | Seed and soil treatment | Crop Health Bioproduct Research Centre, Ghaziabad |
| **Kalisena SD Kalisena SL** | *Aspergillus niger* AN-27 | Seed and soil-borne diseases promotes growth of plants and induces systemic resistance against plant pathogens | Vegetables, pulses, sugar crops, cereals, root crops, etc. | Wettable powder, granules | Seed and soil treatment | Cadila Pharmaceuticals Limited, Ahmedabad |
| **Pant Biocontrol Agent-1** | *T. harzianum* | Soil borne diseases | Vegetables, pulses, root crops, sugar crops, etc. | Wettable powder | Seed, soil and foliar (spray) application | G. B. Pant University of Agriculture Technology, Pantnagar |
| **Pant Biocontrol Agent-2** | *Pseudomonas fluorescens* | Soil borne diseases, sheath rot and panicle blast of rice | Vegetables, pulses, root crops, sugar crops, etc. | Wettable powder | Seed, soil and foliar (spray) | G. B. Pant University of Agriculture Technology, Pantnagar |
| **Trichoguard** | *T. viride* | Fungal pathogens | Cereals, pulses and vegetables | Wettable powder | Seed, soil and seedling dip | Anu Biotech International Ltd., Faridabad |
| **Tricho-X** | *T. viride* | Seed & soil-borne diseases | Nursery crops | Wettable powder | Seed and soil treatment | Excel Industries Limited, Mumbai |
| **AVAILABLE IN WORLD MARKET** | | | | | | |
| **Actinovate** | *Streptomyces lydicus* | Soil-borne disease | Greenhouse and nursery crops, turf | Water-dispersible granule | Drench | Natural Industries, Inc. |
| **AQ10 Biofungicide** | *Ampelomyces quisqualis isolate* M-10 | Powdery mildew | Apples, cucurbits, grapes, ornamentals, strawberries, and tomatoes | Water-dispersible granule | Spray | Ecogen, Inc. |

Table 9.4 (*contd. on* p. 206)

Table 9.4 (*contd. from* p. 205)

| | | | | | | |
|---|---|---|---|---|---|---|
| **Aspire** | *Candida oleophila* I-182 | *Botrytis* spp., *Penicillium* spp. | Citrus, pome fruit | Wettable powder | Post harvest application to fruit as drench, drip or spray | Ecogen, Inc. |
| **Bio-save 10LP, 110** | *Pseudomonas syringae* | *Botrytis cinerea*, *Penicillium* spp., *Mucor pyroformis*, *Geotrichum candidum* | Pome fruit, citrus, cherries, and potatoes | Lyophilized product, frozen cell concent-rated pellets | Pellets, to produce liquid suspension, drench, dip or spray | Village Farms LLC |
| **BlightBan A506** | *Pseudomonas fluorescens* A506 | Frost damage, *Erwinia amylovora*, and russet-inducing bacteria | Almond, apple, apricot, blueberry, cherry, peach, pear, potato, strawberry, tomato | Wettable powder | Bloom time spray of the flower and fruit | NuFarm Inc. |
| **Cedomon** | *Pseudomonas chlororaphis* | Leaf stripe, net blotch, *Fusarium* spot, and others | Barley and oats; potential for other cereals | Seed treatment | Seed dressing | BioAgri AB |
| **ompanion** | *Bacillus subtilis* GB03 other *B. subtilis*, *B. lichenformis*, *B. megaterium* | *Rhizoctonia*, *Pythium*, *Fusarium*, and *Phytophthora* | Greenhouse and nursery | Liquid | Drench at time of seeding and transplanting or as a spray for turf | Growth Products |
| **Contans WG, Intercept WG** | *Coniothyrium minitans* | *Sclerotinia sclerotiorum* and *S. minor* | All agricultural soils | Water dispersible granule | Spray | Prophyta Biologischer Pflanzenschutz GmbH |
| **Deny** | *Burkholderia cepacia* type Wisconsin | *Rhizoctonia*, *Pythium*, *Fusarium*, and disease caused by lesion, spiral, lance, and sting nematodes | Alfalfa, barley, beans, clover, cotton, peas, grain sorghum, vegetable crops, and wheat | Peat-based dried biomass from solid fermentation; aqueous suspension | Applied to seeds with a sticking agent in planter box (aqueous suspension formu-lation is for use in drip irrigation or as a seedling drench) | Stine Microbial Products |

| | | | | | | |
|---|---|---|---|---|---|---|
| **DiTera Biocontrol** | Fermentation product of killed *Myrothecium verrucaria* | Parasitic nematodes | Cole crops, grape, ornamentals, turf, trees | Powder and liquid suspension from fermentation | Applied to soil and incorporated by various methods | Valent Biosciences, Inc. |
| **Galltrol** | *Agrobacterium radiobacter* Strain 84 | Crown gall disease caused by *Agrobacterium tumefaciens* | Fruit, nut, and ornamental nursery stock | Petri plates with pure culture grown on agar | Bacterial mass from one plate transferred to one gallon of non-chlorinated water; suspension applied to seeds, seedlings, cuttings, roots, stems, and as soil drench | AgBioChem, Inc. |
| **HiStick N/T** | *Bacillus subtilis* MBI600 | *Fusarium*, *Rhizoctonia*, *Aspergillus* | Soybean, alfalfa, dry/snap beans, peanuts | ------------ | Slurry, damp and dry inoculation of seed | Becker Underwood Inc.MicroBio Group, Ltd. |
| **Intercept** | *Burkholderia cepacia* | *Rhizoctonia solani*, *Fusarium* spp., *Pythium* sp. | Maize, vegetables, cotton | ------------ | ------------ | Soil Technologies Corp. |
| **Kodiak (several formulations)** | *Bacillus subtilis* GB03 | *Rhizoctonia solani*, *Fusarium* spp., *Alternaria* spp., and *Aspergillus* spp. that attack roots | Cotton, legumes | Dry powder; usually applied with chemical fungicides | Added to a slurry mix for seed treatment; hopper box treatment | Gustafson, Inc. |
| **Messenger** | *Erwinia amylovora* HrpN harpin protein | Many | Field, ornamental, and vegetable crops | Powder | Drench or spray | EDEN Bioscience Corporation |

Table 9.4 (*contd. on* p. 208)

Table 9.4 (*contd. from* p. 207)

| | | | | | | |
|---|---|---|---|---|---|---|
| **Mycostop** | *Streptomyces griseoviridis* strain K61 | *Fusarium* spp., *Alternaria brassicola*, *Phomopsis* spp., *Botrytis* spp., *Pythium* spp., and *Phytophthora* spp. that cause seed, root, and stem rot, and wilt disease | Field, ornamental, and vegetable crops | Powder | Drench, spray or through irrigation system | Kemira Agro Oy |
| **Nogall** | *Agrobacterium radibacter* K1026 | Crown gall disease caused by *Agrobacterium tumefaciens* | Fruit, nut, and ornamental nursery stock | Petri plates with pure culture grown on agar | Bacterial mass from one plate transferred to one gallon of non-chlorinated water; suspension applied to seeds, seedlings, cuttings, roots, stems, and as soil drench | Bio-care Technology, Australia/New Bio-Products, Inc |
| **Primastop** | *Gliocladium catenulatum* | Soil-borne pathogens that cause seed, root and stem rot, and wilt disease | Ornamental, vegetable, and tree crops | Powder | Drench, spray or through irrigation system | Kemira Agro Oy |
| **RootShield, Plant Shield, T-22 Planter box** | *Trichoderma harzianum* Rifai strain KRL-AG2 (T-22) | *Pythium* spp., *R. solani*, *Fusarium* spp. | Trees, shrubs, transplants, all cabbage, tomato, cucumber | Granules or wettable powder ornamentals, | Granules mixed with soil or potting medium; powder mixed with water and added as a soil drench | Bioworks, Inc. |

| **Serenade** | *Bacillus subtilis* QST716. | Powdery mildew, downy mildew, *Cercospora* leaf spot, early blight, late blight, brown rot, fire blight, and others | Cucurbits, grapes, hops, vegetables, peanuts, pome fruits, stone fruits, and others | Wettable powder | Spray | AgraQuest, Inc. |
|---|---|---|---|---|---|---|
| **SoilGard** | *Gliocladium virens* (a.k.a. *Trichoderma virens*) GL-21 | Damping-off and root rot pathogens especially *Rhizoctonia solani* and *Pythium* spp. | Ornamental and food crop plants grown in green houses,nurseries, homes, and interiors capes | Granules | Granules are incorporated in soil or soilless growing media prior to seeding | Certis, Inc. |
| **YiedShield** | *Bacullus pumillus* GB34 | Soil-borne fungal pathogens causing root diseases | Soybean | ------------ | Dry powder slurry mix for seed treatment; hopper box treatment | Gustafson, Inc. added to a |

## FUTURE PROSPECTS

Realistically, biocontrol may not totally replace chemicals in immediate future. However, judicious use of biocontrol agents can significantly reduce use of pesticides and thereby contribute to sustainable development of agriculture.

These days, though biocontrol research is well established, but it has yet to become an integral part of protection technology. Areas awaiting attention of scientists and policy makers include:

1. Biodiversity in Biocontrol Agents. This involves collection, characterization and maintenance of different species/strains of biocontrol agents. This is very important aspect considering the existence of very wide biodiversity in different biocontrol agents. For meaningful research, genera-wise responsibility may be given to different universities/institutes.
2. Improvement of Biocontrol Agents. One major criticism of BCAs is that they act slowly and give limited protection to crops from diseases. For effective disease control, more aggressive strains of BCAs should be sought, *i.e.* which work more quickly and require less inoculum. Virulence determinants should be identified and used in strain selection and quality control. For disease control, priming of inocula, particularly of spores, needs to receive more attention, especially with regard to effective control in the rhizosphere and phyllosphere.
3. Many BCAs that perform well in laboratory are generally less effective in the field. The quality of BCAs prior to use has received very little attention. For effective field performance, the formulations must consistently be able to tolerate a wide range of climatic (fluctuating temperatures, humidity, ultraviolet (UV) light), edaphic (soil types, pH) and biotic (antagonists) factors. The ecological fitness of strains can be improved through physiological manipulation of growth conditions to channel useful endogenous reserves into the inoculum. The physiologically modified inoculum will germinate at humidity slightly lower than unmodified inoculum. This, combined with improved formulations, could greatly improve the field efficacy of BCAs.
4. Four-way relationship between plants, pathogen, biofertilizers and biocontrol agents is little understood. Complete knowledge of this relation is must to ensure durable existence of biological control as a major component of Integrated Disease Management Systems (IDMS). How and why they work and interact with each other must be understood to formulate strategies.
5. Production costs need to be reduced to allow competitive pricing with conventional pesticides. The products must remain viable for up to 2 years under commercial storage conditions and maintain biocontrol efficacy. The end product should be easy to handle and package. Cultural conditions must be identified, without increasing production costs, to overcome problems of loss of biocontrol. For disease control, particular attention needs to be paid to problems of attenuation of virulence. At present, little progress has been made

in this area, partly because the underlying mechanisms of attenuation have not been elucidated.

6. Good results are often obtained in trials carried out with fresh inoculum but when the inocula have been formulated control is often less effective. For any BCA, efficient formulation is necessary to translate laboratory activity into adequate field performances. For BCAs different methods of preparation, from wet pastes to fluidized-bed drying, spray-drying and freeze-drying, have not been investigated exhaustively. During this process additives can be incorporated to enable viability to be conserved. Some progress has been made, but it is evident that investment is needed to improve field efficacy of BCAs and expand their niche (and ultimately market). Furthermore, formulation with appropriate targeting and spraying systems could further improve the consistency and efficacy of BCAs.

7. Depending upon method of multiplication (solid or liquid fermentation based), formulations of fungal biocontrol agents like *Trichoderma* spp. may be based on unicellular structures like conidia and/or multicellular structures like hyphae or clumps of chlamydospores. Aggressiveness of these structures is going to be different. It must be taken into consideration while defining the dosage for application or *cfu* for the registration of the products.

8. There is need of investigations on compatibility of BCAs with other agents, cultural practices and agrochemicals. This will help in the development of more effective and efficient formulations of BCAs. Industries should work closely with researchers and extension service workers in resolving these matters before the products reach the market.

9. Safety is a major concern of all parties developing BCAs. More studies are needed to evaluate the risks involved in the use of BCAs and particular attention should focus on:

   - Allergenic properties
   - Risks of toxic metabolites
   - Genetic recombination and displacement of natural strains
   - Effect on biodiversity (*i.e.* impact on non-target organisms)

10. The formulation type and packaging materials must be similar to those with which the grower is already familiar. Storage stability must be such that product purchased at the start of one season is good for the whole of the season and the next, without special storage requirements. If the shelf life of a BCA is very limited, a distributor may be prepared to buy only small quantities, thus limiting availability, or will only stock products on a consignment basis, which is a major inconvenience to the BCA supplier.

## REFERENCES

Abraham Mathew, K. and Gupta, S. K. 1998. Biological control of root rot of frenchbean caused by *Rhizoctonia solani*. *J. Mycol. Pl. Pathol.* **28**: 202-205.

Agarwal, S. C., Khare M. N. and Agarwal P. S. 1977. Biological control of *Sclerotium rolfsii* causing collar rot of lentil. *Indian Phytopathol.* **30**: 176-177.

Aggarwal, R. 2000. Role of bio-agents in the management of wheat pathogens. *In*: Proceeding of training programe on "Variability in Rust Fungi and Population of Rust Resistance Genes" held at Centre of Advanced Studies in Plant Pathology, IARI, New Delhi. pp. 244-251.

Aggarwal, R. Singh, D. V., Srivastva, K. D. and Bahadur, P., 2000. The potential of antagonists for biocontrol of *Neovossia indica*, causing karnal bunt of wheat. *Indian J. Biol. Contr.*, **9**: 69-70.

Ahmad, J. S. and Baker, R. 1987. Rhizosphere competence of *Trichoderma harzianum. Phytopathology,* **77**: 182-189.

Ahmad, J. S. and Baker, R. 1988. Implications of rhizosphere competence of *Trichoderma harzianum. Can. J. Microbiol.*, **34**: 229-234.

Ait-Lahsen, H., Soler, A., Rey, M., de La Cruz, Monte, E. and Llobell, A. 2001. An antifungal Exo-a-1,3- glucanase (AGN 13.1) from the biocontrol agent *Trichoderma harzianum. Appl. Environ. Microbiol.*, **67**: 5833-5839.

Alagesaboopathi, C. 1994. Biological control of damping-off disease of cotton seedling. *Curr. Sci.*, **66**: 865-868.

Alexander, M. 1982. *Introduction to Soil Microbiology.* Wiley, New York, p. 467.

Alice, D., Ebenezar, E. G. and Sivaprakasam, K., 1996. Biocontrol of *Macrophomina phaseolina* causing root rot of jasmine. *J. Ecobiol.* **8**: 17-20.

Altman, J. 1970. In: Toussoun, T. A., Bega, R. V., and Nelson, P.E. (eds.), *Root Diseases and Soil Borne Pathogens.* University of California Press, Berkely.

Altomare, C., Norvell, W. A., Bjorkman, T. and Harman, G. E. 1999. Solubilization of phosphates and micronutrients by the plant growth promoting biocontrol fungus *Trichoderma harzianum* Rifai 1295-22. Appl. *Environ. Microbiol.*, **65**: 2926-2933.

Amer, G. A., Singh, D. V., Aggrawal, R. and Dureja, Prem, 1998. *Curr. Sci.* **75**: 1393-1396.

Anandraj, M. and Sharma, Y. R. 1994. Biological control of black pepper disease. *Indian Cocoa Arecanut* and *Spices Journal,* **18**: 22-23.

Anderson R. D, Bailey B. A., Taylor, R., Sharon, A., Avni, A., Matto, A. K., Fuchs, Y. 1993. Fungal xylanase elicits ethylene biosynthesis and other defense responses in tobacco. Pages 197-204 *In*: J. C. Pech, A. Latche and C. Balague, (eds.), *Cellular and Molecular Aspects of the Plant Hormone Ethylene.* Kluwer Academic Publishing, Dordrecht, Netherlands.

Anderson, A. J., and Guerra, D. 1985. Responces of bean to root colonization with *Pseudomonas putida* in a hydroponic system. *Phytopathology,* **75**: 992-995.

Anuratha, C. S. and Gnanaminickam, S. S. 1987. *Pseudomonas fluorescens* suppresses development of bacterial blight (BB) symptoms. *International Rice Research Newsletter,* **12**: 17.

Asghari, M. R. and Mayee, C. D. 1991. Comparative efficiency of management of practices on stem and pod rots of groundnut. *Indian Phytopathol.*, **44**(3): 328-332.

Baby, U. I. and Manibhushanrao, K. 1996. Fungal antagonists and VA mycorrhizal fungi for biocontrol of *Rhizoctonia solani*, the rice sheath blight pathogen. *In*: K. Manibhushan Rao and A. Mahadevan, (eds.), *Recent Developments in Biocontrol of Plant Pathogens.* pp. 1-9.

Baby, U. I. and Manibhushnrao, K. 1993. Control of rice sheath blight through the integration of fungal antagonists and organic amendments. *Trop. Agric.,* **70**(3): 240-244.

Backman, P. A., Rodriguez, K. R., and Williams, J. C. 1975. The effect of peanut leaf spot fungicides on the non-target pathogen *Sclerotium rolfsii. Phytopathology,* **65**: 773.

Bae, Y. S. and Knudsen, G. R. 2000. Cotransformation of *Trichoderma harzianum* with β-glucuronidase and green fluorescent protein genes provides a useful tool for monitoring fungal growth and activity in natural soils. *Appl. Environ. Microbiol.*, **66**: 810-815.

Bailey, B. A. and Lumsden, R. D. 1998. Direct effect of *Trichoderma* and *Gliocladium* on plant growth and resistance to pathogens. *In*: G. E. Harman and C. P. Kubicek, (eds.), *Trichoderma* and *Gliocladium* Vol. 2. Taylor and Francis, London, pp. 185-204.

Baker, K. F. 1987. Evolving concepts of biological control of plant pathogens. *Annu. Rev. Phytopathol.*, **25**: 67-85.

Baker, K. F. and Cook, R. J. 1974. *Biological Control of Plant Pathogens*. W. H. Freeman and Co., San Francisco (Reprinted in 1982, American Phytopathological Society, St. Paul, MN).

Baker, R. 1990. An overview of current and future strategies and models for biological control. pp. 375-388 *In*: D. Hornby, (ed.), *Biological Control of Soil Borne Plant Pathogens*. CAB International Wallingford, United Kingdom.

Barber, D. A., and Lynch, J. M. 1977. Microbial growth in the rhizosphere. *Soil Biol. Biochem.*, **9**: 305-308.

Bari, M. A. and Mukhopadhyay, A. N. 1988. Biocontrol efficacy of *Trichoderma* spp. in controlling black scurf of potato. *Indian J. Mycol. Pl. Pathol.*, **19**: 92.

Bari, M. A., Mondal, S. N., Rahman, M. Z., Rahman, M. L. and Ahmad, K. M. 2000. Control of foot and root rot of barley using fungal antagonists. *In*: Proceeding of Indian Phytopathological Society- Golden Jubilee, International Conference on Integrated Plant Disease Management for Sustainable Agriculture, pp. 285-288.

Benftez, T., Limon, J., Delgado-Jarana, J. and Rey, M. 1998. Glucanolytic and other enzymes and their control. *In*: G. E. Harman and C. P. Kubicek, (eds.), *Trichoderma* and *Gliocladium* Vol. 2. Taylor and Francis, London. pp. 101-127.

Bertagnolli, B. L., Dal, Soglio, F. K., and Sinclair, J. B. 1996. Extracellular enzyme profiles of the fungal pathogen Rhizoctonia solani isolate 2B-12 and of two antagonists, *Bacillus megaterium* strain B153-2-2 and *Trichoderma harzianum* isolate Th008. I. Possible correlation with inhibition of growtyh and biocontrol. *Physiol. Mol. Plant Pathol.*, **48**: 145-160.

Bezbarruah, B. and Patgiri, I. 1992. Biocontrol of fungal pathogens of tea (*Camellia sinensis*). *Indian J. Agric. Sci.*, **62**: 354-357.

Bhai, R. S., Thomas, J. and Naidu, R. 1994. Evaluation of carrier media for field application of *Trichoderma* sp. in cardamom growing soils. *J. Plant. Crops.*, **22**(1): 50-52.

Bhargava, Y. R. 1993. Pleiotropic effect of seed pelleting in controlling seed borne fungal disease in *Brassica oleracea* var. *capitata. Adv. Plant Sci.*, **6**: 62-65.

Bhatnagar, H. 1996. Influence of environmental conditions on antagonistic activity of *Trichoderma* sp. against *Fusarium udum. Indian J. Mycol. Pl. Pathol.*, **26**: 58-63.

Bhattacharya, P. and Mukherjee, N. 1990. Rhizoboium challenges the root rot pathogen (*Sclerotium rolfsii*) on groundnut surfaces. *Indian Agricul.*, **34**(2): 63-71.

Bhuyan, S. A., Das, B. C. and Bora, L. C. 1994. Antagonistic effect of *Trichoderma viride, Trichoderma harzianum* and *Aspergillus terreus* on *Rhizoctonia solani* causing sheath blight of rice. *Journal of the Agricultural Science Society of North East India,* **7**(1): 125. 127.

Bidari, V. B. and Gundappagol, R. C. 1997. *Trichoderma viride* in the integrated management of pigeon pea wilt under dry land cultivation. *Advances in Agricultural Research in India,* **7**: 65-69.

Bisset, J. 1991a. A revision of the genus *Trichoderma.* II. Infrageneric classification. *Can. J. Bot.*, **69**: 2357-2372.

Bisset, J. 1991b. A revision of the genus *Trichoderma.* III. Section Pachybasium. *Can. J. Bot.*, **69**: 2373-2417.

Bolar, J. P., Norelli, J. L., Wong, K. W., Hayes, C. K., Harman, G. E. and Alwinckle, H. S. 2000. Expression of endochitinase from *Trichoderma harzianum* in transgenic apple increases resistance to apple scab and reduces vigour. *Phytopathology,* **90**: 1377-1383.

Bora, L. C., Gangopadhyay, S. and Chand, J. N. 1993. Biological control of bacterial leaf spot (*Xanthomonas compestris* pv. *vignaeradiatae*, Dye) of mung bean with phylloplane antagonists. *Indian J. Mycol. Pl. Pathol.,* **23**(2): 162-168.

Broadbent, P., Baker, K. F., Franks, N., Holland, J. 1977. Effect of Bacillus spp. on increased growth of seedlings in steamed and in nontreated soil. *Phytopathology,* **67**: 1027-1034.

Broadbent, P., Baker, K. F., Waterworth, Y. 1971. Bacteria and actinomycetes antagonistic to fungal root pathogens in Australian soils. *Aust. J. Biol. Sci.,* **24**: 925-944.

Broglie, K., Chet, I., Holliday, M., Cressman, R., Biddle, P., Knowlton, S., Mauvais, C. J., and Broglie, R. 1991. *Science,* **254**: 1194-1197.

Budge, S. P., M. C. Quiken, M. P., Fenlon, J. S., and Whipps, J. M. 1995. Use of Coniothyrium minitans and *Gliocladium virens* for biological control of *Sclerotinia sclerotiorum* in glasshouse lettuce. *Biol. Control,* **5**: 513-522.

Burr, T. J., Schroth, M. N., and Suslow, T. V. 1978. Increased potato yields by treatments of seed pieces with specific strains of *Pseudomonas fluorescens* and *P. putida*. *Phytopathology*, **68**: 1377-1383.

Calderon, A. A., Japata, J. M., Munoj, R., Pedreno, M. A. and Barcelo, A. R. 1993. Resveratrol and their production as a part of the hypersensitive like response of grapevine cells to an elicitor from *Trichoderma viride*. *New Phytol.*, **124**: 424-463.

Callan, N. W., Mathre, D. E., Miller, J. B. and Vavrina, C. S. 1997. Biological seed treatments: Factors involved in efficacy. *Hort Sci.*, **32**: 179-183.

Carver, T. L. W., Zeyen, R. J., Bushnell, W. R., and Robbins, M. P. 1994. Inhibition of phenylalanine ammonia lyase and cinnamyl alcohol dehydrogenase increases quantitative susceptibility of barley to powdery mildew (*Erysiphe graminis* D. C.). *Physiol. Mol. Plant Pathol.*, **44**: 261-72.

Chakraborthy, A. and Gupta, P. K. S. 1995. Factors affecting cross protection of fusarium wilt of pigeon pea by soil borne non-pathogenic fungi. *Phytoparasitica*, **23**(4): 323-334.

Chakraborthy, B. N., Das, G., Das, S. K. and Chakraborty, U. 1994. Phyllosphere microflora of tea (*Camellia sinensis* (L.) O. Kuntze) and their interaction with *Glomerella cingulata* the causal agent of brown light disease. *Tea*, **15**(1): 27-34.

Chang, Y. C., Baker, R., Kleifeld, O. and Chet, I. 1986. Increased growth of plants in the presence of the biological control agent *Trichoderma harzianum*. *Plant Dis.*, **70**: 145-148.

Chao, W. L., Nelson, F. B., Harman, G. E., and Hoch, H. C. 1986. Colonization of the rhizosphere by biological control agents applied to seeds. *Phytopathology*, **76**: 60-65.

Chattopadhyay, C. and Sen, B. 1996. Integrated management of fusarium wilt of muskmelon caused by *Fusarium oxysporum*. *Indian J. Mycol. Pl. Pathol.*, **26**(2): 162-170.

Chattopadhyay, S. K. and Nandy, B. 1982. Inhobition of *Helminthosporium oryzae* and *Alternaria solani* by *Streptomyces longisporus* (Kraslinokov) walksman. *Plant* and *Soil*, **69**: 171-175.

Chaturvedi, C. 1986. Biocontrol efficacy of *Trichoderma koningii* on brinjal damping off. M.Sc. (Ag.) Thesis, G. B. Pant University of Agric. & Tech. Pantnagar, INDIA, p. 108.

Chaube, H. S. and Singh, U. S. 1991. Plant Disease Management: Principles and Practices. CRC Press, Boca Raton, U.S.A.

Chaube, H. S., Mishra, D. S., Varshney, S. and Singh, U. S. 2002. Biological control of plant pathogens by fungal antagonists: Historical background, present status and future prospects. *Annu. Rev. Plant Pathol.*, **2**: (In Press).

Chaurasia, R. K. and Bhatt, J. 2000. Biological control of *Phytophthora* foot and leaf rot of betelvine. *In*: Proceeding of Indian Phytopathological Society-Golden Jubilee, International Conference on Integrated Plant Disease Management for Sustainable Agriculture, pp. 353-354.

Chet, I., Hadar, Y., Elad, Y., Katan, J. and Henis, Y. 1979. Biological control of soil borne plant pathogens by *Trichoderma harzianum*. *In*: B. Schippers and W. Gams (eds.), *Soil Borne Plant Pathogens*. Academic Press, NewYork, pp. 581-591.

Chet, I. 1987. *Trichoderma*: Applilcation, mode of action and potential as a bioconrol agent of soil borne plant pathogenic fungi. *In*: I.Chet, (ed.) *Innovative Approaches to Plant Disease Control*. John Wiley and Sons, New York, pp. 137-160.

Chet, I., Harman, G. E., and Baker, R. 1981. *Trichoderma harzianum*: Its hyphal interactions with *Rhizoctonia solani* and *Pythium* spp. *Microbiol. Ecol.*, **7**: 29.

Conway, K. E., and Khan, B. A. 1990. Enhanced growth of borecoli transplants by the biocontrol fungi *Trichoderma harzianum* and *Laetisaria arvalis*. *Phytopathology*, **80**: 434 (Abstr.)

Cook, R. J. and Baker, K. F. 1983. *The Nature and Practices of Biological Control of Plant Pathogens*. APS Books, St. Paul. MN, U.S.A., 599 pp.

Cook, R. J., Bruckart, W. L. and Coulson, J. R. 1996. Safety of mico-organism intended for pest and plant disease management: Framework for scientific evaluation. *Biol. Control*, **7**: 333-351.

Dandurand, L. M., and Knudsen, G. R. 1993. Influence of *Pseudomonas fluorescens* on hyphal growth and biocontrol activity of *Trichoderma harzianum* in the spermosphere and rhizosphere of pea. *Phytopathology*, **83**: 265-270.

Das, B. C. Bora, L. C. and Phookan, A. K. 1995a. Influence of soil pH on *Trichoderma* in suppressing sheath blight of rice. *Journal of the Agricultural Science Society of North East India*, **8**(2): 158-161.

Das, B. C., Bhuyan, S. A. and Bora, L. C. 1995b. Comparative efficacy of *Trichoderma viride* in suppressing sheath blight of rice by different methods of application. *Plant Health,* **1**: 7-11.

Das, B. C., Roy, S. and Bora, L. C. 2000. Biological seed treatment with *Trichoderma* spp. for management of damping off of cabbage caused by *Rhizoctonia solani. In*: Proceeding of Indian Phytopathological Society—Golden Jubilee, International Conference on Integrated Plant Disease Management for Sustainable Agriculture, pp. 409-410.

Datnoff, L. E., Nemec, S., and Pernezny, K. 1995. Biological control of *Fusarium* crown and root rot of tomato in Florida using *Trichoderma harzianum* and *Glomus* intraradices. *Biol. Control,* **5**: 427-431.

Datnoff, L. E., Nemec, S., and Pohronezny, K. 1993. Influence of *Trichoderma harzianum* and *Glomus intraradices* on incidence and severity of *Fusarium* crown and root rot. *Biol. Cultural Tests,* **9**: 78.

De Boer, M., van der Sluis, I., van Loon, L. C., and Bakker, P. A. H. M. 1997. *In vitro* compatibility between fluorescent *Pseudomonas* spp. strains can increase effectivity of *Fusarium* wilt control by combinations of these strains. *In*: A. Ogoshi, K. Kobayashi, Y. Homma, F. Kodama, N. Kondo, and S. Akino, (eds.), *Plant Growth-Promoting Rhizobacteria- Present Status and Future Prospects.* Proc. Int. Workshop on Plant Growth Promoting Rhizobacteria, 4th. Nakanishi Printing, Sapporo, Japan, pp. 380-382.

De la Cruz, J., Pinor-Toro, J. A., Benitez, T., Llobell, A. and Romero, L. C. 1995. A novel endo-β-1, 3-glucanase, BGN 13.1, involved in the mycoparasitism of *Trichoderma harzianum. J. Bacteriol.,* **177**: 6937-6945.

De Meyer, G., Bigirimana, J., Elad, Y. and Hofte, M. 1998. Induced systemic resistance in *Trichoderma harzianum* biocontrol of *Botrytis cineria. Eur. J. Plant Pathol.,* **107**: 279-286.

De, R. K., Chaudhary, R. G. and Naimuddin. 1996. Comparative efficacy of bio-control agents and fungicides for controlling chickpea wilt caused by *Fusarium oxysporum* f. sp. *ciceri. Indian J. Agric. Sci.,* **66**: 370-373.

Dennis, C., and Webster, J. 1971a. Antagonistic properties of species- groups of *Trichoderma.* I. Production of non-volatile antibiotics. *Trans. Brit. Mycol. Soc.,* **57**: 25.

Dennis, C., and Webster, J. 1971b. Antagonistic properties of species-groups of *Trichoderma.* III. Hyphal interactions. *Trans. Brit. Mycol. Soc.,* **57**: 363.

Desai, S., and Schlosser, E. 1999. Parasitism of *Sclrotium rolfsii* by *Trichoderma. Indian Phytopathol.,* **52**: 47.

Deshmukh, P. P., Raut, J. G. and Khan, Y. D. 1994. Effect of *Trichoderma* sp. and fungicides on fungi of sorghum (*Sorghum bicolor*). *Indian J. Agric. Sci.,* **64**: 205-206.

Dileep, C., Dileep Kumar, B. S. and Dube, H. C. 1999. Disease suppression and plant growth promotion of peanut by fluorescent pseudomonad strains, FPC-32 and FPO-4 in soil infested with collar rot fungi, *Aspergillus niger. Indian Phytopathol.,* **52**: 415-416.

Dinakaran, D. and Ramakrishnan, G. 1996. Studies on the control of tomato damping-off with *Trichoderma viride. Plant Dis. Res.,* **11**: 148-150.

Dohroo, N. P. 1995. Integrated management of yellows of ginger. *Indian Phytopathol.,* **48**: 90-92.

Dohroo, N. P. and Gupta, S. K. 1995. *Trichoderma harzianum* in biological control of diseases of vegetable crops- a review. *Agricultural Reviews, Karnal,* **16**(1): 52-56.

Dohroo, N. P., Sharma, S. L. 1984. Biological control of rhizome rot of ginger in storage with *Trichoderma viride. Indian J. Plant Pathol.,* **2**(2): 185-186.

Dube, H. C. 2001. Rhizobacteria in biological control and plant growth promotion. *J. Mycol. Pl. Pathol.,* **31**: 9-21.

Dubey, S. C. 1998. Evaluation of different fungal antagonists, plant extracts and oil cakes against *Thanatephorus cucumeris* causing banded blight of rice. *J. Mycol. Pl. Pathol.,* **28**: 266-269.

Duffy, B. K. and Weller, D. M. 1995. Use of *Gaeumannomyces graminis* var. *graminis* alone and in combination with fluorescent *Pseudomonas* spp. to suppress take-all of wheat. *Plant Dis.,* **79**: 907-911.

Duffy, B. K., Simon, A., and Weller, D. M. 1996. Combinations of *Trichoderma koningii* and fluorescent pseudomonad for control of take-all of wheat. *Phytopathology,* **86**: 188-194.

Duffy, B. K., Simon, A., and Weller, D. M. 1996. Combinations of *Trichoderma koningii* and fluorescent pseudomonad for control of take-all of wheat. *Phytopathology,* **86**: 188-194.

Ebenezar, E. G., Alice, D. and Sivaprakasam, K., 1996. Biological control of damping-off disease in mustard caused by *Pythium aphanidermatum. J. Ecobiol.,* **8**(1): 55-57.

Elad, Y. 1994. Biological control of grape gray mould by *Trichoderma harzianum. Crop Prot.,* **13**: 35-38.

Elad, Y. 1995. Mycoparasitism. *In: Pathogenesis* and *Host Specificity in plant diseases: Histopathological, Biochemical, Genetic* and *Molecular Basis,* Eukaruotes, Vol. II. Pergamon, Elsevier, Oxford, UK, pp. 289-307.

Elad, Y. 2000. Biological control of foliar pathogens by means of *Trichoderma harzianum* and potential modes of action. *Crop Prot.,* **19**: 709-714.

Elad, Y., and Baker, R. 1985. The role of competition for iron and carbon in suppression of chlamydospore germination of Fusarium spp. by Pseudomonas spp. *Phytopathology,* **75**: 1053.

Elad, Y., Chet, I. and Baker, R. 1987. Increased growth response of plants induced by rhizobacteria antagonistic to soil borne pathogenic fungi. *Plant and Soil,* **98**: 325-330.

Elad, Y., Chet, I. and Henis, Y. 1981. A selective medium for improving quantitative isolation of *Trichoderma* spp. from soil. *Phytoparasitica,* **9**: 59-67.

Elad, Y., Chet, I. and Katan, J. 1980. *Trichoderma harzianum:* A biocontrol agent effective against *Sclerotium rolfsii* and *Rhizoctonia solani. Phytopathology,* **70**: 119.

Elad, Y., David, D. R., Levi, T., Kapat, A., Kirshner, B., Guvrin, E. and Levine, A. 1999. *Trichoderma harzianum Trichoderma*-39 mechanisms of biocontrol of foliar pathogens. *In:* H. Lyr, (ed.), *Modern Fungicides and Antifungal Compounds* II. Intercept Ltd. Andover, Hampshire, UK. pp. 459-467.

Elad, Y., Kapat, A. 1999. Role of *Trichoderma harzianum* protease in the biocontrol of *Botrytis cineria. Eur. J. Plant Pathol.,* **105**: 177-189.

Elad, Y., Krishner, B., Nitzani, Y. and Sztejnberg, A. 1998a. Management of powdery mildew and gray mold of cucumber by *Trichoderma harzianum* T39 and *Ampelomyces quisqualis* AQ10. *Biol. Control,* **43**: 241-251.

Elad, Y., Rav David, D., Levi, T., Kapat, A., Kirshner, B., Guvrin, E. and Levine, A. 1998b. *Trichoderma harzianum* T39- mechanisms of biocontrol of foliar pathogens. *In:* H. Lyr, P. E. Russel, H. W. Dehne, H.D. Sisler (eds.), *Modern Fungicides and Antifungal Compounds* II. Intercept Ltd. Andover, Hampshire. UK, pp. 459-467.

Fahima, T., and Henis, Y. 1990. Interactions between pathogens, host and biocontrol agent: *Multiplication* of *T. hamatum* and *T. flavus* on roots of diseased and healthy hosts. *In:* D. Hornby (ed.), *Biological Control of Soil Borne Plant Pathogens.* CAB International, pp. 165-180.

Farrand, S. K., Slota, J. E., Shim, J. S. and Kerr, A. 1985. Tn5 insertions in the agrosin 84 plasmid: The conjugal nature of pAgK84 and the locations of determinants for transfer and agrosin 84 production. *Plasmid,* **13**: 106-117.

Flores, A., Chet, I. and Herrera-Estrella, A. 1997. Improved Biocontrol activity of *Trichoderma harzianum* by overexpression of the proteinase encoding gene *prb 1. Curr. Genet.,* **31**: 30-37.

Fracchia, S., Mujica, M. T., Garcia-Romera, I., Garcia-Garrido, J. M., Martin, J., Ocampo, J. A. and Godeas, A. 1998. Interactions between Glomus mosseae and arbuscular mycorrhizal sporocarp associated saprophytic fungi. *Plant and Soil.,* **200**: 131-137.

Fugro, P. A., Patil, V. H. and Mandokhot, A. M. 2000. Management of *Fusarium* wilt of watermelon. *In:* Proceeding of Indian Phytopathological Society-Golden Jubilee, International Conference on Integrated Plant Disease Management for Sustainable Agriculture, pp. 713-714.

Fukui, R., Fukui, H. and Alvarez, D. M. 1999. Comaparison of single versus multiple bacterial species on biological control of anthurium blight. *Phytopathology,* **89**: 366-373.

Gaikwad, S. J. and Kapgate, D. J. 1990. Biological control of *Sclerotium* root rot of sesamum. PKV *Research Journal,* **14**(1): 87-89.

Gajbe, D. W. and Lanjewar, R. D. 1991. Antagonism of *Aspergillus niger* on some seed borne fungi of two rice cultivars. *PKV Research Journal,* **15**(2): 168-171.

Gandhikumar, N. and Rangnathan, K. 2000a. Evaluation of different substrates on the survival of *Trichoderma viride* and *Trichoderma harzianum*. *In*: Proceeding of Indian Phytopathological Society-Golden Jubilee, International Conference on Integrated Plant Disease Management for Sustainable Agriculture, p. 370.

Gandhikumar, N. and Rangnathan, K. 2000b. Biocontrol of *Fusarium* wilt of coriander. *In*: Proceeding of Indian Phytopathological Society—Golden Jubilee, International Conference on Integrated Plant Disease Management for Sustainable Agriculture, p. 324.

Ganesan, P. and Gnanamanickam S. S. 1987. Biological control of *Sclerotium rolfsii* Sacc. in peanut by inoculation with *Pseudomonas fluorescens*. *Soil Biol. Biochem.*, **19**: 35-38.

Gangopadhyay, S. and Joshi, R. K. 2000. Efficacy of *Trichoderma* in controlling root rot of cotton and chickpea. *In*: Proceeding of Indian Phytopathological Society—Golden Jubilee, International Conference on Integrated Plant Disease Management for Sustainable Agriculture, pp. 325-326.

Garret, S. D. 1965. Towards biological control. *In*: K. F. Baker and W. C. Snyder (eds.), *Ecology of Soil-borne Plant Pathogens*. University of California Press, Berkeley, pp. 4-17.

Geremia, R. A., Goldman, G. H., Jacobs, D., Ardiles, W., Wila, S. B., Van Montagu, M. and Herrera-Estrella, A. 1993. Molecular characterization of the proteinase encoding gene prb1, related to mycoparasitism by *Trichoderma harzianum*. *Mol. Microbiol.*, **8**: 603-613.

Ghosh, S. 1996. Biocontrol characterization of *Trichoderma harzianum*, Rifai, isolate-3 and its protoplast fusion with *Gliocladium virens*, Miller *et al.*,. M.Sc., Thesis, G. B. Pant University of Agric. & Tech. Pantnagar- 263145 (INDIA), p. 75.

Gindrat, D. 1979. Biological soil disinfestations. *In*: D. Mulder (ed), *Soil Disinfestation*. Elsevier, Amsterdam, pp. 251-287.

Gnanamanickam, S. S., Ahmed, S. and Mew, T. W. 1992. Biological control of rice diseases. *Indian Review of Life Sciences*, **12**: 3-22.

Gnanamanickam, S. S., Mew, T. W., Greyson, B. T., Green, M. B. and Copping, L. G. 1990. Biological control of rice diseases (blast and sheath blight) with bacterial antagonists: an alternate strategy for disease management. *Pest management in rice* (conference held by the Society of Chemical Industry, London, U. K. pp. 87-110.

Godara, S. L. and Pathak, V. N. 2000. Integrated disease management of post harvest rots of sweet orange fruits. *In*: Proceeding of Indian Phytopathological Society- Golden Jubilee, International Conference on Integrated Plant Disease Management for Sustainable Agriculture, pp. 757-759.

Gogoi, R. and Roy, A. K. 1996. Effect of soil pH and media on the antagonism of *Aspergillus terreus* to the rice sheath blight fungus. *Indian Phytopathol.*, **49**(1): 32-36.

Gohil, V. P. and Vala, D. G. 1996. Antagonistic effect of microorganisms to *Fusarium moniliforme*. *Madras Agricultural Journal*, **83**(6): 396-397.

Gokulapalan, C. and Nair, M. C. 1992. Phylloplane fungi of rice as mycoparasites of *Rhizoctonia solani*. *Indian Phytopathol.*, **45**(3): 367-368.

Goldman, G. H., Hayas, C. and Harman, G. E. 1994. Molecular and cellular biology of Biocontrol by *Trichoderma harzianum*. *Trends in Biotechnol.*, **12**: 478-482.

Gopinathan, S. 1995. Biological control of *Rhizoctonia* sp. root rot of *Casuarina equisetifolia* seedlings by *Frankia* sp. strains. *Biology and Fertility of Soils*, **20**(4): 221-225.

Goto, M. 1990. Fundamentals of bacterial plant pathology. Academic Press, Inc Harcourt Brace Jovanovich publishers. London, NewYork, Tokyo. pp. 104-141.

Gowda, B. J. and Balasubramanian, R. 1991. Flourescent antibody localization of hyperparasites on uredia of groundnut leaf rust, *Puccinia arachidis*. *Indian J. Microbiol.*, **31**(3): 237-241.

Gowda, B. J. and Balasubramanian, R. 1993. Biological potential of rust of groundnut by *Acremonium obclavatum*. *Can. J. Bot.*, **71**(4): 639-643.

Graham, R. D., and Webb, M. J. 1991. Micronutrients and disease resistance and tolerance in plants. *In*: R. M. Welch, (ed.), *Micronutrients in Agriculture*. Soil Science Society of America, Madison, WI pp. 329-370.

Green, H. and Jensen, 1995. A tool for monitoring *Trichoderma harzianum*. II. The use of GUS transformant for ecological studies in the rhizosphere. *Phytopathology*, **85**: 1436-1440.

Guetsky, R., Dinoor, A., Elad, Y. and Shtienberg, D. 1998a. Microorganisms combinations for the biocontrol of gray mold (*Botrytis cineria*) in strawberries. ((Abstr.) *Phytoparazitica*, **26**: 174.

Guetsky, R., Elad, Y., Shtienberg, D. and Dinoor, A. 1998b. Combinations of microorganisms for the biocontrol of the gray mold (*Botrytis cineria*) in strawberry. *In*: Proc. Int. Congr. Plant Prot., 6th., pp. 106.

Guetsky, R., Shtienberg, D., Elad, Y. and Dinoor, A. 2001. Combining biocontrol agents to reduce the variability of biological control. *Phytopathology*, **91**: 621-627.

Gupta, C. P., Dubey, R. C., Kang, S. C. and Maheshwari, D. K. 2001. Antibiosis mediated necrotrophic effect of *Pseudomonas* GRC. *Curr. Sci.*, **81**: 91-94.

Gupta, I. J. and Cheema, H. S. 1990. Effect of microsclerotia of *Macrophomina phaseolina* and seed dressers on germination and vigour of sesame *seed. Seed Research*, **18**(2): 169-172.

Gupta, S. Arora, D. K. and Srivastava, A. K. 1995. Growth promotion of tomato plants by rhizobacteria and imposition of energy stress on *Rhizoctonia solani*. *Soil Biol. Biochem.*, **27**(8): 1051-1058.

Gupta, V. K. 2000. The concept of integrated disease management in apple. *In*: Proceeding of Indian Phytopathological Society—Golden Jubilee, International Conference on Integrated Plant Disease Management for Sustainable Agriculture, pp. 679-684.

Gupta, V. P. and Sarkar, A. 2000. Biological control of nursery diseases of mulberry. *In*: Proceeding of Indian Phytopathological Society—Golden Jubilee, International Conference on Integrated Plant Disease Management for Sustainable Agriculture, pp. 348-359.

Hadar, Y., Harman, G. E., Taylor, A. E., and Norton, J. M. 1983. Effects of pregermination of pea and cucumber seeds and of seed treatment with *Enterobacter cloacae* on rots caused by *Pythium* spp. *Phytopathology*, **73**: 1322-1325.

Hadwan, H. A. and Khara, H. S. 1990. *In vitro* interaction of *Trichoderma isolates* with *Rhizoctonia solani* causing damping off and fruit rot of tomato. *Indian J. Ecol.*, **17**(2): 125-127.

Haral, A. K. and Konde, R. K. 1983. Biological management of soil borne plant pathogens: effects on nodulation and dry matter of chickpea. *Journal of Maharashtra Agricultural Universities*, **8**(2): 112-113.

Harman, G. E. 2000. Myths and dogmas of Biocontrol: Changes in the perceptions derived from research on *Trichoderma harzianum* T-22. *Plant Dis.*, **84**: 377-393.

Harman, G. E. and Bjöorjman, T. 1998. Potential and existing uses os *Trichoderma* and *Gliocladium* for plant disease control and plant growth enhancement. *In*: G. E. Harman and C. K. Kubicek, (eds.) *Trichoderma* and *Gliocladium*, Vol. 2. Taylor and Francis Ltd., London, pp. 229-265..

Harman, G. E., and Stasz, T. E. 1989. Protoplast fusion for the production of superior biocontrol fungi. *In*: *Microbial Weed Control*, ed. Do TeBeest, New York: Chapman and Hall.

Harman, G. E., Chet, I. and Baker 1980. *Trichoderma hamatum* effects on seed and seedling disease induced in radish and pea induced by *Pythim* spp. and *Rhozoctonia solani*. *Phytopathology*, **70**: 1167-1172.

Harman, G. E., Hayes, C. K., Lorito, M., Broadway, R. M., Di Pietro, A. and Trosma, A. 1993. Chitinolytic enzymes of *Trichoderma harzianum*: Purification of chitobiosidase and endochitinase. *Phytopathology*, **83**: 313-318.

Harman, G. E., Taylor, A. G., and Stasz, T. E. 1989. Combining strains of *Trichoderma harzianum* and solid matrix priming to improve biological seed treatments. *Plant Dis.*, **73**: 631-637.

Hassan, D. G., Zargar, M., and Beigh, G. M. 1997. Biological control of *Fusarium* root rot of common bean (*Phaleolus vulgaris* L.) by using symbiotic *Glomus mosseae* and *Rhizobium leguminosarum*. *Mol. Ecol.*, **34**: 74-80.

Haware, M. P., Lenne J. M. and Mukherjee P. K. 1996. Integrated management of Botrytis gray mold of chickpea. Proceedings of XI. International Botrytis symposium 23-27 June, Wageningen p. 98.

Hayes, C. K., Klemsdal, S., Lorito, M., Di Pietro, A., Peterbauer, C., Nakasa, J. P., Tronsmo, A. and Harman, G. E. 1994. Isolation and sequence of an endochitinase—encoding gene from a cDNA library of *Trichoderma harzianum*. *Gene*, **138**: 143-148.

Hemming, B. C. 1986. Microbial iron interactions in the plant rhizosphere: An overview. *J. Plant Nutr.*, **9**: 505-521.

Henis, Y., Gaffar, A., and Baker, R. 1978. Integrated control of *R. solani* damping off of radish and effect on successive plantings, PCNB and *Trichoderma* on pathogen and disease. *Phytopathology*, **68**: 900-907.

Hornby, D. 1983. Suppressive soils. *Annu. Rev. Phytopathol.*, **21**: 65.

Howell, C. R. 1982. Effect of *Gliocladium virens* on *Pythium ultimum, Rhizoctonia solani* and damping-off of cotton seedlings. *Phytopathology*, **72**: 496-498.

Howell, C. R. 1987. The role of mycoparasitism in the biological control of *Rhizoctonia solani* by *Gliocladium virens. Phytopathology*, **77**: 992-994.

Howell, C. R. 1998. The role of antibiosis in biocontrol. *In*: G. E. Harman and C. P. Kubicek (eds.), *Trichoderma* and *Gliocladium*, Vol. 2 Taylor and Francis, London, pp. 173-184.

Howell, C. R., and Stipanovic, R. D. 1995. Mechanisms in the biocontrol of *Rhizoctonia solani*-induced cooton seedling disease by *Gliocladium virens*: Antibiosis. *Phytopathology*, **85**: 469-472.

Howell, C. R., Beier, R. C. and Stipanovic, R. C. 1988. Production of ammonia by *Enterobacter cloacae* and its possible role in the biological control of *Pythium* preemergence damping off by the bacterium. *Phytopathology*, **78**: 1075-1078.

Howell, C. R., Hanson, L. E., Stipanovic, R. D. and Puckhaber, L. S. 1999. Induction of terpenoid synthesis in cotton roots and control of *Rhizoctonia solani* by seed treatment with *Trichoderma virens. Phytopathology*, **90**: 248-252.

Hubbard, J. P., Harman, G. E. and Hadar, Y. 1983. Effect of soil borne *Pseudomonas* spp. on the biologival control agent *Trichoderma hamatum* on pea seeds. *Phytopathology*, **73**: 655-659.

Huber, D. M., and McCay-Buis, T. S. 1993. A multiple component analysis of the take-all disease of cereals. *Plant Dis.*, **77**: 437-447.

Huber, D. M. and Wilhelm, N. S. 1988. The role of manganese in resistance to plant diseases. *In*: R. D.Graham, R. D.Hannam and N. C. Uren (eds.), *Manganese in Soil and Plants*. Kluwer Academic Publishers, Dordrecht, Netherlands, pp.155-173.

Ischii, H. 1995. Monitoring of fungicide resistance in fungi: Biological to biotechnological approaches. *In*: R. P. Singh and U. S. Singh (eds.), *Molecular Methods in Plant Pathology*. Lewis Publishers, Boca Raton, U.S.A. pp. 493-503.

Islam, K. Z. and Nandi, B. 1985. Control of brown spot of rice by *Bacillus megaterium. Zeitschrift-fur-Pflanzenkrankheiten-und-Pflanzenschutz*, **92**(3): 241-246.

Jacob, C. K., Annajutty Joseph, Jayarathnam, K. and Joseph, A. 1991. Effect of fungal antagonists on *Phellinus noxius* causing brown root disease of *Hevea. Indian Journal of Natural Rubber Research*, **4**(2): 142-145.

Jagadeesh, K. S. and Geeta, G. S. 1994. Effect of *Trichoderma harzianum* grown on different food bases on the biological control of *Sclerotium rolfsii* Sacc. in groundnut. *Environment and Ecology*, **12**(2): 471-473.

Janisiewicz, W. and Bors, B. 1995. Development of a microbial community of bacterial and yeasts antagonists to control wound invading post harvest pathogens of fruits. *Appl. Environ. Microbiol.*, **61**: 3261-3267.

Janisiewicz, W. J. 1988. Biocontrol of postharvest diseases of apples with antagonists mixtures. *Phytopathology*, **78**: 194-198.

Janisiewicz, W. J. 1996. Ecological diversity, niche overlap and coexistance of antagonists used in develping mixtures for biocontrol of post harvest diseases of apples. *Phytopathology*, **86**: 473-479.

Jebakumar, R. Stephen, George, Gilu Lizy, Babu, S., Raghuchander, T., Gopalswamy, G., Vidhyasekaran, P., Samiyappan. R., Raja, J. A. J. and Balasubramanium, P. 2000. Purification and sequencing of a 42-kDa *Trichoderma viride* chitinase isoform effective against *Rhizoctonia solani. Indian Phytopathol.*, **53**: 157-161.

Jeyalakshmi, C., Surairaj, P., Seetharaman, K. and Sivaprakasan, K. 1998. Biocontrol of fruit rot and die-back of chilli using antagonistic micro-organisms. *Indian Phytopathol.*, **51**: 180-183.

Jeyarajan, R. Ramakrishnan G. Dinakaran D and Sridhar R. 1993. Development of product of *Trichoderma viride* and *Bacillus subtilis* for Bio control of root rot disease. *In:* Dwivedi R (ed.), *Biotechnology in India.* Bioved Research Society, Allahabad.

Jharia, H. K. and Singh, M. 2000. Integrated management of sesame diseases. *In:* Proceeding of Indian Phytopathological Society—Golden Jubilee, International Conference on Integrated Plant Disease Management for Sustainable Agriculture, pp. 912-913.

Jindal, K. K. and Thind, B. S. 1990. Microflora of cowpea seeds and its significance in the biological control of seed borne infection of *Xanthomonas compestris* pv. *vignicola. Seed Sci. Technol.*, **18**(2): 393-403.

Jindal, K. K. and Thind, B. S. 1993. Biological control of bacterial blight of cowpea (*Vigna unguiculata* L. Walp.). *Phytopatologia Mediterranea,* **32**(3): 193-200.

Jindal, K. K. and Thind, B. S. 1994. Evaluation of greengram micro-flora for the control of *Xanthomonas compestris* pv. *vignaeradiate,* the incitant of bacterial leaf spot. *Plant Dis. Res.*, **9**(1): 10-19.

Jisha, M. S., and Alagawadi, A. R. 1996. Nutrient uptake and yield of sorghum (*Sorghum bicolor* L. Moench) inoculated with phosphate solubilizing bacteria and cellulolytic fungus in a cotton stalk amended vertisol. *Microbiological Research,* **151**: 213-217.

Johari, B. N., Rao, C. V. S. and Goel, Reeta 1997. Fluorescent Pseudomonads in plant disease management. *In:* K. R. Dadarwal (ed.) *Biotechnological Approaches in Soil Micro-organisms for Sustainable Crop Protection.* Scintific Publisher, Jodhpur, pp. 193-222.

Johnson, K. B., Stockwell, V. O., Mc Laughin, R. J., Sugar, D., Loper, J. E. and Roberts, R. G. 1993. Effects of antagonistic bacteria on establishment of honey bee dispersed *Erwinia amylovora* in pear blossoms and on fire blight control. *Phytopathology,* **83**: 995-1002.

Jones, D. A. and Kerr, A. 1989. Agrobacterium radiobacter K1026, a genetically engineered derivative of strain K84, for biological control of crown gall. *Plant Dis.*, **73**: 15-18.

Jubina, P. A. and Girija, V. K. 1998. Antagonistic rhizobacteria for management of *Phytophthora capsici,* the incitant of foot rot of black pepper. *J. Mycol. Pl. Pathol.*, **28**: 147-153.

Kapadia, M. N., Parsana, G. J. and Koshiya, D. J. 1997. Occurrence of a mycophagous midge *Mycodiplosis* sp. on sugarcane rust in India. *Indian Sugar,* **4**(6): 425.

Kapat, A., Zimand, Y. and Elad, Y. 1998. Effect of two isolates of *Trichoderma harzianum* on the activity of hydrolytic enzymes produced by *Botrytis cineria. Physiol. Mol. Plant Pathol.*, **52**: 127-137.

Karthikeyan, A. 1996. Effect of organic amendments, antagonist *Trichoderma viride* and fungicide on seed and collar rot of groundnut. *Plant Dis. Res.*, **11**(1): 72-74.

Katan J, Dunn M. T. and Papavizas, G. C. 1984. Genetics of fungicide resistance in *Talaromyces flavus. Can. J. Microbiol.*, **30**: 1079-1087.

Katragadda, H. and Murugesan, K. 1996. Hyperparasitic potential of *Trichoderma harzianum* over *Fusarium oxyporum* f. sp. *vasinfectum. Indian J. Microbiol.*, **36**(3): 145-148.

Kaur, N. P. and Mukhopadhyay, A. N. 1992. Integrated control of chickpea wilt complex by *Trichoderma* and chemical methods in India. *Trop. Pest Management,* **38**(4): 372-375.

Kehri, H. K., Sudhir Chandra and Chandra, S. 1991. Antagonism of *Trichoderma viride* to *Macrophomina phaseolina* and its application in the control of dry root rot of mung. *Indian Phytopathol.*, **44**(1): 60-63.

Kerr, A. 1972. Biological control of crown gall: seed inoculation. *J. Appl. Bacteriol.*, **35**: 493-497.

Khilari, K. 1994. Biological control of root rot and wilt disease of chickpea by *Trichoderma koningii* and *Gliocladium virens.* Thesis Ph.D. G. B. Pant University of Agriculture and Technology, Pantnagar, India, 178p.

Kichadi, S. N. and Srinivasa, M. N. 1998. Interaction effects of Glomus fasciculatum and *T. harzianum* on *Sclerotium rolfsii* in presence of biogas spent slurry in tomato Karnataka. *J. Agric. Sciences,* **11**: 419-422.

Kleifeld and Chet, I. 1992. *Trichoderma harzianum*-interaction with plants and effect on growth response. *Plant and Soil,* **144**: 267-272.

Klein, D. A. 1993. Rhizosphere. *In: Encylopedia of Microbiology,* vol. 3. Academic Press Inc. New York, pp. 565-572.

Kloepper, J. W. and Schroth, M. N. 1978. Plant growth promoting rhizobacteria on radishes. *In*: Station de Pathogie Vegetate et Jphytobacteriologie (ed.), Proceedings of the 4th international conference on plant pathogenic bacteria, I.N.R.A., Ronte de Saint Cleament Beaucauze, Angers. Gillbert-Clarey, Tonrs, Volume II, pp. 879-82.

Kloepper, J. W. and Scroth, M. N. 1981. Plant growth promoting rhizobacteria and plant growth under gnotobiotic conditions. *Phytopathology,* **71**: 642-644.

Kloepper, J. W., Hume, D. J., Scher, F. M., Singleton, C., Tipping, B., Laliberte, M., Franley, K., Kutcaw, T., Simonson, C., Lifshitz, R., Zaleska, I. and Lee, L. 1988. Plant Growth Promoting Rhizobacteria on canola (rapeseed). *Plant Dis.,* **72**: 42-46.

Kloepper, J. W., Lifshitz, R. and Zablotowicz, R. M. 1989. Free living bacterial inocula for enhancing crop productivity. *Trends in Biotechnol.,* **7**: 39-44.

Kloepper, J. W., Schroth, M. N. and Miller, T. D. 1980. Effects of rhizosphere colonization by plant growth promoting rhizobacteria on potato plant development and yield. *Phytopathology,* **70**: 1078-1082.

Kloepper, J. W., Zablotowicz, R. M., Tripping, E. M. and Lifshitz, R. 1991. Plant growth promotion mediated by bacterial rhizospohere colonizers. *In*: D. L. Keister and P. B. Cregan (eds.), *The Rhizosphere and Plant Growth.* Kluwer Academic Publ. Dordrecht, pp. 315-326.

Ko, W. H. 1985. Natural suppression of soil-borne plant diseases. *Plant Prot. Bull. Taiwan,* **27**: 171.

Kolte, S. O., Korekar, V. B. and Lokhande, N. M. 1994. Biocontrol of dieback and fruit rot of chillies (*Capsicum annuum*) caused by *Collectorichum capsici* under field conditions. *Orissa Journal of Agricultural Research,* **7**: 80-84.

Krishnamoorthy, A.S. and Bhaskaran, R. 1990. Biological control of damping-off disease of tomato caused by *Pythium indicum. J. Biol. Control.,* **4**(1): 52-54.

Krishnamoorthy, K. and Gnanamanickam, S. S. 1998. Biocontrol of sheath blight with formulated *Pseudomonas putida. Indian Phytopathol.,* **51**: 233-236.

Krishnamurthy, K., Gnanamanickam, S. S. 1997. Biological control of sheath blight of rice: Induction of systemic resistance in rice by plant associated *Pseudomonas sp. Curr. Sci.,* **72**(5): 331-334.

Kuc, J. 1982. Induced immunity to plant disease. *Bioscience,* **32**: 854.

Kuc, J. 1987. Plant immunizaton and its applicability for disease control. *In*: I. Chet (ed.), *Innnovative Approaches in Plant Disease Control.* Wiley-Interscience, New York, pp. 255-274.

Kuc, J. 1995. Induced systemic resistance—An overview. *In*: R. Hammerschmidt and J. Kuc (eds.), *Induced Resistance to Disease in Plants.* Kluwer, Dordrecht pp. 169-175.

Kumar, A. and Gupta, J. P. 2000. Variation in the enzymatic activity of tebuconazole tolerant biotupes of *Trichoderma viride. In*: Proceeding of Indian Phytopathological Society—Golden Jubilee, International Conference on Integrated Plant Disease Management for Sustainable Agriculture, pp. 391-392.

Kumar, R. N. 1993. Biological control of damping-off disease in chir pine. *Indian J. Mycol. Pl. Pathol.,* **23**(3): 237-240.

Kumar, R. N. and Mishra, R. R. 1994. Interaction studies *in vitro* between brown spot pathogen of paddy and certain epiphytic phylloplane fungi. *Plant Cell Incompatibility Newsletter,* **26**: 40-47.

Kundu, P. K. and Nandi, B. 1993. Inhibition of *Rhizoctonia solani* by *Streptomyces arenae* and *S. chibaensis* in soil. *Journal of Mycopathological Research,* **31**(1): 35-42.

Laha, G. S. Singh R. P. and Verma J. P. 1992. Biocontrol of *Rhizoctonia solani* in cotton by fluorescent pseudomonas. *Indian Phytopathol.,* **45**: 412-415.

Laha, G. S. and Verma, J. P. 1998. Role of fluorescent pseudomonads in the suppression of root-rot and damping-off of cotton. *Indian Phytopathol.,* **51**: 275-278.

Lalithakumari, D. 2000. Development of effective technology for strain improvement of Trichoderma spp. *In*: Proceeding of Indian Phytopathological Society—Golden Jubilee, International Conference on Integrated Plant Disease Management for Sustainable Agriculture, pp. 851-859.

Lalithakumari, D., Mrinalini, C., Chandra, A. B. and Annamalai, P. 1996. Strain improvement by protoplast fusion for enhancement of biocontrol potential integrated with fungicide tolerance in *Trichoderma* sp. *Zeitschrift - fur - Pflanzenkrankheiten - und - Pflanzenschutz,* **103**(2): 206-212.

Lam, S. T., and Gaffney, T. D. 1993. Biological activities of bacteria used in plant pathogen control. *In: Biotechnology in Plant Disease Control.* Wiley-Liss, Inc. North Carolina. pp. 291-320.

Leeman, M., den Ouden, F. M., van Pelt, J. A., Cornellissen, C., Matamallagarros, A., Bakker, P. A. H. M. and Schippers, C. 1996. Suppression of *Fusarium* wilt of radish by co-inoculation of fluorescent *Pseudominas* spp. and root colonizing fungi. *Eur. J. Plant Pathol.*, **102**: 21-31.

Leemanceau P, Alabouvette C. 1991. Biological control of *Fusarium* diseases by fluorescent *Pseudomonas* and nonpathogenic *Fusarium. Crop Prot.*, **10**: 279-286.

Leong J. 1986. Siderophores: Their biochemistry and possible role in the biocontrol of plant pathogens. *Annu. Rev. Phytopathol.*, **24**: 187-209.

Lewis J. A., and Papavizas, G. C. 1985. Characteristics of alginate pellets formulated with *Trichoderma* and *Gliocladium* and their effect on the proliferation of the fungi in soil. *Plant Pathol.*, **34**: 571-577.

Lewis J. A., and Papawizas, G. C. 1984. Chlamydospore formation by *Trichoderma* spp. in natural substrates. *Can. J. Microbiol.*, **30**: 1-7.

Lewis J. A., Papavizas G. C. and Connick W. J. 1987. Preparations of pellets containing fungi and nutrient and for control of soil borne plant pathogens. U.S. Patent No. 4, 668 and 512.

Limon, M. C., Lora, J. M., Garcia, I., De la Cruz, J., Llobell, A., Benifez, T. and Pintor-Toro, J. A. 1995. Primery structure and expression of 33kDa chitinase gene from the mycoparasitic fungus *Trichoderma harzianum. Curr. Genet.*, **28**: 478-483.

Lindow, S. E. 1983. The role of bacterial ice nucleation in frost injury to plants. *Annu. Rev. Phytopathol.*, **21**: 363-384.

Liu S. D., 1988. The use of benomyl rasistance mutant of *Trichoderma koningii* as a biocontrol agent against root rot diseases of chrysanthemum and adjuki bean. *Trichoderma News Letter*, **4**: 5 (abstract).

Lo, C. T., Nelson, E. B., Hayes, C. K. and Harman, G. E. 1998. Ecological studies of *Trichoderma harzianum* strain 1295-22 in the rhizosphere and on the phylloplane of creeping bentgrass. *Phytopathology*, **88**: 129-136.

Lokesh, M. S., Hiremath, R. V. and Hedge, R. K. 1987. Seed mycoflora of red gram (*Cajanus cajan* (L.) Mills P.). *Plant Pathology Newsletter*, **5**: 1-2.

Loper, J. E. and Buyer, J. S. 1991. Sideropohores in microbial interactions on plant surfaces. *Mol. Plant Microbe Interaction*, **4**: 5-13.

Lora, J. M., De la Cruz, J., Benifez, T. and Pintor-Toro, J. A. 1995. Molecular characterization and heterologous expression of an endo-β-1, 6-glucanase gene from the mycoparasite fungus *Trichoderma harzianum. Mol. Gen. Genet.*, **247**: 639-645.

Lorito M, Di Pietro A, Hayes CK, Woo SL, Harman CE. 1993a. Antifungal, synergistic interaction between chitinolytic enzymes from *Trichoderma harzianum* and *Enterobacter cloacae. Phytopathology*, **83**: 721-728.

Lorito M, Harman GE, Hayes, C. K., Broadway, R. M., Tronsmo, A., Woo, S. L., Di Pietro, A. 1993b. Chitinolytic enzymes produced by *Trichoderma harzianum*: Antifungal activity of purified endochitinase and chitobiosidase. *Phytopathology*, **83**: 302-307.

Lorito, M, Hayes, C. K., Di Pietro, A., Woo, S. L., Harman, G. E. 1994. Purification, characterization, and synergistic activity of a glucan 1, 3-β-glucosidase and an N-acetyl β-glucosaminidase from *Trichoderma harzianum. Phytopathology*, **84**: 398-405.

Lorito, M. 1998. Chitinolytic enzymes and their genes. *In*: G. E. Harman and C. P. Kubicek (eds.), *Trichoderma* and *Gliocladium*, Vol. 2. Taylor and Francis, London, United Kingdom, p. 73-99.

Lorito, M., Farkas, V., Rebeffat, S., Bodo, B., Kubicek, C. P. 1996a. *J. Bacteriol.*, **178**: 6382-6385.

Lorito, M., Woo, S. L., D'Ambrosio, M., Harman, C. E., Hayes, C. K., Kubicek, C. P. and Scala, F. 1996b. *Mol. Plant Microbe-Interaction*, **9**: 206-213.

Lorito, M., Woo, S. L., Garcia Fernandez, I., Colucci, G. Harman, G. E., Pintor-Toro, J. A., Filippone, E., Mucciflora, S., Lawrence, C. B., Zobina, A., Tuzun, S. and Scala, F. 1998. Genes from mycoparasitic fungi as a source for improving plant resistance to fungal pathogens. *Proc. Natl. Acad. Sci., U.S.A.*, **95**: 7860-7865.

Maheswari, Uma and Ramakrishnan, G. 1994. Effect of seed treatment with *Trichoderma viride* and moisture levels on root rots disease in groundnut. *Madras Agricultural Journal,* **81**(10): 553-555.

Majumdar, V. L. and Pathak, V. N. 1995. Biological control of post harvest diseases of guava fruits by *Trichoderma* spp. *Acta Botanica Indica,* **23**: 263-267.

Majumdar, V. L. and Singh, M. 1995. Antagonistic activity of *Trichoderma* sp. to *Macrophomina phaseolina* (Tassi) Goid *in vitro. Environment* and *Ecology,* **13**(2): 481-482.

Majumdar, V. L., Jat, J. R. and Gour, H. N. 1996. Effects of biocontrol agents on the growth of *Macrophomina phaseolina,* the incitant of blight of moth bean. *Indian J. Mycol. Pl. Pathol.,* **26**(2): 202-203.

Mani, M. T. and Marimuthu, T. 1994. Effect of decomposed coconut coirpith, fungicides and biocontrol agents on damping-off of chillies and dry root rot of black gram. *Indian J. Mycol. Pl. Pathol.,* **24**(1): 20-23.

Marshal, D. S. 1982. Effect of *Trichoderma harzianum* seed treatment and *Rhizoctonia solani* inoculum concentration on damping-off of snapbean in acidic soil. *Plant Dis.,* **66**: 788-789.

Mathre, D. E., Callan, N. W., Johnston, R. H. and Schwand, A. 1994. Factors influencing the control of *Pythium ultimum*—induced seed decay by seed treatment by *Pseudomonas aureofaciens* AB-254. *Crop Prot.,* **13**: 301-307.

Mathre, D. E., Cook, R. J. and Callan, N. W. 1999. From discovery to Use: Traversing the World of Commercializing Biocontrol Agents for Plant Disease Control. *Phytopathology,* **83**: 972-983.

Mazzola, M., Fujimoto, D. K., Thomashow, L. S. and Cook, R. J. 1995. Variation in sensitivity of *Gaeumannomyces graminis* to antibiotics produced by fluorescent *Pseudomonas* spp. and effect on biological control of take-all of wheat. *Appl. Environ. Microbiol.,* **61**: 254-261.

McAllister, C. B., Garcia-Romera, I., Godeas, A. and Ocampo, J. A. 1994. Interactions between *T. koningii, Fusarium solani,* and *Glomus mosseae*: effects on plant growth, arbuscular mycorrhizas and the saprophyte inoculants. *Soil Biol. Biochem.,* **26**: 10, 1363-1367.

McLaren, D. L., Huang, H. C., Kozub, G. C. and Rimmer, S. R. 1994. Biological control of *Sclerotinia* wilt of sunflower with *Talaromyces flavus* and *Coniothyrium minitans. Plant Dis.,* **78**: 231.

Mcquilken, M. P., Whipps, J. M. and Cooke, R. C. 1990. Control of damping-off in cress and sugarbeet by commercial seed coating with *Pythium oligandrum. Plant Pathol.,* **39**: 452-462.

Meena, B., Ramamoorthy, V., Marimuthu, T. and Velazhahan, R. 2000. *Pseudomonas fluorescens* mediated systemic resistance against late leaf spot of groundnut. *J. Mycol. Pl. Pathol.,* **30**: 151-158.

Mehrotra, V. S. 1988. Biological control of *Phytophthora* blight of pigeon pea. M.Sc. (Ag.) Thesis, G. B. Pant University of Agric. & Tech. Pantnagar, INDIA, p. 140.

Menzies, J. D. 1959. Occurrence and transfer of a biological factor in soil that suppresses potato scab. *Phytopathology,* **49**: 648.

Merriman, P. R., Price, R. D., Kollmorgen, J. F., Piggott, T. and Ridge, E. H. 1974. Effect of seed inoculation with bacillus subtilis and *streptomyces griseus* on the growth of cereals and carrots. *Aust. J. Agric. Res.,* **25**: 219-226.

Migheli, Q., Gonzalez-Candelas, L. Dealessi, Camponogara, A. and Raman-Vidal, D. 1998. Transformants of *Trichoderma longibrachiatum* overexpressing the β-1,4-glucanase gene egl1 show enhanced Biocontrol of *Pythium ultimum* on cucumber. *Phytopathology,* **88**: 673-677.

Mihuta-Grimn, L. and Rowe 1986. *Trichoderma* spp. as biocontrol agents of *Rhizoctonia* damping-off of radish in organic soil and comparison of four delivery systems. *Phytopathology,* **76**: 306-312.

Miller, R. H., and May, S. 1991. Legume inoculation: Success and failures. *In*: D. L. Keister and P. B. Cregan (eds.), *The Rhizosphere and Plant Growth.* Kluwer Academic Publishers, Dordrecht, The Netherlands pp. 123-134.

Mishra, D. S. 1998. Comparative efficacy of some biocontrol agents against *Rhizoctonia solani* kuhn, the cause of sheath blight of rice. M.Sc. (Ag.) Thesis, G. B. Pant University of Agric. & Tech. Pantnagar, INDIA, p. 242.

Mishra, D. S. and Sinha, A. P., 2000a. Comparative efficacy of some biocontrol agents applied as seed or soil treatment on seedling infection of rice caused by *Rhizoctonia solani. In*: 52nd Annual

Meeting of Indian Phytopathological Society and National Symposium on "Role of Resistance *in Intensive Agriculture*" held at, Karnal, Haryana, Feb.15-17, 2000 (Abstr.).

Mishra, D. S. and Sinha, A. P. 1997. Biocontrol potential of some biocontrol agents against *Rhizoctonia solani* Kuhn, the cause of sheath blight of rice. *In*: International Conference on "*Integrated Plant Disease Management for Sustainable Agriculture*", held at IARI, New Delhi, 10-15 Nov. 1997 (Abstr).

Mishra, D. S. and Sinha, A. P. 1999b. Effect of seed treatment with fungal and bacterial antagonists on germination and seedling vigour of rice. *In*: 51st annual meeting of Indian Phytopathological Society and National symposium on "*Seed health care and phytosanitation for sustainable agriculture*" held at Lucknow, Feb. 17-19, 1999 (Abstr.).

Mishra, D. S. and Sinha, A. P. 2000b. Plant growth-promoting activity of some fungal and bacterial agents on rice seed germination and seedling growth. *Trop. Agric.*, **77**(3): 188-191.

Mishra, D. S. and Sinha, A. P. 2000c. Potential of some biocontrol agents against *Rhizoctonia solani*. *In*: Proceeding of Indian Phytopathological Society—Golden Jubilee, International Conference on *Integrated Plant Disease Management for Sustainable Agriculture*, p. 352.

Mishra, D. S. and Sinha, A. P. 1998. Plant growth promotion by some biocontrol agents. *In*: Fiftieth annual meeting of Indian Phytopathological Society and National symposium on "*Present scenario in diseases of oilseeds and pulses*", held at Aurangabad, Maharastra, 17-19 Feb. 1998 (Abstr.).

Mishra, D. S., Singh, U. S. and Dwivedi, T. S. 2001a. Comparative efficacy of normal seed treatment and seed bio-priming with commercial formulations of *Trichoderma* spp. *In* : 53rd annual meeting of Indian Phytopathological Society and National symposium on "*Ecofriendly approaches for plant disease management*" held at Chennai, 21-23, 2001.

Mishra, D. S., Singh, U. S. and Dwivedi, T. S. 2001b. Relative efficacy of conidia and chlamydospores based formulations of *Trichoderma* spp. *In*: Biopesticide Conference on "*Emerging trends in Biological Control: BET 2001*" held at Chandigarh, Haryana, Feb. 7-9, 2001, 81p (Abstr.).

Mishra, P. K. 1996. Biological control of *Fusarium* corm rot and yellows of gladiolus. M.Sc (Ag.), Thesis, G. B. Pant University of Agric. & Tech. Pantnagar, INDIA, p. 116.

Mohan, L. and Jeyarajan, R. 1990. An *in vitro* test for evaluating the efficacy of mycoparasites on the sclerotial germination of ergot (*Claviceps fusiformis* Lov.) of pearl millet. *J. Biological Control*, **4**(1): 75-76.

Mondal, G., Agarwal, R. and Srivastava, K. D. 1996. Hyphal interaction between *Trichoderma koningii* and *Ustilago segetum tritici* through scanning electron microscopy. *Curr. Sci.*, **70**(6): 425-426.

Mondal, K. K., Singh, R. P. and Verma, J. P. 1999a. Beneficial effects of indigenous bcotton rhizobacteria on seed germinability, growth promotion and suppression of bacterial blight disease. *Indian Phytopathol.*, **52**: 228-235.

Mondal. Sudhamoy, Srivastva, K. D., Aggarwal, Rasmi and Singh, D. V. 1999b. Mycoparasitic action of some fungi on spot blotch pathogen (*Drechslera sorokiniana*) of wheat. *Indian Phytopathol.*, **52**: 39-43.

Mongia, D. and Sheoraj, 2000. Integrated management of root rot of cotton. *In*: Proceeding of Indian Phytopathological Society—Golden Jubilee, International Conference on Integrated Plant Disease Management for Sustainable Agriculture, pp. 910-911.

Montealegre, J., Varnero, M. T. and Sepulveda, C. 1993. A method for biomass production of *Trichoderma harzianum* strain V: growth evaluation. *Fitopathol.*, **28**: 99-106.

Mukherjee, P. K. 1991. Biological control of Chick-pea wilt complex. Ph.D. Thesis, G. B. Pant University of Agric. & Tech. Pantnagar, INDIA, p. 188.

Mukherjee, P. K. and Haware, M. P. 1993. Biological control of Botrytis gray mould of chickpea. *International Chickpea Newsletter*, **28**: 14-15.

Mukherjee, P. K. and Mukhopadhyay, A. N. 1993. Induction of stable mutants of *Gliocladium virens* by gamma-irradiation. *Indian Phytopathol.*, **46**: 393-397.

Mukherjee, P. K. and Mukhopadhyay, A. N. 1995. *In situ* mycoparasitism of *Gliocladium virens* on *Rhizoctonia solani*. *Indian Phytopathol.*, **48**(1): 101-102.

Mukherjee, P. K., Haware, M. P. and Jayanthi, S. 1995a. Preliminary investigations in integrated biocontrol of *Botrytis* gray mold of chickpea. *Indian Phytopathol.*, **48**(2): 141-149.

Mukherjee, P. K., Haware, M. P. and Raghu, P. 1997. Induction and evaluation of benomyl-tolerent mutants of *Trichoderma viride* for biological control of botrytis gray mould of chickpea. *Indian Phytopathol.*, **50**: 485-489.

Mukherjee, P. K., Mukhopadhyay, A. N., Sarmah, D. K. and Shrestha, S. M. 1995c. Comparative antagonistic properties of *Gliocladium virens* and *Trichoderma harzianum* on *Sclerotium rolfsii* and *Rhizoctonia solani* its relevance to understanding the mechanisms of biocontrol. *J. Phytopathol.*, **143**(5): 275-279.

Mukherjee, P. K., Thomas, P. and Raghu, K. 1995b. Shelf life enhancement of fresh ginger rhizomes at ambient temperatures by combination of gamma irradiation, biocontrol and closed polyethylene bag storage. *Annals of Appl. Biol.*, **127**(2): 375-384.

Mukherjee, P. K., Upadhyay, J. P. and Mukhopadhyay, A. N. 1989. Biological control of Pythium damping off of cauliflower by *Trichoderma harzianum. J. Biol. Control.*, **3**: 119-124.

Mukhopadhyay, A. N. 1994. Biological control of Soil borne fungal plant Pathogens- current status, future prospects and potential limitations. *Indian Phytopathol.*, **47**: 119-126.

Mukhopadhyay, A. N. 1996. Recent innovations in plant disease control by ecofriendly biopesticides. Presidential address, in Agricultural Sciences Section, 83rd Indian Science congress, Patiala.

Mukhopadhyay, A. N. and Mukherjee, P. K. 1998. Biological control of plant diseases: Status in India. *In*: S. P. Singh and S. S. Husain (eds.), *Biological Suppression of Phytopathogens, Nematodes and Weeds*. Project Directorate of Biological Control, Bangalore.

Mukhopadhyay, A. N, Shrestha, S. M. and Mukherjee, P. K. 1992. Biological seed treatment for control of soil borne plant pathogens. *FAO Plant Protection Bulletin*, **40**: 21-30.

Mukhopadhyay, A. N. 1987. Biological control of soil borne plant pathogens by *Trichoderma* spp. *Indian J. Mycol. Pl. Pathol.*, **17**: 1-10.

Mukhopadhyay, A. N., Patel, G. J. and Brahmbhatt, A. 1986. *Trichoderma harzianum*: A potentil agent for tobacco damping-off. *Tobacco Res.*, **12**: 26-35.

Muthamilan, M. and Jeyarajan, R. 1996. Integrated management of Sclerotium root rot of groundnut involving *Trichoderma harzianum, Rhizobium* and cărbendazim. *Indian J. Mycol. Pl. Pathol.*, **26**(2): 204-209.

Nagina, Parmar and Dadarwal, K. R. 1997. Rhizobacteria from the rhizosphere and rhizoplane of chickpea (*Cicer arietinum* L.). *Indian J. Microbiol.*, **37**(4 ): 205-210.

Naik, B. H. L. and Anilkumar, T. B. 1992. Effect of cowpea leaf surface fungi on conidial germination of fungicide resistant strains of *Colletotrichum lindemuthianum. Indian Phytopathol.*, **45**(3): 385-386.

Nakkeeran, S. and Devi, P. R. 1997. Seed borne microflora of pigeonpea and their management. *Plant Dis. Res.*, **12**(2): 197-200.

Nanda, H. P. and Gangopadhyay, S. 1983. Control of rice helminthosporiose with *Bacillus subtilis* antagonistic towards *Bipolaris oryzae. International J. Trop. Plant Dis.*, **1**(1): 25-30.

Narayan, A. and Behera, R. 2000. Antagonistic potential of *Gliocladium virens* and *Streptoverticillium* sp. on selected phytopathogenic fungi. *In*: Proceeding of Indian Phytopathological Society—Golden Jubilee, International Conference on Integrated Plant Disease Management for Sustainable Agriculture, pp. 294-296.

Nautiyal, C. S. 1997. Selection of chickpea rhizosphere competent *Pseudomonas fluorescens* NBRI 1303 antagonistic to *Fusarium oxysporum* f. sp. ciceris, *Rhizoctonia bataticola* and *Pythium* sp. *Curr. Microbiol.*, **35**(1): 52-58.

Neilands, J. B. 1981. Microbial iron compounds. *Annu. Rev. Biochem.*, **50**: 715-731.

Neilands, J. B. and Leong, J. 1986. Sideropohores in relation to plant growth and diseases. *Annu. Rev. Plant Physiol.*, **37**: 187-208.

Nemec, S. 1997. Longevity of microbial biocontrol agents in a planting mix amended with Glomus intraradices. *Biocontrol Science and Technology*, **7**:183-192.

Oliveira, E., Sieverding, E. and Tora, S. 1987. Interaction between three species of VAM fungi and one isolate of *Pseudomonas putida* on cassava. *In*: D. M. Sylvia, L. L. Hung and J. H. Graham (eds.), *Proceedings of the Seventh North American Conference on Mycorrhizae*, University of Florida, Gainesville, pp. 216.

Osburn, R. M., Schroth, M. N., Hencock, N. D. and Hension, M. 1989. Dynamics of sugarbeet root colonization by *Pythium ultimum* and *Pseudomonas* spp.: Effect on seed rot damping off. *Phytopathology,* **79**: 709-716.

Padmanaban, P. and Alexander, K. C. 1990. Biological control of sugarcane root rot disease. *J. Biol. Control,* **4**(2): 135-136.

Padmanabhan, P. and Alexander H. C. 1983. Seedling rot of sugarcane. Extension publication no. 5, Sugarcane Breeding Institute, Coimbatore.

Padmodaya, B. and Reddy, H. R. 1996. Screening of *Trichoderma* spp. against *Fusarium oxysporum* f. sp. *lycopersici* causing wilt in tomato. *Indian J. Mycol. Pl. Pathol.,* **26**(3): 266-270.

Padmodaya, B. and Reddy, H. R. 1998. Screening of antagonists against *Fusarium oxysporum* f. sp. *lycopersici* causing seedling disease and wilt in Tomato. *J. Mycol. Pl. Pathol.,* **28**: 339-341.

Palleroni, N. J., Kunisawa, R., Contopoulou, R. and Dondoroff, M. 1973. Nucleic acid homologies in genus Pseudomonas. *Int. J. Syst. Bacteriol.,* **23**: 333-339.

Pande, A. 1985. Biocontrol characteristics of some moulds. *Biovigyanam,* **11**(1): 14-18.

Pandey, R. R., Arora, D. K. and Dubey, R. C. 1993. Antagonistic interactions between fungal pathogens and phylloplane fungi of guava. *Mycopathologia,* **124**(1): 31-39.

Pandey, V. S. 1996. Studies on population dynamics, plant growth promotion activities, and antagonistic potential of fluorescent Pseudomonas isolated from rhizosphere soil of wheat and chickpea. Ph. D. Thesis, G. B. Pant University of Agric. & Tech. Pantnagar, India, pp. 360.

Papavizas, G. C. and Lewis, J. A. 1982. Introduction and augmentation of microbial antagonists for the control of soil borne plant pathogens. *In:* G. C. Papavizas (ed.), *Biological Control in Crop Production.* Allenhald, Osmum, Granada, USA, pp. 305-322.

Papavizas, G. C., Dunn, M. T., Lewis, J. A. and Beagle-Ristaino, J. E. 1984. Liquuid fermentation technology for experimental production of biocontrol fungi. *Phytopathology,* **74**: 1171-1175.

Papavizas, G. C. and Lewis, J. A. 1983. Physiological and biocontrol characteristics of stable mutants of *Trichoderma viride* resistant to MBC fungicides. *Phytopathology,* **73**: 407-411.

Papavizas, G. C. 1985. *Trichoderma* and *Gliocladium*: Biology and potential for biological control. *Annu. Rev. Phytopathol.,* **23**: 23-54.

Papavizas, G. C. 1987. Genetic manipulation to improve the effectiveness of biocontrol fungi for plant disease control. *In:* I. Chet (ed.), *Innovative Approaches to Plant Disease Control.* Wiley Interscience, N.Y.

Papavizas, G. C. and Lewis, J. A. 1991. Induction of new biotypes of *Trichoderma harzianum* resistant to benomyl and other fungicides. *Phytopathology,* **71**: 247-248.

Parakhia, A. M. and Vaishnav, M. U. 1986. Biocontrol of *Rhizoctonia bataticola. Indian Phytopathol.,* **39**(3): 439-440.

Parashar, R. D., Sindhan, G. S. and Hooda, I. 1992a. Biological control of bacterial blight (*Xanthomonas compestris* pv. *cyanopsidis*) of cluster bean by epiphytes present of leaf surface. *Crop Research,* **5**: 551-558.

Parashar, R. D., Indra Hooda, Sindhan, G. S. and Hooda, I. 1992b. Effect of common fungicides and an antibiotic used for the control of various diseases of cluster bean on the growth of *Xanthomonas compestris* pv. *cyamopsidis* and its antagonistic microorganisms. *Plant Dis. Res.,* **7**(2): 260-262.

Park, C., Paulitz, T. C. and Baker, R. 1988. Biocontrol of *Fusarium* wilt of cucumber resulting from interaction between *Pseudomonas* putida and nonpathogenic isolates of *Fusarium oxysporum. Phytopathology,* **78**: 190-194.

Patel, B. N., Patel, K. D. and Patel, H. R. 1996. Integrated management of damping-off in bidi tobacco nursery. *Tobacco Research,* **22**(1): 14-17.

Patil, P. V., Kachapur, M. R. and Anahosur, K. H. 2000. Role of phyllosphere micro-organisms in the control of sunflower rust caused by *Puccinia helianthii. In:* Proceeding of Indian Phytopathological Society—Golden Jubilee, International Conference on Integrated Plant Disease Management for Sustainable Agriculture, pp. 897-900.

## Plate 9.1

Fungal biocontrol agents *Trichoderma virens* (= *Gliocladium virens*) and *T. harzianum*.
**a.** growth on PDA, **b.** hyphae, **c.** conidiophores and phialides (®), **d.** conidia and **e.** chlamydospores

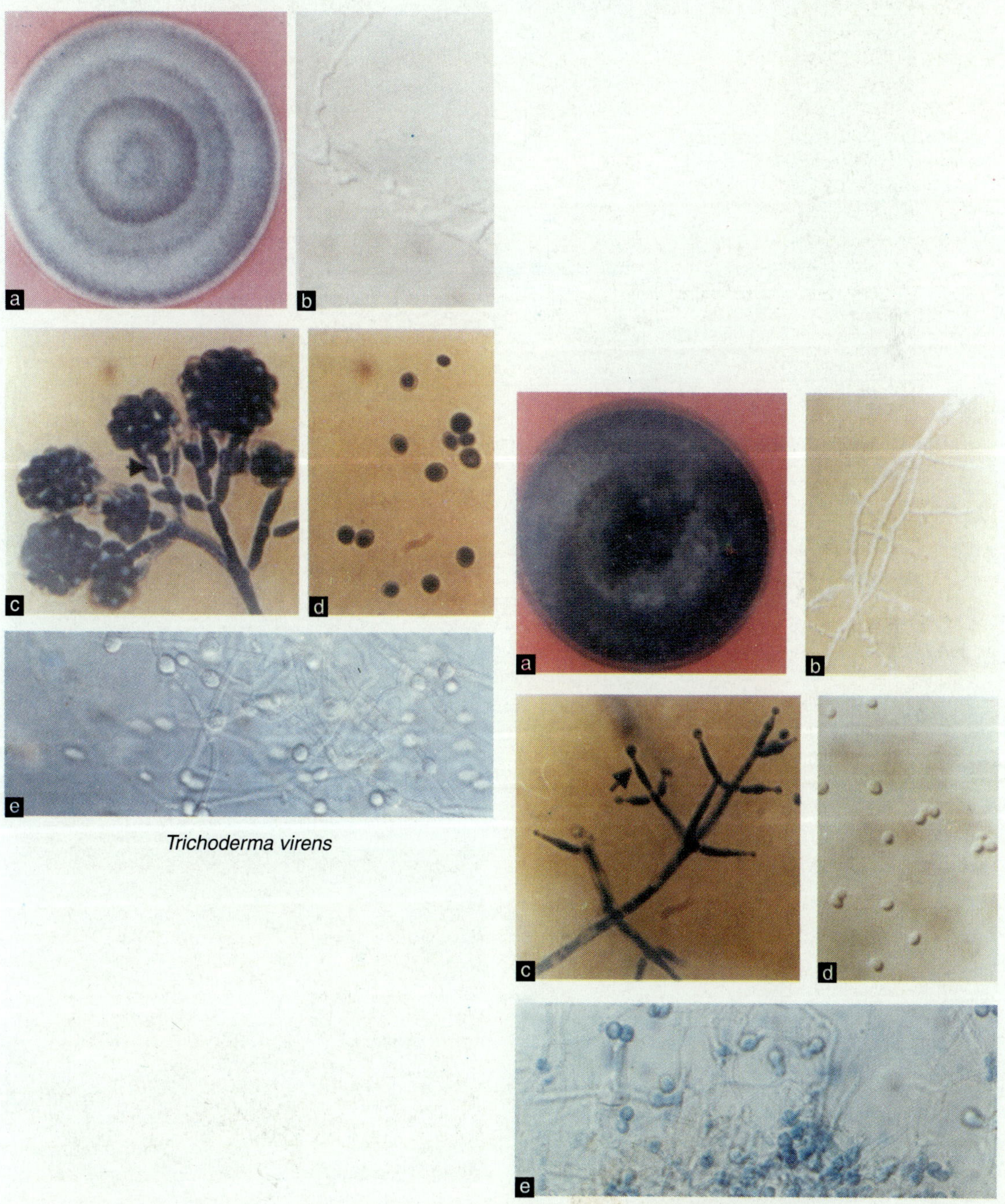


*Trichoderma virens*

*Trichoderma harzianum*

## Plate 9.2

Natural parasitization of *Rhizoctonia solani* by *Trichoderma harzianum* on maize plants (Sharma, 1996)

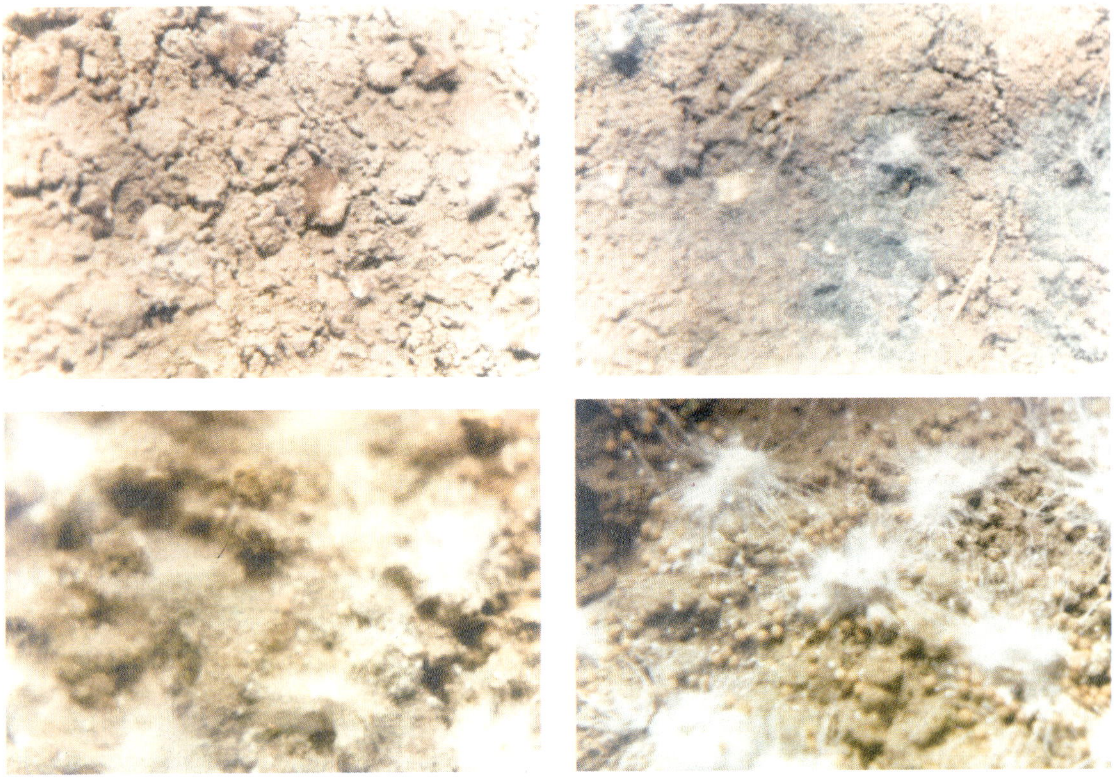

Sclerotial parasitization by *Trichoderma virens* on soil surface

## Plate 9.3

Scanning electron micrographs (SEM) of hyphal interaction between *Trichoderma harzianum* (TH) and *Rhizoctonia solani* (RS).

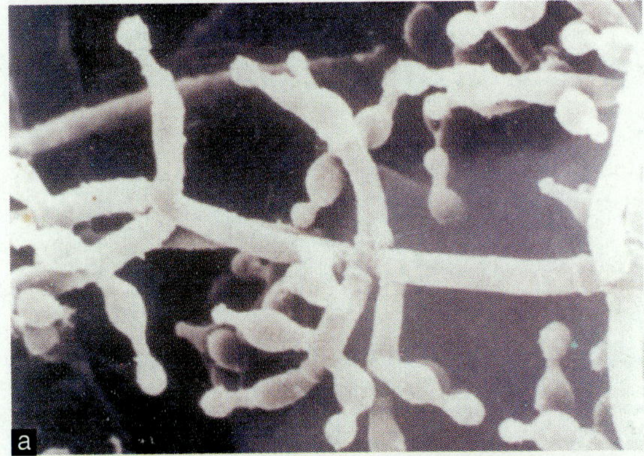


Coniophores and phialides bearing conidia of TH.

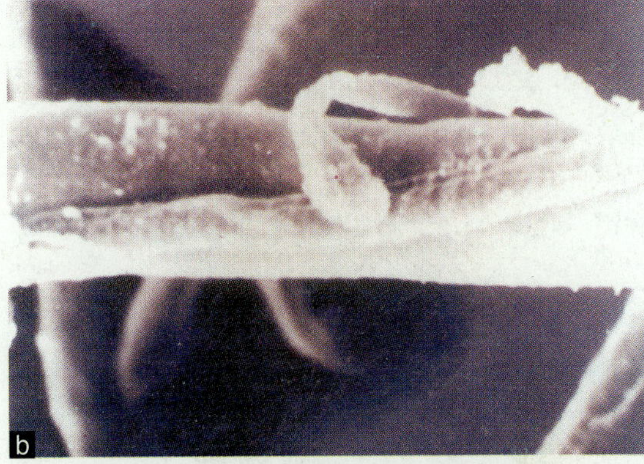


TH hyphae forming appressoria like structure after contact with hyphae of RS.

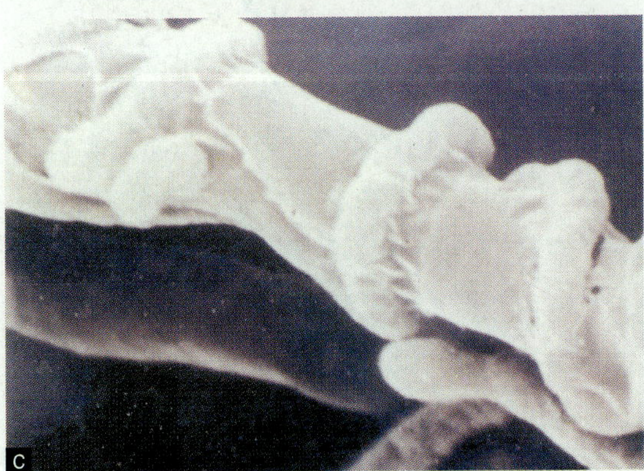


Hypha of TH coils around RS hypha. Depression and degradation of RS hypha at the point of contact.

Extensive coiling of TH hypha around RS hypha.

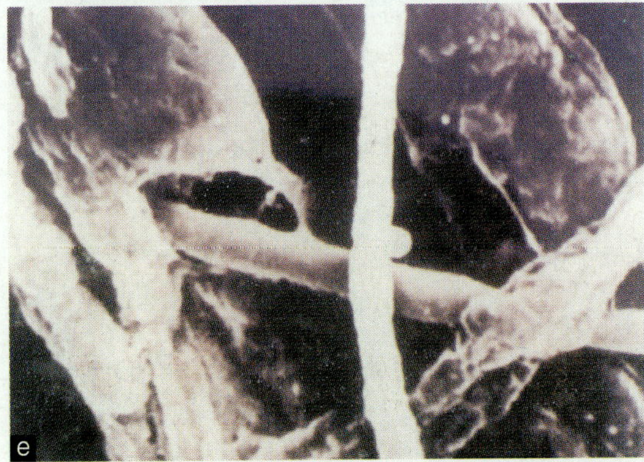


Direct penetration of RS hypha by TH hypha.

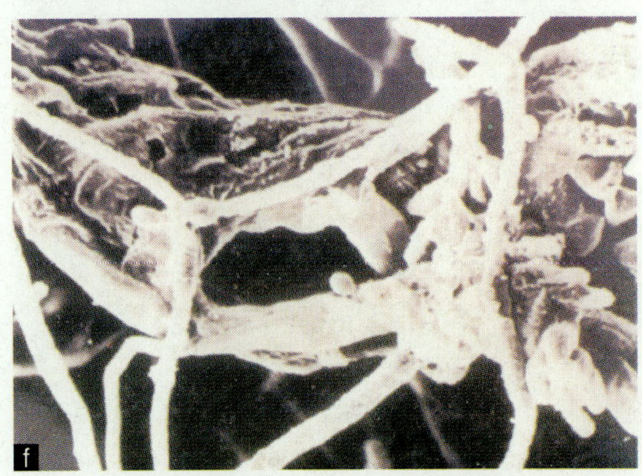


Complete disntegration of RS hypha by TH.

## Plate 9.4

Scanning electron micrographs (SEM) showing parasitization of sclerotia of *Sclerotium rolfsii* (SR) by *Trichoderma virens* (TV).

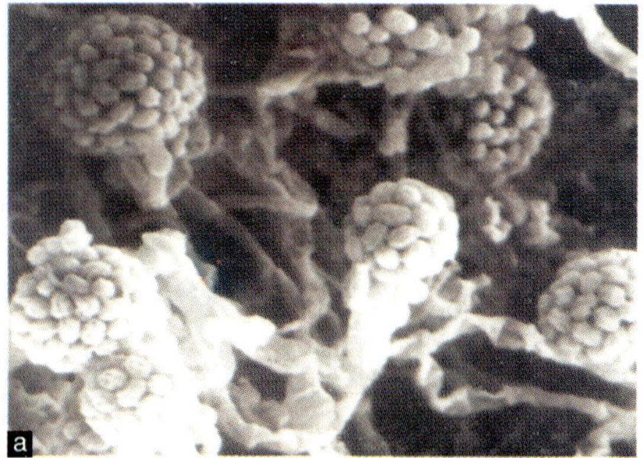


Coniophores and phialides bearing conidial balls of TV.

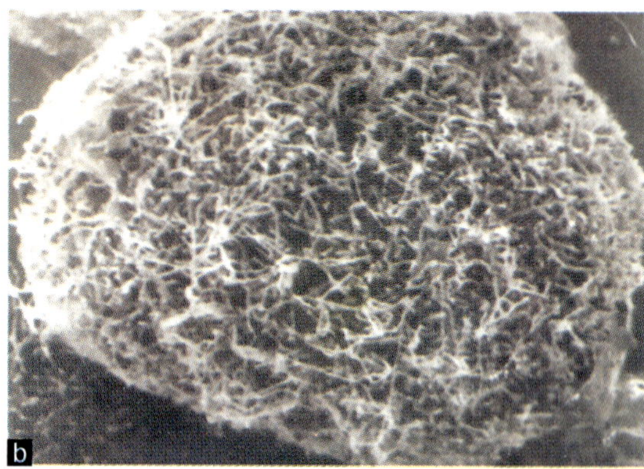


Healthy sclerotium of SR.

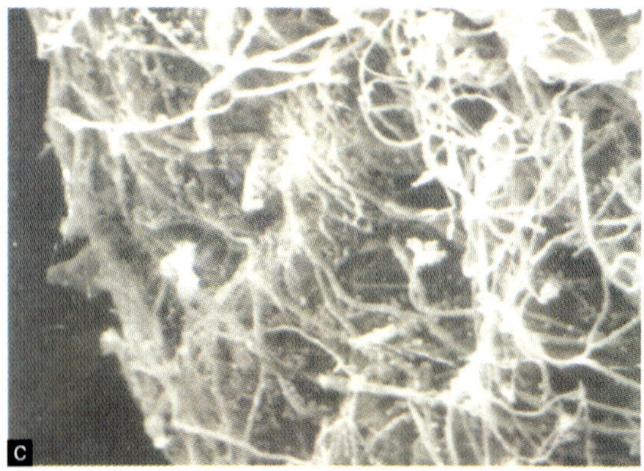


d

Growth and sporulation of TV on the surface of colonized sclerotia of SR.

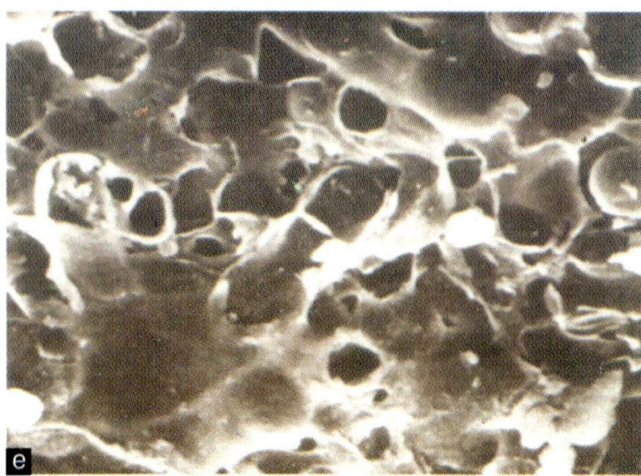


Depressions and holes on colonized sclerotial surface indicating point of entry of TV hyphae and dissolution of sclerotial rind.

Profuse sporulation of TV inside the parasitized sclerotia.

## Plate 9.5

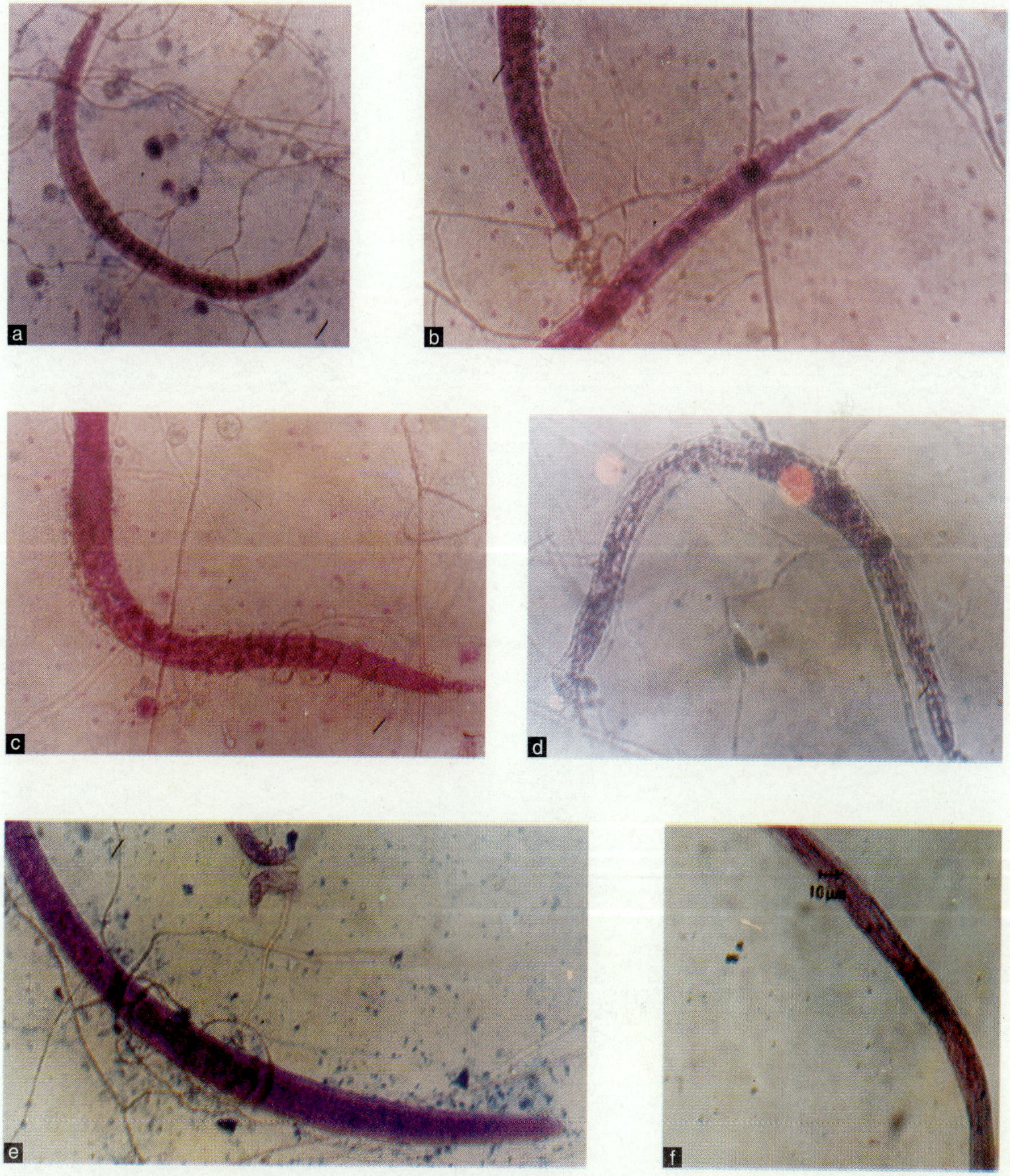

a b c d

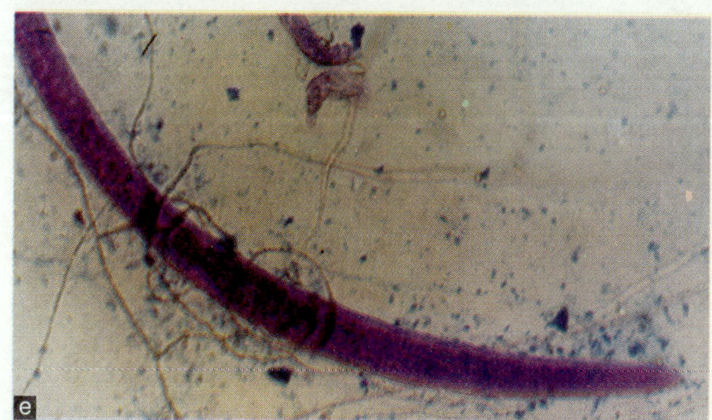


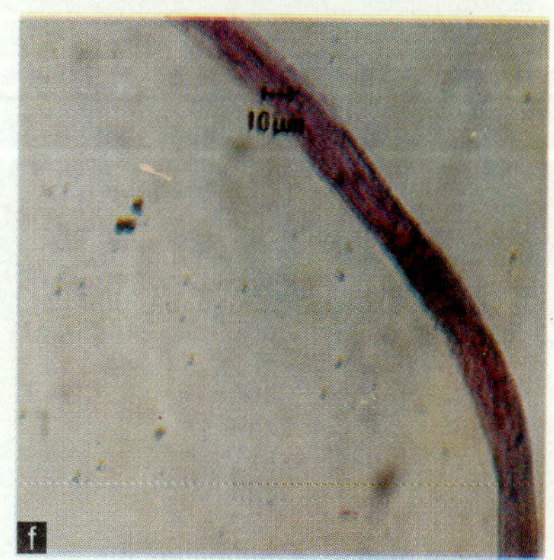


Parasitization of second stage larvae of *Meloidogyne* sp. by *Trichoderma harzianum* (TH). It involves formation of loops and traps (**A-C**), coils around nematode body by the hyphae of TH (**C-E**), penetrates and colonize it (**D-F**).

**Plate 9.6**

Parasitization of *Meloidogyne javanica* by *Trichoderma harzianum.*

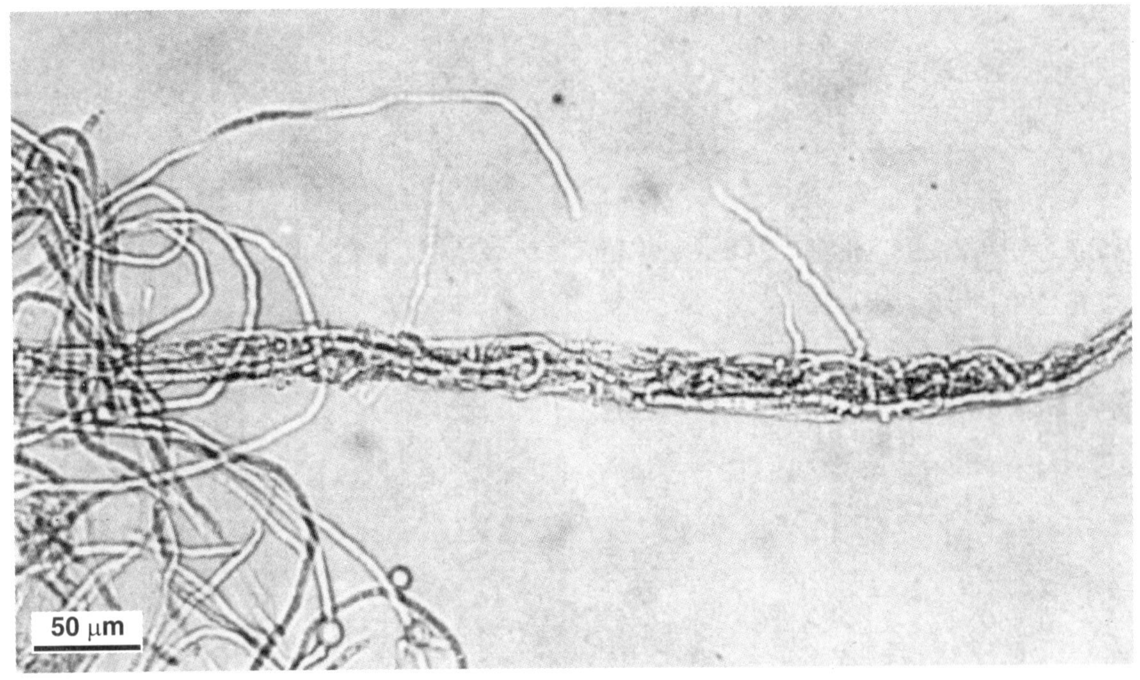


Second stage larva

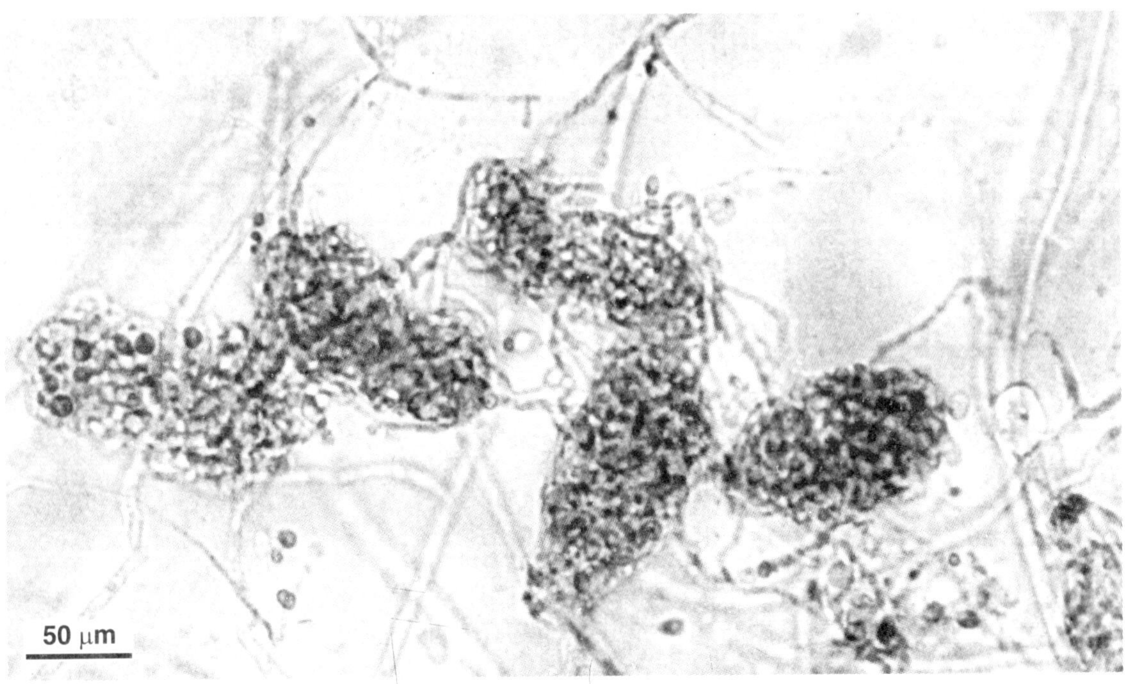


Eggs (Sharon *et al.*, 2001)

Patil, R. K. 1992. Studies on Rhizopus rot and *Botryodiploidia* rot of Mango fruits. Ph.D. Thesis, Rajsthan Agril. University, Bikaner.

Paulitz, T. C. 1990. Biochemical and ecological aspects of competition in biological control. *In:* R. R. Dunn (ed.). *New Directions in Biological Control Alternatives for Suppressing Agricultural Pests and Diseases.* Alan. R. Liss, Inc. Newyork.

Paulitz, T. C., Ahmad, J. S. and Baker, R. 1990. Integration of *Pythium* nunnm and *Trichoderma harzianum* isolate *Trichoderma*-95 for the biological control of *Pythium* damping off of cucumber. *Plant and Soil,* **121**: 243-250.

Phookan, A. K. and Chalia, K. 2000. Biological control of collar rot of brinjal caused by *Sclerotinia sclerotiorum. In*: Proceeding of Indian Phytopathological Society—Golden Jubilee, International Conference on Integrated Plant Disease Management for Sustainable Agriculture, p. 411.

Pierson, E. A. and Weller, D. M. 1994. Use of mixtures of fluorescent pseudomonads to suppress take-all and improve the growth of wheat. *Phytopathology,* **84**: 940-947.

Pieterse, C. M. J., Van Wees, S. C. M., Hoffland, E., Van Pelt, J. A. and Van Loon, L. C. 1996. Systemic resistance in *Arabidopsis* induced by biocontrol bacteria is independent of salicylic acid accumulation and pathogenesis related gene expression. *The Plant Cell,* **8**: 1225-1237.

Prasad, R. D. and Rangeshwaran, R. 1997. Mycelial preparations of *Trichoderma* and *Gliocladium* in biocontrol of *Rhizoctonia solani* infection of chickpea. *International J. Trop. Pl. Dis.,* **15**: 231-236.

Prasad, R. D. and Rangeshwaran, R. 1999. Granular formulation of *Trichoderma* and *Gliocladium* spp. in biocontrol of *Rhizoctonia solani* of chickpea. *J. Mycol. Pl. Pathol.,* **29**: 222-226.

Prasad, R. D. and Rangeshwaran, R. 2000. Shelf life and bioefficacy of *Trichoderma harzianum* formulated in various carrier materials. *Plant Dis. Res.,* **15**: 38-42.

Prasad, R. D., Rangeswaran, R. and Kumar P. Sreerama 1999. Biological control of root and collar rot of sunflower. *J. Mycol. Pl. Pathol.,* **29**: 184-188.

Prasad, R. D., Sreerama Kumar, P. and Narayan, K. 1998. Biological control of *Botrytis* gray mould of rose. *J. Mycol. Pl. Pathol.,* **28**: 61-63.

Prashanthi, S. K., Sreenivasa, M. N. and Kulkarni, S. 1997. Integrated management of root rot disease of safflower caused by *Rhizoctonia bataticola. Environment* and *Ecology,* **15**(4): 800-802.

Press, C. M., Wilson, M., Tuzun, S. and Kloepper, J. W. 1997. Salicylic acid produced by Serratia marcescens 90-166 is not the primary determinant of induced systemic resistance in cucumber or tobacco. *Mol. Plant-Microbe Interact.,* **10**: 761-768.

Punja, Z. K., Raharjo, S. H. T. 1996. Response of transgenic cucumber and carrot plants expressing different chitinase enzymes to inoculation with fungal pathogen *Rhizoctonia solani. Plant Dis.,* **80**: 999-105.

Raaijmakers, J. M., and van der Sluis, I., Koster, M., Bakker, P. A. H. M., Weisbeek, P. J. and Schippers, B. 1995. Utilization of heterologous siderophores and rhizpsphere competence of fluorescent *Pseudomonas spp. Can. J. Microbiol.,* **41**: 126-135.

Raghuchander, T., Samiappan, R. and Arjunan, G. 1993. Biocontrol of *Macrophomina* root rot of mungbean. *Indian Phytopathology,* **46**(4): 379-382.

Raguchander, T., Rajappan, K. and Samiappan, R. 1997. Evaluating methods of application of biocontrol agent in the control of mungbean root rot. *Indian Phytopathol.,* **50**(2): 229-234.

Rajan, F. S., Vedamuthu, P. G. B., Khader, M. D. A. and Jeyarajan, R. 1991. Management of root disease of fenugreek. *Southern Indian Horticulture,* **39**(4): 221-223.

Rajappan, K. 1997. Induction of mutants in *Trichoderma viride* by UV-irradiation. *Plant Dis. Res.,* **12**(1): 1-5.

Rajappan, K., Raguchander, T. and Manickam, K. 1996. Efficacy of UV induced mutants of *Trichoderma viride* against *Sclerotium rolfsii. Plant Dis. Res.,* **11**(1): 97-99.

Ram, P., Mathur, K. and Ram, J. 1997. Response of application methods of biocontrol agents either as rhizome pelleting or as soil application, or as both against rhizome rot of ginger. *Annals of Biology,* **13**(2): 293-296.

Rao, V. K. and Krishnappa, K. 1995. Integrated management of *Meloidogyne incognita, Fusarium oxysporum* f. sp. *ciceri* wilt disease complex in chickpea. *International J. Pest Management,* **41**(4): 234-237.

Rath, M. and Wolf, G. 1992. Biological control of seed rot and damping-off of sugar beet with microbial antagonists. Bulletin OILB/SROP. **15**(1): 113-114.

Rathore, V. R. S., Kusum, Mathur, R., Lodha, B. C. and Mathur, K. 1992. Activity of volatile and non-volatile substances produced by *Trichoderma viride* on ginger rhizome rot pathogens. *Indian Phytopathol.*, **45**(2): 253-254.

Raupach, G. S. and Kloepper, J. W. 1998. Mixtures of plant growth promoting rhizobacteria enhance biological control of multiple cucumber pathogens. *Phytopathology*, **88**: 1158-1164.

Ray, S., Ghosh, M. and Mukherjee, N. 1990. Fluorescent pseudomonads for plant disease control. *J. Mycopathol. Res.*, **28**(2): 135-140.

Raymond, R. N., Muller, G. and Matzanke, B. F. 1984. Complexation of iron by siderophores: A review of their solution and structural chemistry and biological function. *Trop. Curr. Chem.*, **123**: 49-102.

Rehner, S. A. and Samuels, G. J. 1994. Taxonomy and phylogeny of *Gliocladium* analysed from nuclear large subunit ribosomal DNA sequences. *Can. J. Bot.*, **72**: 302-311.

Rehner, S. A. and Samuels, G. J. 1995. Molecular systematics of the Hypocreales: a teleomorph gene phylogeny and the status of their anamorphs. *Can. J. Bot.*, **73**: 816-823.

Rishbeth, J. A. 1963. Stump protection against Fomes annosus III. Inoculation with *Peniophora giggantia. Annu. Appl. Biol.*, **52**: 63.77.

Roberts, D. P., Dery, P. D., Mao, W. and Hebrar, P. K. 1997. Use of a colonization deficient strain of Escherichia coli in strain combinations for enhanced biological control of cucumber seedling diseases. *J. Phytopathol.*, **145**: 461-463.

Rodriguez-kabana, R., Kelley, W. D. and Curl, E. A., 1978. Proteolytic activity of Trichoderma viride in mixed culture with Sclerotium rolfsii in soil. *Can. J. Microbiol.*, **24**: 487-490.

Roy, A. K. 1977. Parasitic activity of *Trichoderma viride* on the sheath blight fungus of rice (*Corticium sasakii*). *Zeischriftfur Pflanzen Krankheifen* and *Pflazenschectz.*, **84**: 675-683.

Ryder, M. H. 1995. Monitoring of Biocontrol agents and genetically engineered microorganisms in the environment: Biotechnological approaches. *In*: R. P. Singh and U. S. Singh, (eds.), *Molecular Methods in Plant Pathology*. Lewis Publishers, Boca Raton, U.S.A. pp. 475-492.

Ryder, M. H., Slota, J. E., Scarim, A. and Farrand, S. K. 1987. Genetic analysis of agrocin84 production and immunity in *Agrobacterium* spp. *J. Bacteriol.*, **169**: 4184-4189.

Saikia, P. and Chowdhary, H. D. 1993. Phylloplane microflora for the control of bacterial leaf blight of rice caused by *Xanthomonas oryzae* pv. *Oryzae. Indian Phytopathol.*, **46**(3): 218-223.

Sakthivel, N. and Gnanamanickam, S. S. 1987. Evaluation of *Pseudomonas fluorescens* for suppression of sheath rot disease and for enhancement of grain yields in rice, *Oryza sativa* L. *Appl. Environ. Microbiol.*, **53**: 2056-2059.

Sakthivel, N. and Gnanamanickam, S. S. 1986. Bacterization of rice with *Pseudomonas fluorescens* reduces sheath rot (ShR) infection. *International Rice Research Newsletter,* **11**(3): 17-18.

Sakthivel, N., Sivamani, E., Unnamalai, N. and Gnanamanickam, S. S. 1987. Plant growth promoting rhizobacteria in enhancing plant growth and suppressing plant pathogens. *Curr. Sci.*, **55**(1): 22-25.

Samuels, G. J., Lieckfeldt, E. and Nirenberg, H. I. 1999. Description of *T. asperellum* sp. nov. and comparison of *T. viride. Sydowia*, **51**: 71-88.

Sanford, G. B. 1926. Some factors affecting the pathogenicity of *Actinomyces scabies. Phytopathology*, **16**: 525-547.

Sangeetha, P., Jeyarajan, R and Panicker, S. 1993. Mass multiplication of biocontrol agent *Trichoderma* spp. *Indian. J. Pl. Pathol.*, **23**: 328-330

Sankar, P. and Jeyarajan, R. 1996a. Biological control of sesamum root rot by seed treatment with *Trichoderma* sp. and *Bacillus subtilis. Indian J. Mycol. Pl. Pathol.*, **26**(2): 217-220.

Sankar, P. and Jeyarajan, R. 1996b. Seed treatment formulation of *Trichoderma* and *Gliocladium* for biological control of *Macrophomina phaseolina* in sesamum. *Indian Phytopathol.*, **49**(2): 148-151.

Saraswathy, N. 2000. *In-vitro* inhibition of *Phytophthora meadii*, the fruit and but rot pathogen of aracanut palm by microbial antagonists. *In*: Proceeding of Indian Phytopathological Society—Golden Jubilee, International Conference on Integrated Plant Disease Management for Sustainable Agriculture, pp. 501-502.

Sathiabama, M. and Balasubramanian, R. 2001. Induction of defence responses in leaves of *Arachis hypogaea* L., by prior treatment with a glucan from *Acremonium obclavatum* W. Gams, a biocontrol agent of rust disease caused by *Puccinia arachidis* Speg. *In*: National Symposium on "Eco-friendly approaches for plant disease management" held at Chennai, Jan. 22-24, 2001.

Sawant, I. S. and Mukhopadhyay, A. N. 1991. Integration of metalaxyl with *Trichoderma harzianum* for the control of pythium damping-off in sugar beet. *Indian Phytopathol.*, **43**(4): 535-541.

Sawant, I. S., Sawant, S. D. and Ganapathy, M. M. 1995a. Collar rot of passion fruit caused by *Rhizoctonia solani* and its control. *Indian Phytopathol.*, **48**(2): 202-205.

Sawant, I. S., Sawant, S. D. and Nanaya, K. A. 1995b. Biological control of *Phytophthora* root rot of coorg mandarin (*Citrus reticulata*) by *Trichoderma* sp. grown on coffee waste. *Indian J. Agric. Sci.*, **65**(11): 842-846.

Schirmbock, M., Lorito, M., Wang, Y. L., Hayes, C. K., Artisan-Atac, I., Scala, F., Harman, G. E., and Kubicek, C. P. 1994. Parallel formation and synergism of hydrolic enzymes and peptaibol antibiotics, molecular mechanisms involved in the antagonistic action of *Trichoderma harzianum* against phytopathogenic fungi. *Appl. Environ. Microbiol.*, **60**: 4364-4370.

Schisler, D. A., Slininger, P. J. and Bothast, R. J. 1997. Effect of antagonist cell concentration and two strain mixtures on biological control of *Fusarium* dry rot of potatoes. *Phytopathology*, **87**: 177-183.

Schneider, R. E. (ed). 1982. *Suppressive Soils and Plant Disease*. Am. Phytopath. Soc., St. Paul, Minn.

Selvakumar, R. and Srivastva, K. D. 2000. Management of spot blotch of wheat using biocontrol agent. *In*: National Conference on Swadeshi Vigyan, held at New Delhi, Dec. 26-28, 2000. 289p. (Abstr.).

Selvakumar, R., Srivastava, K. D., Aggarwal, Rashmi, Singh, D. V. and Dureja, Prem. 2000. Studies on development of *Trichoderma viride* mutants and their effect on *Ustilago segetum tritici*. *Indian Phytopathol.*, **53:** 185-189.

Sen, B. 2000. Biological control: A success story. *Indian Phytopathol.*, **53**: 243-249.

Sharma S. K., Verma, B. R. and Sharma B. K. 1999. Biocontrol of *Sclerotinia sclerotiorum* causing stem rot of chickpea. *Indian Phytopathol.*, **52**: 44-46.

Sharma, B. K. and Singh, B. M. 1990. Biological control of white rot of pea caused by *Sclerotinia sclerotium*. *J. Biol. Control*, **4**(2): 132-134.

Sharma, B. K., Singh, B. M. and Sugha, S. K. 1996. Survival of *Sclerotinia sclerotiorum* (Lib.) de Bary under the influence of biocontrol agents in soil. *Current Research in University of Agricultural Sciences, Banglore*, **25**(3): 46-47.

Sharma, D. D. and Sinha, S. K. 1982. Biological control of red-rot of sugarcane by *Streptomyces dayalbaghesis*. *Indian Phytopathol.*, **35**(1): 174-175.

Sharma, R. C. Kohli, N., Singh, A. and Gill, S. S. 2000. Preliminary studies on biocontrol of *Tilletia barclayana*. *In*: Proceeding of Indian Phytopathological Society—Golden Jubilee, International Conference on Integrated Plant Disease Management for Sustainable Agriculture, pp. 327-328.

Sharma, S. K. and Dohroo, N. P. 1991. Post harvest management of rhizome rot (*Fusarium oxysporum* f. sp. *zingiberi*, Trujillo) of ginger through chemical and antagonists. *Indian Cocoa Arecanut and Spices Journal*, **14**(4): 150-152.

Sharma, S. K. and Gupta, J. S. 1982. Role of *Sterptomyces rochei* against some pathogenic fungi. *Indian J. Mycol. Pl. Pathol.*, **12**(2): 227-228.

Sharma, S. K. and Gupta, V. K. 1996. Potential oe *Trichoderma* species as an antagonist against *Dematophora necatrix* causimg white root rot of apple. *In*: Nat. Sym. on "Management of threatening plant diseases, PAU, Ludhiana, p. 27.

Sharon, E., Bar-Eyal, M., Chet, I., Herrera-Estrella, A., Kleifeld, O. and Spiegel, Y. 2001. Biological control of the root knot nematode *Meloidogyne javanica* by *Trichoderma harzianum*. *Phytopathology*, **91**: 687-693.

Sheela, J., Sivaprakasam, K. and Seethar, K. 1995. Biological control of *Fusarium* wilt of egg plant. *Madras Agricultural Journal*, **82**(3): 199-201.

Shekhawat, G. S., Rajpal Singh, Chakrabarti, S. K. and Singh, R. 1993. Possibility of biological management of potato bacterial wilt with microbial antagonists and latent potato viruses. *Journal of the Indian Potato Association*, **29**(3-4): 219-222.

Shivapratap, H. R., Philip, T. and Sharma, D. D. 1996. *In vitro* antagonism of *Trichoderma* sp. against mulberry leaf spot pathogen, *Cercospora moricola. Indian Journal of Sericulture*, **35**(2): 107-110.

Shrestha, S. M. 1992. Biocontrol potential of *Trichoderma harzianum* and *Gliocladiun virens* on lentil wilt complex. Ph.D. Thesis, G. B. Pant University of Agric. & Tech. Pantnagar, INDIA, pp. 210.

Siddiqui, Z. A. and Mahmood, I. 1993a. Biological control of *Meloidogyne incognita* race 3 and *Macrophomina phaseolina* by *Paecilomyces lilacinus* and *Bacillus subtilis* alone and in combination on chickpea. *Fundamental* and *Applied Nematology*, **16**(3): 215-218.

Siddiqui, Z. A. and Mahmood, I. 1993b. Integrated control of a root-rot disease complex of chickpea by fungal filtrates and green manuring. *Nematologia Mediterranea*, **21**(2): 161-164.

Siddiqui, Z. A. and Mahmood, I. 1995a. Biological control of *Heterodera cajani* and *Fusarium udum by Bacillus subtilis, Bradyrhizobium japonicum* and *Glomus fasciculatum* on pigeonpea. *Fundamental and Applied Nematology*, **18**(6): 559-566.

Siddiqui, Z. A. and Mahmood, I. 1995b. Management of *Meloidogyne incognita* race 3 and *Macrophomina phaseolina* by fungus culture filtrates and *Bacillus subtilis* in chickpea. *Fundamental and Applied Nematology*, **18**(1): 71-76.

Sindhan, G. S., Parashar, R. D. and Hooda, I. 1997a. Biological control of bacterial blight of cluster bean caused by *Xanthomonas axonopodis* pv. cyamopsodis. *Plant Disease Research*, **12**(1): 33-35.

Singh, D. V. 2000. Integrated approach for the control of loose smut of wheat. *In*: Proceeding of Indian Phytopathological Society—Golden Jubilee, International Conference on Integrated Plant Disease Management for Sustainable Agriculture, pp. 657-659.

Singh, D. V. and Srivastva, K. D. 2000. Recent strategies in management of karnal bunt of wheat. *In*: Proceeding of Indian Phytopathological Society—Golden Jubilee, International Conference on Integrated Plant Disease Management for Sustainable Agriculture, pp. 415-420.

Singh, H. B., Kalara, A., Patra, A. K. and Sushilkumar, 2000. Stolon decay of menthol mint caused by Sclerotinia sclerotiorum and its biological control. *In*: Proceeding of Indian Phytopathological Society—Golden Jubilee, International Conference on Integrated Plant Disease Management for Sustainable Agriculture, pp. 386-388.

Singh, R. D. N. and Kaiser, S. A. K. M. 1996. Biocontrol of charcoal rot pathogen (*Macrophomina phaseolina*) of maize with *Fusarium solani* f.sp. *psidii. Advances in Plant Sciences*, **9**(1): 75-80.

Singh, U. S., Mishra, D. S., Singh, Amita, Rohilla, Rashmi and Vishwanath 2003. Induced resistance: present status and future prospects as disease management strategy. *In*: I. O. Koul, G. S. Dhaliwal, S. S. Marwaha, and J. K. Arora, (eds), *Biopesticides and Pest Management* Vol. pp. 262-302.

Singh, R. S., Singh, H. V. and Singh, D. 1997. Effect of fungal antagonists on the growth of chickpea plants and wilt caused by *Fusarium oxyporum* f. sp. *ciceri. Plant Dis. Res.*, **12**(2): 103-107.

Sitther, V. and Gnanamanickam, S. S. 1996. Biological control of blast disease of fingermillet (*Eleusine coracana* L.) and an analysis of fertility of *Magnaporthe grisea. Curr. Sci.*, **71**(2): 144-147.

Sivamani, E., Anuratha, C. S. and Gnanamanickam, S. S. 1987. Toxicity of *Pseudomonas fluorescens* towards bacterial plant pathogens of banana (*Pseudomonas solanacearum*) and rice (*Xanthomonas compestris* pv. *oryzae*). *Curr. Sci.*, **56**(11): 547-548.

Sivan, A. and Chet, I. 1989. The possible role of competition between *Trichoderma harzianum* and *Fusarium oxysporum* on rhizosphere colonization. *Phytopathology*, **79**: 198-203.

Sivan, A., and Chet, I. 1986. Biological control of *Fusarium* spp. in cotton, wheat and muskmelon by *Trichoderma harzianum. J. Phytopathol.*, **116**: 39.

Sneh, B. 1981. Use of rhizosphere chitinolytic bacteria for biological control of *Fusarium oxysporum* f. sp. *dianthi* in carnation. *Phytopath. Z.* **100**: 251-256.

Sneh, B., Dupler, M., Elad, Y. and Baker, R. 1984. Chlamydospore germinaton of *Fusarium oxysporum* f. sp. *cucumerinum* as affected by fluorescent and lytic bacteria from a *Fusarium* suppressive soil. *Phytopathology,* **74**: 1115-1124.

Somasekhara, Y. M., Anilkumar, T. B. and Siddaramaiah, A. L. 1996. Biocontrol of pigeonpea (*Cajanus cajan* (L.) Millsp.) wilt (*Fusarium udum,* Butler). *Mysore J. Agric. Sci.,* **30**(2): 159-163.

Sreenivasa, M. N. 1994. Biological deterrent activities of VA-mycorrhiza and *Trichoderma harzianum* on *Sclerotium rolfsii* at different P-levels in chilli. *Environment* and *Ecology,* **12**(2): 319-321.

Sreenivasaprasad, S. and Manibhushanrao, K. 1993. Efficacy of *Gliocladium virens* and *Trichoderma longibrachiatum* as biological control agents of groundnut root and stem rot disease. *International J. Pest Management,* **39**(2): 167-171.

Stasz, T. E., Harman, G. E. and Weeden, N. F. 1988. Protoplast preparation and fusion in two biocontrol strains of *Trichoderma harzianum. Mycologia,* **80**: 141-150.

Stockwell, V. O., Johnson, K. B. and Loper, J. E. 1996. Compatibility of bacterial antagonists of *Erwinia amylovora* with antibiotics used to control fire blight. *Phytopathology,* **86**: 834-840.

Stone, I. 1980. The origin. A Biographical Novel of Charles Darwin. Doubleday, NewYork.

Sugha, S. K., Sharma, B. K. and Tyagi, P. D. 1993. Factors affecting development of collar rot of gram (*Cicer arietinum*) caused by *Sclerotium rolfsii. Indian J. Agric. Sci.,* **63**(6): 382-385.

Sumitha, R and Gaikwad, S. J. 1995. Checking fusarium wilt of pigeonpea by biocontrol means. *Journal of Soils and Crops,* **5**(2): 163-165.

Sundaram, R. M., 1996. Biocontrol characterization of *Trichoderma harzianum,* Rifai, isolate-1 and its protoplast fusion with *Trichoderma harzianum,* Rifai, isolate-3. M.Sc., Thesis, G. B. Pant University of Agric. & Tech. Pantnagar- 263145 (INDIA), p. 91.

Sung, K. C., Chung, Y. R. 1997. Enhanced suppression of rice sheath blight using combination of bacteria which produce chitinase or antibiotics. *In:* A. Ogoshi, K. Kobayashi, Y. Homma, F. Kodama, N. Kondo, S. Akino (eds.), *Plant Growth Rhizobacteria-Present Status and Future Prospects. Proc. Int. Workshop on Plant Growth Promoting Rhizobacteria,* 4th. pp. 370-372. Sapporo: Nakanishi Printing.

Suslow, T. V. and Schroth, M. N. 1982. Rhizobacteria of sugarbeets: Effect of seed application and root colonization on yield. *Phytopathology,* **72**: 199-206.

Subrahmanyam, P., Reddy, P. M., and Mc Donald, D. 1990. Parasitism of rust, early and late leaf spot pathogens of peanut by *Verticillium lecanii. Peanut Sci.,* **17**: 1-4.

Subrahmanyam, P., Moss, J. P., McDonald, D., Subba Rao, P. V. and Rao, V. R. 1985. Resistance to leaf spot caused by *Cercosporidium personatum* in wild *Arachis* species. *Plant Dis.,* **69**: 951-954.

Suresh, G., Narasimhan, N. S., Masilamani, S., Partho, P. D. and Gopalakrishnan, G. 1997. Antifungal fractions and compounds from uncrushed green leaves of *Azadirachta indica. Phytoparasitica.,* **25**: 33-39.

Tewari, A. K. 1996. Biological Control of chickpea wilt-complex using different formulations of *Gliocladium virens* through seed treatment. Ph.D. Thesis, G. B. Pant University of Agric. & Tech., Pantnagar (INDIA), p. 167.

Thomas, J., Bhai, R. S., Dhanapal, K. and Vijayan, A. K. 2000. Integrated management of small cardamom. *In:* Proceeding of Indian Phytopathological Society—Golden Jubilee, International Conference on Integrated Plant Disease Management for Sustainable Agriculture, p. 481.

Thomas. L., Mallesha, B. C. and Bagyaraj, D. J. 1994. Biological control of damping-off of cardamom by the VA mycorrhizal fungus, *Glomus fasciculatum. Microbiol. Res.,* **149**(4): 413-417.

Thrane, C., Tronsmo, A. and Jenson, D. F. 1997. Endo β-1,3 glucanase and cellulase from *Trichoderma harzianum*: Biological activity against plant pathogenic *Pythium* spp. *Eur. J. Plant Pathol.,* **103**: 331-344.

Troutman, J. L. and Matezka, J. C. 1978. Induced tolerance of Trichoderma viride to benomyl. *Phytopathological News,* **12**, 131 (abstr.)

Turner, J. T. and Backman, P. A. 1986. *Biol. Cult. Tests Control Plant Dis.,* **1**: 49.

Upadhyay, J. P. and Mukhopadhyay, A. N. 1986. Biological control of *Sclerotium rolfsii by Trichoderma harzianum* in sugar beet. Trop. *Pest Management,* **32**(3): 215-220.

Ushamalini, C., Rajappan, K. and Gangadharan, K. 1997a. Inhibition of *Macrophomina phaseolina* and *Fusarium oxysporum* f. sp. *tracheiphilum* by antagonists under *in vitro* conditions. *Plant Dis. Res.*, **12**(2): 168-170.

Ushamalini, C., Rajappan, K., Kousalya Gangadharan. 1997b. Control of cowpea wilt by non-chemical means. *Plant Dis. Res.*, **12**(2): 122-129.

Usman, M., Jaganathan, R. and Dinakaran, D. 1991. Plant disease management on groundnut with naturally occurring plant products. *Madras Agric. J.*, **78**: 152-153.

Utsumi, R., Hadama, T., Noda, M., Toyoda, H., Hashimoto, H. and Ohuchi, S. 1988. Cloning of fusaric acid detoxifying gene from *Cladosporium werneckii*: A new strategy for the prevention of plant diseases. *J. Biotechnol.*, **8**: 311-316.

Van Loon, L. C., Bakker, P. A. H. M., Pieterse, C. M. J. 1998. Systemic resistance induced by rhizosphere bacteria. *Annu. Rev. Phytopathol.*, **36**: 453.

Van Wees, S. C. M., Luizendijk, M., Smoorenberg, I., Van Loon, L. C. and Pieterse, C. M. J. 1999. Rhizobacteria mediated induced systemic resistance in *Arabidopsis* is not associated with direct effect on expression of known defense related genes but stimulates the expression of the jasmonate inducible gene *Atvsp* upon challenge. *Plant Mol. Biol.*, **41**: 537-549.

Varshney, S. 1997. Studies on rhizosphere competence, biocontrol potential and compatibility with VAM and *Trichoderma* sp. of some strains of *Pseudomonas fluorescens* isolated from rhizosphere of tomato. *M.Sc. (Ag.) Thesis*, G. B. Pant University of Agric. & Tech. Pantnagar, INDIA, p. 189.

Varshney, S., and Chaube, H. S. 2001. Mycorrhizal-Rhizobacterial and fungal antagonists: Interactions. *In:* Asha Sinha (ed.) *Microbes and Plants*. New Delhi: Campus Books International, pp. 226-238.

Venkatasubbaiah, P. 1985. Efficacy of *Bacillus subtilis* as a biocontrol for collar rot of coffee pathogen. *Geobios*, **12**(3/4): 101-104.

Venkatasubbaiah, P. and Safeeulla, K. M. 1984. *Aspergillus niger* for biocontrol of *Rhizoctonia solani* on coffee seedlings. *Trop. Pest Management*, **30**(4): 401-406.

Verma, J. P., Singh, R. P., Chowdhary, H. D. and Sinha, P. P. 1983. Usefulness of phylloplane bacteria in the control of bacterial blight of cotton. *Indian Phytopathol.*, **36**(3) 574-577.

Vidhyasekaran, P. and Balasubramanium, P. 1995. Disease management by exploiting pathogenesis related proteins with lytic action. *In*: P. Verma, A. Varma and D. Kumar (eds.), *Detection of Plant Pathogens and their Management*. Angkor Publishers, New Delhi, pp. 259-272.

Vidhyasekaran, P. and Muthamilan, M. 1995. Development of formulations of *Pseudomonas fluorescens* for control of chickpea wilt. *Plant Dis.*, **79**: 782-786.

Vidhyasekaran, P., Balasubramanium, P., Samiyappan, R. and Velazhahan, R. 1996. Genetic engineering approaches for management of crop diseases. *In*: R. K. Upadhyay, K. G. Mukherji and R. L. Rajak (eds.), *IPM System in Agriculture Vol. I Principals and Prospectives*. Aditya Books, New Delhi, pp. 471-502.

Vidhyasekaran, P., Rabindran, R., Muthamilan, M., Nayar, K., Rajappan, K., Subramanian, N. and Vasumathi, K. 1997. Development of a powder formulation of *Pseudomonas fluorescens* for control of rice blast. *Plant Pathol.*, **46**(3): 291-297.

Von Arx, J. A. 1987. Plant pathogenic fungi. *Beihefte zur Nova Hedwigia*, **87**: 288.

Waraitch, K. S. 1987. Efficacy of different fungicides and *Trichoderma harzianum*, Rifai applied as soil drench for the control of root rot of sugar beet (*Beta vulgaris* L.). *Pesticides*, **21**(9): 37-38.

Wei, G., Kloepper, J. W. and Tuzum, S. 1996. Induced systemic resistance to cucumber diseases and increased plant growth by plant growth promoting rhizobacteria under field conditions. *Phytopathology*, **86**: 221-224.

Weindling, R. 1932. *Trichoderma lignorum* as a parasite of other soil fungi. *Phytopathology*, **22**: 834-845.

Weindling, R. 1934. Studies on a lethal principle effective in the parasitic action of *Trichoderma* lignorum on *Rhizoctonia solani* and other soil fungi. *Phytopathology*, **24**: 1153-1169.

Weller, D. M. 1988. Biological control of soil borne plant pathogens in the rhizosphere with bacteria. *Annu. Rev. Phytopathol.*, **26**: 379-407.

Wells, H. D., Bell, D. K., and Jaworski, C. K. 1972. Efficacy of *Trichoderma harzianum* against several pathogens. *Phytopathology,* **62**: 449.

Woo, S. L., Donzelli, B., Scalla, F., Mach, R., Harman, G. E., Kubicek, C. P., Del Sorbo, G. and Lorito, M. 1999. Disruption of the ech42 (endochitinase-encoding) gene affects biocontrol activity in *Trichoderma harzianum. Plant Mol. Plant-Microbe Interact.*, **12**: 419-429.

Wu, W. S. 1977. Antibiotic and mycoparasitic effects of several fungi against seed and soil borne pathogens associated with wheat and oats. *Bot. Bulle. Acad. Sinia.*, **18**: 25-31.

Yedidia, I., Benhamou, N. and Chet, I. 1999. Induction of defense responses in cucumber plants (*Cucumis sativus* L.) by the biocontrol agent *Trichoderma harzianum. Appl. Environ. Microbiol.*, **65**: 1061-1070.

Yehia, A. H., El-Hassan, S. A., and El-Bahadli, A. H. 1985. Biological seed treatment to control Fusarium root rot of broad bean. *Egyptian. J. Phytopathol.*, **14**: 59-66.

Yuen, G. Y., Schroth, M. N. and McCain, A. H. 1985. Reduction of *Fusarium* wilt of carnation with suppressive soils and antagonistic bacteria. *Plant Dis.*, **69**: 1071-1075.

Zeilinger, S., Galhaup, C., Payer, K. L., Woo, S., Mach, R., Fekete-Csaba, L., Lorito, M. and Kubicek, C. P. 1999. Chitinase gene expression during mycoparasitic interaction of *Trichoderma harzianum* with its host. *Fungal Genet. Biol.*, **26**: 131-140.

Zimand, G., Elad, Y. and Chet, I. 1996. Effect of *Trichoderma harzianum* on Botrytis *cineria* pathogenicity. *Phytopathology,* **86**: 1255-1260.

Zhang, S., Reddy, M. S., Kokalis-Burelle, N., Wells, L. W., Nightengale, S. P. and Kloepper, J. W. 2001. Lack of induced systemic resistance in peanut to late leaf spot disease by plant growth-promoting rhizobacteria and chemical elicitors. *Plant Dis.*, **85**: 879-884.

# Potential of Entomopathogenic Nematodes in Integrated Pest Management

**S. S. Hussaini**

## INTRODUCTION

Biological control methods can be used as part of an overall Integrated Pest Management (IPM) program to reduce the legal, environmental, and public safety hazards of chemicals. In addition, it may be a more economical alternative to some insecticides. Some biological control measures can actually prevent economic damage to agricultural crops. Unlike most insecticides, biological controls are often very specific for a particular pest. Other helpful insects, animals, or people can go completely unaffected or undisturbed by their use. There is less danger of impact on the environment and water quality. Concern over chemical pesticides in respect of ground water contamination, residues of food, resistance development, and wild life kills, have increased interest for safer alternatives. Use of natural enemies—parasitoids and insect pathogens—as biological insecticides are considered to be the most viable pest management alternatives. The annual growth increase in microbial insecticides is 10-fold compared to that of chemical insecticides. Entomopathogenic nematodes (EPNs)—steinernematids and heterorhabditids—are lethal insect parasites that are used in biological control (Gaugler & Kaya, 1990; Grewal & Georgis, 1998). The third stage infective juveniles (IJs) serving as potential agents for control of insects with their mutualistically associated bacterium. EPNs possess impressive attributes of parasitoids/predators and pathogens viz., achieve a quick kill, have a broad host range, highly virulent, possess chemoreceptors, can be cultured easily *in vitro*, have a numerical but no functional response, are safe to vertebrates, plants and non targets, have been exempt from registration in USA, are easily applied using standard application equipment, are compatible with many chemical pesticides, and are amenable to genetic selection. Though acknowledged as potential bioagents, several issues contribute to their commercialization. One important issue is the mass production and subsequent formulation and use. Attempt is made to analyze some critical factors in their successful utilization for insect control.

The third stage infective juveniles (IJs) locate suitable insects in soil and invade through natural body openings (mouth, anus and spiracles). On access to the hemocoel, the nematodes release a symbiotic bacterium (*Xenorhabdus* in

*Project Directorate of Biological Control, P.O. Box No, 2491 H.A. Farm Post, Bellary Rd. Bangalogre-560 024.*

Steinememematidae and *Photorhabdus* in Heterorhabditidae) that multiplies rapidly, killing the host within 24-48 h. The IJs feed on bacteria and disintegrated host tissues, grow to adults, and produce two to three generations. When host nutrients are depleted, the nematodes produce next generation IJs that leave the host cadaver and seek new hosts (Poinar 1990). However, limited shelf life is a major obstacle to further expansion of their use (Grewal & Georgis, 1998). Anhydrobiosis is considered as an important means of achieving storage stability. Anhydrobiosis, is a reversible, physiologically arrested, state of dormancy induced by dehydration (Barnett, 1991). It occurs naturally in nematodes as well as other invertebrates, and is believed to be an important survival strategy under drought stress. True anhydrobiotes can loose up to 95-98% of their body water and as desiccation persists, they lower their metabolism to below detectable levels, entering into a state of cryptobiosis (Cooper & Van Guindy, 1971). However, EPNs are capable of only partial anhydrobiosis (Simmons & Poinar, 1973), and are therefore, referred to as quiescent anyhydrobiotes (Womersely, 1990). Earlier efforts on direct contact desiccation and desiccation with the aid of absorbents such as clay to achieve storage stability had only limited success (Georgis *et al.*, 1994). Biological control of insects has progressed significantly since the discovery of infection of Japanese beetle with *Steinernema glaseri* (Glaser, 1932). Nematodes are commercially produced on four continents. Despite progress, the EPNs are not reducing the use of chemical pesticides to any significant degree. They are most often used in niche markets presently.

## VARIATION IN SPECIES AND STRAIN

Differences in efficacy among species and strains have been well documented for predatory insects, parasitoids and a number of entomopathogens. The importance of such interspecific and intraspecific variation has been recognized and demonstrated. Accurate, fast and easy methods for identification of EPNs are required. Since they are specialized to feed by remaining inside the host insect there are very few morphological characters and identification up to species level has always been difficult. Natural host and geographical area of detection was regarded as a major characteristic for identification, leading to designation of several species, which were later considered synonyms. For a species to be considered distinct, morphological, physiological and ecological differences along with reproductive isolation should be detectable when compared with other closely related species. Although, morphological characters help in the identification of species, at times it fails (more so in EPNs). In such cases, additional information on DNA sequence and hybridization data are needed to confirm distinctness. The focus of molecular methods in nematode taxonomy has been to develop novel diagnostic characters for species and infrasubspecific groupings in economically important nematode genera where morphology lacked sufficient discriminatory power. Difference in protein or isozyme phenotype, affinity for antibody, DNA restriction fragment length polymorphism, DNA probe or sequence data for any gene or region of the genome is a potential diagnostic character. Little use has recently been made of protein or immunological techniques in nematode taxonomy. The major focus over last few years has been on DNA analysis.

The morphological characters used in the identification of species sometimes show considerable variations and at times species identification becomes very difficult. In these circumstances the most fundamental test, whether two populations can cross breed to produce fertile offspring, is particularly important both as means of identifying species and as an indicator of those characters that show great divergence between species. Poinar (1967) used hanging drop of insect blood for cross-breeding tests, but technique most commonly used is based on injecting individual *G. mellonella* larvae with one IJ from a stock culture and another from the population being tested (Akhurst & Bedding, 1978). PCR techniques have found wide spread application in molecular taxonomy and effectively replaced the analysis of extracted and purified DNA of EPN by agarose gel electrophoresis and Southern blot technique (Curran & Webster, 1989).

An in-depth knowledge of inter and intraspecific variations in DNA sequence is required. Most of the species descriptions are now appended with DNA data alongwith morphometric and crossbreeding studies (Cabanillas *et al.*, 1994; Tallosi *et al.*, 1995; Elawad *et al.*, 1997; Waturu *et al.*, 1997). Variable morphology and overlapping of characters within the genus, a reliable method is cross breeding for species identification. Molecular techniques are also described reliably distinguishing species of the genera *Steinernema* and *Heterorhabditis* (Joyce *et al.*, 1994; Reid, 1994). In India Poinar *et al.*, (1992) detected *Heterorhabditis indica* in sugarcane fields at Coimbatore. Extensive surveys by PDBC since 1996 detected S. *carpocapsae* from Bangalore, Madurai, Rajahmundry, *S. bicornutum* from Delhi, and *H. indica* from Bangalore, Coimbatore, Chidambaram, Kanyakumari, Aligarh. Detailed RFLP analysis showed the presence of *S. tami* from Jorhat *S. abbasi* from Delhi and unidentified *Steinernema* spp. SSL2 from Aligarh and Coimbatore (Hussaini *et al.*, 2001a). Besides, *S. thermophilum* was recorded from IARI, New Delhi (Ganguly & Singh, 2000). There are presently 30 species of *Steinernema* and 9 of *Heterorhabditis* on record in the World.

## MUTUALISTIC BACTERIA

Penetrating nematodes inoculate bacteria *Xenorhabdus* or *Photorhabdus* spp. respectively into the host by steinernematids and heterorhabditids. The nematode may appear to be little more than a biological syringe for its associated bacterium. Although parasitic EPNs have not severed their nutritional relationship with bacteria, growth and reproduction are dependent upon conditions established in the host cadaver by the bacterium. Bacteria cannot survive in water and soil nor can reach the insect haemocoel on their own. The nematode must carry the bacteria into the hemocoel of an insect host where they multiply rapidly, kill the host by septicemia and serve as an essential food source for the nematode, and the nematodes do not grow and reproduce in the absence of the bacteria (Poinar & Thomas, 1966). Symbiotic bacteria associated with indigenous isolates of *H. indica* and *S. carpocapsae* were isolated and characterized (Nagesh *et al.*, 2001). Phase variation has been observed in this group of bacteria. Pathogenic differences are not found between the two phases. Primary form enhances maturity, reproduction, and production of antibiotics

(Akhurst, 1980; 1982). Phase variation is suggested for survival of bacteria as phase I is more susceptible to phage virus (Akhurst & Boemare, 1990). Specificity of bacteria, bacteria-nematode association has been known. *Steinernema* species reproduce best in the monoxenic culture of their natural symbiont though they can utilize other bacterial species (Akhurst, 1983). Controlled mass culture of bacteria release metabolites that are anti fungal and anti bacterial. Indole derivatives, stilbene derivatives xenorhabdins, xenocoumacins, xeroxodes and nematophins are bioactive. They inhibit *Bacillus subtilis, Staphylococcus epidermidis, S. aureus, Aspergillus fumigatus* and *A. flavus* (Webster *et al.*, 1996). *Xenorhabdus nematophilus* was found to inhibit *Botrytis cinerea, Cerastomella ulmi, C. dryocoetidis, Mucor piriformis, Pythium colaratum, P. ultimum, Penicillium notatum, Rhizoctonia solani, Trichoderma pseudokoningii,* and *Verticillium dahliae* and *Photorhabdus* inhibited *Botrytis cinerea, Cerastomella ulmi, C. dryocoetidis, Mucor piriformis, P. coloratum, P. ultimum, Trichoderma pseudokoningii, Verticillium dahliae* (Chen *et al.*, 1994).

## Molecular Biology

In EPN research has received little emphasis till recently. Most effort has been directed towards the application of molecular methods for nematode identification (Curran 1990; 1993, Joyce *et al.*, 1994, Hashmi *et al.*, 1996). New isolates of *Heterorhabditis* and *Steinernema* species have been collected from around the world and tested for their pathogenicity to various target insects and for tolerance to environmental stress. Genetic variability within species of EPN provides insight into their phylogenetic relationships and population dynamics. Despite the high degree of natural genetic variability among these many species and strains, environmental stability is limited. Although conventional genetic improvement techniques have provided some nematode enhancement (Gaugler *et al.*, 1989a; Gaugler & Campbell 1991; Zioni *et al.*, 1992; Rahimi *et al.*, 1993), the introduction of specific characters require biotechnological approaches. The close relationship of these nematodes with *Coenorhabditis elegans*, the model organism in molecular genetics for nearly three decades, provides an extraordinary opportunity to exploit this new technology. Progress has been made in the genetic transformation, and the functionality of *C. elegans* genes into *H. bacteriophora* (Hashmi *et al.*, 1995a; 1995b; 1996; 1997).

The methodologies of classical genetics and genetic engineering can be used for the genetic improvement of EPNs and their symbiont bacteria. Mutagenesis has the effect of inactivating genes, so it is not a very useful approach for introducing new genetic material into experimental organisms. Mutagenesis is useful, however, for inactivating negative regulators of gene expression and can thus be a means of obtaining the constitutive expression of repressed genes. Screening several thousand IJs for a desirable phenotype can be very time consuming unless a suitable means of mass screening is devised. Lethal screens and behavioural screens provide an easy method of mutant selection. The results of these mutagenesis experiments aimed at isolating EPN strains with improvements in phenotypes relating to environmental tolerances, thermotactic behaviour and IJ longevity are presented, and it is demonstrated that in situations where a suitable and non labour intensive screening method is devised, chemical mutagenesis can provide an accessible, robust and inexpensive means of strain improvement. (Burnell *et al.*, 1999). The success in genetic transformation of EPN opens the way for generating transgenic nematodes carrying genes conferring resistance to various environmental extremes, most notably heat shock genes. (Segal *et al.*, 1999).

While searching for target host in agricultural soils the IJs encounter a variety of substances that hamper their activity. These include residues of various fungicides, herbicides and insecticides. The IJs can withstand many such chemicals, which are commonly used in cultivated soils (Hara & Kaya, 1982,1983; Rovesti & Deseo, 1990; Ishibashi & Takii 1993; Hussaini *et al.*, 2000a). This resistance has been attributed to the thick protective cuticle of the IJs and to their closed oral and anal openings (Mracek *et al.*, 1981) which prevents penetration. However several chemical insecticides or nematicides were found to be highly toxic in lab assays (Hara & Kaya, 1982, 1983; Rovesti & Deseo, 1990; Hussaini *et al.*, 2001b). Exposure to such chemicals may reduce their persistence and activity as biological control agents. Genetic selection has been suggested as a means to enhance tolerance. Successful genetic selection depends on the presence of genetic diversity for the particular trait in the population (heritability, h2) (Glazer *et al.*, 1991). Enhancement of tolerance to nematicide Phenamiphos, Oxamyl and Avermictin in the commercial strain *H. bacteriophora* HP88 was attempted by Glazer *et al.* (1997) and estimated the heritibility for nematicidal resistance in the population, the stability of the trait in selected population was determined and their performance characterized with respect to several key traits relevant to biocontrol efficacy.

## VIRULENCE AND INFECTIVITY

Virulence and infectivity of native populations of *Steinernema* spp. and *H. indica* alone and in combinations were evaluated against *A. ipsilon* in sand and sandy loam soil columns. *H. indica* PDBC EN 13.22 outcompeted *Steinernema* spp. irrespective of soil types, depth and time for mortality. *S. abbasi* PDBC EN 3.1 was found to be promising among the steinernematids. Performance of all the isolates was better in sandy loam soil than in sand at 5 cm depth. The mortality of *A. ipsilon* enhanced with increase in time of exposure. Combination of *S. carpocapsae* PDBC EN 6.11 and *H. indica* PDBC EN 13.22 had an additive effect over their individual populations in both soil types at 10 cm depth (Hussaini *et al.*, 2000a). The nematode isolates differ in their rank for virulence between the stages of the insect and also among the species (Glazer & Navon 1990). Stimulation of isolates, *Steinernema* sp. (SSL2) PDBC EN 13.21, PDBC EN 14.1, *H. indica* PDBC EN 13.22, PDBC EN 14.3 and PDBC EN 6.71 affected with Mg and Mn ions caused increased pathogenicity and progeny production (Hussaini *et al.*, 2001c).

The infectivity of populations of *S. feltiae* and *H. megidis* from Greece (GR) and the UK was compared by dose-response tests (Menti *et al.*, 2000). The two *Steinernema* populations did not differ in their establishment rates but were more infective than *H. megidis* UK 211. The temperature range for infectivity was greater than that for development. However, the optimal temperature for infection and development for all populations was 23° C. Infectivity of *Steinernema* populations was not affected by storage for 12 weeks. However, 12 week-old *H. megidis* UK 211 IJ were less infective than fresh IJ of *H. megidis* GR which showed very low establishment rates at all the doses and temperatures tested, before and after storage. Boff *et al.* (2000) reported that as the storage period of *H. megidis* increased the infectivity, number of active nematodes, and reproduction of IJ decreased both at low and high temperatures.

Effects of temperature and host age on the biocontrol potential of EPNs against the sugarcane rootstalk borer weevil, *Diaprepes abbreviatus* were tested under lab conditions. Older larvae (*i.e.*, 100-day-old) were less susceptible to nematode infection than younger larvae. Nematodes were less virulent at 21° C than at 24 or 27° C. The virulence of *H. indica* was greater than *H. bacteriophora* in 50-day-old *D. abbreviatus* larvae at all temperatures, and greater than the other 2 nematode species in 20-day-old larvae at 24° C. *H. bacteriophora* was more virulent than *S. riobrave* in 20-day-old larvae at 24° C, whereas *S. riobrave* was more virulent at 21° C in 50-day-old larvae. Reproductive potential was greatest in *H. indica* followed by *H. bacteriophora*. The high level of reproduction in heterorhabditid species indicates a potential for nematode recycling in field applications. Hence temperature and host age should be considered critical factors in determining the time of nematode application.

## BIOEFFICIENCY

Bioefficiency tests carried out in India have been confined mostly to lab studies (Table 10.1). In field trials, *S. carpocapsae* (strain DD 136), *H. bacteriophora* (strain Burliar) and *Heterorhabditis* spp. (strains Cherikunnu and Melur) against 4th-instar larvae of *Amsacta albistriga* on groundnut. *S.carpocapsae* was the most effective, followed by *Heterorhabditis* sp. (Cherikunnu). *Heterorhabditis* spp. did not develop in the larvae. The host insect died because of the symbiotic bacteria of the nematodes. *S. carpocapsae* developed in the larvae (Bhaskaran *et al.*,1994 ). At PDBC, indigenous isolates of EPNs were tested against *Leucinodes orbonalis* in lab and field on brinjal. In the field trial, *S. carpocapsae* and *H. indica* @ 0.5-2.0 billion/ac, reduced the borer holes on fruits and increased yields comparable with sprays of neem seed kernel extract. Among the two species, *S. carpocapsae* PDBC EN 6.11 was found more effective (Hussaini *et al.*, 2002). In field tests in Ohio *H. bacteriophora* (NC strain) reduced populations of *Popillio japonica* in turfgrass up to 60%, 34 days after treatment in autumn. Control increased to 96% before pupation the following spring, and was 93-99% of the next larval generation. Application of *S. carpocapsae* (all strain) provided a maximum of 51% control after 34 days, 90% the next spring (290 days after treatment), and 0% after 386 days. In another trial spring application resulted in 68% control 28 days after treatment, and up to 67% of the following generation of larvae in the autumn (138 days after treatment). *H. bacteriophora* (HP88 strain) gave 100% control after 28 days in the spring, and 93-97% control of the next generation of larvae. No adverse effects on non target organisms (mites or Collembola) were observed 28 days after treatments with any of the nematodes. Nematodes reproduced in larvae of *P. japonica*, survived in the field in turfgrass, and influenced target hosts for a longer period of time (Klein & Georgis, 1992).

**TABLE 10.1:** BIOEFFICACY OF ENTOMOPATHOGENIC NEMATODES AGAINST INSECT PESTS

| *Insect Pest* | *Nematode sp.,* | *Observations Lab/Field* | *Reference* |
|---|---|---|---|
| *Scirpophaga incertulas* (Wlk)<br>*Sesamia inferens* (Wlk)<br>*Chilo suppressalis*<br>*Cnaphalocrosis medinalis* (G.)<br>*Orseolia oryzae* | *Sesamia inferens* Wlk (= *N. carpocapsae*) | Lab, Glass house, Field trials | Srinivas and Prasad, 1991 |
| *Tryporyza insertulus* (Wlk.) | *Steinernema carpocapsae* (= *N. carpocapsae*) | Field trials | Rao & Manjunath, 1966 |
| Arctidae<br>Lymantridae<br>Noctuidae<br>Pyralidae | *S. carpocapsae* (DD 136 strain) | Lab tests | Mathur *et al.*, 1971 |
| *Pieris brassicae*<br>*Aphitobis diaperinus*<br>*Oryzaephilus mercator* | *S. feltiae* (= *S. carpocapsae*) | Lab tests | Mathur *et al.*, 1994 |
| *Pseudaletia separata* (Wlk.)<br>*Tryporyza incertulus.* (Wlk.)<br>*Cirphis compta* (Mu.) | *Steinernema carpocapsae* ( = *N. carpocapsae*) | Field trials | Israel *et al.* 1969 |
| *Spodoptera litura* (F.)<br>*Heliothis armigera* (Hb.)<br>*Chilo partellus* (Swinhoe)<br>*Paralellia algira* | *S. feltiae* | Application method in lab tests | Gupta *et al.*, 1987 |
| *Amsacta albistriga* | *Heterorhabditis bacteriophora* | Field trials | Bhaskaran *et al.*, 1994 |
| *Leucinodes orbonalis* (Guen.)<br>*Athalia proxima* (Klug Aulocop)<br>*Aulocophora feveicollis* (Lucas), *S. litura* (F.),<br>*H. armigera* (Hb.), *Diacrisia obliqua* (Wlk.), *Dysdercus cingulatus* (F.) | *S.carpocapsae* (DD 136 strain) | Compatibility with agrochemicals and IPM1 | Singh & Bardhan, 1974 |
| *A. ipsilon* (Huf.)<br>*A. segetum*, (Huf.)<br>*A. biconica*, (Huf.)<br>*Xestia c-nigrum*<br>*Holotrichia* spp. | *S. feltiae* | Occurrence, mortality tests, lab | Singh, 1977, 1982 |

| | | | |
|---|---|---|---|
| *Papilio* spp. | | Lab, Field | Singh, 1993 |
| *Orthacris simulans* (B.)<br>*Draterius* sp.,<br>*Papilio aristolochiae* (Fb.)<br>*Ergolis merione* (Cr.) | *H. bacteriophora* | | Sivakumar *et al.*, 1989 |
| *Agrotis ipsilon* (Huf.) | *S. bicornutum*,<br>*S. carpocapsae* | Encapsulated bait, Lab | Hussaini *et al.*, 2001g |
| *Spodoptera litura* (F.)<br>*Helicoverpa armigera* (Hb.)<br>*Opisina arenosella* (Wlk.)<br>*Plutella xylostella* (L.)<br>*C. cephalonica* (Stainton) | *S. bicornutum*,<br>*S. carpocapsae, H. indica* | Lab tests | PDBC, 2000 |
| *A. ipsilon* (Huf.) | *Steinernema* spp.<br>*H. indica* | Soil application, lab | Hussaini *et al.*, 2000e |
| *A. ipsilon* (Huf.)<br>*C. cephalonica* (Stainton) | *H. bacteriophora*<br>*S. carpocapsae* | Lab | Zaki *et al.*, 2000 |
| *Leucinodes orbonalis* (Guen) | *S. carpocapsae*<br>*H. indica* | Spray, field trials | Hussaini *et al.*, 2002 |
| *Chilo partellus* (Swinhoe) | *Steinernema* spp.,<br>*H. indica* | Lab, field trials | PDBC, 1999 |
| *Tryporyza incertulus* (Wlk). | *Steinernema carpocapsae*<br>(= *N. carpocapsae*) | Microplots | Rao *et al.*, 1971 |
| *Spodoptera litura* (F.) | *S. feltiae*<br>(= *S. carpocapsae*) | Lab tests | Narayanan & Gopalakrish-anan, 1987 |
| *Anomala* sp. | *S. carpocapsae* (DD 136 strain) | Lab tests | Rajeswari Sundarababu *et al.*, 1984 |
| *C. sacchariphagus indicus* | *S. carpocapsae.*,<br>*S. glaseri, H. indica* | Lab tests | Karunakar *et al.*, 1992 |

## Factors Affecting Bioefficacy

Thermal adaptation of EPN-niche breadth for infection, establishment, and reproduction—has been found to vary. The thermal niche breadth for infection, establishment, and reproduction of 12 species and strains of EPN collected from diverse climatic regions was determined (Grewal *et al.*, 1994). *S. riobrave* infected *G. mellonella* larvae at the widest temperature range (10-39° C), and *S. feltiae* at the narrowest (8-30° C ). Thermal niche breadths for establishment within hosts were the widest for *S. glaseri* (10-37° C) and the narrowest for *S. feltiae* (8-30° C). Thermal niche breadth for reproduction was widest for *S. glaseri*, (12-32° C) and the narrowest for *S. carpocapsae* (20-30° C). *S. scapterisci* (20-32° C ), *S. riobrave* (20- 35° C ), and *Steinernema* sp. (20-32° C) were more adapted to warm temperature reproduction and *S. feltiae* to cooler temperatures (10-25° C ). Although heterorhabditids are endemic to warmer climates, the upper thermal limits and temperature optima for reproduction of *H. bacteriophora* and *H. megidis* were cooler than that of some of the steinernematids. Thermal niche breadths did not differ between conspecific populations isolated from different localities, but were different for different species isolated from the same locality. It was concluded that the EPNs have well-defined thermal niches which may be unaffected by their locality. Host plant background of the pest influences the virulence of EPNs. Efficacy varied substantially against insects with polyphagous habit. Presence of allelochemicals can negatively affect herbivore growth and survival. (House and Barlow 1961, Thurston & Fox, 1972). Effect of host plant on the infectivity and progeny production of EPNs in black cutworm, *A. ipsilon* (Plate 10.1) was investigated. Pathogenicity and progeny production of EPN isolates were adversely affected when cut worm larvae were rared on pumpkin. The low susceptibility of cutworm larvae fed on pumpkin may be due to the secondary metabolites present in the host plant (Hussaini *et al.*, 2001d). Similar results were reported on the susceptibility of southern corn rootworm, *Diabrotica undecimpunctata howardi, Sitona lineatus* to EPN (Barbercheck *et al.*,1995) . The significance of host plant effects on the nematodes under field conditions needs further probe.

**Survival**

Soil texture affects nematode dispersal and infectivity and dense roots adversely affect movement and infectivity (Georgis & Poinar, 1983, Choo *et al.*, 1989). The host finding ability of *H. bacteriophora* varied in humus, clay, loam and sand with and without roots (Choo & Kaya 1991). The per cent infection in *G. mellonella* larvae was invariably more in soils with roots and maximum in humus followed by sandy loam and clay, influenced by pore size and presence of roots. Root metabolites served as cues for nematode attraction. The activity and infectivity of indigenous EPN isolates in sand and soil column were compared in relation to soil type and depth. *H. indica* out competed *Steinernema* spp. irrespective of soil depth, types and time for mortality of *A. ipsilon.* Combined populations had an additive effect over single population (Hussaini *et al.*, 2000a). Presence of *S. glaseri* enhanced the performance of *S. carpocapsae* when applied in combination. *S. carpocapsae* and *S. glaseri* together had additive effect against *A. ipsilon* over single population (PDBC, 2000). Survival, movement and infectivity of the EPNs were affected by several factors in soil. Absolute mortality of *G. mellonella* was obtained with *H. indica* PDBCEN 13.22 in both soil types. The activity of *Steinernema* and *Heterorhabditis* populations was higher in sandy loam than in sand. The *H. indica* PDBCEN 13.22 population recorded 100% mortality irrespective of soil depth and the infectivity of *Steinernema* sp. was higher at 5 than at 10 cm depth (80-91%) except for *S. carpocapsae* PDBCEN 13.1 which recorded higher infectivity at both depths (Hussaini & Sankaranarayanan, 2001e).

### Effect of Soil Type and their Persistance in Soil

The survival of *H. bacteriophora* Oswego, *S. carpocapsae* NY001, and *S. glaseri* NCl varied in relation to the bulk density of a sandy loam soil. Survival of *H. bacteriophora* decreased linearly with time (4-70 days) and quadratically with increasing bulk density, whereas *S. glaseri* survival decreased linearly with time, but increased quadratically with increasing bulk density. Survival of *S. carpocapsae* decreased quadratically with time, but was unaffected by bulk density. *H. bacteriophora* and *S. glaseri* infected larvae of the greater wax moth, *G. mellonella* for up to 10 weeks after soil inoculation, and the incidence of infection showed no significant variation in relation to bulk density or time. In contrast, infection rate by *S. carpocapsae* increased with bulk density and decreased with time. The combined effects of soil texture and bulk density on movement of these nematode species generally decreased as the bulk density of 3 soil textures increased. However, the degree to which soils of high bulk density reduced movement differed among species and soil textures: *H. bacteriophora* was the least restricted; whereas, *S. carpocapsae* was the most restricted. All 3 species moved significantly more in sandy loam, than in loam or silty clay loam. *H. bacteriophora* moved at least 18 cm within 4 days of soil inoculation across all bulk densities tested, whereas *S. carpocapsae* moved only 9 cm at the 3 lower densities and <9 cm at the highest soil density. *S. glaseri* showed intermediate levels of movement (Pourtillo., 1999). Persistence of *S. carpocapsae* was significantly greater in crop residue plots than in plots without residue. In crop residue plots that received the higher rate of nematode application, larval mortality did not significantly decrease during the study period (3 to 5 days) and remained above 85%. In nematode-treated plots without crop residue, however, larval mortality fell from over 96% to below 11% and 35% in the first and second trials, respectively. The increased crop residue may have benefited nematode persistence through protection from desiccation or ultraviolet light. We conclude that increased ground cover in cropping systems (e.g., due to reduced tillage) may lead to increased insect pest suppression with entomopathogenic nematodes ( Shapiro *et al.*, 1999).

### Survival Under Storage

At PDBC the storage capacity of different EPN isolates and species was evaluated. *S. carpocapsae* PDBCEN 6.11, PDBCEN 6.61, *S. abbasi* PDBCEN 3.1, *S. bicornutum* PDBCEN 3.2 and *S. tami* PDBCEN 2.1, and *H. indica* PDBCEN 6.71 & PDBCEN 13.3 were stored at room temperature for a period of 8 weeks in distilled water. Storage capacity of *S. bicornutum* and *S. carpocapsae* was found better than *H. indica* (Hussaini *et al.*, 2000b). At 15° C, distilled water was found better media than glycerine and liquid paraffin for all isolates. Liquid paraffin was found most suitable at 8 and 24° C. Storage capacity of steinernematids was better than heterorhabditids in all cases.

### Effect of Temperature on EPNs

Thermal adaptation of EPN, niche breadths for establishment within hosts was the widest for *S. glaseri* (10-37° C) and the narrowest for *S. feltiae* (8-30° C). Although heterorhabditids are endemic to warmer climates, the upper thermal limits and temperature optima for reproduction of *H. bacteriophora* and *H. megidis* were cooler than that of some steinernematids. (Grewal *et al.*, 1994). Absolute mortality of *G. mellonella* and *A. ipsilon* was observed with *S. carpocapsae* PDBCEN 6.11, *S. abbasi* PDBCEN 3.1, *S. tami* PDBCEN 2.1, and *H. indica* PDBCEN 6.71, PDBCEN 13.3 at 32° C. At 25° C absolute mortality in *G.mellonella* was observed after 72 h in all isolates except *S. glaseri*; and in *A. ipsilon* the mortality ranged from 66.7% - 93.3% after 120 h, whereas at 15° C, mortality of both insects drastically reduced. Increase in temperature from 15 C to 32° C was favourable for infection and progeny production (Hussaini *et al.*, 2001f).

## APPLICATION TECHNOLOGY

### Soil

Many factors affect the ability to place quantities of nematodes on or in close proximity to the target host to produce optimal results at the lowest possible cost. To overcome the impact of abiotic and biotic factors on nematode efficacy and persistence, the inundative application of high concentration of a specific nematode species has been used as a primary control strategy. Application of nematodes is mostly targeted to the soil and against cryptic habitats. Inundative and inoculative approaches have been tried (Parkman & Frank, 1992). Timing soil applications of nematodes with the life cycle of target insect is a key factor. Cabanillas and Raulston (1996) found that the efficacy of *S. riobrave* was higher on *Helicoverpa zea* in corn when applied at 200,000 IJ/m$^2$ through furrow irrigation or post irrigation than when nematode were sprayed on to the soil before irrigation. Thus *S. riobrave* was effective in suppressing corn earworm under field conditions of high temperature with irrigation. In the field biotic factors like host susceptibility, pest population levels, host behaviour, different nematode species and host cues affect the nematode behaviour. Other than this susceptibility to environmental extremes reduces their field efficacy (Kaya & Gaugler, 1993). In soil application one or two pre and post application irrigation have been tried to provide enough moisture (Shetlar *et al.*, 1988). As with chemical insecticides, spraying nematodes directly onto the soil surface is the most commonly used application method. This broadcast method provides good coverage and is simple and quick.

Pesta-pelletized *S. carpocapsae* (All strain) were used in soil treatments in the greenhouse against larvae of Western corn rootworm (*Diabrotica virgifera*) and prepupae of Colorado potato beetle (*Leptinotarsa decemlineata*). The pesta-pellets delivered 100,000 living nematodes/g. IJs and their associated bacteria survived the pesta-pellet process, emerged from the pellets in large numbers in the soil, and reduced adult emergence of both pest insects by more than 90%. (Nickle *et al.*, 1994)

Field studies were conducted in Citrus orchards in Florida to determine the efficacy of *S. carpocapsae* (applied as the formulation BioVector at 5 million IJ/tree) and *H. bacteriophora* (applied as the formulation Otinem at 1, 2 and 5 million IJ/tree) for the control of *Diaprepes abbreviatus* and *Pachnaeus litus*. Adult weevil emergence traps were used to evaluate nematode efficacy by catching adult weevils as they emerged from the soil. All 3 rates of Otinem (a commercial formulation) resulted in significant reduction in the number of adults trapped compared to untreated trees, with the lowest rate giving the best level of control. Biovector also reduced adult emergence (by 45%) (Downing *et al.*, 1991).

A preliminary trial by Sitaramaiah, (2002) has indicated the effectiveness of *S. carpocapsae* in tobacco nursery against *S. litura*. EPN can be utilized in tobacco ecosystem on a component of BIPM

Survival of IJ in soil is influenced by pH and oxygen concentration. Populations of *S. carpocapsae* and *S. glaseri* gradually declined during 16 weeks of observation as the soil pH decreased from 8 to 4. Survival of both species dropped sharply after 1 week at pH 10. Survival was similar at pH 4, 6 and 8 during the first 4 weeks, but *S. carpocapsae* survived better than *S. glaseri* at pH 10 for 16 weeks. Both nematodes that had been stored at pH 4, 6 and 8 for 16 weeks, and at pH 10 for 1 or more weeks were not infective to *G. mellonella* larvae. *S. carpocapsae* survival was greater than that of *S. glaseri* at oxygen : nitrogen ratios of 1 : 99, 5 : 95, and 10 : 90 during the first 2 weeks, and declined sharply to less than 20% after 4 weeks.

### Foliar Application

Presently they are being applied through conventional equipment such as high volume sprayers, drip irrigation, food baits or through sound trap (Georgis *et al.*, 1989; Parkman & Frank, 1992). Antidesiccants have been used successfully to retard evaporation of the nematode suspension on foliage in foliar applications of EPN, and thus reduce desiccation of nematodes (Welch & Briand, 1961; Webster & Bronskill, 1968; Shapiro *et al.*, 1985; Glazer & Navon, 1990). Glycerine 10% has been the most effective adjuvant for increasing survival and activity of nematodes on foliage (Nash & Fox, 1969). However with the high cost of glycerine and the risk of phytotoxicity at high temperatures, search for more suitable adjuvant continued. Susceptibility of infective juveniles to UV radiation also hampers their efficacy on leaf surface. Effect of some optical brighteners (OBs) and PABA as UV protectant for entomopathogenic nematodes (EPNs) was tested in the lab. The results indicate the protective effect of PABA and optical brighteners on EPNs. There was no adverse effect of optical brighteners on the nematodes. Suitable UV protectants in the spray formulation will protect the nematodes aginst UV radiation (Hussaini *et al.*, 2001g). Excellent control of Japanese beetle, *P. japonica* and the chaffer, *Cyclocephala borealis* was obtained with 1.25-5.0 billion IJs/ha when plots were irrigated before application and again within 24 hrs after treatment (Downing, 1994). Bauer *et al.*, (1997) studied the effect of a number of adjuvant on EPNs persistence and efficacy against *Plutella xylostella.* In lab TX 7719, Rodspray oil, and Nufilm P provided the best antidesiccant activity and in greenhouse, TX 7719 + Blankophor BBH increased nematode persistence on watercress leaves and efficacy against *P. xylostella* significantly. Addition of phagostimulants enhanced the effectiveness of *S. carpocapsae* against the 4th instar larvae of *S. litura* feeding on sunflower head in lab and field tests (Sezhian *et al.*, 1996). EPNs are usually applied to foliage using standard application mechanics and recent studies have shown that this leads to a very inefficient loading of spray droplets and thus small numbers of nematodes reaching the target area. Considerable improvements have been achieved through optimisation of spray conditions using standard hydraulic equipment and spinning disc (SD) sprayers. The need to reduce the quantity of nematodes and carrier liquid is paramount if EPNs are to compete directly with chemicals. This can only be achieved if the quality of the spray produced is at an optimum for nematode carriage. Here, an assessment is given of droplets suitable for the application of EPNs (carriage droplets) and modifications to a SD apparatus that led to improvement in the spray quality for nematodes. There has been an improvement in the operation of the disc by the discovery and amelioration of a problem unique to this form of apparatus and control agent, namely the clumping of the nematodes during emission. (Piggott *et al.*, 1999).

Richter and Fuxa (1990) found that *S. feltiae* evaluated for control of *S. frugiperda* and *H. zea* in field maize; spraying the nematode resulted in up to 33-43% infection of *S. frugiperda* larvae in autumn and occasionally significant reductions in numbers of *S. frugiperda*. Nematode dosage had a significant effect on per cent infection, but neither spray volume nor the addition of a surfactant affected insect control by the nematode. However, spraying the nematode at a pressure of 0.70 kg/cm$^2$ resulted in a significantly higher percentage first grade marketable ears than in control plots, whereas spraying at 1.76 kg/cm$^2$ did not, regardless of the nematode dose.

## GENETIC MANIPULATION

Molecular biology, in EPNs research has received little emphasis till recently. Most effort has been directed towards the application of molecular methods for nematode identification (Curran 1990; 1993; Joyce *et al.* 1994; Hashmi *et al.*, 1996). Genetic variability within species provides insight into their phylogenetic relationships and population dynamics. Although conventional genetic improvement techniques have provided some nematode enhancement (Gaugler *et al.*, 1989a; 1989b; Zioni *et al.*, 1992; Rahimi *et al.*, 1993), the introduction of specific characters require biotechnological approaches. The close relationship of these nematodes with *Coenorhabditis elegans*, the model organism in molecular genetics, provides an extraordinary opportunity to exploit this new technology. Progress has been made in the genetic transformation, and the functionality of *C. elegans* genes into *H. bacteriophora* have been demonstrated (Hashmi *et al.*, 1995, Gaugler & Hashmi, 1996; Hashmi *et al.*, 1996; Hashmi & Gaugler, 1997). These approaches may fail if the available nematode population do not possess sufficient genetic diversity for the beneficial traits (Glazer *et al.*, 1991) and this may be overcome by surveying natural population for the desired traits (Gaugler, 1987). Selection is employed to find genetically superior nematode species. A heat tolerant strain of *H. bacteriophora* designated IS 5 was discovered in Negev desert, Israel in 1996 and was found superior to HP 88, (Glazer *et al.*, 1997).

## COMPATIBILITY

### Pesticides

EPNs may contribute more if integrated with other methods of control than their use solely as biocontrol agents. Studies on compatibility of EPNs with other methods of control will be appropriate for any IPM strategy against insect pests. Laboratory bioassays conducted to determine the effect of insecticide exposure to EPNs revealed that *Heterorhabditis* spp. were more compatible than *Steinernema* spp. Neem was the best followed by endosulfan and fenvalerate. Quinalphos was deleterious both in terms of nematode survival and progeny production. Among all the pesticides tested neem was found to be the best followed by endosulfan, fenvalerate and quinalphos in terms of compatibility. *Heterorhabditis* population was found to survive better than *Steinernema* populations in general. The data indicated that EPNs are compatible with most of the commonly used pesticides and so could be included as part of BIPM schedule. The bioefficiency of pesticide tolerant strains of *Steinernema* sp. (SSL2) PDBC EN 13.21, PDBC EN 14.1 and *H. indica* 13.22, PDBC EN 14.3, PDBC EN 6.71 were tested in the laboratory against *G. mellonella* and it was not impaired with any of the pesticide exposure. *S. bicornutum* PDBC EN 3.2, *S. tami* PDBCEN 2.1, *Steinernema* sp. PDBCEN 13.1 and *H. indica* PDBC EN 13.3 tolerated twice the recommended dose of endosulfan, malathion, fungicide mancozeb and nematicide, carbofuran. Progeny production of pesticide tolerant strains was also monitored. Progeny production was on par with control for fenvalerte and endosulfan tolerant populations and it was higher than control for Neem tolerant populations. Quinalphos tolerant populations lost their virulence and did not produce any progeny except for *Steinernema* sp. (SSL2) PDBC EN 13.21. *Steinernema* sp. PDBC EN 14.1 and *H. indica.*13.22, PDBC EN 14.3, PDBC EN 6.71 produced more than normal progeny with neem and less with other insecticides (Hussaini., 2001h). Vainio (1994) found that isofenphos plus thiram, permethrin, trifluralin, fluazifop butyl, iprodion applied every season alongwith one inundative release of *S. feltiae* did not have any adverse effect on nematodes and resulted in increased numbers of nematodes in a turnip field. *H. bacteriophora* and *S. feltiae* IJs showed no adverse reaction to insecticides diazinon 25 EC, dimethoate 37%, bromfenvinfos 50% and bromophos EC 40 at concentrations from 0.2 to 0.0001%. The mortality rate of *S. feltiae* varied from 12.3% (dimethoate) to 14.7% (bromophos) and for *H. bacteriophora* from 14.3% (diazinon) to 16.7% (dimethoate). Mortality rates were even lower at 10° C (Jarowska 1990).

Significant differences existed in the levels of tolerance between the heterorhabditids and steinernematids in lab tests. *H. bacteriophora* and *H. heliothidis* were less tolerant to some pesticides than *Steinernema* spp. which showed a higher survival, greater ability to recover and maintain infectivity after pesticide exposure. The normal development of all species was adversely affected after chemical treatment with most pesticides except for *S. glaseri.* This strain was the most tolerant to the toxic effects of pesticides—organophosphates and carbamates and appeared to be the most resistant and thus suitable for integration with pesticides (Sirjusingh *et al.*, 1991).

On sweet potato *S. carpocapsae* was very effective against *Diabrotica* sp. The EPNs provided significant protection from damage by *Conoderus* spp., *Diabrotica balteata, D. undecimpunctata howardi, Systena blanda, S. elongata* and *S. frontalis* in field. Fonofos did reduce damage caused by these insect pests, more so when applied in combination with the nematode. Use of resistant cultivars in combination with the nematode and/or fonofos treatment has been advocated (Schalk *et al.,* 1993). In another study the response of *S. carpocapsae* and *S. feltiae* to 75 commercial pesticides has been assessed. IJs of both species tolerated most of the tested chemicals. The response of the two species to the different pesticides appears to be very similar. Only dodine for the fungicides and alachlor and paraquat for the herbicides seriously affected the juveniles. By contrast a larger proportion of formulations in the insecticide-acaricide-nematicide group were harmful. Parathion, aldicarb, methomyl, flubenzimine, metam sodium and fenamiphos were the most toxic. Overall, results indicate the feasibility of an integrated use of these nematode species and chemical pesticides in crop protection (Rovesti & Deseo 1990).

Vainio and Hokkanen (1990) studied the toxicity of pesticides to *S. feltiae*, *Metarhizium anisopliae* and *Beauveria bassiana*. Bentazone, ioxynil, hexaconazole, cyromazine and buprofezin did not affect *S. feltiae*, but quizalofop-ethyl, tralkoxydim, sulfur and potassium soap were toxic. Pirimicarb, cypermethrin, diazinon, simazine and metalaxyl plus mancozeb did not affect either fungus, but glyphosate, dimethoate, MCPA, vinclozolin, trifluralin, thiram and propiconazole inhibited at least one species.

Mortality of last-instar larvae of *P. japonica* was highest when exposed to isazofos, bendiocarb and chlorpyriphos. Carbaryl and nematodes, *H. bacteriophora* and *S. glaseri*, were less effective treatments. Soil characteristics affecting insecticidal activity were organic matter (chlorpyrifos, bendiocarb and *S. glaseri*) and pH (carbaryl and isazofos). In turf conditions, *S. glaseri* was the most effective treatment, followed by chlorpyrifos, then bendiocarb. The influence of irrigation on improving insecticide efficacy increased with higher soil organic matter. Eradication of *P. japonica* cannot depend entirely on control tactics directed against the immature stages (Cowles & Villani 1994).

## NATURAL ENEMIES

### Pathogens

*S. carpocapsae* and NPV (SeM NPV) in combination produced additive effect for control of *S. exigua* in soybean than either of the organisms alone (Gothama *et al.*, 1995). Progeny of *S. feltiae* contained virus particles in the lumen. Kaya and Burlando (1989) found successful development and reproduction in 68% of moribund larvae of beet armyworm. Therefore, competitive interaction between nematode and NPV in a single host may not occur. *S. carpocapsae* may infect Sl*NPV* infected larva, which is then unsuitable for the virus development since the nematode development will kill the larva in 1-2 days and one nematode is capable of killing the larva.

The reproductive success of *S. carpocapsae* or *H. bacteriophora* in soilborne larvae of *S. exigua* previously exposed to *B. bassiana* was assessed. Treatments with *H. bacteriophora* and *B. bassiana* resulted in higher total mortality of *S. exigua* in soil than treatments with either nematode alone or fungus alone. For *S. carpocapsae* plus *B. bassiana*, insect mortality was not significantly different compared with *S. carpocapsae* alone. In treatments with nematode and fungus, percent mortality of *S. exigua* from *S. carpocapsae* and *H. bacteriophora* was reduced relative to treatment with nematodes alone. These results suggest that inundative release of EPNs where *B. bassiana* occurs may result in greater control of soilborne insect pests than application of nematodes alone (Barbercheck & Kaya, 1991). Gill and Raupp (1994) reported that bagworm, *Thyridopteryx ephemeraeformis* on *Thuja occidentalis* was controlled using 2 formulations of neem, carbaryl, acephate, cyfluthrin, formulations of *S. carpocapsae* and *S. feltiae*, and *Bacillus thuringiensis* var. *kurstaki*. Neem gave the least control (36-56% reduction). The nematodes, either alone or with oil or antidessicant, gave 91-100% control. The synthetic pyrethroid cyfluthrin gave 100% control; carbaryl and acephate also gave acceptable control (83 and 86%, respectively). The biological control agents, *Bacillus* and the nematodes, provided intermediate levels of control. Both species of *Steinernema* were effective.

*S. feltiae* and *H. heliothidis* and the fungus *B. bassiana* possess broad and overlapping host ranges. The impact of *B. bassiana* and nematodes on host period of lethal infection (PLI) and on nematode and fungus progeny production in a single host was investigated. In general, the PLI for larvae exposed to nematodes and *B. bassiana* simultaneously was shorter than that for larvae exposed to either pathogen alone, or exposed to both sequentially. Even though infection with both pathogens decreased host PLI, *B. bassiana* and nematodes rarely coproduced progeny in dually infected hosts. In treatments with nematodes alone, or *B. bassiana* and nematodes applied at the same time or 1 day later, *Xenorhabdus*, the bacterium mutualistically associated with the nematodes, was observed in host haemolymph 12 h after the application of the nematodes. *Xenorhabdus* or nematodes prevented or inhibited the growth of *B. bassiana* in the insect if nematodes were applied within 24 h after the application of *B. bassiana*. *B. bassiana* was detrimental to the development of *S. feltiae* and *H. heliothidis* when applied to the insect more than 48 h before nematodes. Temperature influenced the outcome of development in dually infected larvae. In early sequential treatments *B. bassiana* was more likely to develop to the exclusion of nematodes at 15° C, while nematodes were more likely to develop in these treatments at 22 and 30° C. It is concluded that, even though dual infections can result in a decreased PLI compared to singly infected hosts, antagonistic interactions between *B. bassiana* and EPNs in dually infected hosts can adversely affect pathogen development and progeny production (Barbercheck & Kaya, 1990).

## MASS PRODUCTION AND FORMULATIONS OF EPNs

### Mass Production

One of the factors that make entomopathogenic nematodes successful biocontrol agent is their amenability to mass production in artificial media. For *in vitro* cultivation, storage and transportation of nematodes, oxygen supply is extremely important. In a bioreactor the oxygen uptake rates of *Steinernema* spp. *S. glaseri* and *S. carpocapsae* strains were worked out. However, they were not significantly altered by the agitation speed, which ranged from 50-150 rpm. As nematode size and temperature were increased, the $O_2$ rates also increased. (Kim *et al.*, 1999). Major problems related to EPN mass production in liquid culture remains unsolved (Ehlers, 2001).

### Formulation

Successful control of insect pests through the application of IJs of *H. bacteriophora* and *H. indica* can only be achieved when the nematode material reaches the end user in good condition. Poor storage and post application survival are major obstacles to the exopanded use of EPNs as bioinsecticides. Significant effort has been made in

**TABLE 10.2:** BIOEFFICACY OF EPN AGAINST TARGETED PESTS WORLDWIDE

| *Crop* | *Pest* | *Nematode sp.* | *Dosage* | *% Mortality* | *Reference* |
|---|---|---|---|---|---|
| Potato | Colorado potato beetle, *Leptinotarsa decemlineata* | *S. feltiae* | | 14 | Welch 1958 |
| Cabbage | Cabbage worm | *S. feltiae* | | 73-77 | Welch & Briand, 1961 |
| Maize | Armyworm | *S. feltiae* | 4000 IJ ant | 39 | Landazabel *et al.*, 1973 |
| Chrysanth-emum | Serpentine leafminer | *S. carpo-capsae* | 50 × 10.8 /ha | 64 | Harris *et al* 1990 |
| Vegetables | Serpentine leafminer *L. trifolii* | *S. carpo-capsae* *H. bacterio-phors* | 50 × 10.8 /ha | 93 | Le Beck *et al.*, 1993 |
| Cabbage | Diamondback moth *Plutella xylostella* | *Steinernema* sp., *H. indica* | 100 IJ/larva | 73-100 | Mason & wright, 1997 |
| Cabbage | Diamondback moth *P. xylostella* | *S. carpocap-sae.*, *S. riobrave* *S. feltiae* | 100 IJ/larva | 67-100 | Ratnasinghe & Hague, 1997 |
| Apple | Codling moth *Cydia pamonella* | *S.feltiae* | | 60 | Dutky, 1959 |
| Orchard tress | Borer, *Zeuzera pyrina* | *S.feltiae* | | 85-90 | Deseo, 1982 |
| Maize | Earworm *Heliothis zea* | *S. feltiae* | 40 IJ/ml | 100 | Cabanillas & Raulston, 1994 |
| Paddy | Stem borer *Chilo suppressalis* | *S.carpocap-sae*, *H. bacterio-phora* | 2000 IJ/ml<br>800 IJ/ ml | 69<br>91-100 | Choo *et al.*, 1991 |
| Maize | Rootworm *Diabrotica* sp. | *S. feltiae* | | | Poinar *et al.*, 1983 |
| Raspberry | Blackvine weevil *Otiorhynchus sulcatus* | *S. feltiae* *S. glaseri* | 5 × 10.6 IJ/10 m row | 25 | Georgis & Poinar, 1984 |
| Raspberry | Blackvine weevil *Otiorhynchus sulcatus* | *Heterorhab-ditis* sp. | | 100 | Simons, 1981 |

| | | | | | |
|---|---|---|---|---|---|
| Potato | *L. decemlineata* | *S. feltiae* | | – | Toba *et al.*, 1983 |
| Sugarbeet | Conorhynchys | *S. carpocapsae,* | 2.5 bill IJ/ha | | |
| Litchi | Metarbelid borer *Arbela dea* | Steinernema *carpocapsae* | 8000-10000 /mlinjection/ spraying | 89-100% | Xu and Yang, 1992 |
| Banana | Root weevil *Cosmopolites sordidus* | *S. carpocapsae, S. glaseri, bibionis* | 400-40000 | 100 | Figueroa, 1990 |
| Sweet Potato | Weevil, *Cylas formicarius* | *S. carpocapsae, S. felitae H. bacteriophora* | | | Jannson *et al.*, 1991 |

developing formulation that enhances nematode storage stability. Improved understanbding of the nematode behaviour and physiology has helped in development of improved formulations. Although considerable effort has been expanded in the identification of adjuvants that enhance nematode deposition, retention and survival on foliage, improvements are insignificant to recommend foliar application. Nematode survival tested at temperatures ranging between 5-25° C indicated a maximum survival of *H. indica* at 15° C and the highest mortality at 5° C. *H. bacteriophora* survived best at 25° C. An increase of the salt concentration had positive effects on IJ survival in aqueous suspension. Low pH between 6 and 4 reduced the bacterial growth and prolonged survival of stored dauer juvenile: Of the organic acids, ascorbic, benzoic, citric and sorbic acid, only ascorbic acid had a possible effect on *H. indica* survival. Extracts of the dried spice plants cinnamon, cloves, rosemary and oregano were tested. Enhancement of *H. indica* survival was recorded for cinnamon and cloves. Survival and infectivity of nematodes stored in attapulgite and bentonite clays and sponge were recorded over several weeks at different storage temperatures. Infectivity was not influenced by the different formulation materials, When stored in sponge at 25° C nematodes survived less than one week and the formulation in clay could only prolong this period for another week. At 5° C the survival of *H. bacteriophora* in sponge was superior to that in clay. Whereas *H. indica* survived less well in sponge than in clay at 15° C. Storage in aerated water at 5° C for *H. bacteriophora* and at 15° C for *H. indica* resulted in the lowest mortality. For storage at controlled conditions (temperature, pH and osmolarity) aerated water is superior to all other methods tested and the addition of preservatives will increase survival (Strauch *et al.*, 2000).

## QUALITY OF ENTOMOPATHOGENIC NEMATODES

The quality of commercial nematode products is critical if EPNs are to realize their full potential as biological insecticides. The quality of nematodes produced *in vivo*, *in vitro*, solid or liquid diets, varies. Hence a suitable mass production method should be selected depending on species of nematode. Expanded use of EPNs in biological control cannot be expected unless field efficacy is increased (Gaugler *et al.*, 2000). Matching nematode species might bridge the efficacy gap between the nematodes and chemicals and strains against those insects they are best adapted. Attention should be given to protecting the genetic variability of new isolates, preventing the loss of alleles through laboratory adaptation. Prediction model may have to be developed so that nematodes will be used when and where they are likely to be effective. Distinction to be made between 'lab adapted' and 'field adapted' populations. The competition with chemical pesticides remains fierce due to non-competitive costs compared with chemical pesticides and concerns of inconsistent nematode quality. End users will not adopt biological control agents that do not provide efficacy. Advances in nematode application, timing and delivery, and particularly in selecting optimal target habitats and pests, have narrowed the efficacy gap between chemical and nematode agents. A paradigm for biologicals is required based on realities of biologicals. LOTEK low cost production technology is appropriate for local production. Since more than 70% of the expense producing biopesticides concerns formulation, storage, transport, waste disposal, middlemen, and capital LOTEK using *in vivo* methods eliminates these steps, providing improved costs and local production ensures only "fresh" biologicals are applied, providing improved performance. One primary outlet for this technology could be the existing cottage industry. The ultimate goal is a paradigm shift to grower driven IPMs by developing a simple, efficient mass production system for insecticidal nematodes.

**TABLE 10.3 :** MATRICES USED FOR FORMULATION OF NEMATODES

| Matrix | Matrix | Matrix |
|---|---|---|
| Vermiculite | talc | Charcoal |
| Calcium alginate | Bran | Peat |
| Filtered mud | Compost | Bentonite |
| Kaolin | Rice straw | Wood flour |
| Methyl cellulose | Corn cobb | Coal dust |
| Pulverized lignite | Mineral soil | Sugarcane bagasse |

**TABLE 10.4:** APPLICATION METHODS FOR ENTOMOPATHOGENIC NEMATODES

| *Application Method* | *Reference* |
|---|---|
| Thro overhead sprinkler system | Bari & Kaya, 1984 |
| Drip irrigation | |
| Injection into larval galleries | Abdel Kawy *et al.*, 1992; Deseo, 1982 |
| Cotton swab plug | Foschi & Deseo, 1983 |
| Oil can & backpack sprayer | Lindergren & Bernett, 1982 |
| Drenching or injecting into soil | |
| With liq. fertilizer | Poinar *et al.*, 1983 |
| Bait formulation | Capinera & Hibberd, 1987 |

## CONCLUSION

The characterization of traits related to the control potential of species (strains) of entomopathogenic nematodes is the key for a successful biological pest control with insecticidal nematodes. For commercialisation the adaptation of the nematodes to mass production methods and tolerance towards storage and transportation conditions are essential requisites and the quality of the commercial nematode products is critical to realize their full potential as biological insecticides. The stability and ease of use of current formulations and the excellent quality of nematodes grown in liquid culture are significant steps towards this goal. Aiming for high mortality of the target insects, the genotype of the nematode-bacteria complex and of the insect host are opposed to each other within the limits given by environmental conditions and the physiological state of the antagonist and its host. The possible potential of a one-time liberation of non-indigenous or genetically improved nematode species and strains is emphasized. In India the presence of several indigenous isolates is documented. There is still a need for documenting more isolates to expand the genetic base for further improvements.

## REFERENCES

Abdel Kawy A. G. M., El Bishry M. H. and El Kifl, T. A. H. 1992. Controlling the leopard moth borer, *Zeuzera pyrina* by three entomopathogenic nematode species in the field. *Bulletin of Faculty of Agricultural University, Cairo,* **43**: 769-780.

Akhurst, R. J. 1980. Morphological and functional dimorphism in *Xenorhabdus* spp. bacteria symbiotically associated with the insect pathogenic nematodes, *Neoaplectana and Heterorhabditis. Journal of General Microbiology,* **121**: 303-309.

Akhurst, R. J. 1982. Antibiotic activity of *Xenorhabdias* spp., bacteria symbiotically associated with insect pathogenic nematodes of the families Heterorhabditidae and Steinernematidae. *Journal of General Microbiology,* **128**: 3061-3065

Akhurst, R. J. 1983. Neoaplectanid species: Specificity of association with bacteria of genus *Xenorhabdus. Experimental Parasitology,* **55**: 258-263.

Akhrust, R. J. and Bedding, R. A. 1978. A simple cross-breeding technique to facilitate species determination in the genus *Neoaplectana. Nematologica,* **24**: 328-330.

Akhurst, R. J. and Boemare, B. R. 1990. Biology and taxonomy of *Xenorhabdus. In*: R. Gaugler and H. K. Kaya (eds.), *Entomopathogenic Nematodes in Biological Control.* CRC Press, Boca Raton, Fl., pp. 75-90.

Barbercheck, M. E. and Kaya, H. K. 1990. Interactions between *Beauveria bassiana* and the entomogenous nematodes, *Steinernema feltiae* and *Heterorhabditis heliothidis. Journal of Invertebrate Pathology,* **55**: 225-234.

Barbercheck, M. E. and Kaya, H. K. 1991. Competitive interactions between entomopathogenic nematodes and *Beauveria bassiana* (Deuteromycotina: Hyphomycetes) in soilborne larvae of *Spodoptera exigua* (Lepidoptera: Noctuidae). *Environmental Entomology,* **20**: 2, 707-712.

Barbercheck, M. E., Wang, J., Hirsh, I. S. 1995. Host plant effects on entomopathogenic nematodes. *Journal of Invertebrate Pathology,* **66**: 169-177.

Bari, M. A., and Kaya, H. K. 1984. Evaluation of the entomogenous nematode *Neoaplectana carpocapsae* and the bacterium *Bacillus thuriengiensis* for the suppression of the artichoke plume moth. *Journal of Economic Entomology,* **7**: 225-229.

Barrett, I. 1991. Anhydrobiotic nematodes. *Agricultural Zoology Reviews,* **4**: 161-76.

Bauer, M. E., Kaya, H. K., Gaugler, R. and Tabashnik, B. 1997. Effects of adjuvants on entomopathogenic nematode persistence and efficacy against *Plutella xylostella. Biocontrol Science and Technology,* **7**: 513-525.

Bhaskaran, R. K. M, Sivakumar, C. V and Venugopal, M. S. 1994. Biocontrol potential of entomopathogenic nematode in control of red hairy caterpillar, *Amsacta albistriga* of groundnut. *Indian Journal of Agricultural Science,* **64**: 655-657.

Boff, M. I. C., Wiegers, G. L. and Smits, P. H. 2000. Effect of storage time and temperature on infectivity, reproduction and development of *Heterorhabditis megidis* in *G. mellonella*. *Nematology,* **2**: 635-644

Burnell A. M., Nugent, M. J., O Leary, S. A., Stack, C. M. and Coudert, F. 1999. The use of mutagenesis for strain improvement in entomopathogenic nematodes. *In*: P. Abad, A. Burnell, C. Laumond, N. Boemare (eds.)., *Entomopathogenic Nematodes: Genetic and Molecular Biology of Entomopathogenic Nematodes.* Proceedings held at the Centre de Recherches Agronomiques de Provence-Alpes-Cote d'Azur Institut National de la Recherche Agronomique, Antibes, France, 1 to 5 April, 1997, pp. 113-123.

Cabanillas, H. E. and Raulston, J. R. 1994. Evaluation of the spatial pattern of *Steinernema riobravis* in corn plots. *Journal of Nematology,* **26**: 25-31.

Cabanillas, H. E. and Raulston, J. R. 1996. Evaluation of *Steinernema riobravis, S. carpocapsae* and irrigation timing for the control of corn earworm, *Helicoverpa zea. Journal of Nematology,* **28**: 75-82.

Capinera, J. L. and Hibberd, B. E. 1987. Bait formulations of chemical and microbial insecticides for suppression of crop feeding grasshoppers. *Journal of Agricultural Entomology,* **4**: 337-344.

Chen, G., Dumphy, G. B. and Webster, J. M. 1994. Antifungal activity of two *Xenorhabdus* spp. and *Photorhabdus luminescens,* bacteria associated with *Steinernema* sp. and *Heterorhabditis megidis. Journal of Biocontrol,* **4**: 157-162.

Choo, H .Y. and Kaya, H. K. 1991. Influence of soil texture and presence of roots on host finding by *Heterorhabditis bacteriophora. Journal of Invertebrate Pathology,* **58**: 279-280.

Choo, H. L., Kaya, H. K., Burlando, T. M., and Gaugler, R. 1989. Entomopathogenic nematodes: host-finding ability in the presence of plant roots. *Environmental Entomology,* **18**: 1136-1140.

Choo, H. Y., Kaya, H. K., Kim, J. B., and Park, Y. D. 1991. Evaluation of entomopathogenic nematodes, *Steinernema carpocapsae* (Steinernematidae) and *Heterorhabditis bacteriophora* (Heterorhabditidae) against rice stem borer *Chilo suppressalis* (Walker) (Lepidoptera: Pyralidae). *Korean Journal of Applied Entomology,* **30**: 50-53.

Cooper, A. F. and Van Gundy, S. D. 1971. *In*: B. M. Zuckerman, W. F. Mai, R. A. Rhode, (eds.), *Senescence, Quiescence, and Cryptobiosis, Plant parasitic Nematodes,* vol. 2. New York: Academic Press, 1971. pp. 297-318.

Cowles, R. S and Villani, M. G. 1994. Soil interactions with chemical insecticides and nematodes used for control of Japanese beetle (Coleoptera: Scarabaeidae) larvae. *Journal of Economic Entomology,* **87**: 1014-1021.

Curran, J. 1990 *In*: R. Gaugler & H. K. Kaya (eds.), *Entomopathogenic Nematodes in Biological Control.* CRC Press, Boca Raton, Florida, p. 63.

Curran, J. 1993. *In:* R. Gaugler and H. K. Kaya (eds.), *Entomopathogenic Nematodes in Biological Control.* C.R.C. Press, Boca Raton, Fl, pp. 365.

Curran, J. and Webster, J. M. 1989. Genotypic analysis of *Heterorhabditis* isolates from North Carolina. *Journal of Nematology,* **21**: 140-147.

Deseo, K. V. 1982. prove di lotta col nematoda entomopathogeno (Neoaplectana carpocapsae Weiser) contro i rodilegno *Cossus cossus* L. e *Zeuzera pyrina* L. (Lepidoptera : Cossidae). *Atti Gior. Fitopathol.,* **3**: 3-10.

Downing, A. S. 1994. Effect of irrigation and spray volume on efficacy of entomopathogenic nematodes against white grubs. *Journal of Economic Entomology,* **87**: 643-646.

Downing, A. S., Erickson, C. G., and Kraus, M. J., 1991. Field evaluation of entomopathogenic nematodes against citrus root weevils (Coleoptera: Curculionidae) in Florida citrus. *Florida Entomologist,* **74**: 584-586.

Ehlers, R. 2001. Mass production of Entomopathogenic nematodes for plant protection. *Applied Microbial Technology,* **56**: 623-633.

Elawad, S., Waseem Ahmad and Reid, A. 1997. *Steinernema abbasi* sp.n. from the Sultanate of Oman. *Fundamental and Applied Nematology,* **20**: 1-8.

Figueroa, I. W. 1990. Biocontrol of the banana root borer weevil, *Cosmopolites sordidus* (Germar), with steinernematid nematodes. *Journal of Agricultural University Puerto-Rico.*, **74**: 15-19.

Foschi, S and Deseo, K. V. 1983. Risulti di lotta con nematodi entomopathogeni su *Zeuzera pyrina* L (Lepidopt.; Cossidae) nel 1982. *La Difesa Delle Piante,* **6**: 153-156.

Ganguly, S. and Singh, L. K. 2000. *Steinernema thermophilum* sp.n (Rhabditida: Steinernematidae) from India. *International Journal of Nematology,* **10**: 183-191.

Gaugler, R. 1987. Entomogenous nematodes and their prospects for genetic improvement. *In*: K. Maramorosh (ed.), *Biotechnology in Invertebrate Pathology and Cell Culture.* Academic Press, San Diego, CA, pp. 457-484.

Gaugler, R. and Kaya, H. K. 1990. *Entomopathogenic Nematodes in Biological Control,* CRC Press. Boca Raton, Fl.

Gaugler, R and Hashmi, S. 1996. Genetic engineering of an insect parasite. *In*: J. K. Setlow (ed.), *Genetic Engineering,* **18**: 135-155. Plenum Press, New York.

Gaugler, R., Campbell, J. F. and McGuire, T. R. 1989. Selection for host finding in *Steinernema feltiae. Journal of Invertebrate Pathology,* **54**: 363-372.

Gaugler, R., Grewal, P., Kaya, H. K. and Fiola, D. B. 2000. Quality assessment of commercially produced Entomopathogenic nematodes. *Biological Control Theory and Application in Pest Management,* **17**: 100-109.

Georgis , R., Dunlop, D. B. and Grewal, P. S. 1994. Formulation of intomopathogenic nematodes. *In*: F. R. Hall and J. W. Barry (eds.), *Biorational Pest Control Agents: Formulation and Delivery.* Washington, DC: America.

Georgis, R., Wojcik, W. F. and Shetlar, D. J. 1989. Use of *Steinernema feltiae* in a bait for the control of blackcutworm *Agrotis ipsilon and tawny* mole cricket *Scaptericus visinus. Florida Entomologist,* **72**: 203-204.

Georgis, R. and Poinar, G. O., Jr. 1983. Effect of soil texture on the distribution and infectivity of *Neoaplectana carpocapsae* (Nematoda; Steinernematidae). *Journal of Nematology,* **15**: 2, 308-311.

Georgis, R., and Poinar, G. O Jr. 1984. Field control of the strawberry root weevil, *Nemocestes incomptus,* by neoaplectanid nematodes (Steinernematidae: Nematoda). *Journal of Invertebrate Pathology,* **43**: 130-131.

Gill, S. A. and Raupp, M. J. 1994. Using entomopathogenic nematodes and conventional and biorational pesticides for controlling bagworm. *Journal of Arboriculture,* **20**: 6, 318-322.

Glaser, R. W. 1932. A pathogenic nematode of the Japanese beetle. *Journal of Parasitology,* **18**: 119.

Glazer, I., and Navon, A. 1990. Activity and persistence of entomoparasitic nematodes tested against *Heliothis armigera. Journal of Economic Entomology,* **83**: 1795-1800.

Glazer, I., Gaugler, R. and Segal, D., 1991. Genetics of the nematode *Heterorhabditis bacteriophora* strain HP88: The diversity of beneficial traits. *Journal of Nematology,* **23**: 324-333.

Glazer, I., Salame, L. and Segal, D. 1997. Genetic enhancement of nematode resistance in Entomopathogenic nematodes. *Biocontrol Science and Technology,* **7**: 199-512.

Grewal, P. S., Selvan, S. and Gaugler, R. 1994. Thermal adaptation of entomopathogenic nematodes: niche breadth for infection, establishment, and reproduction. *Journal of Thermal Biology,* **19**: 245-253.

Grewal, P. S. and Georgis, R. 1998. Entomopathogenic nematodes. *In*: F. R. Hall, J. J. Menn (eds.), *Methods in Biotechnology Biopesticides*: Use and delivery, Totowa, NJ: Humana Press, pp. 271-99.

Gupta, M., Desai, P. and Pawar, A. D. 1987. The feasibility of using DD-136 strain of *Steinernema carpocapsae* for the control of insect pests. *Plant Protection Bulletin,* **39**: 16-19.

Hara, A. H. and Kaya, H. K. 1982. Effects of selected insecticides and nematicides on the *in vitro* development of the entomogenous nematode *Neoaplectana carpocapsae. Journal of Nematology,* **14**: 486-491.

Hara, A. H. and Kaya, H. K. 1983. Toxicity of selected organophosphate and carbamate pesticides to infective juveniles of the entomogenous nematode *Neoaplectana carpocapsae* (Rhabditida: Steinernematidae). *Environmental Entomology,* **12**: 496-501

Harris, M. A., Begley, J. W. and Warkentin, D. L. 1990. *Liriomyza trifolii suppression with foliar applications of Steinernema carpocapsae and abamectin. Journal of Economic Entomology,* **83**: 2380-2384.

Hashmi, G. and Gaugler, R. 1998. Genetic diversity in insect-parasitic nematodes (Rhabditida: Heterorhabditidae). *Journal of Invertebrate Pathology,* **72**: 185-189.

Hashmi, G., Glazer, I., and Gaugler, R. 1996. Molecular comparisons of entomopathogenic nematodes using randomly amplified polymorphic DNA (RAPD) markers. *Fundamenatal and Applied Nematology,* **19**: 399-406.

Hashmi, S., Ghazala Hashmi and Gaugler, R. 1995. Genetic transformation of an entomopathogenic nematode by microinjection. *Journal of Invertebrate Patholology,* **66**: 293-296.

Hashmi, G., Hashmi, S., Selvan, S., Grewal, P. S., and Gaugler, R. 1997. Polymorphism in heat shock protein gene (hsp70) in entomopathogenic nematodes (Rhabditida). *Journal of Thermal Biology,* **22**: 143-149.

House, H. L. and Barlow, J. S. 1961. Effects of different diets of a host, *Agria affinis* (Fall.) (Diptera) on the development of a parasitoid. *Canadian Entomologist,* **93**: 1041-1044.

Hussaini, S. S., Singh, S. P., Parthasarathy, R. and Shakeela, V. 2000a. Infectivity of native populations of *Steinernema* spp. and *Heterorhabditis indica* in sand and sandy loam soil columns against *Agrotis ipsilon* (Hüfnagel) *Annals of Plant Protection Sciences,* **8**: 200-205.

Hussaini, S. S., Singh, S. P., Parthasarathy, R. and Shakeela, V. 2000b. Storage effects on activity of native *Steinernema* and *Heterorhabditis* spp. *Indian Journal of Nematology,* **30**: 225-264.

Hussaini, S. S., Ansari, M. A., Ahmad, W. and Subbotin, S. A. 2001a. Identification of some Indian populations of *Steinernema* species by RFLP analysis of the ITS region of rDNA. *International Journal of Nematology,* **11**: 73-76.

Hussaini, S. S., Singh, S. P. and Shakeela, V. 2001b. Compatibility of entomopathogenic nematodes (Steinernematidae, Heterorhabditidae: Rhabditida) with selected pesticides and their influence on some biological traits. *Entomon,* **26**: 37-44.

Hussaini, S. S., Kavita J. Satya and M. Abid Hussain, 2001c. Effect of chemically stimulated entomopathogenic nematods for control of insect pests, Proceedings of the Second National Symposium on IPM in horticultural crops: New Molecules, Biopesticides and Environment, Oct 17-19, 2001 Institution of Agricultural Technologists, Bangalore, pp. 204-206.

Hussaini, S. S., Singh, S. P. and Shakeela, V. 2001d. Effect of different host plants on infectivity and progeny production of entomopathogenic nematodes in *Agrotis ipsilon*, p. 223. *In*: *Proceedings of the Second National Symposium on Integrated Pest Management in Horticultural Crops—New Molecules, Biopesticides and Environment,* October 17-19, 2001, held at Institution of Agricultural technologists, Bangalore.

Hussaini, S. S. and C. Sanakaranarayanan 2001e. Effect of soil type and depth pathogenicity of indeginous isolates of entomopathogenic nematodes. National Seminar on Emerging trends in pests and diseases and their management, Oct 11-13. 2001, p. 57-58. *Journal of Biological Control* (In Press).

Hussaini, S. S., Singh S. P. and Shakeela, V. 2001f. Influence of temperature on infectivity of entomopathogenic nematodes to black cutworm, *Agrotis ipsilon* (Hufnagel) larvae. National Congress on Centenary of Nematology in India—Appraisal and Future plans, Indian Agricultural Research Institute, New Delhi, 5-7, Dec. 2001 p. 120.

Hussaini, S. S., Kavitha, J. Satya and Abid Hussain, M. 2001g. Survival and pathogenicity of indigenous entomopathogenic nematodes in different UV protectants. National Congress on Centenary of Nematology in India—Appraisal and Future plans, Indian Agricultural Research Institute, New Delhi, 5-7, Dec. 2001, p. 120.

Hussaini, S. S., Kavita J. Satya and M. Abid Hussain. 2001h. Tolerance of Entomopathogenic nematode isolates to pesticides and their effect on multiplication. *Current Nematology,* **12**: 29-34.

Hussaini, S. S., Singh, S. P., Nagesh, M. 2002. *In vitro* and field evaluation of some indigenous isolates of *Steinernema* and *Heterorhabditis indica* against shoot and fruit borer, *Leucinodes orbonalis. Indian Journal of Nematology,* **32**:

Ishibashi, N and Takii, S. 1993. Effect of insecticides on movement, nictation, and infectivity of *Steinernema carpocapsae. Journal of Nematology,* **25**: 204-213.

Israel, P., Rao, Y. R. V. J., Prakash Rao, P. S, and Verma, A. 1969. Control of paddy cutworms by DD-136, a parasitic nematode. *Current Science,* **16**: 390-391.

Jannson, R. K., Gaugler, R., Mannion, C. M., Lecrone, S. H., Pavis, C (ed.)., and Kermarrec, A . 1991. Recent advances in biological control of *Cylas formicarius* with entomopathogenic nematodes. Rencontres caraibes en lutte biologique. 1991, 167-182; *In*: Proceedings of the Caribbean meetings on biological control, Guadeloupe, 5-7, November, 1990.

Jarowska, M. 1990. Effect of some insecticides on entomophilic nematodes. *Zeszyty-Problemowe-Postepow-Nauk-Rolniczych.* No. 391, 73-79.

Joyce, S. A., Burnell, A. M., and Powers, T. O. 1994. Characterization of *Heterorhabditis* isolates by PCR amplification of segments of mtDNA and rDNA genes. *Journal of Nematology,* **26**: 260-270.

Karunakar, G., David, H., and Eswaramoorthy, S. 1992. Influence of dosage of *Steinernema carpocapsae, S. glaseri* and *Heterorhabditis indica* on mortality of the host and and multiplication of infective juveniles in sugarcane internode borer, *Chilo saccariphagus indicus. Journal of Biological Control,* **6**: 26-28.

Kaya, H. K. and Gaugler, R. 1993. Entomopathogenic nematodes. *Annual Review of Entomology,* **38**: 181-206.

Kim, D. W., Park, S. H., Kim, D. W. and Park, S. H. 1999. Characteristics of the oxygen uptake rate of entomopathogenic nematodes *Steinernema* spp. *Korean Journal of Applied Entomology,* **38**: 123-128.

Klein, M. G., and Georgis, R. 1992. Persistence of control of Japanese beetle (Coleoptera: Scarabaeidae) larvae with steinernematid and heterorhabditid nematodes. *Journal of Economic Entomology,* **85**: 727-730.

Landazabal, J., Fernandez, F. and Figuiroa, P. A. 1973. Control biologico de *Spodoptera frugiperda* conel nematodo *Neoaplectana carpocapsae* en maiz. *Acta Agron. Palmira,* **23**: 41-70.

Le Beck, L. M., Gaugler, R. Kaya, H. K., Hara, A. H. and Johnson, M. W. 1993. Host stage susceptibility of the leaf miner to the entomopathogenic nematode, *Steinernema carpocapsae. Journal of Invertebrate Pathology,* **62**: 58-63.

Lindegren, J. E. and Barnett, W. W. 1982. Applying parasitic nematodes to control carpenter worms Californian Agriculture. **36**: 7-8.

Mason, J. M., and Wright, D. J., 1997. Potential for the control of *Plutella xylostella* larvae with entomopathogenic nematodes. *Journal of Invertebrate Pathology,* **70**: 234-242.

Mathur, N., Khera, S. and Sharma, N. 1994. A study of infectivity and propagation of *Steinernema feltiae* on some insect pests. *Journal of Parasitology and Applied Animal Biology,* **3**: 47-53.

Mathur, S. B. Jr., Srivastava, P. and Sriviastava, K. L. 1971. Pathogenicity of DD-136 an insect parasitic nematode to five pests of agricultural and horticultural importance. *Proceedings of Nattioan Academy of Sciences* (India), **41**: 325-327.

Menti, H., Wright, D. J and Perry, R. N 2000. Infectivity of populations of the entomopathogenic nematodes *Steinernema feltiae* and *Heterorhabditis megidis* in relation to temperature, age and lipid content. *Nematology,* **2**: 515-521.

Mracek, Z., Weiser, J., and Gerdin, S. 1981. Head and cuticular structures of some species in the family Steinernematidae (Nematoda). *Nematologica,.* **27**: 443-448.

Nagesh, M., Hussaini, S. S. and Singh, S. P 2001. Isolation and characterization of symbiotic bacteria from *Heterorhabditis indica* and *Steinernema carpocapsae. Pest Management in Horticultural Ecosystems,* **7**: 44-49.

Narayanan, K. and Gopalakrishnan, C. 1987. Effect of entomogenous nematode *Steinernema feltiae* (Rhabditida: Steinernematidae) to the pre-pupa, pupa and adult of *Spodoptera litura* (Noctuidae; Lepidoptera). *Indian Journal of Nematology,* **17**: 273-276.

Nash, R. F. and Fox, R. C. 1969. Field control of the pinetip moth by the nematode DD-136. *Journal of Economic Entomology,* **62**: 660-663.

Nickle, W. R., Connick, W. J Jr. and Cantelo, W. W. 1994. Effects of pesta-pelletized *Steinernema carpocapsae* (All) on Western corn rootworms and Colorado potato beetles. *Journal of Nematology,* **26**: 249-250.

Parkman, J. P. and Frank, J. H. 1992. Use of sound trap to inoculate *Steinernema scapterisci* into pest mole cricket population. *Florida Entomologist,* **76**: 75-82.

PDBC, 2000. Survey, identification and utilisation of entomopathogenic nematodes against some lepidopterous and coleopterous insect pests. *Annual Report,* Project Directorate of Biological Control, Bangalore.

Piggott, S., Mason, J., Matthews, G. and Wright, D. J. 1999. Redesigning spray application technology for entomopathogenic nematodes. *Mededelingen Faculteit Landbouwkundige en Toegepaste Biologische-Wetenschappen, Universiteit Gent.* **64**: 3b, 813-820.

Poinar G. O. Jr., Evans, J. S. and Schuster 1983. Field test of the entomopathogenic nematode, *Neoaplectana carpocapsae* for control of corn root worm, *Diabrotica. Protection Ecology,* **5**: 337-342.

Poinar, G. O. Jr. 1990. Taxonomy and biology of Steinernematidae and Heterorhabditidae. *In: Entomopathogenic nematodes in biological control?*

Poinar, G. O. Jr., Karunakar, G. K. and David, H. 1992. *Heterorhabditis indicus* n. sp. (Rhabditida: nematoda) from India: Separation of *Heterorhabditis* spp. by infective juveniles. *Fundamental and Applied Nematology,* **15**: 467-472.

Poinar, G. O., Jr. and Thomas, G. M. 1966. Significance of Achromobacter nematophilus (Achromobacteracae: Eubacteriales) in the development of the nematode, DD-136 (Neoaplectana sp.: Steinernematidae). *Parasitology,* **56**: 386.

Poinar, G. O. Jr. 1967. Description and taxonomic position of the DD-136 nematode (Steinernematidae, Rhabditoidea) and its relationship to Neoaplectana carpocapsae Weiser. *Proceedings of Helminthological Society of Washington,* **34**: 199-209.

Portillo Aguilar, C., Villani, M. G., Tauber, M. J., Tauber, C. A. and Nyrop, J. P. 1999. Entomopathogenic nematode (Rhabditida: Heterorhabditidae and Steinernematidae) response to soil texture and bulk density. *Environmental Entomology,* **28**: 1021-1035.

Rahimi, F. R., Mc Guire, T. R. and Gaugler, R. 1993. Morphological mutant in the entomopathogenic nematode, *Heterorhabditis bacteriophora. Journal of Heredity,* **84**: 475-478.

Rajeswari Sundarababu, Menon, P. P. V. and Vadivelu, S. 1984. Preliminary test with DD-136 for the control of potato chaffer grub, *Anomala* sp. *Indian Journal of Nematology,* **14**: 187-188.

Rao, Y. R. V. J., Prakash Rao, P. S., Verma, A. and Israel, P. 1971. Tests with an insect parasitic nematode DD-136 against the rice stem borer, *Tryporyza incertulus. Indian Journal of Entomology,* **33**: 215-217.

Rao, V. P. and Manjunath, T. M. 1966. DD -136 nematode that can kill many insect pests.*Indian Fmg.,* **16**: 43-44.

Ratanasinghe, G. and Hague, N. G. M. 1997. Efficacy of entomopathogenic nematodes against the diamondback moth, *Plutella xylostella. Pakistan Journal of Nematology,* **15**: 45-53.

Reid, A. P. 1994. Molecular taxonomy of Steinernema. *In*: A. M. Burnell, R. U. Ehlers and J. P. Masson (eds.), *Genetics of Entomopathogenic Nematode-Bacterium Complexes.* COST 812. ECSC-EC, EACE, Brussels, pp. 49-58.

Richter, A. R. and Fuxa, J. R. 1990. Effect of Steinernema feltiae on *Spodoptera frugiperda* and *Heliothis zea* (Lepidoptera: Noctuidae) in corn. *Journal of Economic Entomology,* **83**: 1286-1291

Rothstein, M. 1974. Practical methods for the axenic culture of the free-living nematodes *Turbatrix aceti* and *Caenorhabditis briggsae. Comparative Biochemistry and Physioliology.* **49**: 669.

Rovesti, L and Deseo, K. V. 1990. Compatibility of chemical pesticides with the entomopathogenic nematode, Steinernema carpocapsae Weiser and S. feltiae Filipjev (Nematoda: Steinernematidae). *Nematologica,* **36**: 237-245.

Schalk, J. M., Bohac, J. R., Dukes, P. D. and Martin, W. R. 1993. Potential of non-chemical control strategies for reduction of soil insect damage in sweetpotato. *Journal of. American Society of. Horticultural Science,* **118**: 605-608.

Segal, D., Glazer, I., 1999. Genetic approaches for enhancing beneficial traits in entomopathogenic nematodes. *Japanese Journal of Nematology,* **28**: 101-107.

Sezhian, N., Sivakumar, C. V. and Venugopal, M. S. 1996. Alteration of effectiveness of *Steinernema carpocapsae* against *Spodoptera litura* larvae on sunflower by addition of an insect phagostimulant. *Indian Journal of Nematology,* **26**: 77-81.

**Plate 10.1**

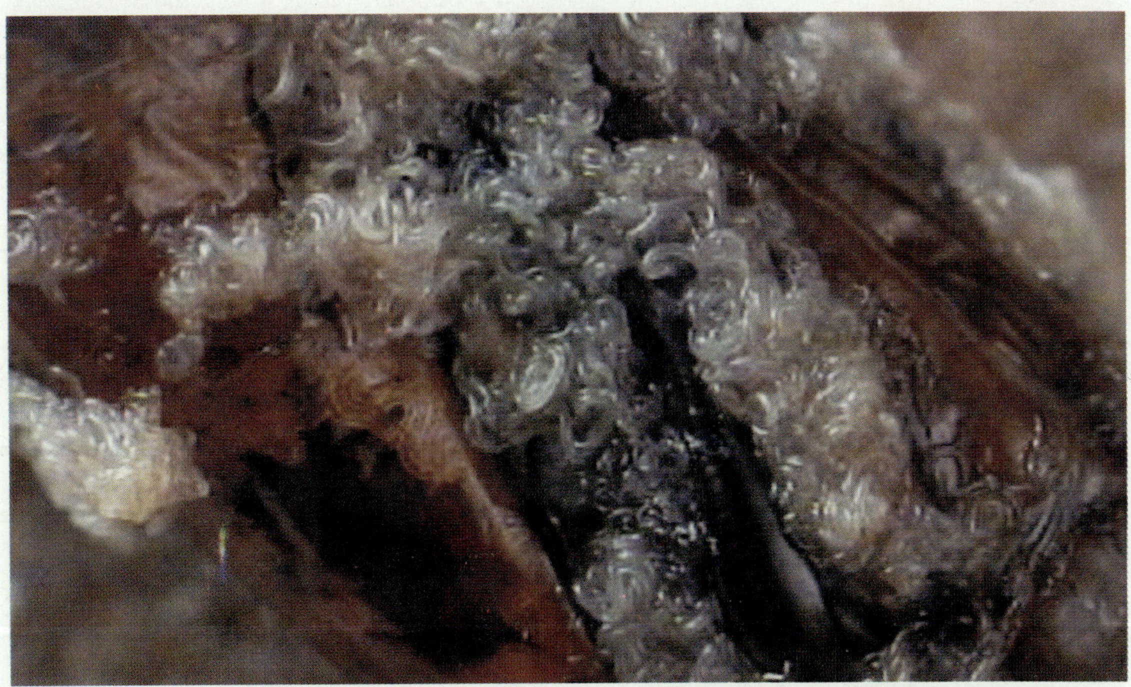

*Agrotis ipsiolon* pupa infected with *Steinernema carpocapsae*

*Helicoverpa armigera* infected with *Steinernema tami*

Shapiro, M., Mc Lane, W. and Bell, R. 1985. Laboratory evaluation of selected chemicals as antidesiccants for the protection of the entomogenous nematode, *Steinernema feltiae* against *Lymantria* dispar. *Journal of Economic Entomology,* **78**: 1437-1441.

Shapiro, D. I., Obrycki, J. J., Lewis, L. C and Jackson, J. J. 1999. Effects of crop residue on the persistence of *Steinernema carpocapsae. Journal of Nematology,* **31**: 517-519.

Shetlar, D. J., Suleman, P. E. and Georgis, R. 1988. Irrigation and use of entomogenous *Neoaplectana* spp. *Heterorhabditis heliothidis* for the control of Japanese beetle grubs in turf grass. *Journal of Economic Entomology,* **81**: 1318-1322.

Simmons, W. R., and Poinar Jr. G. O. 1973. The ability of *Steinernema carpocapsae* (Steinernematidae: Nematoda) to survive extended period of desiccation. *Journal of Invertebrate Pathology,* **22**: 228-30.

Simmons, W. R., 1981. Biological control of *Otiorhynchus sulcatus* with heterorhabditid nematodes in the greenhouse. *Netherlands Journal of Plant Pathology,* **87**: 149-203.

Singh, S. P. 1977. Isolation of an entomophilic nematode from potato cutworms. *Current Science,* **46**: 454-455.

Singh, S. P. 1982. Some observations on potato cutworms and their natural enemies. *Entomon,* **7**: 197-203.

Singh, S. P. 1993. Effectiveness of an indigenous nematode against citrus butterfly. *Journal of Insect Science,* **6**: 107-108.

Singh, J. and Bardhan, V. 1974. Effectiveness of DD-136, an entomophilic nematode against insect pests of agricultural importance. *Current Science,* **43**: 662.

Sirjusingh, C., Mauleon, H., Kermarrec, A., Pavis, C (ed.). and Kermarrec, A. 1991. Compatibility and synergism between entomopathogenic nematodes and pesticides for control of *Cosmopolites sordidus* Germar. Rencontres caraibes en lutte biologique. 1991, 183-192; *In*: Proceedings of the Caribbean Meetings on Biological Control, Guadeloupe, 5-7 November 1990.

Sitaramaiah, S. S., Gunneswara Rao, Hussaini, S. S., Venkateswarlu, P. and Nageswara Rao, S. 2002. Use of entomopathogenic nematode *Steinernema carpocapsae* against *Spodoptera litura* Fab. in tobacco nursery. *Journal of Biocontrol* (In Press).

Sivakumar, C. V., Jayaraj, S. and Subramanian, S. 1989. Observations on Indian population of the entomopathogenic nematode *Heterorhabditis bacteriophora. Journal of Biolical Control,* **2**: 112-113.

Srinivas, P. R. and Prasad, J. S. 1991. Record of DD-136 nematode infection on rice leaf folder, *Cnaphalocrosis medinalis. Indian Journal of Agricultural Sciences,* **61**: 348-349.

Strauch, O. U., Niemann, I., Neumann, A., Schmidt, A. J., Peters, A. and Ehlers, R. U. 2000. Storage and formulation of the entomopathogenic nematodes *Heterorhabditis indica* and *H. bacteriophora. Biocontrol,* **45**: 483-500.

Tallosi, B. A., Peters and Ehlers, R. U. 1995. *Steinernema bicornutum* sp.n. (Rhabditida: Steinernematidae) from Vojvodina, Yugoslavia. *Russian Journal of Nematology,* **3**: 71-80.

Thurston, R. and Fox, P. M. 1972. Inhibition by of emergence of *Apanteles congregatus* from its host, the tobacco hornworm. *Annals of Entomological Society of America,* **65**: 547-550.

Vainio 1994. Effect of pesticides on long term survival of *Steinernema feltiae* in the field. Bull.OILB SROP, **17**: 70-76.

Toba, H. H., Lindgren, J. E., Turner, J. E., and Vail, P. V. 1983. Susceptibility of the Colorado potato beetle and the sugarbeet wireworm to *Steinernema feltiae* and *S. glaseri. Journal of Nematology,* **15**: 597-601.

Vainio, A. 1994. Effect of pesticides on long-term survival of *Steinernema feltiae* in the field. Bull. OILB-SROP. **17**: 70-76.

Vainio, A. and Hokkanen, H. 1990. Side-effects of pesticides on the entomophagous nematode *Steinernema feltiae,* and the entomopathogenic fungi *Metarhizium anisopliae* and *Beauveria bassiana* in the laboratory. Proceedings and abstracts, vth International Colloquium on Invertebrate Pathology and Microbial Control, Adelaide, Australia, 20-24 August 1990, p. 334.

Waturu, C. N., Hunt, D. J. and Reid, A. P. 1997. *Steinernema karii* sp.n (Nematode: Steinernematidae), a new entomopathogenic nematode from Kenya. *International Journal of Nematology,* **7**: 68-75.

Webster, J. M. and Bronskill, J. F. 1968. Use of Gelgard M and an evaporetardant to facilitate control of larch sawfly by nematode-bacterium complex. *Journal of Economic Entomology,* **61**: 1370-1373.

Webster, J. M., Chen, G., Hu, K. Li. J. and Ng. K. 1996. Entomopathogenic Nematodes—The Nematodes for all Reasons (abs). Third International Nematol.Cong. Guadelope, Spain, p.113.

Welch, H. E. 1958. Tests of a nematode and its asssociated bacterium for the control of Colarado potato beetle, *Leptinotarsa decemlineata. Annual Report Entomological Society.,Ontario,* **61**: 1370-1373.

Welch, H. E. and Briand, L. J. 1961. Tests of the nematode DD-136 and an associated bacterium for the control of Colorado potato beetle. *Canadian Entomologist,* **43**: 75.

Womersely C. 1990. Dehydration survival and anhydrobiotic potential. *In*: R. GaUgler, H. K. Kaya (eds.), Entomopathogenic nematodes in biological control. Boca Raton, FL: CRC Press, pp. 117-37.

Xu, J. L., and Yang, P. 1992. The application of the codling moth nematode against the litchi stemborer. *Acta Phytophylacica Sinica,* **19**: 217-222.

Zaki, F. A., Mantoo, M. A. and Shaheena, G. 2000. *In vivo* culturing of entomopathogenic nematode *Heterorhabditis bacteriophora* and *Steinernema carpocapsae* on silk worm *Bombyx mori* and their effect on some lepidopterous insects. *Indian Journal of Nematology,* **30**: 1-4.

Zioni, S., Glazer, I. and Segal, D., 1992. Phenotypic and genetic analysis of a mutant of *Heterorhabditis bacteriophora* strain HP88. *Journal of Nematology,* **24**: 359-364.

# Computer-Based Decision Support Systems for IPM

**A. Dhandapani, Niranjan Singh and O. P. Sharma**

## INTRODUCTION

Integrated Pest Management (IPM), a knowledge-based approach to crop protection, utilizes regular monitoring to determine if and when treatments are needed; employs physical, mechanical, cultural, biological, and educational tactics to keep pest numbers low enough to prevent unacceptable damage or annoyance. IPM emphasizes appropriate decision-making and depends heavily on accurate and timely information for field implementation by practitioners. Knowledge and information are key to make correct pest management decisions. Poor access to IPM knowledge and information has been major constraint in the effective development and implementation of IPM, particularly in India. Management of pests under IPM approach is based on knowledge of the crop, pests, diseases and beneficial organisms that prey on pests. Besides information on pests, a whole lot of information on host plant resistance, agronomic practices, crop rotation and other cultural and agronomic operations are required. Access to such information is greatly facilitated by the use of Information Technology tools in decision-making process for pest management. The IT tools will provide not only a viable opportunity to cover a vast area but also cost effective. The adoption of IPM in the forthcoming years will be increasingly dependent on the efficient utilization of Information technology based decision making tools.

## STEPS OF IPM INVOLVING DECISION MAKING

### Monitoring

The purpose of monitoring is to detect the presence, concentration, and type of pests. Monitoring involves a regular and mechanical procedure to quantify field information needed to make sound pest management decisions. Field observations are used to make immediate IPM decisions as well as record part of the field's history for making rational decisions in the future.

### Identification of Pest

Proper identification of pests is an important aspect of monitoring. Natural enemies that help in keeping pest in check are also present in fields, so it is also very important to identify these friends. Knowledge on specific insects, weeds, disease or nematodes in a field is important for IPM decision-making.

*National Centre for Integrated Pest Management, LBS Building, IARI Campus, New Delhi-110 012.*

### Pest Situation Assessment

In the third step, analyzing information obtained from monitoring and pest identification and determination of the need for pest control. One question is whether or not the damage potential is more costly than the control cost. The economic threshold plays an important role in IPM decisions and is defined as, and when there are enough pests present to warrant treating the crop.

### Pest Management

Finally, if a pest indeed reaches threshold, proper management depending on the assessment has to be applied. This may be physical removal of infested parts/plants, application of bioagents and finally treatment with chemical pesticides.

But there are many information related constraints in decision-making such as Information on various aspects of IPM not readily available at one place, inability to obtain and modify the available information to suit the needs of practitioners and users or lack of proper exchange of information between different research/extension groups etc.

Use of information technology has revolutionized our ability to handle vast knowledge and interpret to solve problems. Computers have made doing routine things faster, more accurate and leave us to concentrate on the analysis of the information and take proper decisions. In the area of plant protection, computers are useful in

- To store, retrieve and analyze data such as survey, surveillance and maintaining of disease/pest incidences.
- Modeling and simulation of pest incidence/forewarning.
- Developing Decision Support Systems, expert systems to pest problems leading to decision-making.

## DECISION SUPPORT SYSTEM (DSS) FOR IPM

Computer-based Decision Support System (DSS) integrates a user-friendly front end to often-complex models, knowledge bases, and database technologies. DSSs are important component of information technology in IPM. Web-based models and DSS are becoming popular due to reduction in software management and distribution costs. Quite often, it was noted that the technology spread or adoption has been severely affected due to complexness. For example, many forewarning models of pests, which utilize several weather parameters and involve calculations such as accumulation of growing degree-days, are not easily understandable to extension specialists or farmers. Several internet-based DSSs have emerged as an essential tool to bridge the gap between science-based technology and end-users who wish to make day-to-day management decisions. DSSs have been developed for industry, medicine, business, meteorology, and agriculture. However, a full-fledged DSS in the area of IPM is still evolving though many individual components of IPM DSS are available. An IPM Decision Support System should provide users all necessary information including pest identification/disease diagnosis, pest/pathogen life histories (cycles), sampling and decision making criteria, sampling threshold calculators, pest/disease developmental models linked to weather networks, biorational pest control methods, plus currently available pesticides, and their safety issues and environmental impacts.

Decision support system can be developed for the use at different level, such as for the use of farmers, extension specialists or district agricultural officer level, research workers, policy managers etc. The farmers want to make decisions based on scouting, monitoring, symptoms etc. for carrying out ideal pest management practices. So, the decision support system for the farmers, must involve options for identification of pests, methods of scouting, monitoring etc. and management options. These must be in a very simple interface so that the farmers can operate themselves. The extension specialists or district agricultural officers will be interested to know the pest forecasting for the regions based on prevailing weather conditions, information on new cultivars, pest management practices etc., so that they can effectively carry out their work. The researchers will like to have decision support systems which can work out complex relationships so that they can optimize.

Decision support systems are used for making decisions on future outcomes. Hence, they carry some risk, hence the decision support system must aid in minimizing this risk. The decision support systems do not provide ready-made answers to the problem but give information based on which the decisions can be made. For example, Sharov and Liebhold (1998) developed a DSS for the spread of gypsy moth. The gypsy moth spread from usually infested area to uninfested area but they do not spread along the population front. Instead, they move to the in-between areas or transition zone through accidental carrying of life stages by human or other organisms and establish local colonies. These isolated colonies tend to grow and become continuously infested in the transition zone thus spreading the population. A decision support system was developed to aid the research workers for optimizing the establishment of pheromone based monitoring of the transition zone. Using GIS and spatial statistical tools, the location of pheromone traps are decided and using the model developed, the locations of transition areas that require immediate attention to curb the isolated colonies are identified. Thus, the decision support system is able to help to optimize the number of pheromone traps, management costs of curtailing the spread of the moth.

A complete DSS for IPM has not been developed but individual DSSs incorporating one or few components have been developed. There are various databases available, which could easily be used as DSSs. In fact, DSSs are developed based on the database. Database is an orderly collection of interrelated data in form of tables stored on a disk so that information required at any time may be easily searched and obtained. There may be different kinds of databases for different types of information. A pest database may contain information about the pests, their identification, symptoms, crops attacked, plant parts affected, time of appearance, control measure, natural enemies, ETL, conducive weather parameters etc. IPM being knowledge intensive, it is necessary to have huge amount of information prior to formulating IPM programme. The pest database can be useful for decision-making by researchers and planners. It can also be useful for extension and training activities. Efforts are on for having a sound database on IPM by different agencies all over the world.

## DATABASES DEVELOPED FOR IPM IN INDIA

### Pest Management Information System

Pest Management Information System (PMIS), a decision support system has been developed at NCIPM (Dhandapani *et al.* 2001) to cater to the need of Master trainers, training organizers, Krishi Vigyan Kendras, progressive farmers. So far, PMIS for cotton, chickpea, Rapeseed-Mustard and Groundnut (Singh *et al.*, 2003) have been released and are available for purchase.

PMIS software is designed for Microsoft® Windows ® based personal computers having one of the operating system Win98/ME/XP/2000.

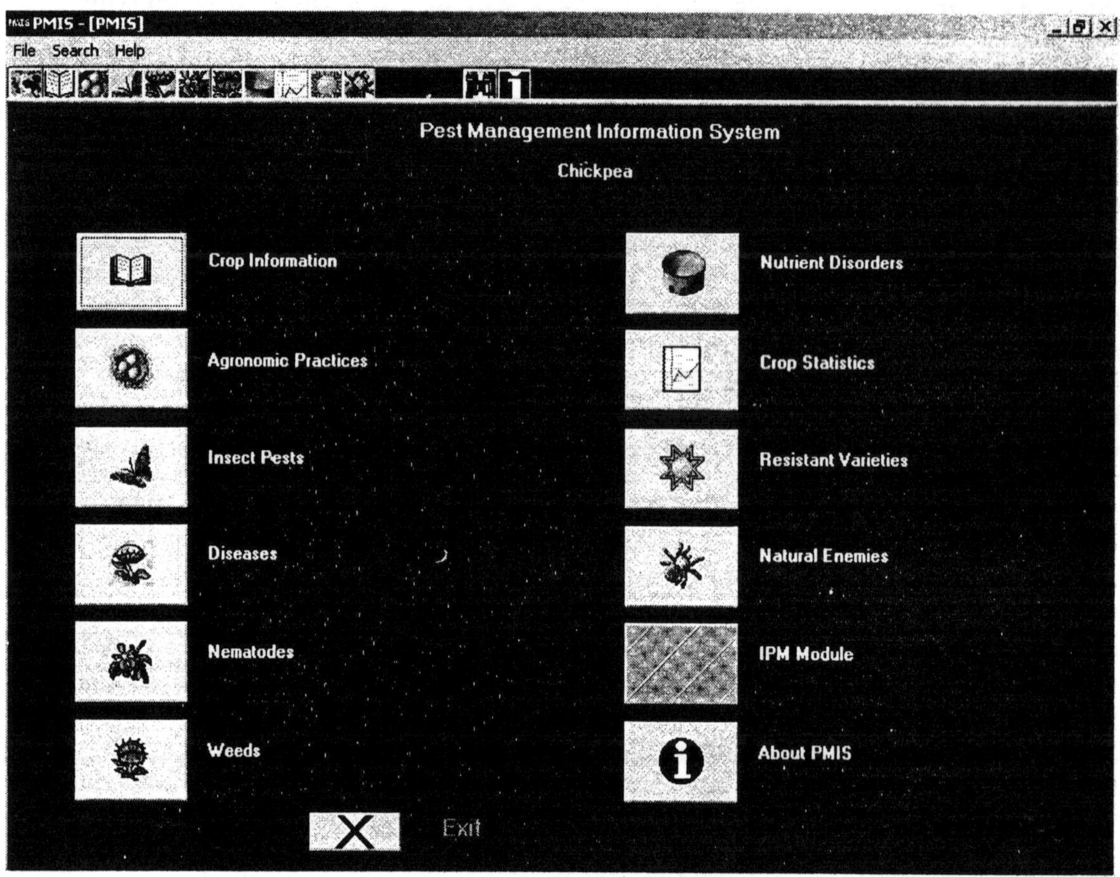


**Fig. 11.1:** Initial screen & PMIS

All the information required for implementing an IPM programme or to adopt IPM program in a particular are included in PMIS. The initial screen of PMIS is shown in Fig. 11.1. By clicking each of the option, one can get details. The crop information provides the information about crop, a photograph of the crop, scientific name etc. The agronomic details page gives the information starting from pre-sowing, seed rate, nutrient requirements (major as well as minor nutrients), harvest, post-harvest details etc. The insect, disease, weeds and nematode pages give the information about the individual pest, identification, photograph showing either the pest or the damage caused by the pest, management options available such as biocontrol, chemical or cultural control. The photographs of pests or the symptoms of the pests can also serve as a field guide for identification. More over, the IPM option available for the particular pest is also provided. If any resistant moderately resistant cultivars or predators/parasitoids available against the pest, the names of such cultivars or predators are shown and the links to the detailed information are also provided. The farmers usually confuse the symptoms of nutrient disorders with the pest symptoms and to clarify this, information about major and minor nutrient symptoms are also provided. A complete IPM module developed for the crop along with the location is also available for ready use. The bioagents page give the complete details about the bioagents and also the pests against which they are useful are also indicated. A search facility is also included to search the PMIS to find out the information quickly. Further, a small help screen is also provided for the benefit of the first time users. Some statistics such as area, production and productivity of the crop in India (state-wise) are also included as a reference.

Thus, PMIS provides an ideal one-stop place where all the information is available. The information provided will be useful in selecting appropriate varieties, agronomic practices and to decide correct management options against the key pest. The target users of PMIS are the Master trainers who can train the other trainers. PMIS can also be useful as a training medium to train the farmers, students, etc. Thus, PMIS can serve both as a training medium as well as a self-learning and referencing tool.

The information contained in PMIS has been collected by the crop experts and the IPM modules are the ones which are validated by NCIPM. The information will be updated as and when required.

There is also an option to change the crop so that the same software can be used for the different crops. Also, the development of PMIS in various crops can be taken up independently. More over, the information can be updated without reloading or modifying the software as only the relevant database files are modified.

The information provided in PMIS is all in English language and thus limiting the scope of the audience, particularly the farmers. The limitations can be overcome if PMIS in Indian languages can be made available. Efforts are on this line and to start with, PMIS-Cotton in Hindi language is being attempted.

## DATABASE ON PRESENT STATUS OF PLANT PROTECTION RECOMMENDATIONS IN INDIA

Frequently, to synthesis IPM package for a location spread across the state where the key pests are same, the package of practices, particularly the plant protection recommendations of individual states will be very useful. Keeping this in mind, the plant protection recommendations of various states in India have been compiled and put in a database to make it as a reference tool. This is also available on the Internet site of the centre so that it is available to all. This database will also be helpful to compare the key pests of each crop in different states and the management options recommended by the individual state.

## COT-IPM Pro

The software COT-IPM pro (Sharma *et al.* 2001) is to enter, store and view the agronomic, pest and weather details for cotton. It is often felt that in a network programme involving multiple partners from different parts of the country, much of the valuable time have been lost in compiling the reports in an uniform pattern so that the situation in different locations can be easily comparable. Further, the computerization will also speed up and automate the need for finding out averages, preparing graphs etc. Keeping this in view, COT-IPM Pro was developed for the use of any agency/institution or a group of agencies in a network engaged in implementing IPM in an area. Uniform reporting can greatly help in identifying the pest problem more systematically. A single farmer to keep up the farm records may use this software. The software can generate reports for individual or group of cotton pests. The reports can be viewed a graphical form and the pests which cross the ETL level are marked so that appropriate decisions can be made to manage those pests. Further, a uniform data sheet is provided to collect pests and natural enemies present in cotton ecosystem. All the pests, major or minor are included. A sample graph generated by the software is shown in Fig. 11.2. However, the COT-IPM pro does not contain any management options. Using COT-IPM pro along with PMIS in cotton will serve a complete decision making tool to manage cotton pests.

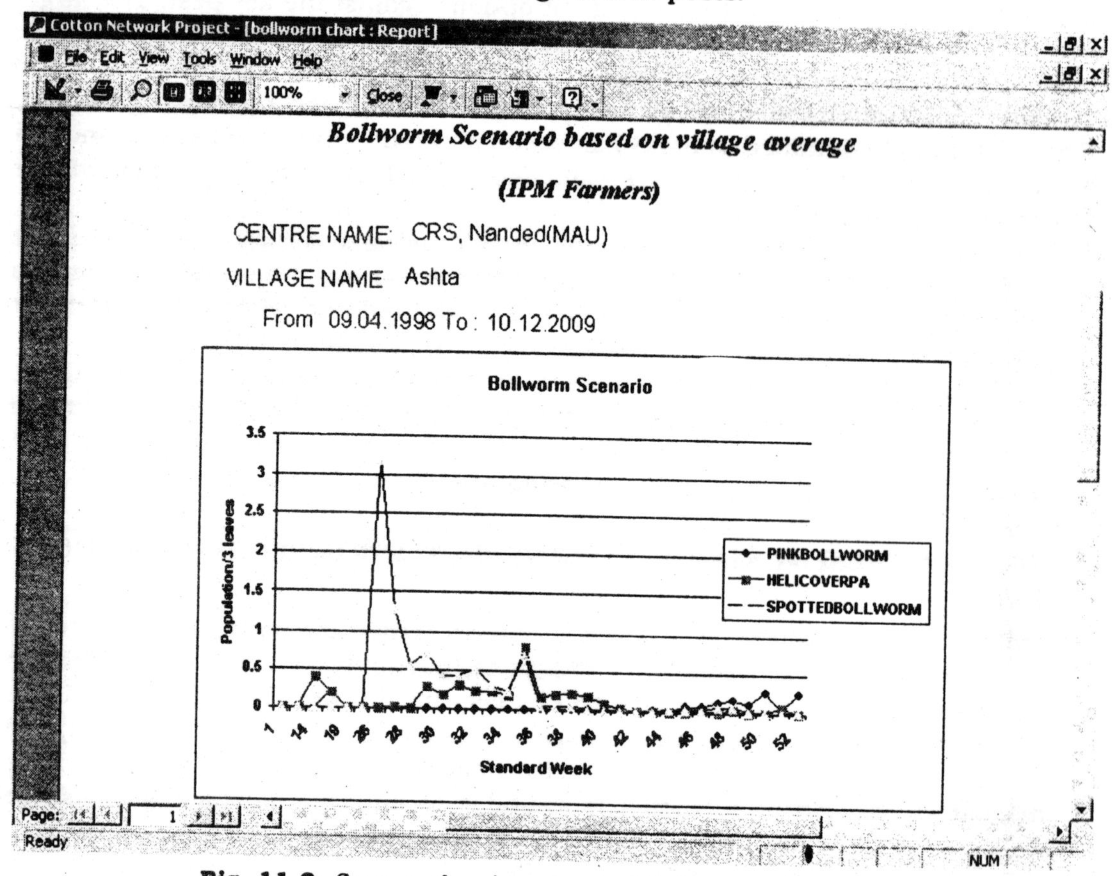


**Fig. 11.2:** Screen showing chart of bollwarm population

For each season, the user has to enter the agronomic details such as variety, date of sowing, fertilizer application with date and dose, spacing followed, irrigation supplied etc. For each date of observation of pests, the data can be entered. Similarly, the weather data can be entered in the software. The report option gives the wide variety of generating reports. The reports can be generated for a single farmer, group of farmers such as IPM or non-IPM. The reports may be simple averages or graphical representations.

The software can act as a repository for storing the pest and weather data from multi-location and can provide long felt need for data to develop pest-forewarning models. The software can also be used for pest monitoring purposes.

The software is developed for Microsoft Windows environment and can be easily loaded in any Microsoft Windows based personal computer.

## Nematode Management Information System

Nematode pests are often considered hidden pests, as they remain neglected in plant protection practices. More often, symptoms of nematode attack are misunderstood as diseases. Nematode Management Information System(NMIS) (Dhadapani *et al.*, 2001) was developed to address the nematode problem in various crops. Here, the different nematodes, classified either as above ground or below ground depending on the symptoms produced. For each nematode, an introduction, symptoms and

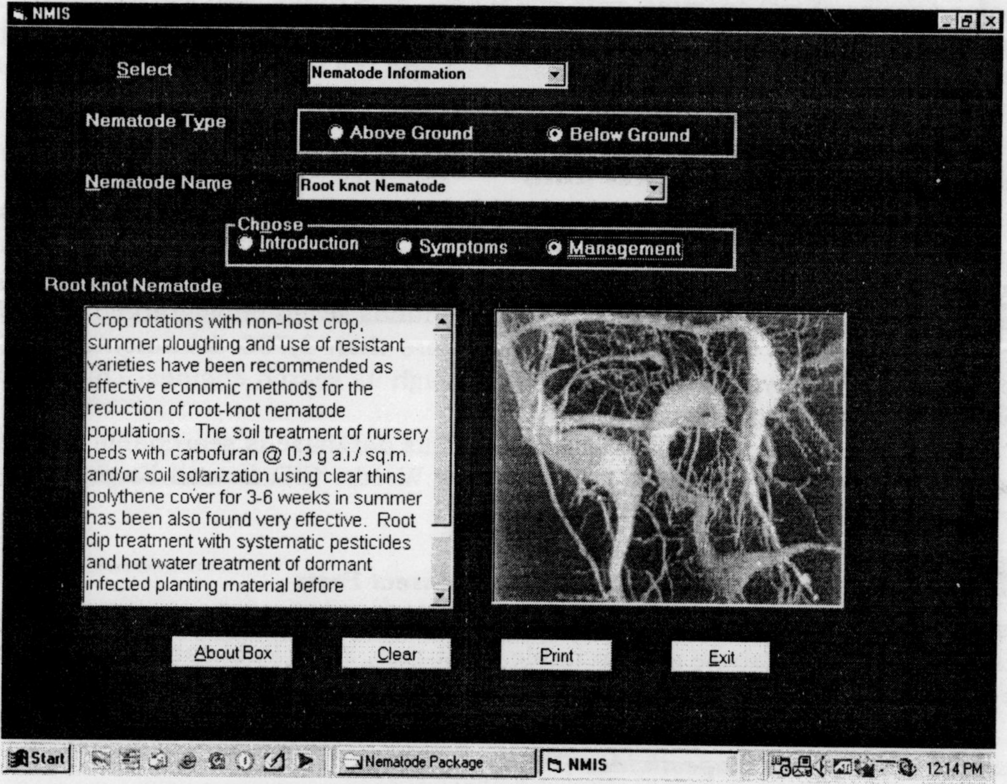


**Fig. 11.3:** Initial screen shot of NMIS

management options are provided. Photographs showing the nematode or its symptoms are also included. Besides, some general information about the nematode problems, losses caused, usual symptoms etc. are also provided. In Nematode infested areas, NMIS will come in handy to tackle the problem. NMIS can also be used a training medium to sensitize the problem of nematodes and a reference material.

As with PMIS, NMIS is also designed to run in Microsoft Windows based environment. Figure 11.3 provides a screen shot of the software showing the management options for root-knot nematode.

### NEMVAR

NEMVAR was developed to provide a tool to select appropriate variety/hybrid in various crops in nematode infested areas. The information against the reaction of different cultivars of important crops were collected from the All-India Coordinated Programme on Nematodes. Each cultivar is either classified as resistant, moderately resistant, susceptible etc. Using this software, one can access the status of any variety with regard to nematode problem. NEMVAR can be used as a ready reconer.

## DATABASES DEVELOPED FOR IPM IN OTHER COUNTRIES

### CABI Crop Protection Compendium

It gives outline information for 1000 insect pest, disease and weed species of the world and their natural enemies, with synonyms, host range, and geographical range (mapped). There are selected agricultural and pest management data for all countries. It has in-depth information on South-East Asia and the Pacific. The Internet address is http://www.cabi.org/compendia/cpc/index.htm.

### Database of Information Resources (DIR)

It is a continuously updated and expanded information retrieval and referral system for the worldwide electronic IPM resources. DIR has three main components including directories of Internet IPM resources, search engines, and informational databases/knowledge bases. Currently, DIR contains seven bibliographic databases, four knowledge bases and a database with more than 3,700 documented Internet resources and their hyperlinks searchable through its search engines. This database is available at http://ippc.orst.edu/DIR).

CID has over 65 unique definitions of IPM. This database is searchable by Author, Year, Publication (Journal/Book Title) and key Words. CID Search Engine now has new features.

### *Bibliographic Database on Cultural Control of Insect Pests*

This database is a component of a website on Cultural Control of Pests (still under construction). The database is searchable by Author, Year, Publication (journal/book title) and Key Words.

### *Database of Microbial Biopesticides (DMB)*

A knowledge base on using pathogens for the control of insect pest and plant diseases.

***Bacillus thuringiensis*—Based Biological Control of Insect Pests**

A knowledge base on practical use of Bt in IPM.

## EXPERT SYSTEMS

An Agricultural Expert System is a Decision Support System for Agricultural Extension Agents who has to decide what advice to be offered to farmers who have to decide what action to take based on it. It can also be used directly by the farmers. It is one of the most efficient extension tools to take the technology from scientists to the farmers directly without any dilution of content which normally creeps in because of the number of agencies involved in normal technology transfer systems.

Decision support programs imitate an expert by involving a client in a problem-solving situation, often providing a recommendation in response to a client's request for help in making a decision. The areas selected for use of Agriculture expert systems are applications to diagnosis the diseases and pests of various crops. In recent years, research and development of the expert system fields of agriculture domain have been paid much attention by many countries, not only by developed countries but also developing countries. The complexity of problems confronting farmers like yield loses, soil erosion, diminishing market prices from international competition, increasing chemical pesticides costs and pest resistance and economic barriers hindering adoption of farming strategies necessitates that they become expert managers of all aspects of their farming operations. On the other hand agricultural researchers need to address problems of farm management and discover new management strategies to promote farm success.. Expert System are Computer programs that are different from conventional computer programs as they solve problems by mimicking human reasoning processes, relying on logic, belief, rules of thumb opinion and experience.

Although there is no general standard for expert systems, most include:

- A knowledge base of domain facts and associated heuristics
- An inference procedure or control structure for utilizing the knowledge base
- A natural language user interface

The knowledge base component includes both Domain facts and Heuristics. Domain constitutes a body of information widely shared and generally publicly available within the domain.

Heuristic knowledge is mostly privately and individually held. It includes rules-of-thumb, judgments, and sometimes, experience based guesses that typically characterize human expert level decision-making. In order for an expert system to solve a problem, a program must have both kinds of knowledge, facts and heuristics, in its knowledge base.

In addition to knowledge base, systems include an inference system or procedure, also commonly called the inference engine. This system contains the general problem solving approach deciding which heuristics are applied to the problem, accessing the appropriate rules in the knowledge base, executing the rule, and determining when an acceptable solution has been found. In fact, the inference system 'runs' an expert system. The remaining components of the expert system permit bi-directional communication. It is known as the input/output system.

The most basic difference of expert systems with that of conventional computer programs is that expert systems manipulate knowledge while conventional programs manipulate data.

## Expert Systems for IPM Developed in India

### *Rice-Crop*

National Institute of Agricultural Extension Management (MANAGE), Hyderabad has developed an expert system to diagnose pests and diseases for rice crop and suggest preventive/curative measures. The rice crop doctor illustrates the use of expert systems broadly in the area of agriculture and more specifically in the area of rice production through development of a prototype, taking into consideration a few major pests and diseases and some deficiency problems limiting rice yield.

### *Indian Institute of Horticultural Research Institute, Bangalore*

The Indian Institute of Horticultural Research Institute, Bangalore, prepared the first software for use by the grape cultivators. This spontaneous response made them to undertake similar software for providing guidance to mushroom cultivators, which became extremely popular and a large number of growers using it regularly for getting solutions to their problems. The Institute has launched into an effort to give a comprehensive package of practices of about 148 horticulture crops for cultivation in the 4 Southern states of Kerala, Tamilnadu, Karnataka and Andhra Pradesh.

### *AGREX*

Center for Informatics Research and Advancement, Kerala has prepared an Expert System called AGREX to help the Agricultural field personnel give timely and correct advice to the farmers. These Expert Systems find extensive use in the areas of fertilizer application, crop protection, irrigation scheduling, diagnosis of diseases in paddy and post harvest technology of fruits and vegetables.

### *Farm Advisory System*

Punjab Agricultural University, Ludhiana, has developed the Farm Advisory System to support agri-business management. The conversation between the system and the user is arranged in such a way that the system asks all the questions from user one by one which it needs to give recommendations on the topic of farm Management. The inputs are encouraging and acceptance by farmers is very good.

## Expert Systems Developed in Other Countries

### *COMAX*

Provides information on integrated crop management in cotton. The system uses a combination of expert derived rules and results generated by the cotton crop simulation model.

### *GOSSYM*

It requires external information such as weather data, soil physical parameters, soil fertility levels, and certain pest management information. Based on this input data, the system makes daily management decision recommendations.

### *POMME*

Provides information about pest and orchard management of apples. External information such as weather data including forecasts and crop symptoms are utilized by the system to generate management decision recommendations.

### *PLANT/ds*

Supports the diagnosis of soybean diseases and can be used by growers and country agents alike.

### *Expert Systems for Cotton Crop Management*

This Expert System provides appropriate management recommendations to cotton growers.

### *CALEX and TAXIM*

This is a blackboard based integrated expert decision support system for agricultural management, developed at University of California and Texas University, Texas respectively. Growers, pest control advisors, consultants and other managers, can use CALEX and TAXIM.

### *Weiping Jin Expert System*

There are fertilizing, irrigating, spraying insecticide process and adopting other measures in crop management, which rely on crop state analysis. However, there is a lot of fuzzy phenomenon in crop state analyse. Then it is necessary to analysis or to measure these fuzzy phenomena by means of fuzzy set theory for crop management. An expert system that can deal with fuzziness has been developed for crop management in PR.China. This paper shows the principal construction of the expert system, CMES, for growers to manage their crop. CMES provides support for crop growth control system (CGCS), *i.e.*, advises growers about optimal population and structure of crop in planting stage and when and what to adopt measures on their crop to keep at optimal state, to avoid Infestation in various stage of growth and development of crop, and finally to obtain the

### *CLIPS Expert System by L. L.M. Rhykerd*

Purdue University agricultural scientists have developed the expert system. This form of artificial intelligence provides an extension tool, which will enable farmers to very economically use a computer program to reach conclusions concerning profitable alfalfa production that normally would require consultation with a forage expert. To date, the management considerations and the sequence in which they were built into the knowledge base are: soil drainage, soil pH, soil P test, soil K test, use of alfalfa crop, chemical weed control, expected longevity of stand, variety recommendation, method and rate of seeding and pure live seed.

## Geographic Information System

A GIS is a set of computer programs that can store, use, and display information about places of interest. Information for any place of interest are soil types, rainfall and temperature patterns, land use, ownership patterns, roads, vegetation types, and topography. A GIS stores two types of data that are found on a map, the geographic definitions of Earth's surface features (spatial reference) and the attributes or qualities that those features possess.

GIS provides pest managers with the capabilities to store, retrieve, process, and display spatially referenced data. It seems only logical that GIS technology will be rapidly embraced because so many questions from insect ecology to pest management have a spatial component. Whether studying the dynamics of host or making prediction of pest problems. Now it is possible to identify two general areas where GIS technology has been used in entomology-applied insect ecology research and insect pest management. Within the general area of applied insect ecology, perhaps the major use of GIS is in the relation of insect outbreaks to environmental features of the landscape. The compilation and interpretation of spatially referenced insect and habitat data is a complex process. Although GIS software is designed to handle this complexity successfully, these systems often are not easy to use. In order to make a GIS more accessible to applied problems, GIS is increasingly being linked as a part of a larger decision support systems (DSSs). These systems typically use a GIS to manage habitat, geophysical, political, and census data. The DSS uses these data, along with other data, as input to mathematical models and other modeling methods to produce useful abstractions or recommendations. These outputs might be maps of high damage hazard or even maps of proposed control areas.

Dynamic sites that include interactive models, GIS (Geographical Information System) based decision systems, real-time weather, and market information are being rapidly developed and made available on the Internet. GIS is another form database with a difference, information are linked to their geographic locations. The use of geographic locations adds another dimension to the information and it is very convenient to analyze and interpret information and drafting policies using GIS. Some specific applications of GIS in the field of IPM are given below.

## Scouting, Monitoring & Mapping Pest Populations

Scouting and monitoring pest populations and making control decisions based on those population estimates is one of the bases for IPM. The ability to accurately and precisely map the density and location of pest populations has obvious advantages, especially in regard to application of control tactics.

Monitoring programs can now digitally map the location of sample sites (taken in the field with a Global Positioning Systems) and the results can be used to interpolate the pest population over the sampled area. This is not a new technique; interpolative techniques, without GIS, have been used to estimate populations. However, GIS will help in not only estimate populations but can be linked to other similar areas throughout a region, resulting in regional maps, which estimate pest populations. This technique is used when constructing state or region wide estimates of pest populations or crop damage.

### Preparation of Pest Distribution Maps

Another important application of GIS is to prepare county wise pest distribution maps. Several such maps are available in India as well as in other countries. Pest distribution maps are prepared using databases on pest, their intensity of attack on different locations over years. The maps for different years of same pest may be overlaid to obtain a composite map. This map will help in identifying hotspots of a particular pest in the country. Further, the map will also help in identifying spread of the pest, which will be very useful in quarantine purposes, and taking remedial actions well in advance. Pest Distribution maps of cotton and Rice crop in India were prepared at NCIPM (Kanojia *et al.* 2002 ) for key pests of these crops, the hotspots are identified.

## INTERNET

The Internet is a worldwide network of networks and computers interconnected for information exchange (Singh *et al.* 2002). The advent of Internet has made the world into a real global village. The Internet has broken the geographic, cultural, religious, government barriers for interested people to come together and exchange information. There is already a large volume of useful IPM information available on the Internet, however, the information is scattered all across the globe. These resources range from topics such as pest identification, biology, control tactics, IPM definitions and basic concepts, to modeling and systems analysis. As awareness of the Internet increases worldwide, more people are participating not only as users of the information but also as creators of new information; as a consequence, the number of both IPM Internet servers and clients is increasing rapidly. Various newsgroups on IPM and agriculture are available in Internet, which facilitates exchange information on IPM. Timely information, such as state pest alerts and changing label information or spray recommendations can be available within minutes of the information being received by the Web site administrators.

### Applications of Internet for IPM

The transfer of research and extension information plays the key role in the promotion and adoption of IPM. Electronic communication provides an effective multidirectional exchange of information. (Bajwa and Kogan). Internet can also be used to collect data from various places, for example monitoring of pests. The data can be processed at a centralized location and the reports can be generated. The advances in computer programming, such as eXtensible Markup Language (XML) provides a new opportunity. For example, the sites providing pest forewarning, can access the weather data from the weather station located nearby the user. The user need not give the weather input and the site will access itself and do the needful for the user. There are many sites, such as http://www.ipm.ucdavis.edu/DISEASE/DATABASE/ available at

University of California at Davis are available. For a complete list, one can refer to Bajwa and Kogan (2000), PPIGB (http://www.pk.uni-bonn.de/ppigb/ppigb.htm) etc. A number of useful addresses have been giving in Table 11.1, which contains useful information for decision making.

**TABLE 11.1:** ADDRESS OF SOME OF USEFUL WEBSITES

| *Organization* | *Website Address* |
|---|---|
| "Ask an Expert" Alberta Agriculture, Food and Rural Development (Canada) | http://www1.agric.gov.ab.ca/staff/ate.nsf |
| "Ask Our Experts!" Virtual Plant & Pest Diagnostic Laboratory, Purdue University (USA). | http://www.ppdl.purdue.edu/ppdl/Ask_Expert.html |
| CABI Crop Protection Compendium | http://www.cabi.org/compendia/cpc/index.htm |
| Central Insecticides Board and Registration Committee (India) | http://cibrc.nic.in/ |
| Database of Information Resources (DIR) | http://ippc.orst.edu/DIR |
| Disease Model database | http://www.ipm.ucdavis.edu/DISEASE/DATABASE |
| Distance Diagnostic Identification System (DDIS) University of Florida, USA. | http://edis.ifas.ufl.edu/TOPIC_DDIS |
| Ecological Database of the World's Insect Pathogens | http://cricket.inhs.uiuc.edu/edwipweb/edwip_search.htm |
| Genome databases for several plant, fungal, and other organisms | http://ars-genome.cornell.edu |
| Indian Council of Agricultural Research | http://www.icar.org.in |
| Insecticide Resistance Action Committee (IRAC) | http://www.irac-online.org/ |
| International Survey of Herbicide-Resistant Weeds | http://www.weedscience.com |
| International agricultural interests from the Consortium for International Crop Protection. | http://www.IPMnet.org |
| National Centre for Integrated Pest Management | http://www.ncipm.org.in |
| NEMABASE | http://ucdnema.ucdavis.edu/imagemap/nemmap/nemabase.htm |
| Plant Viruses Online | http://biology.anu.edu.au/Groups/MES/vide/refs.htm |
| PPIGB (Plant Pathology Internet Guide Book | http://www.pk.uni-bonn.de/ppigb/ppigb.htm |

*Note:* This list is no means neither exhaustive nor complete. Some of the sites mentioned here links to many other sites which can be accessed for any specific information.

## REFERENCES

Bajwa, W. I. and Kogan, M. 2000. Internet-based IPM Informatics and Decision Support. *In*: E. B. Radcliffe and W. D. Hutchison [eds.], *Radcliffe's IPM World Textbook*, URL: http://ipmworld.umn.edu, University of Minnesota, St. Paul, MN.

Dhandapani, A., Singh Niranjan, and Sharma, O. P. 2001. Development of user-friendly software in the area of IPM. *Discussion Papers & proceedings of XII National Conference of Agriculture Research Statisticians*. held at PAU, Ludhiana, November 6-8, 2001, pp. 126-128.

Dhandapani, A. and Singh, Niranjan 2001. Software for Identifications and Management of Nematode in India. ARIS news, July-September, 2001.

Gilman, E. F. and Green, J. L. 1998. Efficient, Collaborative, Inquiry-Driven Electronic Information Systems. *Hort Technology*, **8**(3): 297-300.

Kanojia, A. K., Kumar, S., Prameela Devi, T., Trivedi, T. P., Singh, A., Sundarsarma, K. S., Natarajan, K. and Pawar, A. D. 2002. Distribution maps of Insect Pests and Diseases of cotton crop in India. National Centre for Integrated Pest Management, New Delhi.

Sharma, O. P., Dhandapani, A. and Nagarajan, S., 2001. *COT-IPM Pro: User's Guide*. NCIPM, New Delhi-110 012.

Sharov, A. A. and Liebhold, A. M. 1998. Model of slowing the spread of gypsy moth (Lepidoptera: Lymantriidae) with a barrier zone. *Ecol. Appl.*, **8**: 1170-1179.

Singh, N., Farooqi, M. S. and Dhandapani, A. 2002. Integrated Pest Management and the world wide web. *Agricultural Extension Review*, **14**(6): 9-11.

Singh, Niranjan, Dhandapani, A. and Singh, Saroj 2003. Development of computer-based databases for IPM in oil seed crops. Extended summaries of National Seminar on Stress Management in Oil Seeds for Attaining Self-reliance. *In*: *Vegetable Oils: Need at DOR*. Hyderabad. January 28-30-2003. pp. 142-43.

12

# Development of Forewarning Models for Insect Pests and Diseases of Important Crops

**T. P. Trivedi, D. K. Das and A. Dhandapani**

## INTRODUCTION

Pest forecasting provides opportunity to farmers for preparedness and take timely action to apply bio-agents and pesticides, which ultimately cut down the cost of production and serve as a tool in precision farming. Pest forecasting through mathematical and computer based models deals with perception of the future activity of biotic agents, which adversely affects crop production. Pest forecasting models are essential tools and pre-requisite of IPM as the insect population and disease incidence levels are deciding factors in pest management. One of the earliest forecasting work on plant pest was forecasting of late blight of potato (*Phytophthora infestans*) by Dutch rules (Van Everdingen, 1926) which considered several climatic factors together such as dew during night (at least 4 hours), minimum temperature at night (less than 10° C), mean cloudiness on following day (more than 0.8) and rainfall in the next 24 hours (minimum of 0.1 mm). In India, one of the earliest work on pest forecasting was started by Dr. S Pradhan when he gave the concept of biotic theory of locust population explosion. According to him, temperature was one of the most important factor which determines the duration of various stages in insect life cycle and number of generations. The development of biograph had seen one of the important findings to show the rate of development on different temperature regimes (Pradhan, 1967, 1982). Later, various other models were developed such as wheat stem rust rules (Nagarajan and Singh, 1975) based on climatological parameters.

The main requirement for developing pest forecasting models are data on weather parameters, pest population, natural enemies and crop phenology. The data can be generated through regular monitoring and ecological considerations are foundation of pest management programme (Trivedi, 2001 and Trivedi *et al.*, 2001*a*).

## MONITORING OF PEST

Crop pest surveillance and monitoring are corner stones in pest management programme. Monitoring of pest population through surveillance implies a complete vigilance on pest population, natural enemies, cropping system and weather factors.

An ideal surveillance team should include entomologists, pathologists, nematologists, agricultural meteorologists, modelers and production scientists for collection

*National Centre for Integrated Pest Management, LBS Building, Pusa Campus, New Delhi-110 012.*

of data on various aspects. Monitoring of pest population at regular intervals round the year provides both quantitative and qualitative data.

Agro-ecosystem is also contributing to the population dynamics and the role of fertilizer, spacing, irrigation and crop sequences are major factor influencing the pest population. The knowledge on biology and ecology of the pest are essential element for monitoring the pest population. Population dynamics and role of critical mortality factors, growth rate, inherent behaviour and life processes have to be accounted by developing life table. Quantitative studies viz. sample size, time, sampling scheme, spatial distribution, crops stages need to be studied for estimating the population.

The inter relationship and dependence of plants, pests, natural enemies of pest and weather and their quantification need full understanding. Therefore, forecasting system for pest is mainly developed by using various mathematical models based on biotic and abiotic factors. These models may be deterministic, statistical, system simulation, expert system, schematic or geographical. It would be better, if such models have the input of indigenous technical knowledge of farming community to provide location specific models for the use of crop production managers. The location specific models for polyphagus pests need to be fine tuned based on local factors before field application. These prediction models will make the farmers to prepare against pests and decide the timing of application of bio-agents, pesticides and other approaches in integrated pest management. Government of India has constituted number of committees to strengthen the surveillance, monitoring and forecasting system with multi institutional support. Recommendation of these committees are finding a place to deal with the changing pest scenario in India.

### Monitoring Tools

Various monitoring tools viz. light traps, pheromone traps, manual count of eggs, larvae, visual estimation of crop damage have been used in India and elsewhere. These also include roving and fixed plot observations in different parts of India.

The monitoring of pest has been found useful in the following ways:

1. Identification of geographical distribution, key mortality factors, peak activity, mode of carry over and off-season survival.
2. Conservation of natural enemies.
3. Precision farming.
4. Remote sensing and information system.
5. Preparedness of crop protection managers and farmers.
6. Avoidance of excessive use of pesticides.
7. Reduction in cost of production.
8. Environmental protection.

## DEVELOPMENT OF FORECASTING MODELS

The prerequisite of an economically viable, environmentally sound and easily adoptable pest management programme is precise forewarning of the pest occurrence and peak activity period. The following basic information and methods should be followed for development of dynamic pest prediction system.

### Quantitative Seasonal Studies

Sampling of population, spatial and geographical distribution of pest abundance, seasonal counts in relation to climate, phenology of the crop and topography need to be provided for modeling.

### Life History and Biology of the Pest

The length of life cycle, number of generations in a year, growth index, life span, survival rate, food, habitat, over seasoning, collatoral hosts and intrinsic growth rate in field and simulated laboratory conditions should be available with the working group. The effects of abiotic factors on development of pests, spread and mode of carry over needs to be worked out accurately.

### Ecological Studies of the Pest

Life-table studies of pests are important for better understanding of pest population build-up, natural mortality factor, critical stage, intrinsic growth rate. Life-table of a pest can be used to find the favourable period for mating and emergence, etc. Besides these, the spatial pattern can also provide clues to find the suitable sampling schemes to be used for collecting pest population samples. The migration and immigration of pests alongwith mode of carry over and spread can be used for forecasting of pests.

### Crop Phenology

The different crop cultivars, fertilizers dosages, irrigation and plant spacing influence the phenology of the crop. The population on various phenological stages needs to be studied.

### Natural Enemies

The population of natural enemies present on various time intervals in the crop needs to be worked out precisely for different locations. These natural enemies are playing important role in suppression of pest population. Sometimes due to use of pesticides, the population of natural enemies is drastically reduced and alters the pest population.

### Agro Ecosystems

The changing cropping pattern and diversified crops are emerging as one of the remunerative methods of increasing profitability in some parts of the country. The number of crops and wide range of varieties with different maturity groups are a suitable niche for supporting the build up of *Helicoverpa*. Therefore, the information on cropping pattern and crop sequences needs to be included in the modelling. Population counts on various crop host plants are to be counted regularly. Even the low population is surviving on collateral hosts during off-season.

### Surveillance of Pests

Monitoring for emergence of soil pests or migrating pest through regular monitoring of population through direct count on crop plants, light traps, pheromone traps, wind traps, spore traps and also by drawing soil samples for visual observation of immature stages of pests indicates the pattern of population build up. Even emergence traps fixed in the soil and crops plants also work as a tool. The population of the pests should also be counted on alternate or collateral hosts on periodical intervals for their occurrence on major host plants.

### Modeling of Pest Population

Based on the data available, various modelling options are available to model the pest population with the other factors such as weather, natural enemies present, and crop biology. The relationship between the different components is shown in Fig. 12.1. Some of the successful modelling techniques used in pest forecasting include statistical, mathematical and simulation models. Statistical techniques such as simple linear regression techniques, multiple regression, non-linear models, group method of data handling, Stochastic process and time-series analysis are used in pest forecasting. Mathematical models such as simple growth models like logistic, Gompertz, etc. are widely used in pest forecasting, particularly to forecast disease development and loss assessment. If the model involve the current week pest population data as a dependent variable and previous few weeks weather parameters as independent variables then the model may be used for forecasting purposes.

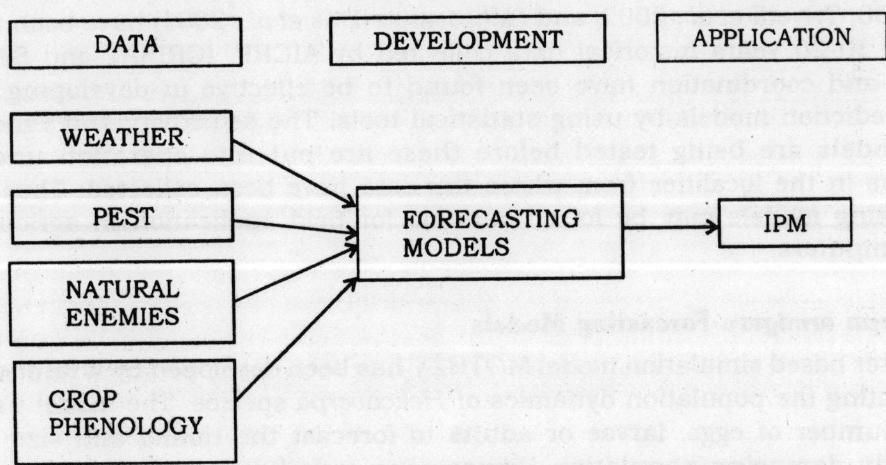


**Fig. 12.1:** Relationship of components of pest forecasting

### Data Requirement

1. Reliable, genuine data on pest population for long period on definite time intervals
2. Weather records of the study sites

3. Crop phenology
4. Population of natural enemies.

### Integration of Research

A working group of plant protection scientists, Agricultural Meteorologists, crop modeler, statisticians and computer scientists in coordination with production and ecological scientists should be formed for development of forewarning system.

## KEY PESTS

The pest forecasting models for key pests need to be developed through collaboration with ICAR institutes, State Agricultural Universities and KVKs. Some of the key pests identified at present for development of forecasting models are:

- *Helicoverpa armigera* (American bollworm/pod borer)
- *Spodoptera litura* (Tobacco caterpillar)
- *Nilaparvata lugens* (Brown plant hopper)
- *Bemisia tabacci* (Whitefly) and Cotton Leaf Curl Virus
- *Xanthomonas oryzae* p. v. *oryzae* (Bacterial Leaf Blight of rice)
- *Ramularia areoli* (Grey Mildew of Cotton).

## PEST FOREWARNING MODELS

Some of the pest forewarning models developed at NCIPM include potato aphid (Trivedi *et al.*, 2000, Trivedi *et al.*, 2002) and *Helicoverpa* (Das *et al.*, 2001) have been taken up by using 10-20 years historical data collected by AICRP, ICRISAT and SAUs. The linkages and coordination have been found to be effective in developing weather based prediction models by using statistical tools. The sensitivity and validation of these models are being tested before these are put into operation under field conditions in the localities from where the data have been collected. These simple and working models may be found suitable for field application in agriculture by using computers.

### *Helicoverpa armigera* Forcasting Models

A computer based simulation model MOTHZV has been developed by Witz *et al.* (1985) for predicting the population dynamics of *Helicoverpa* species. The model uses early season number of eggs, larvae or adults to forecast the timing and size of later, potentially damaging population. Pheromone trap has provided the means for measuring early season number of *Helicoverpa* adults. This pheromone trap data alongwith climatic variable and crop phenology were used as input to the MOTHZV model to predict the timing of future *Helicoverpa* generations for a pilot test on the management of *Helicoverpa* species.

NCIPM has developed the group of plant protection, agrometeorology, statistics and computer scientists for the development of forewarning system for insect pests and diseases for different agro climatic zones of the country. The similar approach with further improvement is working with multi-institutional support under NATP project on weather based forewarning systems for crop pests and diseases with the support of 28 centres situated in 11 states for rice, cotton, pigeonpea, sugarcane, groundnut and mustard ecosystems. Although, some scattered activities were carried out at different locations and forewarning systems have been developed by different agencies in few agro-ecological regions, no attempt was made to cover nationally important pests of major crops in different agro-ecological regions of India.

In India, monthly pheromone trap moth data of 1983-90 alongwith weather data of corresponding period collected from PAU, Ludhiana have been analysed at NCIPM by Das *et al.* (2000) and it was found that there were two major peaks of moth catches in a year. The main peak was during March-April and the second peak was during October every year. During March-April peak, chickpea was the main crop and during October, cotton was grown almost over entire area. The peak population of *Helicoverpa* moth during March-April and October can be predicted in advance by multiple regression models using different weather parameters alongwith previous season's population of *Helicoverpa*. The population density during March-April ($P_{M-A}$) has been regressed with different weather parameters as well as pest population density of previous five months separately and cumulatively. It has been found to depend on total moth catch per trap during previous October to February ($P_{O-F}$), mean monthly relative humidity recorded in the afternoon during previous February ($RHE_F$) and mean monthly minimum temperature of previous February ($Tmin_F$) as follows:

$$P_{M-A} = -1032.65 + 2.06\ P_{O-F} - 34.26RHE_F + 516.74Tmin_F\ (R^2 = 0.75)$$

Apart from weather parameters, the total population cumulated from October to February is another important parameter. The population, which used to undergo diapause from October due to severe winter is emerged again after February.

Similarly, the population density during October ($P_O$) can be predicted in advance with multiple regression using weather parameters as well as pest population of preceding months as follows:

$$P_O = -5.39 + .12\ P_{M-A} + 1.28\ P_J - 0.51\ R_{J-J}\ (R^2 = 0.87)$$

$P_{M-A}$ = Pest population density of March and April,

$P_J$ = Pest population density of June

$R_{J-J}$ = Total amount of rainfall during June and July.

The data collected from ICRISAT, Hyderabad were analysed and a thumb rule has been found out to predict the level of attack during any year using surplus/deficit rainfall of different months and that thumb rule has justified the severity of pod borer attack in different districts of Andhra Pradesh during the winter of 1997-98 (Das *et al.*, 2001).

The surplus or deficit of monsoon rainfall (*i.e.*, the excess or less rainfall of June, July, August and September) which is referred here as 'A' and surplus or deficit rainfall during November which is referred here as 'B' of any place in this region could play the crucial role. A and B can be calculated as:

A = (Actual total rainfall during four monsoon months in a year – Long term average rainfall of that period of that place)

B = (Actual total rainfall during November month in a year – Long term average rainfall of that month of that place)

Positive (+) value of A or B indicates surplus rainfall and negative (–) value indicates rainfall deficit.

| A+B–<br>LOW | A+B+<br>MODERATE |
|---|---|
| A–B–<br>MODERATE | A–B+<br>SEVERE |

***Validation of the Pest Forecasting Models at Different Districts of Andhra Pradesh***

The constructed rule has been tested to predict the disastrous situation in crop damage at different districts of Andhra Pradesh during 1997-98 winter. The actual as well as long term average rainfall data of 1997 of Warrangal, Khammam, Karimnagar, Rangareddy and Mehboobnagar were obtained. Although, the population density data of pod borer were not available, data on the extent of damage were available. The A and B values of the above districts during the winter of 1997-98 showed A–B+ combination (Table 12.1) indicating severe attack or damage of *Helicoverpa armigera* and this was true as cotton, redgram, chillies and sunflower were devastated during this year in the above districts.

**TABLE 12.1:** A AND B PARAMETERS, CROPS AFFECTED AND LEVEL OF DAMAGE BY *Helicoverpa armigera* IN DIFFERENT DISTRICTS OF ANDHRA PRADESH

| *Districts* | *A* | *B* | *Level of Damage* | *Crops Affected* |
|---|---|---|---|---|
| Warrangal | –305.5 | +17.1 | SEVERE | Cotton, pigeon pea, chilles, sunflower |
| Khammam | –142.0 | +9.2 | SEVERE | Cotton |
| Karimnagar | –321.0 | +29.5 | SEVERE | Cotton, pigeon pea, chilles |
| Rangareddy | –213.5 | +17.1 | SEVERE | Cotton, pigeon pea |
| Mehboobnagar | –250.1 | +18.5 | SEVERE | Cotton, pigeon pea |

***Refinement of Thumb Rule for Forecasting of Helicoverpa armigera for Gulbarga (Karnataka)***

The thumb rule developed earlier to predict the level of population of *Helicoverpa armigera* at Andhra Pradesh was put into validation in chickpea-pigeon pea based ecosystem at Gulbarga, Karnataka using the historical as well as current data. After studying the historical data on monthly rainfall and per cent pod damage of Gulbarga, the thumb rule was fine tuned with one modification. To compute B parameter, the rainfall values of October were taken instead of those of November (Das *et al.*, 2001).

**TABLE 12.2:** A AND B PARAMETERS, PER CENT OF POD DAMAGE BY *Helicoverpa armigera*

| *Year* | *A* | *B* | *Predicted Level of Damage* | *Per cent Pod Damage* | *Actual Level of Damage* |
|---|---|---|---|---|---|
| 1989 | +140.9 | –40.5 | LOW | 25.8 | LOW |
| 1990 | +42.6 | +88.8 | MODERATE | 90.7 | SEVERE |
| 1991 | –232.7 | –63.6 | MODERATE | 43.1 | SEVERE |
| 1992 | –180.5 | +12.6 | SEVERE | 100 | SEVERE |
| 1993 | –156.7 | +96.0 | SEVERE | 71.8 | SEVERE |
| 1994 | –354.7 | +145.4 | SEVERE | 65.3 | SEVERE |
| 1995 | –197.5 | +70.6 | SEVERE | 80.2 | SEVERE |
| 1996 | +9.9 | +36.0 | MODERATE | 54.6 | MODERATE |
| 1997 | –126.0 | +23.2 | SEVERE | 99.6 | SEVERE |
| 1998 | +266.6 | +178.4 | MODERATE | 32.5 | MODERATE |

*Assumption*: LOW = <30%, MODERATE = 30-60% and SEVERE = >60% pod damage.

The thumb-rule for predicting *Helicoverpa armigera* in Deccan Region was validated by using the rainfall data of current season of ten taluks of Gulbarga District, Karnataka. The first forecast was made on 30th September and the final forecast for each taluk was given on 30-10-2001. The expected pest population level during the winter months in pigeon pea crop would be very high in 8 out of ten taluks of Gulbarga. The university authorities were also altered about the impending situations.

### *Forewarning System for Kanpur*

The data collected through pheromone traps during the years 1983 to 1988 at Indian Institute of Pulses Research Farms, Kanpur along with the weather data were analyzed. It was found that the maximum population of *H. armigera* was observed during the year 1983 among the observed years with six conspicuous peaks. The highest adult moths were captured during the 12th standard week. On the other hand, during the year 1988 witnessed negligible population. A very small population peak was again observed during the 12th standard week of 1988. The weather data were analyzed and it was found that a sudden rise in the minimum temperature (>5° C) around 7-8 standard weeks associated with a considerable adult population during the current week and previous weeks triggered a major rise in the population around 11-12 standard weeks. This condition was seen during the year 1983 and may be helpful for development of a forewarning system for *H. armigera* during the chickpea growing seasons at Kanpur and adjoining areas.

### Forecasting Model of Potato Aphid, *Myzus persicae*

Data on aphid population per 100 compound leaves and various weather factors from All India Potato Coordinating Centres, Pant Nagar (U.P), Kalyani (W.B.) and Dessa (Gujarat) for the period 1974-75 to 95-96, 1982-83 to 94-95 and 1985-86 to 94-95 respectively have been processed for the development of potato aphid (*Myzus persicae*) forewarning system.

Various non-linear models were tried to develop a suitable model for a particular week. For that purpose, the aphid population of that week over the years have been taken as dependent variables. For independent variables, two weeks-lagged weather variables have been considered using stepwise regression method.

The non-linear models developed for predicting *Myzus persicae* at Kalyani (W.B.) and Deesa (Gujarat) during January I and II weeks were put in to validation trial for the current potato growing season at their respective locations. The weather parameters (Max., Min. temperatures, Relative Humidity ) during December III and IV week obtained through fax message and the forecasted values of expected aphid population were send to the respective centers by fax. The predicted values were below critical level at both the centers. The forecasts were made two weeks in advance. The actual aphid population observed during January I and II week were obtained and found that they were also below ETL. The predicted and observed aphid population at Kalyani and Deesa were given in Table 12.3 below.

**TABLE 12.3:** FORECASTED AND ACTUAL POPULATION OF *Myzus persicae* AT KALYANI AND DEESA DURING JANUARY 2001.

(per 100 compound leaves)

| *Place* | *January I Week* | | *January II Week* | |
|---|---|---|---|---|
| | *Forecasted* | *Actual* | *Forecasted* | *Actual* |
| Kalyani | 3 | 9 | 17 | 14 |
| Deesa | 11 | 2 | 0 | 4 |

It is revealed from the results that both the forecasted and actual values are showing below critical level values (20 aphids/100 compound leaves selected from 34 plants) and no intervention of pest management was required during the current season. The models show their potential to be incorporated in IPM strategy to combat potato aphids in these locations.

Rainfall has negative correlation with tuber moth development at Ootacamund in Tamil Nadu whereas a significant correlation has observed with sunshine hours at Otacamund and negative correlation at Chikballapur in Karnataka. The population of potato tuber moth showed significant positive correlation with weather parameters for two environmentally different locations. This revealed that the population of the pest dependent on multiple weather parameters (Trivedi *et al.*, 1994).

Life table studies of potato tuber moth for six generations in storage and monitoring of its population in field was done by Trivedi and Rajagopal (1991) & Trivedi *et al.*, 1994 *a, b, c*. It was found that the maximum mortality was in first and second instar larvae due to biotic factors whereas temperature below 10° C and above 35° C affects the egg laying of PTM. The population of PTM is also affected due to heavy rain and large sunny days whereas cloudy and dark days favoured the multiplication. The spatial distribution, relationship with weather was also studied, which may serve as a basic for prediction.

The occurrence, spread, mode of carry over of aphids *Myzus persicae* (Sulzer) on potato in different parts of the country was also studied. (Trivedi and Gadewar 1990, Trivedi and Verma 1990, Trivedi and Saxena (1988).

## REMOTE SENSING AND GIS IN PEST FOREWARNING

The use of remote sensing in agriculture was started with the detection of wilt disease in coconut at Kerala coast. But later, the main emphasis was shifted to crop acreage estimation, crop condition assessment and yield forecasting. Some work has been done on forecasting of locusts (*Schistacirca gregaria*) at Regional Remote Sensing Service Centre Jodhpur. The locusts use to oviposit in the sandy desert where moisture is present in the soil. The satellite detection of moist sand as breeding ground and the amount of green vegetation as food in the desert give the possible amount of locust population. The migration of locusts is forecasted using the wind direction.

In case of disease forecasting, it is believed to be possible by remote sensing as the disease inoculated plants increase reflectance particularly in chlorophyll absorption band (0.5-0.7 μm) and water absorption bands (1.45 and 1.95 μm). But the research in this direction is scanty. However, the disease severity assessment and yield loss estimation using changed reflectance pattern of diseased plants were reported by Kanemasu *et al.* (1974). The greenness vegetation index derived from LANDSAT MSS digital data in the four bands has been successfully used to distinguish between diseased wheat in the Pakistan Punjab and the healthy wheat in the Indian Punjab (Nagarajan *et al.*, 1984).

GIS is another tool which can be used effectively for mapping geographical distribution of pests, delineating the hotspot zones. Superimposition with causative abiotic and biotic factors on visual pest maps can be useful for pest forecasting purpose. District wise geographical distribution maps of rice and cotton pests have been prepared at NCIPM (Puri *et al.*, 1997, Kanojia *et al.*, 2001, 2002).

## INFORMATION TECHNOLOGY

The recent advancements made in Information Technology particularly in communication and computing will be highly useful in successful implementation of forecasting models. Different stations can be interconnected with one another and can share the data. The pest forecasting models can be directly used by users with the help of Internet and alongwith the forecast, proper pest management options can be given to all. Moreover, as the costs are coming down, Information Technology would form the essential component of any pest forewarning system.

## ROLE OF OTHER AGENCIES

The pest forewarning system can be improved by linking it with weather forecasting and field level validation. NCMRWF (National Centre for Medium Range Weather Forecasting) is issuing weather forecast 5 days in advance and expected to issue it 7 days in advnace shortly. With the help of this forecasts farmers are advised for different farm operations like, sowing, transplanting, irrigating, harvesting of crops. Advice on plant protection measures are very meagre. This Agro advisory service could be improved, if it can forecast the time of pest attack, its ETL (level of population causes economic loss) value for taking pest management practices. Spraying operation should be done according to forecasted rainfall and wind information.

## LIMITATIONS

The approach for early warning has to be achieved by regular monitoring of pest, weather and crop phenology which is a difficult task. It is location specific and accuracy of the data is must. The validation of the models should be done at a larger area after fine tuning the models. The expertise has to be developed. Also suitable sampling techniques should be developed for counting the pest population.

## CONCLUSIONS

In the present scenario of pest resistance to pesticides, resurgence and high cost of pesticides, emphasis on conservation of natural enemies is of great concern. Therefore, it is mandatory requirement to develop early warning system to provide caution to the farmers regarding the occurrence of pest, peak activity and migration. This will be helpful in developing sustainable pest management system which may be economically viable and socially acceptable. Further, it must be interdisciplinary and participatory approach to achieve long term benefits.

The initiation has been taken up by the ICAR to start NATP Mission Mode Project on Development of Weather Based Forewarning System for Crop Pests and Diseases in cotton, sugarcane, rice, pigeon pea groundnut and mustard.

## REFERENCES

Das, D. K., Trivedi, T. P. and Srivastava, C. P. 2001. Simple rule to predict attack of *Helicoverpa armigera* on crops growing in Andhra Pradesh. *Indian J. Agr. Sci.*, **71**(6): 421-423.

Das, D. K., Trivedi, T. P., Singh, Joginder and Dhandapani, A. 2000. Weather based prediction model of *Helicoverpa armigera* for Integrated Pest Management in cotton-chickpea based agro-ecosystem of Punjab. Paper presented in International Conference on Managing Natural Resources for Sustainable Agricultural Production in the 21st Century. Voluntary Papers-Natural Resources, Vol. 2, February 14-18, 2000, New Delhi, pp. 621-622.

Das, D. K., Yelshetty, Suhas, Trivedi, T. P. and Dhandapani, A. 2001. Refinement and validation of prediction system of *Helicoverpa armigera* at Gulbarga Karnataka. Paper presented in the National Symposium on Plant Protection Strategies for Sustainable Agri-Horticulture. S K University of Agricultural Sciences and Technology. October 12-13, 2001. R S Pura Jammu.

Kanemasu-ET, Schimmelphenning-H, Chin Choy-E, Eversmayer-MG and Lenhart-D. 1974. ERTS-1 Data collection systems used to predict wheat disease severity. *Remote Sensing of Environ.*, **3**: 93-97.

Kanojia, A. K., Singh, R. V. Surender Kumar and Trivedi, T. P. 2001. Geographic information system in IPM: A millenium perspective. *In*: D. Prasad and S. N. Puri (eds.), *Crop Pest amd Disease Management: Challenges for the Millenium.* Ashok Computers, New Delhi.

Kanojia, A. K., Surender Kumar, Prameela Devi, T., Trivedi, T. P., Singh, Amerika, Sundarsarma, K. S., Natrajan, K. and Pawar, A. D. 2002. Distribution maps of insect pests and diseases of cotton crop in India. National Center for Integrated Pest Management, New Delhi. p. 97.

Nagarajan, S. and Singh, H. 1975. Indian stem rust rules—an epidemiological concept on the spread of stem rust of wheat. *Plant Disease Reporter*, **59**: 133-136.

Puri, S. N., Banerjee, T., Baranwal, V. K., Surender Kumar and Sundersarma, K. S. 1997. Distribution maps of insect pests and diseases of rice crop in India. Tech. Bull. National Centre for Integrated Pest Management, New Delhi.

Trivedi, T. P. and Saxena, A. P. 1988. *Aphidius colemani Viereck parasitoid* of *Myzus persicae* Sulzer on potato in Karnataka. *Indian J. Plant Prot.*, **16**: 75-77.

Trivedi, T. P. 1989. Monitoring of potato tuber moth *Phthorimaea operculella* in Karnataka, Mysore. *J. Agric. Sc.*, **23**: 177-180.

Trivedi, T. P. and Verma, K. D. 1990. Population trend of *Myzus persicae* (Sulzer) on different stages of potato crop in Karnataka. *J. Indian Potato Assoc.*, **17**: 65-66.

Trivedi,, T. P. and Gadewar, A. V. 1990. A survey of aphids on potato in Karnataka, Mysore. *J. Agric. Sci.*, **24**: 342-348.

Trivedi, T. P. and Rajagopal, D. 1991. Effect of different temperatures on the development, longevity and fecundity of potato tuber moth. *J. Appl. Zool. Res.*, **2**(1): 43-46.

Trivedi, T. P., Rajagopal, D. and Tandon, P. L. 1994. Environmental correlates of the potato tuber moth *Phthorimaea operculella* (Zeller). *International Journal of Pest Management*, **40**(4): 305-308.

Trivedi, T. P., Rajagopal, D. and Tandon, P. L. 1994. Spatial distribution and sampling of the potato tuber moth. *Phthormaea operculella* (Zeller). *Ann. Enotmol.*, **12**(1): 69-76.

Trivedi, T. P., Rajagopa, D. and Tandon, P. L. 1994. Life Table for establishment of potato tuber moth *Phthorimaea operculella. J. Indian Potato Assoc.*, **21**(1-2): 97-105.

Trivedi, T. P., Puri, S. N., Paul Khurana, S. M., Bhar, L. M. Mehta, S. C., Jain, R. C. and Singh, G. 1998a. Development of forewarning system of aphids. National Seminar on Entomology in 21st Century. April 30-May 2, 1998. Udaipur.

Trivedi T. P., Paul Khurana, S. M., Puri, S. N., Bhar, L. M., Mehta, S. C., Jain, R. C., Singh, G., Choudhary, S. M. and Mohasin, M. 2000. Non-linear models forewarning aphid *Myzus persicae* on potato. *In*: S. M. Paul Khurana (ed.), *Potato Global Research and Development*, Vol. 1. IPA, CPRI, Shimla, India. pp. 472-476.

Trivedi, T. P. 2001. Ecological approaches in integrated pest management. *In*: D. Prasad and S. N. Puri (eds.), *Crop Pest and Disease Management: Challenges for the Millenium.* Ashok Computers, New Delhi.

Trivedi, T. P., Das, D. K. and Dhandapani, A. 2001a. Status of early warning systems in Integrated Pest Management. Plant Protection: New Horizons. (eds.), Bharadwaj S. C. *et.al.* Maharana Pradap University of Agriculture and Technology, Udaipur, India, pp. 20-30.

Trivedi T. P., Paul Khurana, S. M., Puri, S. N., Bhar, L. M., Mehta, S. C., Jain, R. C., Singh, G., Choudhary, S. M., Mohasin, M., Dhandapani, A. and Chona Naveen 2002. Development of forewarning system of aphid *Myzus persicae* (Sulzer) on potato (*Solanum tuberosum*) in India. *Indian J. Agr. Sci.*, **72**(6): 315-19.

Van Everdingen, E. 1926. Het verband de wears gesterdheid ende aardappelzeiekte (*Phytophthora infestans*). *Tijdschr. Plantennziekten.*, **32**: 129-140.

# Disease Forewarning—A Component of IPM System

**A. K. Sharma, M. S. Saharan and J. Kumar**

## INTRODUCTION

Integrated Pest Management (IPM) is a system for accomplishing a specific goal of minimizing the impact of pests by using a variety of procedures and attempting to decrease the overall chemical input into the environment. It is composed of a number of steps: identifying the pest and its life history, establishing economic injury levels, monitoring, scouting and modeling populations, applying management tactics and assessing the success of the programme. As with any system, IPM is influenced by the development of new technology. The degree of the influence depends on how much the technology affects the component steps of the system. Many of the steps in IPM depend heavily on accurate and timely information. Prediction of a plant disease epidemic can promote judicious use of pesticides, agricultural productivity and returns to the management. Disease forecasting allows the prediction of probable outbreaks of disease and therefore, we can decide whether, when and where a particular management practice should be used more effectively. Forecasting involves all the activities in ascertaining and notifying the farmers in a community that conditions are sufficiently favourable for certain diseases that application of control measures will result in economic gain or that the amount of disease expected is unlikely to be enough to justify the expenditure of time, energy and money for control. Generally, farmers need forecasts that can help in decision making for preparing and taking management measures.

In fact, every rational person indulges in prediction or forecasting not only in agriculture but in other spheres of life also. Similarly, every rational farmer needs forecasts on his crops, crop health and the production. When it comes to pest management, he tries to balance three factors—risk, cost and benefit (Kranz and Holz, 1993). Thus forecasting is important in agriculture. Forecasts give rise warning, which means, there is an addressee. Hence, forecasting is intelligence, while warning essentially is the communication, which includes skills beyond the normal aspects of plant protection.

Forecasts are not only to be related to spray scheduling alone. It can forecast, (*i*) whether or not a certain pest/disease will exceed the damage threshold in coming season, (*ii*) first date at which the control threshold will be reached, (*iii*) necessity of the control measures, (*iv*) determination of risk periods, (*v*) crop losses, and (*vi*) the breakdown of resistance in host crop, arrival of new races/pathotypes of pathogens and the need for research for newer resistance genes, etc.

*Directorate of Wheat Research, P.B. No. 158, Agarsain Rd. Karnal (Haryana). 132 001.*

Key elements of a successful forecasting system include accurate prediction for multiple and economically important plant diseases, timely and understandable communication and cost effective remedies. Most existing forecasters are devoted to high value crops because of the reward and savings for effective disease management in those cropping systems. Many of these systems consist of self-contained computer programs and environment. For developing a plant disease forecast, several characteristics of pathogen, host and weather are taken into account. Forecasting is actually "epidemiology applied with courage" or with tact and experience, to satisfy risk aversion of farmers and crop protection staff. In general, for most monocyclic diseases such as root rot diseases and for few polycyclic diseases like apple scab, disease development may be predicted by assessing the amount of initial inoculum. For polycyclic diseases like late blight of potato, disease development can be predicted by assessing the rate of occurrence of the infection cycles. Weather based forecasting systems have been developed for a number of plant diseases (Campbell and Madden, 1990). However, existing forecasters have received only limited acceptance by growers due to scientific and physiological constraints. Among the potential constraints, unacceptable inaccuracy of disease forecasting information and time taken in the information delivery and leftover little action time are the major scientific constraints. Recent progress in weather monitoring and information technologies provide a great opportunity to improve accuracy of forecasting information and quick information delivery. Monitoring of weather conditions within the plant canopy is possible by automated weather stations. Real time weather data can be transmitted from automated weather stations at remote sites to personal computers via telephone, modems or by radio telemetry. The disease forecasting information based on the real time weather data can be delivered immediately to the public via the world wide web. Following are some requirements for practical gain from forecasting:

(1) The disease causes economically significant loss both in terms of quality and quantity of the agricultural produce in the concerned area.
(2) The disease onset, spread and epidemic level is highly dependant on weather variables.
(3) Farmers follow the advice of control measures when required.
(4) Information on weather-disease relationships is fully known.

## APPROACHES OF FORECASTING PLANT DISEASES

Two types of forecasting, *viz.*, short term and long term, are possible if sufficient data on weather, host and pathogen is available. Prediction of disease during the crop season or just before the crop season is called "short term" forecasting while the prediction of disease made years in advance, is called long term forecasting. It is often difficult to detect small populations of most pathogens in the absence of highly susceptible host. Inoculum of soil borne fungi are estimated by extraction from the soil. Airborne fungal spores are estimated by trapping in various devices. It is easier to assess the amount of inoculum present by measuring the number of infections produced on a host within a certain period of time. In some diseases, there is an incubation period during which the host is infected but shows no symptoms. Several plant diseases are forecasted by using the criterion of the amount of initial inoculum e.g., stewart wilt of corn caused by the bacterium *Erwinia stewarti* is predicted by survival percentage of corn flea beetle because bacterium survives the winter in the bodies of the insect. Corn flea beetle is killed by prolonged low temperatures. Therefore, if sum of the mean temperatures for three months from December to January at a given location is less than –1° C, then most of the vectors get killed. So under such situation, there will be no bacterial wilt. Likewise other diseases (downy mildew of tobacco, root rot of pea and fire blight of apple and pear) are also predicted on the basis of initial inoculum assessment. By detecting per cent infected or contaminated seeds in random samples and on the basis of extent of infected seeds, rough estimate of infection of a disease can be made in an area. Primary inoculum of loose smut of wheat, ergot of rye or bajra and ear cockle of wheat can be detected in seed lots by different methods and necessary warnings can be made for use of such seed. However, this type of forecast is of minor importance. Most of the diseases in which forecasting service has helped the farmers are late blight of potato (*Phytophthora infestans* (Mont.)de Bary), blast of rice (*Pyricularia oryzae* Cav.), stripe rust of wheat (*Puccinia striiformis* Westend.) leaf rust of wheat (*Puccinia recondita* Rob.ex Desm.), downy mildew of grapevines (*Plasmopara viticola* Berl and deT.) and apple scab (*Venturia inaequalis*).

## QUANTIFICATION OF DISEASES AND MODELING

Quantitative disease prediction is possible through models and simulations, etc., based on the conceptual concepts. Changes in cultural practices and cropping pattern are of great significance to plant diseases, where in minor pathogen may become a major one and the vice versa. A model is a concise way of representing any system and perception of the reality in a symbolic and simplified form (Campbell *et al.*, 1988). Modeling is a method of representing a system and of summarizing information. Model can also be considered as an instrument or a tool to think, analyze and reason the cause and effect. Models can be quantitative or qualitative. A plant disease model is a mathematical description of the interaction between environment, host and pathogen variables that can result in disease. A model can be presented as a simple rule, an equation, a graph or a table. The output of a model can be a numerical index of disease risk, predicted disease incidence or severity or predicted inoculum development. Kranz (1974) defined model as a verbal statement, a hypothesis, theory or law. Prediction models for forecasting diseases can be made by following approaches.

### Geophytopathological Models

These models involve disease prevalence or severity, space and time. Such models condense years of information and present it in a comprehensive way. The CAB (Commonwealth Agricultural Bureaux)/CMI (Commonweath Mycological Institute) has published a series of world maps showing the distribution of different plant diseases and their intensities.

### Bioclimatic Models

Weather is an important parameter that influences disease development. In the disease triangle, when the susceptible host and virulent pathogen coincide, weather is the only variable that influences epidemic development. Empirical prediction models can be developed by relating weather parameters and disease development. Environmental monitoring has been used to forecast infection periods for plant diseases.

### Late Blight Prediction Model

The potato late blight fungus, *Phytophthora infestans* is known to have one of the highest reproductive rates known for plant diseases. It was the cause of the Irish potato famine. Under favourable weather conditions and in the absence of proper control, it can destroy a field of potatoes in three weeks. A new Mexicon strain of the fungus reached Minnesota in 1995, having resistance against majority of previously used systemic fungicides. Due to its devastating effects and effective fungicides control methods, it is one of those diseases on which forecasting has been tried since long in Britain, Europe and USA (Miller and O'Brien, 1957). In Holland, Van Everdingen (1926) evolved Dutch rules by evaluating several weather parameters which influence *Phytophthora infestans* causing late blight of potato. The Dutch rules are:

1. At night there should be atleast 4 hours of dew
2. Minimum temperature of 10° C or slightly below should prevail
3. Next day, mean cloudiness should be 0.8 or more and
4. Rainfall during the next 24 hours should be at least 0.1 mm.

In Netherlands, control measures are recommended if all above conditions are satisfied under field conditions for a few days. The Dutch rules were modified in many countries with some modifications but the central theme in all these approaches remain unchanged. In the United States, two systems of forecasting were developed by Hyre (1954) and Wallin (1962). The Hyre's system is based on daily rainfall and maximum and minimum temperatures. In Wallin's system, blight forecast is based on temperature and relative humidity. These both systems were used in USA for two decades but they were not widely accepted by the farmers. This led to the development of a computerized programme called 'blitecast' which combines both above systems and provides to the farmers, a late blight control programme tailored to their local conditions.

### Apple Scab Prediction Model

Apple scab caused by *Venturia inaequalis* is one of the major diseases in the Himalayan region of India and Pakistan where the crop is grown. The mycelia overwinter inside the infected plant debris or apple twig. During cold days, the asci present in these dead and decaying plant parts gradually mature and favoured by the early spring rain, release the ascospores. The released windborne ascospores spores get concentrated inside the infected orchard and may reach a concentration of a few thousand spores per cubic metre of air and incite the disease. These ascospores spread little during the first hour of spore discharge. Spore release reaches at maximum after eight hours of sporulation and the released spores are spread by wind turbulence to considerable distances. Ascospores need certain favourable conditions to cause infections on first leaves of apple. Based on two weather parameters by considering that the availability of inoculum is in plenty, the scab severity is predicted by taking into consideration number of hours of leaf wetness and temperature. Mills (1944) monitored air temperature and leaf wetness in order to predict infection periods for the apple scab pathogens *Venturia inaequalis*. Mills (1944) found that when leaf wetness period (hours) multiplied by the then temperature (° C) exceeds 140, then infections are expected. However, this approach is applicable only when mean temperature is 25° C. Jones *et al.* (1980) developed a computerized system to monitor environmental conditions and predict apple scab infection periods based on local conditions.

### *Prediction of Stem Rust in Wheat*

The Indian stem rust rules (Nagarajan and Singh, 1975) is an example of a climatic model. It explains the weather situations that favour the long distance dispersal and deposition of uredospores of *Puccinia graminis tritici* under Indian conditions. They have successfully developed an empirical method for predicting the stem rust appearance. Following steps were taken into consideration for stem rust prediction methods:

1. Rains during November in Central India coupled with southern winds
2. Uredospores presence in rain
3. Check if the Indian stem rust rules are satisfied
4. Weather over the area of uredospore deposition
5. Viability of uredospores

(6) Check if ground conditions are favourable for infection or not.

If all above conditions are satisfied, then infection could occur in 25 to 30 days at locations close to where the cyclone dissipated. Once infections have occurred in Central India, their further spread can be predicted following same rules with deletions of step 1 and 3. Further spread occurs to the east and north India from these established foci. More the number of foci greater the chances of epidemic development. A procedure for predicting the stem rust appearance 30 days in advance has been developed, verified and field evaluated. It is possible now to forecast exactly when and where in Central India, stem rust would appear. The linear model based on artificial field epiphytotics has been developed by Nagarajan and Joshi (1980a). Following the equation given below the disease severities can be predicted seven days in advance.

$$Y = -29.3733 + 1.820\,X1 + 1.7735\,X2 + 0.2516\,X3,$$ where

Y = expected disease severity of seven days

X1 = present level of disease severity

X2 = mean maximum temperature expected for the next 7 days

X3 = mean maximum RH expected in the next 7 days

−29.3733 = constant

### *Prediction of Brown Rust of Wheat in North India*

Nagarajan and Joshi (1980b) developed a bioclimatic approach for predicting brown rust of wheat in North India. In this approach the level of initial inoculum established at a particular time is evaluated. Expecting that the subsequent weather will be favourable for disease development, predictions are made. The following steps form the bioclimatic approach for predicting brown rust.

1. Wheat crop survey should be carried from 15 to 20th January by observing 5 to 6 infection sites at a minimum distance of 25 ± 5 km in North India
2. Amount and number of rainy days during January to mid April over Northwest India should be two times the normal.
3. Weekly mean maximum temperature during March to mid-April should be normal ±1° C.

If susceptible wheat varieties are sown in Indo-Gangetic plains and 1th and 2nd steps are satisfied then severe epidemic would occur. Chester (1942) could make a successful forecasts to predict wheat leaf rust severity in Oklahoma, USA. The warning is issued on 1st April every year based on:

1. Weather on April 1
2. Primary inoculum
3. Weather from December to March
4. Rust intensity on 1st April is the major factor for determining the terminal severity.

### *Disease Prediction Approaches for Karnal Bunt of Wheat*

Attempts to develop a bio-meteorological model to predict KB were not successful in the initial stages because the mean weather of a long period (a month or so) was correlated with KB (Karnal bunt) severity (Aujla *et al.*, 1977; Singh *et al.*, 1990). Nagarajan (1991) overcame this problem by using weather parameters for a much shorter period. The Karnal bunt prediction models for India and Mexico developed by him using multilocation weather and KB data, spanning over more than a decade was better than the previous efforts. Starting from January, weekly mean data on rainy days, amount of rainfall, maximum and minimum RH and temperature was regressed having KB severity as the dependent variable. The multiple regression analysis (MRA) backed by ANOVA, identified the reliable parameters for linear disease prediction. The MRA had an r-value of 0.9 for Indian situations and Mexican conditions. The essential independent variables identified were the same for both the situations except for the time when they were to occur. Their correlation was situation dependent. The Mexican model was field validated for a year and was within the acceptable level of error. Following the disease prediction model explained in the widely circulated report of Nagarajan (1991), several groups established a relationship between weekly weather conditions during flowering or earhead emergence stage with KB (Mavi *et al.*, 1992; Jhorar, *et al.*, 1992; Singh, *et al.*, 1996).

Many of them are yet to be field validated for their reliability in predicting KB. Mavi and co workers used 19 years of weather data from the weather observatory located at the Punjab Agricultural University, Ludhiana, to develop a prediction model. Number of rainy days for the 9th and 10th standard meteorological week (SMW) were positively correlated with KB, whereas sunshine durations for the 9th SMW were negatively correlated. Jhorar *et al.*, (1992) fitted a log-linear function and obtained a high correlation between disease intensity, and both average daily maximum temperature (R = 0.91) and average daily relative humidity (R = 0.93).

Survival of *T. indica* Mitra and the damage there from depends upon the environmental conditions. Interestingly, there is no report of KB occurrence from any of the locations/countries having a temperate climate (USDA, 1997). A comparison of meteorological information of KB infested and non-infested regions of the world indicates that KB has little potential for long-term establishment in the cold temperate climates of the world. The potential for *T. indica* to survive and infect wheat is restricted less by physical requirements for survival of the teliospore than by synchronization of wheat heading with climatic conditions favorable for teliospore germination, secondary sporidial multiplication, penetration and infection. The recent European Plant Protection Organization (EPPO) fact sheet on KB considers temperate and cool areas of western and northern Europe to be at risk for establishment of KB (Smith *et al.*, 1992), although this statement has not been supported with any scientific evidence. Royer and Rytter (1985) considered that because the pathogen is the most severe in those parts of India where cool temperatures (i.e.~ 15° C), high humidity and rainfall prevail, then the summer rainfall and irrigated wheat areas of the Pacific northwestern United States may be at some risk for KB establishment.

While evaluating the environmental risk for KB to occur in Pacific Northwest, Smiley (1997) defined the minimal climatic and plant growth requirements for KB to occur. It was assumed that measurable rain (>3 mm) has to occur on each of two or more successive days, at least 10 mm must be collected within the 2 day interval, and average daily relative humidity above the plant canopy must exceed 70% during both days. Temperature was not a limiting factor because during wheat heading stage the Pacific Northwest always had KB optimum maximum (16 to 26° C) and minimum (7 to 11° C) temperatures. The vast sprinkler irrigated regions of the Pacific Northwest, he surmised, appears to have a higher risk for infection of wheat by *T. indica* than the unirrigated regions (Smiley, 1997). At least 25 countries, including the Russian Federation and Independent Republics, as well as China have put *T. indica* in their quarantine pest list. Russia and China are the two largest wheat importers, and these countries could prohibit wheat from countries having the disease. Since the widely publicised KB disease can act as a non-tarrif barrier in world trade, it has become necessary to put in place a scientifically sound, transparent and acceptable PRA. A computer software has been developed to evaluate the probability of risk of KB (Nagarajan, 2002). It has three parts, "GEOKB", "KBRISK" and "KBSIM" and can predict the probability of occurrence of the disease (KB) in a particular region. It can indicate the disease prone and non-disease prone regions based on various climatological and other factors. The spread of KB to different ecological zones on the Indian subcontinent and its appearance in other geographical areas of the world has been the logic behind the argument (Zhang *et al.*, 1984) that the pathogen possesses great adaptability to different climatic conditions. But in fact, in India KB is confined to the places where it was earlier known to occur in 1970s and has simply not spread to the wheat areas south of Narmada river or to places above the snow line in the Himalayas or to the arid desert of western Rajasthan.

A wheat disease forecasting system for predicting tan spot, leaf blotch, leaf rust and head scab in North Dakota and Minnesota began in 1999. The system composed of regional environmental and airborne fungal spore data, computer and rule based models to predict disease, compilation of results and two methods of information delivery. Tan spot and leaf blotch infection period models were developed from data on healthy potted wheat plants placed in a field environment for 24 hours (Francl, 1995). Leaf infections within this period were predicted with accuracies of more than 80 per cent by back propagation neural network models (De Wolf and Francl, 2000). Model inputs were cumulative growing degree days, daily average temperature and relative humidity, total daily precipitation and wetness hours. The Neural networks (Francl ) play a role in forecasting important wheat diseases.

### *Prediction of Rice Blast*

Rice blast caused by *Pyricularia oryzae* is one of the most important diseases of rice in various parts of the world. Lot of information has been generated on various aspects of crop health and forecasting over the years all over the world. In India, Muralidharan and Venkatarao (1987) developed rice blast outbreak rules with which early warnings can be issued to farmers.

For leaf blast outbreak:

1. Moderate to high incidence of leaf blast in trap nurseries with any locally susceptible cultivar, sown at weekly intervals
2. Continued prevalence of low night temperatures (< 20° C) coupled with high relative humidity (> 90 %) for 7 to 10 days or cloudiness, dew or light drizzle

For neck blast outbreak:

1. A low to moderate leaf blast incidence on crop during tillering stage or atleast in trap nurseries
2. Low night temperatures (< 20° C) during panicle initiation to flowering stage or cloudiness, dewfall or light drizzle during the reproductive phase.

### *Blue Mold of Tobacco and Cucurbit Downy Mildew Prediction*

The North American Plant Disease Forecast Centre (NAPDFC) located at North Carolina State University in Raleigh, NC, provides continent wide internet forecasting support to tobacco and cucurbit growers by tracking the geographic presence and future spread of downy mildew pathogens. The two classical diseases forecasted are: tobacco blue mold (Main and Spurr, 1990) and cucurbit downy mildew (Thomas, 1996). During cool, wet and cloudy weather, large number of asexually produced sporangiospores (conidia) by both pathogens are aerially transported to long distances in the atmospheric boundary layer (Yao *et al.*, 1997). Using the principles and modern methods of aerobiology and biometeorology, the spatial and temporal pathways these spores travel in ABL can be forecasted and the future temporal and spatial spread of the epidemics can be predicted. Biological and environmental factors are used to assess the risk of new distant outbreaks. The principle differences between the NAPDFC forecasting system and previous forecasting system are:

1. Aerial transport of spores inciting new outbreaks are involved
2. The system addresses spore transport and weather on a macroscale involving the entire North American continent.

Blue mold of tobacco also known as *milidiou du tabac* in Europe caused by *Peronospora tabacina* Adam, is a classical disease that develops locally as well as causes macroscale epidemics (Davis *et al.*, 1985). The fungus is highly weather sensitive. During periods of cool, wet and overcast weather, the disease can develop and spread rapidly due to polycyclic nature of the pathogen. When the weather becomes clear, dry and hot, the epidemic usually slows considerably or stops completely. Epidemics of downy mildew of cucurbits caused by *Pseudoperonospora cubensis* resemble with tobacco blue mold in many respects.

## CROP HEALTH MONITORING AND PEST FORECASTS

Crop health monitoring and surveillance activities help in identifying crop health problems early enough so that timely management measures can be undertaken to keep the pest at the lowest level or to have the information that the pests may not warrant intensive crop protection measures. Pest surveillance is the monitoring of the incidence and density of pests of crop, damage sustained and other relevant information about the crop and or pests. Surveillance is the backbone of supervised and integrated pest management as it is the basis of all contingency decisions in crop protection. The current use of surveillance aims primarily at more efficient timing of pesticide application. Some of the successfully implemented surveillance systems have been given hereunder:

### Cooperative Crop Monitoring System (CCMS)

This was developed at Michigan State University in USA during early eighties (Mispagel *et al.*, 1983). It covered diseases, insect-pests, nematodes, vertebrates and weeds of field crops, fruit crops, nursery diseases, vegetables and forest crops. It also provided special service on determination of unknown pests. Transmission of recommendations was done through reports, tables and maps in newsletters like Pest Alert, extension service and other means.

### Pest Management Executive System (PMES)

Pest Management Executive System was developed during the same period by the Michigan State University. This is a computer based data acquisition/information delivery system which was designed with an open structure and for handling of large data sets. Four simulation models are accessible via PMEX. WEEVILCOST is a simple cost benefit model to decide about the benefit of a chemical control of alfalfa weevil.

### Computer-aided Monitoring of Pests/Diseases of Crop Stands—The GDR (East Germany) Model

It was practiced in the erstwhile German Democratic Republic, *i.e.* the East Germany (Spaar and Ebert, 1985). In this system, the sampling was done by the extension workers and the data was transmitted by mail, telephone and telex. Verification, filing and evaluation of data was done by the computer-aided simulation models as well as through traditional handling. The recommendations, based on prediction, were transmitted through mail, telephone, telex, newsletters, leaflets, extension services, etc. This model can be characterized as a highly centralized system with high input of human labour and major emphasis on the surveillance work of high quality. In the later stages, the installation of computer-aided decision making tools on decentralized computers was attempted. However, the programme was shelved when political changes took place in Germany in 1989 (Kranz and Holz, 1993). 'BLITE CAST' is also a part of PMEX, which delivers short term, highly reliable forecasts of potato late blight

### Crop Health Monitoring in India

The Directorate of Plant Protection, Quarantine and Storage (GOI) Faridabad has a well developed network of doing surveys for monitoring the pest situation in various crops in the country. Regular roving surveys are done by this Directorate in various parts of the country through well trained staff, located in its different regional/zonal offices. Major emphasis is laid on the occurrence and severity of various pests in different crops. The information is compiled and distributed in the form a Newsletter. The purpose of these surveys is to monitor the best situation in India. It covers various food crops, but not much emphasis is laid on prediction or forecasting. Also wheat is not dealt in detail.

#### *Wheat Crop Health Monitoring System (WCHMS) in India*

A well developed survey and surveillance programme is in operation in wheat under the All India Coordinated Wheat and Barley Improvement Project. Information on occurrence of pests, especially the diseases like rusts is generated through mobile surveys by various cooperating centers and the Directorate of Wheat Research, and the Trap Plot Nurseries planted throughout the country. For regional monitoring, SAARC Disease Trap Nursery is planted in India and the neighbouring countries. This information is disseminated through monthly "Wheat Crop Health Newsletter" issued by the Crop Protection Programme of the DWR, Karnal. This newsletter is also available on website: http://personal.vsnl.com/dwrweb/ for easy access by those interested in wheat health. The purpose or object of the programme is to monitor the occurrence of various pests, especially the rusts, and surveillance for the occurrence or introduction of new pathotypes/races that may become an issue in future. Hence, it is more for the purposes of strategy planning and preparedness for future. The pathotype analysis of rusts is done by the Directorate of Wheat Research at its regional station, Flowerdale, Shimla. This laboratory is well equipped with facilities required for such investigations. This facility is, perhaps, unique in its kind and the best available in South-East Asia. Because of this approach, the breeding for disease (rust) resistance programme in India is on a firm footing and is the back-bone of Indian agriculture.

Monitoring of wheat crop health during the crop season is done by the cooperating centres of AICW&BIP and DWR, Karnal, as mentioned above, through mobile or roving surveys and the Disease Trap Nurseries. Special teams of wheat pathologists travel several thousand kilometers in the most vulnerable zone, *i.e.* the states of Punjab, Haryana, parts of Jammu and Kashmir, Himachal Pradesh, Western UP and Rajasthan for surveillance of yellow rust. The flow chart of information is depicted in Fig. 13.1.

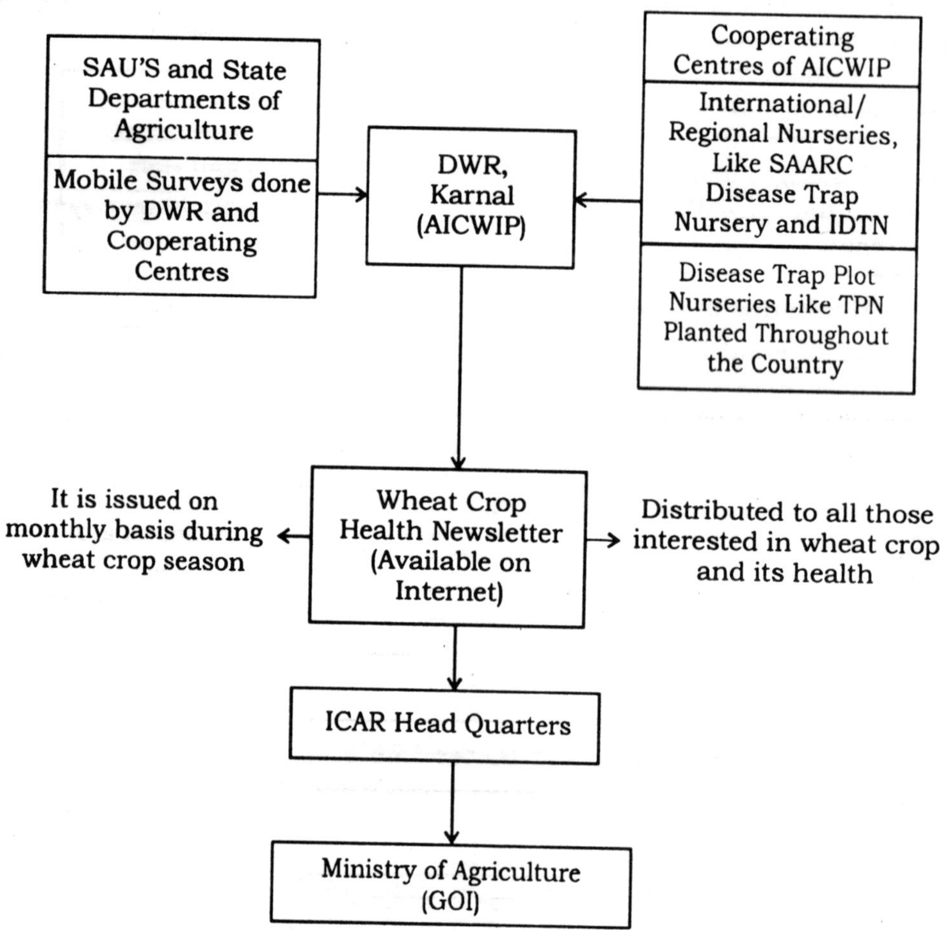


**Fig. 13.1:** Wheat crop health survey and surveillance programme under AICWIP

## Remote Sensing and Crop Surveillance

Remote sensing has been extensively used in disaster and cyclone warning as well as to find out the land use, crop identification and preparing inventory, etc. At present, in India, considerable information has been generated on the use of space-borne remote sensing data for developing yield prediction models in pre-harvest forecasts in wheat, rice, cotton, mustard and groundnut through projects like CAPE (Crop Acerage and Prediction Estimation). Recently, a more precise programme FASAL (Forecasting Agricultural output using Space, Agrometeorology and land based observations) has been developed by the Department of Agriculture and Cooperation (DAC), Ministry of Agriculture (MOA) jointly with Indian Space Research Organization (ISRO) for implementation in near future (Navalgund, 2002). The remote sensing can be used as an additional tool in crop health monitoring. However, the ground truth has to be correlated for reaching a meaningful conclusion. It may not be possible to make prediction on pests in most of the cases, since by the time, the remote sensing sensors pick up the change in colour or canopy of the crop, sufficient damage has already been done. But it can definitely indicate the pests and can help in taking preventive measures in unaffected areas.

## SIMULATIONS

In recent years, information and communication technologies have revolutionized the society. The so-called knowledge community has already influenced markets. As a user, it is difficult to keep track of these fast ongoing changes because information technology has changed completely, the way of handling information. In Plant Pathology, there is an incredible pace of change but the benefits are enormous (Scott, 1997). In field of Plant Pathology, major advantages of Information Technology can be predicted by diagnosis, pest risk assessment, forecasting or alerting the services (Kraska, 1999). Simulation means use of a model under specific set of conditions. The availability of computers has allowed Plant Pathologists to write programs that allow simulation of epidemics of several plant diseases. Simulations with computer is called computer simulation. Simulation models are dynamic as they consider time and reveal epidemic behaviour. Simulation is an art and science of constructing composite models and mimicking one system with another. The first computer based simulator of plant diseases is the EPIDEM (Waggoner and Horsfall, 1969) and EPIMAY (Waggoner *et al.*, 1972). Models to understand the spatial spread of diseases were subsequently developed such as EPIMUL (Kampmeijer and Zadoks, 1977). EPIDEM employed a number of weather factors, viz., temperature, relative humidity, wind speed, sunshine and wetness for predicting early blight of tomato and potato caused by *Alternaria solani* (Ellis and Martin) Jones and Grout. The disease is complex, requiring different optimum weather conditions during the life cycle of pathgen. Waggoner *et al.* (1972) developed a model EPIMAY for southern corn leaf blight caused by *Helminthosporium maydis*. This disease caused heavy losses in the USA in 1970. Similarity between two models is due to the similarity in the life history of two pathogens. Shrum (1975) developed a model EPIDEMIC for stimulating the growth of stripe rust of wheat caused by *Puccinia striiformis*. Kampmeijer and Zadoks (1977) and Zadoks and Kampmeijer (1977) made attempt to model disease epidemics on a time and space scale and developed a model, EPIMUL.

Epidemics Prediction and Prevention (EPIPRE) was developed by Zadoks (1984) and modified over a period of time in the Netherlands by various workers. Creation of this supervising system started in 1977 at the Agricultural University Wagenmgen promoted by the heavy epidemics of stripe rust of wheat caused by *Puccinia striiformis* in 1975 and 1977. This programme envisages the data recording by the farmers, data transmission through telephone or mail and data analysis and verification through computer and transmission of recommendations through mail or telephone (Fig. 13.2). This is perhaps, one of the most successful programme of this type. EPIPRE first started with *Puccinia striiformis,* but later on its use was extended to other wheat diseases such as *P. recondita, Erysiphe graminis* DC., *Septoria nodorum* (Berk) Berk., *S. tritici* Rob. (Zadoks, 1984). Subsequently, computerized predictive systems have been developed for epidemics of several other diseases, for example CERCOS for *Cercospora* blight of celery, MYCOS for *Mycosphaerella* blight of chrysanthemums, EPICORN for southern corn leaf blight caused by *Helminthosporium maydis,* EPIVEN for apple scab caused by *Venturia inaequalis,* FAST for forecasting *Alternaria solani* on tomato and TOMCAST for tomato early blight.

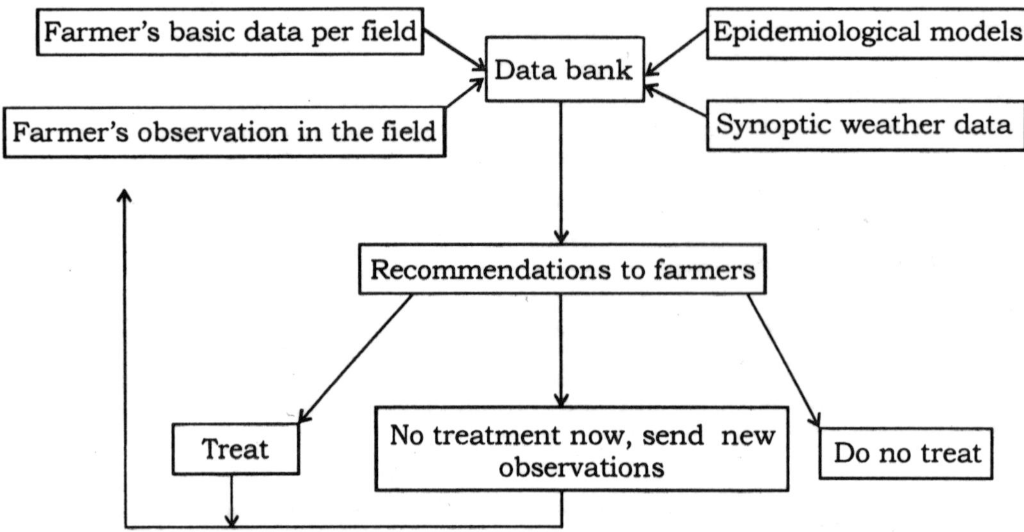


**Fig. 13.2:** Block diagram of EPIPRE (Zadoks, 1981)

Blitecast (Krause *et al.*, 1975) is a computerized potato late blight forecast model being operated in the Eastern USA. This programme written in Fortran, links the Wallin's RH-temperature and the Hyre's rainfall temperature relationship. If late blight inoculum is present in field, only weather is monitored for assessing severity. This model considers that other epidemic components do not play major role. The farmer using blitecast inform the computer center, the following weather parameters recorded in his agro-meteorological observatory installed in between potato rows.

1. Maximum and minimum temperature of the day
2. Number of hours with more than 90 per cent relative humidity
3. The maximum and minimum temperature when relative humidity was 90 per cent
4. Rainfall during the 24 hours to 0.1 cm accuracy.

Within three minutes, the computer analyzes the data and recommendations are issued to farmers when to begin spraying. More recent refinements in late blight forecasting includes also information on the level of resistance in a potato variety to late blight pathogen. The internet and the world wide web represent improvements in information systems. There are two major aspects of monitoring that can be fecilitated by the www. These aspects are monitoring existing populations and projecting possible future populations through online models.

## EXAMPLES OF MODELING RESOURCES ON THE WWW

In the present era of information technology, there are several models available on the world wide web. These can be retrieved and information can be utilized. Some of the examples are:

- University of Wisconsin IPM site has WISDOM, a decision support and record keeping programme for agriculture and Potato Crop Manager (PCM) provides timely recommendations for controlling these pests with minimum pesticide application.
- The Gypsy Moth Home Page at Virginia Tech has a number of models dealing with Gypsy Moth populations
- The USDA-ARS Biological Control of Pest Research Unit has a description of Herme, an object oriented modeling program which does not require the user to learn a complex programming language.
- CALGOS, a cotton simulation model that helps growers predict the possible results of alternative decision on irrigation, nitrogen application and other management practices.
- AgLinks, a free service offered by Clark Consulting International deals with Agriculture modeling links.
- University of California Statewide Integrated Pest Management Project maintains a listing of IPM related Microcomputer software and databases.
- The Cooperative Research Centre for Tropical Pest Management has population simulation models, spatial population models and risk analysis models.

## REFERENCES

Aujla, S. S., Sharma, Y. R., Chand, K. and Sawhney, S. S. 1977. Influence of weather factors on the incidence and epidemiology of Karnal bunt disease of wheat in the Punjab. *Indian J. of Ecology*, **4**: 71-74.

Campbell, C. L. and Madden, L. V. 1990. Forecasting plant diseases. *In*: *Introduction to Plant Disease Epidemiology*. John Wiley 7 Sons, Inc. pp. 423-452.

Campbell, C. L., Reynolds, K. M. and Madden, L. V. 1988. Modeling epidemics of root disease and development of simulators. *In*: J. Kranz and J. Rotem (eds.), *Experimental Techniques in Plant Disease Epidemiology*. Springer-Verlag, Berlin, pp. 253-265.

Davis, J. M., Main, C. E. and Nesmith, W. C. 1985. The biometeorology of blue mold of tobacco. Part II: The evidence for long-range sporangiospore transport. Movement and Dispersal of Agriculturally Important Biotic Agents. Mckenzie *et al.* (eds.), Claitor's Publishing Co., Baton Rouge, LA, pp. 473-498.

Francl, L. J. 1995. Challenge of bioassay plants in a monitored outdoor environment. *Can. J. Plant Path.*, **17**: 138-143.

Hyre, R. A. 1954. Progress in forecasting late blight of potato and tomato. *Plant Dis. Rep.*, **38**: 245-253.

Jhorar, O. P., Mavi, H. S., Sharma, Indu, and Aujla, S. S. 1992. A biometeorological model for forecasting Karnal bunt disease of wheat. *Plant Dis. Res.*, **7**: 204-209.

Jones, A. L., Lillevik, S. L., Fisher, P. D. and Stebbins, T. C. 1980. *Plant Dis.*, **64**: 69-72.

Kranz 1974. The role and scope of mathematical analysis and modeling in epidemiology. *In*: J. Kranj (ed.) *Epidemics of Plant Diseases Mathematical Analysis and Modelling*. Springer, New York.

Kampmeijier, P. and Zadocks, J. C. 1977. EPIMUL a simulator of foci and epidemics in mixtures, multilines and mosaics of resistant and susceptible plants. PUDOC, Wageningen. The Netherlands, p. 50.

Kranz, J. and Holz, F. 1993. Basis of decision-making and planning for IPM. ZEL, Food and Agriculture Development Centre, Feldafing and Zschortan. German Foundation for International Development (DSE): p. 190.

Kraska, T. 1999. Plant pathology and the internet. *In*: H. Lyer, *et al.* (eds.), *Modern Fungicides and Antifungal Compounds* II, Intercept, Andover, pp. 69-73.

Krause, R. A., Massie, L. B. and Hyre, R. A. 1975. BLITECAST, a computerized forecast of potato late blight. *Plant Dis. Rep.*, **59**: 95-98.

Main, C. E. and Spurr, H. W., Jr. 1990. Blue mold disease of tobacco. *In*: *Proc. Internatl. Symposium on Blue Mold of Tobacco*, Raleigh, NC, February 14-17, 1988. Delmar Publishing Co., Charlotte, NC.

Mavi, H. S., Jhorar, O. P., Sharma, Indu, Singh, G., Mahi, G. S., Mathauda, S. S. and Aujla, S. S. 1992. Forecasting Karnal bunt disease of wheat—A meteorological method. *Cereal Res. Comm.*, **20**: 67-74.

Miller, P. R. and O' Brien, M. 1957. Prediction of plant disease epidemics. *Ann. Rev. Microbiol.*, **11**: 77-110.

Mills, W. D. 1944. NY Agricultural Experiment Station, Ithaca, Bulletin, **630**: 4.

Mispagel, M., Gage, S. H., Russel, H. L. 1983. Cooperative crop monitoring system, Michigan State University, Department of Entomology, Michigan (USA).

Muralidharan, K. and Venkatarao, G. 1987. Forecasting outbreak of rice blast disease. *In*: S. Kannaiyan (ed.), *Advances in Rice Pathology*. Tamilnadu Agric. Univ. Coimbatore, India, pp. 111-137.

Nagarajan, S. 1983. *Plant Disease Epidemiology*. Oxford & IBH, New Delhi, pp. 267.

Nagarajan, S. 2002. Pest risk analysis for shipping wheat from Karnal bunt (*Tilletia indica*) infected areas to disease free destinations. Report of a consultancy project of USDA. Directorate of Wheat Research, Karnal-132 001 pp. 1.1-6.11.

Nagarajan, S. and Singh, H. 1975. Indian stem rust rules. An epidemiological concept on the spread of wheat stem rust. *Plant Dis. Reptr.*, **59**: 670-672.

Nagarajan, S. and Joshi, L. M. 1980a. A linear model for a seven day forecast of stem rust severity. *Indian Phytopath*, **31**: 504-506.

Nagarajan, S. and Joshi, L. M. 1980b. Further investigations on predicting wheat rusts appearance in central and peninsular India. *Phytopath. Z.*, **98**: 84-90.

Nagarajan, S. 1991. Epidemiology on Karnal bunt of wheat incited by *Neovossia indica* and an attempt to develop a disease prediction system. Technical Report, Wheat Programme, CIMMYT, Mexico, March, 1991. p. 62.

Navalgund, R. R. (2002). Remote sensing: Pre-requisite for agricultural planning. The Hindu, Survey of Indian Agriculture 2002, Chennai: 203-208.

Royer, M. H. and Ryttter, J. L. 1985. Artificial inoculation of wheat with *Tilletia indica* from Mexico and India. *Plant Dis.*, **69**: 317-319.

Scott, P. R. 1997. The incredible pace of change: information technology in support of plant pathology. *Plant Pathol.*, **46**: 615-635.

Shrum, R. 1975. Simulation of wheat stem rust (*Puccinia striiformis* West) using EPIDEMIC, a flexible plant disease simulator. *Penn. State Univ. Agric. Exp. Stn. Prog. Rep.*, pp. 347-381.

Singh, D. V., Arora, P., Srivastava, K. D., Nagarajan, S. and Aggarwal, R. 1990. Prediction of the frequency and severity of Karnal bunt occurrence in field using climate variables. *Indian J. Plant Prot.*, **18**: 225-229.

Singh, D. V., Srivastava, K. D., Aggarwal, R. and Jain, S. K. 1996. Factors associated with development and spread of Karnal bunt of wheat (*Triticum aestivum*) in north western India. *Indian J. Agri. Sci.*, **66**: 374-83.

Smiley, R. W. 1997. Risk assessment for Karnal Bunt occurrence in the Pacific Northwest. *Plant Dis.*, **81**: 689-692.

Smith, I. M., McNamara, D. G., Scott., P. R. and Harris, K. M.1992. Quarantine pests of Europe. CAB International, Wallingford, U.K., 1992.

Spaar, D. and Ebert, W. 1985. Monitoring and forecasting in plant protection in the Grman Democratic Republic. EPPO Bull., **15**: 299-310.

Thomas, C. E. 1996. Downy mildew. *In*: A. Zitter, Hopkins and C. E. Thomas (eds.), *Fungal Diseases of Aerial Parts, Compendium of Cucurbit Diseases*. American Phytopathological Society, St. Paul.

United States Department of Agriculture 1997. Guideline for Plant Pest Risk Analysis of Imported Commodities. APHIS, Riverside, Maryland, USA p. 263.

Van Everdingen, E. 1926. Het verband de wears gesterdheid ende aardappelzeiekte (*Phytophthora infestans*). *Tijdschr. Plantennziekten*, **32**: 129-140.

Waggoner, P. E. and Horsfall, J. G. 1969. Epidem—A simulator of plant disease written for a computer. *In*: *Bull. Conn. Agric. Expt. Stn. No.* 698. Connecticut, U.S.A., p. 80.

Waggoner, P. E., Horsfall, J. G. and Likens, R. J. 1972. Epimay—A simulator of southern corn leaf blight. *In*: *Bull. Conn. Agric. Expt. Stn. No.* 729. Connecticut, U.S.A., p. 84.

Wallin, J. R. 1962. Summary of recent progress in predicting late blight epidemics in the United States and Canada. *Am. Potato J.*, **39**: 306-312.

Yao, Chengwei, Arya, S. P., Davis, J. M. and Main, C. E. 1997. A numerical model of the transport and diffusion of *Peronospora tabacina* spores in the evolving atmospheric boundary layer. *Atmos. Environ.*, **31**: 1709-1714.

Zadoks, J. C. 1981. EPIPRE: a disease and pest management system for winter wheat developed in the Netherlands. *EPPO Bull.*, **11**: 365-369.

Zadoks, J. C. 1984. Analyzing cost effectiveness of EPIPRE. *EPPO Bull.*, **14**: 401-407.

Zadoks, J. C. and Kampmeijer, P. 1977. The role of crop populations and their deployment, illustrated by means of a simulator EPIMUL 76. *Ann. NY Acad. Sci.*, **287**: 164-190.

Zhang, Z., Lange, L. and Mathur, S. B. 1984. Teliospore survival and plant quarantine significance of *Tilletia indica* (causal agent of Karnal blunt) particularly in relation to China. *European Plant Prot. Bull.*, **14**: 119-126.

14

# Integrated Approaches for Management of Plant Parasitic Nematodes

**H. S. Gaur and Pankaj**

## INTRODUCTION

Nematodes constitute one of the largest and most numerous groups of animals on the planet earth. Most of their species are dependent for food on microfauna and microflora of little economic importance to man; some of them are parasites of animals including insects, fish, birds, cattle and man; while others are parasitic on plants of importance to man. Some nematodes are found worldwide (also termed cosmopolitan) while the distribution of others is restricted by geographical or environmental conditions. The distribution of many species has been influenced by human activities. Some parasites have very broad host ranges while others have very narrow ones.

Although, some species of nematodes can cause significant losses when present in low numbers, most do not cause economically significant damage unless their numbers are unusually high or the plant is also subject to unusual levels of stress caused by other factors. Carefully integrating as many as possible of various components into the management program will help keep most nematode pests below damaging levels, and may simplify the decisions that must be made about selecting and applying nematicides when they are needed. This paper focuses on aspects related to the integrated approach towards management of plant parasitic nematodes in different agro-ecosystems with special reference to the Indian scenario.

## EMERGENCE OF NEMATODES AS PESTS

Nematodes attain an equilibrium population density in the natural undisturbed ecosystems, which remains in harmony with the environmental dynamics and availability of food. Agriculture, on the other hand, involves induction of many unnatural variations, including and associated with the concentration and frequent cycling of a single or a few selected plant types and different agronomic practices to cultivate them. These exclude some organisms but perpetually favour certain others, who eventually attain a pest or pathogen status. The emergence of most of the specialized plant parasites with rather narrow or selective host ranges, including

*Division of Nematology, IARI, Campus New Delhi-110 012, India.*

root-knot, cyst, earcockle, stem, burrowing and citrus nematodes, etc. can be traced back to such adoptions of cropping or planting patterns. A recent example is, the emergence of the root-knot nematodes, *Meloidogyne graminicola* and *M. triticoryzae* as pests of both rice and wheat in some areas of northern India (Gaur *et al.*, 1993*a*, *b*) as a result of the adoption of the rice-wheat cropping system. These nematodes were not known to be present in this part of India before, although *M. graminicola* has been a problem in rice in the eastern and southern India. These root knot nematodes might have been thriving at low population densities on some grasses or other crops and wheat mainly grown in these areas probably supported very small or even undetectable populations, being a winter crop. When rice followed wheat in the summer or rainy season (*kharif*) the nematodes got very favourable hosts in the form of rice and associated graminaceous weeds in the warm and moist season and attained high population densities causing damage significant enough to qualify as pests of rice and to some extent of wheat.

## TARGET PLANT PARASITIC NEMATODE PROBLEMS OF INDIA

Although a large number of species of over 30 genera have been reported to be capable of causing significant quantitative and/or qualitative damage to agriculturally important crops, about 50 of them (Table 14.1) have been recognized to cause considerable economic losses at regional and national levels. Further, polyspecific communities of nematodes, including several cohabiting species of plant parasitic nematodes (Plate 14.1), commonly occur but only some of them have population densities and damage potential of concern. Therefore, such species can be considered as the target species in our attempts to manage them.

## OPTIONS FOR NEMATODE CONTROL

A number of management options based on physical, chemical, biological, and cultural methods have been found effective, to different degrees, in reducing nematode population densities and improving crop performance. None of the methods, except on very small areas or quantities of plant material, have been found sufficient or economic to completely control, or to maintain the population densities at levels below the economic tolerance level. Therefore, reliance has to be placed on a judicious combination of different control options suitable for location specific conditions. The individual options available are shown in Fig. 14.1; their merits and demerits have been discussed by Sethi & Gaur (1986).

The main aim of a control measure is to reduce the pest population density to the minimum possible levels. But the various limitations of cost, environment and safety do not permit attainment of such a goal in the case of most pests, more so in the case of nematodes. Therefore, a suitable management approach is adopted with an objective to maintain nematode population densities at levels below the economic injury threshold or to reduce their levels such as to derive maximum profits out of the management cost incurred.

**TABLE 14.1:** ECONOMICALLY IMPORTANT PLANT PARASITIC NEMATODES OF INDIA

| *Nematode Groups* | *Important Species* | *Crops* | *Regions* |
|---|---|---|---|
| Root knot nematodes | *Meloidogyne incognita,* *M. javanica,* | Vegetables, pulses, fruits, oilseeds, fibre & ornamental crops, medicinal & aromatic plants, spices, condiments | All India |
| | *M. arenaria,* | Groundnut, vegetables | Central and Western India |
| | *M. hapla,* | Vegetables, fruit crops | Temperate regions |
| | *M. graminicola,* | Rice | Most tropical regions |
| | *M. triticoryzae* | Rice, wheat | Northern plains |
| Cyst nematodes | *Heterodera avenae,* | Wheat, barley | North, north-west and Central India |
| | *H. cajani,* | Pulses, vegetables, oilseeds | All India |
| | *H. zeae,* | Maize | North Indian plains |
| | *H. sorghi,* | Sorghum | North Indian plains |
| | *H. oryzicola* | Rice, banana | Southern India |
| | *Globodera rostochiensis,* *G. pallida* | Potato | Nilgiri & adjoining areas of southern India |
| Reniform nematodes | *Rotylenchulus reniformis* | Vegetables, pulses, fruits, fibre and oilseed crops | All India |
| Citrus nematodes | *Tylenchulus semipenetrans* | Citrus | All India |
| Lesion nematodes | *Pratylenchus thornei,* *P. zeae, P. pratensis* *P. loosi* | Cereals and many other crops | All India |
| Burrowing nematodes | *Radopholus similis* | Tea | South India |
| | | Banana, coconut & other plantation crops | Southern and Western India |

| *Nematode Groups* | *Important Species* | *Crops* | *Regions* |
|---|---|---|---|
| Rice root nematodes | *Hirchmanniella oryzae, H. mucronata, H. gracilis* | Rice | All India |
| Rice stem nematodes | *Ditylenchus angustus* | Rice | North and eastern India |
| Lance nematodes | *Hoplolaimus indicus* | Many crops | All India |
| Spiral nematodes | *Helicotylenhus* spp. | Banana and many other crops | All India |
| Stunt nematodes | *Tylenchortynchus* spp., *Merlinius* spp. | Many crops | All India |
| Criconematids | *Macroposthonia* spp., *Hemicriconemoides* spp., *Hemicycliophora* spp., *Paratylenchus* spp., *Caloosia* spp. | Most perennial crops, grasses, trees, rose, grapevines, etc. | All India |
| Dagger nematodes | *Xiphinema* spp. | Most perennial crops grasses, trees, rose, grapevines, etc. | All India |
| Needle nematodes | *Longidorus* spp., *Paralongidorus* spp. | Many perennial plants, trees, forest trees, etc. | All India |
| Stubby root nematodes | *Trichodorus* spp. | Many cereals and other crops | All India |
| Ear cockle nematodes | *Anguina tritici* | Wheat, (barley) | All India |
| White tip nematodes | *Aphelenchoides besseyi* | Rice | North and eastern India |
| Mushroom nematodes | *Aphelenchoides composticola, Ditylenchus myceliophagus* | Mushrooms mushroom houses | Temperate regions, |

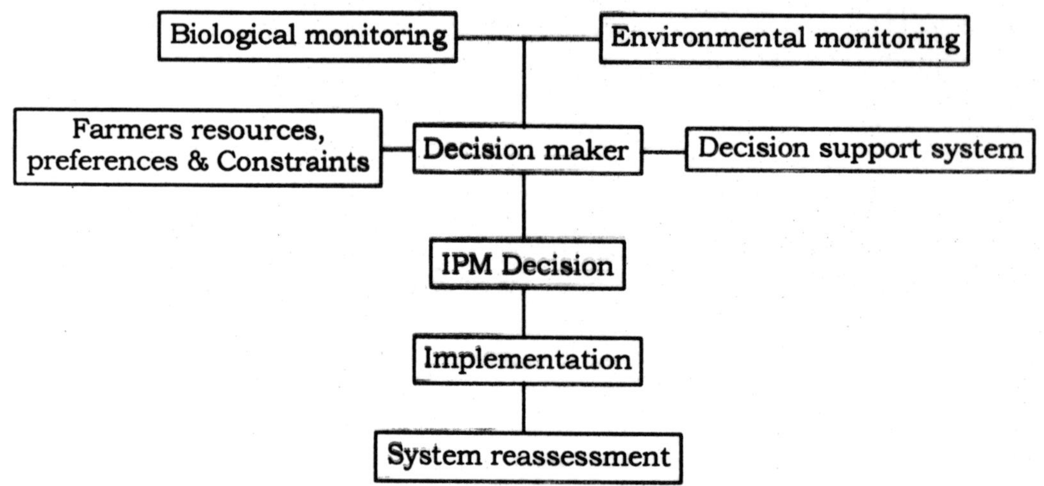


**Fig. 14.1:** Components of the IPM systems management strategy

**TABLE 14.2:** DIFFERENT METHODS OF NEMATODE CONTROL

| *Types of Control Methods* | *Methods in the Category* |
|---|---|
| Cultural Methods | Fallowing, Flooding, Summer ploughing, Time of planting/sowing, Manuring and irrigation, Cover crops, Green manuring, Antagonistic crops, Trap crops, Crop rotation |
| Genetic Methods | Resistant varieties, Tolerant crops/varieties, Genetic engineering |
| Biological Methods | Nematophagous fungi, Parasitic bacteria, Predatory soil fauna (nematodes, mites, collembola, tardigrades, enchytreids) |
| Physical Methods | Solar heat, Steam, Hot water, Irradiation, Electricity |
| Chemical Methods | Fumigation, Systemic nematicides applied to soil as granules, drench, etc. all over or on selected spots, Nematicide sprays, Seed treatment, Bare root dip treatments |
| Botanicals | Neem, Mahua, Karanj used as deoiled seed cakes; leaves, etc. as soil amendment. May possibly serve as source of nematicidal chemicals, Microbial ematicides, antimetabolites, steroids, etc. |

## Ecologically Based Management Approaches

The management of plant parasitic nematodes involves the modification of altered ecosystem by strategic chemical, physical, biological or cultural interference aimed at disrupting the harmony acquired by them with the host and the agroecosystem. Although, chemical nematicides during 1940's were largely responsible for highlighting and demonstrating the losses caused by nematodes as well as the possibilities of their control, yet their costs, meager availability and environmental hazards make nematicides the last of the options in practical nematode management. The emergence of novel nematicides devoid of these unfriendly features, though the target of many a ongoing researches, is not in sight in the near future.

An ecologically and economically sound nematode management approach involves the combined use of a number of measures which may need to be augmented with nematicidal chemicals when quick reduction to very low levels of population density becomes necessary as in the case of very susceptible or high value cash crops.

### *Physiotherapeutic Methods*

Important physical methods include cleaning of seed and other planting materials like tubers, bulbs, rhizomes, rooted cuttings, etc. in dormant state, by winnowing washing, filtration, flotation, paring etc., as appropriate. The use of heat in the form of insulation, heat or hot water treatments to free the planting materials and soil provides some degree of control and prevention of spread of nematodes to uninfested areas. Cleaning of the wheat seed free of ear-cockles caused by *Anguina tritici* has helped many countries to almost eradicate these nematodes. The use of a well controlled product of hot water treatment (40-55° C) and time (1-60 min) kills many nematodes in the planting materials. Prior soaking of dry materials improves the efficacy of the heat treatments. Care must however, be taken to safeguard against the loss of viability of the planting material. Combinations of relatively lower controlled temperature and longer exposure period are usually preferable.

### *Exploitation of Solar Heat*

Exposure of nematode infested soil to solar heat, such as by summer ploughing with soil turning harrows, provides good degree of control of nematodes. However, many nematodes enter into a quiescent anhydrobiotic state in slowly dried soil. Therefore, a light irrigation a few days prior to summer ploughing helps to activate such nematodes making them more vulnerable to heat and desiccation death. Rabbing, *i.e.*, burning of crop residues over soil surface, has been an age-old practice to reduce weeds, insects and pathogens. Turning of soil prior to rabbing can improve efficiency in killing nematodes.

The simple technique of soil solarization, *i.e.*, mulching of moist field soil with a clear thin polyethylene sheet (Katan *et al.*, 1976) for some weeks in hot summer increases the temperature in the upper soil layers by about 5-10° C over normal for several hours daily, which can kill or cause metabolic exhaustion of many nematodes, fungi, bacteria, insects and weeds (Katan, 1981; Gaur & Perry, 1991). The decline in nematode population is correlated to the number of days or hours for which the soil temperature exceeds 40° C (Gaur & Dhingra, 1991). The short wave radiation from the sun easily penetrates the polyethylene sheet to heat the soil but much of the long wave radiation leaving the soil is unable to do so, hence retained under the sheet leading to accumulation of heat. The beneficial microflora and fauna are less affected or recover faster than the plant pathogenic organisms. The antagonistic activity in the soil is also improved. The release of nutrients also promotes plant growth and improves tolerance. This method, though expensive to use over large fields, provides an economical alternative for multiple pest, disease and weed control over small areas, nursery-beds, orchards and forestry plantations and high value crops in regions bestowed with hot summers. In relatively cooler areas, but with sufficient bright sunlight, this method improves antagonistic microbial activity in the soil (Gaur & Perry, 1991). It can be a part of integrated nematode control options (along with chemicals) in the high value crops (Ravindra *et al.*, 2001).

## Cultural Practices

Cultural practices are manipulations of the agro-ecosystem that make the cropping system less friendly to the establishment and proliferation of nematode pest populations. Although they are designed to have positive effects on farm ecology and pest management, negative impacts may also result, due to variations in weather or changes in crop management.

Besides summer ploughing, the most important of the cultural practices are crop rotation and manipulation or augmentation of soil organic matter. Many of the economically important nematodes, like root knot, cyst, reniform, lesion nematodes, etc. have wide but somewhat delineated host ranges. It is often possible to find commercially acceptable and agronomically suitable alternative crops, which may be non-hosts, poor hosts, tolerant or antagonistic crops to the target nematode species. The level of success in nematode management through crop rotation may vary with the year, target nematode and associated plant pathogens, location, weed hosts present and the nature and length of rotation (Trivedi & Barker, 1986; McSorley, 2001). For instance, many dicot crops can be grown as alternatives to wheat, barley, oats, maize, sorghum, etc. to control the cereal cyst or maize cyst or sorghum cyst nematodes. Similarly, several monocots including cereals and some crucifers are poor or non-hosts of the common root-knot and reniform nematodes while many dicots are nonhosts of root-knot nematodes infecting cereals (Trivedi & Barker, 1986). African marigolds, sesame, asparagus, mustard, etc. have been reported to be antagonistic to the root knot, reniform and some other nematodes. These are some examples of alternative crops with good commercial and agroclimatic suitability. The period of rotation, *i.e.*, avoidance of the host crop depends upon the rate of decline of the nematode population in the absence of the host. The nematodes, which do not depend upon the host root diffusates for their hatching decline faster than those which do (Perry, 1987). Usually, a two year rotation against cereal cyst nematodes and a one year rotation against root-knot and reniform nematodes are usually sufficient to bring down the population densities to levels below the economic injury thresholds; although much longer rotations may be necessary to achieve almost total control. The principles and possibilities of crop rotation in nematode management have been elaborated and discussed, time to time (Sethi & Gaur, 1986; Maqbool *et al.*, 1988; Ibrahim & Rezk, 1988; Luc *et al.*, 1990).

Intercropping is the practice of growing two or more crops in the same, alternate, or paired rows in the same area. This technique is particularly appropriate in vegetable production. The advantage of intercropping is that the increased diversity helps "disguise" crops from insect pests, and if done well, may allow for more efficient utilization of limited soil and water resources. Disadvantages may relate to ease of managing two different crop species with potentially different nutrient, water, and light needs, and differences in harvesting time and method in close proximity to each other. Intercropping of certain nematode antagonistic crops such as *Tagetes* spp., sesame, mustard, etc. has been reported to reduce root knot and reniform nematodes. African marigolds (*T. erecta*) have been shown to inhibit the reproduction of nematodes (Davide, 1979; Kimpinski *et al.*, 2000). The use of trap or antagonistic crops as green manure not only reduces nematodes but also improves soil fertility as well as conserve moisture (Nasbaun & Ferris, 1973) in many other ways and also promotes the antagonistic microbial activity. Crops like *Crotalaria spectabilis*, which allow invasion by *Meloidogyne* spp. but do not support development can serve as good trap crops (Patel *et al.*, 1991).

However, in all these alternative cropping methods the control of weeds is essential as most nematodes have a wide host range including several species of weeds as alternative hosts. Some weeds may be found to possess nematode antagonistic characteristics. For instance, *Eclipta alba* a common weed has been found to reduce *M. graminicola* when turned back into soil, although it may serve as a host if allowed to grow too long (Rao *et al.*, 1986). More such weeds may exist, which in addition to reducing nematodes may serve as green manure. Many plants have been reported to have nematicidal properties, the use of their foliage as soil amendment may help in reducing nematode populations. Although the doses required make their use impossible in practical agriculture, these, in available quantities, may serve as an important component of the total nematode management strategy.

Incorporation of organic amendments or manures into soil is known to reduce plant parasitic nematode populations (Jairajpuri *et al.*, 1990; Stirling, 1991) and enhance biocontrol efficacy of *P. lilacinus* in the control of root pathogens (Mehdi *et al.*, 1999; Karthikeyan *et al.*, 2001). Singh (1988) observed a significant negative correlation between population density of *M. incognita* and the natural organic matter content of the soil. Thus, cultural practices helping in the conservation or build up of organic matter status of the soil may help in nematode management. Amendment of soil with non-edible deoiled seed cakes of neem (*Azadirachta indica*), *Melia azadirach,* karanj (*Pongamia glabra*), mahua (*Madhuca indica*), castor (*Ricinus communis*), etc. improve soil fertility and organic matter status besides reducing nematode population density through their constituent or decomposition products which are toxic to nematodes and promotion of the antagonistic microbial activity. The high doses (10-30 q/ha) required are a constraint, but again lower doses in combination with other practices can be advantageous.

Alternate methods like seed treatments were developed in case of seed sown crops (Mojumder & Mishra, 1997; Mojumder, 1999). For transplantable vegetable crops, nursery bed treatments and root dip treatments in different neem products have been tried (Alam, 1993; Mojumder, 1997; Mojumder, 2000). Seed treatments with neem products have been recorded as effective as well as economical for the management in chickpea and pulse crops (Mojumder & Mishra, 1996; Mojumder & Raman, 1996; Mojumder & Basu, 1999; Mojumder & Pankaj, 2002).

Removal or destruction of infected plant materials like roots, rhizomes, tubers, etc. from soil, which was a traditional practice, can help in reducing surviving nematode population densities (Sethi & Gaur, 1986).

Adjustment of sowing or planting time may help in avoiding nematode damage in regions with well defined winters, such as in the north Indian plains. Most tropical plant parasitic nematode species (except ear-cockle, potato cyst and cereal cyst nematodes) are slow in invasion and reproduction during winter than in summer. Late planting of susceptible *rabi* crops therefore, helps the crop to escape early nematode damage (Duncan, 1991). On the same principle early sowing of spring crops in the temperate regions can escape nematode damage to the young crop.

Good crop husbandry practices including tillage, nutrient and moisture management, in general, improve plant tolerance to nematode attack. Proper availability of micronutrients also helps in overcoming some of the nematode damage, eg. *Heterodera avenae* caused more damage to wheat in soils deficient in Mn. The integration of crop management as well as compatible cultural options might be viewed as the basic foundation for successful nematode management and crop production (Trivedi & Barker, 1986).

### Resistance

The resistant varieties of crops would be the cheapest, easy to recommend and most practical method of nematode control. So far, such varieties are rather rare. Nematologists over the years, have reported large numbers of resistant sources. Unfortunately, the effort has not found adequate attention of the plant breeders. The modern techniques of biotechnological gene transfer, cloning and mutation may go a long way in producing desirable nematode resistant cultivars. However, care must be taken of the vast variability and adaptability of nematodes. The varieties found resistant at one location may or may not show resistance to another population of the same nematode species due to prevailing races. Surfacing or emergence of resistance breaking biotypes after a few seasons of selection process is not new to nematodes. Therefore, resistant varieties should form a component of a well planned crop rotation or other nematode management strategy. A number of reviews on the development and deployment of host-plant resistance are available (Roberts, 1992). Varieties have also been developed against limited number of plant parasitic nematodes on relatively narrow range of crops.

### Biological Control

Is the use of living organisms—parasites, predators, or pathogens—to maintain pest populations below economically damaging levels, and may be either *natural or applied.* Recently, there has been much emphasis on the exploitation of biocontrol agents, especially certain bacteria and fungi, against nematodes. Besides, *Pasteuria penetrans*, a bacterium, several fungi like *Dactylella cynopaga, Dactylaria eudermata, Arthrobotrys* spp., *Cytopage* spp. and *Stylopage* spp. etc. have been reported as nematophagous. Also a good number of endoparasitic fungi are known to be egg parasites (*Paecilomyces lilacinus, Verticillium chlamydosporium, Dactylella oviparasitica* and *Cephalosporium* spp.), and parasites of sedentary females (*Nemaphthora gynophilla, Catenaria oxylaris, Glomus* spp., *Fusarium* spp. and *Aspergillus* spp., etc.) have shown great promise under limited experimental conditions (Siddiqui *et al.*, 1996).

*Pasteuria penetrans* has been found equally compatible with the nematicide application. Sekhar and Gill (1991) reported that application of *P. penetrans* in nursery bed in combination with carbofuran @ 1.5 kg a.i./ha was as good as carbofuran applied @ 3 kg a.i./ha in respect to plant growth parameters and nematode reduction. *P. penetrans* deployed as a single measure, may not give consistent or durable control but it may have a role in an integrated approach to nematode management (Souza and Campos, 1997). Although, *Pasteuria* being highly resistant to heat, desiccation and ability to survive for more than two years in soil, qualifies as the most potential biocontrol agent against the root knot nematode infesting vegetable crops, it's incapability to multiply under *in vitro* condition for mass production has created a lacunae in transferring the bacterium on a large scale in field. Efforts are therefore needed to develop a mass multiplication protocol for this bacterium, so that the spores are available in plenty throughout the year.

Among various vasicular-arbuscular mycorrhizae (VAM), the role of *Glomus fasciculatum* against root-knot nematode in tomato and green gram (Ray and Dalei, 1998) and *G. mossae* against *R. reniformis* in tomato has been well documented (Sitaramaiah & Sikora, 1981; Suresh & Bagyaraj, 1984).

As such the mass culturing and release of biocontrol agents at regular intervals may be quite expensive. However, proper establishment and colonization of indigenous or introduced microorganisms is possible by simultaneous modification of the soil environment. Prior testing of such organisms to human and cattle health must of course form a part of the protocol before recommending them.

**Chemical Management**

Nematicides have been found to give quick and demonstrable control of nematodes; these facts have been responsible for the recognition of nematodes as economically important pests and hence, for the establishment of the science of nematology. Several chemicals belonging to diverse groups like halogenated hydrocarbons (DD, EDB, DBCP, MBr, etc.), organophosphates (phorate, phenamiphos, fensulfothion, thionazin, etc.) and oxime carbamates (aldicarb, carbofuran, oxamyl, etc.) have served as nematicides. Many of them also serve as insecticides. However, the large doses required for soil application, high costs, import dependence, environmental hazards and residue problems are the well known limitations of pesticides in general and of nematicides in particular. Consequently, many of the previously recommended nematicides are either not available or have been banned for agricultural use. Presently, mainly phorate and carbofuran are the chemicals used for soil application, mostly as insecticides and sometimes as nematicides in almost all the agriculturally important crops. Their use in main field treatments may be economical only in high value crops. Methyl bromide (MBr) has a limited use for fumigation of infested planting materials. The viable options for the use of nematicides for nematode management are, therefore, their use on smaller areas such as in the nursery-beds, row or spot applications in main fields, in high value cash crops; and their use for preplanting treatment of planting materials, such as seed treatment, seedling dip, rhizome immersion, etc. Carbosulfan has been reported to be effective as seed treatment against root knot nematodes by several workers on brinjal, tomato (Siddiqui *et al.*, 1998a, b), cucumber (Bharali & Phukan, 1997), cotton (Chand & Jain, 1990; Vats *et al.*, 2000), soybean (Prasad, 1998) and sunflower; (Narayana & Prasad, 1999). Direct application of chemicals (Phorate) in the field has also proved to be effective against root knot nematodes in tomato (Sharma & Khan, 1995) and brinjal (Sharma *et al.*, 1997). Similarly, vydate, thionazin, lannate, dimethoate, etc. have been shown effective as bare root dip for seedlings. Used at non-phytotoxic doses, such treatments provide initial protection to the young growing plant when it is most susceptible to the nematodes.

**The Integrated Approach**

Economic and environmental considerations are fundamental to any integrated nematode management approach. The amount of damage to a crop is usually correlated to the population density of parasitic nematodes. Some small population densities are tolerated well by the crops, unless an interaction with other plant pathogens accentuates the damage. The cost of reducing nematode population density to very low levels increases rather exponentially, whereas the additional damage caused by a unit increase in nematode population density tends to decrease as the latter rises above the damage threshold. The intersection of the nematode damage and management cost functions indicates the optimum management level for maximization of profits (Sethi & Gaur, 1986).

The aim of an ecologically sound integrated nematode management approach should be:

- Utilization of several compatible measures,
- Maximization of natural biotic and abiotic environmental resistance,
- Understanding and counteracting nematode survival strategies,
- Minimal use of drastic control measures,
- Increased reliance on location specific and resource compatible management strategy,
- Minimizing input costs in harmony with potential gains,
- Maximization of profit to the grower, and
- Minimization of environmental and health hazards.

Nematodes are usually given a lower priority than most other spectacular pests and diseases. It must be realized that plant parasitic nematodes are endemic and well adapted pests usually causing less spectacular and slow but sure and continuous damage, spreading to larger areas with time. Further, their presence at high densities not only increases the damage caused by the other pathogens but also nematodes may predispose crop cultivars to attack by pathogens to which they may be normally resistant. Hence, a nematode management programme taking care of, or at least supplementary to the control of other major pests and diseases is likely to be more acceptable.

The integrated approach is an entirely a new concept to most of the growers, and they are not as yet willing or able to grasp its significance. They tend to view it as something they should do for someone else benefit. The integrated management is based upon the system approach, follows location specific principle and is environment specific (Pankaj & Sharma, 1998). The field trials are considered to be the pre-requisite for the successful adoption of and INM package.

A low input sustainable integrated nematode management strategy for low and medium value crops in the tropical and subtropical regions is suggested here:

**Summer:** Two or three deep summer ploughing with a soil turning harrow at fortnightly intervals, preferably with a light irrigation between two ploughings; soil solarization of nursery-beds or pit soil using clear thin polyethylene mulch for 3-6 weeks before sowing; application of granular systemic nematicides to nursery-beds; growing of nonhost or antagonistic commercial crop, and ploughing back non-commercial crop residues before monsoon.

**Monsoon:** Green manuring with nonhost or trap crop or application of organic soil amendments/manure.

**Kharif:** Growing nonhost or resistant commercial crops; nematicidal treatment of nursery-beds and seed; spot application of systemic nematicides in high value crops; uprooting and burning of roots of host crops and weeds after harvest.

**Rabi:** Delaying sowing/planting to mid-November (when soil temperature falls to 15-18° C); restricting growing of susceptible or tolerant crops to Rabi season with a suitable period of rotation; removal and burning of roots; ploughing back non-commercial but disease-free crop residues.

The options given above have to be location specific and additional to the normal sanitation and good crop husbandry practices of tillage, manuring, irrigation, weed control, etc.

Incorporation of neem cake, neem leaf/castor leaf/*Pedilanthus* leaf/pongamia leaf each @ 500 g/m and application of spore suspension of *P. penetrans, P. lilacinus* or *V. chlamydosporium* in nursery beds, reduced the incidence of root-knot and reniform nematodes even after transplantation of tomato plants in the main field (Reddy *et al.*, 1997; Rao *et al.*, 1998). Similarly, nematode free healthy brinjal seedlings were obtained from the nursery initially treated with *G. mossae*/*G. fasciculatum* and subsequently by 5% aqueous extract of neem cake/castor cake/neem leaf/calotropis leaf (Rao *et al.*, 1996*a, b*; Rao *et al.*, 1998; Ravindra *et al.*, 2001). Under field conditions, planting of tomato seedlings (raised in nursery beds amended with neem cake (1 kg/m$^2$) and *P. penetrans* (28 × 10$^7$ spores/m$^2$) in pits incorporated with *P. lilacinus* at 0.5 g inoculum per plant gave the least root galling and nematode multiplication rate (Reddy *et al.*, 1997). Integration of various control options for the management of plant parasitic nematode on different agriculturally important crops have been emphasized (Ravindra *et al.*, 2001; Sudha & Sundararaju, 2001).

Intensive fundamental and location specific interdisciplinary research on the ecology of the important nematode pest species is essential to understand the environmental relations, survival strategies and methods of increasing local abiotic and biotic environmental resistance to nematodes still maintaining harmony with the suitable growth conditions for the crop and avoiding environmental hazards. A reasonably good success has already been attained in this area and much more is expected in the coming century. The future may hold in store biomolecular/ biopesticides of plant or microbial origin and their genetically engineered analogues; novel chemicals which may not be toxic but may interfere with chemoreception, establishment of host-parasite relationship or reproduction; and perhaps clones of naturally resistant or genetically engineered crop germplasm. Until then and certainly even after, the integrated approach will be necessary for the management of the most adaptive plant parasites/pathogens—the nematodes.

## REFERENCES


Alam, M. M. 1993. Bioactivity against phytonematodes. *In*: N. S. Randhawa and B. S Parmar (eds.), *Neem Research and Development*. New Delhi, Society of Pesticide Science, pp. 123-143.

AICRP 1992. Achievements 1977-87. All India Coordinated Research Project on Nematode Pests and their Control. pp. 16-26.

Al-Hazmi, A. S. 1988. Relative host suitability of corn and alfalfa cultivars to *Meloidogyne javanica. Pakistan J. Nematol.*, **6**: 101-105.

Bharali, A. and Phukan, P. N. 1997. Efficacy of certain chemicals as seed soaking treatments against *Meloidogyne incognita* on cucumber. *J. Agril. Sci. Soc North East India.*, **10**: 5-8.

Chand, Tand and Jain, R. K. 1990. Chemical control of root-knot nematode (*Meloidogyne incognita*) through seed dressing in cotton. *Indian J. Nematol.*, **20**: 224-226.

Davide, R. G. 1979. Effects of nematicides and *Tagetes erecta* on the control of *Meloidogyne incognita* and on yield of tomato. *Philippine Phytopathol.*, **15**: 141-144.

Duncan, L. W. 1991. Current options for nematode management. *Ann. Rev. Phytopathol.*, **29**: 469-490.

Gaur, H. S. and Perry, R. N. 1991. The use of soil solarization for the control of plant parasitic nematodes. *Nematological Abstract*, **60**: 153-167.

Gaur, H. S. and Dhingra, A. 1991. Management of *Meloidogyne incognita* and *Rotylenchulus reniformis* in nursery beds by soil solarization and organic soil amendments. *Rev Nematol.*, **14**: 189-195.

Gaur, H. S., Saha, M. and Khan, E. 1993a. *Meloidogyne triticoryzae* sp. n. (Nematoda: Meloidogynidae) a root-knot nematode damaging wheat and rice in India. *Ann. Pl. Protec. Sc.*, **1**: 18-26.

Gaur, H. S., Khan, E. and Sehgal, M. 1993b. Occurrence of two species of root-knot nematodes infecting rice, wheat, monocot weeds in northern India. *Ann. Pl. Protec. Sc.*, **1**: 141-142.

Greco, N., D'Addabbo, Brandonisio, A and Zweep, A. 1990. Combined effect of solarization and 1, 3-dichloropropene for the control of *Heterodera carotae. Nematol. Medit.*, **18**: 261-264.

Ibrahim, I. K. A., and Rezk, M. A. 1988. The root-knot nematodes—A major problem in crop production in Egypt. *In*: M. A. Maqbool, A. M. Golden, A. Ghaffar and L. R. Krusberg (eds.), *Advances in Plant Nematology*. Univ. of Karachi, pp. 81-98.

Jain, R. K. and Bhatti, D. S. 1989. An integrated approach for the mnagement of root-knot nematode *Meloidogyne javanica* in tomato. *Indian J. Nematol.*, **19**: 159-161.

Jairajpuri, M. S., Alam, M. M. and Ahmad, I. 1990. *Nematode Biocontrol* Delhi, India, CBS Publ. and Distributors Pvt. Ltd. pp.152.

Katan, J., Greenberger, A., Alon, H. and Grinstein, A. 1976. Solar heating by polyelthylene mulching for the control of diseases caused by soil-borne pathogens. Phytopathology, **66**: 683-688.

Katan, J. 1981. Solar heating (solarization) of soil for control of soil-borne pest. *Ann. Rev. Phytopath.*, **19**: 211-236.

Karthikeyan, G., Sabitha, D and Sivakumar, C. V. 2001. Biological control of *Pythium aphanidermatum-Meloidogyne incognita* disease complex in brinjal with organic amendments. *Madras Agril. J.*, **88**: 40-42.

Kimpinski, J., Arsenault, W. J., Gallant, C. E. and Sanderson, J. B. 2000. The effect of marigolds (*Tagetes spp.*) and other cover crops on *Pasteuria penetrans* and on following potato crops. *Supp. J. Nematol.*, **32**: 531-536.

Luc, M., Sikora, R. A. and Bridge, J. 1990. Plant parasitic nematodes in sub-tropical and tropical agriculture. CAB International. pp. 629.

Maqbool, M. A., Hashmi, S. and Ghaffar, A. 1988. Problem of root-knot nematode in Pakistan and strategies for their control. *In*: M. A. Maqbool, A. M. Golden, A. Ghaffar and L. R. Krusberg (eds.), *Advances in Plant Nematology*. Univ. of Karachi, pp. 229-240.

McSorley, R. 2001. Multiple cropping systems for nematode management—A review. Proc. Soil & Crop Sci. Society of Florida.

Mehdi, F. S., Siddiqui, I. A., Erum, S. and Ali, R. 1999. Effect of *Avicennia marina* and *Paecilomyces lilacinus* on root rot-root knot diseases of tomato. *Pak. J. Biol. Sci.*, **2**: 1462-1466.

Mojumder, V. 1997. Nematode management. *In*: S. S. Narwal, P. Tauro and S. S. Bisla (eds.), *Neem in Sustainable Agriculture*. Jodhpur, Scientific Publishers, pp. 239-253.

Mojumder, V. 1999. Seed soaking of pigeon pea in aqueous extracts of neem products against *Heterodera cajani*. *IARI Neem Newsletter*, **16**: 13-15.

Mojumder, V. 2000. Effect of root dip treatment of tomato in aqueous extracts of neem products against *Meloidogyne incognita*. *Ann. Plant Protection Sciences*, **8**: 272-273.

Mojumder, V. and Basu, R. 1999. Seed coating of chickpea with neem-based pesticidal formulations for the management of *Meloidogyne incognita*. *Indian J. Nematol.*, **29**: 28-33.

Mojumder, V. and Mishra, S. D. 1996. Management of *Meloidogyne incognita* infecting pulse crops through seed treatments with neem products. *In*: R. P. Singh, M. S. Chari, A. K. Raheja and W. Krans (eds.), *Neem and Environment*. Proc. World neem Conference India, Oxford Publication Pvt. Ltd. New Delhi, pp. 699-703.

Mojumder V. and Mishra, S. D. 1997. Neem products for nematode management in pulse crops. Technical Brochure, Division of Nematology IARI, New Delhi, pp.11.

Mojumder, V. and Raman, R. 1996. Comparative efficacy of neem-based nematicidal products for the management of nematode pests of pulse crops (Abstr). International neem Conference Gatton College, Australia, Feb 4-9. pp. 46.

Mojumder, V. and Pankaj 2002. Seed coating of mung bean with neem products for the management of plant parasitic nematodes. *Neem Newsletter*, **19**(1): 66-69.

Narayana, R. and Prasad, D. 1999. Effect of seed soaking in carbosulfan and triazophos on plant growth of sunflower infected with Meloidogyne *incognita*. *Ann Pl. Protec. Sci.*, **7**: 186-189.

Nusbaun, C. J. and Ferris, H. 1973. The role of cropping systems in nematode population management. *Ann. Rev. Phytopathol.*, **11**: 423-440.

Pankaj and Sharma H. K. 1998. IPM strategies for nematode management. *In*: D. Prasad and R. D. Gautam (eds.), *Potential IPM Tactics*. Westvill Publ. House, Paschim Vihar, New Delhi, pp.131-145.

Patel, H. R., Patel, D. J., Patel, C. C and Thakar, N. A. 1991. Management of root-knot nematodes in Periwinkle. *Nematol. Medit.*, **19**: 65-67.

Perry, R. N. 1987. Host-induced hatching of Photoparasitic nematode eggs. *In*: J. A Veech and D. W. Dickson (eds.), *Vistas on Nematology*. Society of Nematologists, Inc. Maryland, pp.159-164.

Prasad, D. 1998. Seed soaking in benfuracarb and triazophos—A prophylactic treatment against *Meloidogyne incognita* on soybean. *Ann. Pl. Protec. Sci.*, **6**: 196-197.

Prasad, D. and Narayana, R. 2001. Effect of seed soaking with carbosulfan and triazophos on the penetration and development of *Meloidogyne incognita* on sunflower. *Indian J. Nematol.*, **31**(1): 64-67.

Rao, M. S., Reddy P. P. and Nagesh, M. 1998. Integrated management of *Meloidogyne incognita* on tomato using *Verticillium chlamydosporium* and *Pasteuria penetrans*. *Pest Management Hort. Ecosys.*, **4**: 32-35.

Rao, M. S., Reddy P. P., Sukhada M., Nagesh, M. and Pankaj 1998. Management of root-knot nematode on egg plant by integrating endomycorrhyza (*Glomus fasciculatum*) and caster cake. *Nematol. Medit.*, **26**: 217-219.

Rao, M. S., Reddy, P. P. and Das, S. M. 1996b. Effect of integration of *Calotropis procera* leaf and *Glomus fasciculatum* on the management of *Meloidogyne incognita* infesting tomato. *Nematologia Mediterranea*, **24**: 59-61.

Rao, M. S., Reddy, P. P., Mittal, A., Chandravadana, M. V. and Nagesh, M. 1996a. Effect of some secondary plant metabolites as seed treatment agents against *M. incognita* on tomato. *Nematol. Medit.*, **24**: 49-51.

Ravindra, H., Onkarappa, T., Narayanaswamy, H., Basavaraja, M. K., Ramaswamy, G. R. and Lokamanya, D. S. 2001. Integrated management of root-knot nematode in FVC tobacco nursery. *Tob. Res.*, **27**(1): 19-23.

Ray, S. and Dalei, B. K. 1998. VAM for root-knot nematode management and increased productivity of grain legumes in Orissa. *Indian J. Nematol.*, **28**: 41-47

Reddy, P. P., Nagesh, M. and Devappa, V. 1997. Effect of integration of *Pasteuria penetrans, Paecilomyces lilacinus* and neem cake for the management of root-knot nematode infecting tomato. *Pest Management Hor. Ecosys.*, **3**: 100-104.

Roberts, P. A. 1992. Current status of the availability, development and use of host resistance to nematodes. *J. Nematol.*, **24**: 213-227.

Roberts, P. A. 1993. Future of Nematology—integration of new and improved management strategies. *J. Nematol.*, **25**: 21-25.

Sekhar, N. S. and Gill, J. S. 1991. Efficacy of *P. penetrans* alone and in combination with carbofuran in controlling *Meloidogyne incognita. Indian J. Nematol.*, **21**: 61-65.

Sethi, C. L. and Gaur, H. S. 1986. Nematode management—An overview. *In*: Gopal Swarup and D. R. Dasgupta (eds.), Plant Parasitic Nematodes of India—Problems and Progress. Allied Pub. Pvt. Ltd. pp. 424-445.

Sharma, R., Dhaliwal, S. S. and Chandurkar, P. S. 1997. Evaluation of chemical and botanical nematicides for nematode management on Brinjal. *Indian J. Pl. Protec.*, **25**: 4-7.

Sharma, G. C. and Khan, M. L. 1995. Efficacy of different chemicals against root-knot nematode (*M. incognita*) infesting tomato *in vivo. Ann. Agril Res.*, **16**: 351-353.

Singh, D. 1991. Studies on the effect on *Tagetes species* on *Meloidogyne javanica* infectivity brinjal (*Solanum melongena*). Ph.D. Thesis, HAU, Hisar, Haryana, India, p. 83.

Siddiqui, M. A., Azam, M. F. and Saxena, S. K. 1998a. Evaluation of chemical pesticides against the root-knot nematode on aubergine. *Tests Agrochem Cultivars*, **19**: 2-3.

Siddiqui, M. A., Azam, M. F. and Saxena, S. K. 1998b. Evaluation of of root-dip treatment with nematicides on development of roor gall and yield (*Meloidogyne incognita*) in tomato and aubergine. *Tests Agrochem Cultivars*, **19**: 2-3.

Siddiqui, Z. A., Mahmood, I and Mahmood, I. 1996. Biological control of plant parasitic nematodes by fungi: A review. *Bioresource Technol.*, **58**: 229-239.

Sitaramaiah, K. and Sikora, R. A. 1981. Mededelmgen van de Faculteit Landbouwetens Chappen Rijksunivesiteet Gent., **45**: 605-702.

Stirling, G. R. 1991. Biological control of plant parasitic nematodes. CAB International, Wallingford, UK. pp. 282.

Sudha, S. and Sundararaju, P. 2001. Integrated approach for the management of burrowing nematode, Radopholus similes in arecanut based cropping system. *Indian J. Nematol.*, **31**(1): 26-33.

Suresh, C. K. and Bhagyars, D. J. 1984. Interaction between a vasicular arbuscular mycorrhiza and root-knot nematode and its effect on growth and chemical composition of tomato. *Nematol. Medit.*, **12**: 31-39.

Souza, J. T. Jr. and Campos, V. P. 1997. Effect of the isolate P1-UFLA of *Pasteuria penetrans* on the first generation of *Meloidogyne javanica* (Treub) Chitwood. *Nematologia Brasiliera.*, **21**: 93-102.

Trivedi, P. C. and Barker, K. R. 1986. Management of nematodes by cultural practices. *Nematropica*, **16**: 213-236.

Vats, R., Singh, J., Jain, R. K., Vats R. and Singh, J. 2000. Management of root-knot nematode (*Meloidogyne incognita*) in cotton through seed dressing with chemicals. *Indian J. Nematol.*, **30**: 90-91.

Young, L. D. 1992. Problems and strategies associated with long term use of nematode resistant cultivars. *J. Nematol.*, **24**: 228-233.

## Plate 14.1

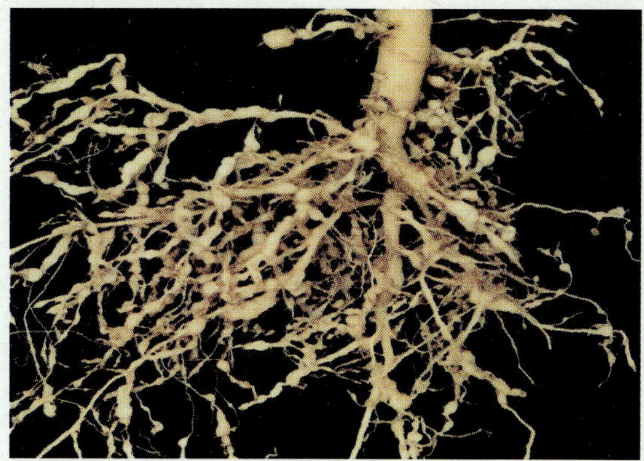

Galls caused by *Meloidogyne incognita* on Brinjal roots

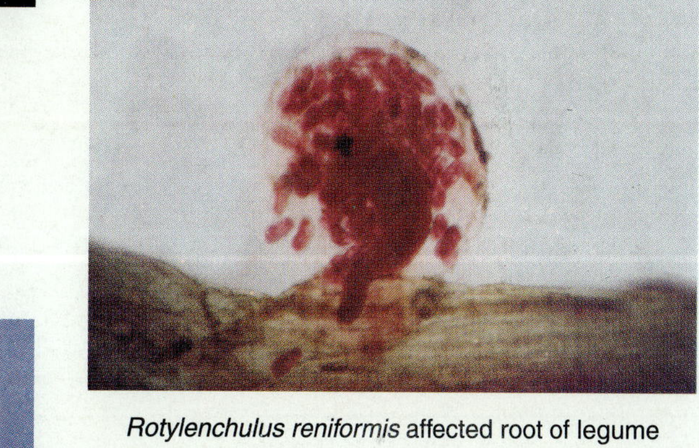

*Rotylenchulus reniformis* affected root of legume

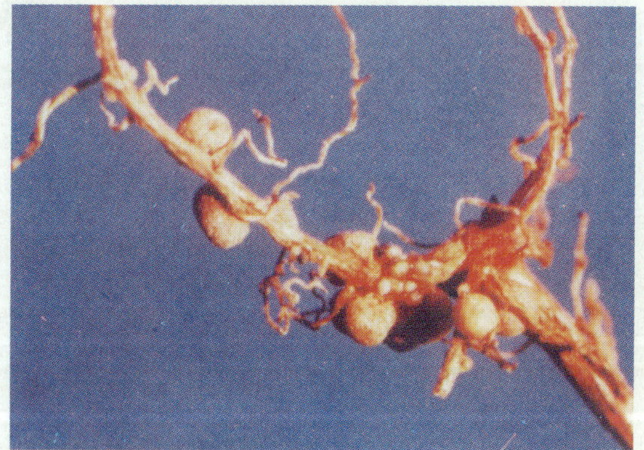

Heavily infested roots with nodules

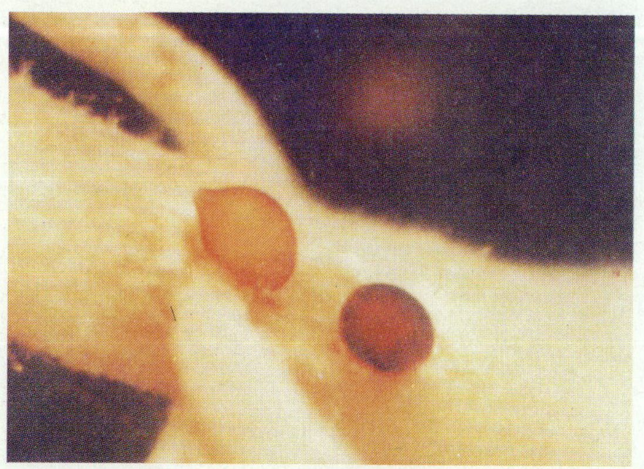

Close up of the nodules

# 15

# Status and Prospects of Integrated Pest Management Strategies for Obnoxious Weeds

**N. T. Yaduraju and J. S. Mishra**

## INTRODUCTION

Weeds are, unwanted plants. A particular plant is a weed only in terms of a human attitude. Plants are considered weeds when they interfere with the utilization of land and water resources or otherwise adversely intrude upon human welfare. Weeds are the major deterrent to the development of more sustainable agriculture systems. They cause enormous losses and sufferings to human beings by way of reduction in crop yield and quality, wastage of human energy and resources and increased expenditure to alleviate the problems caused by them. Weeds also act as alternate host for many insects and pathogens. Common vetch (*Vicia sativa* L.) in chickpea provides shelter to *Helicoverpa armigera*, a major pest of chickpea (Chauhan *et al.*, 1991). Common lambsquarters (*Chenopodium album*) acts as host for mustard aphid. *Ageratum* spp. and *Lantana* spp. provide shelter to white fly which transmits yellow mosaic virus disease in mungbean and soybean. Admixture of weed seeds such as wild rice in rice, wild oat in wheat, *Argemone* in mustard, Chicory in berseem and wild onion in onion impairs the quality of products. Weeds like water hyacinth (*Eichhornia crassipes*) and *Salvinia* spp. impede flow of water in irrigation and drainage channels and even cause flooding and sedimentation. They also affect the fish culture. Weeds like *Parthenium hysterophorus* cause allergy, itching, hay fever, illness to labourers when they come in contact. Thorny weeds like *Argemone maxicana, Amaranthus spinosus, Cirsium arvense, Carthamus oxycantha*, etc., restrict free movement of farm labourers in carrying out the field operations.

## CROP LOSSES DUE TO WEEDS

Weeds are ubiquitous. Their presence in crop field cause considerable reduction in productivity of crops. Unlike insect pests and pathogens, where the effect on crop is visible, the damage done by weeds is often noticed. In addition to direct effect on crop yield, weeds result in considerable reduction in the efficiency of inputs used. The precious and costly inputs such as fertilizers and irrigation water which are otherwise meant for realizing the potential yield will be usurped by the weeds. An attempt has been made to collect the information of losses caused by weeds in some principal crops. Based on the literature published in *Indian Journal of Weed Science* and *Indian Journal of Agronomy* since 1985, the yield losses due to weeds are presented crop-wise in Table 15.1.

*National Research for Weed Science, PB.No.13, Maharajpur, Ashartal, Jabalpur-482 004.*

**TABLE 15.1:** CROP YIELD LOSSES DUE TO WEEDS IN IMPORTANT FIELD CROPS

| *Crop* | *No. of Locations* | *No. of Trials* | *Mean Yield (kg/ha)* | | *Mean Loss (%)* |
|---|---|---|---|---|---|
| | | | *Weed Free* | *Weed Infested* | |
| Rice (DS) | 22 | 28 | 3365 | 1151 | 64.0 |
| Rice (PS/PT) | 20 | 30 | 4549 | 2620 | 43.9 |
| Wheat | 23 | 63 | 3241 | 2226 | 31.6 |
| Maize | 13 | 18 | 4067 | 2056 | 48.8 |
| Groundnut | 20 | 31 | 2486 | 934 | 63.6 |
| Soybean | 21 | 54 | 1986 | 874 | 53.0 |
| Mustard | 12 | 20 | 1433 | 889 | 37.7 |
| Linseed | 4 | 9 | 1110 | 399 | 62.7 |
| Sesamum | 5 | 6 | 616 | 288 | 54.2 |
| Sunflower | 4 | 5 | 1659 | 1117 | 32.2 |
| Pigeonpea | 16 | 21 | 1573 | 774 | 46.7 |
| Mungbean | 7 | 13 | 963 | 516 | 46.3 |
| Urdbean | 15 | 18 | 1001 | 474 | 55.4 |
| Chickpea | 10 | 13 | 1545 | 767 | 48.1 |
| Lentil | 6 | 6 | 1709 | 755 | 58.8 |
| Fieldpea | 9 | 13 | 2094 | 1054 | 47.1 |
| Cotton | 12 | 18 | 1234 | 824 | 60.4 |
| Sugarcane | 8 | 9 | 93.1* | 64.4* | 34.4 |
| Potato | 7 | 10 | 18.3* | 12.8* | 29.0 |

*t/ha, DS-Direct seeded, PS- Puddeled seeded, PT- Puddeled transplanted.

**TABLE 15.2:** WEEDS ACTING AS ALTERNATE HOSTS OF INSECTS AND DISEASES (GUPTA, 1998)

| *Host Weeds* | *Insect/Disease Organisms Hosted* | *Crop Affected* |
|---|---|---|
| **Weeds Hosting Insects** | | |
| *Aeschenomene* sp. | Grasshoppers (Vector of *Colletotrichum*) | Rice |
| *Achyranthus* sp. *Chenopodium album*, *Amaranthus* and *Datura* spp. | Leaf eating caterpillars<br>Gram caterpillar | Lucerne and maize<br>Redgram, cotton, okra, pea and brinjal |
| *Crotolaria* sp. | Hairy caterpillar | Castor |
| *Echinochloa* sp., *Panicum* sp. | Stem borer | Rice |
| *Chenopodium album* | Stalk borer | Tomato, maize |
| *Brassica kaber* | Aphids | Brassica crops and brinjal |
| **Weeds Hosting Diseases/Nematodes** | | |
| *Agropyron* and *Portulaca* spp. | Wilt | Tomato |
| *Cynodon dactylon* and *Digitaria* spp. | Sting nematode | Several vegetables |
| *Commelina* spp. | Certain viral diseases and parasitic nematodes | Banana |
| *Saccharum spontaneum* | Downy mildew | Maize |
| *Solanum* and *Physalis* spp. | Mosaic and cyst nematodes | Solanaceous vegetables, tobacco and cocoa |

In general, impact of weeds on crop yields varies from high input to low input crop production systems. It has been estimated that weeds caused 5% loss in agricultural production in most developed countries, while it caused 10% loss in developed countries and 25% loss in least developing countries (Bhowmik, 1998). The world-wide loss of attainable production of eight principal food and cash crops (rice, wheat, barley, maize, potato, soybean, cotton and coffee) has been estimated to be 76.3 billion US dollar annually (Oerke *et al.*, 1994). An analysis revealed that losses caused by weeds in India were to the tune of 9.28 million tonnes in cereals, 0.78 million tonnes in pulses, 0.57 million tonnes in oilseeds and 7.20 million tonnes in fibre and other commercial crops (Sahoo and Saraswat, 1988). The list of weeds acting as alternate host to insect pests, nematodes and diseases is given in Table 15.2.

## SEED PRODUCTION CAPACITY AND DORMANCY OF WEEDS

A sound knowledge of biology of weeds, with particular reference to their reproduction and survival mechanisms is essential for planning their effective management. The seed production capacity and length of seed survival in soil of few important weeds have been given in Table 15.3.

**TABLE 15.3:** SEED PRODUCTION AND LENGTH OF SEED SURVIVAL OF SOME WEEDS IN SOIL (WILSON, 1988.)

| *Weed Species* | *No. of Seed Produced/ Plant* | *Length of Seed Survival in Undisturbed Soil (years)* |
|---|---|---|
| Ball mustard (*Neslia paniculata*) | 490 | 10 |
| Canada thistle (*Cirsium arvense*) | 680/stem | 21 |
| Common lambsquarters (*Chenopodium album*) | 72450 | 39 |
| Common mullein (*Verbascum thapsus*) | 223200 | 39 |
| Common purslane (*Portulaca oleracea*) | 52300 | 30 |
| Common ragweed (*Ambrosia artemisiifolia*) | 3380 | 39 |
| Common sunflower (*Helianthus annuus*) | 7200 | 1 |
| Curly dock (*Rumex crispus*) | 29500 | 39 |
| Curlycup gumweed (*Grindelia squarrosa*) | 29700 | 10 |
| Dandelion (*Taraxacum officinale*) | 15000 | 6 |
| Devils beggarticks (*Bidens frondosa*) | 7000 | 10 |
| Green foxtail (*Setaria viridis*) | 34000 | 39 |
| Redrot pigweed (*Amaranthus retroflexus*) | 117400 | 10 |
| Wild oat (*Avena fatua*) | 250 | 1 |
| Yellow foxtail (*Setaria glauca*) | 6420 | 30 |

## WEED COMPETITION

Competition is the rivalry between crop and weed for a common demand which becomes short in supply and eventually the demand and supply gap is reflected in the growth and productivity of weed and the crop. The competition occurs when weed and crop grow in a mixed stand, influence their growth mutually reduce growth of some plants in comparison to others (Plate 15.1). Competition is what weed control is all about. Weeds compete with the crop for nutrients, moisture, solar radiation and space when they are limited and reduce the crop yield and quality. Crop-weed competition is largely affected by nature and intensity of weeds, crop species and cultivar, light, moisture, nutrients and management practices (Fig. 15.1).

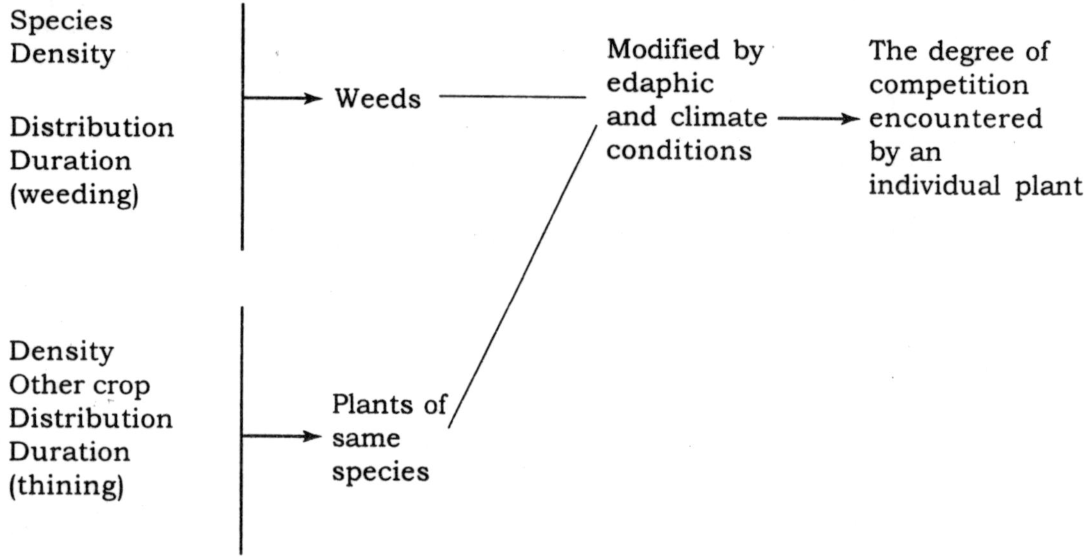


**Fig. 15.1:** Schematic presentation of competition (From Chisaka, 1977 and Bleasdale, 1960)

## Competition for Light

Weeds compete with the crops for light by faster and higher growth, large leaves and climbing devices. The competition for light begins when plants begin to shade each other. Cudney *et al.* (1991) showed that wild oat (*Avena fatua*) reduced light penetration and growth in mixture with wheat by producing greater height growth than wheat. Similarly, in soybean, velvetleaf (*Abutilon theophrasti*) intercepted more light than soybean due to its greater height, growth and dry matter allocation to more branches in the upper layers of the canopy (Akey *et al.*, 1990).

## Competition for Water

Competition for water between weeds and crops reduces soil moisture availability and cause water stress. Weeds are comparatively more tolerant than the crop plants to moisture stress. In general, for producing equal dry matter, weeds transpire more water than do most of our crop plants (Table 15.4). Shahi (1978) determined the consumptive use of water of *Chenopodium album* as 550 mm against 479 mm for wheat. It was further noted that the weeds removed moisture evenly from up to 90 cm soil depth, while the major uptake of moisture by wheat was limited to the top 15 cm of soil. The proliferous growth of weeds, especially perennial ones, such as *Cyperus rotundus*, can severely limit the availability of water to sugarcane in some seasons even in humid regions (Holm *et al.*, 1977). However in some situations, decreased water availability favours crop growth by reducing the impact of competing weeds (Patterson 1995). Thus, under these situations, manipulation of soil moisture may become a reasonable strategy for weed management.

**TABLE 15.4:** TRANSPIRATION COEFFICIENT OF CERTAIN WEEDS AND CROPS (KANITKAR *et al.*, 1960)

| *Weed Species* | *Transpiration Coefficient 'Q'* | *Crop Species* | *Transpiration Coefficient 'Q'* |
|---|---|---|---|
| *Cynodon dactylon* | 813 | *Zea mays* | 352 |
| *Digitaria sanguinalis* | 696 | *Sorghum vulgare* | 394 |
| *Echinochloa colona* | 674 | | |
| *Tridax procumbens* | 1402 | | |

**TABLE 15.5:** NUTRIENT REMOVAL (KG/HA) BY WEEDS AND PULSE CROPS

| *Crops* | *Nitrogen* | | *Phosphorus* | | *Potassium* | | *Reference* |
|---|---|---|---|---|---|---|---|
| | *Crop* | *Weed* | *Crop* | *Weed* | *Crop* | *Weed* | |
| Mungbean (rainy season) | 12.4 | 132.2 | 5.3 | 17.6 | 10.3 | 130.1 | Yadav *et al.* (1985) |
| Mungbean (summer season) | 55.6 | 79.1 | 10.2 | 19.8 | 49.1 | 79.1 | Kundra *et al.* (1991) |
| Urdbean | 73.4 | 76.3 | – | – | – | – | Kumar *et al.* (1985) |
| Pigeonpea | – | 28.4 | – | 23.7 | – | 14.2 | Singh *et al.* (1980) |
| Chickpea | 32.3 | 54.6 | 5.0 | 7.7 | 47.3 | 72.4 | Dadhich and Mali (1991) |
| Peas | 30.6 | 71.6 | 5.8 | 14.4 | 33.1 | 105.0 | Ahlawat *et al.* (1983) |

## Competition for Nutrients

Weeds always remove more nutrients than the crops (Table 15.5). Uncontrolled weeds in any crop remove more quantity of nitrogen and potassium than the phosphorus. In a crop heavily infested with weeds, it seems logical that more fertilizer would reduce nutrient competition. Competition does not occur until the immediate supply falls below the combined demand of both crop and weeds. If supply is increased, competition should decrease. Actually, fertilization usually stimulates weed growth to the crop's detriment. With low fertility, competition is usually for nutrients, however with high fertility, competition is just as vigorous, and primarily for light. The nutrient removal by weeds in different crops is given in Table 15.6.

## Critical Period of Crop-Weed Competition

To optimize herbicide use within a given tillage system and at the same time provide a logical framework for the integration of alternative weed control measures, information on the critical period of weed interference is essential. This information can be used to potentially reduce the need for long term residual control with herbicides, optimize the dose and timeliness of post emergence herbicides, influence of the timing of cover crop seeding and mechanical cultivations. Although duration of the critical period can be affected by numerous factors such as weed species, planting pattern and environmental conditions, an early assessment of this timeframe will provide a guide for future studies in alternative methods of weed control and crop weed interference.

**TABLE 15.6:** NUTRIENT DEPLETION (kg/ha) BY WEEDS IN DIFFERENT FIELD CROPS

| *Crop* | *Nitrogen* | *Phosphorus* | *Potassium* |
|---|---|---|---|
| Paddy (Direct seeded) | 20-37 | 5-14 | 17-48 |
| Paddy (Transplanted) | 11 | 3 | 10 |
| Maize | 23-59 | 6-10 | 16-62 |
| Sorghum | 36-46 | 11-18 | 31-47 |
| Wheat | 20-90 | 2-13 | 28-54 |
| Pigeonpea | 28 | 24 | 14 |
| Greengram | 80-132 | 17-20 | 80-130 |
| Cotton | 67-75 | 20-38 | 30-109 |
| Chickpea | 29-55 | 3-8 | 15-72 |
| Peas | 61-72 | 7-14 | 21-105 |
| Lentil | 39 | 5 | 21 |
| Soybean | 26-65 | 3-11 | 43-102 |
| Groundnut | 15-39 | 5-9 | 21-24 |
| Rapeseed and mustard | 22 | 3 | 12 |
| Linseed | 32 | 3 | 13 |
| Sugarcane | 35-162 | 22-44 | 135-242 |

The time of weed removal has an important effect on growth and yield of the crop. Removing weeds at any time during growing season may not be beneficial. Stage of weed removal is as important as removal *per se*. Therefore, it is necessary to identify the critical period of crop-weed competition to render the weed control practices more effectively. Critical period of weed control is an important consideration in the development of alternative weed management strategies. It can be defined as "the shortest span of time in the ontogeny of crop growth when weeding will result in higher economic returns". Hall *et al.* (1992) described the critical period of weed control as representing the time interval between two separate components. The first component is the maximum length of time that weeds, which emerge with the crop, can remain before they reduce crop yield. The second component is the length of time a crop must be kept weed free after planting so that weeds emerging later do not reduce yield. The two components can be integrated to identify a single critical period of weed control, recognized as the duration over which neither component provides an acceptably low yield loss; weed control must be effective within a period of overlap between the two components. A fundamental principle of plant competition is that early occupants on a soil tend to exclude the later ones. This principle finds application in practical weed control. Weeds are capable of accumulating dry matter faster than the crop plants. Thus, the duration of weed infestation and time of weed removal has a significant influence on crop growth and economic yield. The effect of emergence time and weed duration on crop yield is illustrated in Fig. 15.2. Mishra (1997) reviewed the research work done under AICRP-Weed Control and else where since last 20 years and reported that the critical period varies from 15- 30 days after sowing (DAS) in greengram, blackgram, cowpea and okra; 15-45 DAS in direct seeded rice, maize, sorghum, sunflower, sesame and rapeseed-mustard; 30-45 DAS in transplanted rice, pearl millet, wheat, peas, jute, cauliflower, cabbage and tomato; 20-45 DAS in soybean and potato; 30-60 DAS in castor, lentil, chickpea, Frenchbean, and groundnut; 15-60 DAS in pigeonpea and cotton; 30-75 DAS in onion and 30-120 DAS in sugarcane depending upon nature and intensity of weed flora, agro-climatic situations and management practices.

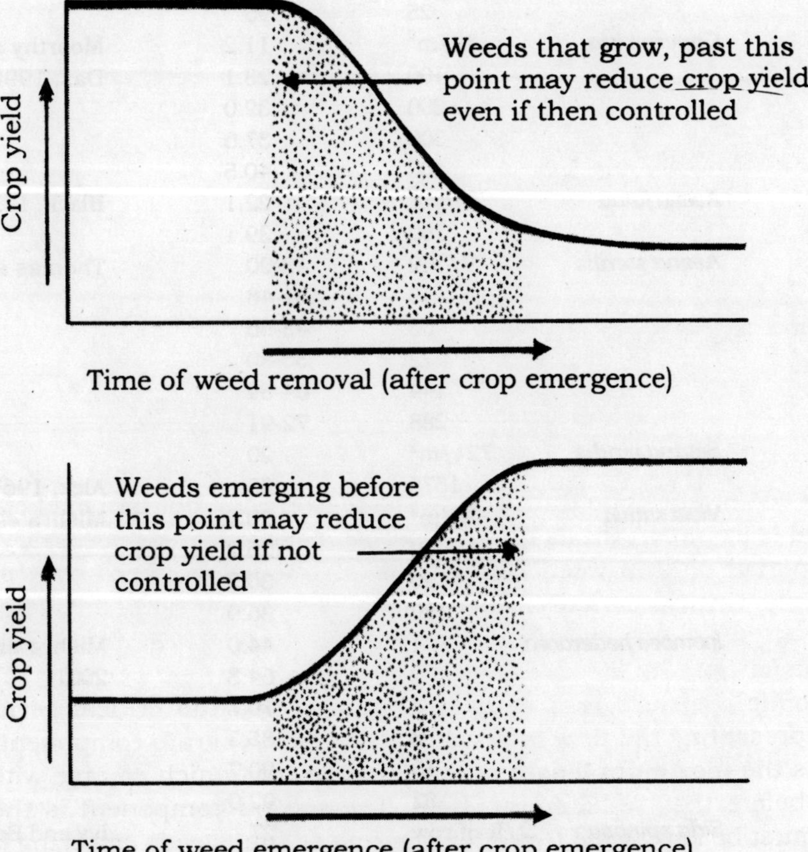


**Fig. 15.2:** The effect of emergences time and weed duration on crop yield. The upper curve shows that weeds allowed to compete with small crop can reduce yield, while the lower curve shows as crop grow they become more competitive, and hence less affected by weeds

## Effect of Weed Density on Crop Yield

It is obvious that increasing weed density decreases yield. However, the weed density-crop yield relationship diverges from linear. A few weeds usually do not affect yield. Weed competition can be represented by a schematic sigmoidal relationship (Fig. 15.3). Data from selected studies depicting increasing weed density effect on crop yield have been given in Table 15.7.

**TABLE 15.7: EFFECT OF WEED DENSITY ON CROP YIELD**

| *Crop* | *Weed* | *Weed Density* | *Per cent Yield Reduction in Control* | *Reference* |
|---|---|---|---|---|
| Rice | *Echinochloa crusgalli* | 1/ft$^2$ | 57 | Smith, 1968 |
| | | 5 | 80 | |
| | | 25 | 95 | |
| | *Cyperus iria* | 40/m$^2$ | 11.2 | Moorthy and Das, 1998 |
| | | 100 | 23.1 | |
| | | 200 | 32.0 | |
| | | 300 | 37.6 | |
| | | 400 | 40.5 | |
| Wheat | *Avena fatua* | 70/yd$^2$ | 22.1 | Black, 1958 |
| | | 160 | 39.1 | |
| | *Avena sterilis* | 9/ m2 | 13-20 | Thomas *et al.* 2000 |
| | | 18 | 31-48 | |
| | | 36 | 43-66 | |
| | | 72 | 55-80 | |
| | | 144 | 64-89 | |
| | | 288 | 72-91 | |
| | *Setaria viridis* | 721/m$^2$ | 20 | |
| | | 1575 | 35 | Alex, 1967 |
| Lentil | *Vicia sativa* | 30/m$^2$ | 20.8 | Mishra *et al.* 1997 |
| | | 60 | 26.2 | |
| | | 120 | 30.3 | |
| | | 180 | 36.9 | |
| Soybean | *Ipomoea hederacea* | 1 | 44.0 | Mishra and Singh, 2001 |
| | | 2 | 64.8 | |
| | | 4 | 70.7 | |
| | | 8 | 85.3 | |
| | | 16 | 90.7 | |
| | | 32 | 92.0 | |
| Cotton | *Sida spinosa* | 2/ft of row | 27 | Ivy and Baker, 1972 |
| | | 4 | 40 | |
| | | 12 | 41 | |

## Modeling of Crop-Weed Interference

The development of an integrated weed management system is a complex task and must be supported by a thorough understanding of crop-weed interference. Computer models can integrate available information and predict the outcome of crop-weed interference. Causens (1985) suggested the hyperbolic weed density yield model which is an empirical regression model widely applied to depict crop yield loss associated with a particular weed density at a specific moment in the growing season. The precision of weed density yield models can be improved by incorporating relative time of emergence or relative leaf area as a factor.

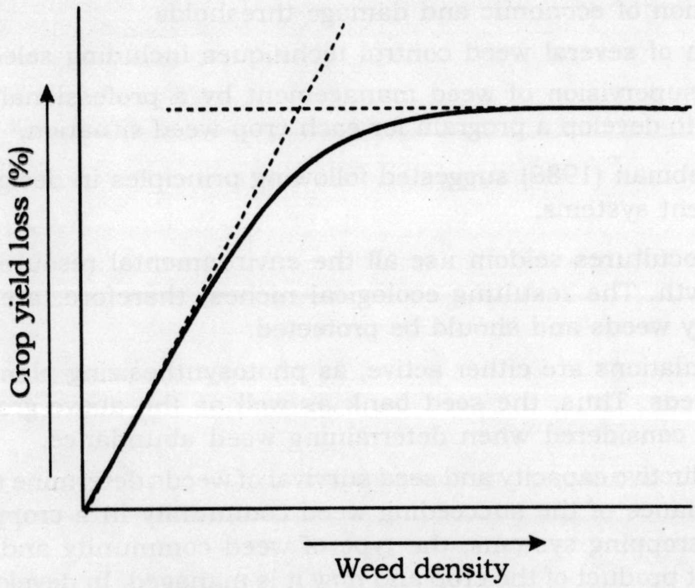


**Fig. 15.3:** The effect of weed density on crop yield

Weed density-yield models are the basis for development of economic weed threshold models that predict the weed density at which specific post-emergence weed control measures are warranted (Causens; 1987). However, the prediction of an economic threshold level can be only as accurate as the underlying weed density-yield model and the cost and efficiency estimate of control.

Population dynamics models can be used for assessing the long term implications of control measures on weed populations. Long-term economic weed threshhold levels can thus be predicted by incorporating weed density-yield models into population dynamic models. Despite these refinements, the general applicability of models based primarily on empirical regressions can be limited by potentially large fluctuations in model parameters due to variability in edaphic, climatic and cultural factors.

## PRINCIPLES FOR WEED MANAGEMENT SYSTEMS

Every weed management programme is only part of a total crop production system. Therefore, any combination of environmental manipulation and cultural techniques to reduce weed abundance must be compatible with other farm objectives. Thus, the interactions between soil, fertility, insects and diseases, and direct weed control procedures may be especially important. However, it is not possible to know everything about every (or any) weed species in order to develop effective weed management strategies. Zimdahl (1993) suggested following components in the development of weed management systems:

- Incorporation of ecological principles
- Use of plant interference and crop-weed competition
- Incorporation of economic and damage thresholds
- Integration of several weed control techniques including selective herbicides
- Frequent supervision of weed management by a professional weed manager employed to develop a program for each crop-weed situation.

Altieri and Liebman (1988) suggested following principles in designing integrated weed management systems.

- Crop monocultures seldom use all the environmental resources available for plant growth. The resulting ecological niches, therefore, are susceptible to invasion by weeds and should be protected.
- Weed populations are either active, as photosynthesizing plants, or dormant, usually seeds. Thus, the seed bank as well as the above-ground vegetation should be considered when determining weed abundance.
- The reproductive capacity and seed survival of weeds determine the composition and abundance of the succeeding weed community in a cropping system. In intensive cropping systems, the type of weed community and its abundance are a direct product of the crop and how it is managed. In developing countries, where mixed cropping is traditionally practiced in contrast to more intensive forms of crop production, the complex cropping patterns appear to disfavor weeds. Additionally, in less intensive cropping systems than those presently practiced in many developed nations, weed management appears to have less relevance than overall cropping practices in determining the weed community composition.
- The cropping pattern can be a powerful agent in reducing weed densities by preemption of environmental resources to crop plants. Weed control tactics, while usually reducing the abundance of weeds, can shift the composition, density, and spatial distribution of weeds in fields. These shifts in the spatial or temporal dynamics of weed communities and populations ultimately may increase weed abundance and, therefore, crop competition over the long term. Although shifts, in species composition often appear inevitable, the practice of growing crops with divergent life cycles and using rotational sequences of crops and weed control tactics are effective strategies to prevent any one weed species from becoming dominant. These practices reduce selection pressure on weed communities and populations.
- Single measurements of weed density are usually not adequate to determine weed impacts. Most crops have thresholds of weed tolerance, expressed as density, amount of biomass, or period of time before significant economic loss

in crop yields results. However, these thresholds vary among cropping systems, weed species, and environmental constraints. The thresholds also may have to be adjusted when criteria other than crop loss are used to determine the economic, ecological, and social effects of weeds.

- Suppressed crop growth cannot always be explained by crop-weed competition. At times, weeds may simply indicate a deteriorated soil or resource base. Allelopathy also may be a mechanism through which weeds affect plant growth, and *vice versa*. In addition, crops and weeds may coexist without crop yields being reduced economically and beneficial effects are possible from some crop-weed associations.
- Weed populations and communities are regulated by a combination of factors (e.g., predation, parasitism, environmental stress, interference, and direct-control methods), and at several stages of the weed's life cycle. Thus, control of weeds can be achieved through direct or indirect means. During direct control the weed plant is physically or chemically removed, while indirect controls rely on biological functions of the crop, the weed, and their associates. Both strategies have been successful, although indirect regulation may be most appropriate for complex cropping systems.

## INTEGRATED WEED MANAGEMENT SYSTEM

Better understanding of weeds will lead to better crop and weed management. A basic principle of weed control is that control measures should be directed at survival mechanisms of weeds in the soil. For annual weeds, the objective is to prevent seed production and to deplete seed reserves. In case of perennials, destruction of underground vegetative organs is sought. Most weed control practices and techniques exploit biological differences between the crop and the weed and are accomplished by manipulations of the shared habitat. Maintenance of the crop in a dominant or superior competitive position in the crop-weed association depend on a differential response of crop and weed to some factor of the habitat which can be modified or manipulated with predictable results. This basic concept underlies effective weed control practice. However, the selection of methods and techniques of agricultural weed control may vary with region, crop, nature of weed infestation and the level of agricultural mechanization. Integrated weed management systems are used as a part of pest management strategies and include:

- Use of multiple-pest-resistant strategies, high yielding, well adapted varieties that resist weed competition also
- Pre-planting seed bed tillage
- Effective seed bed preparation and seeding methods that enhance crop growth and minimize weed growth
- Optimum plant populations including closer spacing in and between rows to optimize crop growth and minimize weed growth
- Use of crops that form a canopy

- Precision placement of fertilizer and timing the fertilizer application for maximum stimulation of crops and minimum stimulation of weeds
- Judicious use of irrigation
- Timely and appropriate cultivations
- Sound crop rotations
- Crop diversification
- Field sanitation
- Harvesting methods that do not spread weed seeds
- Use of biological agents such as insects and pathogens and effective chemical methods.

**Components of Integrated Weed Management**

The weed management in field crops requires an integrated approach that utilizes effective cultural, mechanical, biological, ecological and chemical methods in a mutually supported manner into the crop production system with due consideration of economic, environmental and sociological consequences (Fig. 15.4). Various methods of weed management such as cultural, mechanical, chemical, etc. have been used with different degree of success in different agro-ecological zones and productions system, which are as follows:

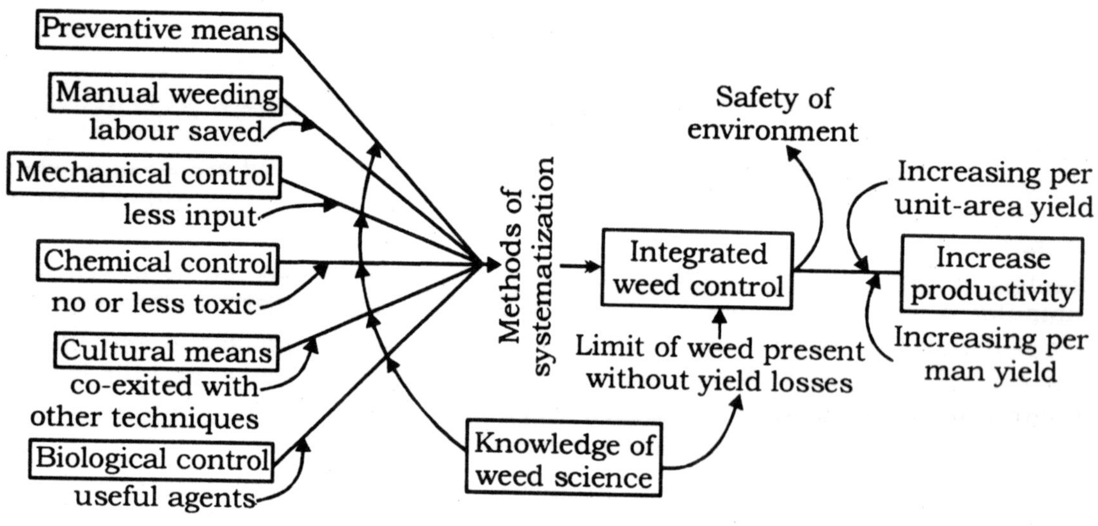


**Fig. 15.4:** A Conceptional model of Integrated weed control, (Noda, 1977)

**Weed Prevention**

Preventive control encompasses all measures taken to forestall the introduction and spread of weeds. Success of a preventive programme varies with species and the amount of effort devoted to control. The prevention of a weed problem is usually easier and less costly than control or eradication. The following measures can be suggested to prevent the introduction of weeds into non-inhabited field:

- Use 'clean' (weed, seed-free) crop seed for planting.
- Use organic manures only after thorough decomposition to kill weed seeds.
- Clean harvesters and tillage implements before moving to non-weed infested area.
- Avoid transportation or use of soil from weed infested area.
- Inspect nursery stock or transplant for seed and vegetative propagules of weeds.
- Remove weeds that are near irrigation ditches, fence rows, right-of-way and other non-crop land.
- Prevent reproduction of weeds.
- Use weed seed screens to filter irrigation water.
- Restrict live stock movement into non-weed infested area.

Other practices used to prevent and avoid potential weed problem at the state, regional or national level are weed laws, seed laws and quarantines.

### *Legal Measures*

Legal measures are necessary to check inter-state and inter-country movement of noxious weeds if the cost of having to control additional alien weeds is to be saved. Unfortunately in most parts of the tropical and sub-tropical world, noxious weeds have not been subjected to strict quarantine laws. This has resulted in the introduction and spread of some of the costliest weeds of the world. Very recently the Indian Plant Quarantine Authorities have made it compulsory to declare plants at the time of disembarking in India. With the establishment of World Trade Organization (WTO), the world market has provided unlimited opportunities of international trade of agricultural products. In order to ensure effective implementation of Plant Quarantine regulations, it is essential that the imported plants and plant materials are free from exotic weeds. Few year back 13 weed species resistant to different herbicides (Table 15.8) were reported in wheat consignment imported from Australia (Mool Chand *et al.*, 2000). It is, therefore, necessary to evolve suitable quarantine measures to prevent the introduction of such herebicide resistant weeds into our country in future.

### Cultural Methods

Despite the great progress made in agriculture, manual and mechanical methods continue to be important weed management practices in many regions of the world. Cultural methods are used to complement manual and mechanical methods. Cultural practices such as method and time of sowing, crop density and geometry, crop species and varieties, method and time of fertilizer application, mulching, crop rotation and intercropping, time of irrigation, soil-solarization, etc., have pronounced effect on crop-weed interference. Cultural practices are manipulated in such a way that they become more favourable for crop growth and less to weeds. They are not only eco-friendly but also reduce the use of costly herbicides.

**TABLE 15.8:** WEED SPECIES INTERCEPTED IN THE WHEAT IMPORTED FROM AUSTRALIA (MOOL CHAND *et al.*, 2000)

| *Weed Species* | *Common Name* | *Family* | *Percent Incidence* | | *Germination (%)* |
|---|---|---|---|---|---|
| | | | *Weight Basis* | *Number Basis* | |
| **A. Not reported in India** | | | | | |
| *Avena fatua** | Wild oat | Poaceae | 0.024 | 0.038 | 60 |
| *A. sterilis** | Sterile oat | Poaceae | 0.0072 | 0.012 | 11 |
| *Brassica caber* | Charlock | Brassicaceae | 0.003 | 0.015 | 80 |
| *Brassica tournefortii** | Wild turnip | Brassicaceae | 0.0054 | 0.031 | 30 |
| *Bromus diandrus* | Great brome | Poaceae | 0.0242 | 0.077 | 20 |
| *Carrichtera annua* | Ward's weed | Brassicaceae | 0.005 | 0.023 | 35 |
| *Carthamus lanatus* | Saffron thistle | Asteraceae | 0.0762 | 0.008 | 40 |
| *Cenchrus pauciflorus* | Sandbur | Poaceae | 0.012 | 0.004 | 58 |
| *Centaurea melitensis* | Maltese cockspur | Asteraceae | 0.017 | 0.115 | 46 |
| *Echium plantagineum** | Paterson's curse | Boraginaceae | 0.023 | 0.012 | 60 |
| *Emex australis* | Spiny emex | Polygonaceae | 0.004 | 0.004 | Nil |
| *Galium tricornutum* | Three-horned bed straw | Rubiaceae | 0.016 | 0.004 | Nil |
| *Heliotropium europaeum* | Common heliotrope | Boraginaceae | 0.00036 | 0.015 | Nil |
| *Hordeum lepornium** | Barley grass | Poaceae | 0.0012 | 0.001 | 30 |
| *Lethospermum arvense* | Corn gromwell | Boraginaceae | 0.013 | 0.008 | 10 |
| *Lolium rigidum** | Annual ryegrass | Poaceae | 0.077 | 0.508 | 40 |
| *Lupinus angustifolius* | Narrow-leaved lupin | Fabaceae | 0.124 | 0.015 | 80 |
| *Malva parviflora* | Dwarf mallow | Malvaceae | 0.005 | 0.038 | 30 |
| *Medicago scutella* | Snail medic | Papilionaceae | 0.001 | 0.008 | 60 |
| *Neslia paniculata* | Ball mustard | Brassicaceae | 0.00014 | 0.004 | Nil |
| *Papaver hybridum* | Rough poppy | Papaveraceae | 0.015 | 0.192 | Nil |
| *Phalaris paradoxa** | Paradoxa grass | Poaceae | 0.002 | 0.015 | 60 |
| *Polygonum convolvulus** | Black bind weed | Polygonaceae | 0.016 | 0.19 | 58 |
| *Raphanus raphanistrum** | Wild radish | Brassicaceae | 0.051 | 0.031 | 60 |
| *Rapistrum rugosum** | Turnip weed | Brassicaceae | 0.009 | 0.038 | 30 |
| *Reseda lutea* | Cut-leaved mignonette | Recedaceae | 0.0007 | 0.0115 | Nil |
| *Rumex crispus* | Curled dock | Polygonaceae | 0.0005 | 0.012 | Nil |
| *Salvia verbenaca* | Wild sage | Lamiaceae | 0.0004 | 0.004 | 10 |
| *Silybum marianum* | Variegated thistle | Asteraceae | 0.002 | 0.004 | 10 |
| *Sisymbrium officinale** | Hedge mustard | Brassicaceae | 0.002 | 0.192 | 10 |
| *Sonchus oleraceus** | Common sawthistle | Asteraceae | 0.002 | 0.384 | 15 |
| *Vicia villosa* | Russian vetch | Papilionaceae | 0.001 | 0.004 | Nil |
| *Vulpia bromoides** | Vulpia | Poaceae | 0.009 | 0.004 | 33 |
| **B. Reported in India** | | | | | |
| *Asphodelus fistulosus* | Onion weed | Liliaceae | 0.001 | 0.015 | 20 |
| *Avena fatua* | Wild oat | Poaceae | 0.024 | 0.038 | 60 |
| *Eucalyptus* sp. | Eucalyptus | Myrtaceae | 0.028 | 0.004 | Nil |
| *Lolium perenne* | Perennial rye grass | Poaceae | 0.077 | 0.508 | 40 |
| *Medicago denticulata* | Burr medic | Papilionaceae | 0.005 | 0.015 | 80 |
| *Phalaris minor** | Canary grass | Poaceae | 0.001 | 0.004 | 72 |
| *Polygonum aviculare* | Knot weed | Polygonaceae | 0.0005 | 0.02 | 13 |
| *Sonchus oleraceus* | Common sawthistle | Asteraceae | 0.002 | 0.384 | 15 |
| *Sorghum halepense* | Johnson grass | Poaceae | 0.0012 | 0.008 | 50 |
| *Tribulus terrestris* | Puncture vine | Zygophyllaceae | 0.0024 | 0.0038 | Nil |
| *Vicia sativa* | Common vetch | Papilionaceae | 0.008 | 0.008 | 55 |

*Herbicide resistant weed species.

In organic agriculture, the approach to weed management involves the whole cropping system. The aim is not the eradication of weeds but to maintain a balance between crop plants and the weeds, with the grower adjusting the balance in favour of the crops whenever possible. Cultural practices that shift the balance of competition towards the crop usually will disfavour weed occurrence and improve crop yields. Crop rotation is at the heart of the organic system and although the method and timing of soil cultivations and choice of crop are usually linked, both contribute in different ways to manipulation of weed population. Any practices that provide vigorous uniform crop establishment usually will assist in reducing weed prevalence. Factors that improve crop competitiveness include:

### *Stale Seed-bed Technique*

The principle of flushing out germinabale weed seeds before cropping forms the basis of the stale or false seed bed technique, in which soil cultivation may take place days or weeks before planting or transplanting a crop. This depletes the seed bank in the surface layer of the soil and reduces subsequent weed emergence. Where light rains occur for an extended period before the onset of the monsoon, or irrigation is available, it may be possible to kill several flushes of weed growth before planting. To ensure success, cropping should be delayed until the main flush of emergence has passed. The emerged weed seedlings may then be killed by flaming or light cultivation or application of contact non-residual herbicides like paraquat. It is vital not to cultivate below the top 1-2 cm soil otherwise a further flush of weeds may emerge.

### *Tillage*

Tillage includes all operations and practices that are carried for the purpose of modifying the physical character of soil so as to provide favourable conditions. A major benefit of tillage is prevention and suppression of weeds. Tillage suppress weeds by breaking, cutting, or tearing from the soil, thus exposing the vegetation to desiccation, and by smothering them. Repeated tillage may deplete weeds from fields by diminishing seed or vegetative propagules in the soil and may also exhaust the food reserves of perennial weeds. Besides weed control, tillage is also important in crop production because of the following reasons:

- Seedbed preparation
- Burial of crop residue
- Control of insects, pathogens and rodents
- Improvement of soil physical conditions
- Incorporation of fertilizers, herbicides and soil amendments.

Weed problem begins with weed seed in soil. It is the tillage which directly affects the weed seed bank by physical mixing of soil and in turn reducing the weed number. Tillage influences the vertical distribution of weed seeds in soil layer. Weed seeds buried deep germinate but fail to emerge due to thick soil layer over it, resulting in death of weed seedling. One of the most important changes occurring in agriculture today is the increased awareness and acceptance by the agricultural community of conservation tillage practices. Conservation tillage, which advocates the maintenance of crop residue cover on 30% of the soil surface, is soundly based within the frame work of sustainable agriculture. Johnson *et al*; (1989) found that the presence of crop residues increased weed suppression and did not result in an increase in herbicide applications.

### *No Tillage and Night Tillage*

A light requirement for seed to be released from dormancy is a wide spread mechanism found in many weed species. This requirement can be satisfied even after a brief exposure to light, such as that resulting from tillage. Thus, germination of weed species whose seed require light should be impeded if a no tillage system were implemented for crop production. Alternatively, it is possible that night cultivation also could result in significant reduction in weed density (Scopel, *et al.*, 1994). The problem of *P. minor* is comparatively less, as the weed seed lying at lower depths does not come to the surface as in case of conventional tillage (Table 15.9). Infestation is also comparatively less due to non-availability of nutrients from well placed fertilizer near to the crop seed. For many burried seeds, it is the exposure to light during soil cultivation that stimulates germination. The exclusion of light during seedbed preparation has been shown to reduce weed emergence. Covering an implement to prevent light reaching the soil at the point of cultivation may be sufficient to reduce weed emergence by up to 70% (Ascard, 1994). However, not all weed species have light-sensitive seeds. Welsh *et al.* (1999) observed the reduced density of *Chenopodium album* by cultivating in darkness.

**TABLE 15.9:** EFFECT OF ZT AND CT PLANTING ON WEED POPULATION (NO./M$^2$) AT 25 DAYS AFTER SOWING (YADURAJU AND MISHRA, 2002)

| *Tillage* | *P. minor* | *A. ludoviciana* | *C. album* | *M. hispida* | *Total* |
|---|---|---|---|---|---|
| Zero | 9.82 | 4.00 | 12.73 | 4.42 | 17.67 |
| Minimum | 11.70 | 2.07 | 11.83 | 3.46 | 17.89 |
| Conventional | 15.16 | 2.11 | 13.52 | 2.60 | 20.80 |
| LSD (P=0.05) | 5.30 | 0.81 | NS | NS | NS |

Data subjected to square root transformation.

### *Furrow Irrigated Raised Bed Planting System (FIRBS)*

In this method crops are grown on raise beds. In this system the problem of *Phalais minor* is very less as the weed seeds lying on top of the raised beds fails to germinate as the top of bed dry out quickly. This method also facilitates mechanical weeding as the area in the furrows can be easily cultivated and even manual weeding can be easily done.

### *Crop Rotation*

Crop rotation is a fundamental tool of integrated weed management. Interest in using crop rotation to control weeds is gaining popularity especially among those focusing on sustainable agriculture. Crop rotation introduces conditions and practices that are not favourable for a specific weed species and thus, growth and reproduction of that weed species are hampered.

Crop rotation under local conditions can be integrated by considering following points in view:

1. There is need to diversify not only cropping system but also farming system to introduce integrated weed management based on cropping system or farming system approach.
2. In the farming system approach, animal component may be integrated with crop component so that introduction of forage crops may help to diversify the weed management. Weed communities in the continuous cropping system tended to have greater total densities and were similar in composition than crop-fallow system (Derksen *et al.*, 1994).
3. Crop rotation allows use of different management options which help in diversity in weed flora.
4. In integrated weed management, the carry over effect of complex weed flora of weedy or weed free fallow should be defined in terms of holistic approach. The weed seed bank in the soil may be reduced or exhausted by crop rotation.

Liebman and Dyck (1993) reported that the success of rotation system for weed suppression appears to be based on the use of crop sequence that create varying patterns of resources competition, allelopathic interference, soil disturbance and mechanical damage to provide an unstable or inhospitable environment that prevents the proliferation of a particular weed species.

The growth and reproduction of a troublesome weed species may be actively discouraged by introducing unfavourable practices in to a rotation. The inclusion of cover crops in the rotation at a time when land might otherwise lie uncropped will suppress weed development, yet maintain soil fertility and prevent erosion. In addition, the decomposing cover crop residues may release allelo-chemical that inhibits the germination and development of weed seeds.

In monocropping system, numerous weed species persist and expand rapidly but crop rotation helps in interrupting life cycle of weeds and prevents any weed species to become dominant e.g. *Sorghum halepense* become predominant weed in continuous maize but can be controlled by rotating with cotton (Dale and Chandler, 1979). Certain weed species often associated with particular crops (eg. Barnyard grass in rice, wild oat and *Phalaris minor* in wheat, dodder in alfalfa etc.). Therefore, population of such weeds usually will increase whenever the crop is grown on the same field continuously for several years. Growing in sequence crops may discourage weed associations with crops that have sharply contrasting growth and cultural requirements. Banga *et al.* (1997) reported higher incidence of *Phalaris minor* in rice-wheat rotation than in other rotations (Table 15.10). Parasitic weeds can also be managed through crop rotation by rotating host crop with trap crops, as they induce germination of weed seeds but they themselves are not parasitized.

**TABLE 15.10:** EFFECT OF CROP DIVERSIFICATION ON POPULATION OF *Phalaris minor* AND WHEAT YIELD (BANGA *et al.*, 1997)

| *Crop Rotation* | *Population of P. minor (no./$m^2$)* | *Wheat Grain yield (kg/ha)* |
|---|---|---|
| Rice-wheat (continuous for 10 years)* | 2350 | 3000 |
| Rice-berseem, rice-wheat | 255 | 4200 |
| Rice-wheat, rice-cotton, cotton-wheat* | 2125 | 3200 |
| Rice-berseem, sorghum-wheat | 190 | 4500 |
| Rice-potato, rice-wheat | 255 | 4000 |
| Cotton-wheat (for 4 years)* | 38 | 4600 |
| Rice-berseem, rice-berseem, rice-wheat | 28 | 5000 |
| Rice-winter maize, sorghum-raya, maize-wheat | 18 | 5500 |
| Maize-sunflower, rice-berseem, rice-wheat | 35 | 5300 |
| Rice-potato, chilly-potato, rice-wheat | 24 | 5400 |
| Rice-wheat (for 5 years), chilly-wheat* | 2421 | 3200 |

*Isoproturon 1.0 kg/ha was also used in wheat at 30-35 days after sowing.

Rotation among crops having drastically dissimilar life cycles or requiring different management practices is useful in disrupting weed cycle. Shankaran and Chinnamuthu (1993) found that *Paspalum dilatum* was nearly eliminated after three crops of rice-maize-mung bean, whereas *Digitaria ciliaris* became dominant. In rice-rice-urdbean system, an increase of 70 per cent in *Cyperus rotundus* population has been reported (Laesino, 1980). *Cuscuta* is one of the important parasitic weeds causing lot of damage in rice-mungbean/urdbean cropping system in coastal Andhra Pradesh, Tamilnadu and parts of Madhya Pradesh. The reports of its infestation is also available in other pulses viz. lentil, chickpea and pigeonpea. The parasitic weeds can be effectively managed through crop rotation by rotating host crop with trap crops, as they induce germination of parasitic weed seeds but they themselves are not parasitised. Due to lack of suitable host, *Cuscuta* seedlings will emerge and die.

**Crop rotation and seed bank dynamics:** The composition and density of weed seed banks are frequently a reflection of long term crop rotations and management systems. Walker and Buchanan (1982) reported changes in the weed flora when mono-cropping has been replaced with crop rotation. However, in any given year the crop species, planting date, herbicide selection and weather patterns may alter species composition of the weed community. Therefore, knowledge of the role of crop rotation in seed bank dynamics would be useful in the refinement of an integrated weed management system.

### *Intercropping*

Intercropping suppresses weeds better than sole cropping and thus provides an opportunity to utilize crops themselves as tools of weed management. When two or more crops are grown together as intercrops, the total weed suppressing ability of a system will be higher than the sole cropping (Rao and Shetty, 1976). Finding an intercrop which will suppress the growth of the weeds but not the crop has been difficult. Two research approaches need to be considered:

(i) eco-physiological studies leading to the manipulation of intercropping systems to obtain better weed control, and

(ii) evaluation of various weed control methods including herbicides for important intercropping systems.

Many short duration pulses like, cowpea, greengram and soybean effectively smoother weeds without causing reduction in the yield of main crop. In wide spaced crops such as pigeonpea, maize, cotton, sorghum and sugarcane, intercropping is a common practice, which besides covering risk will reduce weed infestation. Patel *et al.* (1983) found that intercrops suppressed the weeds and increased the total productivity (Table 15.11). Intercropping of sorghum with cowpea and greengram (Table 15.12) smothered weeds and reduced hand weeding cost (Rao and Shetty, 1981).

**TABLE 15.11:** EFFECT OF INTERCROPPINGIN PIGEONPEA ON WEED AND YIELD OF CROP (PATEL *et al.*, 1983)

| *Crops* | *Weed Dry Weight ($g\ m^{-2}$) at 60 DAS* | *Seed Yield ($kg\ ha^{-1}$)* | |
|---|---|---|---|
| | | *Pigeonpea* | *Intercrop* |
| Pigeonpea – (sole) | 46 | 652 | – |
| Pigeonpea + sorghum | 18 | 593 | 514 |
| Pigeonpea + maize | 28 | 565 | 289 |
| Pigeonpea + rice | 32 | 597 | 125 |
| Pigeonpea + blackgram | 17 | 460 | 587 |
| Pigeonpea + greengram | 13 | 422 | 411 |
| Pigeonpea + groundnut | 29 | 592 | 592 |

Sugarcane is also a wide spaced crop. The row spacing ranges from 60-90 cm and the crop take nearly 3-4 weeks for germination depending upon temperature. Short duration, early canopy forming crops such as French beans, groundnut, soybean, cowpea and greengram can be raised as intercrops to suppress the weeds and to augment the total productivity.

**TABLE 15.12:** EFFECT OF INTERCROPPINGON GRAIN YIELD OF SORGHUM AND WEED DRY WEIGHT AT HARVEST (RAO AND SHETTY, 1981)

| *Treatment* | *Sorghum Grain Yield (kg/ha)* | *Weed Dry Weight ($g/m^2$)* |
|---|---|---|
| Sorghum 1 hand weeding (HW) | 3652 | 78.7 |
| Sorghum 2 HW | 5264 | 17.0 |
| Sorghum + cowpea 1 HW | 4895 | 8.3 |
| Sorghum + greengram 1 HW | 3952 | 14.7 |

### *Mulching*

Mulch is a protective covering of materials maintained or placed on soil surface. Materials used for mulch includes crop residues, straw, leaves, paper plastic films, gravel and dry soil. Mulching the soil surface can prevent weed seeds germination or physically suppress seedling emergence, but is not effective against established perennial weeds. Chemical effect of mulches on weed control includes allelopathy, toxic microbial products and pH changes in soil. Mulching with sugarcane trash at 2-4 inch thickness proved to be very effective in controlling *Cyperus rotundus*, one of the most obnoxious weeds in sugarcane crop during the month of April-June (Mathur, 1960). In maize (Table 15.13), addition of wheat straw mulch reduced the population and dry matter of *Echinichloa* spp., *Panicum capilare* and *Amaranthus albus* (Crutchfield *et al.*, 1986).

**TABLE 15.13:** EFFECT OF WHEAT STRAW MULCH ON WEED POPULATION AND ITS DRY WEIGHT IN MAIZE (MATHUR, 1960)

| *Mulch Level (t/ha)* | *Weed Population ('000/ha)* | *Weed Dry Weight (kg/ha)* |
|---|---|---|
| 0 | 220 | 1500 |
| 1.7 | 160 | 1300 |
| 3.4 | 67 | 950 |
| 5.1 | 57 | 680 |
| 6.8 | 53 | 570 |

A living mulch consists of a dense stand of low growing-species, established before or after the crops. In cereals, an under story of clovers (*Trifolium* spp.) has been shown to improve soil fertility, and reduce pest and disease problems in addition to suppressing weeds (George, *et al.*, 1997). A free-floating fern, *Azolla pinnata*, is used in low land and irrigated rice as a sort of companion crop. This fern has a symbiotic relationship with *Azolla anabenea*, a nitrogen fixing blue green algae. This symbiotic relationship not only contributes up to 100 kg N/ha but also reduces weed growth by forming an *Azolla* blanket over the water surface in a rice crop. The *Azolla* technique suppresses many annual weeds while leaving out certain annuals which have strong culms (eg. Barnyard grass) and perennial weeds.

### *Competitive Crops and Cultivars*

Crops differ in relative growth rate, spreading habit, height, canopy structure and inherent competitive character and accordingly differ in their weed suppressing ability. A quick growing and early canopy-producing crop would be expected to be better competitor against weeds than crops lacking these characters. The competitive ability of wheat cultivars was found to be closely associated with their tallness and early canopy cover (Table 15.14). Tall cultivars apparently intercept more light and reduce weed growth particularly at later stages of crop growth. Seed size within a species also influence the competition through vigorous plants from larger seeds (Spifters and Van Den Berg, 1982). Increased competitive ability of cultivars has been attributed to early emergence, seedling vigour, increased rate of leaf expansion, rapid creation of dense canopy, increased plant height, early root growth and increased root size. Future breeding and variety testing programmes should take factors of crop competitive ability into consideration.

**TABLE 15.15:** GRAIN YIELD OF WHEAT AS INFLUENCED BY CULTIVARS AND WEED CONTROL PRACTICES (BALYAN AND MALIK, 1991)

| *Wheat Cultivars* | *Wheat Yield as Affected by Weed Control Practices* | | |
|---|---|---|---|
| | *Wild Oat Infested* | *Isoproturon 0.75 kg/ha* | *Weed Free* |
| HD 2009 | 2794 (59.8) | 4147 (40.3) | 6948 |
| HD 2285 | 4865 (27.0) | 6692 (No loss) | 6666 |
| S 308 | 3916 (40.22) | 5813 (11.3) | 6551 |
| WH 291 | 4653 (30.3) | 6506 (2.5) | 6676 |
| WH 147 | 5044 (26.7) | 6794 (1.3) | 6884 |

Values in parentheses are per cent yield loss over weed free.

### *Sowing Time*

Planting time considerably influences the occurrence and manifestation of weed species. In timely sown chickpea, the weed population by 30 days is generally quite high to attract manual weeding whereas in late sown chickpea the build up of adequate weed flora is only after 45 days. Delayed sowing of lentil and chickpea is also reported to reduce the infestation of *Orobanche*—a root parasite (Linke and Saxena, 1989). Malik *et al.* (1988) reported that in chickpea, the maximum emergence of most competitive weed, *Chenopodium album* L. occurred when crop was sown on November 5 and declined gradually with delay in sowing. However, in most winter pulses this can not be a viable approach as delayed sowing invariably results in reduced yield. Sinha *et al.* (1988) reported that early sowing (10 August) and closer row spacing (30 cm) reduced the weed growth and increased the dry matter accumulation, LAI, NAR, CGR and grain yield of irrigated pigeonpea at Kalyani (West Bengal).

### *Plant Geometry and Plant Density*

Planting density and pattern modify the crop canopy structure and in turn influence weed smothering ability. Narrow row spacing will bring variation in microclimate viz., light intensity, evaporation and temperature at soil surface. The establishment of a crop with a more uniform and dense plant distribution may result in better use of light, water and nutrients and lead to greater crop competitive ability. Crops grown in narrower rows start competing with weeds at an earlier stage than those in wide rows because of more rapid canopy closure and probably better root distribution. Increased shading at soil surface will smother weed growth. Narrow row spacing are known to suppress the weed growth (Sinha *et al.*, 1988), however, degree of suppression varies greatly. In *Phaseolus vulgaris*, (Tesadale and Frank 1983) found that closer row spacing suppressed weeds effectively than wider row spacing (Table 15.15).

Planting density and pattern modify crop canopy structure and in turn influence weed smothering ability. Narrow row spacing will bring variation in microclimate *viz;* light intensity, evaporation and temperature at soil surface. The increased shading of soil surface will smother weed growth. Increased population of maize (60,000 to 90,000 plants/ha) and decreased spacing were found to reduce the growth of weeds

(Angiras and Singh, 1989; Chaudhary, 1981). Bi-directional sowing and closer row spacing (Table 15.16) were quite effective in suppressing the growth of *Phalaris minor* in wheat (Azad *et al.*, 1988).

**TABLE 15.15:** EFFECT OF ROW SPACING ON CROP CANOPY AND WEED GROWTH IN *Phaseolus vulgaris* (TESADALE AND FRANK 1983)

| *Row Spacing (cm)* | *Crop Canopy (%)* | *Fresh Weed Weight (t ha$^{-1}$)* |
|---|---|---|
| 15 × 15 | 77 | 1.5 |
| 25 × 09 | 78 | 1.3 |
| 36 × 06 | 79 | 2.4 |
| 46 × 05 | 55 | 8.6 |
| 91 × 02 | 61 | 7.5 |

**TABLE 15.16:** EFFECT OF CROSS SOWING AND CLOSER ROW SPACING ON WEED GROWTH AND GRAIN YIELD OF WHEAT (AZAD *et al.*, 1988)

| *Treatment* | *Weed Dry Weight (g/m$^2$)* | *Grain Yield of Wheat (kg/ha)* |
|---|---|---|
| Unweeded | 519 | 2050 |
| Hand weeding | 193 | 2950 |
| Cross sowing | 249 | 2900 |
| Closer spacing (15 cm) | 211 | 2900 |

### *Nutrient Management*

Crops and weeds generally compete for the same nutrient pool. Increasing the levels of soil fertility can alter the competitive interactions between crops and weeds. Resource use by weeds often increases more rapidly with added nutrients, resulting in a greater ability of weeds to compete for other resources. Nitrogen, the major nutrient for which the plants compete could be banded close to the crops row, thus enhancing the crop accessibility to the nutrient. Increasing rates of fertilizer application encourage more weed growth than the crop growth if no weed control measure is followed. Under this situation, it is better to apply fertilizers at lower rates than needed to maximize yields (De Datta, 1977). Inclusion of green manurs as an organic source of nutrient supply not only add nutrients and organic matter in the soil but also suppress the weed growth due to its dense foliage cover on the ground surface and incorporation of existing weeds in the soil. Higher incidence of parasitic weed *Striga* spp. was observed in impoverished soils (Bansinkai, 1955). Application of nitrogen not only reduced the intensity of *Striga* (Table 15.17) but also increased crop yields (Guled, 1982).

### *Water Management*

Proper water management can reduce weeds in both wet and dry seasons. More weeds emerge earlier at high soil moisture than at low moisture level. Many weeds can not germinate under flooded conditions. This is used as weed control method especially in rice crop. Maintaining water submergence in rice field throughout the crop season creates anaerobic condition, which will be unfavourable for weed seed germination (Table 15.18). Method of irrigation also influences the weed density. In rip irrigation the weed density is greatly reduced due to the wetting of soil near the plant base only (Table 15.19). Rest of the area remains dry and free of weeds. In some situations, decreased water availability favours crop growth by reducing the impact of competing weeds (Patterson, 1995). Thus, under these situations, manipulation of soil moisture may become a reasonable strategy for weed management.

**TABLE 15.17:** EFFECT OF NITROGEN AND COMPOST ON *Striga asiatica* POPULATION (AT 90 DAS) AND YIELD OF SORGHUM (GULED, 1982)

| *Treatment* | *Striga Population/ $m^2$* | *Grain Yield (kg/ ha)* |
|---|---|---|
| Control | 166 | 4300 |
| Nitrogen 100 kg/ha | 7 | 6300 |
| Nitrogen 200 kg/ha | 6 | 7000 |
| Nitrogen 300 kg/ha | 3 | 7300 |
| Compost 7.5 t/ha | 131 | 4400 |
| Compost 15 t/ha | 140 | 4700 |
| Compost 7.5 t/ha + 100 kg N/ha | 19 | 5700 |
| Compost 15 t/ha + 100 kg N/ha | 12 | 5800 |

**TABLE 15.18:** EFFECT OF SUBMERGENCE ON WEED EMERGENCE (NO./$M^2$) IN LOW LAND RICE (HOSMANI, 1991)

| *Weed Species* | *Depth of Water Submergence (cm)* | | | |
|---|---|---|---|---|
| | *0* | *2.5* | *12* | *17* |
| *Fimbristylis littoralis* | 794 | 390 | 170 | 0 |
| *Cyperus difformis* | 143 | 155 | 78 | 0 |
| *Cyperus iria* | 28 | 41 | 3 | 0 |
| *Scirpus latifolia* | 21 | 49 | 3 | 1 |
| *Monochoria vaginalis* | 55 | 42 | 38 | 0 |

**TABLE 15.19:** EFFECT OF DRIP AND FURROW IRRIGATION ON WEED INTENSITY IN CABBAGE (KUDARIMANI, 1977)

| *Days after transplanting of cabbage* | *Number of weeds/ $m^2$* | | *Dry weight of weeds (g/ $m^2$)* | |
|---|---|---|---|---|
| | *Drip* | *Furrow* | *Drip* | *Furrow* |
| 30 | 1409 | 1844 | 128 | 157 |
| 60 | 948 | 1530 | 129 | 170 |
| 80 | 352 | 1165 | 44 | 61 |

### Soil Solarization

Solarization is a method of heating the surface by using plastic sheets placed on moist soil to trap the soil radiation. The process would raise the surface soil temperature by 8-10° C as compared to non-solarized soils. A duration of 4-6 weeks is sufficient to give satisfactory control of weeds. Many annuals, some perennials and parasitic weeds are sensitive to this treatment. Besides controlling soil borne pests, soil solarization is reported to enhance the availability of nutrients in soil and favour beneficial microflora, ultimately resulting in increased plant growth response in many crops.

The response to solarization on weeds varies with weed species. Winter weeds are generally more susceptible, whereas summer weeds especially *Cyperus* spp. and *Convolvulus arvenseis* are generally more resistant. In perennials with an established underground systems of deep roots, rhizomes or tubers, failures of solarization is probably due to the limited soil depth, <10 cm, where temperature reaches to lethal levels (Horowitz *et al.*, 1983). Most perennials are capable of regenerating rapidly from partially damaged underground organs.

While a solarization for a mere 10 days gave complete control of *Phalaris minor* and *Avena ludoviciana*-the most dominant grass weeds in winter season crops in India, there was an increase in the population of *M. indica* even at 40-day solarization. The heat tolerance of *M. indica* has been attributed to its thick seed coat.

Parasitic weed broomrape (*Orobanche* spp.) has been effectively controlled with solarization (Meti, 1993; Jacobson *et al.*, 1980). Sauerborn *et al.* (1989) came out with promising data on *Orobanche* control in fababean and lentil with 20-50 days of solarization treatment (Table 15.20).

**TABLE 15.20:** DURATION OF SOLARIZATION ON BROOMRAPE INFESTATION IN FABABEAN AND LENTIL (SAUERBORN *et al.* 1989)

| *Days Solarized* | *Fababean* | | *Lentil* | |
|---|---|---|---|---|
| | *No./m²* | *Weight (g/m²)* | *No./m²* | *Weight (g/m²)* |
| 0 | 115 | 152 | 61 | 33 |
| 20 | 57 | 122 | 32 | · 37 |
| 30 | 33 | 65 | 25 | 35 |
| 40 | 26 | 57 | 22 | 29 |
| 50 | 13 | 41 | 4 | 4 |

Soil solarization for 4-6 weeks in summer not only gave excellent weed control in soybean but also in the succeeding wheat crop (Yaduraju and Ahuja, 1996). The weed control in soybean was better in soil solarization alone than with manual weeding (1 or 2) and pre-emergence application of pendimethalin (0.75-1.5 kg/ha). Soybean yields were significantly higher with soil solarization as compared to pendimethalin. This was attributed to the poor control of *Commelina benghalensis* and *Digera arvensis* with the herbicide. Soil solarization, on the contrary gave excellent control of these weeds.

## Mechanical Method

Weed removal in India is largely restricted to mechanical and cultural methods. Although the farmers are aware of weed problems, they err in their assessment of potential damage the weed may cause mainly because of their fatalistic attitude towards weeds. The weed control they adopt is often inadequate and untimely. Weed control is attempted late when weeds have already inflicted considerable damage on crops. Inadequate labour supply and high wages, force farmers to give weed control the last priority. Inclement soil and weather conditions automatically rule out timely weeding.

Mechanical weed control involves removal of weeds with various tools and implements including manual removal by hand weeding. Inter-cultural operations are performed primarily to destroy the weeds present in the field and create favourable soil conditions for crop growth. Hand hoeing and manual weedings are most common practices performed for weed control in almost all pulse crops. One or two hand weedings at critical crop-weed stage provide satisfactory control of weeds in most of the pulse. Extra weeding may be required if crops are infested with perennial weeds. The use of mechanical weed control demands experience and knowledge of how to use the soil as a weed control agent. Climate and soil type play an important role in the possibilities for mechanical weed control. Monitoring the early development of weeds is necessary for timing of weed harrowing at the optimum stage. Mechanical weeders include cultivating tools such as hoes, harrows, times brush weeders, and cutting tools like mowers. The success of mechanical weeding depends upon the stage of weeds, crop geometry and climatic conditions. Hand weeding may also be used after mechanical inter row weeding to deal with weeds left in crop rows.

## Flame Cultivation

It is another successful alternative method that is catching up in the developed countries in the recent past. Flame cultivation involves the use of liquefied petroleum gas, mostly propane for pre-emergence and post-emergence weed control. Pre-emergence flaming is relatively problem-free, although the timing is critical. Selective flaming in the growing crop requires precision and carries a great risk of damage to the crop. Flaming equipments to burn off weeds has been developed in several countries including Germany, Holland, Sweden and Denmark (Holmoy and Netland, 1994). Selective flaming is performed in a wide variety of crops such as cotton, corn, soybean, and grain sorghum. Flame is used to a limited extent in fruits such as blueberries, raspberries and grapes.

## Biological Control

Biological control of weeds is the deliberate use of natural enemies, primarily insects or fungi, to suppress growth or reduce the population of weed species. The utilization of biological weed control agents in weed management offers many advantages including,

(a) A high degree of specificity for the target weed.

(b) No effects on non target and beneficial plants or man.

(c) Absence of weed resistance development.

(d) Absence of residue build up in the environment.

The two most common approaches are: the classical or inoculative method and the bioherbicide or inaundative strategy. The classical strategy is an ecological approach which relies on the ability of an organism to multiply and spread following small scale release. The organism then remains in balance with the target weed, keeping the latter at an acceptably low level.

The bioherbicide strategy, the second major strategy of biological control of weeds, is to attack a whole weed population with a single, non-persistent application of inoculum. The inoculum inundates the whole of the area infested by a weed to increase the effectiveness of the agent. Generally, the pathogens considered for this strategy are fungi, hence the commonly used name-mycoherbicides. The major mycoherbicide products which are in use are given in Table 15.21.

Eradication of the target population is not possible with biological control. However, rapid and complete weed control is not required, as long as the target weeds are reduced in their vitality and their competitive ability and biological control is complemented by other measures within an IWM system. Consequently, biological control could constitute an important element in the suppression below the economic threshold level of a particular weed population escaping other IWM measures.

The control of pests through biological control agents has been considered as the ideal method for managing pests under organic farming. No doubt, it is environmentally benign and ecologically and socially acceptable. However, their efficacy and economics are questionable. In weed management, their application is limited as the target weeds are many and the bio control agents are not expected to be effective on all of them. Moreover, control of one weed will result in substitution with other weeds, some of which could be more dangerous than the one that has been controlled. The use of insect pests as bio-control agents has application in situations where only one weed is a problem such as in aquatic ecosystem, range lands, forestry or waste lands. The control of *Parthenium hysterophorous* with Mexican beetle *Zygogramma bicolorata* and the control of water hyacinth with weevil *Neochetina* spp. are a couple of successful examples of use of insect pests for weed control (Plate 15.1). The Mexican beetle is very effective on *Parthenium* and excellent control of the weed has been reported from several places in India. However, the insect is active only during the rainy season and it hibernates in soil during the dry and winter months. Several species of fungi have been developed as mycoherbicides (Table 15.21) in developed countries for the management of few problematic weeds. However, they have a number of limitations and their use is limited to a very small area.

**TABLE 15.21:** MYCOHERBICIDE PRODUCTS IN USE (HATZOIS, 1987)

| *Products* | *Agents* | *Target Weeds* |
|---|---|---|
| DeVine | *Phytophthora. palmivora* | *Morrenia odorata* (Strangler vine or milkweed) |
| Collego | *Colletotrichum gloesporoides* f. sp. *aeschynomene* | *Aeschynomene virginica* (Northern jointvetch) |

### *Allelopathy*

Allelopathy has potential in integrated weed management. It is a harmful, direct or indirect, effect of one plant on another through the production of chemicals that enter the environment. Crop plants have the capacity to produce and exude allelochemicals into their surroundings to suppress the growth of weeds in their vicinity. Olofsdotter and Navarez (1996) screened 111 rice cultivars for allelopathic potential against *Echinochloa crus-galli* (L.) in the fields at IRRI and found that 11 cultivars in dry season and 21 in wet season had suppressed the weed growth by more than 50%. Similarly in wheat, Wu *et al.* (1998) reported that out of 38 wheat cultivars screened, some cultivars significantly inhibited both the germination and the radicle growth of *Lolium rigidum* Gaud. The use of allelopathic plants, or substances isolated from them and produced transgenetically, may become an important form of weed control in the future.

## Chemical Method

Weed control through manual/mechanical methods though very effective, has certain limitations such as unavailability of labour during peak period, high labour cost, unfavourable environment particularly in rainy season. etc. Under such conditions, use of herbicides is advantageous and economical. Broadly there are three categories of herbicides which could be used for effective weed control in pulse crops.

**Pre-plant soil incorporation:** The herbicides which have greater toxicity on the emerging crop seedlings and decomposed due to solar radiation are applied before the crop is planted. They are incorporated in the soil up to the depth of 5 cm after the final land preparation. e.g., fluchloralin and trifluralin.

**Pre-emergence application:** Herbicides are applied after sowing but before the emergence of both, the crops and the weeds preferably within 48 hours after sowing., e.g. pendimethalin, alachlor, butachlor, metalachlor, oxadiazon, linuron, etc.

**Post-emergence application:** Herbicides are applied after the emergence of crops or weeds, around 15-25 days after sowing, e.g. 2,4-D, isoproturon, bentazone, chlorimuron-ethyl, sulfosulfuron, clodinafop, fluazifop-p-butyl, etc. The key success with post emergence herbicides is timeliness. Many post emergence herbicides will control weeds only when they are small. Delayed application can also result in yield loss due to early season competition from the weeds. In contrast, applications made too early may miss weeds that have not yet emerged. The optimum application timing varies by herbicide and weed and is affected by several other factors. The introduction of herbicide resistant crops has also greatly increased use of the post emergence application method, especially in soybean.

Herbicides being selective, dependable and effective against target weeds gained popularity in the recent years especially under intensive agriculture. In India use of herbicides for weed management is meager as compared to developed nations. This is mainly due to low purchasing and risk bearing capacity as well as perception of dryland farmers about weeding. Herbicides offer a better alternative to mechanical weeding. The discovery and use of herbicides have revolutionized the agriculture in many developed countries.

It was estimated that losses would rise to nearly 20 billion US dollar annually, if herbicides were no longer available. The estimated net societal loss from banning of only 2,4-D in the U.S. would be 1.638 billion dollar, whereas, banning all phenoxy herbicides would result in a loss of 2.559 billion dollar annually (Burnside *et al.*, 1996). In general, herbicides account for the largest proportion of crop protection chemicals sold on a world-wide scale. Globally, the herbicides constitute 45% of the total pesticides sale and in some countries like the USA, Germany and Australia, the figure is as high as 60-70%. In India, however, the position is different as herbicides form a meagre 16% of total pesticide consumption (Table 15.22). Sharp increase in wages and unavailability of labour as a result of industrialization and urbanization are bound to make herbicides more acceptable to farmers. Currently about 95% of the herbicides is consumed in wheat (42%), rice (30%) and tea plantation (23%). The use pattern might change soon with the introduction and indeginization of more chemicals.

**TABLE 15.22:** PESTICIDE USE IN INDIA, WORLD AND THE USA (SHARMA AND SHARMA, 1999)

| *Pesticide* | *% Total Pesticide* | | | |
|---|---|---|---|---|
| | *India* | | *World* | *USA* |
| | *1988* | *1997* | *1994* | *1998* |
| Herbicide | 5 | 16 | 47 | 55 |
| Insecticide | 76 | 52 | 29 | 32 |
| Fungicide | 18 | 30 | 19 | 7 |
| Others | 5 | 2 | 5 | 6 |

In India, the chemical weed control is mostly prevalent in states of Punjab, Haryana, Western UP, Tamilnadu and Andhra Pradesh. In Punjab and Haryana, the major use of herbicides is in rice and wheat crop, Tamilnadu and Andhra Pradesh (in rice), Madhya Pradesh (in soybean and wheat) and Gujarat (in groundnut and spices). Nearly 75% of rice and 50% of wheat in Punjab and 60% of rice and 40% of wheat in Haryana is using new technology based on herbicide use for weed management. The other area where weed management technology is mostly herbicide based is plantation crops, more specially tea, where mechanical disturbance of the land is discouraged.

Weed management cost is a major input cost in crop production. Herbicides are economical to use in crop production with a larger profit margin. The benefit : cost ratio of controlling weeds in transplanted rice ranged from 16 : 1 to 26 : 1 for herbicides against 3.3 : 1 to 6.3 : 1 for hand weeding (Ampong-Nyarko and De Dutta, 1991). The input cost of herbicide is in general comes to be nearly Rs. 800-1000/ha. This varies from state to state and also on the capacity of the farmers to use herbicides under prevailing weed infestation. The labour cost for doing the mechanical and manual operations do come to around Rs. 1200-1500/ha for one weeding. Where inter row cultivation is done using bullock or tractor power, the cost is around Rs. 400-500/ha. But mechanical weeding is possible only in wider row spaced crops and provides partial weed control between crop rows and weeds in intra-rows remain uncontrolled. It has been observed that the cost of weed management either based on mechanical methods or through herbicides provide minimum of 20% increase in crop yield. In rice, wheat and soybean, the cost of 150-200 kg of produce meets the requirement, while the increase is to the tune of 500-800 kg/ha. This indicates an overall increase of production of respective crops without increasing the cost of operation.

***Advantages of Herbicides***

- Herbicides can kill many weeds that survive by mimicry, e.g. *Phalaris minor* and *Avena* spp. in wheat and *Echinochloa* spp. in rice.
- Herbicides can be safely used where manual weeding damages the crop, e.g. onion, garlic, groundnut, etc.
- Herbicides are more effective on perennial and parasitic weeds.
- Herbicides can effectively be used in closely planted crops where manual and mechanical weeding is not possible.
- Herbicides are safe on erodable and sloppy lands where tillage may accelerate soil and water erosion.
- Herbicides enable early and timely planting of crops.
- Herbicides can be used where physical condition of soil is not conducive to manual weeding, e.g., during rainy spells.
- While one time application of a herbicide is often enough, the manual/ mechanical method is repetitive.
- Herbicides kill weeds *in situ* without permitting their dissemination.
- Herbicides can safely be used to control weeds growing in obstructed situations such as right-of-way, under fruit trees and on undulating lands.
- Herbicides provide timely weed control by controlling weeds at the critical period of their competition.
- In dryland agriculture, effective herbicidal control ensures higher water use by the crops and less crop failure due to drought.
- Planning and management of labour for various agricultural operations in big farms are facilitated by use of herbicides.
- Use of herbicides offers gender equality as manual weeding is largely done by female labourers.
- In many parts of the country the cost of weed control through herbicides is lower than that of manual weeding.

***Concerns***

Despite the above advantages, several concerns have also been made with the indiscriminate use of pesticides. These are as under:

**Weed Shift:** Continuous use of the same herbicide year after year in the same crop in the same area leads to shift in weed flora. For example, due to continuous use of grass killers in rice, particularly in Punjab and Haryana, the weed flora is shifting to sedges like *Cyperus* sp., *Scirpus* sp., *Fimbristylis* sp., *Eleocaris* sp., etc. Similarly, with the successful control of grassy weed *Phalaris minor* in wheat, broad leaved weeds like *Lathyrus sativa, Convolvulus arvensis, Medicago denticulata, Cichorium intybus* and *Cirsium arvense*, are gaining importance. Moreover, pernicious weeds like *Cyperus* spp., *Sorghum halepense, Saccharum spontaneum,* etc. infesting large areas of field crops, defy any solution so far. Similarly, weeds like *Imperata cylindrica, Mikania micrantha, Polygonum* sp., have become important in plantation crops and can't be satisfactorily controlled with any of the existing herbicides. These examples indicate that the existing herbicides though efficient, can't solve all the problems and therefore, new herbicides and their integration with other weed control methods are needed to solve the emerging problems (Plate 15.1).

**Toxicity and Residue Problem:** The indiscriminate use of pesticides leaves behind residues in food and produce. Widespread and increasing use of herbicides is causing concern about potential ecological effects. But still the herbicides are quite safer than the insecticides. In India, around 96% of the herbicides belong to slightly toxic to moderately toxic. Compared to this, more than 70% of the insecticides are highly toxic to extremely toxic. Further, herbicides are never applied directly on grains/fruits which are directly consumed by human beings. A Harvard scientist calculated the risks associated with spraying 2, 4, 5-T- a relatively toxic herbicide ($LD_{50}$ value 300). If a person worked applying 2,4,5-T with a backpack sprayer 5 days a week, 4 months a year, for 30 years, the chances of developing a tumor would be 0.4 per million. In comparison, other risks of developing a tumor are large (Zimdhal, 1993).

With the normal use rate, the quantity of herbicide applied to soil at one time is too small in relation to total soil volume to have any detectable influence on a soil's physical or chemical state. Moreover, the herbicides are applied either before sowing or within one month after sowing of the crop. Results of the experiments conducted under All India Coordinated Research Project on Pesticide Residue and All India Coordinated Research Project on Weed Control indicated that herbicides when applied at recommended doses did not leave any toxic residues either in soil water or in food chain. They provide a long waiting period. The high temperature and rain fall conditions in India would result in quick degradation of the chemicals. Most herbicides have half-lives of less than 30-40 days in the soil.

**Soil Microorganisms:** Because of large populations, short reproductive cycles and great adaptability to environmental change, microorganism populations are very resilient. Nearly all investigations show a positive or negative effect. Reactions such as nitrification are suppressed, but at field use rates, the suppression is not permanent. By and large, herbicides applied at their recommended doses have only temporary effect on nodulation by legume crops. The effect on other soil micro-flora is transient and in the final analysis the crop yield is generally not influenced. There are very few reports of permanent injury to soil micro-flora, soil micro-fauna or invertebrates from herbicides used at normal field use rates.

**Herbicide Resistance:** If the same herbicide, herbicides from the same chemical family, or those with the same mechanism of action are used on the same land for several successive years, development of resistance is more likely. Herbicide resistance is of course a global problem. However, crop and herbicide rotation and herbicide mixtures are important techniques to combat this problem. Integration of many methods of weed management rather than reliance on only herbicides to solve weed problems is an important consideration in the overall management of weeds resistant to herbicides.

Herbicides that are normally available in the Indian market are only listed here (Table 15.23). To increase the spectrum of weed control tank mixing of two or more herbicides may be done but only after expert advice as it may sometimes lead to undesirable side effects.

**TABLE 15.23:** HERBICIDE RECOMMENDATIONS FOR FIELD CROPS

| *Crops* | *Herbicides* | *Dose/Rate (kg ai/ha)* | *Application Time* | *Remarks* |
|---|---|---|---|---|
| **Rice** | | | | |
| **a. Nursery** | Butachlor or Thiobencarb | 1.0-1.5 | 6-7 DAS* | If moisture is less, follow immediately by irrigation |
| | Pendimethalin | 1.0-1.5 | 6-7 DAS | If moisture is less, follow immediately by irrigation |
| **b. Direct seeded upland rice** | Butachlor or Thiobencarb | 1.0-1.5 | Pre-emergence | Apply after the sowing but before emergence of crop. In addition to these herbicides 1 hand weeding may be given at 30-35 DAS |
| | Pendimethalin | 1.0-1.5 | Pre-emergence | |
| | Pretilachlor | 0.50-0.75 | Pre-emergence | |
| **c. Direct seeded puddle and transplanted rice** | Butachlor or Thiobencarb | 1.0-1.5 | 3-5 DAT* | Apply at 3-5 days after transplanting on saturated soil but not flooded for 3 days after application |
| | Pendimethalin | 1.0-1.5 | 3-5 DAT | |
| | Anilophos | 0.40-0.60 | 3-5 DAT | Apply at 3-5 days after transplanting |
| | Fluchloralin | 1.0-1.5 | Pre- trans- | Apply before transplanting on puddled soil |
| | Butachlor, Pendimethalin | 1.0-1.5<br>1.0-1.5 | 3-5 DAT<br>3-5 DAT | Followed by planting |
| | or 2,4-D | 0.5 | 20-25 DAT | Apply 20-25 days after transplanting where sedges and broad weeds are dominant |
| | 2,4-D | 0.75-1.0 | 35-40 DAT/DAS | Controls annual broad leaved weeds and some annual grasses and sedges. Drain before application and reflood where relevant within a few days |

Table 15.23 (*contd. on* p. 350)

Table 15.23 (*contd. from* p. 349)

(*contd. from* p. 349)

| | | | | |
|---|---|---|---|---|
| | Oxadiazon | 0.5-0.75 | Pre-emergence or early Post-emergence | Do not disturb soil surface after application |
| **Wheat** | | | | |
| | Isoproturon | 0.75-1.0 | 30-35 DAS | Apply after first irrigation but in areas in Punjab, Haryana and Western U.P. where isoproturon is not controlling *Phalaris minor*, pendimethalin or sulfosulfuron or lodinafop or diclofop ethyl could be used at the given rates |
| | Pendimethalin | 1.0 | Pre-emergence | Apply on finely prepared seed bed and ensure adequate soil moisture in the surface soil |
| | Diclofop-methyl | 1.0 | 30-35 DAS | After the first irrigation for controlling wild oats and *P. minor* |
| | Clodinafop-propargyl | 0.06 | 30-35 DAS | For controlling wild oats and *P. minor* |
| | Sulfosulfuron | 0.025 | 30-35 DAS | For controlling wild oats and *P. minor* |
| | Fenoxaprop | 0.10 | | For controlling wild oats and *P. minor* |
| | 2,4-D | 0.4-0.6 | 30-35 DAS | Apply after first irrigation for controlling broad leaved weeds only. Should not be used in sensitive cultivars such as HD 2009 |
| **Maize** | Atrazine | 0.75-1.0 | Pre-emergence or early Post-emergence | Apply either prior to emergence of crop or within 2 weeks after emergence Also mixtures of atrazines (0.5 kg/ha) and alachlor (1.0 kg/ha) or pendimethalin (0.5 kg/ha) gives broad spectrum weed control |
| | Alachlor | 2.0-2.5 | Pre-emergence | |
| | Pendimethalin | 1.0-1.5 | Pre-emergence | |
| | 2,4-D | 0.75 | Post-emergence | For the control of broadleaf weeds only |

| | | | | |
|---|---|---|---|---|
| **Sorghum** | | | | |
| | Atrazine | 0.5-0.75 | Pre-emergence | Avoid use of atrazine in Maize, Sorghum and Pearl millet when legumes are grown as intercrops |
| | 2,4-D | 0.75 | 5-6 WAS | For control of *Striga* and broadleaf weeds only |
| | Pendimethalin | 0.75-1.0 | Pre-emergence | |
| **Pearl millet** | | | | |
| | Atrazine | 0.5 | Pre-emergence | Controls most annual weeds |
| | Pendimethalin | 0.75-1.0 | Pre-emergence | Ensure adequate surface moisture for optimal activity |
| **Greengram/ Blackgram/ Pigeonpea** | Fluchloralin | 0.75-1.0 | Pre-planting | Incorporate into the surface soil |
| | Alachlor | 1.0 | Pre-emergence | Should be applied after sowing but before emergence of the crop |
| | Pendimethalin | 0.75-1.0 | Pre-emergence | Some soil moisture in surface soil will enhance herbicide activity |
| **Chicken/ Lentil/Peas** | Fluchloralin | 1.0 | Pre-planting | Incorporate into the surface soil before sowing of the crop |
| | Pendimethalin | 0.75-1.0 | Pre-emergence | Apply after sowing but before emergence of the crop |
| **Groundnut** | Fluchloralin | 1.0 | Pre-planting | Incorporate into the surface soil before sowing of the crop |
| | Alachlor | 1.5-2.0 | Pre-emergence | Apply after sowing but before emergence of the crop |
| | Pendimethalin | 0.75-1.0 | Pre-emergence | |
| **Soybean** | Alachlor | 1.0-2.0 | Pre-emergence | Controls annual grasses and broad leaved weeds |
| | Metalachlor | 1.0-1.5 | Pre-emergence | Controls annual grasses |
| | Fluchloralin | 1.0 | Pre-planting | Incorporate into surface soil immediately after application |
| | Metribuzin | 0.25-0.50 | Pre-emergence | Many annual grasses and broad leaved weeds are controlled |

Table 15.23 (*contd. on* p. 352)

Table 15.23 (*contd. from* p. 351)

| | | | | |
|---|---|---|---|---|
| | Pendimethalin | 0.75-1.0 | Pre-emergence | Incorporate it in dry conditions as pre-plant treatment |
| | Imazethapyr | 0.10 | Post-emergence | Controls broadleaf weeds |
| | Fluazifop-p-butyl | 0.25-0.50 | Post-emergence | Controls grassy weeds |
| | Chlorimuron ethyl | 0.012-0.015 | Post-emergence | Controls broadleaf weeds |
| | Metsulfuron methyl | 0.006 | Post-emergence | Controls broadleaf weeds |
| **Sunflower** | Alachlor | 1.0-2.0 | Pre-emergence | Apply to weed-free soil of fine tilth |
| | Fluchloralin | 1.0 | Pre-planting | Incorporate into surface soil before sowing of the crop |
| | Pendimethalin | 1.0 | Pre-emergence | Apply after sowing but before emergence of the crop |
| | Oxadiazon | 0.5-1.0 | Pre-emergence | Moist soil is essential for activity |
| **Rapeseed-Mustard** | Fluchloralin | 1.0 | Pre-planting | Incorporate into surface soil before sowing of the crop |
| | Pendimethalin | 1.0 | Pre-emergence | Apply before the crop emergence |
| | Isoproturon | 0.75-1.0 | Pre-emergence | Good soil tilth and some soil moisture enhances activities |
| | Oxadiazon | 0.5 | Pre-emergence | |
| **Cotton** | Fluchloralin | 1.0 | Pre-planting | Apply after sowing but before emergence of the crop |
| | Pendimethalin | 1.0 | Pre-emergence | |
| | Oxadiazon | 0.5-0.75 | Pre-emergence | Moist soil is essential for activity |
| | Trifluralin | 0.5-1.0 | Pre-planting | Incorporate into surface soil immediately after application. |
| | Diuron | 0.5-0.75 | Pre-emergence | Do not apply to coarse sandy soil. Crop may be damaged if seed has been treated with systemic insecticide |
| | | | Post emergence | As directed spray when cotton is over 15 cm high |
| **Sugarcane** | Atrazine | 2.0 | Pre-emergence | Good soil tilth and soil moisture enhances the herbicide activity of pre-em. herbicides. Tank mix atrazine with alachlor 2.0 kg/ha for broad spectrum weed control |
| | Atrazine + | 1.0 | Pre-emergence | |

| | | | | |
|---|---|---|---|---|
| | 2,4-D | 1.0 | Post-emergence | Apply 5 weeks after planting |
| | Metribuzin | 1.0-1.5 | Pre-emergence | It can be applied as pre-emergence or early post emergence. Can be mixed with 2,4-D in early post emergence application for broad spectrum weed control |
| **Potato** | Pendimethalin | 1.0 | Pre-emergence | Apply before emergence to crop and weeds |
| | Paraquat | 0.5 | At 5% sprouting | Apply at 5% sprouting. Delay causes phytotoxicity. Does not control weeds which emerge after application |
| | Isoproturon | 0.75-1.0 | Pre-emergence | Apply pre-emergence or early post-emergence |
| | Metribuzin | 0.5 | Pre-emergence | Apply pre-emergence or early post-emergence |
| **Tomato/ Brinjal** | Pendimethalin | 1.0 | Pre-emergence | Apply before transplanting followed by irrigation |
| | Alachlor | 2.0 | Pre-emergence | This should be followed by Ist hand weeding |
| | Fluchloralin | 0.75 | Pre-emergence | 5-6 weeks after planting/ sowing |
| | Fluchloralin<br>Metribuzin<br>(in Tomato) | 1.0<br>0.5 | Pre-emergence or early post-emergence | Should be applied pre-emergence or early post-emergence. Avoid contact with tomato plants |
| **Onion/ Garlic** | Fluchloralin | 1.0 | Pre-emergence | Pre-emergence to weeds at the time of transplanting followed by irrigation |
| | Pendimethalin | 1.0 | Pre-emergence | Apply before or after transplanting and pre-emergence to weeds |
| | Oxyfluorfen | 0.25 | | Apply before or after transplanting and pre-emergence to weeds |
| **Cabbage/ Cauliflower/ Knolkhol** | Fluchloralin | 1.0 | Pre-emergence | Should be applied at the time of planting and followed by irrigation |
| **Beetroot/ Radish/ Carrot** | Pendimethalin | 1.0 | Pre-emergence | Should be applied after transplanting but before the emergence of weeds |

DAS - Days after sowing, WAS - Weeks after sowing; DAT - Days after transplanting

### *Some Points to Note*

- Hand weeding may be given wherever necessary in addition to herbicide treatment.
- Use lower rates in light soils and higher rates in higher soils.
- These recommendations are based on the sole cropping. For herbicide use in inter-cropping system, consult experts.
- Apply herbicide using a sprayer with 500-600 lit/ha water.
- Also spray solutions immediately after preparation. If delay is inevitable, stir the solution or shake the sprayer thoroughly before application to prevent settling down of herbicide in the bottom.
- Flood jet or flat pan nozzle should be used for spraying the herbicide.
- Match the swath correctly. Overlapping of spray may lead to crop phyto-toxicity and gaps may lead to poor control of weeds.
- Separate sprayer need to be used for herbicide and for insecticide spray. If not, then sprayer has to be thoroughly washed with soap water after the herbicide spray before it is used for insecticide spray.
- Avoid spraying on windy days as drifting may damage the neighbouring susceptible crops.
- Do not spray against the wind.
- Avoid smoking or eating during spray application.
- Wash sprayer thoroughly after each spray.
- Handle chemicals carefully. Always keep them away from children and food articles.
- Dispose the empty container by burying in the soil or by burning.
- Use protective clothing (gum boots, gloves, etc.) goggles and mask wherever possible.

### Herbicide Resistant Crops (HRCs) in Weed Management

The development of crops with resistance to specific herbicides represents a powerful new technology for weed control. In recent years, considerable research has been directed towards the introduction of herbicide tolerance or resistance in to normally susceptible crop species (Schultz *et al.* 1990). The first use of herbicide resistant crop was in 1994 with the introduction of IMI (imidazolinone resistant) corn hybrids and STS (sulfonylurea tolerant) soybean varieties. Resistance genes from several other herbicides or herbicide mode of action have been incorporated in to the genetics of corn, soybean, cotton, canola and many other crops and are now commercially available. These include glyphosate resistant corn and soybean, glufosinate (Liberty) resistant corn and soybean and sethoxydim (Post) resistant corn. Harrison (1992) and Dyer *et al.* (1993) indicated the following potential benefits and concerns from the development of herbicide resistant crops.

***Benefits***

- An increased margin of safety with which herbicides can be used and subsequent reductions in crop loss due to herbicide injury.
- Reduced risk of crop damage from residual herbicides used in previous rotational crops.
- Introduction of new herbicides for use on formerly susceptible crops.

***Concerns***

- Potential for increased use of herbicides.
- Abandonment of alternative weed control practices other than herbicides.
- Concern that HRCs may become weed problems or resistance may be transferred (through gene flow) to other species.
- Accelerated selection of resistant weed populations from use of higher rates of herbicides.
- Misuse of herbicides, leading to ground water contamination or other environmental problems.
- General public concern about the release of genetically engineered organisms in to the environment.

## STRATEGY FOR INTEGRATED WEED MANAGEMENT SYSTEM

Integrated weed management (IWM) is a component of integrated crop management (ICM) which transients all disciplines. IWM involves three elements:

(a) Multiple tactics (eg., competitive varieties, cultural practices and herbicide usage)

(b) Weed population maintained at levels below that cause economic damage, and

(c) Conservation of environmental quality.

All crop management practices starting from field preparation to harvesting have implications on weed competition. Judicious use of herbicides, therefore, be given top priority. Lower rates of herbicides integrated with other methods of weed management is invariably more efficient, economical and sustainable than use of higher dose of herbicides alone. The use of herbicides is being scrutinized by many public and private organizations. There is concern about food safety; ground water and atmospheric contamination, increased weed resistance to herbicides, destruction to beneficial organisms and concern about endangered species. IWM has been defined as the application of numerous alternative weed control measures, which include cultural, genetic, mechanical, biological and chemical means of weed control. None of the individual control measures on their own can be expected to provide acceptable levels of weed control. However, if the various components of IWM are implemented in a systematic integrated manner, significant advances in weed control technology can be achieved.

Buchanan (1976) defined integrated weed management (IWM) as combination of the application of many kinds of technologies in a mutually supportive manner. It involves the deliberate selection, integration and implementation of effective weed control measures with due consideration of economic, ecological and sociological consequences". The research approach to the development of an IWM system must take all aspects of the cropping system into consideration. Invariably, each cultural practice influences the competitive ability of both the crop and the weed community leading to a multitude of complex interactions. However, efforts must be made to work within the existing production practice to ensure a greater likelihood of acceptance by the farming community. Although every agronomic practice starting from planting to harvesting of crop has implecations on weed competition, farmers are neither aware of it nor appreciate it. It is important to educate farmers about this. The effect may be small for individual practice but effect would be substantial if all such practices are combined effectively. IWM is a knowledge intensive exercise where scientists may also be discouraged to get involved. In India, at least we are yet to generate information on economic threshold limits (ETL) for different weeds, weed seed dynamics in soil, understanding of eco-physiology of crop-weed competition, weed flora shifts in crops and cropping systems, etc. It is time we started working on these. Besides developing effective IWM packages for different crops and cropping systems, it is very important to demonstrate them to farmers on large scale.

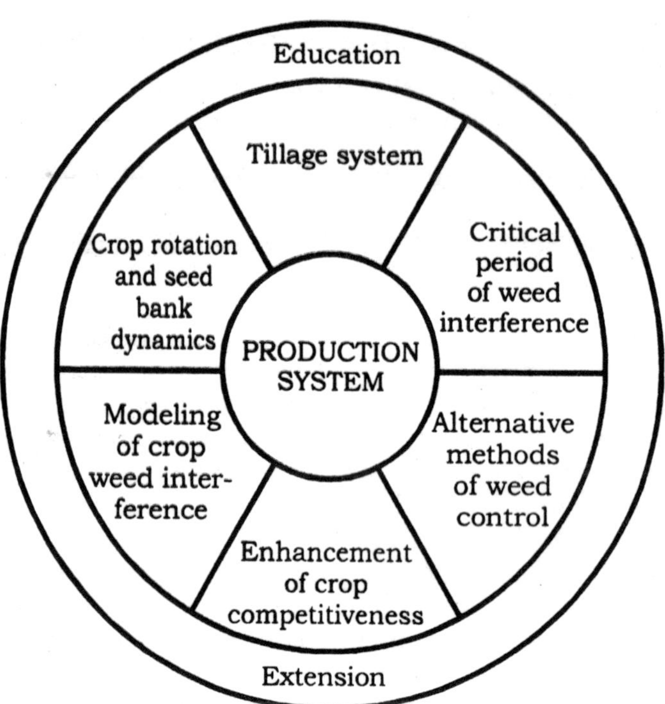


**Fig. 15.5.** Research strategy for the development of an integrated weed management system (Swanton and Weise, 1991)

Thus, it is important to change the existing system in a progressive manner. This progression must be reflected in the research strategy. This would allow for the transfer of specific components through education and extension, while research continues to refine and further develop the system.

## REFERENCES


Ahlawat, I. P. S., Singh, A., and Saraf, C. S. 1983. Studies on weed control in field peas. *Indian Journal of Weed Science,* **15**(2): 217-22.

Akey, W. C., Jurik, T. W. and Dekker, J., 1990. Competition foe light between velvetleaf (*Abutilon theophrasti*) and soybean (*Glycine max.*). *Weed Research,* **30**: 403-411.

Alex, J. F. 1967. Competition between *Setaria viridis* (green foxtail) and wheat seeded with a drill and with a one-way. *Res. Rep., Can. Nat. Weed Comm. West. Sect.* p. 287.

Altieri, M. A., and Liebman, M., (eds.). 1988. *Weed Management in Agro-ecosystems: Ecological Approaches.* CRC Press, Inc., Boca Raton, FL.

Ampong-Nyarko, K., And De Datta, S. K., 1991. *A Hand Book of Weed Control in Rice.* IRRI, Los Banos, Philippines. p. 113.

Angiras, N. N. and Singh, C. M. 1989. *Indian Journal of Weed Science,* **21**(1&2): 69-74.

Ascard, J. 1994. Soil cultivation in darkness reduced weed emergence. *Acta Horticulturae,* 372, *Engineering for Reducing Pesticide Consumption & Operator Hazards,*167-177.

Azad, B. S., Singh, H. and Dubey, A. N. 1988. *Pesticides,* **22**(6): 41-42.

Balyan, R. S. and Malik, R. K. 1991. Competitive ability of wheat cultivars with wild oats. *Weed Science,* **39**(2): 154-158.

Banga, R. S., Yadav, A. and Malik, R. K. 1997. Crop rotation—An effective mean to control resistant *Phalaris minor* in wheat. *Farmers and Parliament,* **33**(3): 16-17.

Bansinkai, J. J. 1955. Witchweed and soil fertility. *Nature,* **175**: 431.

Bhowmik, P. C. 1998. Herbicides in relation to food security and environment: A global perspective. *Proc. First Int. Agronomy Congress,* Nov., 23-27, 1998, New Delhi, India, pp. 244-258.

Black, J. N. 1958. Competition between plants of different initial seed sizes in swards of subterranean clover (*Trifolium subterraneum* L.) with particular reference to leaf area and the light microclimate. *Autralian Journal of Agricultural Research,* **9**: 299-318.

Bleasdale, J. K. A. 1960. Studies on plant competition, pp. 133-142. *In*: J. L. Harper (ed.), *The Biology of Weeds.* Blackwell Sci. Publ., Oxford, Eng. p. 256.

Buchanan, G. A. 1976. Management of weed pests of cotton (*Gossypium hirsutum*). In: *Proceedings of US-USSR Symposium on the Integrated Control of the Arthropod, Disease and Weed Pests of Cotton, Grain, Sorghum and Deciduous Fruits,* Lubbock T.X. pp. 168-84.

Burnside, O. C., Bovey, R. W., Elmore, C. L., Johnson, R., Kanke, E. L., Lembi, C. L., Nalewaja, J. D, Newton, M., Szmedra, P. and Wattenberg, E. V. 1996. *Biologic and Economic Assessment of Benefits from Use of Phenoxy Herbicides in United States.* Special NAPIAP Report No. 1-PA-96, November, 1996, p. 227.

Chaudhary, A. H. 1981. *Experimental Agriculture,* **17**: 389-399.

Chauhan, R., Dahiya, B. and Khokhar, K. S. 1991. Weeding *Vicia sativa* L. to help check pod borer (*Helicoverpa armigera*) damage in chickpea (*Cicer arietinum* L.). *ACIAR Food legume Newsletter,* **15**(3).

Chisaka, H. 1977. Weed damage to crops: Yield loss due to weed competition, *In*: J. D. Fryer and S. Matsunaka (eds.), *Integrated Control of Weeds.* Univ. of Tokyo Press. pp 1-16, 262.

Cousens, R., 1985. A simple model relating yield loss to weed density. *Annals of Applied Biology,* **107**: 239-252.

Cousens, R. D. 1987. Theory and reality of weed control thresholds. *Plant Protection Quarterly,* **2**: 13-20.

Cudney, D. W., Jordan, L. S. and Hall, A. E. 1991. Effect of wild oat (*Avena fatua*) infestation on light infestation and growth rate of wheat (*Triticum aestivum*). *Weed Science,* **39**: 175-179.

Crutchfield, D. A., Wicks, G. A. and Burnside, D. C. 1986. Effect of winter wheat straw mulch level on weed control. *Weed Science*, **34**: 110-114.

Dadhich, S. C. and Mali, A. L. 1991. Effect of herbicides and phosphorus on crop weed competition in chickpea (*Cicer arietinum* L.). *Indian Journal of Agronomy*, **36**: 283-85.

De Datta, S. K. 1977. *Philippine Journal of Weed Science*, **27**: 479-485.

Derksen, D. A., Thomas, A. G., Layfond, G. P., Loeppky, H. A. and Swanton, C. J. 1994. Impact of agronomic practices on weed communities: Fallow within tillage system, *Weed Science*, **42**: 184-194.

Dale, J. E. and Chandler, J. M. 1979. Herbicide-crop rotation for Johnson grass (*Sorghum halepense*) control. *Weed Science*, **27**: 479-486.

Dyer, W. E., Hess, F. D., Holt, J. S. and Duke, S. O. 1993. Potential benefits and risk of herbicide-resistant crops produced by biotechnology. *Horticulture Review*, **15**: 365-408.

George, S. K., Donaldson, G. and Clements R. O. 1997. Cover cereal bi-cropping with reduced agrochemical inputs: The yield and costs. *Aspects of Applied Biology 50, Optimising cereal inputs: its scientific basis*, 487-492.

Guled, M. B. 1982. Effect of manuring and 2,4-D on Striga control in sorghum. *M.Sc.(Ag.) Thesis*, University of Agricultural Sciences, Bangalore.

Gupta, O. P. 1998. *Modern Weed Management.* Agro Botanica, Bikaner, India.

Hall, M. R., Swanton, C. J. and Anderson, G. W. 1992. The critical period of weed control in grain corn (*Zea mays*). *Weed Science*, **40**: 441-447.

Harrison, H. F., Jr. 1992. Developing herbicide-tolerant crop cultivars: Introduction. *Weed Technology*, **6**: 613-614.

Hatzois, K. K. 1987. Biotechnology applications in weed management: Now and in the future. *Advances in Agronomy*, **41**: 325-367.

Holm, L. G., Plucknett, D. L., Pancho, J. V. and Herberger, J. P. 1977. *The World's Worst Weeds: Distribution and Biology.* University Press of Hawaii, Honolulu.

Holmoy, R., and Netland, J. 1994. Band spraying, selective flame weeding and hoeing in late white cabbage, part 1. *Acta Horticulturae* 372, *Engineering for Reducing Pesticide Consumption & Operator Hazards*, pp. 223-234.

Horowitz, Menashe, Regve, Yael, Herzlinger, Geza 1983. Solarization for weed control. *Weed Science*, **31**: 170-179.

Hosmani, M. M. 1991. *Cultural Methods of Weed Management.* University of Agricultural Sciences, Dhrwad.

Ivy, H. W., and Baker, R. S. 1972. Prickly sida control and competition in cotton. *Weed Science*, **20**: 137-139.

Jacobsohn, R., Greenberger, A., Katan, J., Levi, M. and Alon, H. 1980. Control of Egyptian broomrape (*Orobanche aegyptiaca*) and other weeds by means of solar heating of the soil by polyethylene mulching. *Weed Science*, **28**: 312-316.

Johnson, M. D., Wyse, D. L. and Lueschen, W. E. 1989. The influence of herbicide formulation on weed control in four tillage systems. *Weed Science*, **37**: 239-249.

Kanitkar, V. N., *et al.* 1960. *Dry Farming in India.* Indian Council of Agricultural Research, New Delhi (II ed.).

Kudarimani, H. B. 1977. A study on drip irrigation under Dharwad agro-climatic conditions. *M.Sc. (Ag.) Thesis*, University of Agricultural Sciences, Bangalore.

Kumar, V. 1985. Efficacy of herbicides for weed control in Urdbean (*Vigna mungo* L.) M.Sc. (Ag.) Thesis, GBPUA&T, Pantnagar (Nainital). India, p. 116.

Kundra, H. C., Gosal, K. S. and Brar, H. S. 1991. Effect of weed management practices on nutrient uptake by summer mungbean (*Vigna radiata* L.) and associated weeds. *Indian Journal of Weed Science*, **23**(3&4): 31-5.

Laesino, R. Q. 1980. Ph.D., University of IOWA, Ames., pp. 170.

Liebman, M., and Dyck, E. 1993. Crop rotation and intercropping strategies for weed management. *Ecological Applications*, **3**: 92-122.

... H. and Saxena, M. C. (1989). *Proceedings of International Workshop on Orobanche* Oberrenchal. Germany, Aug, 19-22, 1989.

Malik, R. K., Balyan, R. S. and Bhan, V. M. 1988. Effect of herbicides and planting dates on weeds in chickpea. *Indian Journal of Weed Science,* **20**(2): 75-81.

Mathur, P. S. 1960. On the utility of trash mulch in sugarcane fields. *Indian Journal of Sugarcane Research and Development,* **4**: 192-201.

Meti, S. S. 1993. Control of *Orobanche cernua* is *bidi* tobacco by soil solarization M.Sc. Thesis. UAS, Dharwad India.

Mishra, J. S. and Singh, V. P. 2001. Interference of Ivyleaf morningglory (*Ipomoea hederacea*) in soybean. *Indian Journal of Weed Science,* **33**(1&2): 87-88.

Mishra, J. S., Singh, V. P. and Bhan, V. M. 1997. Effect of interference by common vetch (*Vicia sativa*) on yield and yield components of lentil (*Lens culinaris*). *Indian Journal of Agricultural Sciences,* **67**(7): 320-321.

Mool Chand, Rajak, R. L., Shyam Radhey, Reddy, O. R., Vijaykumar, C. S. K. and Indira, M. 2000. Interception of weed seeds in wheat imported from Australia. *Indian Journal of Weed Science,* **32**(3&4): 210-212.

Moorthy, B. T. S. and Das, T. K. 1998. Threshold level of weed umbrella sedge (*Cyperus iria*) in upland rice (*Oryza sativa*) under rainfed direct-seeded condition. *Indian Journal of Agricultural Sciences,* **68**(1): 7-8.

Noda, K., 1977. *In*: J. D. Fryer and S. Matsunaka (eds.), *Integrated Control of Weeds.* University of Tokyo Press, Tokyo, pp. 17-46.

Oerke, E. C., Dehne, H. W., Schonbeck, F. and Weber, A. 1994. *Crop Production and Crop Protection: Estimated Losses in Majoe Food and Cash Crops.* Elsevier, p. 808.

Olofsdotter, M. and Navarez, D. C. 1996. Allelopathic rice for *Echinochloa crus-galli* control. *In*: *Proceedings 2nd International Weed Control Congress,* Copenhagen, Denmark, 1175-1181.

Patel, C. L., Patel, Z. G. and Patel, H. C. 1983. Non-cash technology for minimizing weed growth in pigeonpea. *Indian Journal of Weed Science,* **15**(2): 143-46.

Patterson, D. T. 1995. Effect of environmental stress on weed/crop interactions. *Weed Science,* **43**: 483-490.

Pleasant, J. M. and Schlather, K. J. 1994. Incidence of weed seeds in cow (*Bos* sp.) manure and its importance as a weed source for crop land, *Weed Technology,* **8**: 304-310.

Rao, A. N. and Shetty, S. V. R. 1976. Some biological aspects of intercropping system on crop-weed balance. *Indian Journal of Weed Science,* **8**: 32-34.

Rao, A. N. and Shetty, S. V. R. 1981. Investigations on weed suppressing ability of smother cropping systems in relation to canopy development and light interception. *Proceedings of 8th Asian Pacific Weed Science Society Conference,* pp. 357-364.

Sahoo, K. M. and Saraswat, V. N. 1988. Magnitude of losses in the yields of major crops due to weed competition in India. *Pesticides Information,* **14**(1): 2-9.

Sankaran, S. and Chinnamuthu, C. R. 1993. Integrated weed management in rice based cropping systems. *In: Proceedings of International Symposium. Indian Society of Weed Science,* Hisar, Nov. 18-20, 1993. **I**: 69-74.

Sauerborn J., Linke, K. H., Saxena, M. C. and Koch, W. 1989. Solarization: A physical control method for weeds and parasitic plants (*Orobanche* spp.) in Mediterranean agriculture. *Weed Research,* **29**: 391-397.

Scopel, A. L., Ballare, C. L. and Radosevich, S. R. 1994. Photo-stimulation of seed germination during soil tillage. *New Phytol,* **126**: 145-152.

Schultz, A., Wengenmayer, F. and Goodman, H. M. 1990. Genetic engineering of herbicide resistance in higher plants. *CRC Crit. Rev. Plant Sci.,* **9**: 1-15.

Shahi, H. N. 1978. Competitive effects of *Chenopodium album* for soil moisture and nutrients in wheat. *Indian Pest Control,* **20**(4): 14-16.

Sharma, Vijay P. and Sharma, Pritee 1999. Pesticide use in Indian agriculture: Some issues and Constraints in its growth. *Pestology Special Issue* **XXIII**(2): 242-252.

# 16

# Evolutionary Trends in Pesticide Development

**Madhuban Gopal and Gita Kulshrestha**

## INTRODUCTION

Insecticides, fungicides, herbicides, and plant growth regulators form a group of agrochemicals, or pesticides, which are available to protect crops in order to maintain their yield potential and quality of produce. Recent trend in agrochemicals can be summarized as Reduce Input Approach (RIA). Developed nations have many advantages such as manageable population growth, high literacy and skills, availability of emerging technologies and inputs etc. With the result, the shift is towards the quality of product and production systems rather than on quantity. In the European nations, general trend is to conserve the land use pattern and reduce the use of pesticides by 50 per cent of a base value over a period of 5-10 years. While farmers and consumers are enthusiastic in welcoming such a plan, the following constraints have been identified for redressal: lack of alternatives, inadequate research capacity, inadequate supervision for observance of regulations and absence of clear policy (Jansma *et al.*, 1993). To meet the needs of food security and improved quality of produce new pesticides must have reduced application rates and improved environmental acceptability. Such new molecules, having different mode of action and positive desirable attributes than the older problematic ones, can be recommended for inclusion in the Integrated pest management modules.

## CHEMICAL INSECTICIDES

Since the history about organochlorine, carbamate, organophosphorus and synthetic pyrethriod insecticides is already documented, and recent trend has been modification of synthetic pyrethroids for improved effectiveness (lower rate of application), better properties (safety to fish) and novel usage (soil application), merely relevant references are being provided about older insecticides. Sustained R&D efforts have given way to safer insecticides like malathion, and synthetic pyrethroids which are environmentally more acceptable. Some of these like deltamethrin obtained as a single enantiomer is remarkably potent and effective at lower application rate (2-10 g/ha). β-cyfluthrin is able to control even those insects, which have developed resistance against other pesticides (Sinha and Gopal, 2002). The pyrethroids possess low mammalian toxicity and are safer than organophosphates and carbamates (Elliott,1976; Roy, 2000). The gradual change in mammalian safety ratio (MSR) of newer pesticides marks an improvement over older insecticides.

*Division of Agricultural Chemicals IARI, New Delhi-110 012.*

**Novel Synthetic Pyrethroids**

In the area of insecticides, although a large number of synthetic pyrethroids have been developed as safe and effective molecules but still majority of them are toxic to fish. Recently developed non-ester synthetic pyrethroid insecticides like etofenprox (MTI-500), MTI-800 and some related compounds are found not only safe to fish and possess low mammalian toxicity but also exhibit broad spectrum of activity. Pyrethroid, lambda-cyhalothrin is another potential substitute for DDT in malaria control programme and has already been found useful in countries, like Nepal, Brazil and Indonesia. If $CH_3$ group is replaced by fluoro in cyclpropyl group, the compounds obtained are more effective against rice insects. Pyrethroids having higher volatility, e.g., transfluthrin having vapour pressure of 4 μhPA at 20° C is suitable for controlling household pests. Structure activity studies show that nonconventional silicon and tin derivatives possess better activity than conventional pyrethroid compounds against rice borer and housefly.

The modern synthetic insecticides are highly effective against flies, forestry and timber pests and are capable of checking outbreaks of typhus, bubonic plague and malaria, but repeated applications and misuse are known to induce resistance, which is becoming a serious problem. So far most of the conventional insecticides act on the insect nervous system, pyrethroids on the sodium ion channel whereas organophosphates and carbamates inhibit the enzyme acetylcholinesterase.

**Pyrazolines**

A recent introduction, pyrazolines were reported in 1990 to act through a novel insecticidal mode of action viz., by blocking the Na-channel of neurons. Earlier versions included PH 60-41 and PH 3421. Introduction of carbomethoxy substituent in the angular position enhanced the activity against *Spodoptera*, *Heliothis* and *Plutella* sp. with high level of mammalian safety ratio (MSR). However, these are highly persistent in soil, and therefore, it necessitated the replacement of pyridazine by oxadiazine. Structure activity relationship (SAR) studies revealed the profitability of substitution at the 4 or 5 position of the benzoyl ring, 4-halophenyl or 4-methoxy-carbonyl at the angular position, the Z-substituent being $CF_3O$ and 4-substituent being $CO_2CH_3$, or $COCH_3$. The activity being localized with (+)-enantiomer clearly demonstrated the value of chiral synthesis (McCann *et al.*, 2001). Indoxacarb: oxadiazines has been recently reported as a new class of pyrazoline-type insecticide applied @ 75 g ai/ha.

**2-Arylpyrroles**

This class of insecticides has been developed based on the microbial metabolite dioxapyrrolomycin of *Streptomyces fumanus*. The parent compound had $LD_{50}$ of 14 mg/kg (mouse, oral) but its insecticidal activity, due to the uncoupling of oxidative phosphorylation, held promise by providing a novel mode of action.

Rhone Poulenc introduced a sulfinyl pyrazole insecticide fipronil in 1994. It is a broad-spectrum systemic insecticide with contact and stomach poison activity. It is active against stem borers, leaf miners, hoppers, rootworm termites and mites. It blocks the GABA-regulated chloride channel leading to disruption of CNS activity. Biochemical assays also indicate that fipronil binds to the insect GABA receptor with higher affinity than it does to the vertebrate site. These differences in affinities may account for fipronil's selective toxicity. As a foliar treatment, it is required @ 10-50 g ai/ha (Colliot, 1992).

Halofenozide (Mach 2) is promising as a soil insecticide for controlling white grub and caterpillar. Methoxyfenozide, a new insecticidal ecdysteroid agonist, controls caterpillar pest of families Pyralidae, Pieradae, Tortricidae and Noctuidae (Carlson *et al.*, 2001). It is available as a solid suspension or wettable powder formulation and use rates are expected to range from 30-250 g ai/ha under the trade names Runner$^R$, Intreprid™ and Prodigy™. It binds with very high affinity to the ecodysone receptor complex (EcR: USP) in lepidopteran insects {Kd 0.05nM (Plodia)}, where if functions as a potent agonist, or mimic, of the insect molting hormone, 20-hydroxyecdysone (20E).

Although, new types of insecticides acting on other target sites were developed, their use is restricted because of inherent constraints. Thus compound showing 100% mortality against southern armyworm and tobacco budworm at 10-ppm test concentration holds promise as a new arsenal for pest control (Hunt and Treacy, 1998). Though CL-303, 268 is insecticidal, pharmacodynamics studies revealed that its N-ethoxymethyl derivative coded as CL-303, 630 is selectively safe for mammals because the latter is inactive as an uncoupler of oxidative phosphorylation in rat liver mitochondria. CL-303, 630 is being launched as a proinsecticide. The herbivores break down to insecticidal compound by oxidative N-dealkylation. Foliar application of CL-303, 630 at 60-400 g ai/ha was found very effective in controlling 70 species of phytophagous insects and mites in crops such as cotton, vegetables, tree fruits, citrus, cereals and ornamentals.

## BOTANICAL PESTICIDES

Since the passage of the Food Quality Protection Act in 1996, there has been a strong industry interest in developing "reduced risk" pesticides. Driven in part by the EPA Office of Pesticide Program's Reduced Risk Pesticides Initiative, which offers an expedited review, the industry has been exploring new sources of pesticides, especially in the area of biopesticides. Because the initiative has its roots in food quality concerns, the emphasis has been on registering pesticides for use on food crops: fruits, vegetables, and nuts. The increasing interest in organically grown produce has also driven development of natural-based products registered for food crops. It is hoped that some of these new products find their way to being registered for use on ornamental plants as well. Besides giving the background information, an attempt is made to review some of the products recently registered or under review and testing.

**Biopesticides** (both botanical and bio-organisms) are increasingly becoming popular in insect pest management programmes. The availability of natural products in small quantity, however, is viewed as a serious disadvantage. Attempts have, therefore, been made to develop synthetic analogues of lead molecules though with little success. The total synthesis of azadirachtin, the active component of neem, is still in progress. However, a few simpler analogues of azadirachtin prepared as simpler templates did not show the desired level of insect antifeedant activity. Efforts are being made to explore many unexploited natural products, which might provide new selective and safer pesticides with different biochemical modes of action (Cremlyn, 1990; Mukerji, 1995) to enable us to overcome problem of insect resistance development. The isobutyl amides synthesized by modeling on natural insecticides like piperines appear to afford promising active analogue, effective against insects resistant to pyrethroids.

### Plant Based Insecticides

Another area of exploration for low-risk pesticides has been plant extracts (Hedin *et al.*, 1997). AVA Chemical Ventures has applied for registration of sucrose octanoate esters, a synthetic insecticide based on *Nicotiana.* Natural sucrose esters are difficult and expensive to extract from plants, but AVA developed an easier and less expensive process for synthesizing the esters. The esters are manufactured from sucrose and a caprilic fatty acid ester derived from edible oils such as coconut or palm. Sucrose octanoate dewaxes the outer coating of soft-bodied insects, such as whiteflies, aphids and thrips, causing them to lose water and shrivel. It appears like the same action as fatty acids of potassium salts, commonly known as insecticidal soap. Though it is thought that hard-bodied beneficial insects are not harmed, nevertheless soft-bodied beneficials and larvae might be damaged. Since sucrose fatty acid esters are commonly consumed as food or food components (food emulsifiers and fruit coatings), the EPA is reviewing a petition from AVA for exemption from residue tolerance requirements for speeding up the approval process.

In 1998, Neudorff received approval for the use of canola oil as an active ingredient of insecticide for use on a wide range of insects. Neudorff submitted a product NEU1161, which contains 89.5% canola oil and 0.5% pyrethrins. The company planned two other products, NEU1160 Vegetable Oil Spray (with no pyrethrins) and NEU1161 RTU (with substantially less pyrethrins). It is obvious that these products have the same effect as horticultural oils, which are usually petroleum distillates.

In 1996, IJO Products in Fresno CA registered Jojoba oil as an insecticide against whiteflies (Detur™) and as a fungicide for powdery mildew on grapes and ornamentals (E-Rase™). In October 1999, the EPA released a biopesticide fact sheet for jojoba oil, identifying no risks to humans or the environment. The oil acts as a barrier between the pest and the leaf surface. Jojoba (pronounced ho-ho-ba) oil, extracted from jojoba beans grown in California, Arizona and Mexico, is also used in cosmetics, primarily for moisture control, and lubricants. The availability of jojoba oil as a pesticide will depend on crop production and a growing consumer demand for the oil as a health product.

Cinnacure™, a cinnamon oil extract (cinnamaldehyde) from ProGuard, targets thrips, whitefly, aphids, mites and mite eggs, but also seems to have some effect on fungal diseases, especially powdery mildew. Tests indicated extremely rapid control, within minutes of application. Cinnamaldehyde is broad spectrum and will kill beneficial insects. Although ProGuard received EPA approval in February 1997, commercial availability has been elusive. Recently, Mycotech introduced two cinnamaldehyde products: Valero™ for grapes and Cinnamite™ for vegetables and ornamentals (Julien, 2000).

Neem oil has also been a source of insecticidal products. The neem bitters or limonoids belong to nine basic structure groups: azadirone (from Oil), amoorastaitin (from fresh leaves), vbepinin (from seed oil), vilasinin (from green leaves), gedunin (from seed oil and bark), nimbin (from leaves and seed), nimbolin (from kernel) and salannin (from fresh leaves and seed), and the most valuable aza group (from seed). Using the extract avoids the temperature problem of pure neem oil; the wax content of the oil causes it to congeal at temperatures below 15° C. But tests with crude neem oil have shown it to be effective as a protectant against a number of plant diseases. Green Light's Rose Defense® was one of the first products introduced in the U.S. to use whole neem oil, and has shown some effectiveness in controlling blackspot and powdery mildew, although the product must be mixed in warm water to prevent congealing. Research is underway to produce waxless neem oil. It is expected to see more products in this area.

Many products derived from neem tree, *Azadirachta indica*, Family Melliaceae, and neem seed kernel (NSK) act as insecticide (Schmutterer, 2000). Neem derivatives, of which all azadirachtin, salannin and nimbin are the active principles, produce various effects on insects. They act as antifeedant, egg laying deterrent, interfere in the growth and moulting cycle, even causing morphogenetic defects, reduce female fecundity and impair general fitness and vigour. *Azadirachta* is a steroid-like tetranortriterpenoid and it consists of not only Aza-a but Aza-b, and Aza-h have also been found to have higher activity.

**Nicotinoids**

Nicotine is the most important alkaloid present in steam distillate of tobacco (*Nicotiiana tobacum* and *N. rustica*) leaves. Other closely related alkaloids in the distillate are nornicotine and anabasine. Chemically nicotine is 1-3(1-methyl-2-pyrrolidine) pyridine. The nitrogen of the six membered pyridine ring is weakly basic (pka approximately 3) and the latter five membered pyrrolidine ring moderately basic (pka approximately 8).

Nicotine is a nerve poison killing the insect very rapidly. Its toxicity varies greatly with the mode and form of application. External application of nicotinoids usually causes tremors and convulsions followed by paralysis. The literature on nicotine toxicity and the mode of action of nicotinoids was dealt by Yamamoto (1970).

Pharmacological studies on insects and vertebrates have shown that cholinergic sites are target of nicotine action. Since in insects neuromuscular junction is not cholinergic, it remains insensitive to nicotine poisoning. The central nervous system of insect is cholinergic.

Based on the mark up of the nervous system and correlation between structure and insecticidal activity of nicotinoids (Soeda and Yamamoto, 1968; Yamamoto *et al.*, 1962), it was suggested that nicotine mimics acetycholine by binding with the appropriate receptor at the synapse of insectan central nervous system (Yamamoto, 1965; Yamamoto *et al.*, 1962). Nicotine binds on anionic site at postsynaptic membrane with cationized nitrogen of the pyrrolidine ring. The pyridine ring has some unidentified influence on the nerve membrane (Yamamoto, 1965). It was suggested that nitrogen of pyridine ring acts as hydrogen bond acceptor at a fixed distance from cationized nitrogen of the pyrrolidine ring which is equivalent to the distance between the charged nitrogen of choline moiety of acetylcholine and hydrogen bond formed when the carbonyl oxygen group of this neurotransmitter itself is the acceptor (Corbett, 1974). Based on the structure—insecticidal activity relationships of nicotine, its mode of action was proposed some 30 years ago, which explains why nicotine is more a mammalicide than an insecticide. The newly developed insecticide imidacloprid is lower in mammalian toxicity and higher in insecticidal activity than nicotine. Both compounds share the same essential moiety, but nicotine is ionized while imidacloprid bears a partial positive charge on the active nitrogen atom. The partial positive charge, conferred by a strong electron - withdrawing group, is important for interaction vertebrate nAChRs. Without ionization and with high hydrophobicity, imidacloprid is easily accessible to insect target site.

**Neonicotinoids**

They represent a novel and distinct chemical class of insecticides with remarkable chemical and biological properties. A nitromethylene heterocyclic called nithiazine served as a synthetic precursor for this class of modern insecticides. Extensive research programme started in mid eighties eventually led to the development of commercial products such as imidacloprid (introduced by Bayer AG in 1991), acetamiprid (introduced by Nippon Soda in 1996) and thiamethoxam (introduced by Novartis in 1998). Maienfisch *et al.* (2001) has documented the discovery of thiamethoxam: a second-generation neonicotinoid. Three new products namely thiacloprid (Bayer), clothiamidin (Takeda, Bayer) and dinotefuran (Mitsui Chemicals) are currently under development. Imidacloprod and its many analogs, together with other nicotine mimics, compose a newer group of safer insecticides.

**Rotenoids**

The roots of certain leguminous plants are the source of compounds, which have proved effective toxins against insects. Among these, the chief toxic constituent is rotenone. It is obtained from the roots of *Derris elliptica, D. malaccensis*, etc. Other naturally occurring rotenoids identified from these plants are elliptone, sumatrol, malaccol, toxicarol, etc. Four separate groups form the molecule of rotenone. In insects, rotenone slows down the heartbeat, lowers oxygen consumption and depresses respiratory movements, ultimately leading to flaccid paralysis (Corbett, 1974 and Yamamoto, 1970).

**Pyrethrin and Synthetic Pyrethroids**

They cause a progressive series of poisoning symptoms in insects (Elliott, 1976, 1980; Herve, 1985). These symptoms are hyperactivity, ataxia, convulsions and reversible non-lethal paralysis called knock down (Blum and Kearns, 1956; Burt and Goodchild, 1971a, b; Camougis and Davis, 1971; Clements and May, 1977; Gammon, 1978a; Leake, 1977 and Narahashi, 1971). The knock down effect of pyrethroids, caused by stimulation of central nervous system, is much faster than caused by DDT.

Many synthetic pyrethroids like fenvalerate, cypermethrin, and deltamethrin do not cause symptoms of excitation; they produce ataxia and lethargic symptoms leading to flaccid paralysis (Adams and Miller, 1980; Ford *et al.*, 1977).

The neurophysiological responses to the pyrethroids vary according to the type of nerve element assayed and on their chemical nature and temperature. Like DDT, pyrethroids also show negative temperature co-efficient (Gammon, 1978a, b, 1979). However, the repetitive discharge produced by allethrin in the nerve cord of cockroach has a positive co-efficient (Narahashi, 1971).

## BACTERIA-BASED INSECTICIDES

Among the bacteria-based insecticides/miticides, *Bacillus thuringiensis*, or Bt, as a control for lepidopterous larvae (caterpillars, leafrollers, webworms), miticide abamectin (AgriMek's Avid®), derived from *Streptomyces avermitilis* are well known. Another bacteria-based insecticide is spinosad (a mixture of spinosyn A and spinosyn D) derived from *Saccharopolyspora spinosa*, and registered for control of lepidopterous larvae, sawflies, leafminers and thrips. DowAgroScience markets spinosad under several names (Success®, SpinTor®); Conserve™ is the registered formulation for ornamentals. These macrocyclic lactones, initially from insecticidelly active soil extract, are fast acting, and have a mammalian and environmental profile that is superior to most other synthetic insecticides. These macrolides developed for use on cotton and vegetables are registered as Tracer® and Naturalyte® for insect control (Crouse and Sparks, 1998).

## FUNGI-BASED INSECTICIDES

Mycotech has developed a greenhouse (Botani Gard®) and an outdoor (Mycotrol®) insecticide based on the fungus, *Beauveria bassina*. The fungus enters the insect through the cuticle, and attacks internal organs. The insect stops feeding and dies within a few days. The contact insecticide controls whitefly, aphids, thrips, weevils, mealybugs, leafhoppers and other leaf-feeding insects. Botanigard® is registered for roses.

The fungi derived chemicals are called avermectins. Avermectins affect invertebrates by potentiating the ability of neurotransmitters, such as glutamate and/or GABA, to stimulate an influx of chloride ions into nerve cells. It is currently believed that the anthelmintic properties of the avermectins are due to potentiation and/or direct opening of glutamate-gated chloride channels whereas in insects, it is likely that avermectins bind to multiple sites in insect CI-channels. The CI flux, produced by opening of the channel into neurons, results in loss of cell function and disruption of nerve impulses. Consequently, invertebrates are paralyzed irreversibly and stop feeding. The wide margin of safety for avermectins to mammals is due to: 1) The lack of glu-gated CI-channels in mammals; 2) the low affinity of avermectins for other mammalian ligand-gated CI-channels; and 3) their inability to readily cross the blood-brain barrier. Abamectin shows broad-spectrum insecticidal, nematicidal and miticidal activity with $LC_{90}$ values of 0.02-0.24 ppm against lepidopteran pests. A semisynthetic analogue, 4"-epi-methylamino-4"-deoxyavermectin $B_1$ (emamectin) has been launched as a more efficacious insecticide with recommended rate of application of 56-22.4 g ai/ha. A dihydro derivative of abamectin called ivermectin, finds extensive clinical application as antihelminthes.

## INSECTICIDES OF ANIMAL ORIGIN

Nereistoxin is perhaps the only known insecticide of animal origin. It has been obtained from a marine polychaeteb *Lumbriconereis heteropoda* and is identified as (4-dimethyl-amino) -1,2-dithiole (Corbett, 1974). Using nereistoxin as model, Konishi (1970), Sakai (1972) and Worthing (1983a, b) synthesized many compounds, like cartap, bensultap, thioclam, etc. Regarded as pronereistoxins, these compounds proved effective insecticides against lepidopterous and colepterous pests as they paralyzed the insects without excitation (Hutson and Roberts, 1985).

The insecticidal effect and mode of action of nereistoxin and pronereistoxins have been described by Sakai and Sato (1972). Nereistoxin structurally resembles with acetylcholine. It blocks the synaptic, but not axonal, transmission of cockroach nerves without depolarization probably by acting on acetylcholine receptors on the post-synaptic membrane, as occurs in vertebrates also. The action of this animal toxin quickly immobilizes insects, without convulsive symptoms (Corbett, 1974). The toxic symptoms of nereistoxin and other synthetic analogues differ from those produced by nicotine, which also acts on synaptic receptors. Nereistoxin and synthetic pronereistoxins act on acetylcholine receptors on synapses, blocking the synaptic transmission. Pronereistoxins become effective only after their conversion into nereistoxin in the insect body. Nereistoxin is very weak inhibitor of acetylcholinesterase. Cartap and other pronereistoxins upset the synaptic transmission only when they get converted into nereistoxin in the living tissue of insects (Sakai and Sato, 1972).

Neurotoxic target from scorpion venom: The pentapeptide, cockroach muscle neurotransmitter, proctolin (Lindsey and Jones, 1989) is one such example which along with the toxin generated by insect predators like spider venom could provide alternate future insect control chemicals. The discovery of at least three groups of peptide neurotoxins derived from scorpion venom have shown very high selectivity against insects and are practically inactive on mammals. A joint action of one or other of this group of neurotoxin e.g. LqhaIT and others with synthetic insecticide is proposed as a possible insecticide-resistance mechanism (Stankiewicz *et al.*, 1999).

## SLUG CONTROL PRODUCTS

Sluggo® is an interesting new natural slug control product comprised of iron phosphate and bait additives. When ingested, the slugs stop feeding, become less mobile and begin to die within 3 to 6 days. Any product not ingested biodegrades back into the soil. Iron phosphate is extremely low in mammalian toxicity, and non-toxic to wildlife and pets. The product is marketed to the agricultural industry in 25 and 50-lb bags; a smaller 2.2-lb package is marketed to home gardeners. Western Farm Service markets a similar product under the name "First Choice." Gardens Alive markets iron phosphate slug bait called Escar-Go™. "Worry Free" is a brand that can be found in large hardware stores, and Neudorff of Germany has also registered iron phosphate slug and snail bait.

Flumite-200 is the name of new type of acaricide commercialized by the Hungarian company, CHINOIN Pharmacentical and chemical works. It has a wide spectrum long lasting effect and is selective to phytophagus mites specially at the egg and chrysalis stage.

Abott laboratories have recently commercialized a nematicide Di-Tera from the fungus Myrothecium spp. It gives effective control of nematodes of graphs, citrus and bananas and also induces growth of beneficial microorganism in the rhizosphere.

## REDUCED-RISK PESTICIDES

Novartis has several insecticides in development using a new ingredient, pymetrozine (Fuog *et al.*, 1998). The insecticide is highly selective, targeting aphids, with limited activity against other sucking insects. Pymetrozine paralyzes the insect's salivary pump, eventually resulting in starvation. It has no effect on beneficial insects, and has been given a Reduced Risk status by the EPA. Trade names include Fulfill™, Endeavor™, and Relay 50™.

Uniroyal has registered a new miticide called Floramite™, containing bifenazate, with contact and ingestion action. It is effective against all mite stages, from egg to adult. The product has a 21-day residual activity, and causes minimal damage to beneficials. The EPA has given the product a low (Category IV) toxicity rating.

The pesticide industry is on the threshold of major change. The industry has been exploring biopesticides for the past ten years, and products are finally making their way to the market. Many may be elusive as the market focuses on replacing organophosphates and carbamates, or responds to the growing organic farming industry. But the pattern of pesticide development has shown that the home garden market is not a small one, and we should see a trickle-down of technology from these exciting developments and new products may be seen in future.

The scientists are now working to develop ecofriendly chemicals (Gopal and Mukherjee, 1998) which are safer and more selective in action against the target pest, and do not persist longer than necessary to achieve its objective but without harming the ecosystem.

## SEMIOCHEMICALS

Alternate methods of pest control using semiochemicals and other infochemicals such as pheromones, insect growth hormone mimics, repellents, antifeedants, chitin synthesis inhibitors and chemosterilants are explored during the last twenty years. Some of such novel insect behaviour modifying chemicals possess high selective action against the target insect pests and would not hopefully induce resistance as frequently as conventional insecticides.

Semio chemicals are signaling substances secreted by the insects in the environment to convey behavioural messages between the insect species. The chemicals under this group include pheromones, allomones, kairomones, synomones, and apneumones, which influence and regulate both insect behaviour and physiology. Semiochemicals can also be grouped as intraspecific (pheromones) and interspecific (allelochemicals such as allomones, kairomones etc.) communication chemicals (Walia, 2000).

One of the approaches, which has captured worldwide attention, is the development of novel compounds affecting developmental processes in insects such as insect growth regulators (juvenile hormone mimics, anti-JH compounds, ecdysone agonists and antagonists, chitin synthesis inhibitors), insect behaviour modifying chemicals such as sex attractants, repellents, as well as antifeedants and chemostorilants.

In terms of the chemical structures, most of the brain hormones are believed to be oligopeptides. They are known to regulate all aspects of insect development, reproduction, behaviour, muscle function, homeostasis and metabolism.

Juvenile hormones (JH) are secreted by corpora allata. As long as JH are secreted, the larva will molt into another larva. However, at the end of the last instar, the corpora allata are turned off by some physiological mechanism and secretion of JHs ceases or their concentration falls rapidly. In the absence of sufficient titre, the larva or nymph will metamorphose into a pupa and then into the adults. Thus in order for mature larvae to metamorphose into adult, the concentration of the JH has to decline. The application of JH at this stage can cause death of the insect (Henrick, 1982). It is generally believed that JH-I and JH-II are responsible for controlling metamorphosis by retaining larval character, whereas JH-III reportedly plays a purely gonadotropic role. The promise of practical field application was realized in the commercialization of the compounds methoprene, kinoprene and hydroprene developed by Zoecon Corporation as mosquito growth regulator. Some other potential JH-mimics include epiphenomenona, phenyl geranyl ether and JH-25.

Among the novel JH mimics with relatively high toxicity and potency on agricultural pests are fenoxycarb {(ethyl 2-(4-phenoxphenoxy) ethyl carbamate} and pyriproxyfen (4-phenoxphenoxy) ethoxy pyridine. Fenoxycarb exhibit ovicidal and ovalarvicidal activity and is the first commercial compound recommended for the control of agricultural pests under field conditions (Masner *et al.*, 1987). Pyriproxyfen on the other hand is a potent JH mimic affecting the hormonal balance in insects and cause suppression of embryogenesis, metamorphosis and adult emergence (Itaya 1987; Kawada 1988; Langley 1990; Koechler and Patterson, 1991). The compound has been used successfully for controlling whiteflies in Israeli cotton fields since 1991 (Horowitz and Ishaaya, 1996). NC-170, a new JH mimic belonging to a different class, also exhibits selective JH-like effects on leaf and plant hoppers (Miyake *et al.*, 1991).

Since JH is essential in the early stages of the growth of insects, any compound inhibiting its secretion may provide a useful tool for insect control. Since these compounds induced precocious metamorphosis they were named precocene I and II. The important feature of precocene is that they can readily penetrate into the intact insect, get transported to the corpora allata, and act as a competitive substrate for natural oxidizing enzymes. The generally accepted mode of action of the precocenes in insects is that the electron rich 3,4-double bond is readily epoxidised by cytochrome P-450 linked mono-oxygenase enzymes in the corpora allata to highly reactive and unstable epoxides or quinone methides causing cellular disruption (Pratt *et al.*, 1980; Soderlund *et al.*, 1980)

The advantage of a chemical sterilant over an insecticide can be realized if the chemosterilants is as effective as the toxicant in producing the desired effect. The insect chemosterilants results in the failure of the insect to produce ova and sperm, cause their death after they have been produced or produce mutations/damaged genetic material in ova or sperm. Their examples are apholate, thiotepa, metepa; antimetabolites such as 5-fluorouracil; antibiotics such as mitomycin; cycloheximide; colchicines; tryphenyltin; urea; thiourea; s-triazine compounds etc. (Turner, 1968). The alkylating agents replace hydrogen with an alkyl group in basic genetic material with an effect similar to that of radiation. Chemosterilants are mostly considered unsafe and the possibility of their contact with man or beneficial animals should be avoided. Chemiosterilants have however been used as baits (Hayes and Laws, 1991).

Some of the attractants used successfully in bait traps include siglure, medilure and trimedilure. Certain oviposition lures attract females and induce them to lay eggs. Housefly is attracted to manure and ammonia while female mosquito (*Aedes aegypti*) is attracted towards the specific odour of methyl butyrate, methyl propionate, and ethyl acetate for oviposition purpose. The use of attractants does not appear to be promising since many insect species did not have highly developed olfactory organs, which are the basic receptors of the chemical stimuli.

Periplanone A and Periplanone B are the two sex pheromones isolated from the American cockroach. Most sex pheromones are derivatives (mostly acetate) of unsaturated (Mono, di- or sometimes tri- ) even-carbon straight chain alcaohols. The sex pheromones of the housefly *Musca domestica* called muscalure consist of (Z)-9-tricosene and other hydrocarbon components. Insect pheromones or luring chemicals are highly specific and constitute a key component of integrated pest management. The process of molting is the distinguishing feature of insect growth and development. Periodically the epidermal cells of immature insects become detached from their cuticle. The BH stimulates the prothoraic glands to secrete ecdysones, which in turn act on various cells and promote their growth. Of the two ecdysones, a-ecdysone was isolated from the pupae of silkworm *Bombyx mori*. The second molting hormone b-ecdysone, was later isolated from different sources (Bhan *et al.*, 1980). Several non-steroidal ecdysterioid have been developed recently, the first compound of this series RH-5849 binds to the ecdysteroid receptors, thereby initiating the molting process (Wing, 1988; Wing *et al.*, 1988). Their high selectivity to lepidopteran pests along with their low toxicity to mammals, fish, and ectoparasitoids (Wing and Aller, 1990; Brown, 1994) render these compounds potential agents to be used in IPM programmes for controlling such pest in agricultural crops.

## Chitin

Safe Science, formerly IGG International, has taken a different direction with Elexa™ and Greenleaf™. The company's press releases describe the active ingredient only as "complex carbohydrates derived from naturally occurring substances." The EPA registration, however, lists the active ingredient as chitosan, or deacetylated chitin. Chitin is the substance found in the outer shell of crustaceans and insects and in the cell walls of many fungi, that makes the shell or exoskeleton hard. Chitin also forms a protective membrane that lines the digestive tract of insects and protects them from internal penetration by bacteria or pathogens. In fungi, the thin, threadlike filaments contain chitin. Plants, especially some citrus, develop enzymes called chitinases and chitosanases that degrade chitin, forming a protection against invading insects and fungi. Research has been conducted, injecting plants with cloned chitinase genes, to stimulate production of similar chitinase.

In insects, chitin forms the framework of the cuticle and is also the main constituent of the peritrophicmembrane of the gut, It is chemically known as 2-acetamido-2-deoxy-D-glucose polymer. Hydrolytic enzymes chitinase and chitobiase capable of degrading chitin are also vital in insect molting process. Therefore any interference with chitin synthesis and degradation can lead to derangement of metamorphosis and growth of the organism. These considerations led to the development of several chitin synthesis inhibitors.

### Chitin Synthesis Inhibitors

The practical utility of diflubenzuron, as an IGR in IPM as well as insecticide resistance management of cash crops like cotton, has been widely documented. Newer versions incorporating features that would enable better transport into the target pest as well as delaying of resistance development have been introduced. Except buprofezin, others essentially retain A-ring of diflubenzuron with structural variations in the other ring. Buprofezin launched by Nitron Nohyaku is recommended for the control of scales, whiteflies, plant and leafhoppers. It has unique structure containing 1,3,5-thiadiazine-4-one ring (Decock and Degheela, 1998). In subsequent versions keeping A constant, B has been varied. Benzoylphenyl urea type chitin synthesis inhibitor namely diflubenzuron are getting popular but uneducated poor and risk adverse Indian farmers still prefer to use synthetic insecticides.

## FUNGICIDES

Fungicides are agents of natural or synthetic origin, which act to protect plants against invasion by fungi and/or to eradicate established fungal infection. Major developments in the use of fungicides include (a) the change to systemic fungicides with higher persistence, and (b) the reduction in the amount applied. Since fungicides have relatively higher $LD_{50}$ than insecticides, older molecules are still in vogue. Besides, triazoles that represent the most important systemic fungicides, the recent introduction include strobilurins, anilinopyrimidines, phenylpyrroles and various other groups.

### Inorganic compounds

#### *Bicarbonates*

Fungicides based on sodium or potassium bicarbonate are finally reaching the market. Remedy® (82% potassium bicarbonate) is manufactured by Bonide and sold in a 6-oz bottle that makes 12 gallons of spray. Cleary also markets a similar product under the brand "First Step."

Church and Dwight, manufacturers of Arm & Hammer Baking Soda®, as well as the world's largest producer of potassium bicarbonate, recently revised their EPA registration for ArmiCarb 100®, a fungicide containing potassium bicarbonate, targeting powdery mildew and other diseases on ornamentals and food/feed crops. The revision was a response to increasing use of a potassium bicarbonate product called Kaligreen® (developed by the Japanese company Nichiman and marketed in the US by Monterey Chemical Co.) for powdery mildew on grapes, cucumbers, strawberries, tobacco and roses. Field tests on grapes in California have shown Kaligreen® to be effective when teamed with applications of sterol inhibitors. Kaligreen® (82% potassium bicarbonate) is sold in 2½-lb containers for commercial use.

Bicarbonates damage the cell wall membrane of the powdery mildew spores, leading to dehydration and death of the microorganism. Other studies with Kaligreen® suggest that potassium bicarbonate causes an imbalance of potassium ions in the fungal cell, causing cell wall collapse. For a good review of bicarbonates as a fungicide, refer to "Use of Baking Soda as a Fungicide" on the website for Appropriate Technology Transfer for Rural Areas (ATTRA), http://www.attra.org/attra-pub/baksoda.html

### Copper compounds

Copper compounds are well known effective fungicides. Bordeaux Mixture, a mixture of copper sulfate and lime, is a classic dating back to the late 1800's. More recently, Source Technology Biologicals has been stepping up its promotion of Phyton 27®, containing copper sulphate petahydrate. Phyton 27® is not a new product, but rose growers have been showing more interest in the product. The fungicidal activity of copper is based on its ability to destroy proteins in plants. The trick is to get the copper level high enough to kill fungi, but low enough to avoid injury to the plant. Phyton 27® carries a precautionary statement of DANGER. Copper sulfate is extremely corrosive and can cause irreversible eye damage and skin burns. Other toxicology issues with copper sulfate are available from pesticide information profile on ExToxNet (http://ace.orst.edu/info/extoxnet/pips/coppersu.htm).

### Peroxides

A recent article in the Pensacola Rose Society's newsletter introduced BioSafe's ZeroTol®. The active ingredient of the fungicide/algaecide is hydrogen peroxide. ZeroTol® sanitizes plant tissue of potential pathogens before they can invade the plant cells and cause infection. This process is so unique to the horticultural and agricultural markets that BioSafe was granted a patent by the US Patent Office. The concept is simple, keep the plant and flower surfaces free of bacterial, fungal and viral elements and the plants will stay clean, green and healthy.

Hydrogen peroxide has been used in hydroponics for several years as an algaecide, and sprayed on crops and soil to increase yields and control pests. ZeroTol® is a 27% concentration, while the consumer product in your medicine cabinet is a 3% concentration. There are a number of brands offering a 35% concentration, both food grade and agricultural/industrial grade. BioSafe does not reveal what ZeroTol®'s inert ingredients are, but indicates that the product would meet organic farming standards. ZeroTol™ makes no insecticidal claims, and research tests seem to bear this up, although information from Snow Pond, a hydrogen peroxide distributor, points to tests that support insecticidal claims for hydrogen peroxide. BioSafe Systems markets another hydrogen peroxide called OxiDate™.

Hydrogen peroxide is extremely corrosive, causing irreversible eye damage. ZeroTol® carries a precautionary statement of DANGER. According to the label, the product is toxic to fish and birds, and highly toxic to bees and beneficial insects exposed to direct contact. The inert ingredients added as stabilizers have not been tested for their effect on plants, and the concentration is very low. If drug store product is used, one would have to add 4-8 ounces to a gallon of water. If commercial hydrogen peroxide, but not ZeroTol®, is being used, a food-grade 35% concentration can be recommended. These are sold under various brand names by many health food/ oxygen enhancement firms. For more information on the uses of hydrogen peroxide, factsheets at Snow Pond (http://snow-pond.com) can be consulted.

In August 1999, Biosafe filed an application to register sodium percarbonate as a fungicide, to be marketed under the name TerraCare™. Sodium percarbonate is a disodium carbonate compound combined with hydrogen peroxide. It is a bleaching agent primarily used in laundry and automatic dishwashing detergents, with the added benefits of being an alkali provider and water softener.

### *Phosphates*

LidoChem received EPA approval in 1998 for a fungicide called eKsPunge™, containing potassium dihydrogen phosphate, for use against powdery mildew on a number of crops including roses. Potassium dihydrogen phosphate occurs naturally, and has been used as an agricultural fertilizer and a buffering agent in pesticide formulations. The EPA streamlined approval, finding little to no risk to humans or environment.

UIM Agrochemicals received EPA approval in late 1997 for Foli-R-Fos 400, a fungicide containing mono- and di-potassium salts of phosphorous acid (phosphonic acid), for use against Pythium and Phytophthora on a range of ornamentals and bedding plants. Phosphonic acid is a synthesized compound, not naturally occurring, but the simple inorganic nature of the compound moved it into the process for evaluating low risk pesticides. The ingredient has a low toxicity and a history of safe use in Australia and other countries. Fosetyl Al aluminum salt of ethyl phosphonic acid, is registered for use in India also for controlling diseases caused by Oomycetes.

### Organic Compounds

The multiple-site inhibiting fungicides, which are also called multisite inhibitors acts on various sites in fungal physiology and therefore the fungal resistance to these fungicides is quiet rare in practice. Some compounds are as ferbam, ziram and thiram belonging to dithiocarbamates, and alkylenebis (dithiocarbamates) such as zineb, maneb, mancozeb and propineb, quinnes, such as chloranil and dichlone, N-haloalkylthio derivatives such as captan, and dinitrophenol derivatives, such as dinocap.

Most important specific-site inhibiting and systemic fungicide groups introduced in 1960s were benzimidazole fungicides. The mode of action of benzimidazoles is due to inhibition of fungal mitosis by binding to the fungal tubulin. Benomyl belongs to this group but thiophanate methyl also gets converted to popular fungicide carbendazim, which is methyl benzimidazole-2-yl-carbamate.

N-Arylcarbamates are a group of fungicides having interesting selectivity in their action. Several compounds were found to be fungitoxic to benzimidazole-resistant strains without phytotoxicity. Among them diethofencarb is popular. This class of fungicides acts on fungal cells by inhibiting biosynthesis of fungal sterols. This selectivity in their action signals the importance of sterols in the fungal cells as well as fitness of chemical structures of the fungicides to bind the target sites in the respective fungi.

Sterol biosynthesis inhibitor (SBI) fungicides are practically useful to control diseases such as powdery mildews and rusts, which were rather difficult to control with other fungicides or by other methods. There are several groups in terms of their mode of action, though most agricultural SBI fungicides belong to two main groups; one is the demethylation inhibitor (DMI) group. It includes triazole, imidazole and fungicides having other aryl heterocyclic rings such as pyrimidine and pyridine. The other group includes derivatives of morpholine and its analogues. Morpholines and analogues are assumed to inhibit an isomerization step and a reduction step in fungal sterol biosynthesis. The merit of morpholines was re-evaluated after resistance problems with DMIs became serious in practice, and novel morpholine fungicides and the analogus piperidine fungicides have been developed.

### Acylalanines and Related Fungicides

This class of fungicides is often also called the phenylamide fungicides. Benalaxyl, furalaxyl, metalaxyl and oxadixyl belong to this group. Their mode of action is selective inhibition of biosynthesis of ribosomal RNA (rRNA).

### Phenyl Urea

Pencyuron, a phenyl urea fungicide was also developed and introduced in Japan for the control of rice sheath blight. It is also effective against black scurf of potato and bottom rot of lettuce.

### Anilinopyrimidines

Although the chemical structures of this class of fungicides are relatively simple, they were developed rather recently. Examples are mepanipyrim, pyrimethanil and cyprodinil. Since fungitoxicities of these fungicides were reversed by addition of methionine, inhibition of fungal biosynthesis of methionine by the fungicides was suggested as the mechanism of their action of these fungicides.

### Organophoshorus Fungicides

Examples of this group of phosphorothiolate, phosphorothionate and phosphonate fungicides are pyrazophos, iprobenfos, edifenphos and fosetyl-aluminum.

### Melanin Biosynthesis Inhibitors (MBI)

Pentachlorobenzyl alcohol (PCBA) had little activity *in vitro* but was effective as a preventive treatment for rice blast caused by *Pyricularia oryzae*. Derivatives of pentachlorobenzaldehyde, namely, the oxime and cyanohydrin were similarly effective. They are, however, not used now because their metabolites, *i.e.* penta- and tetra-chlorobenzoic acids, cause indirect phytotoxicity on other crops such as vegetables. Fungicides of various structures were later found to belong to this class. Those now used for rice blast control are Phthalide, tricyclazole and Pyroquilon. Another MBI, carpropamid, was recently developed which has different type of structure i.e. no fused rings. The merit of MBIs over other selective biosynthesis inhibitors is, no resistance and residue problem (Gopal *et al.*, 2002).

Probenazole is also a plant-protecting agent having little fungitoxicity *in vitro.* Seemingly different from that of the MBI fungicides, it induces resistance in the plants against diseases.

### *Dicarboximide*

Fungicides having a common chemical structure, N-(3, 5-dichlorophenyl)-dicaboximide, are called dicarboximide fungicides. Popular among them are chlozolinate, iprodione, procymidone and vinclozolin. They cause disorder of fungal cell structure especially when the cells are growing and multiplying.

### *Phenylpyrrole*

They affect and cause disorder in membrane of the fungi. This class of fungicides, fenpiclonil and fludioxonil, have structures derived from that of an antifungal antibiotic, pyrrolnitrin.

### *Aryl Carboxanilide*

The original fungicides of this class namely carboxin and its sulfone, oxycarboxin were introduced in the late 1960s. Mepronil, flutolanil, thifluzamide and furametpyr inhibit fungal respiration by inhibiting succinate dehydrogenase.

## Bacteria-based Fungicides

An article by Norman Rose in the 1998 American Rose Annual described a spray program using Wilt-Pruf® and a product called Rose Flora™, from Better Flora, based on *Bacillus laterosporus*. The company has developed a number of products based on the same bacteria, including several intended for human, horse and animal consumption that encourage a better balance of bacteria ("flora") in the intestines. The bacteria in Rose Flora™ suppress various pathogenic fungi, including *Pythium*, *Phytophthora* and *Botrytis*, and when used with Wilt-Pruf® or similar anti-transpirants, blackspot and powdery mildew. Additional product information is available at http://www.better-flora.com

Other bacterial fungicides include streptomycin (Agri-mycin®) and oxytetracycline (Mycoshield®), both from Novartis. Mycoshield® is registered for fire blight on pears and bacterial spot of peach and nectarine; Agri-mycin® has broader registered uses, including various bacterial blights, spots and rots. The latter has a registration for rose crown gall in New Jersey.

Agra Quest has been field-testing Serenade™, a biofungicide discovered in their research screening of soil fungi and bacteria. Serenade™ is derived from *Bacillus subtilis*, and purported to be effective against powdery and downy mildews and botrytis, while non-toxic to beneficial insects. The product has been tested on food crops and ornamentals. Agra Quest submitted an EPA registration application.

An 18-member macrolide Soraphen A has been isolated from the myxobacterium *Sorangium cellulosum* by Novarities crop protection group. It is a fungicide which inhibits acetype-Co A carboxylase.

### Fungus-based Fungicides

The most important developments in fungus-based fungicides have been in the strobilurins, extracts of the wood rotting fungus *Strobilurus tencellus*. Strobilurins have a suppressive effect on other fungi, reducing competition for nutrients. Extensive -work in seventies led to the discovery of Strobilurins, a class of fungicides belonging to β-methoxy acrylate, from over 20 species of basidiomycetes. The fungicidal activity stems from their ability to inhibit electron transfer in fungal mitrochondria by binding at a specific site on cytochrome b and inhibit respiration in fungi. This mode of action being novel, heralds the addition of new molecules with the possibility of developing cross-resistance to existing fungicides. The natural strobilurins suffer from unsuitable physico-chemical properties such as photolability, higher volatility etc. and problems associated with their large-scale preparation at an economic level. Three multinational companies Zenneca, BASF and Takeda Chemical Company took up analogue syntheses concurrently, taking strobilurin-A as the prototype.

Zenneca Agrochemicals have announced oxime ether analogues, which are more active, photostable, broad spectrum yet having right lipophilicity. They are required in lower doses.

The three major strobilurins recently released or under development are azoxystrobin (Zeneca's Amistar®, Heritage® and Abound®), kresoxim-methyl (BASF's Sovran® and Cygnus®), and trifloxystrobin (Novartis's Compass™ and Flint™). Strobilurins inhibit electron transfer in mitochondria, disrupting the metabolic processes of the target fungi. Heritage® is registered for use on several turf fungi. Abound® is registered for various fungi on bananas, peanuts, pecans and grapes. Cygnus® is a greenhouse product targeting powdery mildew on roses and other ornamental plants. Research has found that strobilurins are most effective when used in rotation with other fungicide classes, reducing rather than replacing their use.

Among analogues of strobilurin, kresoxim-methyl is hightly effective against powdery mildews, azoxystrobin is a good fungicide against downy mildews and SSF-126 is effective for control of rice blast.

AQ-10, from Ecogen, is a strain of the fungus *Ampelomyces quisqualis*. The product parasitizes powdery mildew. AQ-10 is currently marketed in commercial formulations, but a home garden formulation should be available in the near future. Tests in California have indicated that, on grapes, AQ-10 has limited control by itself, and is intended to be used in rotation with sulfur or sterol inhibitors such as Rally®, Rubigan®, Bayleton®, Procure®, Elite™. Recently, Ecogen has signed an agreement with Plant Health Care to market AQ-10 under a PHC label.

Another fungus-based fungicide is Primastop™, developed by Kemira Agro in Finland, based on *Gliocladium catenulatum.* It is registered in the United States. Kemira Agro also manufactures Mycostop®, an fungicide derived from the soil bacteria *Streptomyces griseoviridis,* and introduced in 1995 as a control for pythium, fusarium and other soil diseases. There are dozens of fungus and bacteria-based fungicides registered for control of various soilborne diseases; a list and brief description of these products is available on the Web at http://mypage.channeli.net/soongu/protection/biocontrol/biocontrol.htm

### Plant-based Fungicides

For fungicides, research has been taking another look at benzaldehyde, the synthetic essence of peach oil, used in flavorings, perfumes, and drugs and as a bee repellent when handling hives. Over ten years ago, benzaldehyde was identified as effective in inhibiting the growth of botrytis. Subsequent research has found that other oil extracts, including thyme, sage, marjoram, lavender, lemongrass, tea tree, melissa, peppermint, pennyroyal, jasmine, wintergreen and hyssop, have a similar effect (thyme oil, in particular). Benzaldehyde is now being studied as a replacement for methyl bromide.

### Plant Defense Inducers

It has been an established observation that plants have defense mechanisms that kick into gear when attached by disease or insects. One method is to wall off the pathogen by killing off surrounding cells, somewhat like a fire line around a forest fire. This is commonly observed as the yellowing around a diseased area, such as with blackspot. But the plant responds further, releasing various chemical compounds that alert the rest of the plant to begin producing other compounds that increase plant resistance to infection or attack at other sites on the plant. These responses are called systemic acquired resistance (SaqR) and induced resistance (IR).

One theory holds that the first salvo in an attack is an oxidative burst, a sudden release of superoxide and hydrogen peroxide. It is believed that the hydrogen peroxide kills the pathogen; the surrounding cells and triggers the production of enzymes and defense compounds. The hydrogen peroxide dissipates in about an hour, but salicylic acid begins to accumulate in the cells.

Salicylic acid is a crystalline solid found in plants, particularly fruit, that is used in various forms to preserve food, antiseptics such as are in mouthwashes and toothpaste, analgesics such as aspirin, and in oil of wintergreen. These are all derivatives or compounds, not salicylic acid itself. At first, scientists observed that a plant sprayed with salicylic acid would begin a systemic acquired resistance response, suggesting that the acid was a translocating signal. Further research, however, seemed to indicate that salicylic acid is not the triggering signal, but may be a necessary component in forming antimicrobial proteins that make up the defensive response.

Experiments in India treating seeds and seedlings with salicylic acid gave results showing 70% protection from downy mildew. Other experiments used polyunsaturated fatty acids, such as arachidonic and linoleic acids, to boost salicylic acid levels, with similar results. Stoller is registering salicylic acid with the EPA under the name Adjust™.

Another chemical, enzothiadiazole or BTH, has been found to mimic salicylic acid, and has been marketed in Germany under the name Bion for use in protecting wheat against mildew. Apparently it is also effective on other plants, but with some danger of phytotoxicity. In the US, Novartis is registering it under the name Actigard™, initially for use on lettuce, tomatoes and tobacco.

Eden Bioscience in Bothell WA is pursuing EPA approval for an all-natural plant stimulant called Messenger™. The product boosts growth, helps block a number of common plant diseases, and helps repel insects and nematodes. The active ingredient is a protein called harpin, found in bacteria that cause pear and apple fire blight. Plants are hypersensitive to a form of the protein that triggers plant defenses, usually within five minutes of application. The plant reaction fights off a broad spectrum of viral, fungal and bacterial infections for two to four weeks.

Eden had been looking at the protein as a defense against plant disease. It was a surprise to find that harpin also stimulated the plants to grow faster and larger, and discouraged insects from living on the plant surface. Field trials revealed growth enhancement of 5 to 30 per cent, with thicker stalks, bigger fruit, earlier ripening, better color.

Currently field trials are being conducted on three dozen crops, from cucumbers and oranges to cotton and roses. The product is used in small quantities, only 2 grams per acre. Messenger™ does not kill diseases or insects, so it does not replace other pesticides. However, it should reduce their use. Research continues in searching for other resistance inducers. In Germany, sodium and potassium phosphates are being studied as inducers on cucumbers, battling anthracnose and powdery mildew.

An extract from *Reynoutria sachalinensis*, or Giant knotweed, induces a localized resistance, and has been found to be effective as a protectant spray against powdery mildew on roses. Like other protectants, such as antitranspirants, it needs to be applied frequently as new growth appears. The extract is marketed under the name Milsana™, originally introduced by BASF as a foliar fertilizer.

Most of these plant defense inducers are effective only against diseases. For insects, the plants produced a different defense involving compounds called jasmonates. Jasmonates seem to play some role in elevating plant steroid hormones that hinder insect development. Jasmonates also have several functions in plant growth regulation, and some influence in disease resistance. But research with spraying jasmonic acid has shown wide variation in effectiveness on different crops. Curiously, salicylic acid seems to counteract the insect-control benefits of jasmonic acid.

**Systemic Acquired Resistance (SAqR)**

Systemic acquired disease resistance is form of induced horizontal resistance. SAqR has been the topic of research for over four decades now. They key feature of SAqR is that the host genetic potential for resistance can be augmented by restricted inoculation of pathogens or certain chemicals that are signals produced by treated plants. Salicylic acid was shown to be one such signal chemical. M/s. Ciba Geigy followed up this lead to come out with certain commercial analogues called synthetic SAR inducers. These are not fungal or fungicides according to the conventional knowledge (Copping, 1998).

Since SAqR is a naturally occurring plant defense mechanism, use of SAqR inducers is expected to lead to long lasting and broad-spectrum disease control. It is more like homeopathic in approach and thus, could benefit marginal farmers.

Geffken at the University of Bonn discovered an oxazolidinone as a lead fungicide and Dupont in synergy with academia reported the development of a new agricultural fungicide famoxadone (Sternberg, *et al.*, 2001) for the control of plant pathogens in the Ascomycete, Basidiomycete, and Oomycete classes that infect grapes, cereals, tomatoes, potato and other crops. Analogue synthesis with careful optimization of each and every substituent position of the prototype molecule coupled with greenhouse and field evaluation led to the development of this fungicide. The mode of action of oxazolidinones was determined to be inhibition of mitochondrial electron transport at Complex-III, thus providing a newer vista for the control of phytopathogenic fungi.

## HERBICIDES

The basic approach for compound design has changed from synthesis of structurally similar herbicides based on structure activity relationship (SAR) to synthesis of enzyme target site directed inhibitors. The evolutionary trend from single toxophoric chemical classes starting from phenoxy alkanoic acids, carbamates, anilides, substituted phenyl ureas, triazines, organophosphorus, pyridines, pyrimidinels dinitroaniline, diphenyl ethers (Kulshrestha and Parmar, 1992) to dual toxophoric classes such as sulphonylureas and imidazolinone etc. classes represent important advances in herbicide development for weed control (Kulshrestha and Parmar, 1992). This recent approach involving the synthesis of enzyme target sited inhibitors has yielded several new classes of potent commercially viable technologies in herbicide chemistry. These herbicides are applied at low dose rate, are biodegradable, have less persistence and possess high mammalian safety. Some of these are presented below:

### Synthetic Herbicides

#### *Phenyltriazolinone Herbicides*

Sulfentrazone was the first extremely active compound of this class commercialized for use in many advance countries. Carfentrazone-ethyl (ethyl 2-chloro-4- [2-chloro-4-fluoro-5- [4-(difluoromethyl)-4, 5-dihydro-3- methyl-5-oxo-1H-1, 2, 4-triazol-1-yl] phenyl]propionate; F-8426), is another herbicide of this group recently commercialized by the FMC Corporation (Agricultural Products Group, Philadelphia, PA 19103, USA). The herbicide is effective as post emergent application at rates as low as 2.2 g/ha

Carfentrazone-ethyl is herbicidally active against morning glories (*Ipomoea* spp.) and velvetleaf (*Abutilon* spp.) that pose serious problems in soybean (*Glycine max* (L.) Merr.) fields of the southern United States. Competition between soybean and velvetleaf may result in as much as 46% yield reduction and infestation by morning glories can reduce soybean yields by 75%. The selectivity of these herbicides is due to rapid metabolism in the crop compared to the weeds.The phenyletriazolinones are potent inhibitors of protoporphyrinogen oxidase (Protox), which causes the accumulation of protoporphyrin IX (Proto IX) in the treated plant tissues that is involved in the light-dependent formation of singlet oxygen responsible for membrane peroxidation.

***Thiazolidinone***

The 5-tert-Butyl-carbamoyloxy-3- (3-trifluoromethyl) phenyl-4-thiazolidinone is a representative of a novel class of Phenyl-lactam-carbamate herbicides. This compound shows potential for the selective pre-emergence control of a range of weed species in soybean. Susceptible weeds include grasses (such as *Setaria virdi*, *Sorghum halepens*, *Bachiaria* spp., *Echinochloa crus-galli* Beauv.) and small-seeded broad-leaved weeds (including *Amaranthus* spp. and *Chenopodium* spp.), though large-seeded broad-leaved weeds (such as *Ipomoea* spp. and *Abutilon* spp) are not controlled. This compound powerfully inhibited the growth and lateral branching of the roots of agar-grown seedlings of susceptible species. The herbicides are a potent inhibitor of [$^3$H] glucose incorporation into the polysaccharide of seedling roots of *Zea mays* and *Setania viridis* but only relatively weakly active on *Glycine max* and *Ipomoea hederacea.* (Sharples *et al.*, 1998). The compound shows excellent crop selectivity at the rates required for control of susceptible weed species.

***Triketones: The Bleaching Herbicides***

Like many other major discoveries, the discovery of the triketones was entirely serendipitous while following a rationale for the synthesis of what would be the 'break-though' molecule for an entire different purpose. Their genesis started with attempts to prepare new inhibitors of acetyl-CoA carboxylase chemically patterned after sethoxydim. In particular, efforts were in attempting to prepare other potential functional mimics of the oximino moiety of sethoxydim. The first target compound, which was prepared, had encouraging herbicidal activity. In an attempt to prepare phenyl analogs using the same reaction procedure, the 2-benzoylcyclohexane-1, 3-diones were obtained instead of the expected product. The triketone prepared was herbicidally inactive. As such, further interest in this class of compounds would normally have terminated. However, at that time an ongoing program to screen for antidotes for soya injury produced by thiocarbamate herbicides, and triketone was found to have antidote properties. Therefore, an analog synthesis program was initiated to optimize this antidoting effect. As part of this effort, the ortho-chloro analog of 2-benzoylcyclohexane-1, 3-dione was prepared . It was found to be quite herbicidally active with unique bleaching symptoms, and the discovery of the triketone herbicides had been made.

Development of bleaching herbicides targeting the inhibition of p-hydroxyphenylpyruvate dioxygenase (HPPD) as a herbicidal mode of action is thus a recent, exciting development in the pesticide science. Discovery of HPPD as an unique and viable herbicide target was first made by Zeneca Agrochemicals in 1982 as part of an investigation of herbicidal 2-benzoyl-1,3-cyclohexanediones, referred to as the triketones. Elucidation of the unique site of action of these compounds was first made in mammalian systems. The HPPD site of action was then subsequently confirmed in plants, and a minimum substructure hypothesis for the inhibition of HPPD was also developed (Hess, 2000). The commercial compound sulcotrione, post-emergent broad-leaf herbicides for use in maize in Europe, eventually resulted from these efforts, along with the development compound ZA1296 for the pre-and post-emergent broad-leaf maize market in the USA. An additional unexpected benefit from this research was the discovery of the pharmaceutical use of these triketones for the treatment of tyrosinaemia, a disorder involving increased concentrations of tyrosine in the blood, with enhanced urinary excretion of tyrosine and tyrosine-related compounds. (Lee *et al.*, 1998)

### *Quinoline Carboxylic Acids*

Substituted quinolinecarboxylic acids are a new class of highly selective auxin herbicides of which quinmerac (7-chloro-3-methylquinoline-8-carboxylic acid) and quinchlorac have been introduced commercially in the recent years. These herbicides effectively control important dicotyledonous weeds, such as cleavers (*Galium aparine* L.) in sugar beet, oilseed rape and wheat. In *Galium*, the compound is taken up via the root and leaves within a few hours of application, and is translocated systemically in the plant. This class of herbicides induced epinastic symptoms on stems and leaves within 5 h of root-treatment, which were followed during the next 20 h by inhibition of root and particularly shoot growth, and a reduction in water consumption. After two to four days, stem necrosis and chlorosis and wilting of the shoot proceeded. Based on the concentrations applied, shoot growth of *Galium* was 33-fold more sensitive to these herbicides than root growth. The levels of the direct biosynthetic precursor, 1-aminocyclopropane-1-carboxylic acid (ACC), and ethylene formation increased, particularly in the shoot tissue. Accumulations of abscisic acid (ABA) proceeded more slowly and reached 70 times that in untreated plants after 48 h. Within 24 h of herbicides exposure, increased ABA resulted in reductions in stomatal aperture, water consumption, photosynthetic carbon dioxide uptake and growth. Thus, the shoot appears to be the predominant target of the biochemical and physiological effects. Studies using intact plants, isolated shoots and cell suspension cultures of *Galium* treated with the ethylene generator, ethephon, or inhibitors of ACC and ABA synthesis, suggested that Quinmerac-stimulated ACC synthesis triggered the accumulation of ABA, mainly from de-novo synthesis. Other Quinmerac-susceptible weed species, such as *Apium graveolens* L., *Conium maculatum* L., *Solanum nigrum* L. and *Veronica* spp, also responded with an increase in ABA concentration which was closely correlated with reductions in root and shoot fresh weight (Grossmann and Scheltrup, 1998).

### *Dimethoxypyrimidinyloxy-methoxyiminoethyl Benzoates*

The most potent compound of this class is pyriminobacmethyl (KIH-6127). The technical grade of this herbicide is a mixture of the E and Z forms it has been found to be particularly effective herbicide against barnyard grass (*Echinochloa oryzicola*) over a wide range of growth stages including pre-emergence application. This compound has excellent safety for transplanted rice crop in flooded paddy conditions. Pyriminobac -methyl was approved in 1996 and was first launched earlier in 1997 as one of the active ingredient of the one-shot rice herbicide Prosper in Japan. The compound inhibits the plant enzyme acetolactate synthase (ALS), during branched chain amino acid biosynthesis.

The synthesis of KIH-6127 yields a mixture of two isomers (in a >9:1) (major/minor) ratio. These isomers have been separated by silica-gel column chromatography, and their stereochemistry was initially determined by NMR spectrometry. The major isomer was tentatively assigned as being the E isomer.

### *Pyrazolephenyl Ethers*

A new class of herbicides generically designated pyrazole phenyl ethers (PPEs) were lately discovered in Monsanto Co. These compounds act by inhibiting protoporphyrinogen oxidase bleaching herbicides as do structurally related nitrodiphenyl ethers (nitroDPEs) (Clark, 1996).

### *Pyrimidinylsalicylates*

A new series of the O-pyrimidinylsalicylates was synthesized and their herbicidal activity was examined. Some of these compounds showed very strong herbicidal activity under pre- and post-emergent treatment conditions against various kinds of grass and broadleaf weeds. Among these compounds, O- (4, 6- dimethoxypyrimidin-2-yl) salicylic acid and its methyl ester were found to exhibit the highest activity. The herbicidal symptoms observed after the treatments included early cessation of plant growth followed by chlorosis, necrosis and plant death. The symptoms were similar to those caused by sulfonylureas and imidazolinones, which inhibit branched-chain amino acid biosynthesis (Nezu *et al.*, 1996).

It was observed that some 2, 4-dimethoxypyrimidines (and triazines) with a phenoxyphenoxy substructure at the 6-position exhibited a marked post-emergent herbicidal activity. Although this compound has good activity against various grass and broadleaf weeds, it is phytotoxic against some crops such as rice, wheat and soybean. During the course of the previous study, substitution patterns in the pyrimidine and the terminal phenyl rings of the compound were studied. In contrast with the ethyl ester, which was herbicidally inactive, its 'regio-isomer' exhibited moderate activity against broadleaf weeds in pre-as well as post-emergent treatments. Symptoms observed on plants of sensitive species after treatment with the regio isomer compound were early cessation of growth followed by necrosis. The activity profiles were similar to those of sulfonylureas, but not to those of the Hill reaction inhibitors. By removing the phenoxy group from the compound, the resulting O-pyrimidinylsalicylate was found to exhibit the highly potent herbicidal activity characteristic of ALS (acetolactate synthase) inhibition.

### *Triazolylphosphonate*

The discovery and exploration of a new class of broad-spectrum post emergent herbicides with a novel mode of action, namely the disruption of histidine biosynthesis via inhibition of imidazoleglycerol phosphate dehydratase (IGPD), are described. Clear structural similarities between the first members, produced during an attempt to produce analogues of glyphosate, and intermediates in histidine biosynthesis were noted. Several series of targets were designed, to mimic both the enzyme substrate and a putative reaction intermediate, and synthesized. Some examples were found to be both extremely potent inhibitors of the enzyme and phloem-mobile herbicides with levels of weed control similar to those shown by glyphosate. It is now well established that many of the most successful commercial herbicides are active via the inhibition of essential amino acid biosnthesis. Phosphonates can provide not only metabolically stable mimics of phosphate enzyme intermediates but also the phloem mobility essential for adequate post-emergent control of regrowth in perennial weed species. Useful herbicidal activity of inhibitors of aromatic amino acid biosynthesis was, in 1981, limited to glyphosate and a very few close analogues, and indeed still is. At that time, there was literature speculation that the mode of action might involve chelation with cations, especially those of transition metals Furthermore, the propensity of 1, 2, 4-triazoles to bind to iron, for example, was already well-known in fungicides inhibiting the cytochrome $P_{450}$ enzyme, lanosterol 14-a-demethylase.

The triazolylphosphonate was designed to have potential binding sites superimposable upon those of glyphosate structure. This did indeed prove to have levels of broad-spectrum phloem-mobile herbicidal activity similar to those of glyphosate. However, unlike glyphosate, it did not inhibit 5-enolpyruvylshikimate 3-phosphae synthase and, indeed, did not otherwise affect aromtic amino acid biosynthesis. There are, moreover, clear structural similarities between intermediates in histidine biosynthesis, in particular (2R, 3S)-imidazoleglycerol phosphate (IGP) and the subsequent acetol phosphate (IAP), the conversion being catalysed by imidazoleglycerol phosphate dehydratase (IGPD). It was rapidly demonstrated that the effects of these compounds could be reversed by application of histidine, both in maize-cell culture and also in certain whole plants, for example *Cynodon dactylon* (L.) Pers. (Bermuda grass).

### *Isoxazolecarboxamides*

A series of unique 3-aryl-5-(haloalkyl)-4-isoxazolecarboxamides have been prepared which exhibit, in both greenhouse and field studies, significant pre-emergent and post-emergent herbicidal activity in the grams per hectare range against broad leaf and narrow leaf weeds. The key step in the formation of the fully substituted isoxazole ring is 1,3-dipolar cycloaddition of a haloalkyl-substituted acetylenic ester and a nitrile oxide intermediate.

Derivatives of aryl-substituted isoxazolecarboxylic acids have provided a rich source of candidates for development as agrochemical and pharmaceutical products (Hamper *et al.*, 1995). Various ester and amide derivatives have been reported as plant growth regulators and agents for control of endoparasites as well as a series of commercial isoxazole penicillins. Recently, fluoroalkyl-substituted isoxazoles have been prepared as intermediates for urea herbicides and analogs of other biologically active serials. In connection with continuing studies of biologically active perhaps aryl substituted heterocycles targeted the synthesis of 3-arylisoxazoles having carboxylate and halo alkyl subsitituents. Using this approach was found a unique series of 3-aryl-5- (halo alkyl)-4-isoxazolecarboxamides having significant herbicidal activity.

### *Substituted Oxazolinones*

A series of novel 3-aryl-5-tert-butyl-4-chloro-4-oxazolin-2ones have been prepared and found to show significant herbicidal activities in the grams per hectare range against broadleaf and narrow leaf weeds (Kudo *et al.*, 1998).

### *Microbial Toxins based Herbicides*

The initiative to use plant pathogens and allelochemicals from pathogens and other microorganisms as biological weed control agents (bioherbicides) began about 30 years ago. Since then, numerous plant pathogens (becteria and fungi) microbial allelochemicals have been and isolated, identified, and tested for their bioherbicidal potential. Pathogens (and in some cases microbial phytotoxins) may be used directly on target weed species, or such allelochemicals may provide unique chemical templates for the synthesis of new herbicide classes with novel molecular modes of action. To date, the most successful microbial products that have led to the development of commercial herbicides are bialaphos (commercially available in Japan) and glufosinate (marketed worldwide). Glufosinate is the ammonium salt of phosphinothricin, which is the active ingredient of bialaphos derived from a nonphytopathogenic *Streptomyces* species. This overview will examine selected advances in the isolation and identification of novel plant pathogens that have weed hosts, and some microbial allelochemicals with phytotoxic properties.

Cyperin is a natural product that has been isolated from fungal cultures of *Preussia fleischhakii, Ascochyta cypericola* and *Phoma sorghina.* The latter two species are pathogens of purple nutsedge (*Cyperus rotandus*) and poke weed (*Phytolacca americana*) respectively. The herbicide is phytotoxic to purple nutsedge and is a potential protox inhibitor.

### *Herbicide Safeners*

Herbicide safeners are chemicals used before, after or as mixture with herbicide to improve crop tolerance to herbicides by regulating the expression of genes involved in herbicide metabolism. With this mode of action, safeners provide a relatively inexpensive and flexible method of improving herbicide selectivity, without incurring the ecological risks.

A score of promising commercial candidates have been developed as herbicide safeners, some of which are shown below in Table 16.1.

**TABLE 16.1:** SAFENERS AND THEIR USAGE

| | *Safener* | *Uses* |
|---|---|---|
| 1. | Cloquintocet-mexyl clodinafop | It is sprayed with propargyl in wheat |
| 2. | Fenchlorazole-ethyl | It is sprayed as mixture with fenoxa propethyl in wheat |
| 3. | Fenclorim | It is sprayed as mixture with pretila chlor in rice |
| 4. | Flurazole | It is used as mixture for seed treatment with alachlor in sorghum |

## FORMULATION OF PESTICIDES

Pesticide formulations are the end user products of pesticide industry. The toxic pesticidal active ingredients is mixed with carriers and auxiliaries into safe products. There are more than 68 formulation types currently in use in pest control in different environments. The particle size of the toxicants in the conventional formulations (e.g., dust, water dispersible powder, granule, emulsifiable) are in the range upto 45 μm in dusts, 5-8 μm in wettable powders. Though the toxicant is dissolved in EC formulations by molecular dispersion in organic solvents, the size of the discontinuous phase *i.e.* the toxicant bearing oil globules in the spray liquid decide the effective particle size. The conventional formulations are effective only when applied under favourable environmental conditions and are quickly lost due to leaching, votality, drift, adsorption to clay and organic matter. To compensate for these losses and obtain effective pest control often these formulations are applied at much higher concentration than what is actually needed. This lead to environmental pollution in air, water, soil and residues in consumable produces (Parmar *et al.*, 2000).

Several advances have been made in pesticide formulation technology by the introduction of controlled release formulations, dry flowables and wet flowable formulations. New ones were introduced in the sixties and eighties, the technological advances are slow and many of the available toxicants are yet to be formulated into viable marketable formulations. The major developments were the replacement of the non-renewable carriers and solvents with natural polymers and water, reduced particle size, and prolonged delivery of the toxicant in the pest environment and the fast degradation of the polymer matrices/carrier materials. The composition of the formulations will reflect the trend.

**TABLE 16.2:** TYPICAL COMPOSITION OF THE COMMON PESTICIDE FORMULATIONS

| *Concentration (% w/w)* | *Wettable Powder (WP)* | *Dry Flowable (WG)* | *Emulsifiable Concentrate (EC)* | *Wet Flowable (SC)* |
|---|---|---|---|---|
| Toxicant | 5-50 | 50-95 | 5-90 | 5.90 |
| Carrier/water* | 40-90 | 0-45 | 40-90 | 5-80* |
| Surfactant | | | | |
| Dispersant | 1-7 | 1-7 | – | 0-2 |
| Wetting agent | 0-2 | 0-2 | – | 1-7 |
| Binder | – | 0-2 | – | – |

The particle size range of the suspension concentrates is much smaller (0, 1-2 μm) than that of the conventional formulations (5-45 μm). The longevity of the toxicant at the application site in the case of controlled release formulations, is much longer (upto 6 months) as compared to the conventional formulations (24 h). The plastic and synthetis polmer used in CR formulations have been replaced with biodegradable natural polymers. No wonder these two formulations are free from many disadvantages of conventional formulations.

**Formulation and Application of Biopesticides**

For the production of biopesticides normal marketing and distribution system cannot be used. The biopesticidal products must be applied close to their place of manufacture and within short time. Several classes of insect pathogens; such as, bacterial and fungal spores, protozoan cysts and inclusion bodies of viruses provide relatively stable product having shelf life of 18 months to 2 years.

Keeping in view the characteristics and quality, the product must be formulated. The formulation has critical effect on the efficacy of biopesticides. The sunlight inactivates most of microbial pesticides; consequently sunlight protectants namely, dyes, carbon black or titanium oxide must be added during the formulation of such products. Similarly, certain microbial product (viz. nematode preparations) requires high humidity. Effective methods should be developed to prevent water loss from such preparations. There is a lot of scope to improve the formulation of microbial pesticides.

The biopesticides are amenable to conventional application methods namely, dispersal as sprays or powders. The biopesticidal product can also be applied as ultra low volume sprays with droplet sizes ranging from 5-30 micron. The effective life of product can be prolonged by application to the underside of foliage (Milstead *et al.*, 1980).

For improving safety, research has progressed on improving selectivity, i.e. enhancing the pesticidal activity on target species while leaving non-target species, including man, more or less untouched. It is calculated by taking ratio of $LD_{50}$ (rat, oral toxicity) to $LD_{50}$ (housefly, topical) for a particular pesticide. For example, the selective toxicity ratio for organochlorine-DDT, organophosphorus-malathion, synthetic pyrethroid-cypermethrin and insect growth regulator (JH analogue)-methoprene have been calculated as 8.4, 55.9, 2873.5 and 1730 000, respectively (Mukherjee and Gopal, 1994). In the process, a higher efficacy resulting in lower rate of application and thereby reduction in load on environment is achieved by using newer pesticides.

When a pesticide interferes with processes that occur only in the target species, only a qualitative selectivity is achieved. For example, interfering with photosynthesis in weeds does not harm mammals, as they do not photosynthesize. Herbicides may, therefore, have a favourable toxicity profile. Browsing for $LD_{50}$ (acute oral, rat) of glyphosate herbicide for example is 5600 mg/kg.

Quantitative selectivity is based on differences between the susceptibility of the target and non-target species towards properties like skin-penetration rate, metabolism and excretion rate. When the target species becomes resistant to a pesticide, a flaw creeps in the value of quantitative selectivity.

Higher pesticidal activity can be achieved by removing the less active or non-active component, e.g. inactive optical isomers from synthetic pyrethroids.

The point about progress in moving from organochlorine-endosulfan, organophosphorus-phorate, synthetic pyrethroid-fenvalerate to a new generation rodenticide flocoumafen with time is explained below. Endosulfan has oral $LD_{50}$ values (70 mg/kg) that place it in the moderately hazardous class of WHO classification. Low no adverse effect level (NOAELs) of 30-mg/kg diet (against rat) in the 2-year feeding studies also points it to be a high toxicity compound. The persistence of organochlorine in the environment was initially viewed as an advantage because it was associated with long-lasting pesticidal activity. However, in light of ecotoxicological ($LD_{50}$ acute oral bird is 205 mg/kg and $LC_{50}$ 0.002 mg/l for fish) consequences, it is now considered a major disadvantage due to residues and a perceived cancer hazard. Organochlorines are being restricted from use in North America as well as in India.

Phorate is classified as extremely hazardous due to its acute toxicity in laboratory animals and its skin penetrating properties. The 90-day feeding studies show NOAEL 6 mg/kg, lower than that of endosulfan. Organophosphates, in particular parathion and malathion have been blamed for many deaths as they along with their metabolites are known to cause irreversible neurological defects in patients recovering from intoxications and cause asthma. Not all organophosphates can be called a safer or ecofriendly pesticides, inspite of their rapid degradation in the environment, albeit showing an improvement from an ecotoxicological point of view.

The pyrethroid fenvalerate is relatively safer, based on acute oral $LD_{50}$ for rat (451 mg/kg). Metabolism and excretion are rapid and other toxicity parameters are also favourable. The lower toxicity of pyrethroids, combined with their slow skin penetration and high value of selective toxicity make synthetic pyrethroids safer to use. Since their excessive use has led to the development of resistance in certain insects, they are recommended to be used in window concept (only one or two times in a season). Skin sensation (tingling) that occurs with over exposure usually disappears within a few hours and leaves no after effects. The sensation acts as a warning signal.

Flocoumafen (Tordoir, 1993) representing new generation of anticoagulants nicknamed as "super-warfarins", has $LD_{50}$ (oral, rat) as 0.25 and $LD_{50}$ (dermal, rat) 0.54 representing extreme toxicity according to the WHO classification, yet these values do not necessarily mean high risk to human health. The 9 day NOAEL is 0.02 ppm for pure substance, but the formulation used to poison bait is almost nontoxic because it contains only 50 ppm (w/w) of the active ingredient. In addition, during product development, a deliberate effort was made to make poisoned bait unattractive to non-target species by incorporating it into wax blocks with a deterrent blue colour and a bitter taste. These measures have rendered a hazardous product safe for practical use. In the unlikely event of intoxication, a specific antidote (vitamin K) is available. No case of human intoxication has been reported.

Guided by better understanding of intrinsic toxicity and data on personal exposure during application, product development can contribute to safety through improved formulations and packaging and advice on handling and personal protection. The comparison of major groups of pesticides shows that with the development of the pyrethroid, a major step forward has been made in the creation of safe pesticides. Similarly, rodenticide is an example of a substance whose high efficacy and sophisticated product development compensate for high toxicity, allowing a final product that is safe for humans.

In order to preempt dumping of toxic chemicals through exports, the FAO has launched an arrangement called voluntary Prior Informed Consent (PIC) among the member countries and brings out a comtemporary list of pesticides that require banning or restriction in import along with an updated status of such chemicals in othr member nations so that any member nation can have an enlightened information on any chemical. A set of operational rules and guidelines are also available for facilitating international movement of safe chemicals. The encyclopadia of agrochemicals published in three volumes is the latest cimpilation available for consultation (Plimmer, 2002).

## REFERENCES


Adams, M. E. and Miller, T. A. 1980. Neural and behavioural correlates of pyrethroid and DDT-type poisoning in the house fly, *Musca domestica* L. *Pestic. Biochem. Physiol.*, **13**: 137-147.

Bhan, P., Soman, S. and Sukh Dev 1980. Insect Juvenile hormone based on bakuchiol. *Agric. Biol. Chem.*, **44**: 1482-1487.

Blum, M. S. and Kearns, C. W. 1956. Temperature and the action of pyrethrum in the American cockroach. *J. Econ. Entomol.*, **49**: 862-865.

Brown, J. J. 1994 Effect of nonsteroidal ecdysone against tebifenozide on host parasitoid interaction. *Arch. Insect Biochem Physiol.*, **26**: 235-248.

Burt, P. E. and Goodchild R. E. 1971a. The site of action of pyrethrin I in the nervous system of the cockroach, *Periplanets americana. Entomol. Exp. Appl.*, **14**: 179-189.

Burt, P. E. and Goodchild R. E. 1971b. The spread of topically applied pyrethrin I from the cuticle to the central nervous system of the cockroach, *Periplanata americana. Entomol. Exp. Appl.*, **14**: 255-269.

Camougis, G. and Davis, W. M. 1971. A comparative study of the neuropharmacological basis of the action of pyrethrin. *Pyrethrum Post*, **11**: 7.

Canning, E. V. 1982. An evaluation of protozoal characteristis in relation to biological control of pests. *Parasitology*, **84**: 1999-149.

Clark R. D. 1996. Synthesis and QSAR of Herbicidal 3-Pyrazolyl a, a, a, - Trifluorotolyl Ethers. *J. Agric. Food Chem.*, **44**: 3643-3652

Clements, A. N. and May, T. E. 1977. The actions of pyrethroids upon the peripheral nervous system and associated organs of locust. *Pestic. Sci.*, **8**: 661-680.

Colliot, F. 1992. Brighton Crop Prof. Conf: Pests and Diseases, 1, 29

Copping, L. 1998. Systemic acquired resistance. *Pesticide Outlook* April 1998: 34-35.

Corbett, J. R. 1974. *The Biochemical Mode of Action of Pesticides.* Academic Press, London.

Cremlyn, R. J. 1990. Future development *In*: *Agrochemicals.* John Wiley & Sons, pp. 361-372.

Crouse, G. D. and Sparks, T. C. 1998. Naturally derived materials as products and leads for insect control: The spinosyns. *Reviews in Toxicology*, **2**: 133-146.

DeCock, A. and Degheele, D. 1998 Burprofezin: a novel chitin synthesis inhibitor affecting specifically planthoppers, whiteflies and scale insects. *In*: I. Ishaaya and D. Degheele (eds.), *Insecticides with Novel Modes of Action.* Narosa Publishing House, New Delhi, India, pp. 74-91.

Elliott, M.1976. Properties and applications of pyrethroids. *Environ. Hlth. Perspect.*, **14**: 3-13.

Elliott. M. 1980. Established pyrethroid insecticides. *Pestic. Sci.*, **11**: 119-128.

Ford. M. G., Reay, R. C., Pert, D. and Ellis, P. E. 1977. Toxicity of pyrethroids to larvae of the Egyptian cotton leaf worm, *Spodoptera littoralis* (boisd.). I. Relative toxicities and knockdown activities of benzyl, and 5-benzyl-3-furylmethylcycle-propanecarboxylates. *Pestic. Sci.*, **8**: 203-210.

Fuog, D., Fergusson, S. J. and Fluckiger, C. 1998. Pymetrozine: a novel insecticide affecting aphids and whiteflies. *In*: (I. Ishaaya and D. Degheele (eds.), *Insecticides with Novel Modes of Action.* Narosa Publishing House, New Delhi, India, pp. 40-49.

Gammon, D. W. 1978a. Neural affects of allethrin on the free walking cockroach, *Periplanata americana*: an investigation using defined doses at 15 and 32° C. *Pestic. Sci.*, **9**: 79-91.

Gammon, D. W. 1978b. Effects of DDT on the cockroach nervous system at three temperatures. *Pestic. Sci.*, **9**: 95-104.

Gammon, D. W. 1979. An analysis of the temperature-dependence of the toxicity of allethrin to the cockroach. *In*: T. Narahashi (ed.), *Neurotoxicology of Insecticides and Pheromones*. pp. 97 - 117.

Carlson, G. R., Dhadialla, T. S., Hunter, R., Jansson, R. K., Christine, S. Jany, Zev Lidert and Slawechi Richard, A. 2001. The Chemical and biological properties of methoxyfenozide, a new insecticidal ecdysteroid agonist. *Pest Management Science*, **57**: 115-119.

Gopal, M. and Mukherjee, I. 1998. Conceptualization of ecofriendly pesticides. *In*: R. D.Gautam and D. Prasad (eds.), *Ecofriendly Pest Suppression*. Westvill Publishing House, New Delhi pp. 25-58.

Gopal, M., Mukherjee, I. and Das, T. K. 2002. Residues of the new fungicide carpropamid in rice (*Oryza sativa*). *Pestology*, **26**: 50-53.

Grossmann, K. and Scheltrup, F. 1998. Studies on the mechanism of selectivity of the auxin herbicide qunmerac. *Pestic. Sci.*, **52**: 111-118.

Hamper B. C., Leschinsky, K. L., Massey, S. S., Bell, C.,L., Brannigan, L.,H. and Prosch, D. 1995. Synthesis and herbicidal activity of aryl-5 (haloalkyl)-4-isoxazolecarboxamides and their derivatives. *J. Agric. Food Chem.*, **43**: 219-228.

Hayes, W. J. Jr, Laws, E. R. 1991. Handbook of Pesticide Toxicology Vol I to III. Academic Press, New York, p. 1576.

Hedin P. A., Hollingworth, R. M., E. P., Miyamoto J. and Thompson, D. G. (eds) 1997. Phytochemicals for Pest Control, Americal Chemical Socieity, Washington, D.C.

Henrick, C. V. A. 1982. JH analogs: structure activity relationships. *In*: Coats, J. R. (ed.), *Insecticidal Mode if Action*. Academic Ptress, New York, pp. 315-402.

Herve, J. J. 1985. Agricultural, public and animal usage. *In*: J. P. Leathey (ed.), *The Pyrethroid Insecticides*. Talyor and Francis, Philadelphia, pp. 343 - 426.

Hess, F. D. 2000. Light-dependent herbicides: an overview. Weed Sciences, **48**: 160-170.

Horowitz, A. R., Ishaaya, I. 1996. Chemical control of *Bemisia tabaci*—management and application *In*: G. Gerling, R. T. Mayer (eds), Bemisia 1995: taxonomy, biology, damage control and management. Inter\cept, Andover, pp. 537-556.

Hunt, D. A. and Treacy, M. F. 1998. Pyrole insecticides: a new class of agriculturally important insecticides functioning as uncouplers of oxidative phosphorylation. *In*: (I. Ishaaya and D. Degheele (eds.), *Insecticides with Novel Modes of Action*. Narosa Publishing House, New Delhi, India, pp. 138-151.

Hutson, D. H. and Robertw, T. R. 1985. *Iinsecticides: Progress in Pesticide Biochemistry and Toxicology* Vol. 5.

Itaya, N. 1987. Insect juvenile hormone analogue as an insect growth regulator. *Sumitomo Pyrethroid World*, **8**: 2-4

Jansma, J. E., van Kuelen, H. and Zadoks, J. C. 1993. Crop protection in the year 2000: A comparison of current policies towards agrochemical usage in four West European countries. *Crop Protection*, **12**: 483-89.

Julien, D. 2000. New Pesticides. American Rose March and April. Northwest Rosarian in 1999; American Rose, March and April, 2000.

Kawada, H. 1988. An insect growth regulator against cockroaches. Sumitomo Pyrethroid World, **11**: 2-4.

Koechler, P. G., Patterson, R. J. 1991. Incorporation of pyriproxyfen in a German cockroach management programme. *J. Econ. Entomol.*, **84**: 917-921.

Konishi, K. 1970. Studies on Organic insecticides part XIII. Synthesis of nereistoxin and related compounds VI. *Agri. Biol. Chem.*, **34**: 1549-1560.

Kulshrestha, G. and Parmar, B. S. 1992. Herbicides: Retrospect and Prospect. *Fusion Asia*, **8**: 28-34.

Langley, P. 1990. Control of the tse tse fly using a juvenile hormone mimic pyriproxifen. *Sumitomo Pyrethroid World*, **15**: 2-5

Leak, L. D. 1977. The action of (S)-allyl-2-methyl-oxocyclopent-2-enyl(IR)-trans-chrysanthemate, (S)-Bioallethrin on single neurons in the central nervous system of the leech, Hirudo medicinalis. Pestic. Sci., **8**: 713-721.

Lindsey, K. and Jones. 1989. M. G. K. Plant Biotechnology in Agriculture, Open Univ. Press, Milton.

Masner, P., Angst, M., Dorn, S. 1987. Fenoxycarb, an insect growth regulator with juvenile hormone activity: A candidate for *Heliothis virescens* control on cotton. *Pestic Sci.*, 18: 89-94.

McCann, S. F., Annis, G. D., Sharpiro, R., Piorows, Ki D. W., Lahm, G. P., Long, J. K., Lee, K. C., Hughes, M. M., Myers, B. J., Giriswold, S. M., Reeves, B. M., March, R. W., Sharpe, P. L., Lowder, P., Barnette, W. E. and Wing, K. D. 2001. The discovery of indoxacarb: oxadiazines as a new class of pyrazoline-type insecticides. *Pest Manag Sc.*, **57**: 153-164.

Milstead, J. E., Odom, D. and Kirby, M. 1980. Control of early larval stage of California Oakworm by low concentrations of *Bacillus thuringiensis* applied\to lower leaf surfaces. *J. Econ. Entomol.*, **73**: 344-345.

Miyake, T. H., Haruyama, H., Ogura, T., Mitsui, T. and Sakurai, A. 1991. Effects of insect juvenile hormone active NC-170 on metamorphosis, oviposition. Aand embryogenesis in leaf hoppers. *J. Pestic Sci.*, **16**: 441-448.

Mukerji, S. K. 1995. Agrochemical Research in India: Priorities must change. *In*: S. Walia and B. S. Parmar (eds.), *Pesticides, Crop Protection and Environment*. Oxford & IBH Publishing Co. Pvt. Ltd., New Delhi, pp. 11-18.

Mukherjee, I. And M. Gopal, 1994. Pesticides for future use. *In*: D. Prasad and H. S. Gaur (eds.), *Soil Environment and Pesticides*. Venus Publishing House, New Delhi, pp. 73, 110.

Narahashi, T. 1971. Effects of insecticides on excitable tisssues. *Adv. Insect Physiol.*, **8**: 1-93.

Nezu, Y., Miyazaki, M., Sugiyama, K., Wada, N., Kajiwara, I. & Miyazawa, T. 1996. Dimethoxypyrimidines as Novel Herbicides. Part 2. Synthesis of Herbicidal Activity of o-Pyrimidinylsalicylates and Analogues. *Pestic. Sci.*, **47**: 115-124

Parmar, B. S., Rengasamy, S. and Kumar, J. 2000. Pesticide formulation advances to meet the challenge challenges of the 21st Century. Division of Agricultural Chemicals, IARI, New Delhi. Nov. 6-15.

Plimmer, J. R. 2002. *Encyclopedia of Agrochemicals*. Culinary and Hospitability Industry Publications Services Texas, USA, p. 163.

Maienfisch, P., Huerlimann, H., Rindlispacher, A., Gsell, L., Dettwiler, H., Haettenschwiler, J., Sieger, E.. and Walti, M. 2001. The discovery of thiamethoxam: a second-generation neonicotinoid 2001 Society of Chemical Industry. *Pest Management Sci.*, **57**: 165-176.

Pratt, G. E. Jennings, R. C., Hamnett, A. F. and Brooks, G. T. 1980. Lethal metabolism of prococene-I to a reactive epoxide by locust *Corpora allata. Nature*, **284**: 5754 320-323.

Roy, N. K. 2000. Potential insecticidal molecules for the future. *In*: Recent Developments in Agrochemicals Research to Meet the Challenges of the 21st Century, Division of agricultural Chemicals, Indian Agricultural Research Institute, New Delhi. Nov. 6-15, 2000.

Sternberg Jeffrey, A., Geffken, D., Adams Jr. J. B., Postages, R., Charlene G Sternberg, Carlton L Campbell and Williamk K Moberg 2001. Famoxadone: the discovery and optimization of a new agricultural fungicide Pest management. *Sci.*, **57**: 143-152 agonist: Effects on a *Drosophila* cell line. Science, Washington DC 241: 467-469.

Sakai, M. 1970. I MMMMNTn: Biochemical toxicology of Insecticides. R. D. O'Brien and I. Yamamoto (eds.) Academic Press, New York, pp. 13-19.

Sakai, M. and Sato, Y. 1972. Metabolic conversion of the nereistoxin-related compounds into nereistoxin as a factor of their insecticidal action. Proc. 2nd Int. Congress of Pesticide Chemistry, London, pp. 455-467.

Schmutterer, H. 2000. The Neem Tree *Azadirachta indica* A. Juss and other Meliaceous Plants. Sources of unique Natural Products for Integrated Pest Management. Medicine, Industry and other purposes, Neem Foundation, Mumbai.

Scoeda, Y. and Yamamoto, I. 1968. Studies on nicotinoids as an insecticide VI. Relation of structure of toxicity of Pyridylalkylamines. *Agri. Biol. Chem.*, **32**: 747-752.

Sharples, K. R., Hawkes, T. R., Mitchell, G., Edwards, L. S., Langford, M. P., Langton, D. W., Rogers, K. M., Townson, J. K. and Wang, Y., A Novel. 1988. Thiazolidinone herbicide is a potent inhibitor of glucose inocrporation into cell wall material. *Pestic. Sci.*, **54**: 368-376.

Sinha, S. and Gopal, M. 2002. Evaluating the safety of beta-cyfluthrin Insecticide for usage in eggplant (*Solanum melongena* L.) *Crop. Bull Environ Contam Toxicol.*, **68**: 406-411.

Sodeurlund, D. M., Messeguarand, A. and Bower, W. S. 1980. Precocene imetabolism in insects: Synthesis of potential metabolites and identification of initial *in vitro* biotranssformation products. *J. Agric. Food Chem.*, **28**(4): 724-731.

Stall, G. B. 1982. Insect control with growth regulators interfering with the endocrine system. *Entomol Exp. Appl.*, **31**: 15-23.

Stankiewicz, M., Grolleau, F., Rochat, H., Zlothin, E., Pelhate, M. and Lapied, B. 1999. Insect background sodium channel as a new target for scorpion alpha toxin. *Pestic. Sci.*, **55**: 1021-1026.

McCann, S. F., Annis, G. D., Shapiro, R., Piotrowski, D. W., Lahm, G. P., Long, K. L., Lee, K. C., Hughes, M. M., Brian, J. M. ers, Sandra, M. Griswold, Bonita, M. Reeves, Robert, W. March, Paula L. Sharpe, Patrick Lowder, William E Barnette and Wing, K. D. 2001. The discovery of indoxacarb: oxadiazines as a new class of pyrazoline-type insecticides 57: 153-164.

Sternberg, J. A., Geffken, D., Adams, J. B., Postages, R., Sternberg, C. G., Campbell, C. L. and Moberg, W. K. 2001. Famoxadone: the discovery and optimization of a new agricultural fungicide. *Pest Manag Sci.*, **57**: 143-152.

Tordoir, W. F. 1993. Development of safe chemical pesticides. *In*: G. Forget, T. Goodman and A. Devillers (eds.), *Impact of Pesticide Use on Health in Developing Countries*. International Development Research Centre, Ottawa, pp. 142-152.

Turner, R. B. 1968. Chemistry of insect chemosterilants. *In*: G. C. La Breque, C. M. Smith (eds.), *Principles of Insect Chemosterilization*. Appleton-Century-Crofts, New York, pp. 159-274.

Walia, S. 2001. Potential fungicidal molecules for the future. *In*: Recent Developments in Agrochemicals Research to Meet the Challenges of the 21st Century, Division of agricultural Chemicals, Indian Agricultural Research Institute, New Delhi. Nov. 6-15, 2000.

Wing, K. D., Aller, H. E. 1990. Ecdysteroid agonists as novel insect growth regulators. *In*: J. E. (ed.), *Pesticides and Alternatives: Innovative Chemical and Biological Approaches to Pest Control.* Elsevier, Amsterdam, pp. 251-257.

Wing, K. D., Slawchki, R. A., Carlson, G. R, 1988, RH-5849, a non-steroidal ecdysone agonist: effects on larval lepidoptera. *Science Washington DC*, **241**: 470-472.

Worthing, Ch. E. 1983a. The Pesticide Manual, pp. 96. The British Crop Protection Council.

Worthing, Ch. E. 1983b. The Pesticide Manual, pp. 527. The British Crop Protection Council

Yamamoto, I. 1965. Nicotinoids as insecticides. *Advan. Pest. Control Res.*, **6**: 231-260

Yamamoto, I. 1970. Mode of action of pyrethroids, nicotinoids and rotinoids. *Ann. Rev. Entomol.*, **15**: 257.272.

Yamamoto, I., Kamimura, H., Yamamoto, R., Sakai, S. and Goda, M.1962. Studies on nicotinoids as an insecticide. I. Relation of structure to toxicity. *Agri. Biol. Chem.*, **26**: 709-716.

# Socioeconomic and Institutional Factors in Promotion of Integrated Pest Management

Pratap S. Birthal

## INTRODUCTION

Over the next quarter of this century foodgrain production in India has to increase at least 2 million tonnes a year to meet the growing domestic demand (Kumar *et al.*, 2003). Increase in the demand for edible oils, fruits, vegetables, etc. is expected to rise faster. Until recently agricultural production increased through area expansion and increasing use of high yielding seeds, chemical fertilizers, pesticides and irrigation water. Now, the prospects of raising production through area expansion and application of existing technologies appear to be severely constrained. Land frontiers are closing down under population pressure, leaving little scope to bring additional land under cultivation. Green revolution technologies have now been widely adopted, and the growth in yields of major crops has started tapering off.

Concurrently, agricultural production continues to be constrained by a number of biotic and abiotic factors. Insect pests, diseases and weeds are major biotic constraints causing considerable damage to the potential agricultural production. According to some estimates pests cause 25 per cent loss in paddy, 5-10 per cent in wheat, 30 per cent in pulses, 35 per cent in oilseeds, 20 per cent in sugarcane and 50 per cent in cotton (Dhaliwal and Arora, 1996). These losses though cannot be eliminated altogether, but can be reduced through effective pest management. Until recently, chemical pesticides were increasingly relied upon to limit the production losses. Pesticide use in India increased from a mere 15 g/ha of gross cropped in 1955-56 to 90 g/ha in 1965-66. Introduction of green revolution technologies in mid-1960s gave a fillip to pesticide use, and in 1975-76 it had increased to 266 g/ha, and reached a peak of 404 g/ha in 1990-91 (Birthal, 2003). Although, there is a paucity of reliable time-series information on pest-induced production losses, anecdotal evidences suggest increase in losses (Pradhan, 1983, Atwal, 1986, Dhaliwal and Arora, 1996), despite increase in the pesticide use. The paradox is explained in terms of rising pest problem, technological failure of chemical pesticides and changes in production systems. Nevertheless, pesticide use has started declining since 1990-91, reaching to 265 g/ha in 1998-99, but without affecting much the agricultural productivity (Birthal, 2003).

*National Centre for Agricultural Economics and Policy Research, Library Avenue Road, New Delhi-110 012.*

The declining trend in pesticide use in agriculture in 1990s can be attributed to the central government's fiscal policy and technological developments in pest management. In 1990s taxes were raised on pesticides and the process of phasing out of subsidies was initiated. Training programmes for both the extension workers and farmers in the methodology of Integrated Pest Management (IPM) were started throughout the country. In fact, the Government of India had adopted IPM as a cardinal principle of plant protection in 1985. Notwithstanding these initiatives, adoption of IPM has not been encouraging. Biopesticides capture about 1 per cent of the agrochemical market. In this context this paper attempts to look into the question why adoption of IPM has been low from the point of view of its technical and economic feasibility/viability, socioeconomic conditions for its adoption, and institutional and policy issues.

## TECHNO-ECONOMIC EFFICACY

For any technology to be a success, it must pass the tests of technical and economic efficiency. Technical efficiency of IPM can be judged on two criteria: change in the pesticide use, and change in yield over the conventional chemical control. As far as the change in pesticide use is concerned it is the basic objective of IPM to reduce pesticide use, and this evidence has been well established under the experimental as well as field conditions. Its effect on yield could be either way. Nevertheless, recent evidences suggest a brighter side of IPM. Evidences compiled by Birthal and Adhiguru (2002) suggest better yield saving potential of IPM over chemical control. The yield advantage has been observed in the range of 1 to 43 per cent in case of rice, 10 to 48 per cent in case of cotton, 16 to 19 per cent in case of sugarcane, 5 to 57 per cent in case of cabbage, and 3 to 12 per cent in case of pulses.

Technical feasibility is a necessary but not a sufficient condition for commercialization and adoption of the technology. The necessary condition is that it should entail at least as much net returns as the conventional technology. Net benefits can be measured in terms of the difference in per hectare net revenue due to application of new technology and/or changes in unit cost of production. A review of the existing evidences suggests reduction in the unit cost of rice production by 0 to 59 per cent, of cotton by 3 to 41 per cent (Table 17.1) and of vegetables by 0 to 27 per cent (Birthal and Adhiguru, 2002).

The magnitude of net benefits however would depend on the type of inputs used in the IPM package, its application rate and price. Birthal (2003) showed that even under experimental conditions some technically feasible IPM packages fail to meet the economic criteria because of higher cost.

*The general inference is that IPM has the potential to substitute chemical pesticides without demanding any additional resources and without any adverse effects on agricultural productivity. Nevertheless, inputs prices are an important determinant of the economics of IPM, and any increase in the prices of critical inputs may upset its economics.*

## SOCIOECONOMIC AND POLICY ISSUES

Despite its techno-economic superiority over conventional chemical control, adoption of IPM remains restricted to hardly 2 per cent of the area. This estimate is based on the informed opinions of the researchers, extension personnel and policy makers. The structure of agrochemical market also suggests a similar level of adoption; biopesticides capture 1 per cent of the agrochemical market (Saxena, 2001). There could be a number of technological, social, economic, institutional and policy factors restricting widespread adoption of IPM.

**TABLE 17.1:** ECONOMIC IMPACT OF IPM

| *Crop* | *Yield Gain (per cent)* | *Cost Reduction (per cent)* | *Location* |
|---|---|---|---|
| Rice | 20 | 14 | Uttar Pradesh |
| | – | 59 | West Bengal |
| | 1 | – | Bihar |
| | 10 | – | Haryana |
| | – | 5 | Punjab |
| | – | 5 | Punjab |
| | – | 13-15 | Andhra Pradesh |
| | – | 20 | Andhra Pradesh |
| | 43 | – | Andhra Pradesh |
| | 29 | 1 | Andhra Pradesh |
| | 3 | 1 | Tamil Nadu |
| | – | 8-14 | Tamil Nadu |
| Cotton | 19 | 20 | Maharashtra |
| | 24 | 13 | Maharashtra |
| | 48 | 3 | Maharashtra |
| | 16 | 12 | Punjab |
| | 18 | 11 | Haryana |
| | 30 | 1 | Rajasthan |
| | 13 | 23 | Gujarat |
| | 11 | 48 | Orissa |
| | – | 41 | Andhra Pradesh |
| | 28 | 34 | Andhra Pradesh |
| | – | 5-17 | Andhra Pradesh |
| | 13 | 23 | Karnataka |
| | 10 | 24 | Tamil Nadu |
| | – | 14-17 | Tamil Nadu |
| Sugarcane | 16 | – | Haryana |
| | 16 | – | Haryana |
| | 19 | – | Bihar |
| Tomato | 26 | – | Karnataka |
| | 26 | 11 | Karnataka |
| Brinjal | – | 27 | Karnataka |
| Cabbage | 57 | 3 | Karnataka |
| | 5 | 0.1 | Tamil Nadu |
| Maize | 10 | – | Bihar |
| Arhar | 3 | – | Bihar |
| Masoor | 3 | – | Bihar |
| Gram | 12 | – | Bihar |

## TECHNOLOGY CHARACTERISTICS

The characteristics of the technology have an important role in farmers' adoption decisions (Adesina and Zinnah, 1993, Lapar and Pandey, 1999). IPM draws heavily on the complementarities and interactions of different methods of pest control (chemical, biological, cultural and mechanical), and each of the components has its own specific characteristics and requirements for application. This makes IPM a complex technology. Generally, farmers adopt those components first that are easily available and yield immediate effect. Biopesticides and bioagents are major components of IPM. Most of the biopesticides and bioagents are host-specific, slow in action and have short shelf-life. Besides, application of some of the components is labour intensive (Birthal *et al.*, 2000). In other words, farmers are risk averse and the technological characteristics as mentioned above create an apprehension among the farming community about their efficacy. These characteristics and complexity of IPM necessitate active involvement of all the stakeholders (researchers, extension workers and farmers) to alleviate apprehensions through participatory/adaptive research trials.

The major issues that the researchers would be confronting in the decades to come include basic research for development of broad-spectrum biological pesticides and improvements in their efficacy and shelf life. At present, problems of insecticide resistance, resurgence and secondary pest outbreak are not reported against biological substitutes. Maintenance of this property would require sustained research efforts. Bio-pesticides based on predators, parasites, viruses, fungi, etc. are sensitive to chemical pesticides. This warrants research emphasis on development of bio-pesticides having compatibility with chemical pesticides. Genetic engineering for resistance breeding will remain a gray area for long. Biotechnology has got tremendous potentialities for developing biopesticides.

### Transfer of Technology

Unlike many other technologies that can be adopted easily without much information requirement by the farmers, IPM is knowledge and information intensive. Its effective implementation requires extension workers to have a sound understanding of the characteristics of the technology, its target host and relationship with natural enemies, and the method of application before it is delivered to the farmers. The farmers should also be educated in these aspects. Lack of understanding of any of these would adversely affect its adoption. The extension worker should act more as a collaborator, consultant, and facilitator in dissemination of the knowledge, and the farmer playing more active role.

In order to achieve this, both the central and state governments have made considerable efforts to impart training to the extension workers. During 1995 and 2000 on an average an extension worker was trained thrice in IPM methodologies. To transfer the skills to the farmers more than 6200 farmers' field schools were established. These efforts however have not trickled down much, as hardly 0.2 per cent of the farmers were trained during this period (Table 17.2).

**TABLE 17.2:** TOTAL NUMBER OF FARMERS' FIELD SCHOOLS ORGANIZED, AND EXTENSION WORKERS AND FARMERS TRAINED IN IPM DURING 1995-96 TO 1999-2000 IN MAJOR STATES

| *State* | *FFS* | *AEOs Trained* | *Ratio of AEOs Trained to Total AEOs* | *Farmers Trained* | *% Farmers Trained** |
|---|---|---|---|---|---|
| Andhra Pradesh | 604 | 1881 | 2.7 | 18104 | 0.20 |
| Assam | 318 | 1556 | 4.4 | 9550 | 0.38 |
| Himachal Pradesh | 124 | 309 | 2.4 | 3360 | 0.40 |
| Karnataka | 404 | 1937 | 3.1 | 13490 | 0.23 |
| Madhya Pradesh | 424 | 1842 | 1.1 | 22706 | 0.33 |
| Maharashtra | 744 | 3712 | 5.4 | 23520 | 0.26 |
| Punjab | 334 | 1904 | 15.0 | 11530 | 1.03 |
| Rajasthan | 292 | 1904 | 3.4 | 11530 | 0.22 |
| Tamilnadu | 245 | 1044 | 1.6 | 6400 | 0.18 |
| Uttar Pradesh | 644 | 2801 | 6.4 | 18896 | 0.09 |
| West Bengal | 216 | 1129 | 4.5 | 7070 | 0.11 |
| Others | 612 | 1166 | 5.1 | 2909 | 0.12 |
| India | 6222 | 26769 | 3.0 | 187283 | 0.19 |

*Number of farmers are assumed equivalent to number of land holdings.
*Source:* Based on information from Directorate of Plant Protection and Quarantine, Ministry of Agriculture, GOI.

## Community Participation

Pest has the characteristics of a detrimental common property resource. It does not recognize spatial boundaries. In other words, successful pest control demands collective efforts. Yet, most of the times pest control efforts are individualistic, giving rise to a number of pest control related problems, such as pest resistance, resurgence and secondary outbreak, destruction of natural enemies of insect pests and other beneficial insects. Collective pest management assumes greater significance in the context of IPM. There are a number of management practices such as observance of synchronicity in sowing dates, use of resistant varieties, crop rotations, etc. that require close cooperation among the farmers. Further, many of IPM inputs are derived from the living organisms, and the application of chemical pesticides in the vicinity of bio-treated field would adversely affect the activities of the biological inputs.

A majority of the farmers is aware of the benefits of collective action, a number of socioeconomic factors act as a disincentive to participate in it. Birthal (2003) empirically examined the factors constraining community participation and found that social heterogeneity was the main hindrance in emergence of a collective approach. The need therefore is to evolve institutional mechanisms that promote community action. The current concept of Farmers' Field School though is based on the principles of collective action, it is often observed that either the groups are not formed, or even if the groups are formed they disappear once the program is withdrawn. These groups need to be sustained by devising an appropriate exit policy. Local bodies such as Panchayats, Non-Governmental Organisations, etc. should be encouraged to shoulder this responsibility. Incentives and awards should be given to those farmers/groups following IPM approach.

### Supply of Biopesticides

Biopesticides capture 2 per cent of the agrochemical market in India despite that mass production standard and techniques have been developed for a number of biopesticides. Further, most of the production takes place in public sector units. Of over 400 biocontrol laboratories in India, 70 per cent are in the domain of public sector. Most of the laboratories are small and cater to the location-specific needs of a small area. The average gross cropped area per biocontrol laboratory is large (Birthal 2003). This shows that supply of biological inputs is a major constraint to widespread adoption of IPM.

The continental dimensions of the agricultural sector offer vast opportunities for the biopesticide industry to increase bio-pesticide production. Certain technical characteristics of bio-pesticides however act as disincentive to the entry of private sector. Unlike chemical pesticides, most of the bio-pesticides are not broad spectrum and are slow in action. Many of these like *Trichogramma* and *Crysoperla* have a short shelf life ranging from a few weeks to few months. Thus, production of biopesticides is fraught with risk. Other constraints in expansion of biopesticide industry are their uncertain demand, lack of appropriate infrastructure for their transportation, storage and marketing. Such problems can partly be overcome by providing incentives to rural unemployed and educated youth to establish small-scale biopesticide production units at village or block level. Measures such as training to the potential entrepreneurs, provision of institutional credit, subsidies, insurance against low off take of inputs due to low pest infestation, and exemption from taxes and duties would stimulate production of bio-pesticides, which is very low (Table 17.3).

**TABLE 17.3:** MARKET SHARE OF BIO-PESTICIDES IN TOTAL AGROCHEMICAL MARKET IN INDIA (%)

| *Pesticides* | *India* | *World* |
|---|---|---|
| Organo-phosphates | 50 | 37 |
| Synthetic pyrethroids | 19 | 22 |
| Organo-chlorines | 16 | 6 |
| Carbamates | 4 | 23 |
| Bio-pesticides | 2 | 12 |
| Others | 10 | 0 |
| **Total** | **100** | **100** |

Like chemical pesticides, setting up of bio-pesticide manufacturing units too under strict registration and quality control requirements. The process of registration is cumbersome and costly, which discourages potential entrepreneurs. Considering the role of biopesticides in protection of environment and human health, registration requirements should be relaxed, but without reconciling the quality standards.

### Enforcement of Pesticide Regulations

In recent years the central government has banned a number of pesticides for use in agriculture in consideration of their adverse effects on environment and human health. Despite many of these are available in the market. For example, DDT and

BHC, which are permitted for use for malaria control, are widely used in agriculture. Further, many pesticides that have been banned elsewhere in the world are available to Indian farmers. Lower prices of such pesticides induce farmers to use them.

### Incentives and Disincentives to Farmers

Cost of application of a technology is an important determinant of its adoption. At present, bulk of the supply of biopesticides comes from public sector, often at subsidized prices. The evidence show that benefits from adoption of IPM are marginal, and an increase in the prices of biopesticides would upset the economics of IPM (Birthal, 2003). Since biopesticides generate considerable social and environmental benefits, the government should think of providing the 'green box' subsidies. Simultaneously the incentives/subsidies, if any, on pesticides be withdrawn and divert the resultant savings towards promotion of IPM. Linking of agricultural credit and insurance to IPM can also facilitate its faster diffusion.

Another alternative is to make production and use of chemical pesticides unattractive through fiscal instruments such as taxes, excise duties, sales taxes, etc. The decline in pesticide use in early 1990s was on account of imposition of heavy taxes on pesticide industry. The pesticide industry, which has established strong market over the last three decades, may resist it, but it may be pursued to switch over to production of safer pesticides and biopesticides.

### Market for Pesticide-Free Products

Economic incentives may not be sustained for a long. Alternative is to develop markets for the pesticide-free or low pesticide residue produce by creating consumer awareness about health benefits of such a produce. At present, there are no premium markets and standards for organic food in India. Since in the short-run there is a possibility of shortfall in yield on switching over to IPM, farmers even if they are willing to adopt IPM may not do so. In developed countries market for pesticide free products is developing and these products fetch premium prices. This however is lacking in India. This would require not only development of certification procedures and labeling system to gain confidence of the consumers. The cost of certification is high for individual farmers. The cost can be brought down considerably following a group approach. The concept of bio-village may help in this. Besides, government should take initiatives to establish certain zones as pesticide free, and procure the produce at a premium price.

Figure 17.1 depicts the trend in pesticide price *vis-à-vis* per hectare pesticide use. There are four distinct phases in this relationship. Till mid 1970s, increase in pesticide price was less than increase in pesticide use. Thereafter, pesticide price increased and the growth in pesticide use slackened. This was due to oil shock in 1974 that led to an increase in the prices of oil-based raw material used in pesticide formulation. The trend continued till 1980-81 (Fig 17.1). During 1980s pesticide price increased at a faster rate, while pesticide use was almost stable. The rising trend in pesticide price became stronger during 1990s. This helped reduce pesticide use considerably. This suggests that farmers are responsive to the pesticide prices. Faster increase in the pesticide price during late 1980s and onward was partly due to gradual withdrawal of the subsidies on pesticides given by the central and state governments under different crop production programs. This phase also coincided with the change in the government policy of plant protection in favour of Integrated Pest Management.

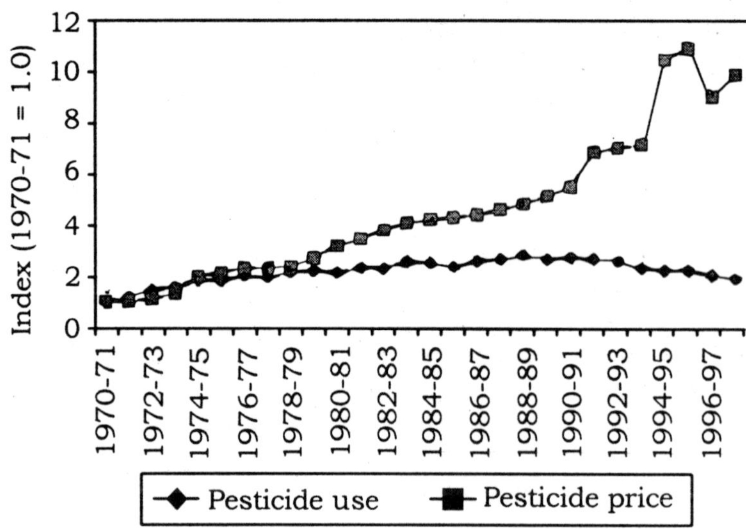


**Fig. 17.1.** Trend in pesticide use and pesticide price

## CONCLUSIONS

India has successfully reduced pesticide consumption without adversely affecting the agricultural productivity. This was facilitated by appropriate policies that discouraged pesticide use, and favoured IPM application. Despite adoption of IPM is low owing to a number of socio-economic, institutional and policy constraints. On the supply side, lack of commercial availability of biopesticides and inappropriate institutional technology transfer mechanisms are the critical impediments to increased application of IPM. The presence of private sector in biopesticide production and marketing is marginal, and needs to be improved through economic incentives. On the demand side, farmers though are aware of technological failure of pesticides to control pests, and their negative externalities to environment and human health, pest risk is too high to experiment with newer approaches to pest management. IPM is a complex process and farmers lack understanding of biological processes of pests and their predators and methods of application of new technology components. The socio-economic environment of farming is also an important factor in adoption of IPM. There are a number of IPM practices that work best when applied by the entire community and in a synchronized mode. This is unlikely to happen without demonstrating benefits of group approach, and external motivation and support to the farmers. Though many technology programs are based on community approach, they do not have any proper exit policy to sustain the group approach. The IPM policy should also provide incentives to farmers to adopt IPM as a cardinal principal of plant protection.

## REFERENCES

Adesina, A. A. and Zinnah, M. M. 1993. Technology characteristics, farmers' perceptions and adoption decisions. *Agricultural Economics*, **9**: 297-311.

Atwal, A. S. 1986. Future of pesticides in plant protection. *In*: G. S. Venkataraman (eds.). *Plant Protection in the Year 2000 A.D.* Indian National Science Academy, New Delhi.

Birthal, P. S. 2003. *Economic Potential of Biological Substitutes for Agrochemicals.* NCAP Policy Paper 18. National Centre for Agricultural Economics and Policy Research, New Delhi.

Birthal, P. S. and Adhiguru, P. 2002. Integrated pest management in India: Problems and prospects. *Journal of Rural Development*, **35**(1): 79-90.

Birthal, P. S., Sharma, O. P. and Kumar, Sant 2000. Economics of integrated pest management: Evidence and issues. *Indian Journal of Agricultural Economics*, **55**(4): 644-659.

Dhaliwal, G. S. and Arora, R. 1996. *Principles of Insect Management.* Commonwealth Publishers, New Delhi.

Kumar, P., Mruthuyunjaya and Birthal, P. S. 2003. Changing consumption pattern in South Asia. Paper presented in the International Workshop on "Agricultural Diversification and Vertical Integration in South Asia" organized by the Federation of Indian Chambers of Commerce and Industry, the International Crops Research Institute for the Semi-Arid Tropics, and the International Food Policy Research Institute at FICCI Federation House, New Delhi, India on 5-6 November 2003.

Lapar, M. L. A. and Pandey, S. 1999. Adoption of soil conservation: The case of the Philippine uplands. *Agricultural Economics*, **21**: 241-256.

Pradhan, S. 1983. *Agricultural Entomology and Pest Control.* Indian Council of Agricultural Research, New Delhi.

Saxena, S. 2001. Pesticide industry in a climate of signal shifts. *Agriculture Today*, April.

# Index

## A



## B



## C

## L



## M



## N



## O



## P



## Q